PRESIDENTIAL ELECTIONS 1789–2008

PRESIDENTIAL ELECTIONS

1789–2008

CQ PRESS

A Division of SAGE
Washington, D.C.

CQ Press
2300 N Street, NW, Suite 800
Washington, DC 20037

Phone: 202-729-1900; toll-free, 1-866-4CQ-PRESS (1-866-427-7737)

Web: www.cqpress.com

Illustration credits and acknowledgments may be found on page 279, which constitutes a continuation of the copyright page.

Cover design: Anne C. Kerns, Anne Likes Red, Inc.
Composition: C&M Digitals (P) Ltd.

♾ The paper used in this publication exceeds the requirements of the American National Standard for Information Sciences—Permanence of Paper for Printed Library Materials, ANSI Z39.48-1992.

Printed and bound in the United States of America

13   12   11   10   09   1   2   3   4   5

Library of Congress Cataloging-in-Publication Data

Presidential elections : 1789-2008.
    p. cm.
 Includes bibliographical references and index.
 ISBN 978-1-60426-541-5 (pbk. : alk. paper) 1. Presidents—United States—Election—History—Chronology. 2. Electoral college—United States—History—Chronology. 3. United States—Politics and government. 4. United States—History—Chronology. I. CQ Press II. Title.

JK528.P75 2010
324.973—dc22

2009040267

★ CONTENTS

★ PREFACE

FROM 1789 TO 2008 there have been fifty-six presidential elections in the United States. The election of the president has evolved into the most dramatic political event in the nation. Every four years the country has undergone a hectic nominating process based on rhetoric, partisan maneuvering, and character analysis as ambitious politicians vie for the nation's most important job.

Over the years the increase in the number of Americans eligible to participate in presidential elections has been one of the most striking measurements of the growth of democracy in the United States. For the first national contest that elected George Washington president, only adult male property holders could vote. During the next century, the electorate was broadened to enfranchise most men. After the Civil War, the Fifteenth Amendment prohibited denying the right to vote "on account of race, color, or previous servitude," but it took another one hundred years and the Twenty-fourth Amendment against poll taxes and other voting restrictions to secure this right for African Americans. The Nineteenth Amendment, ratified in 1920, gave the right to vote to women. The Twenty-third Amendment, ratified in 1961, gave residents of the District of Columbia the right to vote in presidential elections. The Twenty-sixth Amendment, ratified in 1971, lowered the minimum voting age to eighteen.

Despite the continual widening of the base of qualified voters, the last half of the twentieth century witnessed an opposing trend: a decline in electorate turnout. In 1992 more than 100 million Americans went to the polls to cast votes for president, yet that number represented only 71 percent of those registered to vote and only 55 percent of those eligible to vote. The 1996 election, with only 96 million voting, was the first time since 1924 that voter turnout in a presidential race approached 50 percent. Beginning with the 2000 election, however, this trend reversed. That year 105 million voters turned out, and four years later the number rose to 122 million. The number of voters continued to increase in 2008, with a larger number of young and minority voters represented than in the past. Perhaps due to concern over the worsening economy and the ongoing Iraq War, or the nomination of the first African American presidential candidate Barack Obama, the 2008 presidential election saw roughly 131 million people, or 62 percent of the electorate, take to the polls.

The history of presidential elections has been the subject of countless volumes, monographs, and dissertations as well as articles in academic journals. Nevertheless, it is difficult to find a single book that comprehensively and succinctly covers the basic facts and figures on the electoral college, popular vote returns, presidential primaries, nominations of major and minor party candidates, and biographical data on the candidates.

Presidential Elections, 1789–2008 is a unique collection of reference material spanning the time from George Washington's first election as president in 1789 to Obama's election in 2008. It includes popular vote returns for president from 1824 to 1916 obtained from the Inter-University Consortium for Political and Social Research at the University of Michigan. CQ Press has updated this material with data on the presidential elections from 1920 to 2008.

The introduction provides a general overview of the changing presidential selection process and looks at the background of those leaders who have run for and have been elected president. A U.S. Senate seat, a governorship, or the vice presidency continue to be the most popular backgrounds for candidates who are launching presidential bids.

Following a chronology of presidential elections, the next section discusses the origins and development of the presidential primary, which by the 1970s had assumed preeminent importance in the presidential selection process. Overshadowing the caucus method of choosing delegates to a national convention, the primary has become the national stage where the major parties' presidential candidates are chosen.

The expanding role that the popular vote came to play in the election process is examined next. On the first Tuesday after the first Monday in November (a date established in 1845), voters go to the polls to elect the president. Although the voters are actually choosing presidential electors rather than the president, the focus of public attention is the popular vote returns.

Tables provide popular vote returns for the top four candidates for president from 1824 to 2008. These tables are presented in an easily readable format displaying the names and party affiliations of the candidates; state-by-state break-downs of the total vote and percentage for each candidate; the total vote and winning plurality in each state; and the national totals, including the national plurality of the leading popular vote candidate.

The final section of the book examines the constitutional origins and historical development of the Electoral College, the uniquely American system of electing presidents. The section details complex and little-known methods used in the various states through 1832 to choose presidential electors (use of the popular vote began in 1836), recounts historical anomalies in the functioning of the Electoral College, and discusses reasons why a state's electoral votes frequently have been divided among several candidates. It covers the two occasions when a president was elected by the House of Representatives: Thomas Jefferson's close victory over Aaron Burr in 1800 and John Quincy Adams's election from a field of four strong candidates in 1825. It also explains procedures for counting and challenging electoral votes in Congress and describes the famous 1877 Tilden-Hayes contest, which was decided by one electoral vote, and the 2000 Bush-Gore contest, which was decided by five electoral votes. This section concludes with a discussion of presidential disability and the ratification of the Twenty-fifth Amendment to the Constitution.

Electoral maps and tables display all electoral college results since 1789, with electoral vote totals for vice president from 1804 to 2008 listed separately.

The book concludes with a biographical directory of presidential and vice-presidential candidates, a bibliographical list for further reading, and a comprehensive index.

chapter 1

Introduction

THE U.S. SYSTEM OF SELECTING a president and vice president through indirect means is perhaps more complicated than it needs to be. But it has worked with few major repairs for more than two hundred years, generally satisfying the citizenry and meeting the nation's changing needs.

The election happens every four years and permits the peaceful transfer of power or continuation of the status quo for four more years, no matter how bitter or divisive the campaign that preceded it. Indeed, the American electoral system differs from those of other nations and, for all its flaws, is the envy of many other countries. From time to time, however, pressure mounts for abolishing the electoral college system in favor of the direct popular election process used in other major democracies. After each such wave of protest, the demands for reform have gradually faded and the electoral college has survived into the twenty-first century—even weathering the bitter 2000 election and the aftermath of the September 11, 2001, terrorist attack on the United States.

Nevertheless, significant changes have taken place within the system. As the nation and the electorate have grown and technology has evolved, presidential elections have become more expensive. In 2008 preliminary data showed that the candidates alone spent nearly $1.8 billion in the primary and general elections, shattering all previous records. This does not reflect the enormous amounts spent by outside groups. Overall, total outlays were estimated at $3.1 billion.

Because of the high costs, money and its abuses account for the biggest continuing blemish on the system, despite the myriad campaign finance reforms enacted since the 1970s to avoid corruption and lessen the influence of special interests. On the more positive side, presidential nominations have become more open and representative of the voters at large. Party bosses no longer dictate the choice of nominees. Instead, the nominations are won through a hard-fought series of primary elections and party caucuses, where rank-and-file party members have an opportunity to express their preference. Once forums for determining who would head the presidential ticket, national party conventions today perform different functions, including ratification of the nominations won in the primaries.

As televised spectaculars, the conventions remain important to the parties' public relations efforts during the intense weeks before the November election. Although ratings have dropped in recent years, millions of people still watch the conventions on television, and major political parties try to capture and hold as much of that audience as possible. With expert advice they have streamlined the proceedings to showcase their nominees in prime time as the countdown begins to election day. In these final campaign stages, today's nominees usually keep intact the organizations they built to help them survive the primaries. These increasingly professional organizations are made up of the candidate, his or her family, a running mate, polling and political consultants, fund-raisers, media consultants, issues advisers, schedulers, advance persons, and others. Campaign strategies must be carefully managed if the candidate is to move successfully through the primary season, the nominating conventions, and the general election campaign.

WHO RUNS FOR PRESIDENT

Candidates for president or vice president must meet the same few constitutional requirements. They must be at least thirty-five years old and natural-born citizens who have "been fourteen Years a Resident within the United States."

Another requirement, one that affects very few people, is that the candidate must *not* have been elected president twice before. The Twenty-second Amendment, ratified in 1951, limits presidents to two four-year terms. A vice president who succeeds to the presidency and serves more than two years may be elected president only once. Franklin D. Roosevelt, whose breaking of the two-term tradition prompted the term limitation, is the only president who served more than eight years. He died in 1945 at the start of his fourth term.

Democratic senator Barack Obama shakes hands with supporters during his presidential campaign in Los Angeles, California, on February 20, 2007.

More than half (twenty-six) of the nation's presidents have been lawyers, including Barack Obama. He was the forty-fourth president but only the forty-third person to hold the office; (Grover Cleveland is counted twice because he served two separate terms.) Twenty-five presidents served in Congress. Fourteen have been vice presidents. Nineteen presidents have been territorial or state governors. Most presidents have served in the military and three were career generals: Zachary Taylor, Ulysses S. Grant, and Dwight D. Eisenhower. *(See "Roads to the White House," p. 10.)*

Even for well-known public figures, the decision to seek the presidency is a difficult one. The prospective candidates must make complicated calculations about financial and time requirements; they must sort out the tangle of party and state rules and the makeup of the electorate in each state; and they must assess their ability to attract endorsements, recruit a competent staff, and develop an "image" suitable for media presentation. Would-be candidates must also consider the effect a campaign will have on their families, the psychological demands of the office, and possible revelations about their personal lives that might hinder a campaign.

An example of family considerations arose in 1996 from the popularity of retired general Colin L. Powell, the first African American to head the armed forces joint chiefs of staff and one of the architects of the successful 1991 Persian Gulf War. Although polls that year showed Powell would have been a strong contender for the Republican presidential nomination, he declined to seek it, saying he had promised his wife he would stay out of politics. (A pledge he reiterated while serving as secretary of state from

2001 to 2005.) Also in 1996, the man who won the Republican nomination, Robert J. "Bob" Dole, worried that the press would disclose an affair he had while married to his first wife. In his televised debates with President Bill Clinton, who had faced a similar scandal in 1992, Dole did not raise the character issue, reportedly fearing it would open himself to the same criticism. Although Dole's affair was disclosed before the election, it received scant attention and was not a major factor in Dole's defeat.

THE EXPLORATORY STAGE

The first stage in a presidential campaign is the exploratory stage, when the candidates "test the waters" for a try at the nation's highest office. Before announcing, a candidate routinely establishes a political action committee (PAC) to raise money and an exploratory committee to help assess the candidate's chances of challenging the competition. The exploratory advisers identify likely opponents and consider funding prospects and other preliminary factors, and if conditions appear favorable, the committee may form the nucleus of the candidate's campaign organization.

Since 1976, when Jimmy Carter won the presidency after a two-year campaign, candidates have tended to announce their intentions well ahead of the election, in part to have time to build a strong public profile and in part because early fund-raising can be crucial to a campaign. In 2000, with Clinton barred from seeking a third term, the looming White House vacancy drew a large field of Republican candidates. Among the first to form an exploratory committee in 1999 was Elizabeth Dole, wife of the 1996

TABLE 1-1 **U.S. Presidents and Vice Presidents**

President and political party	Born	Died	Age at Inauguration	Native of	Elected from	Term of service	Vice president
George Washington (F)	1732	1799	57	Va.	Va.	April 30, 1789–March 4, 1793	John Adams
George Washington (F)			61			March 4, 1793–March 4, 1797	John Adams
John Adams (F)	1735	1826	61	Mass.	Mass.	March 4, 1797–March 4, 1801	Thomas Jefferson
Thomas Jefferson (DR)	1743	1826	57	Va.	Va.	March 4, 1801–March 4, 1805	Aaron Burr
Thomas Jefferson (DR)			61			March 4, 1805–March 4, 1809	George Clinton
James Madison (DR)	1751	1836	57	Va.	Va.	March 4, 1809–March 4, 1813	George Clinton
James Madison (DR)			61			March 4, 1813–March 4, 1817	Elbridge Gerry
James Monroe (DR)	1758	1831	58	Va.	Va.	March 4, 1817–March 4, 1821	Daniel D. Tompkins
James Monroe (DR)			62			March 4, 1821–March 4, 1825	Daniel D. Tompkins
John Q. Adams (DR)	1767	1848	57	Mass.	Mass.	March 4, 1825–March 4, 1829	John C. Calhoun
Andrew Jackson (D)	1767	1845	61	S.C.	Tenn.	March 4, 1829–March 4, 1833	John C. Calhoun
Andrew Jackson (D)			65			March 4, 1833–March 4, 1837	Martin Van Buren
Martin Van Buren (D)	1782	1862	54	N.Y.	N.Y.	March 4, 1837–March 4, 1841	Richard M. Johnson
W. H. Harrison (W)	1773	1841	68	Va.	Ohio	March 4, 1841–April 4, 1841	John Tyler
John Tyler (W)	1790	1862	51	Va.	Va.	April 6, 1841–March 4, 1845	
James K. Polk (D)	1795	1849	49	N.C.	Tenn.	March 4, 1845–March 4, 1849	George M. Dallas
Zachary Taylor (W)	1784	1850	64	Va.	La.	March 4, 1849–July 9, 1850	Millard Fillmore
Millard Fillmore (W)	1800	1874	50	N.Y.	N.Y.	July 10, 1850–March 4, 1853	
Franklin Pierce (D)	1804	1869	48	N.H.	N.H.	March 4, 1853–March 4, 1857	William R. King
James Buchanan (D)	1791	1868	65	Pa.	Pa.	March 4, 1857–March 4, 1861	John C. Breckinridge
Abraham Lincoln (R)	1809	1865	52	Ky.	Ill.	March 4, 1861–March 4, 1865	Hannibal Hamlin
Abraham Lincoln (R)			56			March 4, 1865–April 15, 1865	Andrew Johnson
Andrew Johnson (R)	1808	1875	56	N.C.	Tenn.	April 15, 1865–March 4, 1869	
Ulysses S. Grant (R)	1822	1885	46	Ohio	Ill.	March 4, 1869–March 4, 1873	Schuyler Colfax
Ulysses S. Grant (R)			50			March 4, 1873–March 4, 1877	Henry Wilson
Rutherford B. Hayes (R)	1822	1893	54	Ohio	Ohio	March 4, 1877–March 4, 1881	William A. Wheeler
James A. Garfield (R)	1831	1881	49	Ohio	Ohio	March 4, 1881–Sept. 19, 1881	Chester A. Arthur
Chester A. Arthur (R)	1830	1886	50	Vt.	N.Y.	Sept. 20, 1881–March 4, 1885	
Grover Cleveland (D)	1837	1908	47	N.J.	N.Y.	March 4, 1885–March 4, 1889	Thomas A. Hendricks
Benjamin Harrison (R)	1833	1901	55	Ohio	Ind.	March 4, 1889–March 4, 1893	Levi P. Morton
Grover Cleveland (D)	1837	1908	55	N.J.	N.Y.	March 4, 1893–March 4, 1897	Adlai E. Stevenson
William McKinley (R)	1843	1901	54	Ohio	Ohio	March 4, 1897–March 4, 1901	Garret A. Hobart
William McKinley (R)			58			March 4, 1901–Sept. 14, 1901	Theodore Roosevelt
Theodore Roosevelt (R)	1858	1919	42	N.Y.	N.Y.	Sept. 14, 1901–March 4, 1905	
Theodore Roosevelt (R)			46			March 4, 1905–March 4, 1909	Charles W. Fairbanks
William H. Taft (R)	1857	1930	51	Ohio	Ohio	March 4, 1909–March 4, 1913	James S. Sherman
Woodrow Wilson (D)	1856	1924	56	Va.	N.J.	March 4, 1913–March 4, 1917	Thomas R. Marshall
Woodrow Wilson (D)			60			March 4, 1917–March 4, 1921	Thomas R. Marshall
Warren G. Harding (R)	1865	1923	55	Ohio	Ohio	March 4, 1921–Aug. 2, 1923	Calvin Coolidge
Calvin Coolidge (R)	1872	1933	51	Vt.	Mass.	Aug. 3, 1923–March 4, 1925	
Calvin Coolidge (R)			52			March 4, 1925–March 4, 1929	Charles G. Dawes
Herbert Hoover (R)	1874	1964	54	Iowa	Calif.	March 4, 1929–March 4, 1933	Charles Curtis
Franklin D. Roosevelt (D)	1882	1945	51	N.Y.	N.Y.	March 4, 1933–Jan. 20, 1937	John N. Garner
Franklin D. Roosevelt (D)			55			Jan. 20, 1937–Jan. 20, 1941	John N. Garner
Franklin D. Roosevelt (D)			59			Jan. 20, 1941–Jan. 20, 1945	Henry A. Wallace
Franklin D. Roosevelt (D)			63			Jan. 20, 1945–April 12, 1945	Harry S. Truman
Harry S. Truman (D)	1884	1972	60	Mo.	Mo.	April 12, 1945–Jan. 20, 1949	
Harry S. Truman (D)			64			Jan. 20, 1949–Jan. 20, 1953	Alben W. Barkley
Dwight D. Eisenhower (R)	1890	1969	62	Texas	N.Y.	Jan. 20, 1953–Jan. 20, 1957	Richard Nixon
Dwight D. Eisenhower (R)			66		Pa.	Jan. 20, 1957–Jan. 20, 1961	Richard Nixon
John F. Kennedy (D)	1917	1963	43	Mass.	Mass.	Jan. 20, 1961–Nov. 22, 1963	Lyndon B. Johnson
Lyndon B. Johnson (D)	1908	1973	55	Texas	Texas	Nov. 22, 1963–Jan. 20, 1965	
Lyndon B. Johnson (D)			56			Jan. 20, 1965–Jan. 20, 1969	Hubert H. Humphrey

(Continued)

TABLE 1-1 **U.S. Presidents and Vice Presidents (continued)**

President and political party	Born	Died	Age at Inauguration	Native of	Elected from	Term of service	Vice president
Richard Nixon (R)	1913	1994	56	Calif.	N.Y.	Jan. 20, 1969–Jan. 20, 1973	Spiro T. Agnew
Richard Nixon (R)			60		Calif.	Jan. 20, 1973–Aug. 9, 1974	Spiro T. Agnew
							Gerald R. Ford
Gerald R. Ford (R)	1913	2006	61	Neb.	Mich.	Aug. 9, 1974–Jan. 20, 1977	Nelson A. Rockefeller
Jimmy Carter (D)	1924		52	Ga.	Ga.	Jan. 20, 1977–Jan. 20, 1981	Walter F. Mondale
Ronald Reagan (R)	1911	2004	69	Ill.	Calif.	Jan. 20, 1981–Jan. 20, 1985	George H.W. Bush
Ronald Reagan (R)			73			Jan. 20, 1985–Jan. 20, 1989	George H.W. Bush
George H.W. Bush (R)	1924		64	Mass.	Texas	Jan. 20, 1989–Jan. 20, 1993	Dan Quayle
Bill Clinton (D)	1946		46	Ark.	Ark.	Jan. 20, 1993–Jan. 20, 1997	Albert Gore Jr.
Bill Clinton (D)			50			Jan. 20, 1997–Jan. 20, 2001	Albert Gore Jr.
George W. Bush (R)	1946		54	Conn.	Texas	Jan. 20, 2001–Jan. 20, 2005	Richard B. Cheney
George W. Bush (R)			58			Jan. 20, 2005–Jan. 20, 2009	Richard B. Cheney
Barack Obama (D)	1961		47	Hawaii	Ill.	Jan. 20, 2009–	Joseph R. Biden Jr.

NOTE: D—Democrat; DR—Democratic-Republican; F—Federalist; R—Republican; W—Whig.

Republican nominee. She decided against running, citing the difficulty of competing against Texas governor George W. Bush's fund-raising powerhouse. Several other prominent Republicans challenged Bush, including Arizona senator John McCain, who won the primaries in New Hampshire and six other states. But he, like the other contenders, eventually ceded the nomination to Bush.

Dole's decision to pull out of the race one year before the election illustrates a characteristic of U.S. presidential elections: they are endurance contests. From start to finish they are much longer, for example, than the few months typically devoted to parliamentary elections in Great Britain. By Labor Day, a good two months before the November election, many American voters are tired of listening to the candidates and have already made up their minds how they will vote.

THE PRIMARY AND CAUCUS SCHEDULE

If a candidate decides to seek a major party nomination, the next step is to enter the primaries and caucuses where Democratic and Republican party members select delegates to their national conventions. The states and the parties have a wide variety of rules for ballot access qualifications and allocation of delegates. Candidates must follow legal requirements to qualify for state contests, and they also have to adapt their campaign strategies to each state's particular circumstances. In 2008 the Democratic Party penalized its state organizations in Florida and Michigan for scheduling primaries earlier than party rules allowed. However, at the national convention in August the party relented and the delegations from both states were seated with full voting rights. Sen. Obama, then the party's presumptive nominee for president, requested that they be seated.

The process of filing to be a presidential candidate can be daunting. In 1988 Rep. Patricia Schroeder of Colorado cited the complexity of state rules as a major factor in her decision not to seek the Democratic presidential nomination. Independent H. Ross Perot made it a condition of his 1992 candidacy that his supporters obtain enough signatures to get his name on the ballot in all fifty states. They succeeded.

Traditionally, the New Hampshire primary and the Iowa caucus are the first delegate-selection events, a head start that gives the two states extraordinary influence over the selection process. (For forty years beginning in 1952, no president was elected without first winning the New Hampshire primary. Bill Clinton broke that precedent in 1992, as did George W. Bush in 2000 and Obama in 2008). Critics have complained that the system is unrepresentative because both states are predominantly rural, with largely white, Anglo-Saxon, Protestant populations. But no serious efforts have been made to change the pattern.

Democratic Party rules prevent other states from scheduling their primaries earlier than the New Hampshire and Iowa events. Republican caucuses are permitted earlier in Alaska, Hawaii, Louisiana, and Guam. For other states and territories, the primary and caucus period begins in late February or early March and ends in early June. The early primaries have grown in importance. Especially when the campaign does not have an obvious front-runner, the early contests single out a possible leader. After several early tests, the field of candidates shrinks. In 2000 both Republican Bush and Democrat Albert "Al" Gore Jr. had secured their party's nomination by mid-March, a feat made possible by the "front loading" of primaries earlier and earlier in presidential election years. In that election year sixteen states held presidential primaries on Super Tuesday, March 7. Although Bush defeated McCain in most of the primaries after New Hampshire, McCain nevertheless received more than five million votes in the 2000 primaries—the most ever amassed by a Republican candidate who did not win the nomination. In 2008, when he won the nomination, McCain received almost ten million primary votes.

In 2004, with President Bush unopposed for renomination, Sen. John F. Kerry of Massachusetts had clinched the Democratic nomination for president by early March, after several of his challengers had dropped out, including Sen. John Edwards of North Carolina, who exited March 3. Kerry later chose Edwards as his running mate.

The 2008 presidential primaries, with Bush ineligible to run for a third term, drew large fields of candidates from both parties—nine Democrats and thirteen Republicans. Most of these had dropped out well before the fall nominating conventions.

THE PRESIDENTIAL NOMINATION

The primary season culminates in the two national party conventions, usually held in late July or August. At these conventions, where guests and reporters outnumber the thousands of delegates, the presidential and vice-presidential nominees are formally selected and a party platform, setting out the party's goals for the next four years, is approved. In recent elections, the convention also has become an important occasion for showcasing party unity after the sometimes divisive primary battles. In 2008 the two major parties held back-to-back conventions in late August and early September. In 2004 and 2008, each party received about $50 million in federal funds for its convention, mostly for security.

The first national convention was held in 1831, and for more than a century afterward state party leaders had the ultimate say in deciding who the presidential nominee would be. As direct primaries took hold in the twentieth century, this influence began to wane. Then in the 1970s and 1980s, the Democrats initiated a series of presidential selection reforms that opened the nominating process. The reforms were expected to result in more open conventions, but instead they led to even more primaries.

Victory in the primaries, however, does not mean the primary leader faces no opposition at the convention. Other candidates may stay in the race because they hope to benefit if the leader falters, or they may use the bloc of delegates committed to them to bargain for specific planks in the platform or to influence the selection of the vice-presidential nominee.

Before the widespread use of primaries, the conventions were more competitive and frenetic than they are

TABLE 1-2 Campaign Lengths for Presidential Candidates, 2008

Aspirants for the White House often begin their campaigns for the nomination months before the nominating conventions, sometimes as long as two years earlier. Candidates for the party that does not hold the White House, or in years where there is no incumbent such as 2008, usually begin the earliest. This table shows the dates on which Democratic and Republican candidates for the 2008 contest officially opened their campaigns and the dates on which they dropped out. For the two winners, Barack Obama and John McCain, the dates listed are the days on which they officially received their party's nomination at the conventions, although their campaigns continued to election day.

	Announcement date	End date
Democrats		
Joseph R. Biden, Del.	Jan. 13, 2007	Jan. 3, 2008
Hillary Clinton, N.Y.	Jan. 20, 2007	June 7, 2008
Christopher Dodd, Conn.	Jan. 11, 2007	Jan. 3, 2008
John Edwards, N.C.	Dec. 28, 2006	Jan. 30, 2008
Mike Gravel, Alaska	April 17, 2006	May 25, 2008
Dennis Kucinich, Ohio	Dec. 12, 2006	Jan. 24, 2008
Barack Obama, Ill.	Feb. 10, 2007	Aug. 27, 2008
Bill Richardson, N.M.	Jan. 27, 2007	Jan. 10, 2008
Tom Vilsack, Iowa	Nov. 30, 2006	Feb. 23, 2007
Republicans		
Sam Brownback, Kan.	Jan. 20, 2007	Oct. 19, 2007
John Cox, Ill.	March 9, 2006	Oct. 28, 2007
Jim Gilmore, Va.	Jan. 9, 2007	July 14, 2007
Rudy Giuliani, N.Y.	Nov. 20, 2007	Jan. 29, 2008
Mike Huckabee, Ark.	Jan. 29, 2007	March 4, 2008
Duncan L. Hunter, Calif.	Jan. 25, 2007	Jan. 22, 2009
Alan Keyes, Md.	Sept. 14, 2007	April 28, 2008
John McCain, Ariz.	April 25, 2007	Sept. 4, 2008
Ron Paul, Texas	March 11, 2008	June 12, 2008
Mitt Romney, Mass.	Feb. 13, 2007	Feb. 7, 2008
Tom Tancredo, Colo.	Jan. 27, 2007	Dec. 20, 2007
Fred Thompson, Tenn.	June 1, 2007	Jan. 22, 2008
Tommy Thompson, Wisc.	Dec. 16, 2006	Aug. 11, 2007

today. All the candidates still in the race had substantial campaign operations at the conventions. Campaign managers and strategists kept in close contact with state delegations. Candidates deployed floor leaders and "whips" to direct voting on the convention floor and to deal with any problems that arose among state delegations. In addition, "floaters" wandered the crowded floor in search of any signs of trouble. Floor leaders, whips, and floaters often wore specially colored clothing or caps so that they could be spotted easily on the convention floor.

This spectacle, however, became a rarity. It has been decades since either major party took more than one ballot to nominate a president. But in 1996 Reform Party founder Perot faced opposition from former Colorado governor Richard D. Lamm. In a two-step procedure the party nominated Perot at the second of two conventions.

At party conventions, nominating speeches mark the beginning of the formal selection process. These remarks are usually followed by a series of short seconding speeches, and all of the speeches are accompanied by floor demonstrations staged by delegates supporting the candidate. For many years a good deal of convention time was taken up by the nomination of favorite sons, candidates nominated by their state's delegation. Such nominations were seldom taken seriously, and since 1972 both parties have instituted rules that have effectively stopped them.

In recent years, the balloting for the presidential nominee has been anticlimactic. More attention focuses on whom the presidential nominee will select as a running mate. Even then, much of the suspense has been removed because the leading presidential candidates may have named their running mates well before the convention begins. That was not the case in 2008, when Republican nominee John McCain, just before the convention, surprised the political world by choosing a woman, the little-known Alaska governor, Sarah Palin, as his running mate.

With the young, politically moderate, all-southern ticket of Clinton and Gore in 1992 an obvious exception, the choice of the vice-presidential candidate often has been motivated by an effort to balance the ticket geographically. For years, a balanced ticket was one that boasted an easterner and a midwesterner. More recently, the balance has shifted so that the split is more often between a northerner and a southerner. Some examples: Democrats John F. Kennedy of Massachusetts and Lyndon B. Johnson of Texas in 1960, Johnson and Hubert H. Humphrey of Minnesota in 1964, Jimmy Carter of Georgia and Walter F. Mondale of Minnesota in 1976, Kerry of Massachusetts and Edwards of North Carolina in 2004, and Obama of Illinois and Joseph R. Biden Jr. of Delaware in 2008; and Republicans Barry Goldwater of Arizona and William E. Miller of New York in 1964, George W. Bush of Texas and Richard B. Cheney of Wyoming in 2000, and McCain of Arizona and Palin of Alaska in 2008.

Ideology also plays a part in the balance. A liberal presidential candidate may be paired with a more conservative running mate to attract a broader base of voters. Or the choice of the vice-presidential candidate may be used to appease party factions who are unhappy with the presidential candidate. Additionally, governors generally choose running mates with Washington credentials, such as senators. With the increasing number of vice presidents who go on to be president, more attention is given to the abilities of the person who is chosen, and more prominent figures are willing to accept the nomination.

The method for nominating the vice-presidential candidate mirrors the procedure for presidential nominations. The climax of the convention then occurs with the two nominees' acceptance speeches and their first appearance together, with their families, on the podium.

GENERAL ELECTION CAMPAIGN

The traditional opening of the presidential election campaign is Labor Day, just two months before the general election on the first Tuesday after the first Monday in November. In recent years, however, candidates have been unwilling to wait until Labor Day to capitalize on their postconvention bounce in the polls.

The campaign organization for the general election is usually an extension of the nomination organization, and it is separate from the national and state party organizations. Nominees normally have the prerogative of naming their party's national committee chair to help coordinate the campaign.

The national campaign committee, usually based in Washington, D.C., receives its funding from the Federal Election Commission (FEC). In exchange for federal funding, the campaign must agree not to spend more than it receives from the FEC. From 1975, when federal funding of elections began, to 2004 all major party nominees accepted the government funds for their general election campaigns. In 2008, however, Democrat Obama rejected public money for the fall campaign so that he could continue his highly successful fund-raising operation. Republican McCain accepted the federal funds and accused Obama of reneging on his pledge to do the same. Neither candidate took the checkoff money for their primary campaigns. A president running for reelection has inherent advantages that may tilt the balance in the incumbent's favor. The incumbent already has the stature of the presidency and is able to influence media coverage by using official presidential actions and "pork-barrel politics" to appeal to specific constituencies. The president also benefits from the public's reluctance to reject a tested national leader for an unknown quantity.

In times of economic or foreign policy difficulties, however, the president's prominence can have negative effects on the campaign. President Carter's bid for a second term was plagued by both a sagging economy and Iran's continued holding of U.S. citizens as hostages. In 1992, after achieving record-high approval ratings for success in the Gulf War, President George H.W. Bush saw his reelection hopes dashed by an economic recession, which he was slow to acknowledge and which the Democrats used to advantage with their emphasis on "it's the economy, stupid."

Debates

Now almost taken for granted, presidential and vice-presidential candidate debates are a relatively recent phenomenon. Until the second half of the twentieth century, White House nominees did not debate. Richard Nixon and Kennedy began the debate tradition on September 26, 1960, with the first of four televised meetings. When Abraham Lincoln and Stephen A. Douglas held their famed debates in

TABLE 1-3 "Minority" Presidents

Under the U.S. electoral system, there have been eighteen presidential elections (decided by either the electoral college itself or by the House of Representatives) where the victor did not receive a majority of the popular votes cast in the election. Four of these presidents—John Quincy Adams in 1824, Rutherford B. Hayes in 1876, Benjamin Harrison in 1888, and George W. Bush in 2000—actually trailed their opponents in the popular vote.

The following table shows the percentage of the popular vote received by candidates in the eighteen elections in which a "minority" president (designated by boldface type) was elected:

Year Elected	Candidate	Percentage of Popular Vote	Candidate	Percentage of Popular Vote	Candidate	Percentage of Popular Vote	Candidate	Percentage of Popular Vote
1824	Jackson	41.34	**Adams**	30.92	Clay	12.99	Crawford	11.17
1844	**Polk**	49.54	Clay	48.08	Birney	2.30		
1848	**Taylor**	47.28	Cass	42.49	Van Buren	10.12		
1856	**Buchanan**	45.28	Fremont	33.11	Fillmore	21.53		
1860	**Lincoln**	39.82	Douglas	29.46	Breckinridge	18.09	Bell	12.61
1876	Tilden	50.97	**Hayes**	47.95	Cooper	0.97		
1880	**Garfield**	48.27	Hancock	48.25	Weaver	3.32	Others	.15
1884	**Cleveland**	48.50	Blaine	48.25	Butler	1.74	St. John	1.47
1888	Cleveland	48.62	**Harrison**	47.82	Fisk	2.19	Streeter	1.29
1892	**Cleveland**	46.05	Harrison	42.96	Weaver	8.50	Others	2.25
1912	**Wilson**	41.84	T. Roosevelt	27.39	Taft	23.18	Debs	5.99
1916	**Wilson**	49.24	Hughes	46.11	Benson	3.18	Others	1.46
1948	**Truman**	49.52	Dewey	45.12	Thurmond	2.40	Wallace	2.38
1960	**Kennedy**	49.72	Nixon	49.55	Others	0.72		
1968	**Nixon**	43.42	Humphrey	42.72	Wallace	13.53	Others	.33
1992	**Clinton**	43.01	G.H.W. Bush	37.45	Perot	18.91	Others	.64
1996	**Clinton**	49.24	Dole	40.71	Perot	8.40	Others	1.65
2000	Gore	48.38	**G.W. Bush**	47.87	Nader	2.74	Others	1.01

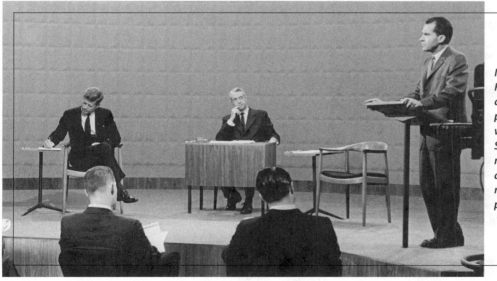

In 1960 Vice President Richard Nixon speaks during the first televised presidential debate while his opponent, Sen. John F. Kennedy, takes notes. Since 1976 televised debates have become a regular part of each presidential campaign.

1858 they were Senate candidates; they did not debate as presidential candidates two years later.

There were no debates from 1960 until 1976, when President Gerald R. Ford, running behind in the polls, agreed to debate the Democratic nominee, former Georgia governor Carter. The relatively unknown Carter gained stature in the exchange when Ford made a gaffe by saying he did not believe East European nations were under Soviet Union control. Since 1976 all major party nominees have debated on live television. Independent candidate Perot was included in the presidential debates in 1992, but he was excluded as the Reform Party nominee in 1996.

Unlike formal, academic debates, the presidential confrontations have been loosely structured, at first with a panel

Democratic senator Joe Biden and Republican governor Sarah Palin deliberate during the vice presidential debate at Washington University on October 2, 2008.

of journalists or audience members asking the questions. Beginning in 1992, debate sponsors began having a journalist moderator question the candidates, with the audience sometimes allowed to participate. Throughout, there have been no judges to award points and therefore no way to determine who "won" or "lost" except by public opinion polling. Media commentators make immediate assessments of winners and losers, however, and their judgments undoubtedly influence the public's opinion about which candidate "won" the debate.

With one exception, vice-presidential nominees have debated since 1976 when Ford's running mate Bob Dole faced Democrat Mondale. There was no debate in 1980 between Vice President Mondale and the Republican nominee, George H.W. Bush. The nominees in 2000, Republican Cheney and Democrat Joseph I. Lieberman, debated once. In 2004 Vice President Cheney and Edwards, the Democratic nominee, also debated once, as did 2008 nominees Palin and Biden.

Early in the presidential debate era, the television networks or the League of Women Voters sponsored the debates. Since 1988 they have been sponsored by the bipartisan Commission on Presidential Debates.

The Popular Vote

The United States' winner-take-all electoral college system gives presidential and vice-presidential nominees an incentive to campaign where the votes are. Because in most states the leading vote-getter wins all that state's electoral votes, the system encourages nominees to win as many populous states as possible. Nominees generally spend most of their time in closely contested states, and just enough time in "likely win" states to ensure victory. Appearances in unfavorable states are usually symbolic efforts to show that the candidate is not conceding anything.

In the electoral college, states have votes equal to their representation in Congress: two for the senators and at least one for the representatives, for a total of 538 votes. (The District of Columbia has the three votes it would have if it were a state.) Two states, Maine and Nebraska, permit splitting their electoral votes between the statewide winner and the winner in each of the congressional districts (two in Maine, three in Nebraska). No such split had occurred until 2008, when Obama won one district and one electoral vote in Nebraska. *(See "Electoral College," p. 9; and Chapter 5, The Electoral College.)*

Four times in U.S. history—most recently in 2000—the winner of the presidential popular vote has lost the electoral college vote. In these and other close presidential races, a shift of a few hundred votes within one or two states could have changed the result of the election. In the most notable example, in 2000 Bush won Florida's twenty-five electoral votes by a scant 537 votes out of more than six million popular votes cast. After the Supreme Court halted Gore's requested manual recount, those 537 votes gave Bush the bare electoral vote majority he needed to win.

The disputed Florida election brought renewed calls for abolition or reform of the electoral college system. But it also spurred demands for modernization of methods of casting, recording, and reporting of the popular vote throughout the United States. The election brought to light that 37 percent of all U.S. registered voters were still being required to use outmoded punch-card voting systems similar to those blamed for much of the difficulty in Florida. By 2004, largely to avoid a repeat of the Florida fiasco, many states and counties had modernized their voting systems, cutting in half the percentage of voters using punch-card systems.

Previously, little attention had been paid nationally to voting systems. Each state or locality was free to purchase whatever type of system it wanted or could afford, although the FEC set standards for such equipment and recommended purchase of systems that met those standards.

Campaign finance reform and efforts to make registration easier and increase voter participation received higher priority from most groups in the final decades of the twentieth century. The National Voter Registration Act of 1993, the motor-voter act, which enabled people to obtain registration forms when they picked up driver's licenses, was an example of laws that helped put millions more people on the voting rolls. Yet the changes did not necessarily translate into higher turnouts at the polls.

By 2008 most jurisdictions had modernized their voting systems, with many using some form of optical scanning in which the voters uses a marker to fill in their ballots, which can then be read by the machine. Some such systems leave a "paper trail," whereby the ballots can be stored and recounted if necessary. The 2008 elections elicited few complaints nationwide about the voting technology. Nevertheless, the most persistent complaints were over systems that lacked a paper trail for verifying the election result at a particular polling place. After 2008, states and manufacturers continued to work to address these complaints.

Similarly, actions to expand the electorate took place at both the state and federal levels. Voting qualifications varied widely because the U.S. Constitution (Article I, Section 2) permits the states to set their own voting standards. Early in the nation's history, the states dropped their property qualifications for voting, but some retained literacy tests as late as 1970.

On the federal level the Constitution has been amended five times to circumvent state qualifications denying the franchise to certain categories of people. The Fourteenth Amendment, ratified in 1868, directed Congress to reduce the number of representatives from any state that disfranchised adult male citizens for any reason other than commission of a crime. However, no such reduction was ever made. The Fifteenth Amendment, ratified in 1870, prohibited denial of the right to vote "on account of race, color or previous condition of servitude," and the Nineteenth Amendment in 1920 prohibited denial of that right "on account of sex." The Twenty-fourth Amendment, which came into effect in 1964, barred denial of the right to vote in any federal election "by reason of failure to pay any poll tax or other tax." Finally, in 1971 the Twenty-sixth Amendment lowered the voting age to eighteen in federal, state, and local elections.

Congress in the 1950s and 1960s enacted a series of statutes to enforce the Fifteenth Amendment's guarantee against racial discrimination in voting. A law passed in 1970 nullified state residence requirements of longer than thirty days for voting in presidential elections, suspended literacy tests for a five-year period (the suspension was made permanent in 1975), and lowered the minimum voting age to eighteen years from twenty-one, the requirement then in effect in most states. A 1970 Supreme Court ruling upheld the voting-age change for federal elections but invalidated it for state and local elections. In the same decision the Court upheld the provision on residence requirements and sustained the suspension of literacy tests with respect to both state and local elections. The Twenty-sixth Amendment was ratified six months after the Court's decision.

The right to vote in presidential elections was extended to citizens of the District of Columbia by the Twenty-third Amendment ratified in 1961. District residents had been disfranchised from national elections except for a brief period in the 1870s when they elected a nonvoting delegate to the House of Representatives. In 1970 Congress took another step toward full suffrage for District residents by again authorizing the election of a nonvoting delegate to the House.

Through the various state or federal reforms, virtually all citizens aged eighteen or over were eligible to vote at the beginning of the twenty-first century. By 2001, following the decennial census, the U.S. Census Bureau estimated the nation's voting-age population at 205.8 million. But a relatively low 105.4 million voted in the 2000 presidential election, for a turnout rate of 51.2 percent. The numbers improved in the 2004 election when 122.3 million, or 56.7 percent, voted for president, the highest turnout since 1968. In 2008 the presidential turnout was slightly higher at 131.3 million, or 56.8 percent of the voting-age population.

Because the United States does not register voters nationally, reliable figures on the number of registered voters were not available until motor-voter required states to report the numbers to the FEC. In 1996 the states reported a total of 146.2 million registered voters. Using that figure, only about 71.0 percent of voting-age citizens were registered in 2000, and the turnout was about 72.1 percent.

ELECTORAL COLLEGE

Even after the winner has declared victory and the loser has conceded defeat, at least two more steps must be taken before a president-elect is officially declared. The first occurs on the first Monday after the second Wednesday in December. On that day electors meet in their respective state capitals to cast their votes for president.

Each state has as many electors as it has members of Congress. Typically, slates of electors are pledged before the popular election to each of the presidential nominees. The presidential nominee who wins the state wins that state's electors. Although the Constitution does not require electors to remain faithful to their pledge of support for a particular candidate, many states have laws to that effect. Such laws, however, are generally regarded as unenforceable and likely unconstitutional. There have been several instances in which "faithless electors" did not vote for their party's nominee.

The second step occurs when the electors' ballots are opened and counted before a joint session of Congress in early January. The candidate who wins a majority of the vote is declared the president-elect and is inaugurated three weeks later on January 20. The counting of electoral votes by a joint session of Congress is normally a routine affair. But in 2001 a number of Democratic House members attempted unsuccessfully to have Florida's controversial twenty-five electoral votes for George W. Bush thrown out. Likewise, in 2005 several House Democrats and one Democratic senator, Barbara Boxer of California, failed to block the counting of Ohio's twenty electoral votes on grounds that thousands of mostly minority voters had been disfranchised by numerous irregularities. By contrast, the electoral vote counting on January 8, 2009, was conducted without incident. Obama and Biden each received 365 electoral votes to 173 each for McCain and Palin.

In the rare event that no presidential candidate receives a majority of the electoral college vote, the election is thrown into the House of Representatives. If no vice-presidential candidate receives a majority of the electoral college vote, the Senate makes the selection.

TERM OF OFFICE

A president's term begins with inauguration at noon on January 20 following the November election. Until the Twentieth Amendment was ratified in 1933, presidents were not inaugurated until March 4, leaving a four-month hiatus between the election and the inauguration. The briefer interval established by the so-called lame-duck amendment shortened the period in which the nation had, in effect, two presidents—the outgoing president and an incoming president-elect. Yet the amendment allowed time for an orderly transition between the old and the new administrations.

The Twentieth Amendment took effect in 1933 after President Franklin Roosevelt and Vice President John Nance Garner had been sworn in. In 1937, at the beginning of their second terms, they became the first president and vice president inaugurated on January 20.

ROADS TO THE WHITE HOUSE

The earliest tradition concerning the path to the presidency developed around the secretary of state, who was considered the preeminent cabinet officer and therefore the most important person in the executive branch after the president. Thomas Jefferson was George Washington's first secretary of state. Although he left the cabinet early in Washington's second term, he went on to become leader of the newly formed Democratic-Republican Party and its candidate for president in 1796, 1800, and 1804. Losing to John Adams in 1796, Jefferson came back to win four years later.

In turn, James Madison, Jefferson's secretary of state for two terms, won the presidency in 1808. Madison had been a close ally of Jefferson's in the political struggles of the 1790s and served throughout Jefferson's two presidential terms as secretary of state (1801–1809). During his first term as president, Madison appointed fellow Virginian James Monroe as his secretary of state. And following in what was rapidly becoming a tradition, Monroe went on to the presidency in 1816, serving two terms (1817–1825).

Throughout Monroe's terms, the secretary of state was John Quincy Adams, son of former president John Adams. At the end of Monroe's second term, five major candidates entered the race to succeed him. Three were cabinet officers, including Adams. After none of the candidates acquired a majority in the electoral college, the House of Representatives chose Secretary of State Adams.

Adams was the last secretary of state to go directly from his cabinet post to the White House. After him, only two secretaries of state made it to the White House at all—Martin Van Buren, who was secretary of state under President Andrew Jackson from 1829 to 1831 and president from 1837 to 1841, and James Buchanan, who served as secretary of state from 1845 to 1849 under President James K. Polk and as president from 1857 to 1861.

Two other institutions died at approximately the same time as the cabinet tradition—the Virginia dynasty and "King Caucus," a derogatory term referring to the congressional party caucuses that met throughout the early 1800s to designate presidential nominees.

After the four Virginians who occupied the presidency during the first thirty-six years of the Republic—Washington, Jefferson, Madison, and Monroe—there have been no elected presidents who were born in and made their careers in Virginia. John Tyler was born there but succeeded to the presidency from the vice presidency in 1841 and was not renominated. Three other presidents were born in Virginia but made their careers elsewhere—William Henry Harrison, Zachary Taylor, and Woodrow Wilson.

During its heyday, the Washington-centered mentality of King Caucus had virtually guaranteed that cabinet officers should be among those most often nominated by the party in power. But the caucus came under attack as being undemocratic and unrepresentative and ceased to function as a presidential nominating mechanism after 1824. It was eventually replaced by the national party conventions, bodies that are not connected with Congress and that, as of the 2008 presidential election, had never met in the national capital.

Military Men

The next cycle of American politics, from the presidency of Jackson (1829–1837) to the Civil War, saw a variety of backgrounds qualify candidates for the presidency. One of the most prevalent was the military. Jackson, who ran in 1824 (unsuccessfully), 1828, and 1832, was a general in the War of 1812, gaining near-heroic stature by his defeat of the British at the Battle of New Orleans in January 1815. Like most military officers who rose to the presidency, however, Jackson was only a part-time military man. As a politician, he had served in the U.S. House during Washington's presidency and in the Senate during the administration of John Adams, as well as later under Monroe and John Quincy Adams.

Other candidates during this era who were or had been military officers included William Henry Harrison, a Whig candidate in 1836 and 1840; Taylor, the Whig candidate in 1848; Winfield Scott, the 1852 Whig candidate; Franklin Pierce, the Democratic nominee in 1852; and John C. Fremont in 1856, the Republican Party's first presidential candidate. From 1824 through 1856, all but one presidential election (1844) featured a major candidate with a military background.

Career general Ulysses S. Grant was elected president in 1868 and 1872.

Like Jackson, Harrison had a mixed military and political career. A member of a distinguished Virginia family, he was the son of a signer of the Declaration of Independence. Harrison served in Congress during the John Adams administration and again under Madison, Monroe, and John Quincy Adams. In between, he battled American Indians and the British during the War of 1812.

Taylor and Scott led victorious armies in the Mexican War. Pierce also had a command in the Mexican War, although he had been primarily a politician, with service in both the House and the Senate during the 1830s and 1840s. Fremont was famous as an explorer as well as for a dashing military campaign through California during the Mexican War. Later, he was a U.S. senator from the young state of California (1850–1851).

The smoldering political conflicts of the 1840s and 1850s probably contributed to the naming of military men for the presidency. Generals usually had escaped involvement in national politics and had avoided taking stands on the issues that divided the country—slavery, expansion, the currency, and the tariff. In 1840, for example, the Whigs adopted no platform or statement of principle; they simply nominated Harrison and assumed that his personal popularity plus the resentments against Van Buren's administration would suffice for Whig victory. They were correct.

Later on, the nature of the Civil War almost automatically led at least one of the parties to choose a military officer as presidential standard-bearer every four years. To have been on the "right" side during the war—fighting to save the Union and destroy slavery—was a major political asset in the North and Midwest, where tens of thousands of war veterans were effectively organized in the Grand Army of the Republic (GAR). The GAR became part of the backbone of the Republican Party during the last third of the nineteenth century.

Consequently, it became customary for Republicans to have a Civil War officer at the head of their ticket. Except for James G. Blaine in 1884, every Republican presidential nominee from 1868 to 1900 had served as an officer in the Union Army during the Civil War. Blaine, who had spent the war years as a Maine state legislator and a member of the U.S. House, lost the election to Grover Cleveland.

Of all the late-nineteenth-century Republican nominees, however, only Ulysses S. Grant, who was elected president in 1868 and 1872, was a professional military man. The others—Rutherford B. Hayes in 1876, James A. Garfield in 1880, Benjamin Harrison in 1888 and 1892, and William McKinley in 1896 and 1900—were civilians who volunteered for Civil War service. Two of them—Hayes and Garfield—were elected to the House while serving in the army. At the time of their presidential nominations, Hayes was governor of Ohio, Garfield was minority leader of the U.S. House and a senator-elect, Harrison was a former senator from Indiana, and McKinley was a former governor of Ohio.

WHAT THEY DID BEFORE THEY BECAME PRESIDENT

This list gives the terms of office for each president and the public jobs each held before becoming president.

George Washington. 1759–1774, Virginia House of Burgesses; 1774–1775, delegate to Continental Congress; 1775–1783, commanding general of Continental Army; 1787, president, Constitutional Convention; 1789–1797, president.

John Adams. 1771, Massachusetts colonial legislature; 1774–1778, Continental Congress; 1778, minister to France; 1779, delegate to Massachusetts constitutional convention; 1780–1782, minister to the Netherlands; 1785–1788, minister to Great Britain; 1789–1797, vice president; 1797–1801, president.

Thomas Jefferson. 1769–1774, Virginia House of Burgesses; 1775, delegate to Continental Congress; 1775, delegate to Virginia convention; 1776, delegate to Continental Congress; 1776–1779, Virginia House of Delegates; 1779–1781, governor of Virginia; 1784–1789, envoy and minister to France; 1789–1793, secretary of state; 1797–1801, vice president; 1801–1809, president.

James Madison. 1774, Colonial Committee of Safety; 1776, delegate to Virginia convention; 1776–1777, Virginia House of Delegates; 1777, Virginia State Council; 1778, Virginia Executive Council; 1779–1783, Continental Congress; 1784–1786, Virginia House of Delegates; 1786–1788, Continental Congress; 1787, delegate to Constitutional Convention; 1789–1797, U.S. House (Va.); 1801–1809, secretary of state; 1809–1817, president.

James Monroe. 1780, Virginia House of Delegates; 1781–1783, governor's council; 1783–1786, Continental Congress; 1786, Virginia House of Delegates; 1787, delegate to Constitutional Convention; 1790–1794, U.S. Senate (Va.); 1794–1796, minister to France; 1799–1803, governor of Virginia; 1803, minister to England and France; 1804, minister to Spain; 1810, Virginia House of Delegates; 1811, governor of Virginia; 1811–1817, secretary of state; 1814–1815, secretary of war; 1817–1825, president.

John Quincy Adams. 1794–1796, minister to Netherlands; 1796–1797, minister to Portugal; 1797–1801, minister to Prussia; 1802, Massachusetts Senate; 1803–1808, U.S. Senate (Mass.); 1809–1814, minister to Russia; 1815–1817, minister to Great Britain; 1817–1825, secretary of state; 1825–1829, president.

Andrew Jackson. 1788, solicitor for western North Carolina; 1796, delegate to Tennessee constitutional convention; 1796–1797, U.S. House (Tenn.); 1797–98, U.S. Senate (Tenn.); 1798–1804, Tennessee Supreme Court; 1807, Tennessee Senate; 1812, commander, U.S. militia; 1814, U.S. Army; 1821, territorial governor of Florida; 1823–1825, U.S. Senate (Tenn.); 1829–1837, president.

Martin Van Buren. 1813–1820, New York Senate; 1815–1819, New York attorney general; 1821–1828, U.S. Senate (N.Y.); 1829, governor of New York; 1829–1831, secretary of state; 1831, minister to Great Britain; 1833–1837, vice president; 1837–1841, president.

William Henry Harrison. 1798–1799, secretary of Northwest Territory; 1799–1800, U.S. House (territorial delegate); 1801–1813, territorial governor of Indiana; 1812–1814, U.S. Army; 1816–1819, U.S. House (Ohio); 1819–1821, Ohio Senate; 1825–1828, U.S. Senate (Ohio); 1828, minister to Colombia; 1841, president.

John Tyler. 1811–1816, Virginia House of Delegates; 1816, Virginia State Council; 1817–1821, U.S. House (Va.); 1823–1825, Virginia House of Delegates; 1825–1827, governor of Virginia; 1827–1836, U.S. Senate (Va.); 1838–1839, Virginia House of Delegates; 1841, vice president; 1841–1845, president.

James Knox Polk. 1821–1823, chief clerk, Tennessee Senate; 1823–1825, Tennessee House; 1825–1839, U.S. House (Tenn.); 1839–1841, governor of Tennessee; 1845–1849, president.

Zachary Taylor. 1808–1849, U.S. Army; 1849–1850, president.

Millard Fillmore. 1828–1831, New York Assembly; 1833–1835, U.S. House (N.Y.); 1837–1843, U.S. House (N.Y.); 1848–1849, New York controller; 1849–1850, vice president; 1850–1853, president.

Franklin Pierce. 1829–1833, New Hampshire House; 1833–1837, U.S. House (N.H.); 1837–1842, U.S. Senate (N.H.); 1846–1848, U.S. Army; 1850, delegate to New Hampshire constitutional convention; 1853–1857, president.

James Buchanan. 1814–1815, Pennsylvania House; 1821–1831, U.S. House (Pa.); 1832–1833, minister to Russia; 1834–1845, U.S. Senate (Pa.); 1845–1849, secretary of state; 1853–1856, minister to Great Britain; 1857–1861, president.

Abraham Lincoln. 1833, postmaster, New Salem, Illinois; 1835–1840, Illinois General Assembly; 1847–1849, U.S. House (Ill.); 1861–1865, president.

Andrew Johnson. 1828–1829, alderman, Greeneville, Tenn.; 1830–1833, mayor, Greeneville, Tenn.; 1835–1837, Tennessee House; 1839–1841, Tennessee House; 1841, Tennessee Senate; 1843–1853, U.S. House (Tenn.); 1853–1857, governor of Tennessee; 1857–1862, U.S. Senate (Tenn.); 1862–1865, military governor of Tennessee; 1865, vice president; 1865–1869, president.

Ulysses S. Grant. 1843–1854, U.S. Army; 1861–1865, general, U.S. Army; 1867–1868, secretary of war; 1869–1877, president.

The Democrats, who had been split over the war, had few prominent military veterans to choose from. Only twice between 1860 and 1900 did the Democrats pick a Civil War officer as their nominee, and both lost. In 1864, during the war, the Democrats nominated Gen. George B. McClellan, the Union military commander who had fallen out with President Abraham Lincoln. In 1880 Gen. Winfield Scott Hancock of Pennsylvania was the Democrats' choice.

New York and Indiana

From the Civil War to the midtwentieth century, several governors or former governors of New York were

Rutherford B. Hayes. 1857–1859, Cincinnati city solicitor; 1861–1865, U.S. Army; 1865–1867, U.S. House (Ohio); 1868–1872, governor of Ohio; 1876–1877, governor of Ohio; 1877–1881, president.

James A. Garfield. 1859, Ohio Senate; 1861–1863, U.S. Army; 1863–1880, U.S. House (Ohio); 1881, president.

Chester A. Arthur. 1871–1878, collector for Port of New York; 1881, vice president; 1881–1885, president.

Grover Cleveland. 1863–1865, assistant district attorney of Erie County, N.Y.; 1871–1873, sheriff of Erie County, N.Y.; 1882, mayor of Buffalo, N.Y.; 1883–1885, governor of New York; 1885–1889, president; 1893–1897, president.

Benjamin Harrison. 1862–1865, U.S. Army; 1864–1868, reporter of decisions, Indiana Supreme Court; 1879, member, Mississippi River Commission; 1881–1887, U.S. Senate (Ind.); 1889–1893, president.

William McKinley. 1861–1865, U.S. Army; 1869–1871, prosecutor, Stark County, Ohio; 1877–1883, U.S. House (Ohio); 1885–1891, U.S. House (Ohio); 1892–1896, governor of Ohio; 1897–1901, president.

Theodore Roosevelt. 1882–1884, New York State Assembly; 1889–1895, U.S. Civil Service Commission; 1895, president of New York City board of police commissioners; 1897, assistant secretary of the Navy; 1898, U.S. Army; 1899–1901, governor of New York; 1901, vice president; 1901–1909, president.

William Howard Taft. 1881–1882, assistant prosecutor, Cincinnati; 1887, assistant city solicitor, Cincinnati; 1887–1890, Cincinnati Superior Court; 1890–1892, U.S. solicitor general; 1892–1900, U.S. Circuit Court; 1900–1901, president of Philippines Commission; 1901–1904, governor general, Philippine Islands; 1904–1908, secretary of war; 1907, provisional governor of Cuba; 1909–1913, president.

Woodrow Wilson. 1911–1913, governor of New Jersey; 1913–1921, president.

Warren G. Harding. 1895, auditor of Marion County, Ohio; 1899–1903, Ohio Senate; 1904–1905, lieutenant governor of Ohio; 1915–1921, U.S. Senate (Ohio); 1921–1923, president.

Calvin Coolidge. 1899, city council of Northampton, Mass.; 1900–1901, city solicitor of Northampton, Mass.; 1903–1904, clerk of the courts, Hampshire County, Mass.; 1907–1908, Massachusetts House; 1910–1911, mayor of Northampton, Mass.; 1912–1915, Massachusetts Senate; 1916–1918, lieutenant governor of Massachusetts; 1919–1920, governor of Massachusetts; 1921–1923, vice president; 1923–1929, president.

Herbert Hoover. 1914–1915, chairman of American Committee in London; 1915–1918, chairman, Commission for the Relief of Belgium; 1917–1919, U.S. food administrator; 1919, chairman, Supreme Economic Conference in Paris; 1920, chairman, European Relief Council; 1921–1928, secretary of commerce; 1929–1933, president.

Franklin D. Roosevelt. 1911–1913, New York Senate; 1913–1920, assistant secretary of the Navy; 1929–1933, governor of New York; 1933–1945, president.

Harry S. Truman. 1926–1934, administrative judge, court of Jackson County, Missouri; 1935–1945 U.S. Senate (Mo.); 1945, vice president; 1945–1953, president.

Dwight D. Eisenhower. 1915–1948, U.S. Army; 1950–1952, commander of NATO forces in Europe; 1953–1961, president.

John F. Kennedy. 1941–1945, U.S. Navy; 1947–1953, U.S. House (Mass.); 1953–1961, U.S. Senate (Mass.); 1961–1963, president.

Lyndon B. Johnson. 1935–1937, Texas director of National Youth Administration; 1937–1948, U.S. House (Texas); 1949–1961, U.S. Senate (Texas); 1961–1963, vice president; 1963–1969, president.

Richard M. Nixon. 1942–1946, U.S. Navy; 1947–1951, U.S. House (Calif.); 1951–1953, U.S. Senate (Calif.); 1953–1961, vice president; 1969–1974, president.

Gerald R. Ford. 1949–1973, U.S. House (Mich.); 1973–1974, vice president; 1974–1977, president.

Jimmy Carter. 1946–1953, U.S. Navy; 1955–1962, chairman, Sumter County (Ga.) Board of Education; 1963–1967, Georgia Senate; 1971–1975, governor of Georgia; 1977–1981, president.

Ronald Reagan. 1967–1975, governor of California; 1981–1989, president.

George H.W. Bush. 1942–1945, U.S. Navy; 1967–1971, U.S. House (Texas); 1971–1973, ambassador to the United Nations; 1974–1975, chief of U.S. Liaison Office, Beijing, People's Republic of China; 1976–1977, director of Central Intelligence Agency; 1981–1989, vice president; 1989–1993, president.

Bill Clinton. 1977–1979, attorney general of Arkansas; 1979–1981, governor of Arkansas; 1983–1993, governor of Arkansas; 1993–2001 president.

George W. Bush. 1995–2000, governor of Texas; 2001–2009, president.

Barack Obama. 1997–2004, Illinois State Senate; 2005–2008, U.S. Senate (Ill.); 2009– , president.

Democratic standard bearers. The 1868 nominee was Horatio Seymour, who had been governor there 1853–1855 and again 1863–1865. In 1876 the Democrats chose Samuel J. Tilden, New York's reform governor who was battling Tammany Hall. In 1884 Cleveland, another New York reform governor, captured the Democratic nomination. He went on to become the first Democrat to win the White House in twenty-eight years. Cleveland was again the Democratic nominee in 1888 and 1892.

Besides being the most populous state, New York was a swing state in presidential politics. During the period from Reconstruction through the turn of the century, most southern states voted Democratic, although the Republicans usually carried Pennsylvania, the Midwest, and New England. A New Yorker appeared as the nominee for president or vice president of at least one of the major parties in every election from 1868 through 1892.

This general tradition was maintained through the candidacy of Thomas E. Dewey, Republican governor of New York, in 1948. Only twice between 1868 and 1948 was there no New Yorker on the national ticket of at least one of the major parties—for president or vice president. Once, in 1944, both major party presidential nominees, Democrat Franklin Roosevelt and Republican Dewey, were from New York.

From 1952 to 2008, however, no New Yorkers were nominated by a major party for president and only three for vice president. The latter three were Rep. William E. Miller, R, in 1964; Rep. Geraldine A. Ferraro, D, in 1984; and Rep. Jack Kemp, R, in 1996. Dwight D. Eisenhower in 1952 and Richard Nixon in 1968 were technically residents of New York but were generally identified with other states. President Gerald R. Ford's vice president, Nelson A. Rockefeller, was a former governor of New York, but he was appointed to the vice presidency. He was not asked to be on the ticket when Ford ran in 1976.

Another major swing state in the years from the Civil War through World War I was Indiana. In most elections during this period a prominent Indianan found his way onto one of the major party's national tickets. In the thirteen presidential elections between 1868 and 1916, an Indianan appeared ten times on at least one of the major parties' national tickets. However, from 1916 to 2008 only two Indianans, Wendell Willkie in 1940 and Dan Quayle in 1988 and 1992, were major party nominees.

Governors

From 1900 to 1956 Democrats tended to favor governors for the presidential nomination, whether from New York or elsewhere. Democratic governors who received their party's presidential nomination included Wilson of New Jersey in 1912, James M. Cox of Ohio in 1920, Alfred E. Smith of New York in 1928, Franklin Roosevelt of New York in 1932, and Adlai E. Stevenson of Illinois in 1952.

During the same period, Republican presidential nominees had a wide variety of backgrounds. There were two cabinet officers (Secretary of War William Howard Taft in 1908 and Secretary of Commerce Herbert Hoover in 1928), a Supreme Court justice (Charles Evans Hughes in 1916), a U.S. senator (Warren G. Harding in 1920), two governors (Alfred M. Landon of Kansas in 1936 and Dewey of New York in 1944 and 1948), a private lawyer (Willkie in 1940), and a general (Eisenhower in 1952 and 1956). Calvin Coolidge of Massachusetts, the 1924 nominee, and Theodore Roosevelt of New York, the 1904 nominee, who

succeeded to the presidency from the vice presidency, had been governors of their respective states.

Curiously, the two world wars did not produce a plethora of military candidates. The only general besides Eisenhower who made a strong bid for a presidential nomination was Gen. Leonard Wood, who had commands in the Spanish-American War and World War I. Wood led on five ballots at the 1920 Republican National Convention before losing out on the tenth ballot to Harding. Otherwise only a few military men were even mentioned for the presidency in the twentieth century—most notably Gen. Douglas MacArthur in the 1940s and 1950s (he got little support at Republican conventions) and Colin Powell in the 1990s.

Senators and Former Vice Presidents

An abrupt change took place in 1960 with the nominations of John F. Kennedy, a senator, and Nixon, a former senator and sitting vice president. It was only the second time in the twentieth century that an incumbent U.S. senator was nominated for the presidency. The first time was in 1920 when the Republicans nominated Harding from Ohio. In the nineteenth century the phenomenon also had been rare, with National-Republican Henry Clay in 1832, Democrat Lewis Cass in 1848, and Democrat Douglas in 1860 the only incumbent senators nominated for president by official party conventions. Republican Garfield was a senator-elect at the time of his election in 1880. Beginning with Kennedy's ascension from the Senate to the White House in 1960, senators dominated presidential campaigns until 1976. During those sixteen years every major party nominee was a senator or former senator.

The nomination of Nixon, like the nomination of Kennedy, was also a sign of things to come. It was the first time since 1860 and only the third time in the history of party nominating conventions that an incumbent vice president was chosen for the presidency. Beginning in 1960 the vice presidency, like the Senate, became a presidential training ground. Vice President Hubert H. Humphrey was chosen by the Democrats for president in 1968. That same year the Republicans renominated Nixon, who went on to win the presidency eight years after being vice president.

Vice President Spiro T. Agnew was the leading contender for the 1976 Republican presidential nomination before his resignation in October 1973. In 1984 former vice president Walter Mondale, who had served under Jimmy Carter, emerged as the Democratic choice for the presidential nomination. When George H.W. Bush won the presidency in 1988, after filling the second spot under Ronald Reagan for eight years, it marked the first time a sitting vice president had been elected president since Van Buren in 1836. Democratic Vice President Al Gore tried to duplicate Bush's success in 2000. He won the popular vote but lost in the electoral college to Bush's son, George W. Bush.

Even defeated vice-presidential nominees have been considered for the nomination—witness Henry Cabot Lodge Jr. of Massachusetts in 1964; Edmund S. Muskie of Maine in 1972; Sargent Shriver of Maryland in 1976; Bob Dole of Kansas in 1980, 1988, and 1996 (when he was the Republican nominee); Joseph I. Lieberman of Connecticut in 2004; John Edwards of North Carolina in 2008.

Only four senators or former senators secured the top spot on a major party ticket between 1976 and 2004—Mondale in 1984, Dole in 1996, Gore in 2000, and John Kerry in 2004—and all suffered defeat. Several senators were also tapped as vice-presidential running mates: Mondale with Carter and Dole with Ford in 1976; Lloyd Bentsen with Dukakis and Quayle with George H. W. Bush in 1988; Gore with Bill Clinton in 1992; Lieberman with Gore in 2000, and Edwards with Kerry in 2004.

In the 2008 election senators dominated the presidential primaries and the general election. Six of the nine Democratic candidates were senators or former senators. Sen. Hillary Rodham Clinton of New York and Sen. Barack Obama of Illinois were the top two contenders over a field that included Sen. Joseph Biden of Delaware, Sen. Christopher Dodd of Connecticut, and former senators Edwards of North Carolina and Mike Gravel of Alaska. In the Republican contest Sen. John McCain of Arizona quickly bested twelve other candidates including Sen. Sam Brownback of Kansas and former senator Fred Thompson of Tennessee. However the most historical aspect of the 2008 presidential race was the fact that for the first time a woman, Clinton, and an African American, Obama, vied for the top of a major party ticket, with Obama eventually winning the nomination and the presidency.

Governors Reconsidered

The 1976 campaign saw the reemergence of governors as leading contenders in the nomination sweepstakes. Between 1976 and 2004 governors or former governors won seven out of eight presidential elections. Although there was no shortage of senators in the 1976 races, it was the governors who attracted the most attention. Former California governor Reagan came close to depriving incumbent Ford of the Republican presidential nomination. The Democratic nominee and eventual winner, former Georgia governor Carter, faced a dramatic last-minute challenge from the governor of California at the time, Edmund G. "Jerry" Brown Jr. In 1980 Reagan (the Republican nominee), Carter (the Democratic nominee), and Brown were candidates again along with former Democratic Texas governor John B. Connally. In 1984 former Florida governor Reubin Askew vied unsuccessfully for the Democratic presidential nomination as incumbent Reagan easily gained his reelection.

In 1988 and 1992 the field of Democratic presidential candidates contained a near equal mix of governors and senators, but two Democratic governors established momentum early in the primaries. In 1988 Massachusetts governor Michael S. Dukakis won enough delegates by June to take the Democratic nomination, but he lost to Vice President George H. W. Bush in the November general election. In 1992 Arkansas governor Clinton fought off several Democratic contenders—including another challenge from Brown of California—to secure the nomination. Clinton went on to defeat Bush in 1992 and Dole in 1996. In 2000 Bush's son, George W. Bush, governor of Texas, locked up the Republican nomination in March and then defeated Vice President Gore who had moved to the top of the Democratic ticket. In the 2004 campaign, two governors joined the crowded Democratic field: former Florida governor and sitting senator Daniel Robert "Bob" Graham and Vermont governor Howard Dean. Dean became the early Democratic front-runner before losing the nomination to Massachusetts senator Kerry, who had also served previously as lieutenant governor. Bush prevailed over Kerry in the November election.

In 2008 four of the thirteen Republican candidates for president were former governors—Jim Gilmore of Virginia, Mike Huckabee of Arkansas, Mitt Romney of Massachusetts, and Tommy Thompson of Wisconsin. A sitting governor, Sarah Palin of Alaska, became the party's candidate for vice president. Among Democrats, Gov. Bill Richardson of New Mexico and Tom Vilsack of Iowa were the only sitting or former governors among the presidential candidates.

chapter 2

Chronology of Presidential Elections

IN THE EARLY YEARS of the Republic, the American colonists and their leaders were ambivalent about the concept of democracy. On the one hand, Americans searched for ways to prevent the kind of tyranny they had experienced at the hand of elite rulers such as King George of England. On the other hand, political elites feared the instability that might result from mass participation in politics. This ambivalence was evident in the compromise for presidential selection worked out at the Constitutional Convention in 1787 and in the halting steps the nation took toward party competition.

The presidential selection process has changed significantly since George Washington was elected to his first term in 1789. The electoral college is still the center of the system, but all of the related institutions and processes are dramatically different, in part because the constitutional provisions for presidential selection are so vague.

The major features of the electoral system have developed over time as a process of trial and error. The Constitution contains no provisions for organizing political parties, nominating candidates, or campaigning for office. The Framers assumed, incorrectly, that the selection process would be a reasoned one that would transcend petty partisanship. The original provision for balloting by the electoral college was flawed and had to be superseded by the Twelfth Amendment in 1804.

Until the eighteenth century, competitive elections were rare. The nation's first legislative body, the Virginia House of Burgesses, had largely single-candidate elections until the 1700s, and later, even when the elections for state legislatures attracted more than one candidate, there was little active campaigning. It was only with the decline of homogeneous communities and the end of elite control over politics that election contests began to occur.

The very concept of the political party—a way to organize electoral coalitions—was viewed with distrust by the nation's earliest leaders. As George Washington described the dangers of parties in a letter: "A fire not to be quenched; it demands a uniform vigilance to prevent its bursting into a flame, lest instead of warming it should consume."[1] Only after the experience of factional debate in Congress, where bitter strife developed over issues such as banking, tariffs, and slavery, did the idea of parties seem necessary and capable of control.

EMERGENCE OF THE ELECTORAL PROCESS

The method of choosing presidential and vice-presidential candidates has moved through four distinct phases, according to political scientist Richard P. McCormick.[2] The first phase was a period marked by uncertain and hazardous rules that lasted until the Twelfth Amendment was ratified in 1804. The second phase, continuing through 1820, saw the decline of the Federalists as a national force and the dominance of the Democratic-Republicans. This phase is associated with "King Caucus"—the nomination of candidates by congressional caucuses. In the third phase, King Caucus was replaced by factional politics and unsettled rules for selecting candidates. The fourth phase—still in effect today—evolved between 1832 and 1844. It is characterized by a two-party system that nominates candidates by national conventions. In recent years, however, the conventions have been rendered obsolete by mass politics, which takes the form of mass media presentations of candidates to the public and mass participation of party members in primary elections.

Washington's First Election: 1789

Establishment of the rules for democratic decision making in the United States occurred inauspiciously. The states completed their separate ratifications of the Constitution in July 1788—nearly nine months after the close of the Constitutional Convention in Philadelphia. The Continental Congress then decided that New York City would serve as the seat of government. There, on September 13, 1788, Congress passed a resolution requiring the states to appoint electors on the first Wednesday in January, the electors to assemble and vote in their respective states on the first Wednesday in February, and the new government to convene on the first Wednesday in March.

Under the Constitution, the method of choosing electors was left up to the individual state legislatures. *(See "Methods of Choosing Electors," p. 190.)* The requirement that all electors be chosen on the same day proved to be troublesome for the states. Some did not have time to call elections. In New York, for example, where electors were to have been chosen by the legislature, dissension between the two houses led to a stalemate and prevented the state from participating in the election.

No formal nomination of candidates took place in 1788. Nevertheless, it had been widely anticipated since the Constitutional Convention the previous year that George Washington of Virginia, the reluctant hero of the Revolutionary War, would be president. The only real question was who would be the vice president. Leaders of the Federalists, a group organized in the fall of 1787 to achieve ratification of the Constitution, ultimately decided to support John Adams of Massachusetts.

The inherent flaws of the electoral system became evident quickly. Under the Constitution, each elector was to cast two votes for president. The two votes had to be for different persons, and the two candidates could not both receive votes from a common home state. The individual receiving the votes of a majority of the electors was to be named president, and the person receiving the second highest total was to be named vice president. Because no distinction was made between balloting for president and vice president, it was possible for more than one candidate to receive an equal number of votes, thereby throwing the election into the House of Representatives. It also was possible that a candidate for vice president—through fluke or machination—actually could end up with the most votes and become president.

The Federalist leader Alexander Hamilton recognized the danger, and his personal animosity toward Adams aggravated his concern. In response, he plotted to siphon away votes from Adams. In a letter to James Wilson of Pennsylvania, Hamilton wrote: "Everybody is aware of that defect in the constitution which renders it possible that the man intended for vice president may in fact turn up president." To prevent such a crisis, Hamilton recommended that several votes that would otherwise have gone to Adams be thrown away on other candidates: "I have proposed to friends in Connecticut to throw away 2 [votes], to others in New Jersey to throw away an equal number and I submit to you whether it would not be well to lose three or four in Pennsylvania."[3]

Hamilton's efforts were successful. Washington was unanimously elected president with sixty-nine electoral votes. Adams, however, won the vice presidency with only thirty-four electoral votes. Just two states—New Hampshire and his own Massachusetts—voted solidly for him. Because in other states Federalist leaders withheld support from Adams and sometimes worked against him, he did not receive *any* votes from Delaware, Georgia, Maryland, and South Carolina, and he received only one vote from New Jersey. The remaining votes were spread among ten other candidates, including John Jay, John Hancock, Robert Harrison, John Rutledge, and George Clinton.

Although the new government was supposed to open its doors on March 4, 1789, not enough members of Congress had arrived in New York City by that date to achieve a quorum. When the Senate finally convened on April 6 and counted the electoral votes, a messenger was dispatched on horseback to deliver the news to President-elect Washington at his home in Mount Vernon, Virginia. He received the news on April 14. Washington then set out for New York where he was sworn in on April 30.

Before the end of Washington's first term as president, political divisions developed that would lead to a party system. James Madison emerged as the de facto opposition leader in Congress. Seventeen members of the House of Representatives regularly sided with Madison, and a bloc of fifteen supported the administration. The other dozen or so members of the House switched back and forth between the administration's and Madison's faction.[4]

The election of 1789 demonstrated the potential for partisanship and intrigue in presidential contests. It also revealed the weaknesses of the existing election calendar (which had made it difficult for New York to participate in the election) and reminded participants of the danger of the constitutional "defect" in the selection process that made it possible for the person intended to be vice president to become president.

Washington's Reelection: 1792

Washington remained first in the hearts of his countrymen when his first term as president drew to a close in 1792. But the facade of national unity was showing signs of crumbling as bitter oppositional factions began to develop. From this arose a system of electoral competition.

Washington won a second unanimous term as president in 1792, but the election did produce competition for vice president. An overtly partisan contest broke out when the Democratic-Republicans, as one faction was now known, decided to challenge the Federalist Adams. Some of Adams's approving statements about the British angered populists, who campaigned behind the scenes against him. Adams managed to win, but not before bitter partisan identities had developed in response to the nation's only unanimous administration.

The election was different from the 1789 one in another way as well. The election calendar was changed and made more flexible by an act of Congress that allowed states to choose electors within a thirty-four-day span before the first Wednesday in December when the electors met to vote. The new law remained in effect until 1845.

Thomas Jefferson, the leader of the Democratic-Republicans, chose not to run for vice president in 1792, in part because he came from the same state as President Washington. Because electors could vote for only one candidate from their state, Jefferson was tacitly precluded from receiving the large electoral vote of Virginia. Besides, a "balanced ticket" required regional diversity. Instead, Democratic-Republican leaders from New York, Pennsylvania, Virginia, and South Carolina chose New York governor George Clinton as their candidate at a meeting in Philadelphia in October 1792. The endorsement of Clinton was a milestone in the evolution of the presidential nominating process and a step away from the Framers' original understanding of the selection process.

Both Washington and Adams were reelected, but Clinton scored well in the electoral college. Adams received 77 electoral votes to Clinton's 50 (with four votes going to Jefferson and one to Sen. Aaron Burr of New York), and Washington was reelected president by a unanimous electoral vote of 132.

The political tensions brought out by the Adams-Clinton contest became even tauter as policy controversies arose. Jefferson resigned as secretary of state in 1793 in protest over Secretary of the Treasury Hamilton's growing influence in foreign affairs. Jefferson complained: "In place of that noble love of liberty and Republican government which carried us triumphantly through the war, an Anglican, Monarchical, and Aristocratical party has sprung up, whose avowed subject is to draw over us the substance as they have already done the forms of the British government." Even Washington was subject to attacks. A Pennsylvania politician wondered aloud if Washington had not "become the tyrant instead of the saviour of his country."[5]

News of the French Revolution's period of terror divided the nation's political leaders. Federalists recoiled in horror with the news of a democratic revolution gone awry, while democrats such as Jefferson expressed sympathy for France's struggle. The U.S. government's use of troops to suppress the Whiskey Rebellion of 1794, approval of the Jay Treaty of 1794, and maneuvering between the warring French and British also polarized the young nation into factions. State-level Democratic-Republican societies formed during this period in opposition to the Federalists.

The First Succession: 1796

Washington decided not to run for president again in 1796, even though the Constitution did not bar a third term and public sentiment supported it. With Washington out of the race, the United States witnessed its first partisan contest for president. Washington's Farewell Address, published in summer 1796, was "a signal, like dropping a hat, for the party racers to start."[6]

On the Democratic-Republican side, Jefferson faced no opposition as the presidential candidate; a consensus of

John Adams, the Federalist presidential candidate, won the election of 1796 despite opposition by some members of his own party, including Alexander Hamilton. Democratic-Republican Thomas Jefferson won the vice presidency. The Twelfth Amendment (1804) precluded future split-ticket administrations.

party leaders selected him to run in 1796. But a caucus of Democratic-Republican senators was unable to agree on a running mate, producing a tie vote for Burr of New York and Sen. Pierce Butler of South Carolina that ended with a walkout by Butler's supporters. As a result, there was no formal Democratic-Republican candidate to run with Jefferson.

The Federalists, by contrast, held what historian Roy F. Nichols has described as a "quasi caucus" of the party's members of Congress in Philadelphia in May 1796.[7] The gathering chose Vice President Adams and Minister to Great Britain Thomas Pinckney of South Carolina as the Federalist presidential and vice-presidential candidates. The choice of Adams was not surprising because he was Washington's vice president. Nevertheless, Adams was unpopular in the South, and he continued to be disliked by Hamilton. As a result, Hamilton tried to use the "defect" in the Constitution to make Pinckney president instead of Adams. He urged northern electors to give equal support to Adams and Pinckney in the hopes that the South would not vote for Adams and that Pinckney would therefore win the most votes.

Had the northern electors followed Hamilton's advice, Pinckney might have won the presidency. Instead, eighteen votes were thrown to other Federalists (thereby preventing a Pinckney claim to the presidency), giving Adams the presidency with seventy-one electoral votes. Pinckney—with fifty-nine votes—was not even able to win the vice presidency. Jefferson—the candidate of the opposing Democratic-Republican ticket—came in second with sixty-eight votes and became Adams's vice president. Although the results again played up the defects in the constitutional procedure for electing presidents, Federalists and Democratic-Republicans did not seem unduly concerned that the president and vice president were of opposing parties. Both sides felt that they had prevented the opposition from gaining total victory.

For the first and last time, a foreign figure played an active and public role in the election. French ambassador Pierre Adet promoted Jefferson's campaign in appearances and in written statements. Whether the Adet effort helped or hurt Jefferson is uncertain. The effort aroused supporters of France but angered others who favored Great Britain or resented outside interference.

Jefferson's Revenge: 1800

The election of 1800 was the first in which both parties used congressional caucuses to nominate candidates for their tickets. Such caucuses were an important innovation in the presidential selection process because they formalized partisan alignments in Congress and demonstrated the emergence of organized political parties.

President Adams was hated bitterly by farmers, populists, and states' rights advocates. In one of the nation's first professionally run smear campaigns, Adams was denounced as a "hideous hermaphroditical character which has neither the force and firmness of a man, nor the gentleness and sensibility of a woman."[8]

Federalist members of Congress met in the Senate chamber in Philadelphia on May 3, 1800, to choose their candidates. As in previous presidential election years, Federalists were divided in their support of Adams, yet they felt they had to nominate him because he was the incumbent president. Their ambivalence toward Adams was revealed, however, when they nominated both Adams and Maj. Gen. Charles Cotesworth Pinckney of South Carolina without giving preference to one or the other for president. Pinckney was the elder brother of the Federalist vice-presidential candidate in 1796.

The choice of Pinckney was made at Hamilton's insistence. Once again Hamilton was plotting to use the constitutional defect against Adams. In 1796 South Carolina had voted for an all-southern ticket—Jefferson and Thomas Pinckney—even though the two were of opposing parties. Hamilton hoped that South Carolina would vote the same

way in 1800, and that all other Federalist electors could be persuaded to vote for Adams and Charles Pinckney. That would give Pinckney more votes than Adams, thus making him president.

Although the deliberations of the Federalist caucus were secret, the existence of the meeting was not. It was described by the local Democratic-Republican paper, the Philadelphia *Aurora,* as a "Jacobinical conclave." Further denunciations by the paper's editor, Benjamin F. Bache, earned him a personal rebuke from the U.S. Senate.

The Democratic-Republicans once again chose Jefferson as the presidential candidate by consensus. On May 11 a caucus of Democratic-Republican members of Congress met at Marache's boarding house in Philadelphia to choose a running mate. Their unanimous choice was Burr.

Although there was no such thing as a formal party platform in 1800, Jefferson wrote fairly detailed statements of principle in letters to various correspondents. Among other things, the Democratic-Republicans believed in states' rights, a small national government, and a relatively weak executive. They opposed standing armies in peacetime, a large naval force, and alliances with other countries. They also denounced the Alien and Sedition Acts, which had been passed by the Federalists in 1798, ostensibly to protect the nation from subversives given the threat of war with France.

The presidential election in 1800 witnessed other signs of formal public campaigning. Tickets listing the names of Democratic-Republican electors were printed and distributed in a number of states, including New York, Massachusetts, Pennsylvania, and Delaware. Speeches in behalf of the candidates increased markedly. Partisan newspapers also helped to spread the party positions—the number of newspapers in the United States had grown dramatically in the last decade of the century, from 91 to 234.[9] Despite attempts by the Federalist Party to muzzle the opposition press with the passage of the Sedition Act of 1798, partisan newspapers on both sides actively defamed the opposition. Ultimately, the Sedition Act worked against the Federalists by turning the Democratic-Republicans into public champions of a free press.

Increased partisan activity spurred voter participation. Because electors still were chosen indirectly in twelve of the sixteen states, voters often expressed themselves through state legislative elections as a means of influencing future presidential elections.[10] The seeds were being sown for a new phase in the development of the presidential election process.

A harbinger of Democratic-Republican success came in May when the New York state party won state legislative elections. Burr managed the campaign in the state, building a machine with ward and precinct organizations. Burr's efforts showed the importance of large-scale mobilization—a lesson that would not be lost on the party in future years.

When the electors voted in December, the constitutional defect did not work as Hamilton had hoped. Instead of resulting in a Pinckney victory, the defect produced an unexpected tie vote between the two Democratic-Republican candidates, Jefferson and Burr—each of whom had seventy-three electoral votes. Adams came in third with sixty-five, and Pinckney followed with sixty-four. In accord with the Constitution, the election was thrown into the Federalist-controlled House of Representatives.

Some Federalists felt that Burr was the lesser of the two evils and plotted to elect him president instead of Jefferson, even though Jefferson was clearly the presidential candidate. Hamilton helped to squelch the idea as he preferred Jefferson over Burr. After thirty-six ballots, Jefferson carried a majority in the House of Representatives. The crisis—which could have fatally wounded the nation by calling into question the legitimacy of the new president—was over. Jefferson was elected president and Burr, vice president.

The near disaster brought about by the constitutional defect led to the passage of the Twelfth Amendment to the Constitution in September 1804. It called for electors to vote for president and vice president on separate ballots, thereby clarifying who was the presidential candidate and eliminating the possibility of a tie between the principal candidate and the running mate.

Jefferson's Reelection: 1804

By the 1804 election, President Jefferson had grudgingly accepted the emergence of a party system. Indeed, the president wrote that year: "The party division in this country is certainly not among its pleasant features. To a certain degree it will always exist."[11]

Jefferson's record—lower taxes, a reduced national debt, repeal of the Alien and Sedition Acts, and purchase of the Louisiana Territory from France—assured him of a second term. Particularly important was Jefferson's willingness to expand the nation's reach and power with the Louisiana Purchase, which compromised his philosophical preference for a small republic. The opposition's case against Jefferson was personal. But the voters were not convinced of the need to make a change.

The 1804 election was the first one held after the Twelfth Amendment went into effect, requiring electors to cast separate votes for president and vice president. Therefore as of that election, parties always specifically designated their presidential and vice-presidential candidates.

The Democratic-Republicans retained the caucus system of nomination in 1804, as they did for the next two decades, and for the first time they publicly reported their deliberations. When the party caucus met on February 25,

This 1807 anti-Jefferson cartoon compares Washington and Jefferson in contrasting images of good and evil.

1804, it attracted 108 of the party's senators and representatives.

President Jefferson was renominated by acclamation, but Vice President Burr, who had fallen out with his party, was not considered for a second term. On the first nominating roll call publicly reported in U.S. political history, New York governor George Clinton was chosen by the caucus to run for vice president. He received sixty-seven votes and easily defeated Sen. John Breckinridge of Kentucky, who collected twenty votes. To "avoid unpleasant discussions" no names were placed in nomination and the vote was conducted by secret ballot.

Before adjourning, the caucus appointed a thirteen-member committee to conduct the campaign and promote the success of Democratic-Republican candidates. A forerunner of party national committees, the new campaign group included members of both the House and Senate, but with no two persons from the same state. Because the Twelfth Amendment had not yet been passed when the caucus met, the committee was designed to "manage" the vote of Democratic-Republican electors to ensure that the events of 1800 were not repeated. In fact, that precaution was not necessary because the Twelfth Amendment was ratified in September—well before the electors voted.

By 1804 the Federalist Party had deteriorated badly. The new era of dominance by the Virginia-led Democratic-Republicans had begun. The Federalists did not even hold a congressional caucus to elect their nominees. Instead, Federalist leaders informally chose Charles Cotesworth Pinckney for president and Rufus King of New York for vice president. How the Federalists formulated this ticket is not clear. There is no record in 1804 of any formal meeting to nominate Federalist candidates.

The Federalists then mounted a disorganized and dispirited national campaign. Despite concerted efforts to win at least the votes of New England, the Federalists failed miserably. Pinckney received only 14 electoral votes—those of Connecticut and Delaware, plus 2 from Maryland. Jefferson, the Democratic-Republican candidate, was the overwhelming victor with 162 electoral votes.

Madison's Victory: 1808

Following Washington's precedent, Jefferson refused to seek a third term of office. The nation was bitterly divided over Jefferson's policy toward France and Britain. In an attempt to stay out of their war, Jefferson had supported a trade embargo so that neither country would seize American ships. But the embargo only undermined U.S. business interests. Under political attack, Jefferson decided to return to his beloved home of Monticello near Charlottesville, Virginia.

Despite the unpopularity of the administration's European policy, Jefferson's secretary of state and chosen successor, Madison, won the presidency in 1808. Jefferson's

retirement provided a serious test to the authority of the Democratic-Republican congressional caucus to select presidential candidates. The caucus met on January 23, 1808, after, for the first time, a formal call was issued. Sen. Stephen R. Bradley of Vermont, chairman of the 1804 caucus, issued the call to all 146 Democratic-Republicans in Congress and several Federalists sympathetic to the Democratic-Republican cause. A few party leaders questioned Bradley's authority to call the caucus, but various reports indicate that between eighty-nine and ninety-four members of Congress attended.

As in 1804, the balloting took place without names being formally placed in nomination. Madison easily won the presidential nomination with eighty-three votes. Despite earlier support for future secretary of state James Monroe among Democratic-Republicans in Virginia, and Vice President Clinton's desire to be president, each won only three votes at the caucus. But the caucus overwhelmingly renominated Clinton as vice president, giving him seventy-nine votes; runner-up John Langdon of New Hampshire collected five votes.

The Democratic-Republican caucus also repeated its practice of appointing a committee to conduct the campaign. Membership was expanded from thirteen to fifteen House and Senate members, and it was formally called the "committee of correspondence and arrangement." The committee was authorized to fill vacancies on the national ticket, should any occur. Before the caucus adjourned, it passed a resolution defending the caucus system as "the most practicable mode of consulting and respecting the interest and wishes of all." Later caucuses adopted similar resolutions throughout the history of the system.

Still, the Democratic-Republicans suffered divisions as 40 percent of their members of Congress had refused to attend the nominating caucus. Monroe refused to withdraw from the presidential race even after his defeat in the caucus. Clinton, although nominated for vice presidency, was angry at not being nominated for president—so much so that he publicly denounced the caucus, as did Monroe's supporters. Pro-Clinton newspapers in New York launched harsh attacks on Madison and even suggested a Clinton-Monroe ticket. Some Clinton supporters went so far as to hope that Federalists would nominate Clinton for president later in the year. But such a thought was unpalatable to the Federalists, who ultimately nominated Charles Cotesworth Pinckney.

The Federalists chose their ticket at a secret meeting of party leaders in New York City in August 1808. Initially, the meeting was called by the Federalist members of the Massachusetts legislature. Twenty-five to thirty party leaders from seven states, all north of the Potomac River except South Carolina, attended the national meeting. Despite the suggestion from Massachusetts representatives that Clinton be nominated, the gathering decided to run the same ticket they had chosen in 1804: Pinckney and King.

The Federalists did not actively publicize their ticket. The party itself was divided and devoid of leadership. Indeed, many Virginia Federalists formally endorsed Monroe, even though he was a Democratic-Republican. Others preferred to align themselves with Clinton.

In the end, Madison achieved a wide margin of victory with 122 electoral votes; Pinckney came in second with 47 votes. Monroe received no electoral votes. For the sake of future party unity, Democratic-Republicans had retained Clinton as their vice-presidential nominee even though he had tried to subvert Madison's candidacy. Clinton won, receiving 113 electoral votes for vice president. He even received 6 electoral votes from New York for president.

Madison's Reelection: 1812

The winds of war were sweeping through presidential politics when Madison sought a second term in 1812. In response to constant agitation by "war hawks," the president asked Congress on June 1 for a declaration of war against Great Britain. Madison, benefiting from the public's willingness to rally in times of national emergency, swept to a second term. The Federalists did not field a candidate but supported a dissident from Madison's party.

The possibility of war had long hung over the United States. Great Britain had taken American ships captive for years—boarding the vessels, taking cargo, and intimidating seamen. Anti-British political forces also charged that the British had encouraged Native Americans in their attacks against settlers in the North and West.

The Democratic-Republican Party held its quadrennial nominating caucus on May 18, 1812. Only eighty-three of the 178 Democratic-Republicans in Congress participated. The New England and New York delegations in particular were poorly represented. Many of the New Yorkers supported the candidacy of their state's lieutenant governor, DeWitt Clinton (George Clinton's nephew), who also was maneuvering for the Federalist nomination. New England was noticeably upset with Madison's foreign policy, which was leading to war with England. Others did not attend the caucus because they opposed the system in principle.

Madison won a near-unanimous renomination in the caucus, receiving eighty-two votes. John Langdon of New Hampshire got the vice-presidential nomination by a wide margin, collecting sixty-four votes to sixteen for Gov. Elbridge Gerry of Massachusetts. But Langdon declined the nomination, citing his age (seventy) as the reason. The Democratic-Republicans held a second caucus on June 8 to select another vice-presidential candidate. Gerry was the clear winner with seventy-four votes, and he responded with a formal letter of acceptance. Ten members of Congress who had not been present at the first caucus also took the opportunity to endorse Madison's presidential candidacy.

Democratic-Republicans from New York were unwilling to accept the choice of Madison. They held their own caucus, composed of nearly all party members from the New York state legislature, where they unanimously nominated Clinton, who responded with a written "Address" that was a precursor to party platforms. Clinton won the endorsement of the Federalists as well.

As they had four years earlier, the Federalists convened a three-day secret meeting in New York City. The September meeting was more than twice the size of the 1808 gathering, with seventy representatives from eleven states attending. Delegates were sent to the conference by Federalist general committees, with all but nine of the delegates coming from the New England and Middle Atlantic states.

Debate centered on whether to run a separate Federalist ticket or to endorse Clinton. After much debate, they decided to endorse Clinton, and they nominated Jared Ingersoll of Pennsylvania for vice president. Originally, the caucus's decision was meant to be kept a secret, but leaks eventually were reported by Democratic-Republican newspapers.

The presidential election of 1812 was the first wartime contest for power in the United States. The Federalists, calling Madison a dupe of French emperor Napoleon Bonaparte, aligned themselves with the cause of peace and unimpeded commerce. In some northern states the Federalists even adopted the Peace Party label.

Despite all the opposition, President Madison beat Clinton by an electoral vote count of 128–89. The vote reflected the growing split between southern agricultural states, which supported Madison, and northern commercial states, which supported Clinton. Indeed, the common bond that held the Clinton coalition together was a hatred of Virginia—the kingmaker of the Democratic-Republican Party.

The 1812 race was the last real campaign by the Federalists. Disgraced by their obstructionist tactics during the war, isolated by their talk of secession from the Union, and unable to coordinate a national campaign, the Federalists faded from a system increasingly marked by permanent party competition.

Monroe's Victory: 1816

Monroe, President Madison's old foe who had left the Democratic-Republican Party in 1808, seemed like an unlikely presidential candidate for the party in 1816. But not only did Monroe return to the Democratic-Republican fold, he also won the White House without any opposition.

The inconclusive War of 1812 colored American politics for years. The United States and Great Britain fought to a stalemate, and then both sides offered conditions for ending the war that the other would not accept. The British, for example, demanded control over the Great Lakes and Mississippi River for commerce, as well as the creation of a

Native American state in the Northwest. In the end, both parties simply accepted the end of hostilities. An American representative said the treaty was "a truce rather than a peace."[12] Inconclusive or not, the war sparked a generation of nationalism. Rufus King revived the Federalist Party in 1816 with his race for the governorship of New York. But he lost the race and afterward found the job of maintaining the party a "fruitless struggle." Efforts were made to convene another secret meeting in Philadelphia to nominate candidates for president and vice president, yet the party held no such meeting. With the Federalists not running candidates, nomination by the Democratic-Republican caucus was tantamount to election.

Despite his opposition to Madison in 1808, Monroe had been accepted back into the Democratic-Republican fold in the years that followed. In 1811 Madison had named him secretary of state; by 1816 he was Madison's heir apparent. But many states were increasingly jealous of the Virginia dynasty that had held a grip on the presidency since 1804. Democratic-Republicans in such states opposed Monroe (himself a Virginian) and favored Secretary of War William H. Crawford of Georgia.

A Democratic-Republican caucus met in the House chamber on March 12, 1816, but only fifty-eight members of Congress—mostly Crawford supporters—attended. With the expectation of better attendance, a second caucus was held on March 16. It drew 119 of the 141 Democratic-Republicans in Congress. There, Monroe narrowly defeated Crawford by a vote of 65–54. Forty of Crawford's votes came from five states: Georgia, Kentucky, New Jersey, New York, and North Carolina. The vice-presidential nomination went to New York governor Daniel D. Tompkins, who easily outdistanced Pennsylvania governor Simon Snyder, 85–30.

The nominations of Monroe and Tompkins revived a Virginia–New York alliance that extended back to the late eighteenth century. With the lone exception of 1812, every Democratic-Republican ticket from 1800 to 1820 was composed of a presidential candidate from Virginia and a vice-presidential candidate from New York.

With the Federalist Party still in disarray, the Democratic-Republican ticket won easily. Monroe received 183 electoral votes. The three states that had chosen Federalist electors—Connecticut, Delaware, and Massachusetts—cast their 34 electoral votes for King.

Although the collapse of the Federalists ensured Democratic-Republican rule, it also increased intraparty friction and spurred further attacks on the caucus system. Twenty-two Democratic-Republican members of Congress had not attended the second party caucus, and at least fifteen were known to be opposed to the system. Mass meetings around the country protested the caucus system.[13] Opponents asserted that the writers of the Constitution did not envision the caucus, that presidential nominating should not be a function of Congress, and that the caucus system encouraged candidates to curry the favor of Congress.

Monroe's Reelection: 1820

The 1820 election took place during the "Era of Good Feeling," a phrase coined by a Boston publication, the *Columbian Centinel,* to describe a brief period of virtual one-party rule in the United States. But that phrase glosses over serious sectional divisions that were growing during Monroe's presidency. The divisions, however, did not prevent Monroe from winning another term.

Sectional strife was on the brink of eruption during Monroe's first term over the admission of Missouri as a new state. Tensions between northern and southern states had simmered for years. The emotional core of the struggle was slavery. Therefore whichever region controlled Congress might decide whether slavery was extended into new territories—and the shape of the nation's economy and culture—for years to come.

In the Senate, there was a tenuous balance between the two regions—eleven free states and eleven slave states—but the admission of Missouri threatened that balance. The two sides finally agreed to a compromise in which both Missouri and Maine would apply for statehood at the same time, Maine as a free state and Missouri as a slave state. Monroe remained neutral in the debate leading up to the compromise. Despite a financial panic in 1819, he retained overwhelming popular support, bolstered by peace and a wave of nationalistic feeling that overshadowed any partisan divisions.

While the United States struggled over the slavery issue, President Monroe embarked on a bold new foreign policy. Still smarting over the British presence in North America that had resulted in the War of 1812, the president declared that the United States would view any European attempts to colonize the Western Hemisphere as acts of hostility. The Monroe Doctrine claimed the hemisphere as the preserve of the United States. It was the boldest venture yet of the nation into foreign policy and permanently defined America's role in world affairs.

Although several rival Democratic-Republican candidates aspired to win the presidency when Monroe retired in 1824, none wanted to challenge his reelection in 1820. A nominating caucus was called for early March, but fewer than fifty of the Democratic-Republican Party's 191 members of Congress showed up. The caucus voted unanimously to make no nominations and passed a resolution explaining that it was inexpedient to do so because so few of the party's members were in attendance. Although Monroe and Tompkins were not formally renominated, electoral slates were filed in their behalf.

Because the Federalist Party was finally dead, Monroe ran virtually unopposed. Even John Adams, the last Federalist president, voted for Monroe as an elector from Massachusetts.

Only one elector, a Democratic-Republican from New Hampshire, cast a vote against Monroe, supporting instead John Quincy Adams, son of the former president.

Last of the Old Order: 1824

The 1824 election, in an odd way, represented everything that the Framers of the Constitution had hoped to see. Without a permanent party system, a number of candidates vied for the presidency. Unable to win an electoral majority, the top three finishers saw their names submitted to the House of Representatives for a final decision. The candidate representative of elite interests and sensibilities and who had House ties won.

But if the 1824 election of John Quincy Adams represented something old, it also represented something new. The popular vote winner and House loser, Andrew Jackson, protested loudly that the election had been stolen from the people. In fact, soon he would mobilize the Democratic Party around a populist rallying cry. American politics would never be the same.

In 1824, as in 1820, only one working party existed in the United States: the Democratic-Republican. But that party had an abundance of candidates competing for the presidency: Secretary of State Adams of Massachusetts, Senator Jackson of Tennessee, Secretary of War John C. Calhoun of South Carolina, House Speaker Henry Clay of Kentucky, and Secretary of the Treasury William H. Crawford. The number of candidates, coupled with the growing democratization of the U.S. political system, led to the demise of King Caucus in 1824.

Early on, Crawford was the leading candidate. He had strong southern support and appeared likely to win the support of New York's Democratic-Republicans. Because it was assumed that he would win a caucus if one were held, Crawford's opponents joined the growing list of caucus opponents. But Crawford's apparent invincibility suddenly ended in September 1823 when he suffered a paralytic stroke. Nearly blind and unable even to sign his name, he was incapacitated and stayed in seclusion for months.

In early February 1824, eleven Democratic-Republican members of Congress issued a call for a caucus to be held in the middle of the month. Their call was countered by twenty-four other members of Congress from fifteen states who deemed it "inexpedient under existing circumstances" to hold a caucus. They claimed that 181 members of Congress were resolved not to attend if a caucus were held.

The caucus convened in mid-February, but only sixty-six members of Congress showed up. Three-quarters of those attending came from just four states—Georgia, New York, North Carolina, and Virginia. Despite his illness, Crawford won the caucus nomination with sixty-four votes. Albert Gallatin of Pennsylvania was selected for vice president with fifty-seven votes. The caucus adopted a resolution defending its actions as "the best means of collecting and concentrating the feelings and wishes of the people of the Union upon this important subject." The caucus also appointed a committee to write an address to the people. As written, the text of the address viewed with alarm the "dismemberment" of the Democratic-Republican Party.

In fact, the action of the caucus just aggravated splits in the party. Because so few members of Congress attended the caucus—almost all of them Crawford supporters—opponents could argue that the choice was not even representative of the Democratic-Republicans serving in Congress. Crawford was roundly criticized as being an illegitimate candidate. His opponents derided King Caucus, and his physical condition made it even easier for them to reject his nomination. As it stood, other candidates simply refused to follow the caucus's decision. Never again were candidates chosen by the caucus system.

With the caucus devoid of power and the party lacking unity or leadership, there was no chance of rallying behind a single ticket. In addition, many political issues proved to be divisive. Western expansion and protective tariffs, for example, benefited some parts of the country but hurt others. Thus the various candidates came to represent sectional interests.

The candidates themselves recognized that such a crowded field was dangerous. The election would be thrown into the House of Representatives if no candidate received a majority. The candidates therefore made efforts to join forces. Adams tried to lure Jackson as his running mate. Adams was a short, stocky, aloof, well-educated New Englander who came from a family of Federalists, while Jackson was a tall, thin, hot-tempered war hero with little formal education who came to epitomize a new brand of populist democracy. In trying to recruit Jackson onto their team, Adams's supporters envisaged a ticket of "the writer and the fighter." Jackson would have nothing of it.

In the meantime, Crawford dropped Gallatin as his vice-presidential running mate. His supporters then tried to persuade Clay to drop his quest for the presidency and join the Crawford team. They hinted that Crawford's physical condition was such that he would probably not finish out a term of office if elected (in fact, he lived ten more years). But Clay was not swayed. Calhoun then dropped his race for the presidency and joined efforts with Jackson.

Four candidates remained in the field, and each collected electoral votes. None, however, received a majority. Jackson received the most with ninety-nine, followed by Adams with eighty-four, Crawford with forty-one, and Clay with thirty-seven. Therefore the election was thrown into the House of Representatives.

In accordance with the Twelfth Amendment, the names of the top three candidates—Jackson, Adams, and Crawford—were placed before the House. Clay, who had come in fourth and was Speaker of the House, would play a major role in tipping the balance in favor of one of the candidates.

In contrast to Jackson, Adams actively lobbied for support, and the Capitol rocked with rumors of corruption. Clay informed Adams in January that he would support the New Englander in the House election—a major blow to Jackson. Shortly thereafter, a letter in a Philadelphia newspaper alleged that Adams had offered Clay the post of secretary of state in return for his support. Adams went on to win the House election narrowly by carrying thirteen out of twenty-four state delegations. Jackson came in second with seven, and Crawford third with the remaining four. Consequently, the candidate who won the most electoral votes and the most popular votes did not win the presidency.

Jackson was furious at what he considered to be unfair bargaining between Adams and Clay. He felt that the will of the people had been thwarted, and he seethed when President Adams proceeded to name Clay secretary of state as rumor had indicated he would. In this way, the events of 1824 kindled the flame of popular democracy. The stage was set for a rematch between Adams and Jackson in 1828.

AGE OF JACKSON

Andrew Jackson was in many ways the perfect man to usher in an age of popular politics, although his rhetoric was more populist than his style of governing. The textbook version of U.S. history depicts Jackson as a coarse man of the frontier, a war hero, a battler of banks and moneyed interests, and a leader of the unschooled and exploited men who built a mass party on patronage and charismatic leadership. Jackson, from Tennessee, was the first politician to break the Virginia dynasty that had governed the country since the Revolution. After his bitter defeat in the 1824 election, Jackson fought back and grabbed the reins of government in the turbulent election of 1828. These two elections signaled the passing of elite politics and the rise of popular politics. In 1828 Jackson roused the people to turn Adams and his aristocratic clique out of office.

But the Jacksonian folklore has serious flaws. Jackson traveled in elite business circles, for example, and one of his greatest contributions as president was the creation of a more rationally organized bureaucracy.[14] Still, the textbook depiction of Jackson suffices to show some trends in U.S. politics, including the development of a stable mass party system, sectionalism, urbanization, and shifts in the debate about U.S. expansionism.

While President John Quincy Adams was struggling with warring factions in Washington, an opposition force was gathering strength and, in fact, was able to deal the president a number of humiliating defeats. Adams's desire for a national program of roads and canals, education, and

After losing the election of 1824 to John Quincy Adams, Andrew Jackson soundly defeated Adams in 1828. A hero of the 1812 Battle of New Orleans, Jackson held strong appeal to the common man.

research in the arts and sciences antagonized even the most nationalistic groups in the country. U.S. participation in a conference of countries from the Western Hemisphere and the imposition of a tariff (a tax on imported goods designed either to raise revenues or to protect domestic industries from foreign competition) also were divisive issues. But even though Adams was under constant personal attack, the opposition was divided on the same issues. The opposition was united, however, behind "Old Hickory."[15]

Jackson, hero of the Battle of New Orleans in the War of 1812, had a strong appeal to the common man even though he traveled in the circles of southern gentlemen. People who met with Jackson talked of his unerring "intuition" about people and politics. Jackson's decision to push for reforms of the punishment of debtors was an important gesture to small businesspeople and workers who were held to a kind of indentured servitude to their creditors. Sen. Martin Van Buren of New York, Jackson's strongest supporter in the Northeast, said the people "were his blood relations—the only blood relations he had."[16]

Jackson's First Victory: 1828

Jackson and his running mate, John C. Calhoun, easily beat Adams in their 1828 rematch; Jackson won 178 electoral votes, and Adams won 83. (Calhoun also had been vice president under John Quincy Adams.) Of the popular vote, Jackson received 643,000 votes (56.0 percent) to Adams's 501,000 (43.6 percent). Sectional splits showed in the vote distribution. Adams held all but 1 of New England's electoral votes, all of Delaware's and New Jersey's, 16 of New York's 36 votes, and 6 of Maryland's 11 votes. Jackson took all the rest—the South and the West. The election, then, was decided by the newly enfranchised voters in the burgeoning regions of the country. The U.S. electorate, however, was expanding not only in the West but also in the original states. Between 1824 and 1856 voter participation grew from 3.8 percent to 16.7 percent of the total population.[17]

Jackson had only begun to exert electoral influence with his revenge victory over Adams. The expanded pool of politically involved citizens that had brought Jackson victory also brought him demands for patronage jobs with the federal government. Van Buren, a master machine politician from New York State, tutored the beleaguered new president in dealing with the office seekers. Jackson replaced fewer than one-fifth of the government's employees, which he defended as a perfectly reasonable "rotation in office" that would keep the ranks of the bureaucracy fresh. But the effect of his system was greater. Appointees of previous administrations were able to retain their jobs only when they expressed loyalty to Jackson and his party. Far more important than any government turnover, Jackson's spoils system inaugurated an age in which mass party loyalty was a paramount concern in politics.

The increased importance of loyalty, to the president and to the party, became clear with Jackson's dispute with Vice President Calhoun and the subsequent purging of the cabinet. A growing feud between Jackson and Calhoun came to a head when a personal letter in which Calhoun criticized Jackson's conduct of the Seminole Indian campaign and the 1818 invasion of Florida became public. In a letter to Calhoun during the cabinet crisis, Jackson wrote: "Et tu, Brute." A purge of Calhoun men in the cabinet followed the incident. Secretary of State Van Buren enabled the president to make the purge when he and Secretary of War John Eaton, both Jackson allies, resigned their posts; the president then called on the whole cabinet to quit.

The central element of the Jacksonian program was expansion. Much like twentieth-century politicians who would talk about economic growth as the key to opportunity, Jackson maintained that movement West "enlarg[ed] the area of freedom."[18] The administration fought to decentralize the management of expansion. Jackson railed against the "corrupt bargain" between the government and banks, joint-stock companies, and monopolies, which, he said, were squeezing out the average person seeking opportunity.

Indeed, Jackson opposed the Bank of the United States and promoted state banks because of his desire to free finance capital from central control. In his first term, the president carried on a long-running battle with Nicholas Biddle, the head of the Bank of the United States, and with Congress over the status of the bank. Alexander Hamilton

This 1836 cartoon depicts Jackson attacking the Bank of the United States with his veto stick. Vice President Van Buren, center, helps to kill the monster, whose heads represent Nicholas Biddle, president of the bank, and directors of the state branches.

had created the bank to manage the nation's monetary policy and investment, but Jackson opposed it as a tool of the eastern financial establishment. Jackson may have failed to close the bank, but he did manage to strip it of much of its basic authority and functions by placing its deposits in a number of regional institutions.

Jackson's presidency was activist from the beginning. His administration negotiated treaties with France, the Ottoman Empire, Russia, and Mexico. Jackson himself established a distinctive interpretation of federalism when he vetoed a number of public improvement bills as unconstitutional infringements of local affairs. He also called for a tariff that would yield revenues for dispersal to the states for their public projects—an early form of "revenue sharing." Jackson also signed the Indian Removal Act of 1830, which provided for settlement of the territory west of the Mississippi River. Late in his first term, Jackson's strong stand defeated the South Carolina legislature's claim that it could "nullify," or declare "null and void," federal tariff legislation that the state disliked.

Jackson's Reelection: 1832

There was never any doubt that Jackson would be renominated in 1832; in fact, several state legislatures endorsed him before the convention. Jackson's political strength was also underscored with the introduction of a quintessentially party-oriented institution: the national party convention. Jacksonians from New Hampshire proposed the Democratic convention of 1832, and the president and his advisers jumped at the opportunity. The only previous national convention had been held by the Anti-Masonic Party in 1831. Conventions had been the principal means of selecting candidates for local offices since the early part of the century. Especially when compared with the caucus system that preceded it, the convention system was a democratic leap forward.

The convention system enabled the parties to gather partisans from all geographic areas, and it welded them together as a cohesive unit that ultimately was accountable to the electorate, if only in a plebiscitary way. Voters had the opportunity to give approval or disapproval to a party program with one vote. Historian Eugene H. Roseboom has written: "It was representative in character; it divorced nominations from congressional control and added to the independence of the executive; it permitted an authoritative formulation of a party program; and it concentrated the party's strength behind a single ticket, the product of compromise of personal rivalries and group or sectional interests."[19]

Given Jackson's popularity in 1832, the purpose of the convention was to rally behind the president and select a new vice-presidential candidate. Van Buren got the nomination, despite lingering resistance from Calhoun supporters and various "favorite sons" (prominent state and local leaders of state party organizations).

As in 1828, Jackson's political opposition was fragmented. The Whigs—the opposition party that had developed from grassroots protests in the North and West against Jackson's tariff and development policies—held their national convention in Baltimore in December 1831 and unanimously nominated Henry Clay of Kentucky for president. Eighteen states used a variety of selection procedures to determine who would be their convention delegates. The party's platform sharply criticized the Jackson administration's patronage practices, relations with Great Britain, and ill-tempered congressional relations, as well as Supreme Court decisions.

In the election, the incumbent easily dispatched the opposition. "The news from the voting states blows over us like a great cold storm," wrote Rufus Choate, a prominent lawyer, to a friend.[20] Despite last-minute maneuvering to unite the opposition to Jackson and a well-financed campaign by the Bank of the United States, the president won 219 electoral votes to Clay's 49, Independent John Floyd's 11, and Anti-Mason William Wirt's 7. Jackson won all but seven states. Clay won Kentucky, Massachusetts, Rhode Island, Connecticut, and Delaware, plus five electors from Maryland. Jackson won 702,000 popular votes to Clay's 484,000 and Wirt's 101,000.[21]

Jackson, who finally left the political stage in 1837, changed the face of U.S. politics. Even if his pretensions to being an everyman were overstated, he opened up the system to mass participation, and he forced politicians to listen to popular demands. He developed the notion of a strong party organization. He fought, and eventually defeated, the national bank by withdrawing its funds and placing them in state banks. He strongly opposed two forces that could have torn the nation apart—the nullification principle of state sovereignty and the Supreme Court's bid for broader discretion over political issues (that is, to review legislation and state actions)—by simply proclaiming the law to be "unauthorized by the Constitution" and "therefore null and void."

Van Buren's Win: 1836

Many historians consider the election of 1836 to be the most important event in the development of the party system. Van Buren, a Democratic follower of Jackson and a theorist on the role of political parties in a democratic system, easily won the election against an uncoordinated Whig Party. The defeat eventually persuaded Whig leaders of the need for a permanent organization for political competition. The emergence of two permanent parties extinguished the American suspicion of the morality of a party system based on unabashed competition for the levers of power.

Van Buren, who had allied with Jackson during the cabinet controversies and promoted his philosophy of parties and patronage, received the Democratic nomination in 1836 at a convention packed with Jackson administration appointees. The vice-presidential nomination of Richard M. Johnson of Kentucky, whose earlier relationship with a mulatto woman caused controversy, damaged the ticket in the South, but the Democrats won anyway.

The Whigs' campaign strategy was to run several favorite sons to prevent any candidate from getting a majority of the electoral votes, thereby throwing the election into the House of Representatives. As one Whig put it: "The disease [Democratic rule] is to be treated as a local disorder—apply local remedies."[22] The Whig expectation was that one of two favorite sons—Gen. William Henry Harrison of Ohio or Hugh Lawson White of Tennessee—would be selected by the House after the electoral college vote proved inconclusive.

Van Buren, however, had Jackson's machine and his personal backing and was able to overcome the Whigs' local strategy. Thus in this race, the last for the White House before presidential elections became dominated by two national parties, Van Buren took 170 electoral votes—22 more than he needed for election. Of the Whig candidates, Harrison received 73 electoral votes; White, 26; and Daniel Webster of Massachusetts, 14. Willie Mangum, an Independent Democrat from North Carolina, received 11 electoral votes from the South Carolina legislature, which was hostile to White because of his role in nullification politics. Van Buren won 764,000 popular votes (50.8 percent); Harrison, 551,000 (36.6 percent); White, 146,000 (9.7 percent); and Webster, 41,000 (2.7 percent). For the only time in history, the Senate selected the vice president, Van Buren's running mate Johnson, who had fallen one vote shy of election by the electoral college. In the Senate, Johnson defeated Francis Granger by a 33–16 vote.

Van Buren was besieged with problems practically from the minute he took the oath of office in March 1837. About midway through his term, the economy crashed after years of feverish business growth, overspeculation in land and business, huge private debt accumulation, and unregulated financial and trade practices. Van Buren's approach to the economic crisis alternated between stubborn refusal to fix a mess that he had not created and action that was guaranteed to antagonize key interest groups.

When Van Buren moved to create an independent treasury to insulate the federal government from state financial institutions, he was opposed by conservative Democrats who were supporters of the state financial institutions that Jackson had promoted in his legendary national bank battles. When Van Buren was not hit from the right, he was hit from the left. The nascent labor movement called for protection of jobs and wages and made protests against monopoly and privilege.

IDEA OF A PARTY SYSTEM

Whatever problems Martin Van Buren had in governing, he should receive credit at least for helping to establish the principle of party government in the United States. That principle, much derided in the early days of the nation's history, now enjoys widespread allegiance.

Van Buren's arguments for a party system—contained in his book, *An Inquiry into the Origin and Course of Political Parties in the United States*—were similar to the economic principle of Adam Smith, which had held that the pursuit of selfish ends redounded to the good of the entire community. American leaders from George Washington through John Quincy Adams had believed that self-interested factions endangered the functioning and virtue of the Republic. These leaders also had warned against the dangers of democracy, which they often called "mob rule." In the worst possible scenario, permanent parties with strong ideological stances appealed to the mass public for support, undermining the ability of national leaders to guide public virtue.[23]

The basic tension that Van Buren had to resolve was the system's need for stability and responsible leadership and the parties' imperative to gain office. How could a party's selfish desire to run the government and award patronage and contracts to political allies benefit the whole system?

Van Buren argued that the absence of parties—that is, collections of people from disparate backgrounds—resulted in a system of personal politics that fueled demagogy, perpetual campaigns, and a lack of accountability. Personal presidential politics was more polarizing than the politics of consensus or of coalition building. Presidents should be able to do their job without constant carping from outsiders who fancied themselves prospective presidents. Mass parties with certain partisan principles would enable presidents to get the backing they needed to do their work.

Moreover the existence of two parties would enable the nation to move beyond its many cleavages—that is, toward the general interest and away from simple clashes of particular interests. Competition among parties, like competition among economic enterprises, would bring about a situation in which disparate demands would be promoted by a party. The key was to achieve a balance of competing forces. Summarizing Van Buren, political scientist James W. Ceaser has written:

> Established parties ... may stand "over" the raw electoral cleavages, possessing some leeway or discretion about which potential issues and electoral divisions will be emphasized and which will be suppressed or kept at the fringes. This discretion is exercised according to the interests of the organizations and the judgement of their leaders. But it is important to keep in mind that the degree of this discretion is limited.... Their discretion is always threatened or held in check by the possibility that they might be displaced by a new party having as its goal the advancement of a certain policy.... When a sufficiently powerful and enduring issue exists, an impartial reading of American party history suggests that the party system in the end will have to respond to it, regardless of how the established parties initially react.[24]

The Age of Jackson brought a fundamental shift from republican to democratic values as the nation's territory and activities expanded. Republicanism was the product of a variety of strains of thought—from the Romans Cicero and Tacitus and the Greek Polybius to the Frenchman Charles Montesquieu—that stressed the need for a balancing of interests to produce public virtue. Republicans worried about excess in any single form of governance, particularly "mob rule." For them, *democracy* was a term of derision. That is why the Constitution contained many buffers against this and other forms of excess.

Republicanism declined in many stages. A greater stress on the individual's role in society, embodied in the work of Adam Smith and David Hume, restricted the kinds of issues open to public deliberation. At the same time, the pace of economic change undermined established patterns. As the nation demanded large-scale projects (such as canals and railways), and as rival factions looked to the mobilization of larger and larger parts of the electorate to augment their strength, democratic rhetoric gained respectability. Mass party participation became a vehicle for pursuing civic virtue and balance, and the notion of a constant opposition party gained strength. If the democratic process had enough constitutional "checks," political thinkers now reasoned, the harmful "mob" aspects of democracy could be tempered. The development of the Jacksonian party as a way of arbitrating interests was the final stage in republican decline and democratic ascendance.

Political scientist Russell Hanson has noted that the new democratic ethos sprang from one of the same goals as the old republican ethos: development of a public spirit by rising above particular restraints. "Support for popular sovereignty became the lowest common denominator for a Democratic Party composed of interests seeking liberation from a variety of sectionally specific restraints on the 'will of the people.'"[25]

A two-party system persisted as the nation drifted toward civil war, but it was not a simple two-party system. The Democrats and Whigs competed for the presidency and other political offices until 1856, when the Republican Party fielded its first national ticket and made the Whigs obsolete. But the parties were so unstable that their many elements were constantly forming and breaking up coalitions—and threatening to bolt from the system itself. Moreover, a series of third parties entered the national electoral arena for short periods, applying or relieving pressures on the two major parties.[26]

Only by examining the parties and their various factions and struggles can one understand the presidential contests in the two decades before the Civil War, and the way that the Civil War revealed the basic fault lines of U.S. politics.

The Whigs' Victory: 1840

The Whigs developed to fill the role of their British namesake, which had been to mount a republican opposition to the royal ruling power. When the rise of Andrew Jackson and his supposedly imperial presidency threatened the "balance" of the United States, the Whigs rose to restore that balance. The Whigs saw Jackson's Democrats as a faction of the most dangerous variety—a majority faction that had the ability to trample liberties in its mad scramble for spoils.

The key to Whiggery was the notion of balanced development. The Whigs opposed the war with Mexico and other expansionist programs because they feared the perils of overextending the nation's abilities and getting entangled with foreign powers. They favored internal improvements, but only as a way of maintaining balance and staving off the corruption of the Jackson era. The protective tariff was central to the Whigs' program of internal development and protection from outsiders. According to Hanson,

> Even in America, which was uniquely blessed by an abundance of natural resources and a citizenry of hardy stock, there was need for informed guidance and direction of progress. For the Whigs, government was the primary agent of this progress. Government represented a strong and positive force to be used in calling forth a richer society from the unsettled possibilities of America. In the economic realm this meant that government was responsible for providing the essential conditions for a sound economy, namely, a reliable currency, ample credit, and the impetus for internal improvements. In the social realm, the government was responsible for promoting virtue in its citizenry through education and exhortation.[27]

The Whigs' desire for balance and compromise was intended to give the party a national rather than a sectional identity. Moreover, their tendency to nominate widely popular military heroes helped to create at least the illusion of a party of national dimensions. A series of Senate battles with President Jackson, especially the tariff battles of 1833, which resulted in an unsatisfying compromise, gave impetus to grassroots organizations in the North and West and to Southern Democratic opponents. In fact, the Whigs developed first in the South where voters were dissatisfied with Jackson's selection of Van Buren as his running mate. There, loose coalitions elected candidates in the 1834 and 1835 state and congressional elections. Westerners also organized to oppose the Democratic Party, which was headed by a New Yorker.

The first serious Whig presidential contest was a loss, but an encouraging one. In 1836 the Whig tickets headed by William Henry Harrison and others had shown surprising appeal in the loss to the Democrat Van Buren. The Whigs had won Jackson's home state of Tennessee and neighboring Georgia, as well as three border slave states, and were strong competitors elsewhere. Harrison had carried the old North-west (now the Midwest) and had come close in northern states such as Pennsylvania.

Because of the rise of the antislavery "conscience Whigs," the Whigs eventually moved to a completely different base of support—the North rather than the South and West—but their early organizing at least broke the Democratic stranglehold on the latter two regions. The Whigs nominated Harrison in 1840 after a nomination struggle with Henry Clay. A Clay supporter, John Tyler of Virginia, was the vice-presidential nominee. This time, the popular if politically inexperienced hero of the War of 1812 won his ticket to the White House. Harrison defeated the incumbent Van Buren in an electoral vote landslide, receiving 234 of the 294 electoral votes—all the states except Alabama, Arkansas, Illinois, Missouri, New Hampshire, South Carolina, and Virginia. For the popular vote, Harrison won 1.3 million (52.9 percent) to Van Buren's 1.1 million (46.8 percent).

According to political scientist Richard P. McCormick,

> The campaign of 1840 brought the American party system at last to fruition. In every region of the country, and indeed in every state, politics was conducted within the framework of a two-party system, and in all but a handful of states the parties were so closely balanced as to be competitive. In broad terms, it was the contest for the presidency that shaped this party system and defined its essential purpose.[28]

Harrison's campaign was as vague as his government experience was unimpressive. The image of Harrison as a sort of frontier everyman—which received its popular expression when a Baltimore newspaper mocked him as a sedentary man who would sit in a log cabin and drink cider rather than perform great deeds of leadership—was the theme of numerous parades and mass meetings. On issues from banking and currency to slavery, Harrison spoke in generalities. Harrison's strategist acknowledged that he advised the candidate to "say not a single word about his principles or creed. Let him say nothing—promise nothing."[29]

As it happened, Harrison did not have an opportunity to do much as president besides discipline the aggressive Clay. Clay had assumed that he and the rest of the congressional leadership would play the leading role in the government, but Harrison quickly dispelled that notion in a note rebuking him. But one month after his inauguration, the sixty-eight-year-old Harrison developed pneumonia and died. On April 6, 1841, the burdens of the presidency fell on Vice President Tyler, who became the first to assume the office after the death of a president.

The rift between the White House and Congress widened under Tyler. Clay acted as if he were prime minister during a special session of Congress, pushing through a legislative program that included a recharter of the long-controversial Bank of the United States, higher import taxes, and distribution of proceeds from land sales to the states. Tyler, a lifetime states' rights advocate, vetoed two bills for a national bank, and the Whigs in Congress and his cabinet began a bitter feud with the president. In 1842 Clay left the Senate to promote his presidential aspirations, and everyone in the cabinet except Secretary of State Daniel Webster quit. Tyler was all alone, but he did manage to defeat the Whig program in his four years as president.

Polk's Dark-Horse Victory: 1844

The Democrats were transformed into a well-organized party by Jackson and Van Buren between 1828 and 1836. But, as with the Whigs, the Democratic Party became vulnerable because of the irreconcilable differences among many of its parts.

From the beginning, the Democratic Party had contained contradictory elements. According to political scientist James L. Sundquist: "The party had been formed originally as an alliance between Southern planters and New Yorkers and had always spanned both regions. Northern men of abolitionist sympathies were accustomed to sitting with slaveholders in presidential cabinets and collaborating with them in the halls of Congress."[30] But northern Democrats went so far as to organize antiabolitionist rallies in their cities and towns, and newspapers and churches also defended slavery.

The deepest Democratic divisions—which eventually would lead to the failure not only of the party but also of the nation—were the regional differences based on slavery. But other, more complex divisions also affected the operation of the Democratic Party. When the party was able to reconcile or even delay action on the divisive issues, it won. When the divisions burst into the open, the party was in trouble.

James K. Polk of Tennessee, the first "dark-horse" candidate in history, defeated the Whig Henry Clay in 1844 by supporting an expansionist program and winning the support of the solid South. One of the key issues in the campaign was whether Texas should be admitted to the Union and, if so, whether it should be a slave or free state. President Van Buren in 1840 had opposed annexation—opposition that may have cost him the presidency—and the Democrats and Whigs hedged on the issue for the next eight years. In 1844 Polk endorsed the annexation of Texas as a slave state; that was enough for him to lock up the South.

During the 1844 nominating convention, the Democrats finessed the sectional dangers of the Texas issue by combining it with a call for occupying Oregon and eventually bringing that state into the Union. The Democrats also appealed to Pennsylvania and the rest of the Northeast by supporting a high tariff. Both parties spoke out against the growing foreign elements in the cities, but the Whigs were more effective because of the Democrats' swelling immigrant ranks.

In the election, the Democrat Polk defeated the Whig Clay, winning 1.34 million votes (49.5 percent) to Clay's 1.30 million (48.1 percent) and 170 electoral votes to Clay's 105. Clay received his strongest support from five northeastern states and five border slave states. Of the expansionist Northwest, only Ohio fell in the Clay column.

The Liberty Party—an abolitionist party formed out of more than two hundred antislavery societies in time for the 1840 election—may have been the deciding factor in the 1844 race. Although the party received only 2.3 percent of the popular vote and no electoral votes, it was strong enough in New York to prevent the Whigs from winning that state's crucial thirty-six electoral votes. Those votes went to the Democrat Polk rather than to the Whig Clay.

The depth of the Democrats' divisions were agonizingly evident even when the party won elections and started to pass out spoils and make policy. Like Harrison, the Whig who had won the presidency four years before, President Polk faced the antagonisms of party factions when he began making appointments after his 1844 win. Westerners were angry when they were shut out of the cabinet and Polk vetoed a rivers and harbors bill. Supporters of both Van Buren and John Calhoun were angry that their faction did not win more prominent positions. Northeasterners were upset at tariff cuts. The New York split between the reformist "Barnburners" and the party-regular "Hunkers"—who disagreed on every issue, including banks, currency, internal improvements, and political reforms—also disrupted the administration.

Creating still more dissension was the war with Mexico (1846–1848), fought because of the dispute over the Texas border and the possible annexation of California. Northerners resented the country's fighting Mexico over a slave state.

Whig Success under Taylor: 1848

In 1848 the Whigs recaptured the White House behind another military hero, Gen. Zachary Taylor, who was vague on most political issues. Hailing from Louisiana, where he was a slave owner, Taylor defeated the irrepressible Clay and Gen. Winfield Scott for the nomination on the fourth convention ballot. His running mate was New Yorker Millard Fillmore. Clay mounted an impressive public campaign that drew large crowds, but the Whigs had lost too many times with Clay.

The Whigs were so determined to avoid sectional and other splits that they not only nominated the popular Taylor but also eschewed writing a platform. Despite such extreme measures to maintain unity, the convention was disturbed by squabbles between pro- and antislavery forces on the question of the Wilmot Proviso, which would ban slavery in any territory the United States obtained from Mexico.

At the Democratic national convention, Sen. Lewis Cass of Michigan defeated Sen. James Buchanan of Pennsylvania and Supreme Court Justice Levi Woodbury for the presidential nomination, and Gen. William Butler was picked as his running mate. (The Democratic incumbent Polk had declared after taking his office that he would not seek a second term.) But the convention experienced splits between two New York factions: the Barnburners, who were part of the antislavery movement, and the more conservative Hunkers, who had ties to Southerners. The Barnburners finally defected from the party to become part of the Free Soil Party.

The Democrats behind Cass praised the administration of the beleaguered Polk, defended the war with Mexico, congratulated the French Republic that emerged from the wave of revolution in Europe, and did everything it could to avoid the nasty slavery issue. The nomination of Cass—a "doughface," or northerner with southern principles—was expected to appeal to both sides of the simmering issue.

But Taylor defeated Cass, winning 1.4 million popular votes (47.3 percent) to Cass's 1.2 million (42.5 percent). New York Democrat Van Buren, the former president, running on the Free Soil ticket, won 291,500 votes (10 percent) but no electoral votes. Taylor received 163 electoral votes to Cass's 127, with a strong showing in the North. Taylor won Connecticut, Massachusetts, New Jersey, New York, Pennsylvania, Rhode Island, and Vermont in the North; Delaware, Kentucky, Maryland, North Carolina, and Tennessee in the border states; and Florida, Georgia, and Louisiana in the Deep South. This combination was enough to beat Cass's coalition of seven slave states, six northwestern states, and two New England states.

On July 10, 1850, Fillmore succeeded to the presidency when Taylor died suddenly. After consuming too many refreshments at a Fourth of July celebration, Taylor had developed cramps and then a fatal illness, probably typhoid fever.

Despite this turn of events, Fillmore was unable to secure the party nomination two years later, in 1852, although he had an early lead in convention polling. Gen. Scott won the nomination, and the Whigs entered into permanent decline.

SLAVERY DIVIDES THE NATION

The Whigs' electoral strategy with dealing with the nation's disagreements was to select military heroes as candidates and take vague stances on issues. When divisive issues erupted, however, the party suffered.

The tariff issue and their mildly probusiness stance gave the Whigs strength in the North. But, like the Democrats, they also needed to attract support in the South—a goal they sought by trying to keep the slavery question out of their rhetoric. The Whigs could count on being competitive in the border slave states but not in the rest of Dixie. In 1844 Henry Clay had won only the northern rim of slave states (Delaware, Kentucky, Maryland, North Carolina, and Tennessee).

The abolitionist movement, which may be dated to the founding of William Lloyd Garrison's newspaper, the *Liberator,* in 1831, posed problems for the Whigs that eventually proved fatal. The antislavery belt developed in the Whigs' strongest territory—New England—and westward into the modern-day Midwest. Abolitionism was largely an upper- or middle-class and religious cause. But it also became a partisan issue: the Whigs, the party out of power for years, needed an issue with which to confront the Democrats, and slavery was a useful one, even if the Whigs' antislavery stance in the North contradicted their accommodating stance in the South.

As Sundquist has noted, both the Whig and Democratic parties in the pre–Civil War era attempted to ignore the slavery issue, but the Whigs had less room to maneuver. The Democrats' agrarian and populist position gave them the solid South as a foundation, and they could make a variety of antiabolitionist appeals to the rest of the electorate. Democrats could argue that their support for slavery in the South was compatible with their many "moderate" positions. The appeal of Senators Stephen A. Douglas of Illinois and James Buchanan rested on such a coalition-building strategy. The Whigs, however, included vociferous opponents of slavery who could not be reconciled easily with "moderate" positions. Abolitionism had upper-class and religious roots that were difficult to use as a foundation. The support the Whigs were able to retain in the South was based on their positions on local issues. In sum, the Whigs did not have the same potential to build a national party organization as the Democrats.

Because both parties contained slavery sympathizers and opponents, neither was willing to take a principled stand against the institution, particularly where it already existed. This was not the case, however, for issues such as westward expansion, banking questions, public improvements, the tariff, and foreign relations, where their differences were more evident. But third parties such as the Liberty and Free Soil parties had no such hesitations about pressing the slavery issue. In fact, sectional cleavages were so strong that in 1836 Congress passed a "gag rule" that forbade the reading of antislavery statements in Congress. Such attempts to silence abolitionist fervor were in vain, however, because politics was entering an age of mass communication and organization. The slavery issue would become irrepressible.

The slavery issue split the Whigs badly with the controversy over the admission of Texas to the Union in 1845. A splinter group of young party members calling themselves the "Conscience Whigs" argued for a straightforward statement of principle against slavery. An opposition group, "Cotton Whigs," wanted to defuse the slavery issue by ignoring moral arguments and simply calling for a halt to annexation. The party split became complete with Clay's Compromise of 1850, which admitted California as a free state, ended slave trade in the District of Columbia, and admitted Texas but reduced its size by splitting off the New Mexico territory. After agitation from Conscience Whigs and General Winfield Scott's nomination in 1852, the party was irreparably rent by the slavery issue.

The 1852 Whig convention platform contained several statements supporting states' rights and the principles behind Clay's compromise[31]—concessions made by northern Whigs to win southern support for their presidential favorite, General Scott. But when no Whigs voted for the Kansas-Nebraska Act in 1854, which permitted new states to determine individually the slavery question, the Whigs' remaining ties to Dixie were severed.

The Whigs' strength in the Northwest was almost nonexistent. Only Ohio, in 1844, went for the Whigs even once over the course of the 1844, 1848, and 1852 presidential elections. Previously strong ties between the "lake region" and the South deteriorated as immigrants and others moved from the Northeast to the Northwest and, after the completion of railroad links, the two regions developed strong economic ties.

The Whigs' last gasp came in 1852, when Scott was demolished by Democrat Franklin Pierce, who won all thirty-one states except two in New England (Massachusetts and Vermont) and two border states (Kentucky and Tennessee). In 1856 the Whigs split their votes among Democrat Buchanan, former Whig Millard Fillmore, and Republican John C. Fremont. At that time, not all Whigs were ready yet to join the nascent Republican Party because of the extremism of some of the party's abolitionists. But the majority of Whigs folded into the Republicans in 1860 when Republican presidential candidate Abraham Lincoln avoided a white "backlash" by insisting that he supported slavery where it existed and opposed its spread only because of how it would affect the economic fortunes of poor northern whites.

The Democrats suffered a North-South cleavage that Lincoln exploited in the 1860 election against Douglas. Southern Democrats were intent on protecting slavery, and control of Congress was necessary to their strategy. They believed that extension of slavery to the new states joining the Union was needed to maintain their congressional strength. In short, the extension of slavery was the issue that most divided the Democratic Party.

Northern Democrats were willing to allow Dixie to maintain its peculiar institution but were scared about their electoral prospects if slavery should expand. At first they rallied to Douglas's doctrine of "popular sovereignty" (under which the people of new states could decide whether to adopt slavery), but they became nervous when Lincoln hammered away at his argument that any unchecked slavery threatened the freedom of whites as well as blacks. Lincoln argued that Democrats such as Douglas wanted to make slavery a national, rather than an individual state, institution.

Lincoln planted seeds of doubt about partial solutions to the slavery extension question by asserting that slavery could extend to whites if it were nationalized: "If free negroes should be made *things*, how long, think you, before they will begin to make *things* out of poor white men?"[32] Lincoln also maintained that the extension of slavery into new territories would close off those areas for whites seeking upward mobility: "The whole nation is interested that the best use be made of these Territories. We want them for homes of free white people. This they cannot be, to any considerable extent, if slavery shall be planted within them."[33]

Following Lincoln's lead, the growing movement against the extension of slavery was based on a concern for the upward mobility of labor. Rather than stressing the common interests of blacks and poor, northern, white laborers, the antiextension movement played up the competition between the two groups. Horace Greeley's vision of the frontier as "the great regulator of the relations of Labor and Capital, the safety valve of our industrial and social engine" left little room for the extension of slavery into the new territories.[34]

Democrat Pierce's Victory: 1852

Clay's congressional compromise on slavery in the territories, known as the Compromise of 1850, turned out to be the major reason for the Democrats' 1852 victory. The compromise addressed the slavery question in all of the new U.S. territories by making concessions to both sides of the struggle. For the North, California would be admitted as a free state, and the slave trade (but not slavery itself) would be abolished in the District of Columbia. For the South, fugitive slave laws would be strengthened, and the New Mexico territory would be divided into two states where the voters, exercising popular sovereignty, would decide the slave issue.

The compromise was designed to settle the issue of slavery in new territories once and for all. But the slavery issue could not be contained by region; it had an increasingly important "spillover" effect. Because of concerns about the congressional balance of power and the difficulties of enforcing slavery provisions such as the fugitive slave law in states that opposed slavery, it was impossible to isolate the slavery question into particular regions as Clay intended.

President Zachary Taylor had stalled action on the compromise for months and even suggested that California and New Mexico might become independent nations. But his successor, Fillmore, had thrown his support behind the compromise. The Whigs were divided on the proposal.

General Scott won the Whig nomination in 1852 after platform concessions to the party's southern delegation. Scott's appeal was always limited to the North, while Fillmore appealed to the South and Daniel Webster appealed to New England. Scott won on the fifty-third ballot.

Pierce, governor of New Hampshire, a dark-horse candidate who gained fame with his Mexican War record, won the Democratic nomination in 1852. His vice-presidential running mate was Sen. William Rufus de Vane King of Alabama. The party held together a coalition of groups with contradictory positions on the slavery issue and regional affairs. The convention, meeting in Baltimore, pledged to "abide by, and adhere to" Clay's compromise and to do what it could to smother the slavery issue.

Attempts to inject issues of economics and foreign affairs into the election failed, and the campaign degenerated into squabbles over personalities. Pierce easily won with 1.6 million popular votes (50.8 percent) to Scott's 1.4 million (43.9 percent). Pierce carried twenty-seven states and 254 electoral votes to Scott's four states and 42 electoral votes. Free-Soil candidate John P. Hale took 4.9 percent of the popular vote and won no electoral votes.

The Democrats' Bruising Victory: 1856

By 1856 the national parties were coming apart. The North-South split had eliminated the Whigs as a national party and was rendering the Democrats into two camps, damaging the party's chances for winning national elections in the decades ahead. A new national party, the Republican Party, emerged from the remnants of the Whigs and dissatisfied members of other factions.

Congress had opened the slavery issue by passing the Kansas-Nebraska Act of 1854. The act declared "null and void" the Missouri Compromise of 1820, which had prohibited slavery in new territories north of the 36"30' parallel except in Missouri. The 1854 legislation created two territories (Kansas and Nebraska) from the original Nebraska territory and left the slavery issue to be determined by popular sovereignty there and in the Utah and New Mexico territories.

The Kansas-Nebraska Act was a vehicle to spur the development of the West. Such development was part of a long-standing American approach to creating opportunity and freedom via growth. Senator Douglas of Illinois—the promoter of the law and the main advocate of popular sovereignty—held that the law was necessary if the country was to be bound together by rail and telegraph lines and was to drive Great Britain from the continent. The latter goal was based on the widely held suspicion that Britain was exploiting the slavery issue to distract American politics and stunt the growth of the nation.

Whatever the economic motives for unification, the Kansas-Nebraska Act was bitterly divisive. Northern state legislatures passed resolutions denouncing the law. The development of sectional parties continued. A flood of new settlers into Kansas, and the violence that accompanied balloting over whether Kansas was to be a free or a slave state, further inflamed passions. Neighboring Missourians took part in the controversy, arguing that their status as slave owners would be undermined if Kansas voted to be free.

After an 1854 meeting in Ripon, Wisconsin, where the party was first proposed, the Republican Party developed quickly. The Republicans had developed a strong grassroots organization in the Northwest after the Kansas-Nebraska Act passed in 1854 and attracted disgruntled abolitionists, Whigs, Know-Nothings, Northern Democrats, and members of the Liberty and Free Soil parties who were troubled by the possible extension of slavery. Uncertainty about how the extension of slavery would affect laborers who sought opportunity in the territories also helped to unite the new coalition.

The first Republican nominating convention met in Philadelphia in 1856 with delegates from all of the free states, four border states, three territories, and the District of Columbia. The party's opposition to slavery was far from unanimous, but its willingness to address rather than suppress the issue enabled it to redefine the political dialogue. Besides strong antislavery statements, the party platform contained proposals for several internal improvements advantageous to the North. The party did not offer anything to the solidly Democratic South. To win a national election, it would have to sweep the North. Col. John Charles Fremont was named the Republicans' first presidential candidate. Former Whig senator William Dayton of New Jersey received the vice-presidential nomination.

The Democrats, in endorsing the Kansas-Nebraska Act in 1856, continued rapidly on the path of becoming a southern party. Meeting in Cincinnati, Ohio, after seventeen roll-call votes, the party nominated the pro-South Buchanan as presidential candidate. John Breckinridge of Kentucky, who later served as a Confederate general, was Buchanan's running mate. The Democrats' platform stressed limited federal government and sought compromises on slavery. Benefiting from close wins in Buchanan's home state of Pennsylvania and in New Jersey, and in western states such as Illinois, Indiana, and California, the Democrats won the White House. But the only strong region for the Democrats was the South. Buchanan won all the slave states except Maryland. Overall, Buchanan won 1.8 million popular votes (45.3 percent) to Fremont's 1.3 million (33.1 percent). The electoral college gave Buchanan a 174–114 victory.

The nativist American Party—or the "Know-Nothings," as they were called—nominated former Whig president Fillmore, but the party was never able to move beyond an urban strength based on parochial resistance to immigration and Catholicism. Fillmore won only the state of Maryland; overall, he got 873,000 popular votes (21.5 percent) and 8 electoral votes.

The Fateful Election: 1860

When the time came for the 1860 presidential campaign, the Democrats had become hopelessly split over slavery. The biggest sticking point was the Supreme Court's infamous 1857 *Dred Scott* decision, which, by decreeing that Congress had no power to prohibit slavery in a territory, was just what Southerners favoring popular sovereignty wanted. Yet it also created uncertainty about any legislature's authority over slavery. If Congress could not regulate slavery, could state legislatures? Illinois senator Douglas insisted on state resolution of the slavery issue. However, the Democratic administration of President Buchanan had waged war on Douglas earlier by ousting his allies from the federal bureaucracy for opposing the administration's pro-southern stance on the Kansas issue. Jefferson Davis of Mississippi, who later became president of the Confederate States of America, led Southern Democrats in Congress who argued that Congress had the right to promote and protect slavery in new territories.

At the Democratic convention in Charleston, South Carolina, Douglas managed several moderate platform victories, defeating resolutions that called for acceptance of the *Dred Scott* decision and protection of slavery in the territories. But Douglas's success prompted delegates from ten southern states to bolt the convention. After disputes over quorum rules and fifty-seven ballots, the Democrats were unable to muster the necessary two-thirds majority for Douglas. The convention therefore adjourned, reassembled in Baltimore in June, and faced disputes about the seating of delegates that caused further defections from the South. With southern radicals effectively eliminated from the convention, Douglas swept to a unanimous nomination victory.

Meanwhile, the southern defectors held their own Democratic convention in June and nominated Vice President Breckinridge for the presidency. The Southern Democrats insisted that they were the backbone of the party and could win the White House as they had been strong enough to elect Buchanan four years before. The Constitutional Union Party, which developed as a futile attempt to repair the nation's geographic divisions, nominated moderate John Bell of Tennessee.

With the *Dred Scott* decision as a rallying point for popular control of government, and the Democrats in disarray, the Republicans held a frenzied convention in Chicago. After the convention blocked several radical candidates, Lincoln, the former U.S. representative of Illinois, emerged as the compromise choice. Although Lincoln had lost the

Stephen Douglas, at five feet and four inches, was the 1860 Democratic candidate for president.

1858 Senate race to Douglas two years earlier, his stance against the expansion of slavery into the territories had made him a national figure. The fact that Lincoln was widely supported throughout Illinois also had improved his chances at the Chicago convention.

None of the four major candidates seeking the presidency, however, could compete seriously throughout the nation. The two Southerners, Breckinridge and Bell, were doomed from the start, because the South's electoral vote total was significantly below that of the North. The presidential winner was likely to be a candidate from the North, the region with the most electoral votes—that is, either Lincoln, a Republican, or Douglas, a Democrat.

Lincoln won easily with a total of 180 electoral votes to Breckinridge's 72, Bell's 39, and Douglas's 12. Lincoln's closest competitor in the popular vote was Douglas. Lincoln had 1.9 million northern popular votes (40.0 percent); Douglas had 1.4 million (29.5 percent) spread out geographically. The two other principal candidates received much less support, which was concentrated in the South: Breckinridge won 848,000 popular votes (18.1 percent); Bell, 591,000 (12.6 percent).

Thanks to the wide-ranging Republican coalition—one that eluded the Whigs in their last years of existence—Lincoln was able to count on strength in the areas that Fremont had won in 1856: New England and the upper Northwest, as well as New York and Ohio. Lincoln's political ties to Illinois, where he practiced law and began his public career, would help in Illinois and Indiana, and his background as a former Whig was a plus in the Ohio valley. The coal and iron regions of Pennsylvania and Ohio were attracted to the party's high-tariff policy. Urban immigrants, particularly Germans, were attracted by the Republican support of homestead (frontier settlement) legislation and the Lincoln campaign's "Vote Yourself a Farm" appeal.[35] The vice-presidential selection of Hannibal Hamlin of Maine, a former Democrat, broadened the coalition beyond partisan lines. Lincoln's oft-stated desire not to challenge slavery where it then existed was an appeal to border states.

The Republicans succeeded in 1860 because they were able to pull together a variety of potentially warring factions. But above all else the Republicans stood against the extension of slavery into new territories. By accepting slavery where it already existed but warning against the spread of the system, the Republicans divided the Democrats and picked up support from a diverse array of otherwise contentious factions—abolitionists, moderate abolitionists, and whites who feared for their position in the economy. Moreover, the *Dred Scott* decision enabled the Republicans to rail publicly against the high court in the tradition of Jefferson and Jackson. While opposing the Democratic doctrine of popular sovereignty, the Republicans picked up some states' rights sympathizers by having a middle-ground slavery stance.

Because some Southerners had vowed to secede from the Union if Lincoln won the election, in the period before Lincoln's inauguration congressional committees sought to put together a compromise that would save the nation from civil war. They failed, however, because of Lincoln's refusal to abandon his policy of containing slavery. He rejected proposals for popular sovereignty or a slave-free geographic division of western states, and he would not comment on proposals for constitutional amendments or popular referenda on the issue.

After Lincoln was elected, South Carolina, Louisiana, Mississippi, Alabama, Georgia, Texas, and Florida seceded from the Union and on February 7, 1861, adopted a constitution forming the Confederate States of America. After a protracted standoff between Union soldiers who held Fort Sumter and the Confederate soldiers who controlled South Carolina, the Confederates fired on the fort. Virginia, Arkansas, North Carolina, and Tennessee then joined the Confederacy on April 13, 1861, and the Civil War was under way.

The Civil War Election: 1864

The Union's military difficulties in 1861 and 1862 created resentment against and impatience with President Lincoln. The splits that developed in the Republican Party seemed to imperil his chances for renomination and reelection.

From the beginning of his administration, Lincoln suffered because of the difficulty he had finding a general who could successfully prosecute the war. Repeated military setbacks and stalemates—such as the Battles of Fredericksburg and Chancellorsville, Confederate general Robert E. Lee's escape after the battle of Antietam (Sharpsburg), and heavy casualties in the drive to Richmond—hurt the Republicans. Publicized conflicts with Union generals such as George McClellan caused further damage. In addition to the military problems, the president's announcement in September 1862 of the emancipation of slaves in rebellious states (the Emancipation Proclamation) created legal and political controversy.

In the 1862 midterm elections, the Republicans experienced widespread losses in congressional and state elections. Among the more bitter defeats for Lincoln was Democrat John Stuart's victory in the president's old congressional district in Illinois. By the time of the presidential election, Stuart, a former law partner of the president, was an ardent political foe.

The military frustrations gave rise to deep divisions within Lincoln's cabinet. Treasury Secretary Salmon P. Chase was a constant critic of Lincoln's capacity to serve as commander in chief, and the Philadelphia banker Jay Gould briefly led a movement for Chase's nomination for president in 1864. Chase withdrew only after the Lincoln forces dealt him a severe blow at the party caucus in his home state of Ohio. Other radicals met in Cleveland in May 1864 and

Republican presidential candidate Abraham Lincoln stood tall at six feet and four inches.

PRESIDENT OF THE CONFEDERACY

In 1861, two weeks before Abraham Lincoln was inaugurated in Washington, D.C., as the sixteenth president of the United States, another president was inaugurated in Montgomery, Alabama. On February 18, 1861, Jefferson Davis became the first and only president of the Confederate States of America.

Davis was born in Christian (now Todd) County, Kentucky, on June 3, 1808. He was the youngest of the ten children of Samuel and Jane Davis, who moved their family to a small Mississippi plantation when Jefferson was a boy. He attended private schools and Transylvania University in Lexington, Kentucky, before his oldest brother, Joseph, secured his appointment to West Point in 1824.

After graduating from the academy, Davis was stationed in Wisconsin under Col. Zachary Taylor. There he saw action in the Black Hawk War during the early 1830s and fell in love with Taylor's daughter, Sarah Knox. In 1835 he left the army, married Sarah, and settled on a one-thousand-acre plantation in Mississippi, which was given to him by his brother Joseph. Tragically, Sarah died from malaria three months after the wedding, and for several years Davis devoted himself to developing his land and wealth.

In 1845 Davis married Varina Howell, a member of the Mississippi aristocracy, and was elected to the U.S. House of Representatives. He served in Washington less than a year before the Mexican War began, and he gave up his seat to accept a commission as a colonel. He became a national hero when his company made a stand at the Battle of Buena Vista that was said to have saved Gen. Zachary Taylor's army from defeat.

In 1847 he left the army and was elected to the Senate. He served there until 1851, when he ran unsuccessfully for governor of Mississippi. He returned to Washington in 1853 after being appointed secretary of war by President Franklin Pierce. Davis was credited with strengthening the armed forces during his time in office. He also was influential in bringing about the Gadsden Purchase from Mexico in 1853, which added southern areas of present-day Arizona and New Mexico to the United States.

In 1857 Davis was reelected to the Senate. Although he became a leading spokesperson for the South, he did not advocate secession until 1860 when it had become inevitable. Davis hoped to be appointed commanding general of the South's army, but instead he was chosen as president by a convention of the seceding states.

Davis believed his first priority as president was to preserve Southern independence. He tried to secure French and British assistance for the Confederacy, but he was largely unsuccessful. Similar to what Lincoln did with the Northern army, Davis helped develop military strategy and on occasion interfered with the

Jefferson Davis

plans of his generals. In managing the war effort, Davis was hampered by his paradoxical position. The South could fight most effectively as a unified nation run by the central government in Richmond, but the Southern states had succeeded in part to preserve their rights as independent states. Davis took actions, including the suspension of *habeas corpus* and the establishment of conscription, that were regarded as despotic by many Southerners.

When the Union's victory appeared imminent in early 1865, Davis fled south from Richmond and was captured by federal troops. He was indicted for treason and imprisoned for two years, but he never stood trial. He lived in Canada and Europe for several years before retiring to Mississippi. There he wrote his *Rise and Fall of the Confederate Government,* which was published in 1881. He died in New Orleans on December 6, 1889.

---

named John Fremont to run against Lincoln in the fall. Fremont withdrew only after a series of Union military victories strengthened Lincoln's political standing.

The president manipulated the Republican convention in Baltimore brilliantly, ensuring not only his renomination but also the selection of pro-Union governor Andrew Johnson of Union-occupied Tennessee—a lifelong Democrat—as the vice-presidential candidate. Lincoln professed

indifference about a possible running mate. "Wish not to interfere about V.P. Cannot interfere about platform," he said in a letter. "Convention must judge for itself." [36] Nevertheless, he maneuvered to build support for Johnson. Johnson's selection was in accord with the desire of the party, which also called itself the Union Party as a way to attract Democrats and to develop nationwide unity. Yet Lincoln's reelection drive was so uncertain that he obliged his cabinet in August 1864 to sign a statement pledging an orderly transition of power if he lost. The statement read: "This morning, as for some days past, it seems exceedingly probable that this Administration will not be reelected. Then it will be my duty to so cooperate with the President-elect, as to save the Union between the election and the inauguration; as he will have secured his election on such ground that he cannot possibly save it afterwards."[37]

The man for whom Lincoln anticipated arranging a wartime transition was Democratic nominee George McClellan, whom Lincoln had fired as general in January 1863. McClellan had won the Democratic nomination with the strong backing of "peace Democrats" such as Clement L. Vallandigham of Ohio, who was arrested by Union general Ambrose E. Burnside after making a series of antiwar speeches. (Vallandigham later took up exile in Canada.) McClellan's running mate was Rep. George Pendleton of Ohio, who after the war would sponsor landmark civil service reform legislation.

Although popular with his soldiers, General McClellan had not won a single major battle of the war despite many infusions of extra troops. Yet he blamed Lincoln for the losses. Indeed, he was a vocal critic of the administration. McClellan's presidential campaign was built around a call for a cease-fire and a convention to restore the Union. He and his fellow peace Democrats also criticized the administration's violation of civil liberties and other unconstitutional actions.

Lincoln's fortunes improved in the two months before the election. When Gen. William Tecumseh Sherman took Atlanta after a scorched-earth march through the South, the Confederacy was left badly divided geographically. The military victory cut off the Gulf states from the Confederate capital of Richmond. Gen. Philip Sheridan had had important successes in the Shenandoah Valley, and Gen. Ulysses S. Grant had fared well in Virginia.

Not only did the Democrats face a Republican Party reconstituted for the war election as the Union Party and united by recent military victories, but McClellan also had a difficult time developing consistent campaign themes. He was at various times conciliatory toward the Confederacy and solicitous of the soldiers who fought for the Union. The balancing problem was underscored by the inclusion of both war and peace songs in the *McClellan Campaign Songster,* a piece of campaign literature.[38] McClellan also had a difficult time selling his message to northern industrialists who were profiting from munitions procurement.

Not until the arrival of election results from three state elections on October 11 were Lincoln and the Unionists confident that they would win the national election in November. Republican victories in Indiana, Ohio, and Pennsylvania were the first concrete indications that Lincoln's fortunes had turned around.

Lincoln overwhelmed McClellan by winning all of the loyal states except Delaware, Kentucky, and New Jersey for a 212–21 electoral vote victory. Lincoln garnered 2.2 million popular votes (55.0 percent) to McClellan's 1.8 million (45.0 percent). The electoral votes of Louisiana and Tennessee, the first Confederate states to return to the Union, were not accepted by Congress.

POSTWAR RADICALISM

The end of the Civil War left the nation almost as divided as it had been in the antebellum years. Concerns about punishment of the rebel states, the status of the freedmen, and economic development replaced slavery as the principal sources of disagreement.

The nation undoubtedly would have experienced bitter splits no matter who had served as chief executive, but the assassination of President Abraham Lincoln on April 14, 1865, shortly after the Confederate surrender, created a crisis of leadership. Lincoln's vice president, Andrew Johnson, ascended to the presidency and quickly came into conflict with the radical Northern Republicans who controlled Congress. Johnson, a Democrat from Tennessee, was stubborn, which only aggravated the troubles that were inevitable anyway because of his party and regional background.

Johnson intended to continue Lincoln's plans for the reconstruction of the North and South "with malice toward none"; he chafed at the notion of the South as a conquered territory. A states' rights politician, Johnson attempted to put together a coalition of moderates from all parts of the country that would bring about a quick reconciliation between his administration and Congress.

But Congress was intent on establishing political institutions that would respect the rights of former slaves and promote economic growth and vowed to use military occupation to destroy the South's old political elite.[39] Thus Johnson and Congress fought over bills that would extend the life of the Freedmen's Bureau (an agency established to help blacks make the transition from slavery to citizenship) and guarantee the franchise and equal protection to blacks, with the result that Johnson vetoed both bills. Johnson also opposed the Fourteenth Amendment, which guaranteed equal protection, as well as the stipulation that Confederate states approve the amendment as a condition of their readmission to the Union.

When the Radical Republicans took over Congress in the 1866 midterm elections, the war with Johnson began in earnest. In March 1867 Congress established limited military rule in recalcitrant Southern states and in May passed the Tenure of Office Act limiting the president's right to dismiss his appointees. Johnson contemptuously disregarded the tenure act and fired Edwin Stanton, his secretary of war. For this action Johnson was impeached by the House and tried by the Senate. When the Senate voted in May 1868, he avoided the two-thirds total needed for conviction by a single vote (35–19).

The Grant Victories: 1868 and 1872

Ulysses S. Grant was more than a concerned citizen during the dispute between Johnson and Congress. Despite its portrayal in many history books as a clear instance of congressional abuse of power, the affair was more complicated. All of the players in the drama negotiated their way with care, and almost none of them escaped without major scars. Grant was a central figure, and his style of maneuvering was dictated by his ambition to succeed Johnson as president.

Radical Republicans in Congress achieved a lasting victory when they secured passage of the Civil Rights Act of 1866 over President Johnson's veto, but they were increasingly disturbed by reports that the statute was not being enforced. A congressional investigation of violence against blacks in Memphis concluded that the Freedmen's Bureau

The 1872 Republican campaign called voters' attention to the humble backgrounds of presidential candidate Ulysses S. Grant and his running mate, Henry Wilson.

could not enforce civil rights without help. Radicals began to look to Secretary of War Stanton to enforce the law that the president clearly disliked and repeatedly subverted. When Stanton indicated that he would carry out the law in the Confederacy as Congress intended, Johnson began to think about replacing him. At this point Congress passed the Tenure of Office Act over Johnson's veto in May 1867, reasoning that its constitutional "advise and consent" powers over appointments could be extended to removal as well. Johnson, however, decided to test the law's constitutionality.

In replacing Stanton, Johnson's concern—and indeed the concern of all involved—was who could assume the secretary of war post with minimal threat to Johnson's position. The president first considered General Sherman but decided to appoint Grant on a temporary basis. Originally a Democrat and supporter of moderate policies toward the South, Grant worried about appearing too close to the unpopular president. As a result, after vaguely assuring Johnson that he would accept a temporary appointment, Grant hedged. He increasingly expressed support for the notion that appointees should interpret and obey laws according to congressional intent. Eventually Grant told the president in a letter that he could not accept the appointment.

After the drama of Johnson's impeachment in 1868, Grant was in a good position to seek the White House. He had avoided allying himself with controversy during both Johnson's search for a replacement for Stanton and the ensuing impeachment battle. In fact, he and Chief Justice Salmon Chase were the only ones not tainted by the affair. Grant even managed to maintain his public posture of disinterested duty. Thus during one of the nation's ugliest political episodes, Grant looked clean. He was ready for a presidential campaign.

As Johnson endured his Senate impeachment trial in March, Grant won his first electoral victory. A New Hampshire congressional campaign, which normally would favor the Democrat, became an early Grant referendum when Republican candidate Donald Sickles told voters that a vote for a Republican was a vote for Grant; Sickles won. Just before the Republican convention in May, a Soldiers and Sailors Convention "nominated" Grant. Yet he avoided an excessively military image when he vowed to reduce the size of the standing army. Grant was on his way.

Grant won the presidential nomination without opposition. The real battle at the 1868 Republican convention was for the vice-presidential nomination. Schuyler Colfax of Indiana, the Speaker of the House, won on the sixth ballot; eleven candidates received votes on the initial roll call.

The Democrats had a difficult time finding a nominee. Johnson sought the Democratic nomination, but his appeal was to the South. (Because many Southern states were still outside the Union, Northern politicians were selecting the nominee.) Chief Justice Chase, highly regarded for his fairness during Johnson's Senate trial, was a possibility, but his strong stand for black suffrage was a barrier. Sen. Thomas A. Hendricks of Indiana was strong in the East, and George Pendleton of Ohio, the party's vice-presidential candidate four years earlier, was strong in the West. Gen. Winfield Scott Hancock of Pennsylvania presented the opportunity of running one military hero against another.

After twenty-three bitter ballots in a sweltering New York City, Horatio Seymour, the national party chair and popular war governor of New York, accepted the Democratic nomination against his will. Gen. Francis P. Blair Jr. of Missouri was the vice-presidential nominee. The party platform called for the rapid reentry of Confederate states to the Union, state authority over suffrage questions, and the "Ohio Idea," which promised an inflationary money supply that would help the indebted South.

Both sides were well financed in the election, but the Republicans had the edge. The Republican Party's probusiness positions on the tariff, railroad grants, and the currency attracted millions of dollars. Newspapers and magazines tended to be pro-Republican because of their urban business orientations.

Grant, who ran his campaign from his home in Galena, Illinois, was vague about issues ranging from the currency to voting rights. Appearances in Colorado with fellow generals Sherman and Sheridan were taken to be endorsements. Everything seemed to go Grant's way. Even the traditional campaign gossip about the sexual activities of candidates did not hurt him. Charges that Grant was excessively problack—"I am Captain Grant of the Black Marines, the stupidest man that was ever seen" were the lyrics of one ditty[40]—helped him with the recently enfranchised citizens. Without the black vote, Grant probably would have lost the popular vote and perhaps the electoral vote. Results from October state elections that favored the Republicans created a brief movement for Seymour and Blair to quit the contest so that the Democrats could name a new ticket. Instead, Seymour took the October results as an incentive to get on the campaign stump. Seymour was a good speaker, but he still came up short.

Grant defeated Seymour by 3.0 million (52.7 percent) to 2.7 million votes (47.3 percent). The electoral vote tally was 214 for Grant and 80 for Seymour. Finally, Grant won all but eight of the thirty-four states taking part in the election. He benefited from Radical Republican reconstructionist sentiment in the North and newly enfranchised blacks in the South.

With Grant's ascension to the presidency in 1869, the Republican Party entered a new era—what the German sociologist Max Weber would have called a shift from "charismatic" to "rational" institutional authority. In other words, the party shifted its devotion from a great moral cause to its own survival as an organization. It had begun as a coalition of activists fervently opposed to the expansion of slavery (many opposed slavery itself) and to the rebellion of Southern states from the Union. The Republicans' 1868 victory under Grant was the first not dominated wholly by crisis conditions.

The Republicans had a strong base of support: eastern bankers, manufacturers, railroad tycoons, and land speculators. With the old Confederacy under the control of military governments and with blacks given the franchise, the Republicans had strength in the South. The West was restive, however, because of depressed farm prices, high taxes, and debt. The industrial-agrarian split between North and South before the Civil War would be resumed as an East-West split in the years after the war.

The Republican leadership itself was changing. Age was claiming a number of the early Republican leaders, such as Thaddeus Stevens, William Seward, Benjamin Wade, Charles Sumner, James Grimes, Stanton, and Chase. New party leaders included Senators Roscoe Conkling of New York, Oliver Morton of Indiana, Simon Cameron of Pennsylvania, and Zachariah Chandler of Michigan, and Representatives Benjamin Butler of Massachusetts, John Logan of Illinois, James A. Garfield of Ohio, and James G. Blaine of Maine.

As for the new Grant administration, it was undistinguished. The new president's inaugural address—spoken without the traditional company of the outgoing president because Grant had neglected to respond to Johnson's polite letters—was decent but uninspiring. Grant vowed that "all laws will be faithfully executed, whether they meet my approval or not," that debtors would not be tolerated, and that blacks should get the vote throughout the country and Indians should be offered "civilization and ultimate citizenship."[41] With a few important exceptions, cabinet positions went to old Grant cronies.

In 1869 the nation experienced a financial panic when financiers Jay Gould and Jim Fisk attempted to corner the world's gold market. Their scheme led to "Black Friday," September 24, 1869. Gould and Fisk had met with President Grant and had urged him not to sell government gold, therefore keeping the price of gold high. At the last minute, however, Grant decided to reject their advice and dumped $4 million worth of gold on the market. That dumping caused a severe drop in gold prices, breaking up the Gould-Fisk conspiracy but also causing tremendous losses for thousands of speculators. It was the worst disaster on Wall Street up to that time. Although it did not cause a depression, the South and West were hard hit by the financial retrenchment program that followed. Tariff rates remained high on most manufactured goods, despite tentative efforts to reform the system.

The spoils system was in full swing during the Grant years. Grant himself was not involved in the scramble for booty, but his family and aides were often shameless in their greed. When Grant learned that liberal Republicans were planning an independent presidential campaign against him in 1872, he took the edge off the spoils issue by creating the Civil Service Reform Commission, but his neglect of the commission made it ineffective.

Before the 1872 election, the *New York Sun* exposed the Crédit Mobilier scandal. The newspaper reported that the firm's board of directors had many of the same members as the Union Pacific Railroad Company, which hired it to build a transcontinental route, and that Crédit Mobilier had paid its board exorbitant profits. To avoid a public investigation, Crédit Mobilier offered stock to Vice President Colfax and Representative (later president) Garfield. Colfax lost his place on the Republican ticket for his role in the scandal; Sen. Henry Wilson of New Hampshire took his position as the vice-presidential candidate in 1872.

Liberal Republicans, unhappy with protective tariffs, spoils, and the uneven administration of the Southern states, bolted the party in 1872. The group was interested in policies such as civil service and free trade that would promote individual virtue in a laissez-faire economic system. The reformers thought they had a chance to win. The German-born senator Carl Schurz of Missouri wrote to a friend that "the administration with its train of offices and office-mongers [is] the great incubus pressing upon the party.... The superstition that Grant is the necessary man is rapidly giving way. The spell is broken, and we have only to push through the breach."[42]

Candidates for the nomination from this group of Republicans included former ambassador to Great Britain Charles Francis Adams, son of President John Quincy Adams and grandson of President John Adams; Supreme Court Justice David Davis; Chief Justice Salmon Chase; Sen. Lyman Trumbull of Illinois; and Horace Greeley, editor of the *New York Tribune*. Greeley won the nomination on the sixth ballot and ran as a Democrat and Liberal Republican. The Democrats were so weak that they did not field a candidate of their own. They endorsed the Greeley ticket. (Charles O'Conor of New York was nominated by a group of "Non-coalition Democrats" for president. He did not accept the nomination.)

Since his early days as a newspaper reporter, when he described President Van Buren as an effeminate failure, Greeley had won fame as a pungent social critic. He was a crusading, abolitionist editor and a dedicated reformer, but his rumpled appearance and unpolished speaking style made him appear "unpresidential." Greeley was unable to parlay an amalgam of promises to various interest groups—blacks, soldiers, immigrants, and laborers—into a victory over Grant. Groups that Greeley actively courted found him wanting for a variety of reasons, and even though Greeley advocated the tariff favored by the North, he could not cut into Grant's northeastern strength. One Republican cartoon that revealed Greeley's difficult task showed a fence on

which sat a laborer, skeptical because of Greeley's stand against strikes, and a black, concerned because of Greeley's advocacy of amnesty for Confederates. Sitting on the sidelines was a German, upset with Greeley's prohibitionist stance: "Oh! Yaw! You would take my Lager away, den you must get widout me along!"[43]

Even though he went on the stump and delivered a series of impressive speeches, Greeley never had a chance. Republican gubernatorial victories in North Carolina in August and in Pennsylvania, Ohio, and Indiana in October were clear harbingers that the Republican Party would do well in November. Grant took the entire North and the newly admitted South with 3.6 million popular votes (55.6 percent). Greeley won three border states, as well as Tennessee, Texas, and Georgia, with 2.8 million popular votes (43.9 percent). Less than a month after the election, Greeley died. Of the electoral votes, which were cast after Greeley's death, Grant received 286; the Democrats' 63 electoral votes were scattered among various candidates, and 17 Democratic electoral votes were not cast.

Compromise: 1876

The pattern of Republican, northern, and business domination of presidential politics was institutionalized in the 1876 election. Republican Rutherford B. Hayes, the three-time governor of Ohio, lost the popular vote and had a questionable hold on the electoral college vote, but he managed to beat Democrat Samuel J. Tilden for the presidency when the election was settled by a special commission created by Congress. (Hayes won 4.0 million votes to Tilden's 4.3 million—48.0 and 51.0 percent of the popular vote, respectively.) Perhaps the most controversial election outcome in history, some feared it would set off a second civil war.

The problem arose when the vote tallies in Florida, South Carolina, and Louisiana were called into question. Violence had accompanied the voting in all three states, but President Grant had not sent in federal troops to ensure fair balloting. On those states hung the electoral outcome. There was good reason to be suspicious of any vote count in those and other Southern states. While the Republicans had controlled the balloting places and mounted vigorous drives to get blacks to the polls, the Democrats had used physical intimidation and bribery to keep blacks away. The bitterness between northern interests and southern whites was apparent in the violence that often took place at polls.

When state election board recounts and investigations did not settle the question of the vote tallies, Congress took up the matter. An electoral commission made up of five senators (three majority-party Republicans, two minority Democrats), five representatives (three majority-party Democrats, two minority Republicans), and five Supreme Court justices (two from each party, one independent) assembled to hear complaints about the disputed states. At the last minute the independent justice disqualified himself, and his place was taken by a Republican who was accepted by Democrats because they considered him to be the most independent of the Republican justices. Weeks of bargaining followed, during which the Republican vote totals of the disputed states were confirmed and the Southern Democrats extracted promises of financial aid and political independence from the federal government.

When the validity of the Florida vote count for Hayes was challenged, the commission responded that it did not have the capacity to judge the actual conduct of the balloting, only the validity of the certificates presented to Congress. That decision gave the state to Hayes. Challenges to the vote counts of Louisiana, South Carolina, and Oregon were dismissed in a similar way, so Hayes was awarded the presidency by a single electoral vote, 185 to 184.

The compromise not only settled the partisan dispute between Hayes and Tilden but also established a rigid alignment of political interests that would dominate U.S. politics for the next half-century. Although Democrats won occasional victories, the Republican, eastern, conservative, business-oriented establishment held sway over the system until Franklin Roosevelt's election in 1932.

The institutional form of the regional splits created by the compromise remained much longer. Historian C. Vann Woodward has argued that secret wheeling and dealing among congressional and party leaders institutionally divided the political system by party, region, economic interest, and governmental branches. Northern Republican industrial interests were given control of the presidential election process, and southern Democratic agricultural interests were given autonomy over their regional politics, which led to domination of Congress.[44] This alignment was not completely dislodged until the passage of important civil rights legislation in the 1960s.

To reward southern Democrats for throwing the 1876 election to the Republican Hayes, northern politicians agreed to pull federal troops out of the South and to allow southern whites to take over the governments. Within months Southern states were erecting a powerful edifice of racial discrimination that would last until the 1960s. Former South Carolina governor Daniel H. Chamberlain, a Republican, later summed up the deal:

> What is the president's Southern policy? [I]t consists in the abandonment of Southern Republicans and especially the colored race, to the control and rule not only of the Democratic Party, but of that class of the South which regarded slavery as a Divine Institution, which waged four years of destructive war for its perpetuation, which steadily opposed citizenship and suffrage for the negro—in a word, a class whose traditions, principles, and history are opposed to every step and feature of what Republicans call our national progress since 1860.[45]

AGE OF REPUBLICANISM

From 1860 to 1908, the Republicans won eleven elections; the Democrats won only two. Only Grover Cleveland could put together Democratic wins, and he was as conservative on most issues as the Republicans of the period. Presidential election winners after the Great Compromise were Rutherford B. Hayes (1876), James A. Garfield (1880), Cleveland (1884), Benjamin Harrison (1888), Cleveland (1892), William McKinley (1896 and 1900), Theodore Roosevelt (1904), and William Howard Taft (1908).

The political aspirants of the day were required to adhere to the creed of high tariffs, laissez-faire economics, and tight money. Tight money policies—the restricted issuance of currency, which favored bankers and other established interests but hurt debtors and those seeking more rapid expansion of some kinds of investment and spending—provided rare openings for effective Democratic resistance to Republican hegemony. Resistance did develop, however, when the scramble for tariff protections created obvious inequities among businesses and hardships for the consumer. Yet populist uprisings, such as Democrat William Jennings Bryan's 1896 campaign, faltered because of strong mobilization by the Republicans and divisions within the Democratic ranks. Bryan failed to bring a likely Democratic constituency—the worker—into the fold. Eastern business owners were able to portray their interest in industrial growth as a common concern with labor and Bryan's western agrarian alliance as a danger to that growth.

Although the Republican Party dominated presidential politics, the parties were well balanced in Congress and in state governments until the class and sectional cleavages of the 1890s. The Senate was split evenly in 1881, 37–37, and two years later the Republicans had a 38–36 edge. The Democrats had made gains in northern congressional races, and Republicans were making smaller gains in the South. The House tended to provide a majority for whichever party held the White House.

Garfield Carries the Republican Banner: 1880

Hayes honored his pledge to serve only one term, setting off a scramble for both parties' nominations in 1880. When the early momentum for a third term for Grant faltered, the Republican contest became a battle between Grant, Sen. James G. Blaine of Maine, and Treasury secretary John Sherman of Ohio. Grant was able to muster a first-ballot plurality but could not attract new supporters as the balloting proceeded. A stalemate between Blaine and Sherman ensued.

Rep. Garfield of Ohio, a former preacher who was impressive in his oratory and organization for Sherman, was the compromise choice for the nomination. He selected as his running mate Chester A. Arthur, the collector of the Port of New York, an important patronage job.

The Democrats named Gen. Winfield Hancock of Pennsylvania and former Indiana representative William English to head their ticket. The Democratic platform advocated the gold standard, a low tariff designed to raise revenue, civil service reform, restrictions on Chinese immigration, and a belated criticism of the 1876 deal that gave the presidency to Hayes. Except for the tariff and 1876 questions, the Democrats' platform was close to the Republicans' statement of principles.

The regional breakdown of support, with most of the North and West falling in Garfield's camp and the South lining up behind Hancock, gave the presidency to Garfield. The popular vote was close—4.45 million (48.27 percent) to 4.44 million (48.25 percent)—but Garfield won a 214–155 electoral vote victory.

The festering issue of patronage and civil service came to a head shortly after Garfield's inauguration. On July 2, 1881, Charles Guiteau, a man later described as a "disappointed office-seeker," shot Garfield while he was en route to Williams College to deliver a commencement address. Garfield died in September, and Arthur became president.

The outstanding feature of Arthur's presidency was the easy passage of the Pendleton Act—legislation that set up a commission to regulate the provision of federal jobs and the behavior of civil servants. The number of federal workers removed from the patronage system was at first small, but successive presidents widened the coverage of nonpartisan workers so that today less than 1 percent of all federal workers are appointed by the president.[46] The tariff question also emerged as crucial during the Arthur presidency. The Tariff Act of 1883 "gave little or no relief to the consumer and took care of every important industrial interest."[47] The Democrats opposed the bill and later worked for the gradual lowering of rates, but they failed. The tariff would be a major issue in later elections.

Democrat Cleveland Wins: 1884

Arthur wanted the Republican nomination in 1884, and his record as stand-in for the assassinated Garfield arguably should have earned him the nod—even though no successor president during the nineteenth century had been nominated by his party. Not only was he an important player in civil service reform and the tariff issue, but he initiated modernization of the navy and vetoed the Chinese Exclusion Act of 1882, which prohibited Chinese laborers from entering the United States for ten years. His veto of the $19 million rivers and harbors bill was a model of fiscal probity.

Blaine of Maine—secretary of state in Arthur's administration—stood in the president's way. After months of public appeals by old-line Republicans interested in stronger leadership and more generous patronage from their party, Blaine quit his administration position and opposed Arthur for the nomination.

The fiery oratory of 1884 Republican candidate James G. Blaine captured the imagination of the political establishment, but it was not enough to win him the election over Democrat Grover Cleveland.

Blaine was the most charismatic figure of the period. A former teacher, editor, state legislator, and member of Congress, Blaine's fiery oratory captured the imagination of the political establishment. He had made a national name for himself when he opposed an 1876 congressional resolution expressing forgiveness to Civil War rebels including the Confederate president, Jefferson Davis. Col. Robert G. Ingersoll, a rising political figure in the Republican Party, said of Blaine: "Like an armed warrior, like a plumed knight,

James G. Blaine marched down the halls of the American Congress and threw his shining lance full and fair against the brazen forehead of every traitor to his country."[48] The sobriquet "Plumed Knight" caught on.

The Republican convention in Chicago praised Arthur's administration and fudged the tariff issue. The tariff that passed in 1883 was the product of the efforts of swarms of lobbyists for private interests. The Republican platform promised better protection for raw wool interests, angered by their treatment in 1883, and a generally protective stance for domestic industry. The platform also called for an international currency conference, railway regulation, a national agency for labor affairs, and further improvements in the navy.

At a frenzied convention, Blaine took the lead over Arthur on the first ballot. Old-line party leaders quickly united behind Blaine, while Arthur was unable to consolidate the support of reform Republicans still skeptical of his leadership abilities from his days as a patronage politician and collector of the Port of New York. Blaine won the nomination on the fourth ballot. Gen. John Logan of Illinois received the vice-presidential nomination.

The Democrats nominated Cleveland after skirmishes with Sen. Thomas F. Bayard Jr. of Delaware and Sen. Thomas A. Hendricks of Indiana. Hendricks, whose liberal expansionist currency stance would balance the more conservative stance of Cleveland, was named the vice-presidential candidate. The Democratic platform vaguely promised reform of the tariff laws to make them fairer and, even more vaguely, promised a more honest and efficient administration.

Cleveland was a former teacher, lawyer, assistant district attorney, and reform mayor of Buffalo who had won the governorship of New York only two years before. Members of both parties consistently underestimated Cleveland's intellect and resolve. As governor, he had made enemies through his vetoes of low public transit fares and aid to sectarian schools. He also had defied Tammany Hall, the Democratic Party organization that dominated New York politics, especially in New York City.

Cleveland's nomination signaled a triumph for the "educational politics" characteristic of urban progressivism. (Progressives took a patriarchal view of politics in which elites assumed an obligation to better their social underlings through education and various social services.) In a move away from the highly partisan and vitriolic campaigns of the post–Civil War era, Cleveland and other disciples of former New York governor Samuel Tilden promoted their program through a "literary bureau" that distributed pamphlets describing the party's policy positions. Campaign themes were developed at the national level and disseminated via the mails and meetings with the many professional and community organizations. The educational style was adopted by Republican candidate Harrison in 1888.[49]

In contrast, Blaine's campaign was one of the dirtiest in U.S. history. He first attempted to spark sectional antagonisms with his "bloody shirt" warnings that the South was trying to reassert its rebel ways through Cleveland. Blaine also tried to rouse the fears of business with claims that Cleveland would institute free trade policies damaging to domestic industries. But that appeal failed because the Democratic platform's plank on the tariff laws specifically supported protection of those interests. Finally, Blaine tried to make a scandal of Cleveland's admission that he had fathered a child out of wedlock years before. Cleveland was charged, among other things, with kidnapping and immuring both the mother and child to cover up the story.

The campaign eventually turned on Cleveland's victory in New York, which resulted from a number of blunders by Blaine. One blunder had occurred years before, when Blaine mocked New York party boss Roscoe Conkling: "The contempt of that large-minded gentleman is so wilted, his haughty disdain, his grandiloquent swell, his majestic, supereminent overpowering, turkey-gobbler strut, has been so crushing to myself that I know it was an act of the greatest temerity to venture upon a controversy with him."[50] Conkling was so peeved by the turkey image that he spent his whole career battling Blaine, including the presidential campaign of 1884. Even Blaine's running mate, Logan, sympathized with Conkling in the dispute.

The other Blaine faux pas occurred a week before the election when a Protestant minister praised Blaine and proclaimed, "We are Republicans, and do not propose to leave our party and identify ourselves with the party whose antecedents have been rum, Romanism, and rebellion." Blaine did not divorce himself from the remark, which angered New York Democrats—and ethnic voters everywhere—and cost him many votes. Later the same day Blaine attended a formal dinner with a number of wealthy persons that became known as "the millionaires dinner." That event belied Blaine's claim to speak for ordinary people.

Of Irish background, Blaine appealed to Irish immigrants in New York for their votes. But Cleveland countered Blaine's Irish tactic by obtaining the last-minute endorsement of the powerful Tammany leader Edward Kelly. On the Saturday before the election, he attended a parade in New York City that attracted 40,000 people chanting: "Blaine, Blaine, James G. Blaine, the Monumental Liar from the State of Maine!" With the help of an economic downturn and the "Mugwumps"—independents and liberal Republicans offended by Blaine—Cleveland won the presidency.

The race, however, was close. Cleveland received 4.9 million votes (48.5 percent) to Blaine's 4.8 million (48.3 percent). He won the solid South, Indiana, Connecticut, New Jersey, and, most important, New York (although by only 1,047 out of 1.13 million votes cast). Still, the election controversy did not end with the balloting. The *New York*

Tribune originally reported that Blaine had won the race, fueling fears about an election deadlock similar to the Hayes-Tilden contest of 1876. But Cleveland received 219 electoral votes to Blaine's 182, making the Democrat the clear winner.

Cleveland's first two years in the White House were productive. His inaugural address and cabinet selections elicited wide praise. His style of leadership—examined closely in the newspapers—appeared refreshingly unassuming. The Cleveland agenda included issues such as tariff reform (cutting rates on the "necessaries of life"), modernization of the navy, civil service, expansion, and land law reform. The president oversaw passage of the Presidential Succession Act and the Electoral Count Act, changes in currency policy, and labor controversies.

Just as he had done during his terms as mayor of Buffalo and governor of New York, Cleveland icily refused to compromise his values. This steadfastness proved to be a problem, however, when Cleveland entered the White House. Thousands of Democratic Party workers went to Washington seeking jobs in the new administration only to be disappointed. "Ah, I suppose you mean that I should appoint two horse thieves a day instead of one," Cleveland said in response to one party leader.[51] In vetoing pension bills, Cleveland called their sponsors "blood-suckers," "coffee-boilers," "pension leeches," and "bums."[52] The president appeared just as aloof to labor when a record number of strikes and disturbances swept the nation in 1886; the federal troops that Cleveland sent to the Haymarket riot in Chicago killed thirty people.

When Cleveland did bend to political realities, his timing was off. After standing firm against patronage when party enthusiasm for reform was at its height, Cleveland disappointed reformers when he allowed lieutenants such as First Assistant Postmaster Adlai E. Stevenson to distribute favors.

The biggest controversy of the Cleveland administration involved tariffs. Concerned about federal budget surpluses that threatened to stall economic activity, Cleveland prodded the House of Representatives to pass tariff reductions. The Senate responded with a protective (high) tariff measure.

The Republican Recovery: 1888

The tariff issue propelled the two parties into the 1888 election. At their national convention the Democrats nominated Cleveland by acclamation and chose seventy-five-year-old judge Allen G. Thurman of Ohio for the vice presidency. The Democrats tried to soften their low-tariff image by promising that open trade would open world markets to domestic industries. Lower tariffs were said to be necessary for avoiding disastrous federal budget surpluses, preventing the development of monopolies, and ensuring consumers reasonable prices for basic goods.

Captioned "Another Voice for Cleveland," this 1884 cartoon played on Cleveland's admission that he had fathered an illegitimate son.

As for the Republicans, a politics-weary Blaine sent word from Florence and Paris that he would not be a candidate in 1888, leaving the race open to some lesser political lights, including Sen. John Sherman of Ohio, Gov. Russell Alger of Michigan, Sen. William Allison of Iowa, and Sen. Harrison of Indiana. At the Republican national convention Sherman led the early balloting but quickly lost ground to Alger and Harrison. After extensive backroom maneuvering, including a last-minute plea by party members to Blaine to accept the nomination, Harrison, who had the backing of state party bosses, won on the ninth ballot. Levi Morton, a banker, got the vice-presidential nomination.

Harrison, a senator from Indiana, was a former Civil War brigadier and the grandson of President William Henry Harrison. Characterized by a scandal-free if colorless demeanor, Harrison was a good speaker, but he often appeared aloof. One historian wrote: "Those who talked with him were met with a frigid look from two expressionless steel grey eyes; and their remarks were sometimes answered in a few chill monosyllables devoid of the slightest note of interest."[53] Harrison pledged a modernized navy, civil service reforms, and the traditional Republican policies to protect trusts and restrict U.S. markets.

The election turned, as in 1884, on New York and Indiana—both states with extensive evidence of voter intimidation and manipulation of vote counts. Harrison won the two states narrowly—New York by only 14,373 votes out of the 1.3 million cast—and captured the White House. Except for Connecticut and New Jersey, Harrison swept the North and West. Cleveland won the South. Overall, Harrison won 5.4 million popular votes (47.8 percent) and 233 electoral votes; Cleveland won 5.5 million popular votes (48.6 percent) and 168 electoral votes.

Cleveland left the White House with an unusual amount of good will among the public because of his honest tariff campaign. His popularity increased during the next four years as the economy hit slumps and as the former president, while practicing law, delivered speeches calling for a more egalitarian brand of politics. Cleveland would be back in 1892 for vindication.

With a majority in Congress and a president in the White House—the first time the party had accomplished such a feat in a dozen years—the Republicans went about their business briskly after the election. Postmaster General John Wanamaker dispensed patronage with zeal. President Harrison signed into law the McKinley Tariff Act and the Sherman Silver Purchase Act. The former raised duties on manufactured goods to their highest level ever but also included provisions for negotiating with other countries to bring the rates down. The silver act loosened the money supply, which stimulated economic activity but angered creditors and bankers (money, when it is more readily available, is worth less).

Cleveland's Comeback: 1892

The 1890 midterm elections brought huge Democratic gains. Voters all over the country—but especially in the depressed farm belt—rebelled against the inflation that high tariffs brought. The Republicans held on to the Senate, but the new House of Representatives had 235 Democrats, 88 Republicans, and 9 Farmers' Alliance members. The brief experiment with party government ended with two years of stalemate.

President Harrison evoked widespread discontent in 1892 for both his demeanor and his policies, but no Republican could mount an effective challenge. Through their strong party government, Republicans had cast their lot with Harrison and had few places to turn for an alternative. Political wizard Mark Hanna, a wealthy coal magnate who had become a powerful behind-the-scenes Republican strategist, promoted Ohio governor William McKinley, and Secretary of State Blaine became an alternative when he abruptly quit the administration just before the Republican convention. But Harrison received a first-ballot nomination. Former minister to France Whitelaw Reid of New York got the vice-presidential nomination.

In the battle for the Democratic nomination, Cleveland enjoyed widespread backing among rank-and-file voters, but party leaders were suspicious. New York governor David B. Hill got a head start when he called a "snap" state

convention and won the delegation. An "anti-snapper" convention from New York sent a rival delegation to the national party convention. Democrats across the country rebelled at Hill's move and rapidly switched their support to Cleveland.

Another problem for Cleveland was the rising sentiment in agrarian states for free and unlimited coinage of silver—a way of boosting sagging farm prices by inducing inflation in the overall economy. Cleveland always had opposed this solution. The former president's consistent, principled stance on the issue not only added to his reputation for integrity but also kept business- and finance-dominated northeastern states in the Democratic camp. Cleveland defeated Hill for the nomination on the first ballot and selected his former first assistant postmaster Adlai Stevenson of Illinois as his running mate.

The fall campaign was uneventful. Historian Eugene Roseboom wrote: "Honest bearded Benjamin Harrison confronting honest mustached Grover Cleveland in a tariff debate was a repeat performance that did not inspire parades with torches or the chanting of campaign ditties.... Democrats, out of power, could assail Republican tariff policy without clarifying their own position."[54]

Cleveland won easily. He received 5.6 million popular votes (46.1 percent) to Harrison's 5.2 million (43.0 percent) and 277 electoral votes to Harrison's 145. Populist general James B. Weaver, advocating expansion of currency and limits on interest rates, won 1.0 million popular votes (8.5 percent) and 22 electoral votes.

AGE OF REFORM

Throughout the period dominated by Republican conservatism—from Ulysses S. Grant's election in 1868 to William McKinley's 1895 win—movements for the reform of political and economic institutions gathered strength at all levels of the American political system. The so-called populists and progressives did not overturn the system, as their rhetoric sometimes suggested, but over time they made major changes in the operation and discourse of U.S. politics.

Depending on the time and place, Americans who called themselves "populists" and "progressives" promoted such contradictory notions as strict morals and free spirits, tight money and loose money, redistribution to the masses and control of the economy by elites, federal intervention and local control of politics, the opening and closing of electoral participation, technological progress and a return to a long-gone pastoral ideal, individualism and community action, ethnic celebration and immigration barriers, scientific investigation and religion, and internationalism and isolationism.

Reformism was the response to the pressures of national expansion, urban development, and growth. Both major parties had adopted probusiness, laissez-faire policies in the latter part of the nineteenth century; indeed, the parties seemed to exist mainly to ensure the terrain was suitable for economic expansion. But the lack of any program to deal with the undesired consequences of explosive growth led to an accumulation of problems that demanded attention. The most obvious problems evolved on the opposite ends of the rural-urban continuum: on the farms and in the cities.

The farm problem developed as the United States became a major economic power in the world. Agriculture expanded on a vast scale to feed the booming cities and, with international trade, to bring foreign capital to the United States. By 1880 the value of U.S. wheat and flour exports nearly equaled that of cotton exports.[55] As agriculture became part of the international market, farmers became dependent not only on the vagaries of the weather but also on the fluctuations of currency in the larger economy.

In the thirty years after the Civil War, prices for farm staples fell steadily. A debt that could have been paid by producing one thousand bushels of grain immediately after the war required three thousand bushels in 1895. The more farmers produced to meet their obligations, the more prices fell to exacerbate their problems. A solution to the problem required confronting a wide array of issues, including tight money, bankers who charged 20 percent interest for loans, monopolies among farm equipment producers, high tariffs, railroad price gouging, shipping inflation, warehouse monopolies, and land speculation. Throughout the farm belt, particularly in the West, tens of thousands of farmers developed an "intense class consciousness."[56]

All these issues received attention from a variety of third parties and independent organizations, but the two major parties usually were inattentive. The Granger Movement of the 1870s, for example, took hold in several farm states and elected new legislatures and high state officials. The Greenback Party attempted to merge a labor-farmer alliance with a doctrine of silver use for public debts. Later, the Farmers' Alliance politicized the same issues. In 1892 the Populist Party had won 8.5 percent of the vote on a platform calling for free coinage of silver.

Another site of growing reformist strength was the city. The dominance of machines of both parties in the cities established an electoral system based on patronage but stubbornly opposed to any coherent program for addressing urban ills such as poverty, poor housing, unsanitary conditions, transportation, education, and unfair workplace practices. Electoral fraud spurred mostly middle-class reformers to devise new electoral and city government machinery, while social problems incited some insurgent class politics.[57] The labor movement developed strength during this period.[58]

Other parts of the progressive agenda developed with a greater understanding of the nationalization of the economic and political systems. The wider sphere of economic activities created calls for regulation of corporations, railroads, and banks, as well as attention to health and environmental concerns and product safety.

Until the ascendance of William Jennings Bryan, the Democratic presidential nominee in 1896, 1900, and 1908, the reformers had been unable to capture a major party. Partly because political activism was based at the state and local level, neither national party had adopted the reformers' widely variegated program as its own. But the depression of 1888 caused the populist forces to pull together more than they had during previous economic downturns, probably because of the accumulated effects of inaction. The earlier panic of 1873 had created a sectional rather than a party split, with the Democrats eventually adopting a more conservative stance on the debate over whether the currency should be expanded to spur economic activity and redistribute social burdens.[59]

The Republican presidential candidates in the post–Civil War years steadfastly opposed the class-oriented proposals of the progressive movement, especially the loose-money demands. The only Democrat to win the presidency since the Civil War was Cleveland, a stubborn advocate of hard money and other conservative economic policies, in 1884 and 1892. President Cleveland vetoed dozens of private pension bills, only grudgingly accepted railroad regulation, and did not address domestic problems in any comprehensive way. Cleveland's public statements on the currency question were especially strong. He called the use of silver "a dangerous and reckless experiment" that was "unpatriotic."[60] On the question of labor, Cleveland was just as conservative: he called out federal troops to put down the Pullman strike of 1894 and regularly preached about the evils of disorder that the labor movement seemed to foster.

Despite the complexity of the agriculture issue, the most concerted populist action concentrated on the currency question. The drive to overturn the prevailing conventional economic thought by moving from a gold (tight) to a gold and silver (loose) money standard captured the imagination of the entire farm belt stretching from the Southeast to the prairie and silver-producing states of the West. The silver standard was a very simple answer to the problem of farm prices: "If money was scarce, the farmer reasoned, then the logical thing was to increase the money supply."[61]

Republican McKinley Triumphs: 1896 and 1900

Gold runs on banks, manipulation of the gold crisis by J. P. Morgan and other leading financiers, Supreme Court decisions favoring corporations, and antilabor actions all stirred up resentment in the South and West. The silver sentiment escalated. The Democratic convention in 1896 called for the issuance of silver and rejected a resolution praising President Cleveland.[62] The movement for a silver currency found an eloquent advocate in Bryan, a member of the House of Representatives from Nebraska, who defeated Richard P. Bland of Missouri for the 1896

Democratic presidential nomination on the strength of his fiery "Cross of Gold" speech.

The speech was one of the most emotional and successful in U.S. history. Bryan attacked eastern financiers and businessmen who exploited farmers. Using a theme to which his fall campaign would return, Bryan sought to expand the traditional Democratic conception of the independent working man to include farmers and factory workers.[63] In his speech's fortissimo, Bryan declared: "You shall not press down upon the brow of labor this crown of thorns, you shall not crucify mankind upon a cross of gold."[64]

In 1896 the Republicans nominated Ohio governor McKinley after brilliant maneuvering by his manager, Mark Hanna. Hanna's chief strengths were fund-raising and his mastery over state party organizations.

McKinley had little difficulty defeating Bryan. McKinley outspent the prairie populist by as much as ten-to-one, and he attracted the disaffected progold wing of the Democratic Party.[65] The Grand Old Party (or GOP as it was by then called) platform called for retention of the gold standard unless international negotiations could produce a bimetallic (silver and gold) currency system. The platform also called for restored tariff protections and an aggressive foreign policy in the Western Hemisphere.

Bryan's campaign was a political hurricane. He spent just $650,000, most of it donated by silver interests, compared with the millions McKinley spent. But Bryan traveled 18,000 miles and gave 600 speeches, and his campaign staffers put out an impressive quantity of literature. Several million copies of *Coin's Financial School*, a prosilver pamphlet, were distributed during fall 1896. Other silverites also maintained busy speaking schedules in the fall.

Bryan's appeal to industrial workers to join his coalition of independent businesspeople failed, largely because they depended for their livelihoods on the very eastern interests that Bryan attacked. McKinley won not only the East but also the small cities and towns in Bryan's southern and western belt of support. Bryan was unable to win rural areas in the East. McKinley won the popular vote 7.1 million (51.0 percent) to 6.5 million (46.7 percent) and the electoral vote 271–176.

The effect of the 1896 presidential election was lasting. James Sundquist wrote: "For 20 years the two-party system had been based on dead issues of the past. It had offered the voters no means of expressing a choice on the crucial issues of domestic policy around which the country had been polarizing…. Then suddenly, with the nomination of Bryan in 1896, the party system took on meaning once again."[66]

The new Republican coalition included residents of cities, where capital and labor were both reasonably content with the economic growth that the GOP tariff policy promoted; farmers in the East and Midwest, who had strong ties to the "party of Lincoln" and who had come to favor high tariffs; Catholic, German Lutheran, and other liturgical Christian denominations; and some border states. Sundquist noted: "It was the persistence of the Civil War attachments that made the realignment of the North so largely a one-way movement—pro-Republican."[67]

After 1896 the competitive party balance that had prevailed for years gave way to lopsided party strength according to region—Democrats in the South, Republicans in the North. Strong opposition parties disappeared in all regions of the country, vesting political power in the hands of those already part of the system.

As political scientist E. E. Schattschneider has observed:

The 1896 party cleavage resulted from the tremendous reaction of conservatives in both major parties to the Populist movement…. [S]outhern conservatives reacted so strongly that they were willing to revive the tensions and animosities of the Civil War and the Reconstruction in order to set up a one-party sectional southern political monopoly in which nearly all Negroes and many poor whites were disenfranchised. One of the most important consequences of the creation of the Solid South was that it severed permanently the connection between the western and the southern wings of the Populist movement.[68]

Conservative Republicans won the White House in all but two (1912 and 1916) of the nine elections from 1896 to 1928. During this period the country experienced economic prosperity that blunted the possible activism of workers and the previous activism of farmers. With good harvests and rising commodity prices, the agrarian revolt fizzled. The development of new ore extraction methods and discovery of new gold deposits made calls for silver to expand the currency supply superfluous. The Spanish-American War in 1898, which McKinley reluctantly entered and the burgeoning mass media publicized, created a patriotic fervor.

McKinley's reelection in 1900 was even stronger than his 1896 election. He won 7.2 million popular votes (51.7 percent) to Bryan's 6.4 million (45.5 percent), and 292 electoral votes to Bryan's 155. McKinley swept to victory with all states except the South and the silver states of the West (Colorado, Montana, Idaho, and Nevada).

Rise of Theodore Roosevelt: 1904

Because Vice President Garret A. Hobart died in office in 1899, the Republicans selected New York's progressive governor, Theodore Roosevelt, to share the ticket with McKinley in the 1900 election. Roosevelt, an independent-minded environmentalist and trust-buster, was promoted for vice president by New York GOP boss Thomas Platt, who wanted to rid the state of him and his progressive politics. Roosevelt was reluctant to take the job: "I am a comparatively young man yet and I like to work…. It would not entertain me to preside in the Senate."[69] He accepted, however, when a convention movement and McKinley prevailed on him.

When McKinley was assassinated in 1901 and Roosevelt became president, presidential politics came under the influence of a variant of the progressive movement. As Gabriel Kolko and other historians have demonstrated, Roosevelt's administration was friendly to many of the GOP's traditional conservative allies. But Roosevelt's rhetoric and his legacy of regulation and conservation had strong progressive or reformist elements.[70]

Roosevelt's leadership of the progressives was an example of generational politics. (As each generation assumes control over political and social structures, it stamps those institutions with its distinctive style and ethos.) The new president grew up in an era in which economic expansion was straining the nation's fabric, causing political figures to seek idealistic but pragmatic solutions to a wide variety of problems. The previous generation had grown up in a simpler age when "politics were devoid of substance, built around appeals to tradition and old loyalties and aimed at patronage."[71]

Roosevelt steered his party toward conservation of natural resources, enforcement of antitrust laws, promotion of the concerns of labor, and railroad regulation. The government's suit to dissolve the Northern Securities Company under the Sherman Anti-Trust Act and Roosevelt's intervention in the anthracite coal miners' strike, both in 1902, established the tenor for an activist presidency. TR (the first president identified by his initials) also used his office as a "bully pulpit" to promote his progressive ideology.

Facing his first election at the top of the ticket, Roosevelt had no trouble winning the Republican nomination in 1904. The party's convention, arranged in advance at the White House, unanimously voted for Roosevelt and his platform of trust-busting, tariffs, labor relations, and activist foreign policy. Sen. Charles W. Fairbanks of Indiana was the GOP vice-presidential nominee.

To oppose the rambunctious Roosevelt, the Democrats selected a sober-visaged judge. Alton Parker, the chief justice of the New York State Court of Appeals, received the backing of the Democratic Party's conservative establishment when former president Cleveland turned down entreaties to make a fourth presidential run. Parker was opposed by William Randolph Hearst, a member of Congress and newspaper magnate. Bryan forced the party to adopt a liberal platform, as a balance to the conservative judge.

The Roosevelt victory was a landslide. He won 7.6 million votes (56.4 percent) to Parker's 5.1 million (37.6 percent) and carried all but the southern states. Roosevelt won 336 electoral votes to Parker's 140. Both houses of Congress were overwhelmingly Republican. President Roosevelt pledged not to seek another term because he had already served most of McKinley's second term. He occupied himself with his progressive agenda and groomed his secretary of war, William Howard Taft, as his successor.

Roosevelt Picks Taft: 1908

Roosevelt appeared to be genuinely dismayed by talk in 1907 of a possible third term, so he made public shows of his support for Taft. Because he also was able to line up state delegations for Taft, the nomination was never in doubt. Taft, through Roosevelt, was particularly strong among Republicans in the South. Attempts to restrict southern representation and pass a more liberal party platform were defeated.

Taft had impressive governmental experience. Before joining Roosevelt's cabinet, he had been a Cincinnati judge, U.S. solicitor general, federal circuit judge, head of the U.S. Commission on the Philippines, and the first civil governor of the Philippines.

Roosevelt's only problem in pushing Taft at the convention was avoiding a stampede in his own favor. Despite a highly disciplined convention, the galleries demonstrated wildly for Roosevelt. But Taft—a newcomer to electoral politics—easily won the nomination on the first ballot. He had 702 votes to the runner-up Philander C. Knox's 68. Rep. James S. Sherman of New York was selected as his running mate.

The Democrats nominated William Jennings Bryan for the third time. The electoral disaster that befell Judge Parker in 1904 was said to be evidence that the party needed an aggressive challenger to the Republicans rather than another conservative candidate. The Democrats were bereft of new talent, especially in competitive states in the East and Midwest, and turned to Bryan despite his disastrous campaign record and the warnings of former president Cleveland.

Taft campaigned on the Roosevelt record. Bryan called for government ownership of railroads and other liberal measures—such as a lower tariff, campaign finance reform, a graduated income tax, labor reforms, and greater enforcement of antitrust and other business regulations.

With Roosevelt and Taft promoting much of the progressive agenda, Bryan's message was no longer distinctive, and Taft won easily. He gathered 7.7 million popular votes (51.6 percent) to Bryan's 6.4 million (43.1 percent), and 321 electoral votes to Bryan's 162. The North, most of the West, and the border states went into the Republican column.

Wilson and the Divided Republicans: 1912 and 1916

Taft was not, by temperament, an ideal executive. His lifelong ambition had been to serve on the Supreme Court, and his disciplined legal mind and collegial nature eventually would enable him to become one of the high court's most able chief justices. (He was appointed to the Court by President Warren G. Harding in 1921.) But Taft foundered in the presidency. He carried out Roosevelt's program of business regulation and conservation, yet Roosevelt responded not

Woodrow Wilson traveled widely in the 1912 election campaign. His dynamic presence and reformist rhetoric appealed to the crowds who came to hear.

with gratitude but with a series of nasty statements and plans for a campaign against Taft.

The tariff issue proved to be Taft's early trouble spot. Taft was committed to reducing tariffs, but he was less cautious than Roosevelt, who had fudged the divisive issue. As a result, Taft quickly became embroiled in a fight with Congress, which wanted to raise tariffs. The Senate remolded House legislation to push up various duties, and Taft publicly promoted the legislation after he managed to secure new corporate taxes and tariff reductions for raw materials. Overall, then, Taft proved ineffective and indecisive on the tariff issue and, as a consequence, began losing his party.

The Glavis-Ballinger affair further muddied the image of the administration. The scandal broke when the chief forester of the Interior Department, Gifford Pinchot, charged that Secretary Richard A. Ballinger had betrayed the cause of conservation and had even engaged in corrupt practices regarding minerals and water power. Pinchot also charged that Ballinger had wrongly fired another Interior official, Louis Glavis, for trying to expose the scandal. Pinchot took his complaints directly to Taft, but Taft sided with Ballinger and urged Pinchot to drop the matter. After an

indignant Pinchot went public with the issue, Taft fired him, fueling suspicion of a cover-up at Interior. The incident was a major embarrassment to Taft because of the priority that conservation had received under Roosevelt and because of the inevitable complaints that Taft was betraying his mentor on the issue.[72]

Divisions within the Republican Party eventually created rival Taft and Roosevelt factions. Tariffs, Arizona's new state constitution (which included a provision for recall of the governor which Taft opposed), treaties, and antitrust issues split the former president and the sitting president. In many ways, the dispute was over personalities. Taft carried out Roosevelt's program but lacked his fervor and decisiveness. In a still conservative age, progressives felt they needed more aggressive leadership than the judicially tempered Taft would ever give them.

Roosevelt spent more than a year of Taft's term hunting in Africa, but he was an active speaker and campaigner when he returned to the United States. He gave a detailed accounting of his philosophy of government in a 1912 speech in Columbus, Ohio, calling for binding votes on public issues, recall of elected officials, and curbs on judicial power. When a dump-Taft movement decided in 1911 that Wisconsin senator Robert La Follette had no chance to defeat the president for the GOP nomination, party discontents turned to the energetic and still young (fifty-two years) Roosevelt.

Roosevelt made an all-out effort for the Republican nomination, entering twelve primaries and winning all but three. More specifically, Roosevelt won 278 delegates in states with primaries to Taft's 48 and La Follette's 36. In today's system, Roosevelt probably would have marched to a first-ballot nomination. (Today, more delegates are allocated by popular votes than by the party organizations, which then dominated the process.) Three crucial Republican states—Pennsylvania, Illinois, and Ohio—went for Roosevelt. He clearly, then, had great popular appeal and vote-getting ability—perhaps more than ever.

But Taft won the nomination. The president controlled the party machinery, and most of the convention's delegates were sent by the state party machines. Roosevelt challenged the credentials of Taft delegates at the Chicago convention, and the nomination's outcome turned on battles over almost one-fourth of the delegates. The fight went to the floor of the convention, but Taft's smooth operation defeated Roosevelt. Roosevelt appeared at the convention to buoy his forces and cry foul.

After the defeat, Roosevelt urged his supporters to continue their fight, which motivated some bolting progressive delegates to organize a convention in August to mount a third-party effort. The bolters formed the Progressive Party. When Roosevelt remarked to a reporter during the GOP convention, "I'm feeling like a bull moose," his vigorous campaign had a symbol.

With the Republicans divided, the Democrats saw their first opportunity to win the presidency since Cleveland in 1892. As the 1912 Democratic convention in Baltimore neared, several national candidates and favorite sons were vying for the nomination. The front-runner was House Speaker James Beauchamp "Champ" Clark of Missouri, a party regular who had party organization support and years of experience to recommend him.

Gov. Woodrow Wilson of New Jersey—who held a doctorate in political science and who had moved into politics after a distinguished career as professor and president at Princeton University—was another strong candidate. Wilson's virtues were the opposite of Clark's. He did not have an extensive political record for opponents to attack, and he was supported enthusiastically because of his dynamic presence and reformist rhetoric. Although the New Jersey machine had brought Wilson into politics, he quickly asserted his independence and became something of a crusader.

As a newcomer to national politics, Wilson both refreshed and alienated Democratic crowds in speeches before the convention. He came out strongly for the "radical" platform of referendum, initiative, and recall, prompting a newspaper to report: "The boldness, the directness, the incisiveness, the fearlessness, and the force of the 'Virginian-Jerseyan's' words crashed at times through the throng like a series of thunderbolt jolts."[73] But Wilson's embrace of the progressive agenda and attacks on business alienated many southerners; even the delegates from Wilson's home state of Virginia opposed him at the convention.

Other Democratic candidates were the conservative representative Oscar Underwood of Alabama, author of a historic tariff act; another conservative, Gov. Judson Harmon of Ohio; and four favorite-son governors. Clark appeared to have won the nomination when a Tammany bloc of delegates moved to support him after he won a tenth-ballot majority. The requirement for a two-thirds majority, however, gave other candidates time to maneuver. Wilson almost dropped out of the race, but Bryan's late transfer of his support from Clark to Wilson created a bandwagon effect for Wilson. On the forty-sixth ballot, Wilson accumulated the necessary two-thirds of delegates for the nomination. Gov. Thomas Marshall of Indiana, one of the favorite-son candidates, was picked to be the vice-presidential nominee because Underwood, Wilson's choice, would not accept it.

The Democratic platform was progressive. It called for tariff reduction, utility regulation, banking reforms, legislation to curb monopolies, a national income tax, direct election of senators, campaign finance reforms, and a national presidential primary. Roosevelt actually praised Wilson as "an able man" in the early fall and said he might not have started a third-party effort if he had known Wilson would be the Democrats' candidate. But Wilson and Roosevelt eventually criticized each other's approach to government, especially after Wilson expressed reservations about government activism.[74]

Wilson easily won the election, receiving 435 electoral votes to Roosevelt's 88 and Taft's 8. The Republican split obviously helped Wilson; if Roosevelt and Taft had combined their totals of 4.1 million votes (27.4 percent) and 3.5 million votes (23.2 percent), they would have topped Wilson's 6.3 million (41.8 percent). Yet even though Wilson was a minority president, there was a clear Democratic trend since the Democrats had taken over the House and replaced several Republican governors in the 1910 midterm elections. It was the worst showing ever for an incumbent president—third place with only two states.

Whatever the strength of Wilson's "mandate," he acted as though he had won by a landslide. His first term was one of the most productive in U.S. history. With the Democrats in control of Congress, and with a shrewd political adviser in Col. Edward M. House, Wilson adopted a reform agenda that had been percolating at various levels of government for years. He broke precedent by delivering his first State of the Union message to Congress in person. At the center of the message was a call for reductions in tariff rates. After a bitter fight that raged for a month, Wilson went public with a demand that members of Congress reveal their property holdings. The revelations, in response to public pressure, showed close links between their holdings and the kinds of tariff protections on the books. Congress soon was shamed into passing tariff cuts of 15 percent. More than 100 items were placed on a free-trade list for the first time.

Wilson also addressed other areas successfully: taxes (institution of a graduated income tax in 1913, which replaced reliance on tariffs and various excise and user taxes); banking regulation (the Glass-Owen Act of 1913, which created the Federal Reserve system); antitrust legislation (the Clayton Anti-Trust Act of 1914, creation of the Federal Trade Commission in 1914); labor relations (Section 6 of the Sherman Anti-Trust Act, which exempted unions from antitrust strictures); agriculture (the Smith-Lever Act of 1914, the Federal Farm Loan Act of 1916); conservation (creation of the National Park Service in 1916); and the judiciary (the appointment of Louis Brandeis to the Supreme Court).

Despite his strong leadership—highlighted by his stirring oratory—Wilson still faced the prospect in 1916 of a tough reelection. He had won the presidency in 1912 with only 41.8 percent of the popular vote, and the escalating war in Europe was beginning to disturb the American process of steady economic growth.

Public opinion on the Great War was volatile, largely because more than a third of the U.S. population was either foreign born or the offspring of foreign-born parents. Some 11 million Americans surveyed in the 1910 census were of direct German or Austrian descent, and another five million were from Ireland. Many other immigrants were Russian, Italian, Hungarian, British, and French. Wilson sought to diffuse feelings for the immigrants' native lands when he denounced "hyphenism"—the tendency of many citizens to identify themselves with appellations that linked their ethnic origins and American status—but politicians at lower levels tailored their campaigns to specific nationality voting blocs.[75]

Wilson and Vice President Marshall won renomination without any opposition. The most significant event of the Democratic convention was the passage of the platform, which indicated the party's main campaign theme. By calling for national universal suffrage, Wilson helped himself in the eleven western states where women already had won the vote. The platform praised "the splendid diplomatic victories of our great president, who has preserved the vital interests of our government and its citizens, and kept us out of war." The latter phrase would be repeated endlessly during the fall.[76]

The Republicans gave the presidential nomination to Supreme Court Justice Charles Evans Hughes. Hughes was silent in the months before the convention, but a number of party leaders lined up enough delegates for him to win a third-ballot nomination. Other potential candidates in 1916 included former president Roosevelt, former senator Elihu Root of New York, former vice president Fairbanks, and Senators John Weeks, Albert Cummins, and Lawrence Sherman. Fairbanks won the vice-presidential nomination.

Prosperity and reformism limited the campaign themes available to the Republicans. The GOP railed against Wilson's foreign policy as "shifty expedients" and "phrasemaking" that put the United States in danger of entering the war. Hughes turned out to be a bad campaigner, but he bridged the gap between conservative and progressive Republicans that had cost the party the 1912 election. Wilson was occupied with Congress throughout the summer of 1916, but he emerged to give a series of speeches in the fall. Democratic strategists, meanwhile, conceived and executed a masterful strategy to return Wilson to the White House. The Democrats concentrated all their resources on "swing states" and ignored states they thought Wilson was sure to lose. Illinois, for example, was ignored since it was a certain Republican state. Bryan, Wilson's secretary of state, toured the West.

Wilson won one of the closest elections in history. California, an uncertain state, ensured Wilson's victory when, because of the urban vote, it went the president's way late in the campaign. The margin of victory was 3,420 votes in that state. The president defeated Hughes by a margin of 9.1 million (49.2 percent) to 8.5 million popular votes (46.1 percent). The electoral college gave Wilson 277 votes and Hughes 254.

Even though Wilson's campaign in 1916 was based on his determination to stay out of the Great War, the United States entered the war in 1917. Wilson's conduct of the war won him the status of war hero, but his diplomatic efforts after the war failed. Wilson was the architect of the Treaty of Versailles, which created a League of Nations to prevent future wars. But Wilson was unable to induce the Senate to approve the treaty, and he left office in 1921 a broken and dispirited man.

"RETURN TO NORMALCY" AND THE ROARING TWENTIES

After the tumult of Woodrow Wilson's domestic reforms, World War I, and the divisive battle over the Versailles treaty, the time was ripe for a period of conservatism and Republican government. Deep resentment had developed toward Wilson and the Democratic Party, and the Democrats themselves were divided over many issues, including economic regulation, Prohibition, and race relations.

Blessed with good luck, substantial financial backing, and a strong trend toward split-ticket voting, beginning in the 1920s the Republicans were able to resume their dominance over national politics with three successful presidential campaigns: Warren G. Harding in 1920, Calvin Coolidge in 1924, and Herbert C. Hoover in 1928.

The 1920s are usually pictured as a time of steady, unexciting politics. The conservatives dominated the federal government, and occupying the White House were men who spoke of "normalcy" and a noninterventionist brand of politics in both domestic and foreign affairs. One of the symbols of the age was President Coolidge's program of tax cuts, which reduced the rates on the wealthy. The wartime Revenue Act of 1918 had driven tax rates to the highest point in U.S. history—77 percent in the highest brackets. In 1921, 1923, and 1926, Secretary of the Treasury Andrew Mellon presented to Congress proposals to cut taxes, the most controversial being the reduction in the maximum surtax from 77 to 25 percent. Congress eventually cut the surtax to 40 percent in 1924 and 20 percent in 1926.[77]

But the sober men who filled the presidency in the twenties met challenges from progressives of both parties in Congress and in the state governments. On a wide range of issues—including relief of the poor, subsidies for the depressed farm sector, regulation of utilities, immigration, race relations, states' rights, tax cuts, and Prohibition—the conservative presidents encountered strong challenges. They frequently responded by vetoing legislation, but such an expedient would not prevent the pressures for a more activist government from developing.

Harding and "Normalcy": 1920

Harding, a product of the GOP machine of Ohio, emerged from a crowded and largely unknown pack to win the Republican nomination in 1920 at a convention dominated by economic interests such as oil, railroads, and steel. The

Democratic presidential candidate James M. Cox of Ohio, left, and vice-presidential candidate Franklin D. Roosevelt (one year before he was stricken with polio) campaign in the 1920 election. They lost to Republican presidential candidate Warren G. Harding and his running mate, Gov. Calvin Coolidge of Massachusetts.

early candidates were Gen. Leonard Wood, an old Roosevelt ally; Gov. Frank Lowden of Illinois, who married into the Pullman family and therefore had ample financing for a campaign; and Sen. Hiram Johnson of California, whose progressive and isolationist stances put him in good stead with voters in many states. A dozen favorite sons hoped that a deadlocked convention might bring the nomination their way. All of the candidates were on hand in Chicago to maneuver for the nomination.

While Wood, Johnson, and Lowden performed reasonably well in the primaries, Harding won only his home state of Ohio and did not arouse much popular enthusiasm. But under the direction of a shrewd campaign manager, Harry Daugherty, Harding gained the support of the party's bosses and won the nomination on the tenth ballot after a brief interview with them in the "smoke-filled room" that was synonymous with boss control. Governor Coolidge of Massachusetts, a favorite-son contender for president, became Harding's vice-presidential candidate.

The Democrats selected Gov. James Cox, also from Ohio, after lengthy platform battles and balloting for the nomination. Early ballots put former Treasury secretary William G. McAdoo and Attorney General Mitchell Palmer in the lead, but Cox gained steadily and had the nomination by the forty-fourth roll call. The convention then rapidly selected thirty-eight-year-old Franklin D. Roosevelt of New York, the assistant secretary of the navy, to be Cox's running mate.

The image of Wilson hung over the convention and would hang over the fall campaign. The Democratic platform praised Wilson's conduct of the war and his domestic reform program. But the results in the November election indicated deep unease over the Democratic administration.

Harding amassed 16.1 million popular votes (60.3 percent) to Cox's 9.1 million (34.2 percent), and 404 electoral votes to Cox's 127. Harding carried the North and West including Oklahoma and all of the southern and border states except Tennessee and Kentucky.

Harding's landslide victory was termed "election by disgust" by political analysts. The wartime sacrifices demanded under Wilson were widely perceived as the cause of Harding's victory rather than a desire for the ideology or policy proposals that Harding was offering. The *New York Post* editorialized: "We are in the backwash from the mighty spiritual and physical effort to which America girded herself when she won the war for the Allies.... The war has not been repudiated, though the administration that fought it has been overwhelmed. We are now in the chill that comes with the doctor's bills."[78]

The electorate's ability to shift allegiances from the Republicans to the Democrats and back again—from one period to the next, and from one level of government to the next—suggested a dissolution of partisan alignments. The addition of women to the electorate after passage of the Nineteenth Amendment in 1920 and the increasing independence among all voters induced uncertainty. National exhaustion from the war and the lack of sharp ideological differences between the candidates produced apathy. The electorate's instability was suggested by the divisions within both parties on high-profile issues such as Prohibition, the League of Nations, agricultural policies, and other social and economic matters—among them, technical assistance and trust busting. The appearance of numerous "blocs" in both parties represented "little if anything more than a transitory alignment upon a particular vote or issue."[79]

The shifts in control of congressional and state offices also indicated electoral instability. The Democrats had had comfortable control of Congress under Wilson, but in 1920 the Republicans gained a majority of 301 to 131 in the House and 59 to 37 in the Senate. Impressive liberal gains in congressional and state elections in the midterm election of 1922 appeared to be a slap at the Harding administration. The high turnover of votes also indicated unstable party affiliations: the 14.2 percentage point increase in the Republican vote between the 1916 and 1920 presidential elections was the largest since the Civil War, another time of turmoil.[80]

President Harding died on August 2, 1923, of a heart attack, just as revelations of kickbacks and favoritism in the administration began to surface and several members of the administration quit and two committed suicide. The investigation into the so-called Teapot Dome scandal—so named after the site of naval oil reserves that were transferred to private hands in exchange for bribes—would last five years. The Democrats hoped to make the scandal a major issue in the 1924 election, but Democratic complicity in the wrongdoing and the personal integrity of Harding's successor, Calvin Coolidge, defused the issue.

Coolidge Cleans Up: 1924

President Coolidge fired Attorney General Harry M. Daugherty and other members of Harding's clique and projected an image of puritan cleanliness. Coolidge—a taciturn man who had slowly climbed the political ladder in Massachusetts from city council member to city solicitor, mayor, state legislator, lieutenant governor, and governor before he became vice president—expounded a deeply individualistic Yankee philosophy that helped to separate him from the corrupt men in the Harding White House.

Except for appointing as attorney general Harlan Fiske Stone, former dean of the Columbia University School of Law, Coolidge allowed others to finish cleaning up the mess left behind by Harding. The new president was concerned about unnecessarily alienating himself from party leaders.

By the time Coolidge sought the presidency on his own in 1924, the economy had rebounded. One of the most conservative presidents ever, Coolidge's platform called for additional tax cuts but said nothing substantive about increasingly salient agriculture and labor issues. Coolidge

President Calvin Coolidge stands by radio equipment used on an automobile during his 1924 campaign.

also pushed an isolationist foreign policy plank. He won the nomination on the first ballot.

While the Republicans were able to "Keep Cool with Coolidge," the Democrats spent sixteen days in a seemingly endless attempt to pick a nominee in New York's sweltering Madison Square Garden. A fight developed because the party was badly split between its northeastern urban bloc and its more conservative southern and western rural bloc. New York governor Alfred E. Smith and former Treasury secretary William McAdoo of California were the key combatants at the convention until the delegates were freed from the instructions of party bosses on the one-hundredth ballot.

Suspicions between the two regional blocs were intense. A platform plank denouncing the Ku Klux Klan created the most controversy. Northerners wanted an explicit repudiation of the society that preached hatred of blacks, Catholics, and Jews; in the end, southerners would settle only for a vaguely worded rebuke. (The Klan had infiltrated the party in many rural areas.) Another divisive issue was Prohibition, with northerners attacking the initiative and southerners supporting it. These sectional splits would cripple the Democrats in the 1924 and 1928 elections.

After the delegates were freed from instructions, a stampede developed for John W. Davis of West Virginia, a lawyer with Wall Street connections. The ticket was balanced with the vice-presidential selection of Charles W. Bryan of Nebraska, the younger brother of three-time presidential candidate William Jennings Bryan.

The Progressive candidacy of Robert La Follette complicated the calculations of voters, particularly those on the liberal end of the political spectrum. Because the Democrats had a nearly impenetrable hold on the South, La Follette was not given a reasonable chance of winning. But the conservatism of both Coolidge and Davis meant that La Follette was the only liberal in the race. Still, many liberals voted for

Davis or even Coolidge because of the fear of an inconclusive election that would have to be resolved in the House of Representatives.

Coolidge won the election easily, with the Democrats polling their smallest percentage ever. Coolidge won 54.1 percent of the vote, Davis won 28.8 percent, and La Follette won 16.6 percent. Coolidge attracted 15.7 million popular votes and 382 electoral votes; Davis, 8.4 million and 136; and La Follette, 4.8 million and 13.

On August 2, 1927, when Coolidge announced his decision not to seek reelection by passing out a brief note to reporters and then refusing further comment, the Republicans began jockeying for the nomination for the 1928 election.

Hoover Succession: 1928

Secretary of Commerce Hoover was the obvious choice to replace Coolidge at the head of the GOP ticket. A native of Iowa who learned mining engineering at Stanford University, Hoover was immensely popular with most of the party. Hoover's administration of Belgian relief and food distribution programs during World War I had earned him the status of statesman and humanitarian.

Hoover began working for the nomination soon after Coolidge dropped out, spending $400,000 in the nominating phase of the election. He won the nomination on the first ballot over Governors Frank Lowden of Illinois and Charles Curtis of Kansas. Curtis was named Hoover's running mate.

Hoover was religious in his zeal for what he called "the American system" of free enterprise and individualism. He did not see any inconsistency in having the government vigorously support businesses with tax breaks, tariffs, public provision of infrastructures, and police protection, while at the same time denying relief to people in need. Hoover appeared to be less rigid than Coolidge, however. He proposed creation of a special farm board and said he would consider legislation to protect labor unions from abuses in the use of court injunctions.

Al Smith, the Tammany-schooled governor of New York, was the Democratic nominee. Smith had the support of all the party's northern states, and he won a first-ballot nomination. Sen. Joseph T. Robinson of Arkansas was the vice-presidential candidate.

Smith's candidacy polarized the electorate, particularly the South. He was the first Catholic to be nominated for president by a major party, and he endured religious slurs throughout the fall. Moreover, he favored repeal of Prohibition, still a divisive issue, and he was an urbanite, a problem for a nation that had nurtured a rural ideal since Thomas Jefferson. Because he also was a machine politician, he presented a problem for anyone outside (and many people inside) the nation's great cities. He also was a strong opponent of the Klan, which put him in trouble in the South. Finally, he was an unabashed liberal who proposed public works, farm relief programs, stronger protection of workers, and regulation of banking and industry.

During the fall campaign, Hoover acted like the incumbent and Smith barnstormed the country, trying in vain to pick up support in the South and West. The 1928 campaign was the first with extensive radio coverage, and

In 1932 World War I veterans, seeking early receipt of their service bonuses, staged a protest by setting up camps near the Capitol. President Herbert C. Hoover ordered federal troops, headed by Gen. Douglas MacArthur, to disperse the veterans with tear gas.

Hoover generally fared better than Smith on the airwaves. Hoover, the small-town boy who made good, represented fulfillment of the American Dream; Smith, the inner-city boy who made good, also embodied that ideal, but he had too many ethnic traits for much of the nation to realize it.

The November election produced another Republican landslide. Hoover carried forty states with 21.4 million popular votes (58.2 percent) and 444 electoral votes, while Smith carried only eight states with 15.0 million popular votes (40.8 percent) and 87 electoral votes. As disastrous as the election appeared to be for the Democrats, it put them in position to build a wide-ranging coalition in future years.

Smith carried only six southern states, but the defection of the others was temporary. More important to the Democrats' long-range fortunes was the movement of cities into the Democratic column, where they would stay for the rest of the century. Immigrants in cities were expanding their vision from local politics to the national stage for the first time. In all, Smith diverted 122 northern counties from the GOP to the Democratic Party. Catholics, whose turnout previously had been low, turned out in record numbers. Smith also seemed to pick up some of the Progressive farm vote that La Follette had tapped before; in Wisconsin, for example, the Democratic vote jumped from 68,000 to 450,000 from 1924 to 1928. Finally, Smith's candidacy put the Democrats solidly in the "wet" column, just as the national temper began to resent Prohibition.

President Hoover impressed political observers with his managerial skills and "coordinating mind." With passage of the Agricultural Marketing Act in June 1929, the administration appeared to address the most pressing economic problem for the business-minded president. He met some legislative setbacks, but, overall, the Great Engineer appeared to be in good political condition as the nation looked back over his record when Congress began its recess in summer 1929.

The national economic and social fiesta that had begun at the close of World War I came to an abrupt end on October 29, 1929. After climbing to dizzying new heights for months, the stock market crashed. First described by economists and politicians as a temporary interruption of the good times, the crash quickly led to a wave of business and bank failures, mortgage foreclosures, wage cuts, layoffs, and a crisis of political leadership. By the end of Hoover's term in 1933, more than 12 million workers had lost their jobs; the unemployment rate was approximately 25 percent. An October 1931 advertisement for 6,000 jobs in the Soviet Union brought 100,000 American applications.[81]

President Hoover, who had celebrated his inauguration with a prediction that poverty and hunger were near an end, did not know how to cope with the crisis. In a special session that Hoover called, Congress created the Federal Farm Board to coordinate marketing of agricultural products, but Hoover steadfastly opposed further moves, especially subsidies. In 1930 Hoover signed the Smoot-Hawley Tariff Act to protect manufacturers, but, true to the predictions of economists and bankers, the tariff only aggravated economic conditions by hurting foreign trade.

Hoover later approved agricultural relief and public works programs and established the Reconstruction Finance Corporation. The president refused to approve direct relief to the unemployed and businesses, but he did approve some loans and aid to specific sectors of the economy.

Despite his earnest and tireless efforts, Hoover became a figure of widespread enmity. The low point of his distinguished career came when World War I veterans petitioned for early receipt of their service bonuses, which, by contract, were not to be paid until 1945. They set up camp in Washington, singing old war songs and carrying placards that bore their pleas. The "Bonus Army" numbered 20,000 at its height. When Hoover feared a protracted protest, he ordered federal troops to take over buildings where some veterans were camping. In two skirmishes, two veterans were killed. The president then sent in Gen. Douglas MacArthur with tanks, infantry, and cavalry soldiers. (MacArthur's junior officers included Dwight D. Eisenhower and George Patton.) After successfully removing the veterans, the military forces overran nearby veterans' camps in a rain of fire and tear gas. Thousands of veterans and their families fled the burning district.

The administration's tough stance against a defeated, ragtag band of former war heroes shocked and embittered the nation. The barricaded White House and administration statements about "insurrectionists" symbolized a dangerous gulf between the government and the people.

Partly because of the economic crisis he did not create, but also because of his dour and unimaginative demeanor, Hoover probably never had a chance to win reelection. The 1930 midterm elections indicated a loss of confidence in the administration. The House went Democratic, 219 to 214, and the Senate came within a seat of going Democratic as well.

Those election results did not convey the bitterness and despair that the Depression would aggravate before the next presidential campaign. Hoover was mercilessly ridiculed in newspapers and in Democratic speeches. The Democratic Party coordinated a comprehensive anti-Hoover campaign that made the president politically impotent.

"The New Deal" Election: 1932

Franklin D. Roosevelt, fifth cousin to Theodore Roosevelt, was the perfect candidate to oppose Hoover. The New York governor had been an activist in state politics, first opposing the state's Tammany machine and then pioneering many relief and reconstruction programs that Hoover refused to expand to the national scale. Roosevelt had been the party's vice-presidential candidate twelve years earlier,

Franklin D. Roosevelt campaigns by car in West Virginia, October 19, 1932.

and he had served in the federal government as assistant secretary of the navy.

Perhaps more important than any of his political accomplishments were FDR's image of strength and optimism and his deft handling of hot issues and disparate members of the potential Democratic coalition. Although he was a polio victim, Roosevelt often smiled—a devastating contrast to Hoover. (Gutzon Borglum, the sculptor, wrote: "If you put a rose in Hoover's hand, it would wilt."[82]) Roosevelt was able to campaign for the presidency without putting forth a comprehensive program: the simple promise of a change in leadership was enough.

Some observers found the man from Hyde Park wanting. Journalist Walter Lippmann, for example, complained that Roosevelt was "a pleasant man who, without any important qualifications for the office, would like very much to be president."[83] But those detractors and a large field of Democratic candidates were not able to keep Roosevelt from his "rendezvous with destiny."[84]

The Democratic field included the 1928 Democratic standard-bearer, Smith; Speaker of the House John Nance Garner; Gov. Albert Ritchie of Maryland; Gov. George White of Ohio; Gov. Harry Byrd of Virginia; and former senator James Reed of Missouri. Most considered Smith more of a "stalking horse" for the anti-FDR forces than a serious candidate on his own. Garner had impressive backing from the newspaper magnate William Randolph Hearst and former Democratic candidate William McAdoo.

The many favorite sons in the race threatened to deadlock the convention and deny the nomination to the front-runner, as they had done so often in the past. Roosevelt had difficulty with his region of the country because of his opposition to the Tammany machine in New York. Acquiring the required two-thirds vote of delegates for the nomination was difficult for Roosevelt or any other candidate, but FDR eventually won on the fourth ballot when he promised the vice-presidential slot to Garner.

In U.S. political history, Franklin Roosevelt was the first candidate to appear before the convention that nominated him. In an acceptance speech to the conventioneers who had staged wild rallies in his support, Roosevelt made passing reference to the "new deal" that his administration would offer Americans. That phrase, picked up in a newspaper cartoon the next day, came to symbolize the renewal for which Americans yearned as riots and radicalism seemed to threaten the nation's spirit and the legitimacy of its institutions.

Roosevelt conducted an active fall campaign, traveling 23,000 miles in forty-one states to quell suspicions that his physical handicaps would deter him from performing his job. Besides barnstorming the nation, Roosevelt took to the radio airwaves—he was the first sophisticated electronic media candidate—where he conveyed a sense of warmth and confidence. He also showed an intellectual bent and an open mind when he called on academics and professionals—the famed "brain trust"—for their expert advice on the issues.

Roosevelt won 22.8 million votes (57.4 percent) to Hoover's 15.8 million (39.6 percent). Forty-two of the forty-eight states and 472 of the 531 electoral votes went for Roosevelt. The election was a landslide and a realignment of the major forces in U.S. politics.

NEW DEAL COALITION

The profound effect of Franklin D. Roosevelt's victory on U.S. politics can hardly be overstated. The New Deal coalition that Roosevelt assembled shaped the political discourse and electoral competition of the United States until the late 1960s. In many respects, that coalition is a central element of politics today.

The new Democratic coalition brought together a disparate group of interests: southerners, African Americans, immigrants, farmers, capital-intensive producers, international businessmen, financiers, urbanites, trade unions, intellectuals, Catholics, and Jews. Rexford Tugwell called it "the most miscellaneous coalition in history."[85] These blocs were not always in perfect harmony—for example, the Democrats juggled the demands of blacks and white southerners with great difficulty—but they were solid building blocks for national political dominance.

The dominance was impressive. Between 1932 and 1964, the Democrats won seven of nine presidential elections. The only successful Republican, Dwight D. Eisenhower, could just as easily have run as a Democrat. Party leaders in fact asked him to run as a Democrat in 1948 and 1952, and his name was entered in some Democratic primaries in 1952.

The strength of Roosevelt's rule was attributable partly to the president's personality. He could be soothing. When he gave his first "fireside chat" about the banking crisis, the nation responded with cooperation; the raids and violence at banks ended in a matter of weeks. More important than his soothing nature was his ability to experiment and shift gears. Professor James David Barber described Roosevelt's many public postures:

> Founder of the New Deal, modern American democracy's closest approximation to a common political philosophy, Roosevelt came on the scene as the least philosophical of men—"a chameleon in plaid," Hoover called him. Firm fighter of yet another Great War, Roosevelt appeared to H. L. Mencken in 1932 as "far too feeble and wishy-washy a fellow to make a really effective fight." Architect of world organization, he introduced himself as totally concerned with America's domestic drama. His name is inseparable from his generation's great social revolution; in 1932, nearly all the heavy thinkers scoffed at him as just another placebo politician—a "pill to cure an earthquake," said Professor [Harold] Laski.[86]

More important than personality was what Roosevelt had to offer the many groups in his coalition. As historian Richard Hofstadter has noted, the New Deal was "a series of improvisations, many adopted very suddenly, many contradictory."[87] The Roosevelt credo was: "Save the people and the nation, and if we have to change our minds twice a day to accomplish that end, we should do it."[88]

Until the vast expenditures of World War II, there was not enough pump-priming to end the Depression, but Roosevelt's initiatives touched almost everyone affected by the slump.[89] For the jobless, there were unemployment insurance and public works programs such as the Works Progress Administration and the Civilian Conservation Corps. For the poor, there were categorical aid programs. For westerners, there were conservation measures. For the banks, there was the famous holiday that stopped runs on holdings, and there were currency and securities reforms. For farmers, there were incentives and price supports and cooperatives. For the aged, there was Social Security. For southeasterners, there was the Tennessee Valley Authority. For southern whites, there was a hands-off policy on race matters. For blacks, there were sympathy and jobs programs. For those living in rural areas, there was electrification. For families, there were home loans. For the weary worker eager for a few rounds at the local tavern, there was the repeal of Prohibition. For laborers, there was acknowledgment of the right to negotiate for their share of the national wealth. For business, there were the Federal Emergency Relief Act and the National Industrial Recovery Act, as well as diplomatic negotiation to reduce trade barriers.

The remarkably divergent interests in the coalition were underscored by the politics of race. Blacks moved en masse to the Democratic Party from their traditional position in the "Party of Lincoln," partly because of Hoover's failure but also because of the inclusive rhetoric of the New Deal. Yet Roosevelt was too concerned about his bloc of southern support to accept even antilynching legislation.

Scholars have argued that the New Deal coalition did not indicate a wholesale shift in existing political loyalties, but rather that new groups such as urbanites and blacks had joined an already stable alliance to tip the competitive balance of U.S. parties. The political discourse in the United States changed not because all or even most groups changed their behavior but because new groups and issues became involved.[90]

The core of Roosevelt's winning coalition was easy to describe: "Southern white Protestants, Catholics, and non-Southern white Protestants of the lowest socioeconomic stratum together accounted for roughly three-fourths of all Americans of voting age in 1940 who thought of themselves as Democrats. By way of contrast, these three groups provided only about 40 percent of the smaller cadre of Republican identifiers."[91] Within the Democratic coalition, there were both new and old elements.

Although the Democratic Party encompassed new constituencies and addressed new issues, it retained many of its traditional supporters. The segregated "Jim Crow" South had consistently been in the Democratic column; in 1896, for example, the South's percentage support for Democrat William Jennings Bryan exceeded that of the rest of the nation by 15.3 points. Even in 1928, when Al Smith's Catholicism reduced support for the Democrats to under 50 percent for the first time, the Deep South supported the Democrats more than the border South did.[92] To the South, the Democrats were reliably the party of white supremacy and agricultural interests, while Republicans favored the industrial interests of the North.

Outside the South, the Democratic Party was the party of immigrants and Catholics. Since Andrew Jackson's day, the overwhelmingly Democratic voting patterns of Catholics had contrasted with the split vote of Protestants in the United States. The Catholic-Protestant divisions represented "not so much religious as more general ethnocultural traditions."[93] The Democratic hold on the Catholic vote was reinforced by the heavy immigration into northern cities in the last half of the nineteenth century. While the anti-Catholic Ku Klux Klan received Democratic backing in the South, it received Republican backing in the North, pushing northern Catholics decisively into the Democratic Party.

A steady base in the Democratic Party consisted of laborers and the poor. From the first party machines in the early nineteenth century to Bryan's campaign on behalf of the depressed farm belt in 1896 to Woodrow Wilson's acceptance of labor bargaining in 1914, the Democrats had shown sympathy for the less-privileged classes. Such sympathies often were constricted by prejudice or conservatism, but the Democrats offered more hope of representation than the business-oriented Republicans. Roosevelt solidified the support of the poor and laboring classes.[94] Sundquist has written: "The party system undoubtedly reflected some degree of class before the realignment, but there can be little doubt that it was accentuated by the event. It was in the New Deal era that tight bonds were formed between organized labor and the Democratic Party, that ties equally close if less formal and overt were formed between business and the GOP, and that politics for the first time since 1896 sharply accented class issues."[95] Roosevelt consistently received the support of more than two-thirds of the voters of low socioeconomic status.[96]

New converts to the Democratic Party included blacks and Jews. The inclusion of blacks into the New Deal coalition underscored a "multiplier effect" at work within thriving interest group politics. The Republicans received the black vote in the seventeen elections from Reconstruction to 1932. That year, Roosevelt received 35 percent of the black vote, but his black support was as low as 23 percent in Chicago and 29 percent in Cincinnati.[97] Even though Roosevelt did little to promote black interests in the South, where most blacks lived but could not vote, the black vote for him

increased to 70 percent in 1936 and 1940. Migration of blacks to the North and the spillover effects of Roosevelt's many domestic programs brought blacks to the Democratic Party.

Jews, who had voted Republican since their numbers swelled during immigration around the turn of the century, turned to the Democrats as they became the more liberal party. Roosevelt got 85 percent of the Jewish vote in 1936 and 84 percent in 1940. New Deal assistance programs and Roosevelt's efforts to fight Nazism appealed to Jews, but perhaps more important was "the historic pattern of discrimination which forced or disposed Jews to oppose conservative parties."[98] The class division that split other social groups was absent in the Jewish population.

In many ways, the whole of the New Deal was greater than the sum of its parts. Political scientist Samuel Beer has argued that two long-competing visions of U.S. politics—the national idea and the democratic idea—at last came together during Roosevelt's administration. With the New Deal, the Democratic Party was able to combine its traditional concern for local, individualistic interests with a national vision. By bringing "locked-out" groups into the system, the Democrats enhanced both nation building and individual freedoms. The parts, put together, created a stronger whole. Beer quotes the French sociologist Emile Durkheim: "The image of the one who completes us becomes inseparable from ours.... It thus becomes an integral and permanent part of our conscience...."[99]

The political genius of "interest-group liberalism"[100] was not just that it offered something to everyone, but that it created a new age of consumerism in which everyone's interest was in economic growth rather than structural change. The general good was defined as growth. The potentially divisive competition over restricted and unequally distributed resources was avoided with a general acceptance of growth as the common goal. When there was growth, everyone could get a little more. That public philosophy became a permanent part of American political discourse.

Roosevelt's First Reelection: 1936

Roosevelt's coalition and leadership were so strong that he became the only president to win more than two elections. He won four elections and served a little more than twelve years in the White House before dying in office at the start of his fourth term.

Roosevelt's four electoral triumphs caused Republicans to fume about his "imperial" presidency; all they could do in response to FDR was to promote a constitutional amendment to limit presidents to two terms. But more important than this perception was the way Roosevelt shaped the U.S. political agenda. For many people of the time, it was difficult to imagine the United States under any other leader.

President Franklin D. Roosevelt's Republican opponents during his three successful reelection campaigns were, from left: Gov. Alfred M. Landon of Kansas in 1936; former Democrat and business executive Wendell L. Willkie in 1940; and Gov. Thomas E. Dewey of New York in 1944. Dewey ran again and lost against President Truman in 1948.

It is possible that Roosevelt could have forged an even stronger liberal coalition than he did. But Roosevelt was a pragmatist above all else and alternately angered and wooed such groups as business, labor, farmers, and the military. For example, Roosevelt kept his distance from Upton Sinclair's populist campaign for governor of California in 1934. Because he threatened business interests, Sinclair was the target of a sustained personal attack by business and other conservative forces in the state in what one authority has called the first media campaign in American history. Sinclair's losing effort, the historian Greg Mitchell argued, undermined the power of reformers nationally.[101]

Roosevelt's three successful reelection drives evoked a changing response from Republicans. Roosevelt's first reelection opponent, in 1936, was Gov. Alfred M. Landon of Kansas, who strongly criticized every aspect of the New Deal. After 1936, Republican candidates did not criticize federal intervention in economic and social affairs but rather the speed and the skill of Democratic intervention. In the third election the Republicans argued that Roosevelt was a "warmonger" because he tilted toward Great Britain in World War II. The GOP also argued in the third and fourth elections that Roosevelt threatened to become a "dictator" by exceeding the traditional two-term limit.

Landon was the early favorite for the Republican nomination in 1936. Sen. Charles McNary of Oregon, Sen. Arthur Vandenberg of Michigan, and *Chicago Daily News* publisher Frank Knox provided weak opposition. A Republican bolter for Theodore Roosevelt's "Bull Moose" candidacy in 1912, Landon was consistently to the left of the GOP. Historian James MacGregor Burns observed: "Landon had just the qualities of common sense, homely competence,

cautious liberalism and rocklike 'soundness' that the Republicans hoped would appeal to a people tiring, it was hoped, of the antics and heroics in the White House."[102]

In 1936 the Republicans could not have stated their opposition to the popular New Deal in any stronger terms. The platform read: "America is in peril. The welfare of American men and women and the future of our youth are at stake. We dedicate ourselves to the preservation of their political liberty, their individual opportunity, and their character as free citizens, which today for the first time are threatened by government itself."[103]

The Republicans called for ending a wide range of government regulations, returning relief to state and local governments, replacing Social Security, balancing the budget, and changing tariff and currency policies. Landon's only innovation was to call for a constitutional amendment allowing the states to regulate the labor of women and children; the Supreme Court had struck down a New York minimum wage law in 1935. After Landon won the nomination on the first ballot, he selected Knox as his running mate.

The only time the two presidential candidates met was at a meeting Roosevelt called with state governors in Des Moines to discuss farm relief and a recent drought. FDR hoped to put Landon on the spot about farm relief. But Landon turned out to be the aggressor, demanding that FDR address the dire situation of 100,000 starving farmers in Oklahoma. FDR responded that he had some federal agencies working on programs "just as fast as the Lord will let them." When Landon said that such an answer was small consolation, Roosevelt retorted: "What more can you say to the hungry farmer, governor? The machinery will be put in gear just as fast as the Lord will let *you*?"[104]

Landon's campaign possessed a lavish war chest of $9 million, benefited from the defections of Democratic stalwarts such as John Davis and Al Smith (the party's presidential nominees in 1924 and 1928) and well-coordinated campaign work by business lobbies, and engaged in smear campaigns that portrayed Social Security as a simple "pay reduction" measure and Roosevelt as physically and mentally ill. Landon also argued that New Deal spending was just another form of spoils politics, a charge Roosevelt addressed by folding postmasters into the civil service system.

The only important innovation at the Democratic convention was the repeal of the party's requirement that a candidate receive two-thirds of the delegates to win the nomination. After some arm twisting, southern delegates backed the change, but the governor of Texas wondered aloud if the change was designed for a third Roosevelt run in 1940. Roosevelt was renominated without opposition. He asked Vice President John Nance Garner to run with him a second time.

In response to Landon's GOP nomination and agitation by leaders of the left and right—including Huey Long of Louisiana, Father Charles E. Coughlin of Detroit, Dr. Francis Townsend of California (who espoused a federal pension plan for senior citizens), and the Socialist Norman Thomas of New York—President Roosevelt in his acceptance speech launched a rhetorical war against "economic royalists" who opposed his programs. He dropped the idea of a "unity" campaign in favor of a partisan ideological attack intended to gain a mandate for a variety of stalled programs rather than a personal vote of confidence.[105]

At first, Roosevelt had planned a low-key campaign of "conciliation," but when Landon got the GOP nomination he decided to wage the more aggressive campaign. After all, Landon had run an impressive nominating campaign and was thought to appeal to American pinings for governmental stability. In the early stages of the fall campaign, Roosevelt pretended not to be a partisan politician. He crisscrossed the country making "official" inspections of drought states and public works programs and delivering speeches on electrical power, conservation, and social welfare programs, among other topics. Roosevelt assigned Postmaster General James Farley the task of addressing party rifts and Republican charges of spoils.

At the end of September, Roosevelt assumed the role of partisan leader. The president answered Republican charges point by point, then lashed out at the Republicans in biting, sarcastic terms. As the campaign progressed and Roosevelt sensed a strong response from the large crowds to his attacks, the attacks became stronger. At the close of the campaign, he said:

We have not come this far without a struggle and I assure you that we cannot go further without a struggle. For twelve years, our nation was afflicted with a hear-nothing, see-nothing, do-nothing government. The nation looked to the government but the government looked away. Nine mocking years with the golden calf and three long years of the scourge! Nine crazy years at the ticker and three long years at the breadlines! Nine mad years of mirage and three long years of despair! And, my friends, powerful influences strive today to restore that kind of government with its doctrine that that government is best which is most indifferent to mankind.… Never before in all of our history have these forces been so united against one candidate as they stand today. They are unanimous in their hate for me—and I welcome their hatred.[106]

Especially to sophisticated campaign technicians of the modern age, a poll that predicted a big Landon victory provides some amusement. The *Literary Digest*, which had predicted past elections with accuracy, conducted a postcard poll of its readers that pointed toward a Landon landslide. But the heavy middle- and upper-class bias of the magazine's readership meant that the views of the voters on the lower rungs of the economic ladder were left out of the sample. To this day, the poll is cited as the prime example of bad survey group selection.

The failure of the *Literary Digest*'s survey pointed to the most salient aspect of the election results: the heavy class divisions among the voters. Polls showed that class divisions widened starting around the midpoint of Roosevelt's first term. The broad support Roosevelt had enjoyed because of a common economic disaster had hardened along class lines by the time of the 1936 election.

In the 1936 election, Roosevelt won 27.7 million popular votes (60.8 percent) to Landon's 16.7 million (36.5 percent). Roosevelt carried all but two of the forty-eight states, and he took 523 of the 531 electoral votes. In addition, the Senate's Democratic majority increased to 75 of 96 seats, and the House majority increased to 333 of 435 seats. Roosevelt even ran ahead of candidates—such as gubernatorial candidate Herbert Lehman of New York—who had been recruited to boost his vote totals in various states. In fact, the Democratic victory was almost too overwhelming, Roosevelt suggested, because it would encourage Democrats to fight among themselves rather than with Republicans.

Roosevelt's Third Term: 1940

Soon after his 1936 landslide, Roosevelt tempted fate with a proposal that would have increased the size of the Supreme Court from nine to fifteen members in order to "pack" the Court with justices closer to the president's political philosophy. In 1935 and 1936 the high court had struck down important New Deal initiatives such as the Agriculture Adjustment Act, the National Recovery Administration, and the tax on food processing.

Roosevelt shrouded his proposal in statements of concern about the capacities of some of the Court's older justices. In a fireside speech, Roosevelt said the Court's failure to keep pace with the other "horses" in the "three-horse team" of the federal government constituted a "quiet crisis."[107] The elderly chief justice, Charles Evans Hughes, belied that charge with the energy he brought to the tribunal. But Roosevelt refused to compromise on the bill, and it became an executive-legislative dispute. The proposal was widely seen as a brazen power play, and Congress defeated it by summer 1937.

Nevertheless, President Roosevelt eventually got the judicial approval he wanted for his initiatives—what wags called "the switch in time that saved nine." The Court appeared to shift its philosophy during the court-packing affair, and, before long, enough justices had retired so that Roosevelt could put his stamp on the Court.

Other problems awaited Roosevelt in the second term. Splits in the labor movement gave rise to violence during organizing drives, and the president responded haltingly. After his rift with business over the full range of New Deal policies, Roosevelt appeared to be drifting. Conservatives in Congress were more assertive than ever in opposing the "socialist" measures of the Roosevelt years. The only major New Deal legislation in the second term was the Fair Labor Standards Act of 1938, which abolished child labor and set a minimum wage and an official rate of time-and-a-half for overtime.

As Roosevelt looked toward a third term in 1940, the widening war in Europe posed a difficult problem. Nazi Germany had invaded the Rhineland, Poland, France, Norway, Denmark, Holland, Belgium, and Luxembourg and had made alliances with Italy and the Soviet Union. Japan had invaded China. Adolph Hitler launched the Battle of Britain in summer 1940; all-night air raids of London came soon afterward.

British prime minister Winston Churchill desperately petitioned Roosevelt to provide fifty naval destroyers. Britain's need for the destroyers was so great that Roosevelt balked at asking Congress for help. He reasoned that congressional action probably would take three months, and isolationists might even block action, dealing a crippling blow to Britain. After lengthy debate within the administration, Roosevelt agreed to send Churchill the destroyers as part of a "lend-lease" agreement. The United States received British bases in the Caribbean as part of the deal.

A favorite parlor game as the 1940 election approached was guessing whom Roosevelt might tap as his successor. Roosevelt publicly maintained that he did not want another term, but he refused to issue a definitive statement begging off the race. Despite the historic precedent against third terms, Roosevelt wanted to remain president. To avoid the appearance of overzealousness, however, Roosevelt wanted the Democrats to draft him in 1940.

While the nation waited for Roosevelt to act, Vice President Garner announced his candidacy for his boss's job. Postmaster General Farley and Secretary of State Cordell Hull also wanted to be president, and Roosevelt gave both vague assurances of support. Roosevelt, whose relations with Garner had soured since the court-packing episode (which Garner opposed), simply watched the vice president struggle to gain a respectable public profile. The Farley and Hull prospects withered without the help of the old master.

From a distance, Roosevelt watched state Democratic delegations declare their support. Polls showed Roosevelt's fortunes rising with the deepening European crisis. Just before the GOP convention, Roosevelt appointed Republicans Henry Stimson and Frank Knox to his cabinet. But Roosevelt did not reveal his plans for 1940, even to his closest aides. The president did not forbid aides such as Harry Hopkins to work on a draft, but he did not get involved because he wanted the Democrats to call on him and not the other way around.

At the Chicago convention, Sen. Alben Barkley told the delegates: "The president has never had, and has not today, any desire or purpose to continue in the office of president.... He wishes in all earnestness and sincerity to make it clear that all the delegates of this convention are free to vote for any candidate."[108] The statement was followed by an hour-long demonstration and Roosevelt's first-ballot nomination.

The convention mood turned sour, however, when Roosevelt announced that he wanted the liberal secretary of agriculture, Henry Wallace, as his running mate. The announcement disgruntled delegates who already had lined up behind other candidates. But Wallace eventually beat Alabama representative William Bankhead, his strongest opponent for the nomination.

The Republicans mounted their strongest challenge to Roosevelt in 1940, largely based on the charge that Roosevelt was moving the United States toward involvement in the world war. Several moves toward military preparedness had failed at the hands of isolationists in Congress. When Roosevelt asked for increases in defense spending after Gen. Francisco Franco's victory in Spain and Germany's annexing of Austria in 1938, critics asserted that the president was attempting to cover up domestic failures with foreign adventures. Roosevelt pressed on, however, and Congress passed the Selective Service Act and increases in military spending in 1940.

The Republican field in 1940 included several fresh faces: Sen. Robert A. Taft of Ohio, son of the former president; District Attorney Thomas E. Dewey of New York City; and Sen. Charles L. McNary of Oregon and Sen. Arthur H. Vandenberg of Michigan who had been considered long shots for the Republican nomination in 1936. The freshest face of all was Wendell L. Willkie, a utility executive who had never run for political office. A large, affable man, former

Democrat Willkie had barnstormed the country for seven years speaking in opposition to the New Deal.[109] Hundreds of "Willkie clubs" sprang up in summer 1940, and a number of publications, including Henry Luce's *Time* magazine, chronicled Willkie's career and encouraged the Willkie groundswell. Despite concern about Willkie's lack of political experience, which led to a "stop Willkie" movement, the Indianan won a sixth-ballot nomination by acclamation. Senator McNary, the Republicans' Senate floor leader, reluctantly accepted the vice-presidential nomination.

Traveling 30,000 miles in thirty-four states, Willkie gave some 540 speeches. By the time his campaign ended, his already husky voice had turned hoarse. The Republicans spent lavishly and organized grassroots clubs for Willkie across the country. "No Third Term" campaign buttons were popular with Wilkie supporters. Charges against Roosevelt of managerial incompetence, "warmongering," and imperial ambitions punctuated the Willkie effort. A dramatic moment came when labor leader John L. Lewis called on workers to back Willkie.

After a period of strictly "presidential" behavior, Roosevelt took to the campaign trail with partisan vigor. He answered Willkie's warmongering charges with a promise never to involve the United States in "foreign wars" (which left Roosevelt free to respond to a direct attack).

The alienation of some Democratic and independent voters was symbolized by Vice President Garner, who did not even vote. Roosevelt won, but by the slimmest popular vote margin of any race since 1912. He received 27.3 million popular votes (54.7 percent) to Willkie's 22.3 million (44.8 percent). The electoral vote tally was 449–82.

The War and Its Legacy: 1944

Roosevelt's third term and fourth election were dominated by World War II. Japan attacked U.S. bases at Pearl Harbor, Hawaii, on December 7, 1941. The president, speaking before Congress, declared the date of the surprise attack "a day that will live in infamy." Congress shook off its isolationist inclinations and declared war. A few days after Pearl Harbor, Germany and Italy declared war on the United States, confronting the nation with a two-front war.

The war did for the economy what the New Deal, by itself, could not: it brought economic prosperity. The number of unemployed workers fell from eight million to one million between 1940 and 1944. The boom brought seven million more people, half of them women, into the job market. Inflation, worker shortages, and occasional shortages in raw materials posed problems for wartime agencies. The number of U.S. families paying taxes quadrupled, and by 1945 tax revenues were twenty times their 1940 level. Budget deficits reached new heights.[110]

The fighting in Europe and Asia was grim for the first two years of the president's new term. Isolationist sentiment again built up in Congress, with the Midwest proving the region most resistant to Roosevelt's foreign policy. Criticism of how the Roosevelt administration was managing U.S. participation in the wars on both fronts was rampant. The administration won key congressional votes on the war but faced stubborn resistance on domestic measures. In the 1942 midterm elections, the Republicans gained ten seats in the Senate and forty-seven seats in the House—a major repudiation of Roosevelt.

After several setbacks, the Allied forces won impressive victories. Roosevelt and Churchill worked closely together. Allied forces, led by General Eisenhower, routed the Axis powers in North Africa in 1942. The Soviet Union beat back a Nazi assault on Stalingrad in the winter of 1942–1943. The Allies invaded and occupied Italy in 1943 before crossing the English Channel to confront the Nazis in France in 1944. In September 1944 British and American troops entered Germany. In the Pacific war, American offensives protected Australia in 1942 and secured the Philippines in 1944.

Despite the bitter opposition that prevailed through much of his third term, Roosevelt had no trouble winning a fourth term in 1944. The Allies found greater success on the battlefield and on the sea, and the nation did not appear willing to risk untested leadership to prosecute the war. The Republicans turned to the governor of New York, Thomas Dewey. Willkie wanted another shot at the White House, and his bestselling book *One World* put him in the public eye, but old-line conservatives blamed him for the 1940 election defeat. Governors John Bricker of Ohio and Harold Stassen of Minnesota and Gen. Douglas MacArthur were the other hopefuls.

Dewey's primary victories over Willkie in the Wisconsin, Nebraska, and Oregon primaries ended Willkie's public career. Dewey was too far in front to stop. At the convention he won a nearly unanimous first-ballot nomination after Bricker and Stassen dropped out. After Gov. Earl Warren of California refused the vice-presidential nomination, Bricker accepted it.

The party platform extolled the virtues of free enterprise but did not criticize the concept of the New Deal and even made bids for the votes of blacks and women. In his acceptance speech Dewey criticized "stubborn men grown old and tired and quarrelsome in office."[111]

The 1944 election marked the early resistance of the South to the modern Democratic Party. Roosevelt was a shoo-in for the nomination, but southerners wanted a replacement for Wallace as vice president, restoration of the two-thirds nominating rule, and a platform declaration of white supremacy. Dissatisfied southerners threatened to bolt the party in November, but when the party adopted only a vague civil rights plank in its platform, southern discontent dissipated. The rest of the platform called for an internationalist thrust in foreign policy and further New Deal–style reforms domestically.

Roosevelt expressed support for Wallace but said he would allow the convention to pick his running mate. Wallace gave a stirring convention speech but disturbed conservatives with his stand against the poll tax and for equal opportunity for all "regardless of race or sex." Sen. Harry S. Truman of Missouri, who had won fame as a critic of defense spending, beat Wallace for the vice-presidential nomination on the second ballot.

The Democratic campaign was dominated by references to the need for wartime unity and reminders of the Republican rule under Hoover. One leaflet bore the words "Lest We Forget" and a photograph of an unemployed man selling apples in front of a "Hoover Club"; an inset photograph showed Dewey conferring with former president Hoover. The Republicans spent nearly as much money in 1944 as they had in the record-setting 1936 election.

Roosevelt won with 25.6 million popular votes (53.4 percent) to Dewey's 22.0 million (45.9 percent). The electoral vote was 432 to 99. But President Roosevelt, who reshaped U.S. politics at all levels, did not have the opportunity to see the end of the war or to participate in the making of the postwar world. On April 12, 1945, less than three months after his fourth inauguration, he collapsed while sitting for a portrait in Warm Springs, Georgia, and died a few hours later.

Truman Presidency: 1948

The shock of President Roosevelt's death was perhaps greatest for the former haberdasher and machine politician who succeeded him. Truman had been a last-minute choice as FDR's running mate the previous year, and he never became a part of Roosevelt's inner circle. Truman did not know about the most important military program of the age—the Manhattan Project, which, in a race with the Nazis, was developing a nuclear bomb in secrecy in the out-of-the-way places of Oak Ridge, Tennessee; Hanford, Washington; and Los Alamos, New Mexico.

Truman also faced a problem of stature. Roosevelt had done nothing less than redefine the presidency in his twelve years in office. He not only effected a partisan realignment in U.S. politics, but he changed the very scope of government activity. As would become clear during the Eisenhower presidency, even Republicans had come to accept, grudgingly, the notion that the government ought to play an active role in stimulating the economy and addressing the needs of specific constituency groups.

Another problem facing Truman: many people could not fathom a presidency without Roosevelt. One member of the White House staff said later: "It was all so sudden, I had completely forgotten about Mr. Truman. Stunned, I realized that I simply couldn't comprehend the presidency as something separate from Roosevelt. The presidency, the White House, the war, our lives—they were all Roosevelt."[112] Other aides could not bring themselves to call Truman "Mr. President," as if so doing would dishonor the late president.

Truman's personality could not have presented a greater contrast to that of Roosevelt. Plain-speaking, blunt, middle-class, midwestern, high school educated, wheeling-and-dealing, and surrounded by old pals from the Pendergast machine of Missouri (the Democratic organization that dominated politics in the state), Truman offended people who had been accustomed to the charisma of Roosevelt. The new first lady, Bess Truman, also paled in comparison to her predecessor, the dynamic, more public Eleanor Roosevelt. Nevertheless, Truman showed absolute loyalty to the New Deal, but that would never be enough for many old Roosevelt hands and a nation entering a difficult period of postwar readjustment.

By the time the 1948 election neared, Truman was in grave political shape. He brought former president Hoover back from exile for special projects—one of the many ways he rankled the sensibilities of former Roosevelt aides and Eleanor Roosevelt. Truman also professed a desire to "keep my feet on the ground" and avoid the "crackpots and lunatic fringe" that had surrounded FDR.[113] Toward that end he got rid of Commerce Secretary Henry Wallace and others. The independent journalist I. F. Stone wrote of Truman's personnel moves: "The little nameplates outside the little doors … began to change. In Justice, Treasury, Commerce and elsewhere, the New Dealers began to be replaced by the kind of men one was accustomed to meeting in county courthouses."[114]

The politics of postwar adjustment was difficult. The Republican 80th Congress, elected in 1946, sought to dismantle many New Deal programs, and it frustrated anti-inflation efforts. Truman, then, had to duel with Congress, vetoing 250 bills (eleven vetoes were overridden). Tentative civil rights initiatives disgruntled the South. Labor unrest was on the rise. Truman's efforts to "contain" Soviet geopolitical ambitions not only created splits among Democrats but also brought attacks from Republican isolationists. To make matters worse, Truman was said to have performed inadequately at Potsdam, the conference of World War II victors held in the summer of 1945 that established many geographic borders in Europe.

The situation was so bad that Roosevelt's own son promoted General Eisenhower and Supreme Court Justice William O. Douglas for a 1948 run for the Democratic nomination against Truman. Truman, in other words, was doing a good job antagonizing both the left and the right. In August 1948 the Democratic convention appeared to reflect a dangerously polarized nation. The convention began with a feeling of desperation when Eisenhower and Douglas refused to run. Then a "states' rights" plank offered by southern delegates was defeated, and, after strong speeches by Minneapolis mayor Hubert H. Humphrey and others, a

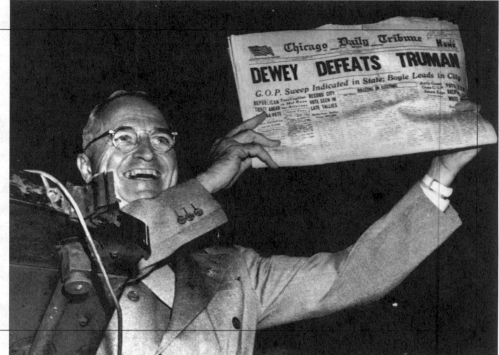

In 1948 pollsters and the media fed Republican candidate Thomas Dewey's overconfidence in his campaign to unseat President Harry S. Truman. Truman had the last laugh on the press and his opponent.

strong northern civil rights plank passed. The party's New Deal and northern machine elements decided that southern defection would be less damaging than northern defection.

Defect is just what some southerners did. The "Dixie-crats," under the leadership of South Carolina's governor J. Strom Thurmond, left the convention to conduct their fall campaign. Thurmond's candidacy ran under the Democratic Party label in four states (Alabama, Louisiana, Mississippi, and South Carolina) and under the States' Rights Democratic Party elsewhere in the South. Meanwhile, the party's left wing, behind Henry Wallace, protested Truman's Marshall Plan (a multimillion-dollar program to rebuild the economies of western Europe), military buildup, and confrontational stance toward the Soviet Union. It, too, ran its own fall campaign under the banner of the Progressive Citizens of America (the Progressive Party).

The seeds of Dixie defection were planted long before the convention. In 1947 the President's Committee on Civil Rights issued a report calling for the protection of the rights of all minorities. It was just the kind of spark southern segregationists needed to begin a dump-Truman drive and to organize their own campaign in 1948. The Southern Governors Conference in March 1948 recommended that southern states send delegates to the Democratic convention and electors to the electoral college who would refuse to back a pro–civil rights candidate.

As political scientist V. O. Key Jr. has shown, the degree of resistance to civil rights in southern states depended on two basic factors: the proportion of blacks in the population

and the strength of the two-party system. Key argued that the existence of a large black population led to stronger Democratic measures against black enfranchisement and led whites to support the Democratic Party in greater numbers. "To them [the whites in such districts], a single Negro vote threatened the whole caste system."[115] Alabama, Louisiana, Mississippi, and South Carolina ended up voting for the Thurmond ticket. Other southern states found broader economic and political issues more compelling than race and voted for Truman.[116]

Many of FDR's old political allies eventually got behind Truman, but the president's election prospects looked bleak. Some support was grudging—Eleanor Roosevelt offered a straightforward endorsement only to rebut newspaper reports that she favored the Republicans. While the Democratic Party was badly fractured, the Republican Party united behind Dewey.

Dewey, who had been the 1944 GOP candidate, survived a large field in 1948 to become the nominee once again. Senator Taft of Ohio was the main threat, but his isolationism and dull public demeanor were liabilities. The most spirited opposition came from Governor Stassen of Minnesota, who appealed to the more liberal and internationalist wing of the party. An anathema to party bosses, Stassen proved his strength in a series of primary victories. Other candidates or potential convention contenders included Generals Eisenhower and MacArthur, Governor Warren, and Senator Vandenberg. Polls showed all of the Republicans but Taft beating Truman.[117]

Dewey gained the preconvention momentum he needed with an impressive primary victory over Stassen in Oregon. He spent three weeks in the state, while Stassen frittered away his time and resources with a hopeless challenge to Taft in the Ohio primary. Dewey was especially tough in a primary debate with Stassen about communism. With these successes, as well as his impressive organizational strength and mastery over convention mechanics, Dewey won the presidential nomination on the third ballot. Warren was selected as the vice-presidential nominee.

Dewey was part of a new breed of Republican leaders—pragmatic and accepting of the New Deal and the international role that the United States would play in the postwar era. He expressed support for the basic tenets of postwar liberalism, including Social Security, civil rights, and the United Nations. In the 1948 campaign, Dewey planned to put himself above the slashing attack style of President Truman. His constant calls for national unity—spoken in a baritone voice and perfect English—expressed broad public acceptance of the vast changes in U.S. politics over the previous twenty years.

From the beginning of the campaign, the media and professional politicians gave Truman little chance of retaining the White House. Early polls showed Dewey with such a strong lead that pollsters simply stopped surveying voters. But the polls failed because of a bias in the way the questions were asked and a presumption that the large undecided vote would cast their ballots in the same way as the rest of the population, when it in fact heavily favored Truman.[118]

Dewey was so certain of victory that he ran as if he were the incumbent. He made a series of bland, almost diplomatic statements rather than energetic campaign speeches. Dewey appeared confident that his advice to one audience—"Vote your own interests"—would attract an amalgam of disaffected groups. Never even mentioning the president's name, Dewey calmly canvassed the country and just smiled when people called him "President Dewey." Dewey was careful to avoid the overaggressive posture that he thought had ruined his 1944 campaign against Roosevelt. He even made some initial cabinet and policy decisions.

Truman's strategy from the beginning was simply to mobilize the New Deal coalition. The biggest danger was apathy, he and campaign aide Clark Clifford reasoned, so the best strategy was to give the voters a reason to go to the polling booths. Because the Democrats were the majority party, they had to concentrate mainly on getting their long-time supporters to the polls.

Truman ran a scrappy and blunt underdog campaign that could have been mistaken for an outsider's effort. Truman was the president, but he ran against the Washington establishment. Crisscrossing the nation on a whistle-stop train tour, Truman traveled 31,000 miles and spoke before six million people. He turned his record of vetoes into an asset,

claiming that the "do-nothing" Republican 80th Congress made him do it. He assailed the conservative Republican record on inflation, housing, labor, farm issues, and foreign affairs. The president drew large crowds—sometimes many times the size of Dewey's crowds—but he was virtually the only political professional who thought he would win.

Truman himself predicted in October that he had 229 solid electoral votes to Dewey's 109 and Thurmond's 9; 189 votes, he said could go either way. The best anyone would say about the Truman campaign was that its fighting spirit improved the Democrats' chances to win the Senate. Truman answered the Republicans' claims of liberalism and reformism by criticizing the GOP for obstructing his policies. Truman's outsider taunt was constant: "that no-account, do-nothing, Republican 80th Congress!"[119]

Despite the *Chicago Tribune*'s now-famous headline—"Dewey Defeats Truman"—President Truman prevailed. Early returns put Truman in front, but it was expected that the later-reporting western states would give Dewey the win. When California and Ohio went into the Truman column midmorning on Wednesday, Dewey conceded defeat.

Considering the Democratic defections, Truman's appeal was widespread. He won twenty-eight states with 24.11 million votes (49.51 percent) and might have won more in the South and North with a united party—as it was, Thurmond won 22 percent of the vote in the South. Dewey won 21.97 million votes (45.12 percent), and Thurmond polled 1.17 million votes (2.40 percent). Henry Wallace won 1.16 million votes (2.38 percent) but no electoral votes. Wallace's candidacy may have cost Truman New York, Michigan, and Maryland. Yet Wallace may have done Truman a favor by freeing him from the taint of being the most liberal candidate in a time when the electorate was weary of liberalism. Particularly because the Republicans did not have a midwesterner on their ticket and talked about cutting back agricultural subsidies, farmers felt safer with Truman. In all, Truman won 303 electoral votes, Dewey, 189, and Thurmond, 39.

The Democratic defections may have helped Truman by making him the candidate of the center. The Wallace campaign freed the president from suspicions on the right, and the Thurmond defection strengthened Truman's more liberal northern constituency. In addition, the defections may have inspired Democratic voters to turn out in larger numbers than they would have had victory seemed certain.

In the end the election mostly confirmed long-held partisan allegiances. In the words of political scientist Angus Campbell and his colleagues, it was a "maintaining" election: "The electorate responded to current elements in politics very much in terms of its existing partisan loyalties. Apparently very little of the political landscape attracted strong feeling in that year. But what feeling there was seemed to be governed largely by antecedent attachments to one of the two major parties."[120]

"I Like Ike": 1952

Truman's political fortunes worsened during his second term to the extent that he decided belatedly against making a bid for the Democratic nomination. In 1952, for the first time in twenty-four years, neither party had an incumbent president as its nominee.

The Democrats suffered from a weariness that is bound to affect any party that has been in power for twenty years. Problems and opponents' frustrated ambitions were piling up, and in General Eisenhower the Republicans were able to recruit a candidate with universal appeal who was coveted by both parties. The national mood in the years before the 1952 election was sour. The nation was tiring of price controls, recurring scandals among members of the White House staff, and the Korean War, which the Truman administration had begun in 1950 but did not appear interested in either winning or pulling U.S. troops out of. The Republicans asked for a chance to "clean up the mess" in Washington and punctuated their appeals with the question: "Had enough?"

The Truman administration had met with repeated frustration in dealing with Congress. On civil rights, tariffs, taxes, labor reform, and the sensationalized question of communist sympathizers in the government, Truman had had to cope with a stubborn Democratic Congress, which, in turn, became more stubborn after Republican gains in the 1950 midterm elections. When Truman seized control of the steel mills because he said the steelworkers' strike threatened the nation's security, he was rebuffed by the Supreme Court.[121]

Truman's biggest problems, however, had concerned cronyism and war. Republicans in congressional investigations and on the stump had hammered away at conflict-of-interest scandals in Truman's administration, creating nationwide sentiment to "clean up" Washington with a new administration. Meanwhile, the United States was mired in a stalemate in Korea—a distant war that was being fought inconclusively under the aegis of the United Nations, with uncertain goals (was it to protect South Korea or to defeat North Korea as well?) and uncertain enemies (was the People's Republic of China an opponent as well as North Korea?). Truman evoked ire with his firing of General MacArthur, who wanted to take the war into China, and with the slow movement toward a settlement. Just as the nation had tired of sacrifices in World War I under Woodrow Wilson, it had tired of sacrifices under Truman.

General Eisenhower—who had just left the presidency of Columbia University to take charge of the forces of the North Atlantic Treaty Organization (NATO)—was recruited by Republicans to run when it appeared that other GOP candidates lacked the national appeal to win the White House. Senator Taft was running again, but his isolationism was considered a liability in the postwar age of internationalism.

Stassen, MacArthur, and Warren were other likely Republican candidates.

Eisenhower's popular appeal was revealed when he attracted 50.4 percent of the vote in the New Hampshire primary to Taft's 38.7 percent and Stassen's 7.1 percent. Eisenhower performed well in the northeast area primaries, and Taft generally performed well in the Midwest. A write-in campaign for Eisenhower almost upset Stassen in his home state of Minnesota.

When the GOP convention finally met in Chicago, Taft had the lead in convention delegates. In crucial delegate-seating contests, many of them played out on national television, Eisenhower defeated Taft and won the right to seat pro-Eisenhower insurgents from the South. Taft had relied on the old strategy of mobilizing state machines, but such tactics looked unsavory on television. Eisenhower had undisputed popular appeal, and he won on the first ballot after his early lead turned into a stampede.

Eisenhower selected Sen. Richard Nixon of California as his running mate. The thirty-nine-year-old conservative had won national recognition with his activities on the controversial House Committee on Un-American Activities, which investigated the alleged Soviet ties of Alger Hiss, a former State Department official. Hiss would serve time for a perjury conviction.

The Democrats moved haltingly toward putting together a ticket. Truman did not announce his decision to stay out of the race until April, after two primary losses. Sen. Estes Kefauver of Tennessee, who had gained fame with his televised hearings on organized crime, ran an aggressive primary campaign and entered the convention with the lead in delegates. Other candidates included Gov. Averell Harriman of New York, Vice President Alben Barkley, Sen. Robert Kerr of Oklahoma, and Sen. Richard Russell of Georgia.

The eventual nominee was Gov. Adlai Stevenson of Illinois, grandson of Grover Cleveland's second vice president. Stevenson had had experience in the navy and State departments before running for governor. President Truman had privately recruited Stevenson for the race—at first unsuccessfully. Then Truman and Illinois backers set up a draft movement for Stevenson, which the governor disavowed until the last minute. Kefauver was the early leader in convention balloting, but Stevenson, always close, pulled into the lead on the third ballot.

Stevenson's campaign was an eloquent call to arms for liberals and reformers. Years later Democrats would recall that the campaign had inspired the generation that would take the reins of power under John F. Kennedy in 1960. Democratic politics at all levels in the 1950s and 1960s would revolve around battles between party regulars and reformers.

Stevenson did not have a chance, however, against the popular Eisenhower. Some southern states bolted the

Democratic Party, and the Republicans hammered away at the misdeeds of the Democratic administration under Truman. Such issues as the 1949 communist revolution in China ("Who lost China?"), the protracted Korean War, administration corruption, and the alleged communist infiltration of the government captured the nation's attention more than Stevenson's oratory.

More than anything, however, the desire for party change rather than policy change determined the election. The Republican evocation of the theme of "Corruption, Korea, and Communism" did not challenge the policies that the Democrats offered the nation as much as the way they executed those policies. Eisenhower was a proven administrator and was free of the taint of everyday U.S. politics. Stevenson was a reformer himself, but his campaign had the conspicuous backing of President Truman. Stevenson's divorce and his public support of Hiss were constant if only vaguely stated issues.

The campaign's biggest controversy developed when newspaper reports alleged that Nixon had used a "secret fund" provided by California millionaires to pay for travel and other expenses. To a Democratic Party weary of charges of impropriety, the revelation offered an opportunity to accuse Nixon of being beholden to special interests. Nixon admitted the existence of the fund but maintained that he used the money solely for travel and that his family did not accept personal gifts.

Nixon originally reacted to the story by asserting that it was a communist smear. When Eisenhower would not publicly back his running mate, speculation developed that Ike would ask Nixon to leave the ticket—and the Republican *New York Herald Tribune* openly called for him to drop out. When Nixon decided to confront his accusers with a television speech, campaign aides told him he would be dropped if the public reaction was not favorable.

Nixon's speech was remarkable. He denied any impropriety and stated that the Stevenson campaign was hypocritical in its criticisms because it had similar funds. More specifically, Nixon denied that he had accepted such gifts as a mink coat for his wife, Pat; he said that his wife wore a "Republican cloth coat." He acknowledged, however, receiving a pet dog named Checkers from a Texas admirer: "And you know, the kids love that dog, and I just want to say this right now, that regardless of what they say about it, we're going to keep it."[122] His folksy message and appeal for telegrams created a wave of sympathy, which Eisenhower rewarded with a pledge of support. The crisis was over.

In a personal victory—surveys showed that the nation still favored the programs of the New Deal but simply wanted to put the cronyism, sacrifices, and Korean War behind it—Eisenhower swept to the White House. Ike won the entire North and West, parts of the South, and some border states—a total of thirty-nine states to Stevenson's

nine. His 442 electoral votes and 33.9 million popular votes (55.1 percent) overwhelmed Stevenson's 89 electoral votes and 27.3 million popular votes (44.4 percent). The election of 1956 would bring more of the same.

Eisenhower's Reelection: 1956

Despite his age (sixty-six) and having had a heart attack in 1955, Eisenhower was the strong favorite to be the GOP nominee for another term. Close cooperation with the Democratic congressional leadership and a "hidden-hand" leadership style seemed to comport with the electorate's wishes for normalcy.[123] The White House staff was ably run by the chief of staff, Sherman Adams, and foreign policy was supervised by Secretary of State John Foster Dulles. The genius of Eisenhower's management style was his use of aides as "lightning rods" for unpopular policies.

Even without lightning rods, Eisenhower probably would have fared well. The economy was booming, and Eisenhower had quickly brought the Korean War to a close. His nuclear policy gave the nation a "bigger bang for the buck" in defense spending and kept the troop requirements low. Federal housing and highway programs gave impetus to suburbanization, now considered part of the middle-class American Dream. Issues that would in the future become divisive, such as civil rights, were muffled.

The only unsettled Republican issue was whether Nixon would again be the vice-presidential candidate. Eisenhower offered him a cabinet post, and Stassen mounted a campaign to replace Nixon with Massachusetts governor Christian Herter. After some hesitation, however, Eisenhower stood by his controversial running mate.

In the Democratic camp, Kefauver challenged Stevenson for the right to face Eisenhower in the fall. After impressive primary victories in New Hampshire and Minnesota for Kefauver, the Stevenson campaign fought back with a string of primary wins in states as varied as California, Florida, and Oregon.

Former president Truman endorsed New York governor Harriman—not Stevenson—at the opening of the Democratic convention. A variety of other favorite sons entered the race. But with the help of Eleanor Roosevelt, Stevenson was able to win the nomination for a second time. Stevenson won on the first ballot.

Stevenson left the vice-presidential slot open to the convention delegates. Kefauver eventually won, after battling Senators John Kennedy, Albert A. Gore, and Hubert Humphrey and New York mayor Robert Wagner. The open contest highlighted the future national political potential of Kennedy, who, according to later accounts, mainly intended not to win the second spot on the ticket but to gain visibility for a 1960 presidential run.

The campaign was bereft of real issues. Eisenhower's campaigning was a tempered appeal to American values and bipartisan consensus. Nixon was left the job of hacking away at the opposition; he called Stevenson "Adlai the Appeaser" and a "Ph.D. graduate of Dean Acheson's cowardly College of Communist Containment."[124] Overall, however, the campaign was an example of what James David Barber has called "the politics of conciliation," with little conflict or desire for change.

Whether or not the electorate was "asleep," as frustrated critics charged, Eisenhower nailed down another strong victory. He won forty-two states, 457 electoral votes, and 35.6 million popular votes (57.4 percent), compared with Stevenson's six states, 73 electoral votes, and 26.0 million popular votes (42.0 percent). In an unprecedented development, however, both houses of Congress went to the opposition.

Kennedy and the Politics of Change: 1960

The periodic national desire for change came at the expense of the Republicans in 1960, when Massachusetts senator Kennedy became the youngest person ever elected president by defeating Vice President Nixon. The presidential election was foreshadowed by the 1958 midterm election, when the Democrats made impressive gains in Congress. An economic recession and generational politics created the first major shift toward liberalism since the administration of Franklin D. Roosevelt. The "Class of '58" decisively changed the discourse of U.S. politics. After the election the Democrats held 64 of 98 Senate seats and 283 of 436 House seats, and thirty-five states had Democratic governors. The time appeared ripe for reopening issues that had long been stifled such as civil rights, urban problems, and education.[125]

The 1960 Democratic field was dominated by senators—Kennedy, Lyndon B. Johnson of Texas, Humphrey of Minnesota, and Stuart Symington of Missouri. Each had important advantages and disadvantages. Kennedy was from a wealthy and politically minded family, but his Catholicism and undistinguished Senate record were liabilities. Johnson was a masterful majority leader, but no southerner had won the White House since James K. Polk in 1844. Humphrey was popular in the Midwest, but he lacked financial backing and was considered too loquacious and liberal. Symington had a strong Senate record and Truman's backing, but he was considered colorless, and Truman's backing carried liabilities.

Former Illinois governor Adlai Stevenson, the party's nominee in 1952 and 1956, stood on the sidelines, hoping that a convention deadlock or draft movement would bring him another chance for the White House. Early speculation was that the convention would be deadlocked and a compromise candidate would have to emerge. It appeared likely that the nomination would go to Symington, Johnson, Humphrey, or to one of the two senior candidates, Stevenson and Kefauver; the other candidates were good bets for the vice-presidential slot.

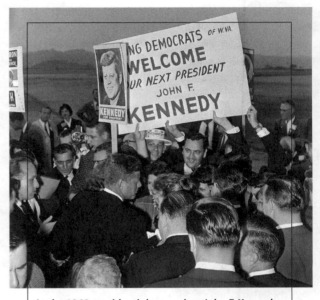

In the 1960 presidential campaign, John F. Kennedy, seen here greeting supporters in Charleston, worked hard to win the West Virginia primary. His victory in this overwhelmingly Protestant state blunted the issue of his Catholicism and set him on the way to a first-ballot nomination.

Kennedy presented the most intriguing candidacy. He was the son of Joseph P. Kennedy, the millionaire who had been Roosevelt's ambassador to Britain before their bitter break over U.S. involvement in World War II. John Kennedy also was an Ivy League graduate (of Harvard University), a war hero (described in the book *P.T. 109*), and a Pulitzer Prize winner (for *Profiles in Courage*). With an experienced campaign staff, he had won an overwhelming reelection to the Senate in 1958. Moreover, he had been planning a run for the White House for years.

There were Kennedy skeptics, however. No Catholic except Alfred Smith had been a major party nominee, and Smith's bitter loss and the anti-Catholic sentiments he aroused in 1928 made political professionals wary of naming another Catholic. Some considered Kennedy, at age forty-three, to be too young. Others focused on the influence of Joseph Kennedy, who had bankrolled his son's political career.[126] Truman's comment captured the crux of Kennedy's liabilities: "It's not the Pope I'm afraid of, it's the Pop."[127]

To address the doubts, Kennedy entered political primaries that would enable him to demonstrate vote-getting ability and to confront the religion problem. The two key primaries were Wisconsin and West Virginia. In Wisconsin, Kennedy would answer the charge that he was too conservative. But the Kennedy strategists were divided about whether he should oppose Senator Humphrey of neighboring Minnesota. Wisconsin's growing independence in party politics eventually convinced them, however, that it would present a low risk in return for the possibility of beating Humphrey in his native region. In West Virginia, Kennedy would attempt to blunt the religion issue by attracting the votes of an overwhelmingly Protestant electorate.

In the end, Kennedy defeated Humphrey in Wisconsin. Kennedy's impressive campaign treasury enabled him to staff offices in eight of the ten congressional districts in the state; Humphrey had only two offices. Humphrey maintained that the defeat stemmed from crossover Republican Catholic votes and was therefore illegitimate. (Most of the state's Catholics, who made up 31 percent of the population, belonged to the GOP.) But to Kennedy and many political observers, it was still an important victory.

Humphrey wanted to even the score in West Virginia. If Humphrey had quit the campaign and left Kennedy with no opponents, as many advised him to do, a Kennedy victory would have attracted little attention.[128] But Kennedy was able to use the Appalachian state as a way to deflect the religion issue as well as the "can't win" problem. Kennedy had a thorough organization in West Virginia, and he worked hard. He had commissioned polls in the state as far back as 1958 in anticipation of the presidential race.

Kennedy's handling of the religion question in the primaries was shrewd and would be repeated in the fall campaign. He framed the question as one of tolerance— which put Humphrey on the defensive because he had never tried to exploit the religion issue. Kennedy had his campaign workers plant questions about how his religious beliefs would affect his loyalty to the nation, to which the candidate replied with a stock answer: "When any man stands on the steps of the Capitol and takes the oath of office as president, he is swearing to uphold the separation of church and state; he puts one hand on the Bible and raises the other hand to God as he takes the oath. And if he breaks the oath, he is not only committing a crime against the Constitution, for which the Congress can impeach him—but he is committing a sin against God."[129]

Kennedy's direct confrontation of the religion issue worked to his benefit. Kennedy had the money to get his message across: his television expenditures alone in the state totaled $34,000, while Humphrey had only $25,000 for the whole primary campaign in West Virginia.[130] Early polls gave Humphrey wide leads, and interviews elicited strong reservations about Kennedy's Catholicism. As the commercials aired and the primary neared, the lead became smaller, and voters privately said they would vote for Kennedy.

JFK, as he asked headline writers to call him instead of the youthful-sounding "Jack," easily won the primary, taking 61 percent of the vote to Humphrey's 39 percent. He was on his way to a first-ballot nomination.

The Kennedy campaign staffers managed the Democratic convention with consummate skill. Had they failed to gain a majority on the first ballot, pressure might have developed for another candidate. But the Kennedy team efficiently lobbied delegations to augment support; the vice-presidential slot was vaguely offered to several politicians. In the end, Lyndon Johnson was the surprise choice for running mate. Even Kennedy supporters had doubts about Johnson, but the selection of the southerner was a classic ticket-balancing move.[131]

Central to Kennedy's winning campaign was his younger brother Robert F. Kennedy. A former counsel to Republican senator Joseph McCarthy, Robert developed into the consummate political operative. He was JFK's confidant, chief strategist, delegate counter, fund-raiser, taskmaster, and persuader. Biographer Arthur M. Schlesinger Jr. wrote that Robert Kennedy's strength "lay in his capacity to address a specific situation, to assemble an able staff, to inspire and flog them into exceptional deeds, and to prevail through sheer force of momentum."[132]

Vice President Nixon was the overwhelming choice for the Republican nomination. Nelson A. Rockefeller, elected governor of New York in 1958, was a liberal alternative, but he announced in 1959 that he would not run. There was a brief surge for Rockefeller when he criticized the party and its "leading candidate," but meetings with Nixon settled the differences. Some conservatives were disgruntled with Nixon, but their efforts for Sen. Barry Goldwater of Arizona would have to wait until 1964.

Nixon selected United Nations Ambassador Henry Cabot Lodge as his running mate, and the party platform and rhetoric stressed the need for experience in a dangerous world. Nixon promised to continue President Eisenhower's policies. He attempted to portray Kennedy as an inexperienced upstart, even though he was Kennedy's senior by only four years and the two had entered Congress the same year. Nixon led in the polls at the traditional Labor Day start of the fall campaign.

Kennedy's campaign was based on a promise to "get the nation moving again" after eight years of calm Republican rule. Specifically, he assured voters that he would lead the nation out of a recession. The gross national product increased at a rate of only 2.25 percent annually between 1955 and 1959. Economists puzzled over the simultaneously high unemployment and high inflation rates.[133] Kennedy repeatedly called for two related changes in national policy: pump up the economy and increase defense spending dramatically.

The Democrat faced up to the religion issue again with an eloquent speech before the Greater Houston Ministerial Association, and he attracted attention from civil rights leaders when he offered moral and legal support to the Reverend Martin Luther King Jr. after King was arrested for taking part in a sit-in at an Atlanta restaurant. While Kennedy appealed to the party's more liberal and moderate wing, Johnson toured the South to appeal to regional pride and to assuage fears about an activist government.

The high point of the campaign came on September 26, 1960, when the candidates debated on national television before 70 million viewers. Kennedy was well rested and tanned; he had spent the week before the debate with friends and associates. Nixon was tired from two solid weeks of campaigning; he had spent the preparation period by himself. Their appearances alone greatly influenced the public's perception of the debates.

Kennedy's main objective had been simply to look relaxed and "up to" the presidency. He had little to lose. Nixon was always confident of his debating skills, and he performed well in the give-and-take of the debate. But the rules of debating—the way "points" are allocated—are not the same for formal debating and televised encounters. Kennedy's managers prepared their candidate better for the staging of the debate. Nixon's five-o'clock shadow reinforced the cartoon image of him as darkly sinister. As a result of all these factors, polls of radio listeners found that Nixon had "won" the debate, but polls of the more numerous television viewers found that Kennedy had "won." Historian Theodore H. White wrote: "It was the picture image that had done it—and in 1960 it was television that had won the nation away from sound to images, and that was that."[134]

While Kennedy called for a more activist and imaginative approach to world problems, Nixon stressed the candidates' similarities so much that their differences paled into insignificance. Kennedy called for a crusade to eliminate want and to confront tyranny. Nixon responded: "I can subscribe completely to the spirit that Senator Kennedy has expressed tonight."[135] With ideology an unimportant part of the debate, the images of personal character the candidates were able to project gained in importance.

The candidates held three more debates, addressing issues such as Fidel Castro's Cuba, whether the United States should defend the Chinese offshore islands of Quemoy and Matsu in the event of a military strike by China, and relations with Nikita Khrushchev's Soviet Union. None of the debates had the effect of the first, which neutralized Nixon's quasi-incumbency advantage. Nor was Nixon greatly helped by President Eisenhower, who did not campaign for his protégé until late in the campaign.

The election results were so close that Nixon did not concede his defeat until the afternoon of the day after the election. After a vacation in Florida and Nassau, Nixon returned to Washington on November 19 to consider a series of charges that voter fraud had cost him the election. A shift of between 11,000 and 13,000 votes in a total of five or six states could have given Nixon the electoral vote triumph. Nixon said he decided against demanding a recount because it would take "at least a year and a half" and would throw the federal government into turmoil.[136] Other commentators have pointed out that had Nixon, for instance, challenged voting irregularities in Illinois in Democratic precincts in Chicago, irregularities in Republican rural areas of the state could have been challenged by Kennedy.

When the electoral college voted, Kennedy won 303 electoral votes to Nixon's 219. Democratic senator Harry F. Byrd of Virginia attracted 15 electoral votes. Kennedy won twenty-three states to Nixon's twenty-six. (Six Alabama electors and all eight Mississippi electors, elected as "unpledged Democrats," as well as one Republican elector from Oklahoma cast their votes for Byrd.) The overall popular vote went 34.2 million for Kennedy and 34.1 million for Nixon. The margin was about two-tenths of 1 percent, or 118,574 votes. Moreover, the margins in many states were close. Kennedy won Illinois by 8,858 votes and Texas by 46,242 votes. Despite statements that the religion question would hurt Kennedy, it probably helped him by mobilizing Catholics on his behalf. Gallup polls showed that 78 percent of Catholics voted for JFK. Although Catholics were a traditional Democratic constituent group—supporting the party by margins of three or four to one—they had shown support for Republicans Eisenhower and Senator McCarthy.[137] In addition, Kennedy put together a predictable coalition: he won the support of voters in the Northeast, in most of the South, and in cities, plus blacks and union workers. Upper New England, the Midwest, and the West went primarily to Nixon.

After the election, Kennedy and Goldwater discussed, in an informal way, how they would conduct their campaigns for the presidency in 1964. The two expected to win their parties' nominations easily, and they talked about crisscrossing the nation in head-to-head debates, which would set a new standard for national campaigns.[138]

The Kennedy-Goldwater campaign never came to be, however. On November 22, 1963, while riding in a motorcade in Dallas, Texas, President Kennedy was assassinated by a gunman named Lee Harvey Oswald.[139] Vice President Johnson assumed the presidency.[140]

In his brief administration, Kennedy had compiled a record disappointing even to many of his supporters. The Bay of Pigs fiasco in which a Central Intelligence Agency plan—begun under Eisenhower—to overthrow the Cuban government failed miserably, the inability to obtain passage of landmark civil rights legislation, budget deficits and a drain of gold supplies from the United States, confrontations with the Soviet Union in Cuba, Hungary, and Berlin, and the nascent U.S. involvement in the Vietnam War created doubts about the young president's control of the government.

Kennedy had, however, made a start on many important issues. Arms control initiatives such as the test ban treaty, economic growth through tax cuts, modernization of the military, the successful management of the Cuban Missile Crisis, civil rights and other domestic initiatives, the

Peace Corps and Alliance for Progress, and growing world stature all offered hope for the second term. It would fall to Johnson, the legendary former Senate majority leader, to bring the Kennedy plans to fruition. First acting as the loyal servant of the slain president, then on his own, Johnson was able to bring to legislative enactment many of the initiatives long cherished by liberals—most notably the Civil Rights Act of 1964, which was considerably stronger than the Kennedy bill that had stalled in Congress.

"All the Way with LBJ": 1964

From the time of his sad but graceful ascension to the White House, Johnson was never in doubt as the Democrats' 1964 nominee. He was expected to select an eastern or midwestern liberal as his running mate, and he did so when he tapped Senator Humphrey of Minnesota at the convention, which his campaign organization stage-managed down to the last detail. The only dissent from Democratic unity was provided by Gov. George C. Wallace of Alabama, whose segregationist campaign took advantage of a backlash against the civil rights movement. Wallace entered three primaries against Johnson-allied favorite sons, and he polled 43 percent of the vote in Maryland. Wallace talked about mounting a third-party bid in the fall, but he backed off.

The Republicans were divided into two bitter camps led by Senator Goldwater of Arizona, the eventual nominee, and by Governor Rockefeller of New York. The nomination contest was a struggle for the soul of the party. Other active and inactive candidates included Ambassador to Vietnam Henry Cabot Lodge, former vice president Nixon, and Gov. William Scranton of Pennsylvania. After a New Hampshire primary victory by Lodge, achieved through a well-organized write-in drive while he was still ambassador to Vietnam, Goldwater and Rockefeller scrapped through a series of primaries. The moderate Lodge later helped Scranton in a late effort to recruit uncommitted delegates to stop Goldwater, but by then it was too late. Goldwater lined up strong delegate support to get the nomination before the primary season even began, but he needed to use the primaries to show that he had vote-getting ability. The state organizations that backed him also needed evidence that his conservative message would find popular acceptance.

In the "mixed" nominating system then in place, candidates were able to pick and choose the primaries that best suited their strategies. Front-runners avoided risks, and long shots entered high-visibility and often risky contests as a way to attract the attention of party professionals. As expected, Goldwater won widespread support in the southern state conventions and had strong primary showings in Illinois and Indiana. Rockefeller beat Lodge in Oregon, but the decisive test came when Goldwater narrowly upset Rockefeller in California.

In accepting the 1964 Republican nomination, Sen. Barry Goldwater called for a moral crusade, declaring, "Extremism in defense of liberty is no vice; moderation in pursuit of justice is no virtue."

More important than the confusing preconvention contests was the rhetoric. Both the conservative Goldwater and the liberal Rockefeller vowed to save the party from the other's ideology. Goldwater, who rode the bestseller success of his *Conscience of a Conservative* to hero worship among conservatives, made a vigorous case against New Deal politics and for American sway in world politics: "I don't give a tinker's damn what the rest of the world thinks about the United States, as long as we keep strong militarily."[141] Rockefeller implied that Goldwater would risk nuclear war and would recklessly dismantle basic social programs.

The nominating contest was a regional as well as an ideological struggle. The westerner Goldwater—backed by labor-intensive manufacturers, small business and agricultural enterprises, and domestic oil producers—opposed internationalist banking and commercial interests.[142] Goldwater made eastern media the objects of scorn. Rockefeller and his family, of course, represented the apex of the eastern establishment. Because of his strategy, Goldwater isolated his campaign from the manufacturing and financial interests that had been at the center of American economic growth for a generation.

Bitter battles over the party platform and unseemly heckling of Rockefeller displayed the party's divisions at the convention. When the conservatives won the nomination and the platform, there was no reconciliation. Goldwater selected Rep. William Miller of New York, another conservative, as his running mate and vowed to purge the party of liberal and moderate elements.

In a defiant acceptance speech, Goldwater painted a picture of the United States as inept in international affairs and morally corrupt in domestic pursuits, and he vowed an all-out crusade to change the situation: "Tonight there is violence in our streets, corruption in our highest offices, aimlessness among our youth, anxiety among our elderly, and there's a virtual despair among the many who look beyond the material successes toward the inner meaning of their lives.... Extremism in defense of liberty is no vice; moderation in pursuit of justice is no virtue."[143]

To a nation experiencing prosperity and unaware of the true proportions of its involvement in Vietnam, the "choice, not an echo" that Goldwater offered was a moral crusade. But the American consensus was built on material, consumer foundations, and an "outsider" appeal would have to wait until the system's foundations became unstable.

The divided GOP made for easy pickings for Johnson. The fall campaign was dominated by Goldwater's gaffes, which started long before the campaign began. He said, for example, that troops committed to NATO in Europe probably could be cut by at least one-third if NATO "commanders" had the authority to use tactical nuclear weapons in an emergency.[144] Goldwater also proposed a number of changes in the Social Security system, called for selling off the Tennessee Valley Authority, criticized the civil rights movement, and denounced the Supreme Court, the National Labor Relations Board, and the federal bureaucracy. Except for the use of nuclear weapons and changes in Social Security, most of Goldwater's proposals when taken alone were not shocking. But the sum of his proposals—and his sometimes halting explanations—scared many voters.

President Johnson campaigned actively to win a mandate for an activist new term. He traveled throughout the country making speeches to build a consensus for his domestic programs as well as his reelection. Johnson resisted Goldwater's frequent calls for televised debates. The nation's prosperity was probably enough to keep the president in the White House.[145]

Johnson desperately wanted a personal mandate to pursue a variety of domestic programs that fell under the rubric of the "Great Society"—a term that Johnson used in a 1964 commencement address (borrowed from a book of the same title by British socialist Graham Wallas). The desired landslide—underscored by his campaign slogan, "All the Way with LBJ"—was essential to initiatives in civil rights, health care, community action, education, welfare, housing, and jobs creation. Central to the landslide was not only economic prosperity but also peace in the world's trouble spots. Johnson therefore ran as a "peace" candidate.

But while he was trying to build a coalition that would sustain his domestic initiatives, Johnson faced an increasingly difficult dilemma about the U.S. role in Vietnam. The United States had been involved in opposing Ho Chi Minh's revolution against French colonial rule in the 1940s and 1950s, and under Presidents Eisenhower and Kennedy the United States had made a commitment to the leaders of South Vietnam (created after the failure of the 1954 Geneva

accord) as a bastion against communist expansion in Asia. But talk of war would likely imperil the domestic initiatives of the Great Society.

So while Johnson was campaigning as the peace candidate in 1964, he also was preparing for a major increase in U.S. involvement in Vietnam. As early as February 1964, the administration began elaborate covert operations in Southeast Asia and prepared a resolution to give the president a "blank check" in Vietnam.[146] By June the resolution was ready, and the Pentagon had chosen ninety-four bombing targets in North Vietnam and made provisions for bombing support systems on the ground. But on June 15, Johnson decided to delay major offensives until after the election.[147] In August Johnson sent to Congress what would be known as the Tonkin Gulf resolution, which granted the president broad authority to wage war in Vietnam. The resolution passed quickly and nearly unanimously—after all, the president had instructed congressional leaders to get an overwhelming majority so his policy would be bipartisan.

Johnson also seized on Rockefeller's use of the peace issue during the Republican primaries against Goldwater. He alluded to some of Goldwater's scarier statements about war, and he pledged that "we are not about to send American boys nine or ten thousand miles away from home to do what Asian boys ought to be doing for themselves."[148] A week before the election Johnson said: "The only real issue in this campaign, the only one you ought to get concerned about, is who can best keep the peace."[149]

Johnson's popular vote landslide was the largest in U.S. history. He won 61 percent of the popular vote to Goldwater's 38 percent (or 43.1 million to 27.2 million votes). In the electoral college Johnson received 486 votes to Goldwater's 52, and he carried forty-four states—all but Goldwater's home state of Arizona and five deep South states. In addition, the Democratic Party amassed huge majorities in both the Senate (67–33) and the House of Representatives (295–140).

On election day, Johnson created a working group to study "immediately and intensively" the U.S. options in Southeast Asia.[150] The war was increasing far beyond what most supporters of the Tonkin Gulf resolution or "peace" supporters of the president imagined. In 1965 alone the number of U.S. troops in Vietnam increased from 15,000 to nearly 200,000.[151]

BREAKUP OF CONSENSUS

A long period of uncertainty in American politics began sometime after Lyndon B. Johnson's landslide victory over Barry Goldwater in 1964. By 1968 some 30,000 Americans had been killed in action in Vietnam, and television was bringing the war into the living rooms of American families. Despite repeated assertions that the United States was defeating the North Vietnamese enemy, U.S. bombing efforts and ground troops did not break the resolve of the communists in the North or their sympathizers who had infiltrated the South. The corrupt South Vietnamese government and army appeared to lack the will to fight the war on their own.

In the United States, the opposition to the war developed as the casualties mounted, and the administration experienced a "credibility gap" because of its statements about the war. Before the United States left Vietnam in 1975, 55,000 Americans had died in combat. Perhaps more important than the number of casualties—about the same as in the Korean War—was the long-term commitment that the United States appeared to have made with little evidence of progress. The "quagmire," as *New York Times* reporter David Halberstam called the war, was perhaps typified by the program of intense U.S. bombing raids that were judged by many experts to be ineffectual against the North's guerrilla warfare strategy.[152]

As opposition to the war grew among an increasingly vocal and well-organized minority, strains developed in Johnson's economic and domestic programs. Starting with the riots in the Watts section of Los Angeles in 1965, urban areas sizzled with resentment of the mainstream liberal establishment. Detroit, Newark, and many major U.S. cities erupted in other riots that burned miles of city streets and caused millions of dollars in damage. The assassination of civil rights leader Martin Luther King Jr. in Memphis in April 1968 led to riots throughout the nation. Even before the riots, however, a conservative reaction against the Great Society had developed.

The activities of the Great Society were many and varied. Most prominent were the Civil Rights Act of 1964, the Voting Rights Act of 1965, Head Start, Model Cities, mass transit legislation, food stamps, Medicare and Medicaid, the Elementary and Secondary Education Act, college loans, and housing programs that included subsidies for the poor.

The conservative backlash was apparent before many programs had time to do their work. Efforts such as the Model Cities program and the Community Action Program, which mandated that poverty programs promote "maximum feasible participation" by the poor themselves, often were badly organized. The programs also created new struggles over jurisdiction in cities that already were notorious for divisive politics. Liberal efforts that predated the Great Society, such as school desegregation, only added to the tensions in cities.

The alarming increase in street crime in the late 1960s contributed to changing political attitudes. Even though African Americans and the poor were the chief victims of the increase, the issue was salient for conservative whites. Many tied the breakdown in order to the growth of the welfare state caused by the Great Society. The crime rate seemed

to many to be nothing less than ingratitude on the part of the poor. James Sundquist wrote: "While increasing millions were supported by welfare, rising state and local taxes made the citizen more and more aware of who paid the bill. And while he armed himself for protection against thieves or militants, the liberals were trying to pass legislation to take away his guns."[153]

The crime problem was an important element in both national and metropolitan politics. Polls taken in the late 1960s showed that half the women and a fifth of the men in the country were afraid to walk alone in their own neighborhoods at night.[154] In Alabama, Gov. George Wallace was drawing increased support from groups rooted in prejudice and resentment. The fear of crime also would be an important element in Richard Nixon's 1968 campaign.

"Nixon Now": 1968

With the nation divided over the war and domestic policy, the Democrats entered the 1968 campaign in an increasingly perilous state. In December 1967 Sen. Eugene McCarthy of Minnesota challenged President Johnson for the Democratic nomination, a campaign driven by McCarthy's antiwar stance. McCarthy did unexpectedly well against Johnson's write-in candidacy in the New Hampshire primary on March 12, 1968, drawing 41.9 percent of the vote to Johnson's 49.6 percent. Seeing the president's weakness, Sen. Robert F. Kennedy of New York declared his antiwar candidacy on March 16. Anticipating a devastating defeat in the upcoming Wisconsin primary, Johnson unexpectedly announced his withdrawal from the campaign in a televised address March 31.

Vice President Hubert Humphrey took Johnson's place as the administration's candidate. Humphrey, however, did not enter the primaries, which quickly turned into a duel between McCarthy and Kennedy. In April McCarthy won three primaries where Kennedy was only a write-in candidate. In May Kennedy won the Indiana and Nebraska primaries before losing Oregon to McCarthy. Appearing to gain the upper hand when he won in California on June 4, Kennedy was shot after making his acceptance speech in Los Angeles and died June 6. Kennedy's death threw the Democratic Party into turmoil.

At the chaotic party convention in Chicago, a site Johnson had chosen for what he thought would be his renomination, Humphrey emerged as the Democratic Party's candidate on the strength of endorsements from state party organizations. Although he did not participate in the party's primaries (the last major party nominee to do so), the vice president took the nomination on the first ballot after Chicago Mayor Richard Daley committed the Illinois delegation to him. Humphrey won with support from the traditional elements of the Democratic coalition—labor, African Americans, urban voters—plus the backers of

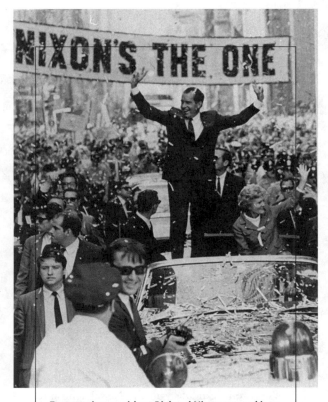

Former vice president Richard Nixon tapped into widespread discontent over the Vietnam War and domestic turmoil to win the 1968 presidential election, one of the closest in U.S. history.

President Johnson. Humphrey appealed to many of the party's "moderates" on the issue of the Vietnam War.

Preliminary battles over rules and delegate seating, the representativeness of the party, and the Vietnam War caused ugly skirmishes on the convention floor. The party's platform eventually endorsed the administration's war policy, including bombing, but strong opposition to this plank left the Democrats divided.[155]

The real story of that convention, however, was outside the convention halls where demonstrations for civil rights and an end to the war met brutal rejection from the police. After three days of sometimes harsh verbal and physical battles with antiwar demonstrators in city parks, graphically broadcast on television and extensively reported in newspapers, the police charged a group of protesters who planned a march on the convention. Theodore H. White described the scene that played on national television:

> Like a fist jolting, like a piston exploding from its chamber, comes a hurtling column of police from off Balbo into the intersection, and all things happen too fast: first the charge as the police wedge cleaves through the mob; then screams, whistles, confusion, people running off into Grant Park, across bridges, into hotel lobbies. And

as the scene clears, there are little knots in the open clearing—police clubbing youngsters, police dragging youngsters, police rushing them by their elbows, their heels dragging, to patrol wagons, prodding recalcitrants who refuse to enter quietly.[156]

Humphrey and his running mate, Sen. Edmund S. Muskie of Maine, faced an uphill fight.

The Republicans united behind Richard Nixon, the 1960 nominee whose political career had seemed at an end after he lost the 1962 California gubernatorial election. The GOP did not have to deal with any of the divisiveness of the 1964 Goldwater-Rockefeller battle.

Nixon outspent Humphrey two-to-one. He also followed a carefully devised script that avoided the exhausting schedule of his 1960 campaign and capitalized on the national discontent created by the Vietnam War, urban riots, political assassinations, and popular concern about the speed of change wrought by the Great Society. Nixon traveled the high road in his own campaign by calling for the nation to unite and heal its wounds. Nixon's main offer was change. "I must say the man who helped us get into trouble is not the man to get us out."[157] Nixon gave few major addresses, preferring instead interviews with local newspapers and broadcasters.

As President Johnson resisted calls for a halt in the bombing of North Vietnam, Nixon said he had a "secret plan" to end the war. He appealed to weary Democrats with his pledge of an activist administration and alternative approaches to dealing with some of the problems the Great Society addressed. Nixon promised to give African Americans, in his words, "a piece of the action with a program to encourage entrepreneurial activity in cities." The "new Nixon" appeared willing to deal with the Soviet Union, which he had scorned earlier in his career. Meanwhile, his vice-presidential nominee, Gov. Spiro T. Agnew of Maryland, offered a slashing critique of the Democrats to middle-class and blue-collar Americans who resented the civil rights laws, government bureaucracy, Vietnam War protesters, and the young protest generation.

Alabama governor Wallace, heading up one of the strongest third-party campaigns in U.S. history, ran as an antiestablishment conservative, railing away at desegregation, crime, taxes, opponents of the war in Vietnam, social programs, and "pointy-head" bureaucrats and "intellectual morons." His American Independent Party, mainstream politicians feared, might win enough states to deny a majority to either Nixon or Humphrey, throwing the contest into the House where Wallace could have held the balance of power.[158]

Humphrey, however, made steady inroads into Nixon's support by disassociating himself from Johnson's Vietnam policies. Johnson on November 1 ordered a halt to all bombing of North Vietnam, but this change in policy was not enough to win the election for Humphrey.

The 1968 election was one of the closest in U.S. history. Nixon's victory was not confirmed until the day after the election when California, Ohio, and Illinois—each with close counts—finally went into the Nixon column. Nixon attracted 31.8 million votes (43.4 percent of all votes cast); Humphrey, 31.3 million votes (42.7 percent); and Wallace, 9.9 million votes (13.5 percent). Nixon won thirty-two states and 301 electoral votes, compared with Humphrey's thirteen states and 191 electoral votes. Nixon won six southern states (Wallace won five others), all of the West except Texas, Washington, and Hawaii, and all the midwestern states except Michigan and Minnesota. Humphrey won all of the East except New Hampshire, Vermont, New Jersey, and Delaware, plus West Virginia, Maryland, and the District of Columbia.

The turmoil of 1968 transformed the nominating process. Democrats, in the aftermath of the chaos of their 1968 convention, adopted rules to make primaries the center of the nominating process. The Chicago convention, dominated by party professionals at the expense of many important constituencies—African Americans, women, youth—had nominated a candidate who did not compete in any primaries. The key reform was a limit on the number of delegates that state committees could choose—after 1968, no more than 10 percent of the delegation.

Nixon's Reelection: 1972

Sen. George S. McGovern of South Dakota was the miracle candidate of 1972, but his miracle did not last long enough. Maine Sen. Edmund Muskie, the vice-presidential nominee in 1968, was the early favorite to win the Democratic nomination.

No fewer than fifteen entered the race, twelve with serious hopes of winning or influencing the final selection. Some twenty-two primaries to choose 60 percent of the party's delegates—a third more than in 1968—were scheduled over four months. The marathon would be decided by accidents, media strategy, and a confusing array of voter choices that changed with each new development.

Muskie was badly damaged before the New Hampshire primary when he appeared to cry while lashing back at the *Manchester Union Leader*'s strong and unrelenting attacks on his campaign and on his outspoken wife, Jane. Muskie won New Hampshire's primary with 46.4 percent of the vote, which was considered a "disappointing" showing. McGovern, the antiwar candidate, won 37.1 percent of the vote. Political pundits anointed him the real winner.

After New Hampshire, the Democrats battled through the summer. In the popular primary vote before the late summer California primary, McGovern actually stood in third place behind Wallace and Humphrey but delegate allocation rules gave him edge. McGovern had 560 delegates to Humphrey's 311. Wallace had 324 delegates, but he was

paralyzed after being shot in a Maryland shopping center on May 15, 1972, essentially taking him out of contention.

The big McGovern-Humphrey showdown was California, which McGovern won by five percentage points. McGovern also won a majority of the delegates in New Jersey, South Dakota, and New Mexico on the last day of the primary season.[159]

After platform battles over welfare, busing, and the Vietnam War, McGovern won the nomination handily. But the unfocused organization of the conventions at the time, which parties in later years were to correct, prevented McGovern from delivering his acceptance speech—one of the best speech of his career—until almost three o'clock in the morning, when most television viewers already were in bed.

He selected Sen. Thomas Eagleton of Missouri as his running mate after several others declined. This was another public relations disaster. Rumors began circulating that Eagleton had been hospitalized for exhaustion in the early 1960s. Eagleton finally told the McGovern campaign that he had been hospitalized three times for nervous exhaustion and fatigue, and his treatment included electroshock therapy. Despite McGovern's public statement that he was "1,000 percent for Tom Eagleton, and I have no intention of dropping him," Eagleton left the ticket less than two weeks after his nomination. McGovern eventually replaced Eagleton with his sixth choice, R. Sargent Shriver, former executive of the Peace Corps and Office of Economic Opportunity. But the aura of confusion that surrounded the Eagleton affair and the search for a new vice-presidential candidate hurt the campaign badly. The columnist Tom Braden likened it to a school teacher who could not control the class: "Nice people, too. One looks back with sympathy and a sense of shame. But at the time—was it that they were too nice?—their classes were a shambles. The erasers flew when they turned their backs."[160]

President Nixon and Vice President Agnew were easily renominated and Nixon was in full command of the fall campaign. He paraded a litany of accomplishments—peace talks in Paris over the Vietnam War, a diplomatic opening to China, an arms limitation treaty with the Soviet Union, and a number of domestic initiatives.

Nixon won all but Massachusetts and the District of Columbia in the fall election. His popular vote margin was 47.2 million to McGovern's 29.2 million; the electoral college cast 520 votes for Nixon and only 17 for McGovern. Nixon's 60.7 percent share of the popular vote stood second only to Johnson's 61.1 percent in 1964.

On the surface, it appeared in 1972 that American politics was entering an age of calm consensus. At the time of the election the economy was temporarily strong. Moreover, opposition to the Vietnam War had faded as the two sides negotiated in Paris to end the conflict, and the United States had signed an important nuclear arms treaty with the

Soviet Union and had made important diplomatic moves with that country and the People's Republic of China. Nixon's landslide victory appeared to be a mandate and a vote of confidence.

But trouble loomed. The war in Vietnam continued, as did the antiwar protests, and generational cleavages remained. The economy experienced the first of many "shocks" in 1973 when the Organization of Petroleum Exporting Countries (OPEC) agreed to ban oil exports to the United States. The economic turmoil that resulted in the United States was topped off with a wage and price freeze. In addition, a warlike atmosphere existed between the White House and the media, as well as other individuals and organization that the administration, and Nixon himself, perceived as enemies. But none of these issues compared to the developing Watergate scandal. All of these tensions combined to create a dark side to U.S. politics in the 1970s.[161]

The Watergate affair, most observers thought, was the worst political scandal in U.S. history. For the first time, a president was forced to leave office before his term expired. President Nixon resigned on August 9, 1974, when it became apparent that the House of Representatives would impeach him for "high crimes and misdemeanors" and the Senate would convict him. In addition, a number of Nixon aides, including his first attorney general and campaign manager, John Mitchell, would spend time in jail because of the scandal.

At its simplest, the Watergate affair was a simple burglary, followed by a cover-up by President Nixon and his aides. In the summer of 1972, several employees of the Committee to Re-elect the President were arrested when breaking into and bugging the Democratic National Committee's offices at the posh Watergate complex in Washington. The break-in was not a major issue in the 1972 election, but the next year a Senate committee began an investigation of the entire affair.

During the investigation, a presidential aide revealed that Nixon had secretly taped Oval Office conversations with aides. These tapes became the center of the Watergate battle with Nixon resisting their release and investigators demanding them. Nixon did eventually hand over some of the tapes but not all. Then, in summer 1974, the Supreme Court ruled that Nixon had to surrender even more tapes, which indicated that he had played an active role in covering up the Watergate scandal. Nixon resigned the presidency when his impeachment and conviction appeared certain after he lost all semblance of Republican support in Congress. The impeachment articles charged him with obstruction of justice, abuse of presidential powers, and contempt of Congress.

Many scholars of the Watergate affair maintain that the illegal campaign activities were just part of a tapestry of illegal activities in the Nixon administration—including

secretly bombing Cambodia, accepting millions of dollars in illegal campaign contributions, offering government favors in return for contributions, "laundering" money through third parties, wiretapping and burglarizing a wide variety of people thought to be unsupportive of the president, offering executive clemency to convicted campaign workers, engaging in "dirty tricks" to discredit other political figures, compromising criminal investigations by giving information to the people under scrutiny, and using government funds to renovate the president's private residence.[162]

In 1973 Nixon's vice president, Spiro Agnew, resigned after pleading "no contest" to charges of taking bribes while he was governor of Maryland. After Agnew's resignation on October 10, 1973, Nixon named House Minority Leader Gerald R. Ford, a longtime GOP stalwart, to become vice president under the Twenty-fifth Amendment. Ford, who had never entered a national election, then became president after Nixon's resignation and quickly attracted the support of the American public with his modest, earnest disposition. He responded to the widespread feeling that Nixon's isolation in the Oval Office had contributed to his downfall by promising to work closely with Congress and to meet with the press regularly.

One month after becoming president, however, Ford granted Nixon a full pardon for all crimes he may have committed while president. Ford testified before Congress that he believed Nixon had suffered enough and that the nation would have been badly torn if a former president were brought to court to face criminal charges. Critics asserted that Ford had made a "deal" in which Nixon resigned the presidency in exchange for the pardon.[163] Ford selected former New York governor Nelson Rockefeller to be his vice president. Rockefeller received Senate and House confirmation on December 10 and 19, respectively. Ford's pardon, which drew widespread public condemnation, was later seen as a significant factor in his loss in the presidential race of 1976, which was won by Georgia Gov. Jimmy Carter.

Election of "Jimmy Who?": 1976

With the benefit of the Watergate scandal and Ford's pardon of Nixon, the Democrats won resounding victories in the 1974 midterm elections. The Democrats gained fifty-two House seats and four Senate seats creating stronger majorities and reducing the number of members with allegiance to the old system of organizing congressional business.

The moralistic zeal of the "Watergate class" forced major changes on Congress as well as on the presidency and the nation's process of pluralistic political bargaining. The new crop of legislators was so large that it was able to undermine the seniority system that had ordered the way Congress had operated for years. The new system of committee assignments led to a proliferation of subcommittees on which most members had prominent roles. That, in turn,

Virtually unknown to the country at the outset of the campaign, former Georgia governor Jimmy Carter emerged from a field of candidates to win the Democratic nomination and the presidency. His casual and honest approach appealed to many voters.

created a fragmented policymaking process—less susceptible to coercion by presidents and party leaders but more susceptible to interest group politics.[164]

The 1976 campaign was the first governed by campaign finance reform legislation enacted in 1971 and 1974. The Federal Election Campaign Act (FECA) of 1971 limited campaign expenditures and required disclosure of campaign receipts and expenditures. The Revenue Act of 1971 created a tax check-off that enabled taxpayers to allocate $1 of their taxes for public financing of elections. The FECA amendments of 1974 limited spending and donations for both primary and general election campaigns, established a system of partial public funding of elections, and created the Federal Election Commission to monitor campaign activities.

The Democrats and their eventual nominee, former Georgia governor Jimmy Carter, continued to exploit the nation's discontent through the 1976 election. Ronald Reagan, a former movie actor and California governor, added to the Republican Party's vulnerability by waging a stubborn primary campaign against President Ford.

The Democrats appeared headed for a long and bitter nomination struggle for the third time in a row. A few candidates—such as senators Henry Jackson of Washington and Birch Bayh of Indiana and Gov. George Wallace of Alabama—had greater stature than others, but their appeal was limited to specific factions of the Democratic coalition. Other candidates included Rep. Morris Udall of Arizona, Sen. Fred Harris of Oklahoma, Sen. Frank Church of Idaho, and Gov. Edmund G. "Jerry" Brown Jr. of California. Church and Brown entered the race late, and Hubert Humphrey of Minnesota and Sen. Edward M. Kennedy of Massachusetts awaited a draft in the event of a deadlocked convention.

The moderate Carter, whose name recognition in polls stood in single figures when the campaign began, executed a brilliant campaign strategy to win the nomination on the first ballot. Constructing strong organizations for the Iowa caucuses and the New Hampshire primary, Carter won both contests by slim margins. Although liberal candidates Udall and Bayh together polled more votes than Carter, it was Carter who received cover billings on national magazines and live interviews on morning television talk shows.[165] Within a matter of days, Carter went from long shot to front-runner. Carter had strong challenges from others in the remaining primaries but gathered ample delegates and endorsements by the time of the Democratic convention in New York for a first-ballot nomination.

The GOP was divided between Ford and Reagan. Ford won the early contests, but Reagan scored big wins in the North Carolina and Texas primaries. Reagan was put on the defensive with his proposals for transferring welfare obligations to the states, but when he focused on foreign policy he had success. For example, he attacked Ford for his policy of détente with the Soviet Union and his negotiation of a treaty that would forfeit U.S. control of the Panama Canal.

Carter emerged from the Democratic convention with a wide lead over Ford, but the race was too close to call by election day. A number of gaffes—such as an interview Carter gave to *Playboy* magazine, his ambiguous statements about abortion, and his confused observations on tax reform—hurt the Democratic contender.[166] Ford also gained in the polls when he began to use the patronage powers of the presidency and effectively contrasted his twenty-seven years of Washington experience to Carter's four years as governor of Georgia.

For the first time since 1960, the major candidates took part in televised debates. As the outsider, Carter helped himself by demonstrating a good grasp of national issues and by appealing to Democrats to vote the party line. Ford hurt himself with a claim that eastern European nations did not consider themselves to be under the control of the Soviet Union.[67] The remark was intended to be testimony to the Europeans' sense of national identity, but it was interpreted as evidence of the president's naiveté.

Carter's main advantage was regional pride. The Democrats had long since lost their hold over the South, but Carter gained widespread support as the first candidate nominated from the region on his own in more than a century. The Democratic Party's many factions—including such big city mayors as Richard Daley of Chicago and Abraham Beame of New York, civil rights activists, and organized labor—put on a rare display of unity.

Carter defeated Ford by a slim margin, winning 40.8 million votes (50.1 percent) to Ford's 39.1 million (48.0 percent). In the electoral college, 297 votes went to Carter,

240 to Ford. Carter won by pulling together the frazzled New Deal coalition of industrial and urban voters, African Americans, Jews, and southerners. Ford won the West, and Carter won the South, except Virginia. Ford won all the states from the Mississippi River westward except Texas and Hawaii, plus states in his native Midwest like Iowa, Illinois, Michigan, and Indiana. Ford also won Connecticut and the three northernmost New England states—New Hampshire, Vermont, and Maine.

Carter's Uncertain Leadership: 1980

After his election, President Carter's ability to hold the coalition together was limited. The growing influence of the mass media, the fragmenting effects of interest groups, poor relations with Congress, and difficult issues that cut across many different sectors—inflation and unemployment, long gasoline lines from restricted oil imports, and the more general energy crisis, the Iran crisis in which revolutionary militants seized the U.S. embassy and held Americans hostage for the remainder of Carter's term, relations with the Soviet Union, and budget austerity moves such as proposed cutbacks in water projects and social welfare—all damaged Carter's governing ability.

As the 1980 election approached, voters were poised to reject a president for the fourth time in a row including Ford's 1976 loss, Nixon's resignation, and Johnson withdrawal. Carter appeared to have lost all but his institutional strength: he controlled party processes, such as the primary schedule; he had access to key financial support and skilled political operatives; and he shaped much of the political agenda. But opponents were attacking from both wings: Massachusetts senator Kennedy on the left, and Ronald Reagan and others from the right. As a result, Carter was unable to forge a lasting consensus on important issues. Kennedy, however, was unable to develop campaign themes or to adequately answer questions about his personal conduct in the 1969 Chappaquiddick incident in which a woman died after a car he was driving went off a bridge.

Carter won the nomination on the first ballot despite a variety of stop-Carter efforts. But his campaign entered the fall contest as a wounded army unable to generate much enthusiasm from the troops.

The Republicans united early behind Reagan. By April 22, 1980, less than two months after the New Hampshire primary, six candidates had dropped out of the race, and George H. W. Bush, Reagan's only surviving competitor, was significantly behind in the delegate count. Reagan's campaign experienced an early scare when Bush beat Reagan in the Iowa caucuses, but Reagan rebounded, changed campaign managers and tactics, and won a string of primaries and caucuses. By the time of the convention, Reagan was the consensus candidate, and he improved party unity by adding Bush to the fall ticket.

Reagan called on the electorate to replace politics that he said was marked by "pastels," or compromising and uncertain policies, with "bold colors." Reagan's proposed bold strokes included a 30 percent reduction in marginal income tax rates based on a "supply-side" economic theory—which even Bush had said was a dangerous kind of "voodoo economics"—and massive increases in military expenditures. At the same time Reagan criticized Carter's alleged vacillation and his commitment to liberal policies.

President Carter, who was vulnerable as the hostage crisis neared its first anniversary (on November 4, election day) and high inflation and unemployment rates persisted, attempted to portray Reagan as a dangerous, heartless, and inexperienced amateur.

Carter strategists also were concerned about the independent candidacy of Rep. John B. Anderson of Illinois, a moderate who dropped out of the Republican race when it became clear that conservatives would dominate that party. After some stronger support in the polls, Anderson stood at about 10 percent for the final two months of the campaign. Carter was concerned that Anderson would take more votes from him than from Reagan, even though analysis of Anderson support suggested otherwise.[168]

Polls before election day predicted a close race. Reagan, however, won all but six states and took the White House in an electoral landslide, 489 electoral votes to 49. Reagan won 51 percent of the vote, while Carter managed 41 percent and Anderson 7 percent. Even more surprising than Reagan's electoral landslide was the Republican takeover of the Senate. Newly formed conservative groups targeted several Senate liberals, creating the biggest Senate turnover since 1958. The Republicans now held the Senate by a 53–46 margin.

President Reagan was able to parlay his claims of an electoral mandate into wide-ranging changes in tax, budget, and military policies. Among other things, he won passage of a three-year, 25 percent cut in tax rates that would reduce federal revenues by $196 billion annually by the time the three-stage program was in place. He also secured omnibus legislation that cut the domestic budget by $140 billion over four years and increased defense spending by $181 billion over the same period. The media hailed Reagan as the most successful handler of Congress since Lyndon B. Johnson.

NEW CONSERVATIVE DISCOURSE

Ronald Reagan's rise ushered in a new period of conservatism in the American political discourse. The vigorous conservative campaigns for the presidency and Congress were accompanied by a host of new "think tanks" and publications with a restyled set of philosophical and policy pronouncements.

A celebrated event of the conservative revival was the publication in 1980 of George Gilder's *Wealth and Poverty*, a far-reaching attack on welfare state policies that rested on supply-side economic theory. Gilder argued that free markets and low taxes promoted not only economic efficiency and growth but also other benefits such as family strength and artistic creativity. Gilder's book was a central element of Reagan's campaign for major tax cuts.[169] But the supply-side arguments of Gilder and others were only the most visible signs of the conservative movement. Reagan's criticism of the Supreme Court decisions on abortion and school prayer helped to bring evangelical Christians into the political process. Businesses and conservative philanthropists, meanwhile, sponsored an unprecedented level of public policy research that shaped the debate of elections and government policy.[170]

Reagan's political appeal, according to scholar Garry Wills, turned on his ability to blend contradictory elements of American culture such as capitalism, conservatism, and individualism. While Reagan decried the decline of "traditional American values," for example, he extolled the dynamic economic system that demanded constant change. Wills wrote: "There are so many contradictions in this larger construct that one cannot risk entertaining serious challenge to any of its details. In Reagan, luckily, all these clashes are resolved. He is the ideal past, the successful present, the hopeful future all in one."[171]

Using the "bully pulpit" of the presidency, Reagan was able to overwhelm his opponents with his vision. When Democrats criticized specific Reagan policies, Reagan deflated them with expressions of disdain for "little men with loud voices [that] cry doom."[172] Jeane Kirkpatrick's depiction of Democrats as the "blame America first crowd" neatly expressed the way the Reagan rhetoric foreclosed debate on major policy issues such as the budget and trade deficits, military spending, the U.S. role in the third world, and U.S.-Soviet relations.

By the time the 1984 campaign took place, much of the nation had adopted Reagan's terms of debate. The Democratic candidate that year, Walter F. Mondale, in the first debate congratulated Reagan for restoring national pride and suggested not that Reagan should be ousted but rather that he be given a graceful retirement. Mondale's campaign was basically conservative: he did not propose a single new social program and called the federal budget deficit the nation's top problem.

Reagan's Landslide: 1984

Reagan's popularity dipped to 44 percent in 1983—about the average for modern presidents—but it rebounded when the economy later picked up.[173] As the 1984 election approached, Reagan faced no opposition from Republicans, but a large field of Democrats sought the right to oppose him in the fall.

The Democrats' early front-runner was former vice president Walter Mondale, who had accumulated a wide

Democrat Walter Mondale and Republican Ronald Reagan shake hands prior to the presidential debate. While Mondale performed well in the first presidential debate, Reagan's overwhelming popularity brought him an easy victory in the 1984 election.

range of endorsements (AFL-CIO, National Education Association, United Mine Workers, and the National Organization for Women) and an impressive campaign treasury. The more conservative senator John Glenn of Ohio, the first American to orbit the earth, was considered a strong challenger. Other candidates included senators Gary Hart of Colorado, Alan Cranston of California, and Ernest Hollings of South Carolina, civil rights leader Jesse Jackson, former presidential candidate George McGovern, and former Florida governor Reubin Askew.

The early results eliminated all but Mondale, Hart, and Jackson just sixteen days after the New Hampshire primary. Hart became the serious challenger to Mondale when he finished second in Iowa and first in New Hampshire, creating substantial of media coverage. After Mondale recovered, the two fought head-to-head until the convention. Jackson, the second African American to run for the presidency, stayed in the race to promote his liberal party agenda.[174]

After interviewing a wide range of candidates, Mondale selected Rep. Geraldine A. Ferraro of New York as his running mate—the first woman ever to receive a major party nomination for national office. Ferraro's vice-presidential candidacy was plagued by controversy over her husband's questionable real estate, trusteeship, and tax practices and her stand on abortion. The controversies hindered the Democratic campaign's effort to articulate its vision for the nation.[175]

Mondale ran a generally conservative campaign, concentrating on a proposed tax increase to address the unprecedented budget deficit of more than $200 billion and proposing no new social programs. Mondale criticized Reagan's record on the arms race, but he did not outline basic disagreements on other foreign affairs issues. He charged that Reagan, the oldest president in history, was lazy and out of touch. Only late in the campaign, when his speeches became unabashedly liberal and combative, did Mondale create any excitement. He never was never within ten percentage points of Reagan in the polls. Reagan's campaign was a series of rallies with masses of colorful balloons and confident talk about the United States "standing tall" in domestic and world affairs. Reagan was so sure of victory that he made a last-minute trip to Mondale's home state of Minnesota with the hope of completing a fifty-state sweep of the nation.

As it was, Reagan won forty-nine states, with two-to-one margins in eight states. Mondale won only the District of Columbia and his home state of Minnesota, where he beat Reagan by only two-tenths of a percentage point. In the popular vote, Reagan won 54.5 million votes (58.8 percent) to Mondale's 37.6 million (40.6 percent). In the electoral college, he received 525 votes to Mondale's 13 votes.

Reagan's two landslides and the conservative discourse of his administration led many experts to wonder if they were witnessing a "realignment"—a major shift in political alliances among a variety of social, economic, and ethnic groups.[176] The trend during the 1970s and 1980s appeared to be one of a Democratic hold on congressional and state elections and Republican dominance of presidential elections. Some experts pointed to the electorate's ticket-splitting tendencies as evidence of "dealignment"—a breakdown of the old system without development of an entirely new system.[177]

Bush's Ascendancy: 1988

The election of 1988 was the first after 1968 in which an incumbent president did not run. With no major figure and no major issues, the campaign was an usual affair. Fourteen candidates struggled to develop an identity with the voters, and the campaign lurched from one symbolic issue to the next, never developing the overarching themes of previous campaigns.

In the absence of any major new issues, and in a time of general peace and prosperity, Republican vice president George H.W. Bush won the presidency. Bush defeated Democratic Massachusetts governor Michael S. Dukakis by a margin of 54 percent to 46 percent—48.9 million votes to 41.8 million votes. Bush's electoral vote margin was more impressive, 426–111. A negative campaign and limited voter registration efforts resulted in the lowest voter turnout rate since the 1920 and 1924 race percentages of 49 percent of

After two popular terms as president, Ronald Reagan and wife Nancy pass leadership of the "Reagan Revolution" to newly inaugurated President George H.W. Bush and wife Barbara in 1989.

voting age citizens. Just a little more than 50 percent of those voters cast ballots for president in 1988.

Bush, benefiting from the Nixon-Reagan presidential coalition, won all the states of the old Confederacy, the entire West except Oregon and Washington, and several northern industrial states. Dukakis originally had hoped to crack the South by selecting a favorite son, Sen. Lloyd M. Bentsen Jr. of Texas, as his running mate, but that tactic failed. Dukakis lost crucial states that he had fought for to the end, such as California, Pennsylvania, Illinois, Ohio, and Missouri. He won New York, Massachusetts, Wisconsin, Minnesota, Oregon, Washington, West Virginia, Iowa, Rhode Island, Hawaii, and the District of Columbia.

President Ronald Reagan's retirement after two full terms created a political void. Perhaps the most popular president since Dwight D. Eisenhower in the 1950s, Reagan's dominance of national politics left little room for other figures to establish presidential stature.

Reagan's fiscal and social policies reduced the possibility for candidates to offer ambitious new programs. The national government's huge budget deficits—which exceeded $200 billion, compared with about $73 billion in the last year of the Carter administration—checked any grandiose new spending plans. The Reagan debt had exceeded the debt of the previous thirty-eight presidents.

Reagan also had reshaped the dialogue on foreign affairs. He maintained strong opposition to the Soviet Union and other "Marxist" nations with his policies in Nicaragua, Afghanistan, and Angola. He also had projected an image of strength with military action in Libya and Grenada. At the same time, however, he had co-opted his critics by meeting with Soviet leader Mikhail Gorbachev several times and signing a nuclear arms control agreement. Reagan even asserted that the Gorbachev regime was fundamentally different from previous Soviet regimes, which he had called the "evil empire."

The one issue that threatened Bush throughout 1988 was the Iran-contra scandal. Revelations that the Reagan administration had traded arms to Iran in exchange for the release of hostages held in Lebanon, then used the proceeds illegally to fund the war in Nicaragua, raised questions about Bush's role in the matter. Administration officials admitted lying to Congress, destroying evidence, and operating outside normal government channels; one top official even attempted suicide. The question of Bush's involvement in the affair, however, fizzled after months of inconclusive questioning.

Dukakis selected conservative senator Lloyd Bentsen of Texas as his running mate before the Atlanta Democratic convention. No Democrat had won the presidency without winning Texas since the state became part of the nation in 1845, a tradition that continued in 1988.

The July convention was a success for the Democrats. After a week of Bush-bashing and Democratic conciliation, Dukakis gave an effective acceptance speech peppered with statements in Spanish and Greek. Dukakis left the convention with a double-digit lead over Bush in the polls.

The Republican convention in August did not start out as well. Bush announced his vice-presidential selection, Sen. James Danforth "Dan" Quayle of Indiana, when he arrived in New Orleans. After revelations that Quayle had avoided military service in the Vietnam War by enlisting in the Indiana National Guard, many Republicans criticized Bush's choice. Some even said that Quayle might have to be dropped from the ticket.[178] By the end of the convention, however, the Republicans had weathered the storm. Bush delivered a crisp address, which provided the appealing self-portrait the vice president needed, and moved into the fall campaign for a close battle with Dukakis.

Bush took the offensive immediately after the August GOP convention and hit Dukakis as a "liberal" out of touch with American "values." The Bush campaign's "Willie Horton" commercial—which told of a black prisoner raping a woman while out on a weekend release program—was particularly controversial. As Bush pounded away at these symbolic issues (effectively drowning out other major issues such as the national debt, trade deficit, housing, education, U.S.-Soviet relations, the environment, and ethics in government), Dukakis's "negative" ratings with voters soared. Roger Ailes, Bush's media adviser, admitted that the Bush camp knew it would have to define Dukakis. The Bush thus campaign spent its time "avoiding mistakes, staying on the attack, and giving them [media] pictures," Ailes said.[179]

Not believing the attacks would affect his standing with undecided voters—and believing they might even hurt Bush—Dukakis did not respond forcefully to the frontal assault until October. By then, however, Bush had effectively defined Dukakis as a newcomer to national politics. Dukakis's counteroffensive in the last two weeks of the campaign came too late. As Dukakis fell behind Bush, his campaign pinned its hopes on two nationally televised debates. Dukakis performed well in the first debate, but Bush appeared to "win" the second debate. Dukakis failed to gain on Bush.

After months of inconsistent and confusing strategy, Dukakis finally developed a strong appeal in the last two weeks of the campaign. He told voters he was on their side and portrayed Bush as a toady to the wealthy. Dukakis said the middle class had been "squeezed" by the policies of the Reagan administration and that the Democrats would provide good jobs, affordable housing and health care, and tough enforcement of environmental protection laws.

But it was not enough. Bush, who had made a fortune in the oil business before entering politics and was the son of a former U.S. senator, persuaded more voters that his experience and values were what they wanted in the very personal choice of a president.

CLINTON ERA

In March 1991, in the aftermath of the U.S.-led victory over Iraq in the Persian Gulf War, President George H.W. Bush received the highest approval ratings since opinion polling began: around 90 percent of respondents said they approved of his performance as president. But just a year later, Bush was struggling to keep his job—and he failed.

Bill Clinton's victory over Bush in 1992 could have been viewed, on the one hand, as a dramatic shift in American politics. Touting his campaign slogan of "change," the forty-six-year-old Arkansas governor repeatedly blasted the Republican White House for its inattention to domestic problems such as the budget deficit, health care, welfare, civil rights, crime, trade, and economic investment. President Bush, Clinton said, was too obsessed with foreign policy and unconcerned with domestic affairs.

On the other hand, Clinton's election could have been viewed as an aberration. Only the second Democrat elected president since 1968, Clinton got only 43 percent of the vote in a three-candidate race. Voters said they voted against Bush, not for Clinton. The independent candidacy of Texas billionaire H. Ross Perot may have cost Bush the election, as much by tarnishing his reputation as by taking away the votes of the angry middle class. Even people who supported Clinton expressed reservations about his character. Voters reacted warily to reports of Clinton's avoidance of military service in Vietnam, marital infidelity, and conflicts of interest while governor, and to his evasiveness about smoking marijuana as a student. On policy questions, Clinton was well informed, but sometimes he appeared insincere. A label pinned on Clinton in Arkansas—"Slick Willie"—stuck.

President Bush began the election cycle looking unbeatable. Coasting on the apparent success of his leadership during the Gulf War, Bush appeared to have the strength to lead the United States into what he called the "new world order." In 1989 the countries of the so-called Soviet bloc—East Germany, Poland, Czechoslovakia, Romania, Hungary—had broken from communist rule in a series of nonviolent revolutions. In August 1991 an attempted coup against Mikhail Gorbachev's "perestroika" government in the Soviet Union had failed. Afterward, the Soviet regime—Communist Party and all—had collapsed. The Bush presidency had overseen the most remarkable realignment of world politics since World War II.

Indeed, Bush took credit for presiding over the dramatic changes, but those American "victories" also undermined his position. The Republican Party had dominated recent presidential politics at least partly because of its hawkish policies during the cold war. With the end of the Soviet threat, the GOP no longer had a "gut" issue to use against the Democrats. Bush had a hard time adjusting.

Despite high polling numbers, President Bush faced serious challenges from the start. Despite three decades in public life, Bush had never conveyed a coherent identity or campaign theme. His advisers planned to "narrowcast" messages to selected groups until the summer, when Bush would deliver his big "what-I-stand-for" speech. But by that time, Bush's opponent had defined him as weak and unprincipled. His attempt to divert attention to Clinton's foibles only intensified Bush's image as uncertain of his own values and goals.[180]

By spring 1992 Bush's base had crumbled. The president had decided to "sit" on his high popularity ratings and win reelection by avoiding mistakes. Bush's chief of staff, John Sununu, summed up the strategy: "There's not another single piece of legislation that needs to be passed in the next two years for this president. In fact, if Congress wants to

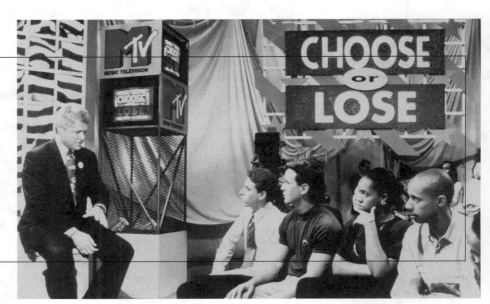

Democratic presidential candidate Bill Clinton talks with young people on a program hosted by the MTV cable channel. The 1992 campaign was revolutionary in the way candidates used nontraditional media to reach voters.

come together, adjourn, and leave, it's all right with us."[181] The results of this strategy were devastating. In May 1992 a poll found that 76 percent of the public disapproved of the way Bush was handling the economy.[182] His overall approval rating dropped an unprecedented 57 percentage points from the end of the Gulf War to the beginning of the 1992 GOP convention.

A bitter anti-incumbent mood dominated the new campaign year. Nationwide, reformers promoted the idea of term limits for elected officials as a way to sweep out career politicians.[183] Perot, who had parlayed his wealth into a number of headline-grabbing exploits over the years, became a viable independent candidate.[184] His pithy statements about how to "fix" government captured the imagination of the public.

Pennsylvania voters sent a warning shot to the White House when they rejected the 1991 Senate candidacy of Bush's friend and first attorney general, Richard Thornburgh. Democrat Harris Wofford, appointed to the seat that had opened with the death of Sen. John Heinz in April 1991, won on a platform of national health care and a return to domestic priorities—themes that Clinton reprised in 1992.

Bush's major domestic initiative—the budget law passed in October 1990—angered the Republican Party's right wing. Conservatives had long distrusted Bush because of his past moderate positions on taxes, abortion, civil rights, and social programs. The budget act, which increased taxes by $150 billion, broke the pledge of "no new taxes" that Bush had taken in the 1988 presidential campaign.

As the recession and other domestic crises deepened, the president seemed increasingly out of touch. Bush's reported confusion over the use of bar codes at a grocery store symbolized his elite background and isolation. After race riots in Los Angeles drew the nation's attention to the severity of poverty, Bush was photographed teaching baffled-looking urban youths how to use a fishing pole. In a political environment couched in symbolism, these images did not help the candidate.

Bush had begun his term with less party support than any president in history—the Democrats controlled the Senate by ten seats and the House by eighty-five seats. As a result, Bush's legislative initiatives were routinely labeled "dead on arrival." In 1989, for the first time, the Senate rejected an incoming president's cabinet nominee when it voted down former senator John G. Tower's bid to be secretary of defense. In his dealings with Capitol Hill, Bush had vacillated between confrontation and compromise. In fact, Bush regularly tussled with Congress, vetoing forty-four bills between 1989 and 1992.

Three-Way Race: 1992

The Democratic field grew slowly. Besides Clinton, the field included former Massachusetts senator Paul E. Tsongas,

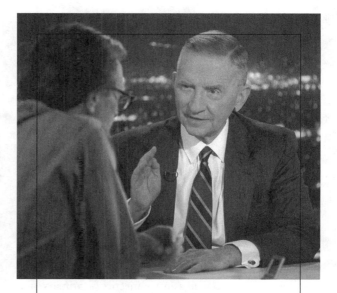

Independent H. Ross Perot mounted his 1992 campaign for presidency by relying on his own money and appearing on television talk shows, such as here with Larry King.

former governor Edmund G. "Jerry" Brown Jr. of California, senators Thomas Harkin of Iowa and Robert Kerrey of Nebraska, and Gov. L. Douglas Wilder of Virginia. Wilder dropped out, however, before the first contest and others faded in the March primaries. Clinton won the "invisible primaries" before the formal balloting began; he attracted $3.3 million in contributions by the end of 1991.[185]

By calling himself a "new Democrat," Clinton hoped to separate himself from some of the rejected Democratic candidates of the past: Jimmy Carter, Walter Mondale, and Michael Dukakis. In keeping with this strategy, Clinton promised to move beyond liberal orthodoxy and "reinvent government."[186] His record in Arkansas suggested a willingness to oppose liberal nostrums on issues such as the death penalty, economic growth, and public education.

The centerpiece of Clinton's strategy was to appeal to the "forgotten middle class." Suburbanites, the working class, and southerners and westerners had abandoned the Democratic Party since the late 1960s. Unfortunately for the Democrats, these groups composed a growing part of the electorate. In fact, many pundits argued that these groups gave the Republicans a "lock" on the presidency.[187] Clinton's goal, then, was to forge a new ideological center and "pick" the lock.

Clinton led the polling before the New Hampshire primary until he ran into trouble when the media questioned his character. A woman claimed that she and Clinton had had an affair, and Clinton was reported to have misled an Army Reserves recruiter as part of a scheme to avoid service in Vietnam. But Clinton hit back. Appearing on the television news magazine *60 Minutes* after the January 1992 Super Bowl game, Clinton admitted he had "caused pain" in his marriage but said he and his wife had solved their problems. Hillary Clinton's appearance with her husband seemed to close the matter.

Tsongas and Brown won the occasional contest after New Hampshire, but Clinton rolled to the nomination starting with his March 3 victory in the Georgia primary. Clinton's sweep of southern states on "Super Tuesday," March 10, and his decisive wins in Michigan and Illinois on March 17 practically clinched the nomination.

Clinton won thirty-one state primaries with 51.8 percent of the vote; Tsongas, four states with 18.1 percent; and Brown, two states with 20.1 percent.[188] Democratic leaders nevertheless searched for an alternative, worried about Clinton's ability to confront the character issue. In March almost half the Democratic voters in Connecticut's primary said Clinton lacked the "honesty or integrity" to be president.[189] Party professionals, however, became resigned to Clinton's nomination.

President Bush faced an unusually pointed challenge from conservative columnist and former White House aide Patrick J. Buchanan, who charged that Bush had betrayed the conservative faith. His main point of attack was the 1990 tax increase. Although in the end Bush won New Hampshire, the media focused on the 37 percent of the vote that the underdog Buchanan received. But Buchanan thereafter never matched his New Hampshire numbers.

The campaign of the Texas billionaire, H. Ross Perot, unsettled Republicans' plans to build on their base in the South and West. Perot's folksy antigovernment rhetoric appealed to voters in the suburbs and high-growth areas of the 1980s—the heart of the GOP base since Richard Nixon's 1968 campaign. Perot waged an aggressive campaign on the television talk show circuit and said he would spend up to $100 million of his own money. But as his unofficial campaign progressed, the media raised doubts about his background and grasp of government. By summer more people viewed Perot unfavorably than favorably.

Perot dropped out of the campaign before he had a chance to announce his entry formally. He pointed out that Clinton's selection of well-respected Gore as his running mate indicated that the Democrats were "getting their act together." He also recognized that his campaign might split the vote badly and send the election into the House of Representatives.

Perot resumed his campaign in the fall, blaming his temporary exit on a Republican "dirty tricks" effort to smear his family. By then the critical reporting had faded. But it was too late for Perot because his erratic behavior had driven away supporters and curious voters alike.

Even though Perot had no real chance to win, his campaign was significant. He spent $60 million of his money,

mostly to purchase half-hour television advertisements. Some of the ads, dubbed "infomercials," won critical acclaim for their plain talk about the dangers of the federal budget deficit. Perot's bluntness lent credibility to his relentless attacks on Bush.

The communications revolution changed the way the candidates reached voters as candidates appeared in settings once considered undignified for potential presidents. Television talk shows provided a way for candidates to bypass the establishment media. The blurred lines between news and entertainment were perhaps most evident on cable television in the rock music MTV channel's ongoing coverage of the presidential campaign. New outlets were especially important for candidates facing credibility problems in mainstream media (Clinton) and for the insurgents (Perot and Brown).

Clinton parroted Perot's rhetoric about the evils of special-interest influence in Washington and promised reforms of the campaign finance system. Clinton, however, also raised money aggressively. The Democrats raised $71 million in 1992, $9 million more than the Republicans.[190] Clinton's selection of moderate senator Gore of Tennessee as a running mate was central to his fall strategy. Gore's service in Vietnam and military expertise countered Clinton's suspect status in foreign policy. Moreover, Gore's Washington experience going back to 1976 helped Clinton to compensate for his lack of federal government experience. Finally, Gore's reputation as an intellectual—he wrote an acclaimed book about the environment in 1992[191]—contrasted with Vice President Dan Quayle's lightweight reputation.

The Republican convention in Houston was a turning point in the campaign. Strategists decided to shore up Bush's right-wing support and raise doubts about Clinton's character. The party's platform committee was dominated by the right-wing Christian Coalition. Speeches by Patrick Buchanan, Pat Robertson, and Marilyn Quayle, questioning the Democrats' patriotism and arguing for a rollback of civil liberties, played badly. Bush's lost convention opportunity was apparent in the meager 3 percentage point "bounce" in poll support, compared with Clinton's 17 to 20 percent increase after the Democratic convention.[192]

Clinton ran a sophisticated general election campaign, coordinated from the "war room" in Little Rock by strategists, led by James Carville, who choreographed every aspect of the campaign, from television commercials to talk show appearances to speechwriting to the bus tours of small towns. The campaign professionals were especially adept at answering charges from the opposition. When Bush attacked, Clintonites issued instant, detailed responses. The quick response prevented Bush's charges from dominating the news cycle.

The Bush-Quayle fall campaign was erratic. Early on, it focused on "family values," critiquing the Democrats as elitists out of touch with ordinary people. Then Bush used the powers of incumbency by announcing billions of dollars in grants to different states. All along, Bush criticized Clinton's character and experience. But the personal attacks often appeared shrill; at one point, he called Clinton and Gore "bozos" and said "my dog Millie" would be better at foreign policy than they. Bush criticized Clinton's visit to the Soviet Union as a student and suggested that he wanted to import British-style socialism to the United States.

Bush's credibility came under fire in the campaign's final days when a special prosecutor indicted former defense secretary Caspar Weinberger and released a memorandum that indicated Bush had participated in the an arms for hostages scandal—the Iran-contra affair—much more actively than he had acknowledged.

The Clinton-Gore ticket gave the Democrats a solid base in the border states on which to build. With Arkansas and Tennessee in the Democratic camp, the Democrats built outward into the old Confederacy (Georgia, Louisiana, Kentucky), north into the industrial states (Illinois, Michigan, Ohio), and west and north into the farm states (Iowa, Minnesota, Wisconsin). The Democrats had consistently lost those states in presidential elections in the past generation, despite strong support in congressional and statewide races. The Democrats also built on their core of support in the Northeast (winning all the states from Maine to West Virginia) and capitalized on disgruntlement with Bush in the West (California, Colorado, Hawaii, Montana, Nevada, New Mexico, Oregon, and Washington went for Clinton). That was enough to "pick" the Republican "lock" on the electoral college.

Clinton took only 43 percent of the popular vote but garnered 370 electoral votes. This compared with Bush's 38 percent of the popular vote and 168 electoral votes. Perot's 19 percent share of the vote was the largest percentage a third party had won since 1912, but he did not win any electoral votes. The hard anti-incumbent mood of the electorate, stoked by Perot, helped to produce the highest voter turnout rate since 1960. Some 55 percent of voting-age citizens participated in the election.

Clinton's Reelection: 1996

In 1994 many voters sent a strong message of disapproval with President Clinton's record by electing a Republican Congress. That dramatic event led many political analysts to conclude that Clinton would be a one-term president but they did not anticipate that the new GOP Congress, led prominently by controversial House Speaker Newt Gingrich of Georgia, would incorrectly interpret the 1994 election results as a mandate for their conservative ideological agenda and then push for substantial—and unpopular—policy reform. This miscalculation provided President Clinton with a new opportunity to redefine himself and to rehabilitate his political future.

President Bill Clinton and Vice President Al Gore accept their renomination at the Democratic National Convention in August 1996. In the general election Clinton became the first Democratic president reelected to a second term since Franklin Roosevelt in 1936.

While the Republicans strove aggressively for conservative policy change, Clinton adopted more moderate positions and portrayed himself as a check against the "extremism" of the GOP agenda. That tack proved successful by the end of 1995. With the president and Republican legislators feuding over spending priorities, Congress failed to pass a budget in time to avoid two temporary government shutdowns. As the impasse persisted, the Republican Congress began to get the blame from voters, and the president benefited from the comparison. This budgetary standoff against Congress was perhaps the single most important event to Clinton's political rehabilitation.

The president entered the 1996 election season with renewed political strength and high approval ratings. In addition to the political miscalculations of the majority in Congress, Clinton benefited from a strengthening economy. In addition, he did not face a challenge for renomination, while the GOP nomination contest was an expensive, highly negative, and divisive process.

From the beginning Senate Majority Leader Robert J. "Bob" Dole of Kansas was the clear front-runner for the Republican Party's nomination. He had the broadest party support of any announced candidate, the most prominent endorsements, and the best grassroots campaign organization. Although there never was any serious doubt that he would be the Republican nominee, for several months Dole had to fight off a large group of presidential contenders.

Dole's eventual nomination—even after losing the traditionally crucial battleground primary in New Hampshire to television commentator Pat Buchanan—did not ensure a united Republican Party to challenge the president. Although Dole had long supported the antiabortion stance of many in his party, social conservatives who made up a crucial bloc of the Republican vote were not convinced of his commitment to their cause while party moderates worried that Dole would allow the Christian right to force his campaign to adopt positions enabling Democrats to once again capitalize on the "extremism" charge.[193]

Even after his nomination was ensured, Dole's campaign failed for weeks to capture the public's attention. In part he appeared too much a part of the GOP agenda in Congress that Democrats had successfully defined as harshly conservative. Dole in June resigned from the Senate to campaign full time for the presidency.

At his nominating convention in San Diego, Dole performed a tough balancing act in keeping warring moderates and social conservatives from dividing the party. Dole especially sought to avoid the kind of negative publicity that had surrounded "family values night" at the 1992 GOP convention in Houston.[194] The Republicans struck an awkward compromise: although the party platform was conservative and kept the antiabortion plank, the convention that the country saw on television was moderate in tone and did not feature prime-time addresses by controversial figures such as Buchanan and television evangelist Pat Robertson.

Throughout the campaign season, Clinton often seemed to be running against the unpopular Gingrich and the Republican Congress more than he was taking on Dole. What made Clinton's campaign so strong, in part, was his governing strategy of what one key aide called "triangulation": that is, separating himself from the unpopular elements of both political parties and establishing a less partisan identity at the center of the political spectrum. To achieve that end, Clinton adopted a number of policy initiatives that were conservative, but also largely popular. He signed a welfare reform bill that liberals in his party opposed, pushed for imposition of a V-chip in televisions to allow parents to screen program content for children and for a television program rating system, proposed a balanced budget by the year 2002, and extolled his record in reducing the federal budget deficit. Clinton also stayed true to his Democratic roots by opposing congressional efforts to reduce Medicare spending and weaken environmental regulation and by proposing new government programs to make college education more affordable.

Clinton's strategy was effective. He took away from Dole's campaign a number of issues that usually help Republican presidential candidates, such as welfare reform, deficit reduction, and family values. He kept his Democratic base by positioning himself as the only viable check against the "extremism" of the Republican Congress.

Billionaire Perot, who ran again under the Reform Party banner, also benefited somewhat from the negative Clinton press. Although he had never been a serious factor in 1996 as he had been as an independent candidate in 1992—and as a result was excluded from the presidential debates—Perot's support increased by several percentage points in the late polls. But in the end, Perot had little impact on the elections. Because of a perceived strong economy and a substantial reduction in the federal debt, the public frustration with the two major parties that had given growth to Perot's candidacy in 1992 simply did not exist in 1996.

Clinton easily won reelection with 49.2 percent of the popular vote and 379 electoral votes to Dole's 40.7 percent and 159 electoral votes. Reform Party candidate Perot polled 8.4 percent of the vote, less than half of his 1992 total, and once again received no electoral votes.[195] Clinton's victory made him the first Democrat to win reelection since Franklin D. Roosevelt won his second term in 1936. He became the first Democrat to be elected to the presidency along with a Republican-controlled Congress. Clinton won every state he had captured in 1992, except for Georgia, Montana, and Colorado. However, he picked up Florida and Arizona—becoming the first Democratic presidential candidate to win Florida since 1976 and first to win Arizona since 1948. The so-called gender gap was key to Clinton's victory: while the male vote was evenly split between the two candidates, Clinton won the female vote by 16 percent, the largest margin ever. Clinton also beat Dole among every age group and was the clear choice of minorities: he received 80 percent of the black vote and 70 percent of the Hispanic vote.[196]

Yet three facts remained discouraging for Clinton. First, for the second straight election he had failed to win a majority of the popular vote. Second, voter turnout was less than 50 percent, the lowest since 1924. Third, Democrats failed to regain control of Congress, despite the unpopularity of Gingrich and many of his Republican colleagues. Given this scenario, it was difficult for the president to credibly claim that he had achieved any kind of mandate from the American people.

Perhaps most remarkable in 1996 was how little had changed despite expenditures of about $500 million by the two major parties. Political analysts referred to the 1996 elections as reaffirming the status quo, an important difference from both the 1992 and 1994 elections in which voters expressed frustration with the existing political arrangement and sought substantial changes in their government.

NEW CENTURY, OLD PARTISANSHIP

The last presidential election of the twentieth century, the closest in forty years, brought the nation to the brink of a constitutional crisis that was narrowly averted only after an unprecedented thirty-six days of rancorous arguing and litigation over who won, Democrat Al Gore or Republican

George W. Bush. The eventual outcome, with Texas governor Bush the official winner, did little to unite the electorate, which had split a hundred million votes almost evenly between the two major party candidates.

Although Gore, the departing vice president, clearly won the national popular vote in the 2000 race by more than a half-million votes, Bush claimed the 25 electoral votes of Florida, where the election had been extremely close. Ultimately the state certified Bush as the popular vote winner in Florida, raising the GOP candidate's nationwide electoral vote total to 271, one more than he needed to win. Gore unsuccessfully contested the election on grounds that the state had stopped the recounts prematurely, leaving thousands of machine-processed ballots not subjected to the scrutiny of human eyes in a hand recount.

In the end, a sharply divided U.S. Supreme Court halted the Florida count, effectively deciding the election in Bush's favor. It was the first time the Court had taken up a disputed presidential election. In a historic election studded with anomalies, "firsts," and ironies, the Court for the first time immediately released audio tapes of its hearings on the suit.

The tumult focused new attention on proposals to abolish or reform the electoral college system. It brought to light the need to modernize the problem-prone voting systems still in use in many states besides Florida. It also exposed serious flaws in the technology that broadcast media rely on to project election results minutes after the polls have closed. Repercussions of the event would be felt for many years to come.

Bush's victory marked the fourth time in U.S. history that the popular vote loser gained the presidency. The first such election, in 1824, was won by John Quincy Adams, who, like Bush (son of former president George H. W. Bush), was the son of a president, John Adams. Although Andrew Jackson won the 1824 popular vote, none of the four candidates received the required electoral vote majority and the House of Representatives decided the election in Adams's favor. All four candidates represented factions of the Democratic-Republican Party. In an 1828 rematch with Adams, Jackson won the presidency under the banner that became the modern day Democratic Party. (See "Last of the Old Order: 1824," p. 25.)

The second contested presidential election, in 1876, was more analogous to the Bush-Gore dispute in that it too involved charges of irregularities in the election process. New York Democrat Samuel J. Tilden won the national vote against Ohio Republican Rutherford B. Hayes, but controversies over the popular votes in three southern states, including Florida, led to rival sets of electoral vote results being sent to Congress from the three states. Lacking a procedure for resolving the dispute, Congress formed a bipartisan special commission, including Supreme Court justices,

that gave the votes to Hayes in return for concessions to the South. Hayes thereby won the presidency by a single electoral vote, a margin only one vote lower than Bush's. (See "Compromise: 1876," p. 42.)

In 1887 Congress enacted the Electoral Vote Count Act, specifying procedures for settling electoral vote disputes. One year later Republican Benjamin Harrison won the 1888 presidential election even though Democrat Grover Cleveland received more popular votes. The 1887 act did not come into play, however, because Harrison decisively won the electoral college vote, 233 to 168. (See "The Republican Recovery: 1888," p. 46; and Chapter 5, The Electoral College.)

Had the Supreme Court not intervened in 2000, it was conceivable that Florida might have sent competing sets of electors' votes to Congress. Although that did not happen, the rules of the 1887 act thwarted efforts by some House members to challenge Florida's electoral votes. In one of the ironies of the election, it fell to Gore as Senate president to reject his supporters' objections.

Favorites Win Nomination

From the outset, the election was Gore's to lose. It is almost axiomatic that the party in power retains the White House in times of peace and prosperity. Gore stood to inherit the advantage of running on Clinton's successes, especially an economy that had gone from record federal deficits to record surpluses, which opened the prospect of retiring the $3.7 trillion national debt while safeguarding popular but expensive social programs. Clinton could also claim legislative successes in welfare reform and the North American Free Trade Agreement (NAFTA) as well as foreign policy efforts in Bosnia, Kosovo, Northern Ireland, and the Middle East.

Despite his high job approval ratings, Clinton himself was a handicap for Gore. Republicans tried to tie Gore closely to the GOP's view of Clinton administration shortcomings, particularly Clinton's December 1998 impeachment for lying under oath about his affair with White House intern Monica Lewinsky. The Republicans' strategy was to run against "Clinton-Gore" rather than against Gore alone.

The 2000 primary season was lackluster, dominated by Gore for the Democrats and Bush for the Republicans. Both locked up their nominations early. Gore had to face a strong nomination challenge from former New Jersey senator Bill Bradley. Bradley, failing to win a single primary in the opening round, dropped out of the race in early March.

Gore's need to distance himself from Clinton's indiscretions was implicit in his choice of Joseph I. Lieberman as his running mate. An Orthodox Jew, the first of his faith to run on a major party ticket, Lieberman was known for speaking

George W. Bush and Al Gore compete for moderator Jim Lehrer's attention during the final presidential debate held October 17, 2000, in St. Louis. Although Gore was given a slight edge in most disinterested postdebate analyses of who won or lost, Bush did better than expected, and, presenting a more likable persona, improved his standing with voters over the course of the three debates.

out on moral issues and family values. Although he voted in the Senate to acquit Clinton, Lieberman had publicly taken the president to task for his dalliance with Lewinsky.

Bush entered the race in early 1999 and quickly established himself as the favorite of the Republican establishment and its campaign donors. Without a sitting Democratic president to compete against, the contest attracted a dozen hopefuls for the GOP nomination, but even before the kickoff Iowa caucuses in January 2000 half of the field dropped out.

By early February, Bush, publisher Malcolm S. "Steve" Forbes Jr., and Sen. John McCain of Arizona remained the only serious contenders. Forbes, who finished third in New Hampshire, ended his campaign after a less impressive showing in Delaware. McCain was perceived as a moderate despite a solid conservative voting record in the Senate. This, and his penchant for bluntness, appealed to many non-Republicans, who could vote in the growing number of open or semi-open GOP primaries. McCain upset Bush in the New Hampshire and Michigan primaries, but Bush went on to win a cluster of March 7 primaries. In all, McCain defeated Bush in seven of the eighteen primaries he entered, but Bush won enough convention delegates to clinch the nomination in March. Bush chose Richard B. Cheney, the former representative from Wyoming and defense secretary under Bush's father, for his running mate.

The Green Party candidate, consumer advocate Ralph Nader, threatened to take votes from Democrats. He received almost 1 percent of the presidential vote in 1996 and was aiming for 5 percent in 2000.

With polls continuing to show the electorate almost evenly divided, the major party race settled down to basically a personality contest between two Ivy Leaguers—Gore (Harvard) and Bush (Yale). The public perceived Bush as personable but perhaps not so intelligent as Gore, despite Bush's master's degree from Harvard's business school.

Gore's primary asset was his experience, sixteen years in Congress and eight years in the vice presidency, against Bush's six years as Texas governor. But being vice president was no guarantee of success. Only four sitting vice presidents, including Bush's father in 1988, had been elected president.

With the cold war over and much of the electorate economically better off than they were eight years earlier, traditionally Democratic pocketbook and social issues dominated the campaign—Social Security, education, health care, abortion rights, and gun control. The huge federal surpluses fueled the money issues, with Bush pushing for tax cuts and heavier outlays for antimissile research and development.

Some Gore supporters thought the vice president distanced himself too much from Clinton, thereby sacrificing the opportunity to share credit for the booming economy and other positive aspects of the Clinton legacy. Clinton himself was said to feel "underused" by the Gore campaign. By the final weeks of the campaign Gore became less reluctant to run on Clinton's record, but it was too late to make much of an impression on undecided voters.

Cliff-Hanger Election: 2000

The election had been expected to be close. Bush and Gore ran neck-and-neck in public opinion polls, right up to election day. Problems with the crucial Florida vote erupted almost immediately on election day November 7, 2000. Voters in Palm Beach County reported difficulties with an unusual "butterfly" punch-card ballot. Some Democratic voters there thought that they had inadvertently voted for Reform Party nominee Pat Buchanan instead of for Gore. In some of the other twenty-four counties using outmoded punch-card systems, but with regular ballot forms, voters said they were unable to punch out the hole for the candidate of their choice.

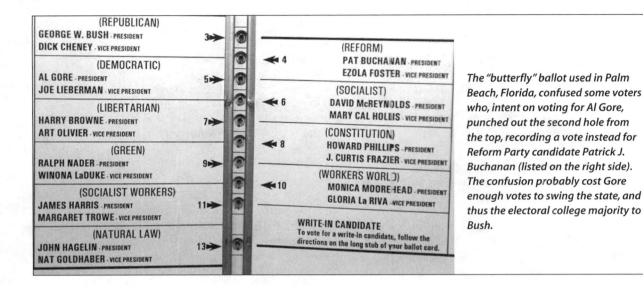

The "butterfly" ballot used in Palm Beach, Florida, confused some voters who, intent on voting for Al Gore, punched out the second hole from the top, recording a vote instead for Reform Party candidate Patrick J. Buchanan (listed on the right side). The confusion probably cost Gore enough votes to swing the state, and thus the electoral college majority to Bush.

Within hours, as news of the problems spread, people around the world became familiar with the obscure noun *chad,* singular or plural, meaning the tiny piece of paper that is pushed out in a punch-card system. If the chad is only dented (dimpled) or partially dislodged, the voting machine may not register the punch as a vote. Therein lay the basis for much of the contention in the days and weeks that were to follow.

Besides leading nationwide in the popular vote, Gore outside of Florida led in the electoral college vote, 267 to 246 (after the counting of the absentee vote in Oregon and New Mexico concluded several days later). The entire 2000 presidential election therefore hung on the final results of the popular vote in Florida, which would determine the winner of the state's twenty-five electoral votes.

The close election triggered an automatic machine recount, showing Bush ahead by about 300 votes in Florida. But the Gore camp focused on the thousands of votes that the machines rejected as under-voted, showing no vote for president, or over-voted, showing more than one vote for presidential candidates. Only a manual count of those ballots could discern votes that the machines could not detect, Gore lawyers argued."

In what may have been a tactical mistake, Gore did not request an immediate statewide revote or recount. Instead his lawyers fought to keep hand counts going where Gore was picking up votes, in mostly Democratic counties such as Broward, Miami-Dade, and Volusia, and in Palm Beach County where the butterfly-ballot had recorded an unlikely 3,407 votes for Pat Buchanan, three times more than he received elsewhere in the state. Buchanan himself said it appeared he received votes meant for Gore. Just as fiercely, the Bush forces fought to stop the hand counts. They argued that the votes had been legally counted and recounted, including military and other absentee ballots

that favored Bush, and that the canvassers had no uniform standards for gauging the difference between a vote and a nonvote on a punch-card ballot. Allowing more time for recounts, they said, would be changing the rules after the game started.

During the weeks of contentious legal maneuvering over the Florida vote, partisan tempers flared throughout the United States. Large groups of demonstrators in Florida and Washington, D.C., shouted at the television cameras and waved signs supporting Bush and his vice-presidential choice, Cheney, or Gore and his running mate, Lieberman.

But it was a race against the calendar, and Katherine Harris was the timekeeper. Harris, Florida's secretary of state and former cochair of Bush's campaign in the state, announced November 13 that counties had until the following day, the date set in state law, to submit their returns, without any manual recount figures. Lawsuits stayed Harris's hand, however, and the manual counts proceeded by fits and starts until Sunday, November 26, under an extension granted by the seven-member Florida supreme court, made up mostly of Democratic appointees. That evening Harris ceremoniously "certified" Bush as the Florida winner by 537 votes out of six million cast.

The battle was by no means over, however. Gore formally contested the election and Bush meanwhile protested the deadline extension to the U.S. Supreme Court, which heard the arguments December 1. In Tallahassee, after hearing two days of televised testimony, Leon County Circuit Judge N. Sanders Sauls ruled that Gore failed to prove the need for manual recounts. Gore's witnesses had testified that "chad buildup" and poorly maintained equipment could prevent voters from cleanly punching out a machine-read ballot. Gore received another setback the same day, December 4, when the U.S. Supreme Court returned the deadline-extension case to the Florida high court for clarification.

COUNTDOWN IN FLORIDA

The following is a day-by-day chronology of the events surrounding the disputed presidential election results from Florida in the 2000 race between Republican George W. Bush and Democrat Al Gore.

November 7, 2000. Election in Florida too close to call, with Bush holding narrow lead. TV networks retract premature reports declaring Gore winner of state's twenty-five electoral votes.

November 8–10. Gore calls Bush to concede early November 8 then calls back to withdraw concession. Gore seeks hand recounts in four largely Democratic counties. Bush has unofficial 1,784-vote lead November 9. After all but one of Florida's sixty-seven counties complete machine recount required by state law, Bush lead falls to 327 votes.

November 11–14. Broward, Miami-Dade, Palm Beach, and Volusia counties undertake manual recounts requested by Gore; federal court on November 13 rejects Bush bid to block hand counts; Volusia finishes recount November 14.

November 13. Florida secretary of state Katherine Harris says she will enforce state law deadline of November 14 for counties to submit returns and will not include manual recounts; election boards in Volusia and Palm Beach counties ask state court judge to overturn deadline.

November 14–16. Leon County Circuit Judge Terry P. Lewis says Harris must justify her position on deadline; Harris reaffirms decision November 15; Lewis hears new round of arguments November 16.

November 17. Lewis upholds Harris's decision to disregard manual recounts, but Florida supreme court bars certification of state results pending oral arguments on November 20; federal appeals court rejects Bush suit over manual recounts.

November 18. Bush lead grows to 930 votes with absentee ballots; Bush campaign criticizes Democrats for challenging absentee votes from military.

November 21. Florida supreme court rules manual recounts must be included in presidential race if submitted to Harris by 5:00 p.m., Sunday, November 26.

November 22–24. Bush running mate Richard B. Cheney has heart attack, leaves Washington hospital two days later after surgery to insert stent in artery. Shouting, fist-waving crowd, including Republican congressional aides, tries to enter private room where recounts resume in Miami-Dade. County stops recount, pleading too little time and denying intimidation by the demonstrators. State supreme court on November 23 rejects Gore suit to force Miami-Dade to resume counting. U.S. Supreme Court agrees to hear Bush appeal of Florida supreme court action allowing extended deadline for certifying presidential race.

November 25–26. Manual recounts: Broward finishes November 25; Palm Beach falls just short of completion November 26. Harris announces November 26 that state elections canvassing board certifies Bush as winner by 537-vote margin; Bush claims victory, says he and Cheney are "honored and humbled" to have won Florida's electoral votes.

November 27–29. Gore formally contests the Florida election on November 27. He sues in Leon County Circuit Court, in Tallahassee, claiming the number of legal votes "improperly rejected" and illegal votes counted in Nassau, Palm Beach, and Miami-Dade counties is enough to change outcome. Judge N. Sanders Sauls orders ballots brought to Tallahassee for possible counting. More than one million ballots are trucked with police escort to the state capital.

December 1. U.S. Supreme Court hears Bush appeal of deadline extension. Florida justices refuse to order revote requested in Palm Beach County because of controversial "butterfly ballot" used there.

December 2–3. Judge Sauls hears testimony on whether 13,000 ballots from Miami-Dade and Palm Beach counties should be manually counted. Both sides call witnesses on reliability of punch-card voting systems.

December 4. Sauls rejects Gore's request for manual recount and refuses to decertify Bush as winner. U.S. Supreme Court asks state high court to explain its November 21 action allowing manual recounting and extending deadlines.

December 8–9. Florida justices order hand count of ballots on which machines found no vote for president. U.S. Supreme Court unexpectedly halts the hand counts the next day.

December 10–11. U.S. Supreme Court receives briefs and hears arguments in *Bush v. Gore.*

December 12. U.S. Supreme Court splits 5–4 in ruling for Bush against further hand counts. Florida legislature convenes special session to meet the federal deadline for designating presidential electors. Twenty states miss the deadline by a few days.

December 13. Gore concedes election, congratulates Bush and jokingly adds "and I promised him that this time I wouldn't call him back."

December 18. Presidential electors meet in state capitals to cast votes.

January 6, 2001. Congress meets in joint session to count electoral votes. As Senate president, Vice President Gore presides over his own defeat. Twenty Gore supporters, mostly Congressional Black Caucus members, try to block Florida's votes but Gore rejects each representative's objection because none has also been signed by a senator as the 1887 Electoral Vote Count Act requires. One District of Columbia elector, Barbara Lett-Simmons, withholds her vote from Gore in protest of the District's lack of representation in Congress. Final electoral vote tally is 271 for Bush, 266 for Gore with one abstention.

January 20. Inauguration of Bush as president and Cheney as vice president. Largely nonviolent protests mar--but do not disrupt--the inaugural parade.

Gore scored a short-lived victory December 8 when the Florida court by a 4–3 vote ordered a resumption of the hand counts, only to have the U.S. Supreme Court quickly halt them the following day, pending its decision in *Bush v. Gore*. In its 5–4 decision, handed down December 12, the Court majority ruled for Bush that the lack of uniform standards for manual recounts denied "equal protection of the laws" to Florida voters. The Court split along ideological lines in the unsigned decision. In the majority were conservatives William Rehnquist, Antonin Scalia, Clarence Thomas, Anthony Kennedy, and Sandra Day O'Connor. Dissenting were liberals or moderates Stephen Breyer, Ruth Bader Ginsburg, David Souter, and John Paul Stevens.

The Court action left 42,000 Florida under-votes unexamined, including 35,000 from the punch-card counties, but it effectively resolved the 2000 presidential race and possibly averted a constitutional crisis that might have arisen had the dispute resulted in Florida's sending two sets of electoral votes to Congress. The state legislature had already designated a slate of electors committed to Bush. Faced with a hopeless situation, Gore folded his campaign and conceded December 13.

When the presidential electors met in their states December 18 to cast their ballots, one District of Columbia elector, Barbara Lett-Simmons, withheld her vote from Gore in protest of the District's lack of representation in Congress. This reduced Gore's electoral vote total to 266 against 271 for Bush. Gore received 51.0 million votes (48.4 percent) to 50.5 million (47.9 percent) for Bush. Gore's lead in the popular vote was 539,947. Nader's 2.8 million votes amounted to 2.7 percent of the total. Buchanan received less than 1 percent with 447,798 votes.

An embarrassing loss to Gore was his home state of Tennessee and its eleven electoral votes. Had he won there he would have had an electoral vote majority and the Florida vote would have been irrelevant. Likewise, had Gore received a fraction of the Nader vote in several close states, including Florida, he would have been over the top in electoral votes. Political analyst Rhodes Cook, however, pointed out while Nader may have siphoned off Gore voters in Florida and elsewhere, Reform Party candidate Pat Buchanan, whose supporters traditionally lean Republican, may have prevented Bush from winning a few states that went closely for Gore. "[T]here were 30 additional electoral votes that Bush may have won if Buchanan had not been in the race, compared to 29 more electoral votes that may have gone to Gore if Nader had not run. In short, the effect of the two third-party candidates on the electoral vote was essentially a wash.[197]

Nationwide, African Americans voted nine to one for Gore. On January 6, 2001, twenty House members, mostly members of the Congressional Black Caucus, tried to disqualify Florida's electoral votes as Congress met in joint session to count the electoral votes. As Senate president by virtue of his being U.S. vice president, Gore one by one ruled the objections out of order because they had not been signed by a senator as required by law. None of the 100 members of the new Senate, evenly divided between Republicans and Democrats, including presidential spouse Hillary Rodham Clinton of New York, had signed a challenge to the Florida votes. Gore in his concession had asked his supporters to accept the Court verdict and the "finality of the outcome."

The lingering bitterness put a damper on the inauguration of Bush as the forty-third U.S. president on January 20, 2001. On the cold, rainy Saturday, thousands of protesters, under tight security, lined the Pennsylvania Avenue parade route to the White House. They were noisy and visible, but there were relatively few arrests and clashes with the police. Long and bitter as it was, the thirty-six-day 2000 election "night" was shorter and perhaps less vitriolic than its 1876 counterpart, which extended from November 7 to two days before inauguration, then in March. Because March 4, 1877, fell on a Sunday, President Hayes was sworn in privately at the White House and the public ceremonies took place quietly on Monday.

Similarly, the nation witnessed another peaceful transfer of power with the Bush-Cheney inauguration. As historian David McCullough phrased it, the peacefulness was typical of past inaugurations but perhaps for a different reason. "As close as it was, this election was not about visceral issues like slavery or war—things people are really passionate about," McCullough said. "The nation is closely divided, certainly, but we seem to be divided over which party controls the middle of the political spectrum. I'm not sure it's happened quite like that before."[198]

Effect of 2001 Terrorist Attacks

Entering the White House in January 2001, Bush moved rapidly on his priorities and managed to push through a $1.35 billion tax cut—a key campaign pledge; additional tax cuts followed in subsequent years. Despite his pledge to be "a uniter, not a divider," education reform was the only major bipartisan legislation the president passed in 2001. The new administration faced a sharply divided Congress. Although Democrats had made some gains, Republicans retained a narrow majority in the House. The 2000 elections had caused a 50–50 split in the Senate as the Democrats had picked up five seats. Because Cheney, as vice president, could cast tie-breaking votes, the chamber was still under effective Republican control. But in May, after Republican James Jeffords of Vermont opted to leave his party and become an Independent who caucused with the Democrats, the Democrats took control of the Senate.

Vice President Cheney played a key role in the Bush White House. Cheney added gravitas and a seasoned foreign policy background to the inner circle of a president regarded by many as lacking in international experience. Cheney had a history of heart trouble, and in June 2001, after tests that showed occasional irregular heartbeats, he had a pacemaker implanted.

The events of September 11, 2001, altered the course of Bush's first term in office. A presidency that had seemed more focused on domestic issues suddenly was faced with the worst terrorist attack on U.S. soil in the country's history. That morning, terrorists hijacked four U.S. planes, crashing two of them into the Twin Towers of the World Trade Center, a Manhattan landmark, and one of them into the Pentagon, just outside Washington, D.C., in Virginia. The fourth plane crashed in a Pennsylvania field. Everyone aboard the planes was killed; several thousand more died on the ground; the towers collapsed.

The unprecedented, massive attacks on U.S. soil shifted the Bush administration's focus to a "war on terrorism." The president, whose popularity ratings had been dropping before the attacks, saw it rocket upward to a historic 90 percent as the country rallied behind him. His visit to Ground Zero in New York several days after the attacks, where he spoke with rescue workers, was seen as a high point of his first year in office.

One impact of September 11 was a heightened sense of security affecting the entire country and the way the government functioned. For example, although Cheney remained an important part of the president's circle of advisers, for security reasons, he often traveled to what was called an "undisclosed location." Public tours of the White House were suspended temporarily and a part of E Street, close to the building, was shut down.

Another change involved the shape of the federal government bureaucracy. Bush called for a White House Office of Homeland Security, to be headed by former Pennsylvania governor Thomas Ridge. While Bush originally opposed the idea of a new federal Department of Homeland Security, he changed his mind and joined Democratic-led calls for its creation. Bush signed a bill in late 2002 creating the department, which officially came into existence on March 1, 2003. The reorganization was the largest in the federal government since the late 1940s and involved the merging of a variety of agencies, including the Secret Service, the Coast Guard, and the Immigration and Naturalization Service.

A third outgrowth of the terrorist attacks was the actual "war on terror" itself. The United States that had basked in a post–cold war hiatus in which international concerns took a back seat found itself in the midst of a full-fledged war. A strongly supportive Congress approved a $40 billion emergency appropriation, as well as a resolution that authorized using force against terrorist groups and countries that backed them. U.S. forces attacked Afghanistan, toppling the Taliban government that had supported September 11 mastermind Osama bin Laden and his al Qaeda terrorist network, and began to prepare for a possible invasion of Iraq.

In 2002 and into 2003, the Bush administration pushed for military action against the Iraqi regime of Saddam Hussein. Bush's father had fought a war against Iraq more than a decade earlier, but Saddam remained in power. The George W. Bush administration sought to link Saddam to Osama bin Laden and al Qaeda. In addition, the White House focused on what it called Saddam's "weapons of mass destruction." In fall 2002 Congress approved military action against Iraq. The U.N. Security Council unanimously backed a resolution seeking stringent weapons inspections in Iraq by the international body and granting Saddam a final chance to disarm. In February 2003 Secretary of State Colin Powell delivered a forceful slide presentation to the United Nations, laying out the administration's case for war.

The war began on March 19, 2003, with a "coalition of the willing," in Bush's words, with the most prominent member—Britain—joining the United States in its attack on Iraq. However, many other countries that had joined Bush's father in the first Gulf War, including France, opted out of this one. Saddam's regime fell within several weeks, and on May 1 Bush triumphantly spoke on the U.S.S. *Abraham Lincoln,* in front of a banner reading "Mission Accomplished," to declare the end of large-scale combat operations in Iraq.

The terrorist attacks also affected the U.S. economy, which already had been faltering. The budget surplus in effect when Bush came into office, $86 billion in fiscal year 2000, turned into a deficit. By fiscal year 2004, the deficit had reached $412 billion.[199]

In addition to his foreign policy concerns, the president devoted much of 2002 to campaigning for Republican candidates around the country. Generally, midterm elections had resulted in losses for the president's party, the only twentieth-century exceptions being in 1934 and 1998. Also incumbent presidents usually do not throw themselves into off-year elections. But Bush's hard work paid off, and the Republicans picked up seats in both the House and Senate, maintaining control of the House and—even more important—winning back control of the Senate. Still, the Republican margin in both chambers was narrow, and Congress continued to be bitterly divided during the next two years.

No sooner were the 2002 midterm elections over than attention shifted to the 2004 presidential contest, in which Bush was seeking election to a second term. Unlike his father, who in his 1992 reelection bid had seen a tough primary challenge from conservative challengers, Bush faced no primary opposition. During Bush's 2004 reelection campaign, issues of terrorism and the new term "homeland security" were at the forefront. Bush successfully used his incumbency to portray an image of strength in the face of the terrorist enemy, despite a lackluster economy and the growing unpopularity of his venture into Iraq.

Bush's Reelection: 2004

For much of 2001 and 2002, many political observers had assumed that Gore would run for president again in 2004 in a rematch with Bush. But in December 2002, Gore declared that he would not run for president, leaving the Democratic without a leading candidate.

A large groups of contenders immediately jumped in, including Sen. Lieberman of Connecticut, Gore's vice-presidential running mate in 2000; John F. Kerry, a long-serving senator from Massachusetts who had made his name in the early 1970s as a decorated Vietnam veteran who turned against the war; and Sen. John Edwards, the charismatic first-term senator from North Carolina who had been a successful trial lawyer. A number of others joined also including former Vermont governor Howard Dean.

The sputtering economy at home and, in particular, the war in Iraq became the major issues in the primary campaign. Lieberman was a hawk on Iraq. Kerry had voted for the congressional authorization for the use of force against Iraq, but he later voted against an $87 billion supplemental authorization, which laid the foundation for Bush's later criticism of the senator as a "flip-flopper." Although Bush had declared an end to major combat activities in Iraq, violence continued there, and U.S. military forces were to extend their tours amid increasing casualties. Dean and others forged strong antiwar positions, and as 2003 wound on, Dean's antiwar stance—in addition to his innovative use of the Internet to raise money—propelled him to the front of the pack. The 2004 election marked the first time the Internet became a primary source of fund-raising for political campaigns.

Dean had been the front-runner at the end of 2003, but the momentum shifted as the 2004 caucuses and primaries began. Kerry and Edward gained strength while the others faded and one by one dropped out. With more primary wins, Kerry locked up the nomination and selected Edwards, who had performed well in the primaries and attracted a popular following, as his running mate.

The Kerry campaign, as did the Bush campaign, decided against taking federal matching funds during the primaries. Kerry raised $234.6 million during that period. After their conventions, each candidate was given $74.6 million in public financing for the general election.

The Democrats held their convention in late July, in Kerry's home town of Boston—the first time the city had hosted a convention. Kerry focused on his Vietnam-era service, rather than his Senate record. The convention was later remembered for another event: the keynote address delivered by future president Barack Obama of Illinois, who was running at that time for the U.S. Senate. His speech was a spectacular success, overshadowing even the primary figures present. Obama went on to win his Senate race that year to become the third African American senator since Reconstruction.

Kerry emerged from his convention without much of a "bounce," or rise in the polls; the race was still close. In August, a group called Swift Boat Veterans for Truth began airing anti-Kerry ads attacking the candidate's service in Vietnam. Kerry was slow to respond to the ads; the Bush campaign, meanwhile, while saying it had nothing to do with the ads, was equally slow to condemn them. In addition, the Bush campaign was having success with its portrayal of Kerry as a "flip-flopper" who switched positions at will on the Iraq war and would not provide a steady hand in the White House at a time of national crisis.

Bush kept Cheney on the ticket for the 2004 campaign, although some observers speculated the president might select a more popular figure. Cheney had been out of the public eye for much of the time since the September 11 attacks. In addition, his former company, Halliburton, was involved in controversy, including an investigation by the Securities and Exchange Commission (SEC). Halliburton eventually agreed to pay a penalty of $7.5 million in a settlement with the SEC. Cheney's history of heart trouble also was a factor. But Bush relied on Cheney, and the vice president was an enthusiastic campaigner on the trail, focusing much of his attention on what he described as Kerry's weakness regarding the terrorist threat.

The president opted to forego federal matching funds during the primary phase of the campaign, which allowed him to raise as much money as he could. In total, he raised $269.6 million during the primaries. The Republicans held their convention from August 30 to September 2, later than usual, in New York City, the site of the September 11, 2001, attack. At the convention, the focus was on the president's success in fighting global terrorism. Bush emerged from the convention with an average bounce of six percentage points.

The three major networks chose not to broadcast much of either convention in 2004, accelerating a decline in network coverage of conventions. But various cable-news outlets, such as CNN, C-SPAN, MSNBC, and Fox News Channel, covered the events, as did public broadcasting.

Kerry's service in Vietnam continued to be an issue, as press reports focused on additional Swift Boat ads. But Bush's Vietnam era career also was examined as news organizations looked into his National Guard service and tried to pin down whether the future president had performed his duty adequately or had received preferential treatment. No definitive report ever emerged.

In the wake of the Republican convention, Bush held his lead in many polls, leading analysts to predict an easier-than-expected win for the president. The Democratic challenger seemed unable to capitalize on either the worsening situation in Iraq or the less-than-robust economy. In Iraq, insurgents continued to mount a terror campaign, and the weapons of mass destruction—a key rationale for the Bush administration's invasion of

Iraq—had not been found. In addition, the U.S. military was suffering the fallout from a scandal uncovered that spring involving U.S. soldiers abusing Iraqi prisoners at Iraq's Abu Ghraib prison.

In the first of three presidential debates, Kerry came through as poised and intelligent, improving his image. Bush, meanwhile, seemed to grimace and scowl as his opponent spoke, and the president often appeared less focused in his answers than did the Democrat. Kerry received a postdebate "bounce" that turned the contest back into a horse race. The other debates were more even.

In the days leading up to November 2, 2004, polls showed a tight race between Bush and Kerry with the election probably dependent on a handful of competitive states including New Hampshire, Ohio, Michigan, Wisconsin, Minnesota, Iowa, New Mexico, Nevada, and Florida. When voters went to the polls in November, the tally was close, as most of the states lined up as they had in 2000. Bush carried Florida, the state that had proved so troublesome four years earlier. Ohio—a Bush state in 2000—was harder to predict, although Bush appeared to be holding a narrow lead, and most of the networks declined to call a winner overnight. The next day, November 3, Kerry, convinced that Bush's margin of more than 100,000 votes in Ohio could not be overcome, conceded the election to Bush. Republicans also welcomed the news that they had, for the second election in a row, picked up seats in the House and Senate, solidifying their control on Washington.

Bush won 51 percent of the vote to Kerry's 48 percent and an electoral college majority of 286–252. (One elector from Minnesota ended up voting for Edwards, so the final total was 286–251.) The election of 2004 involved more fund-raising and spending than any other presidential contest in U.S. history. According to the Federal Election Commission, private and public spending during 2004 on presidential candidates and national conventions totaled a little more than $1 billion, "56 percent more than comparable activity during the 2000 campaign."[200]

Bush was sworn in for his second term on January 20, 2005, by Supreme Court Chief Justice William Rehnquist, then ill with cancer. Because it was the first presidential inauguration since September 11, 2001, the central area of Washington, D.C., was locked down under unprecedented security. Access to the parade route along Pennsylvania Avenue was limited; the blocks close to the route were cordoned off with high metal barriers. Two thousand out-of-town police officers united with about 4,000 local officers in the effort.[201] In his inaugural address, Bush called for an expansion of freedom across the world. As befitted a president known for his early-to-bed routines, Bush attended the inaugural balls that night but still managed to get home to the White House by 10:00 p.m., an hour and 22 minutes ahead of schedule.[202]

Democrats Take Back Congress: 2006

Although President Bush won a close but clear reelection victory and was still working with a Republican-controlled Congress, his second term would prove difficult. In the first year of that term, Bush faced problems on the domestic as well as the international front, causing his popularity to slide.

One defining moment for the Bush administration in 2005 was its response to Hurricane Katrina, a monster storm that hit the U.S. Gulf Coast in late August, causing major damage along the seaboard and devastating the low-lying city of New Orleans. The flooding caused more than a thousand deaths and led to thousands of displaced residents leaving the city. The administration, particularly the Federal Emergency Management Agency (FEMA), was widely criticized for responding too slowly and too clumsily to the disaster.

Bush also had little success with a top domestic priority that year: changes to the Social Security system to encourage investment in private accounts. Democrats were successful in labeling the plan risky, and Bush never gained momentum with the public or even the GOP Congress. Another event that backfired on Republicans was the case of Terri Schiavo, a Florida woman who had been in a coma for many years. Her husband sought to remove the feeding tube that was keeping her alive, while her parents wanted her to remain on it. Top Republican officials backed keeping Schiavo alive, pushing through legislation that Bush signed, but eventually court decisions led to the tube's being removed, and Schiavo died on March 31, 2005.

Meanwhile, Bush's top political advisor, Karl Rove, and Vice President Cheney's top aide, Lewis "Scooter" Libby, were implicated in an ongoing investigation relating to the leaking of the identity of CIA agent Valerie Plame to the media during Bush's first term, causing more political headaches for the White House. Libby was later convicted in 2007 for his role in the matter.

In addition, the Iraq war was going poorly. The country was increasingly unsafe, with roadside bombs targeting U.S. troops and American casualties rising. Although Iraq had held elections in January, by the end of 2005 the situation had deteriorated, with violence on the upswing; growing numbers of Americans thought the invasion of Iraq had been a mistake. The fallout from the Abu Ghraib torture scandal continued.

Bush was successful, however, in putting a more rightward-leaning stamp on the Supreme Court, by appointing two relatively young conservative justices. John G. Roberts Jr. was fifty when he took his seat as chief justice in September 2005, and Samuel Alito was fifty-five when he became a associate justice in January 2006. While Roberts replaced a conservative chief justice, William Rehnquist, Alito replaced a moderate, Sandra Day O'Connor, who had been a swing vote in many key decisions.

Overall Bush was not the positive factor for Republicans in Congress that he had been four years earlier when he helped his party win additional seats in a midterm election. In addition Republicans in Congress had to deal with numerous unfolding ethical scandals. In the largest congressional bribery scheme to date, Rep. Randy "Duke" Cunningham of California in November 2005 resigned after pleading guilty to taking more than $2.4 million in bribes from defense contractors. A bigger scandal had erupted a few months earlier in August 2005 when Republican lobbyist Jack Abramoff, who had ties to many GOP politicians, was indicted for wire fraud. In 2006 House Majority Leader Tom DeLay of Texas and Rep. Bob Ney of Ohio, who were connected to Abramoff, were among those who had resigned their seats under ethical clouds. Ney eventually was sentenced to prison. Finally, two months before the election, Republican Mark Foley of Florida resigned his House seat after it became known that he sent inappropriate e-mails to congressional pages.

As the election neared, political observers expected gains for Democrats, but few predicted the Democratic sweep that gave the party control of both the House and Senate. The Democrats emerged with a substantial margin in the House, 233–202, but with just a one vote majority in the Senate. The 51–49 majority included two independents. In the House, Nancy Pelosi of California was elected Speaker, the first woman to hold that office.

With Democrats controlling the committee chairmanships, Bush faced a tough final two years in office, with little chance that his priorities would get much attention. Indeed, as the 110th Congress began that January, attention already had shifted to the 2008 presidential race and the battle to succeed the increasingly unpopular president.

Obama Leads Democrats: 2008

Both the Republican and Democratic parties, leading up to the 2008 presidential race with no incumbent, featured large candidate fields, with a range of personalities and political backgrounds. On the GOP side, there was no obvious front-runner, in contrast to Bush's dominance of the field in 2000. The candidates included longtime Arizona senator John McCain, a Vietnam War veteran and former prisoner of war who had mounted a spirited, independent-minded effort in 2000; former Massachusetts governor Mitt Romney, a wealthy entrepreneur and businessman who headed the 2002 Olympic Games in Salt Lake City; former Arkansas governor Mike Huckabee, who also was a Baptist minister; and former New York mayor Rudolph "Rudy" Giuliani, who had become a household name in the aftermath of the September 11, 2001, attacks on his city.

Huckabee unexpectedly won the Iowa caucuses, the nation's first. The important New Hampshire primary followed with McCain winning, beating Romney who had been governor of neighboring Massachusetts. Romney won

President-elect Barack Obama meets with President George W. Bush in November 2008, discussing the economic crisis and other pressing issues during the transition period.

Michigan, his boyhood state where his father was once governor, and the Nevada primary. But McCain gained strength thereafter, essentially locking up the nomination with big wins in the major wave of primaries in February and March.

The Democratic side was large also, but with a single front-runner: Sen. Hillary Rodham Clinton of New York. Clinton already had made history by becoming the first first lady to win a Senate seat, in 2000, as her husband's second term as president was ending. She won reelection in 2006. Many women were thrilled at the prospect of a female candidate leading the Democratic pack for the White House.

But despite Clinton's prominence, a host of other candidates jumped into the race, including Sen. Obama of Illinois. A young African American first-term senator, Obama also had been spoken of as a possible presence on a national ticket since his leap to prominence at the 2004 Democratic National Convention, where he gave a dramatic and widely praised keynote address. Obama won his Illinois Senate seat that year, and in January 2007 announced that he was forming a presidential exploratory committee. Like Clinton, Obama generated much excitement. His youth—he was born in 1961—and his unusual family background—his mother a white Kansan, his father a black Kenyan, and Obama's childhood in Hawaii and Indonesia—made for a captivating campaign story. Obama initially did not have widespread backing in the African American community because many black Americans had been fond of President Clinton and had transferred that favorable opinion to his wife. But Obama, whose campaign skillfully employed the Internet to win support, quickly gained traction among young people.

Former North Carolina senator John Edwards, John Kerry's running mate in 2004, was an early favorite. Other candidates included New Mexico governor Bill Richardson, Delaware senator Joseph R. Biden, Connecticut senator Chris Dodd, Ohio representative Dennis Kucinich, and former Alaska senator Mike Gravel. Most competed aggressively in the early period but quickly faded as the campaign became a race between Clinton and Obama.

The Obama campaign worked hard on grassroots efforts, and the underdog candidate's team continued to be known for its technological savvy and its appeal to youthful voters. A well-organized group, the Obama campaign made a strong pitch in Iowa, a predominately white state with a tiny black population. On January 3, Obama won the Iowa caucuses, with Edwards just edging Clinton for second place; the Illinois senator demonstrated that a black candidate could triumph in an overwhelmingly white area.

In New Hampshire Clinton won a narrow victory with Obama second. The battle between the two was fully joined. Clinton was running as the candidate of experience, while Obama focused on a theme of change. A crucial issue was the Iraq war. Clinton voted for it in 2003 while Obama had

opposed it from its earliest days when he was still a state senator, giving him additional credibility among the party's antiwar activists. Clinton contrasted her years of experience with Obama's relative lack of time on the national and world political stage. Clinton, who still retained the backing of many female supporters, sought to win working-class voters and those with fewer years of formal education. She racked up solid victories in states such as Pennsylvania and Ohio, with large white working-class populations. Although large numbers of African Americans initially backed Clinton, many gradually shifted to Obama's camp.

Obama, unlike Clinton, waged a national campaign, focusing on smaller caucus and primary contests as well as the large battleground states. With this strategy he continued to pile up delegates throughout February and March, essentially collecting so many that Clinton had an almost impossible task of overtaking him. Nevertheless, the remarkable contest continued until the last primaries in June before being conclusively settled in Obama's favor.

The Democrats held their convention from August 25–28 in Denver, the second time that city had hosted a Democratic convention. Both former President Clinton and his wife gave Obama strong endorsements. Hillary Clinton even made the magnanimous gesture of halting the roll call of states in the middle to call for Obama's nomination by acclamation, which the delegates did. Most of the proceedings took place at an indoor convention hall, but Obama delivered his acceptance speech on the last night at Denver's football stadium, to accommodate a larger crowd of approximately 80,000.

Obama's moment was quickly eclipsed when, the day after his speech, McCain announced his choice of running mate: Alaska governor Sarah Palin. Reporters scrambled to learn more about the little-known Palin, who had served as governor for less than two years and previously was mayor of the small town of Wasilla, Alaska. Palin, a conservative, quickly became a controversial figure. A charismatic politician who referred to herself as a "hockey mom" and used folksy expressions such as "you betcha," Palin drew strong support from the GOP's conservative base, one of McCain's objectives in picking her over more conventional choices. Her selection marked another historic first in an election season filled with them: she was the first woman on a national Republican ticket. Democrats in 1984 had nominated Geraldine Ferraro as their vice-presidential candidate.

The four-day Republican convention opened the following Monday, August 31, in St. Paul, Minnesota. But the first day's events were curtailed as a major hurricane headed toward the U.S. Gulf Coast. Republicans did not want to remind voters about the controversial government response to Katrina in 2005. The convention resumed full-scale activities on Tuesday. The most-awaited event was Palin's

Wednesday night speech, viewed as a success for the Alaska governor and the McCain ticket overall. McCain's speech on the convention's closing day, Thursday, came as something of an anticlimax.

Palin's selection gave a lift to the GOP ticket in national polls. The McCain campaign also saw an upsurge in contributions, many apparently from members of the conservative Republican base. However, the presence of a woman on the GOP ticket did not seem to shift many disappointed Clinton supporters to the GOP ticket. Additionally, while Palin energized members of the Republican Party, her missteps and panned media interviews seemed to have a negative effect on the rest of the populace.

In mid-September, the country's economy, which had been sputtering, began a major meltdown, turning into the most serious financial crisis since the Great Depression of the 1930s. The stock market plummeted, and a series of major financial institutions either went bankrupt or were bailed out by the federal government. The economy soon replaced the Iraq war as the leading issue in the campaign. Against that backdrop, Obama began to make gains in the polls, as dispirited voters sought a change from the Republican-controlled White House.

The presidential and vice-presidential candidates participated in a series of widely anticipated televised debates, as had become the custom. While the debates rarely present an opportunity for a knockout blow, Obama had the most to lose if he came off looking unpresidential alongside the older, more experienced McCain. Obama, with his calm demeanor, confidence, and grasp of the facts, proved up to the task and a majority of viewers felt he won the debates, if only slightly. The vice-presidential debate also garnered a lot of attention, but in that meeting observers gave the more experienced Biden the nod over the well-rehearsed, folksy Palin. Yet no debate moved either campaign significantly forward or backward.

As the fall campaign season progressed, the economy deteriorated still further. The Bush administration and Congress put together a $700 billion rescue package designed to help financial institutions considered "too big to fail." The declining economic situation continued to benefit the Obama campaign, which maintained slight leads in national polls as well as in many of the battleground states. McCain's postconvention, post-Palin-selection bounce had dissipated, and the Republican campaign turned more negative as the weeks went on.

The McCain campaign's frustration also stemmed from its relative lack of campaign funds. McCain had opted to take federal campaign matching funds for the general election, meaning that he received $84.1 million for the general election phase of the campaign, but he could not raise additional funds. Obama, meanwhile, opted out of the federal matching system—the first major party candidate to do so during the general election phase since the system had been set up—allowing him to build up a huge sum of money from which to draw when he needed to boost campaign advertising in one key state or another, which McCain's people could not match. Obama's campaign raised approximately $742 million in total and spent approximately $712 million, compared to McCain's total figures of approximately $367 raised and $326 spent, according to the Center for Responsive Politics. Obama's use of the Internet to accomplish this was foreshadowed by Howard Dean in his unsuccessful campaign four years earlier.

In 2004 Bush had won a narrow victory by capturing a few crucial swing states, such as Ohio and Florida. This time, as the election grew closer, Obama was slightly ahead in many competitive states, including some that Bush had won in 2004. For example, Virginia and North Carolina, which had not gone Democratic in decades, were polling slightly for Obama. To counteract the Democratic inroads into Republican states, the McCain forces made a big push in Pennsylvania, which Kerry had won in 2004, a state that Clinton had won in the primaries.

November 4 saw substantial voter turnouts—the highest since the 1960s—as Americans sought to participate in what was shaping up to be a milestone for the country. Obama not only won all the traditional Democratic-leaning states that Kerry won, such as Pennsylvania, but was also able to pull out victories in states that Kerry had been unable to win. Among the "Bush states" that Obama won were Florida, Virginia, North Carolina, Ohio, Indiana, and Colorado. Obama won 69.5 million votes (53 percent) to McCain's 59.9 million votes (46 percent) and his electoral college victory was 365 to McCain's 173. That night, Obama appeared with his family to deliver a speech at an emotional mass rally in Chicago's Grant Park.

In addition to Obama's historic victory, Democrats picked up additional seats in Congress, getting them close to sixty Senate seats, the number needed to halt a filibuster, while padding their House majority. Against the backdrop of Bush's unpopularity, the economic collapse, and the ongoing wars in Iraq and Afghanistan, Republicans had had their worst showing in many years.

The country woke up the next morning to the once-unbelievable reality that an African American had won the country's highest office and with his family would take up residence in the White House. The international reaction was positive, a contrast to the negative image the United States and President Bush had in the wake of the Iraq War.

Throughout the two-and-a-half month transition period, the Bush administration and the Obama team worked together with Congress to come up with potential solutions for the economic situation. Obama was more reticent when it came to international issues, opting for the most part to remain silent until he was in the White House.

During the transition Obama surprised many by selecting his primary rival Clinton to be secretary of state. Other cabinet appointments included former Justice Department official Eric Holder as attorney general and, in a bipartisan nod, Republican holdover Robert Gates as defense secretary. But not all nominations went smoothly. Treasury secretary nominee Timothy Geithner was confirmed by the Senate 64–30 only after acknowledging his failure to pay payroll taxes in previous years. The same embarrassing issue of failing to pay federal income taxes sunk the nomination of former Senate majority leader Tom Daschle to be secretary of health and human services. The position was seen as key for Obama, who made health care reform a major campaign theme. Obama would eventually nominate Kansas governor Kathleen Sebelius for the cabinet post.

Washington prepared for a record-breaking turnout, and unprecedented security measures for Obama's inauguration on January 20, 2009. The entire National Mall was filled, with huge television screens placed along its length, as approximately 1.8 million people gathered to see the inauguration, which occurred without incident under clear and sunny skies but in exceptionally cold temperatures. In anxious economic times, the new president strove to reassure the American people: "Today I say to you that the challenges we face are real, they are serious and they are many. They will not be met easily or in a short span of time. But know this America: They will be met."[203]

★

NOTES

1. A. James Reichley, *The Life of the Parties: A History of American Political Parties* (New York: Free Press, 1992), 17.

2. Richard P. McCormick, *The Presidential Game: The Origins of American Presidential Politics* (New York: Oxford University Press, 1982), chap. 1.

3. Ibid., 33–34.

4. Reichley, *Life of the Parties*, 42.

5. Ibid., 49.

6. Robert J. Dinkin, *Campaigning in America: A History of Election Practices* (New York: Greenwood Press, 1989), 18.

7. Roy F. Nichols, *The Invention of the American Political Parties* (New York: Macmillan, 1967), 192.

8. Bruce L. Felkner, *Political Mischief: Smear, Sabotage, and Reform in U.S. Elections* (New York: Praeger, 1992), 31.

9. Dinkin, *Campaigning in America*, 15, 18.

10. Edward Stanwood, *A History of the Presidency* (Boston: Houghton Mifflin, 1898), 63.

11. John F. Hoadley, *Origins of American Party Politics, 1789–1803* (Lexington: University Press of Kentucky, 1986), 191.

12. T. Harry Williams, *The History of American Wars: From Colonial Times to World War I* (New York: Knopf, 1981), 134.

13. Stanwood, *History of the Presidency*, 110.

14. Matthew A. Crenson, *The Federal Machine* (Baltimore, Md.: Johns Hopkins University Press, 1971), 11–30.

15. Jackson biographer Robert V. Remini explains the nickname "Old Hickory." In an arduous five-hundred-mile march, Jackson gave his three horses to wounded soldiers and marched on foot with his troops to give them moral support. The soldiers serving under him agreed that their general was as tough as hickory. "Not much later," Remini writes, "they started calling him 'Hickory' as a sign of their respect and regard; then the affectionate 'Old' was added to give Jackson a nickname ... that admirably served him thereafter throughout his military and political wars." Robert V. Remini, *Andrew Jackson* (New York: Harper and Row, 1969), 54.

16. Arthur M. Schlesinger Jr., *The Age of Jackson* (New York: New American Library, 1945), 34.

17. *Guide to Congress*, 5th ed. (Washington, D.C.: CQ Press, 2000), 807.

18. Russell L. Hanson, *The Democratic Imagination in America: Conversations with Our Past* (Princeton, N.J.: Princeton University Press, 1985), 125.

19. Eugene H. Roseboom, *A History of Presidential Elections* (New York: Macmillan, 1970), 106.

20. Schlesinger, *Age of Jackson*, 55.

21. Estimates of vote totals vary, especially in the years before standardized methods of balloting. Discrepancies developed because of disputes about stuffing ballot boxes, the eligibility of some voters, absentee ballots, and simple counting and reporting difficulties in the premedia age.

22. Roseboom, *History of Presidential Elections*, 112.

23. Hanson, *Democratic Imagination*, 54–120.

24. Ibid., 140–141.

25. Ibid., 136.

26. See Albert O. Hirschman, *Exit, Voice, and Loyalty* (Cambridge, Mass.: Harvard University Press, 1970).

27. Hanson, *Democratic Imagination*, 138.

28. Richard P. McCormick, "Political Development and the Second Party System," in *The American Party Systems: Stages of Development*, ed. William Nisbet Chambers and Walter Dean Burnham (New York: Oxford University Press, 1967), 102.

29. Paul Taylor, *See How They Run: Electing a President in the Age of Mediaocracy* (New York: Knopf, 1991), 4.

30. James L. Sundquist, *Dynamics of the Party System*, rev. ed. (Washington, D.C.: Brookings, 1983), 51.

31. Roseboom, *History of Presidential Elections*, 143.

32. Richard Hofstadter, *The American Political Tradition* (New York: Vintage, 1948), 113.

33. Ibid.

34. Hanson, *Democratic Imagination*, 176.

35. Roseboom, *History of Presidential Elections*, 177–181.

36. Paul N. Angle, ed., *The Lincoln Reader* (New York: Pocket Books, 1954), 523.

37. Ibid., 531.

38. Roseboom, *History of Presidential Elections*, 201.

39. Eric Foner, *Reconstruction: America's Unfinished Revolution, 1863–1877* (New York: Harper and Row, 1988).

40. William S. McFeely, *Grant* (New York: Norton, 1981), 283.

41. Ibid., 288–289.

42. Ibid., 381.

43. Bernhard Bailyn et al., *The Great Republic: A History of the American People* (Boston: Little, Brown, 1977), 802.

44. C. Vann Woodward, *Reunion and Reaction* (New York: Doubleday Anchor Books, 1951).

45. Kenneth M. Stampp, *The Era of Reconstruction, 1865–1877* (New York: Vintage, 1965), 210–211.

46. Michael Nelson, "A Short, Ironic History of American National Bureaucracy," *Journal of Politics* 44 (winter 1982): 747–777.

47. Roseboom, *History of Presidential Elections*, 264.

48. Harry Thurston Peck, *Twenty Years of the Republic, 1885–1905* (New York: Dodd, Mead, 1906), 20.

49. Michael E. McGerr, *The Decline of Popular Politics: The American North, 1865–1928* (New York: Oxford University Press, 1986), 82–106.

50. Peck, *Twenty Years of the Republic*, 41.

51. Ibid., 78.

52. Ibid., 144.

53. Ibid., 169.

54. Roseboom, *History of Presidential Elections*, 290.

55. Bailyn et al., *Great Republic*, 786.

56. Sundquist, *Dynamics of the Party System*, 107.

57. For a concise account of the machine reform struggle, see Dennis R. Judd, *The Politics of American Cities* (Boston: Little, Brown, 1984), 50–110.

58. See David Montgomery, *The Fall of the House of Labor* (New York: Cambridge University Press, 1987).

59. Sundquist, *Dynamics of the Party System*, 116–118.

60. Ibid., 143, 152.

61. Hofstadter, *American Political Tradition*, 187.

62. Sundquist, *Dynamics of the Party System*, 149–152.

63. Hofstadter, *American Political Tradition*, 192–193.

64. See "William Jennings Bryan, Cross of Gold Speech," in *Great Issues in American History: From Reconstruction to the Present Day, 1864–1969*, ed. Richard Hofstadter (New York: Vintage, 1969), 166–173.

65. Jasper B. Shannon, *Money and Politics* (New York: Random House, 1959), 30–32.

66. Sundquist, *Dynamics of the Party System*, 158.

67. Ibid., 169; for a general discussion of the 1896 election's resulting realignment, see pages 160–169.

68. E. E. Schattschneider, *The Semisovereign People* (Hinsdale, Ill.: Dryden Press, 1975), 76–77.

69. Edmund Morris, *The Rise of Theodore Roosevelt* (New York: Ballantine, 1979), 718.

70. See Gabriel Kolko, *The Triumph of Conservatism* (New York: Free Press, 1963).

71. Sundquist, *Dynamics of the Party System*, 176.

72. See Alpheus I. Mason, *Bureaucracy Convicts Itself* (New York: Viking Press, 1941); and James Penick Jr., *Progressive Politics and Conservation* (Chicago: University of Chicago Press, 1968).

73. August Heckscher, *Woodrow Wilson* (New York: Scribner's, 1991), 231–232.

74. Ibid., 259.

75. J. Leonard Bates, *The United States, 1898–1928* (New York: McGraw-Hill, 1976), 187.

76. Roseboom, *History of Presidential Elections*, 384.

77. John L. Shover, ed., *Politics of the Nineteen Twenties* (Waltham, Mass.: Ginn-Blaisdell, 1970), 148.

78. Ibid., 4.

79. Ibid., 12.

80. Ibid., 10.

81. James David Barber, *The Pulse of Politics: Electing Presidents in the Media Age* (New York: Norton, 1980), 239.

82. William E. Leuchtenberg, *Franklin D. Roosevelt and the New Deal* (New York: Harper and Row, 1963), 13.

83. Frank Friedel, *Franklin D. Roosevelt: The Triumph* (Boston: Little, Brown, 1956), 248–249.

84. Barber, *Pulse of Politics*, 243.

85. Ibid., 244.

86. Ibid., 238.

87. Hofstadter, *American Political Tradition*, 332.

88. Barber, *Pulse of Politics*, 244.

89. See Robert Lekachman, *The Age of Keynes* (New York: Random House, 1966).

90. Schattschneider argues in *The Semisovereign People* that the key element of any conflict is the extent to which the protagonists are able to control how many people get involved. Every "scope of conflict" has a bias. The size of the group involved in the conflict is almost always open to change. Schattschneider writes: "A look at political literature shows that there has indeed been a long-standing struggle between the conflicting tendencies toward the privatization and socialization of conflict" (p. 7). The New Deal was a stage of socialization of conflict.

91. Everett Carll Ladd Jr. and Charles D. Hadley, *Transformations of the American Party System* (New York: Norton, 1978), 86.

92. Ibid., 43.

93. Ibid., 46.

94. Ibid., 64–74, 112; Sundquist, *Dynamics of the Party System*, 214–224.

95. Sundquist, *Dynamics of the Party System*, 217.

96. Ladd and Hadley, *Transformations*, 82.

97. Ibid., 58–59.

98. Ibid., 63.

99. Samuel H. Beer, "Liberalism and the National Interest," *Public Interest*, no. 1 (fall 1966): 81.

100. Theodore J. Lowi, *The End of Liberalism* (New York: Norton, 1969). See also Hanson, *Democratic Imagination*, 257–292.

101. Greg Mitchell, *The Campaign of the Century: Upton Sinclair's Race for Governor of California and the Birth of Modern Media Politics* (New York: Random House, 1992).

102. James MacGregor Burns, *Roosevelt: The Lion and the Fox* (New York: Harcourt Brace and World, 1956), 282–283.

103. Roseboom, *History of Presidential Elections*, 447.

104. Burns, *Roosevelt*, 277–278.

105. Ibid., 269–271.

106. Ibid., 282–283.

107. Ibid., 300.

108. Ibid., 427.

109. Barber, *Pulse of Politics*. This book tells the story behind the Willkie movement and the role played by Henry R. Luce, the founder of Time Inc.

110. See Lekachman, *Age of Keynes*, especially chaps. 5 and 6.

111. Roseboom, *History of Presidential Elections*, 483.

112. William E. Leuchtenberg, *In the Shadow of F.D.R.: From Harry Truman to Ronald Reagan* (Ithaca, N.Y.: Cornell University Press, 1983), 1–2.

113. Ibid., 15.

114. Ibid., 21.

115. V. O. Key Jr., *Southern Politics in State and Nation* (Knoxville: University of Tennessee Press, 1984), 649.

116. Ibid., 330–344.

117. Barber, *Pulse of Politics*, 50.

118. Nelson W. Polsby and Aaron Wildavsky, *Presidential Elections* (New York: Scribner's, 1984), 205–206.

119. Barber, *Pulse of Politics*, 61.

120. Angus Campbell, Philip E. Convers, Warren E. Miller, and Donald E. Stokes, *The American Voter* (New York: Wiley, 1960), 532.

121. Richard Neustadt, *Presidential Power* (New York: Wiley, 1980), 10, 12–14, 16, 18, 19, 22–25, 43, 67–68, 178.

122. Garry Wills, *Nixon Agonistes* (New York: New American Library, 1969), 91.

123. Fred Greenstein, *The Hidden-Hand Presidency* (New York: Basic Books, 1982).

124. Barber, *Pulse of Politics,* 269.

125. Eric F. Goldman quipped, "The returns, as the gangsters said, made even Alf Landon look good," in *The Crucial Decade* (New York: Vintage, 1960), 326.

126. The elder Kennedy always had planned for his sons to enter national politics. He originally pushed his eldest son, Joseph Jr., but the son died in combat in World War II. John was next; he ran for Congress in 1946. Robert, the third Kennedy son, served as an aide to Sen. Joseph McCarthy before managing John's 1960 presidential campaign and serving as his attorney general. Edward, the youngest, worked on the 1960 campaign and won his first Senate race in 1962.

127. Merle Miller, *Plain Speaking* (New York: Berkeley, 1974), 199.

128. Theodore H. White, *The Making of the President 1960* (New York: Atheneum, 1961), 114–116.

129. Ibid., 128.

130. Ibid., 130.

131. Ibid., 198–204.

132. Arthur M. Schlesinger Jr., *Robert F. Kennedy and His Times* (Boston: Houghton Mifflin, 1978), 193.

133. Henry Fairlie, *The Kennedy Promise* (New York: Dell, 1972), 30–31.

134. White, *Making of the President 1960,* 329.

135. Ibid., 327.

136. Richard M. Nixon, *Six Crises* (Garden City, N.Y.: Doubleday, 1962), 412.

137. White, *Making of the President 1960, 397–401.*

138. Sen. Barry Goldwater, letter to the author, January 25, 1988.

139. The Warren Commission, appointed by Johnson, concluded that Oswald acted alone, but Oswald himself was killed before he had a chance to give full testimony. Many experts dispute the Warren Commission conclusion.

140. The Kennedy assassination fomented passage of the Twenty-fifth Amendment, which provides for a more orderly system of replacement. Previously, when a vice president ascended to the White House after the death or removal of a president, the vice presidency was left vacant. The amendment provides for presidential appointment of a vice president to fill the vacant spot. It also provides for at least temporary replacement of the president in the case of disability. The latter provision developed out of a concern that the country could have become leaderless had Kennedy been physically or mentally impaired but not killed.

141. Barber, *Pulse of Politics,* 167.

142. Thomas Ferguson and Joel Rogers, *Right Turn: The Decline of the Democrats and the Future of American Politics* (New York: Hill and Wang, 1986), 53.

143. Theodore H. White, *The Making of the President 1964* (New York: New American Library, 1965), 261.

144. Ibid., 353.

145. The central importance of economic conditions to electoral politics is widely documented. See, for example, Stanley Kelley Jr., *Interpreting Elections* (Princeton, N.J.: Princeton University Press, 1983); Edward R. Tufte, *Political Control of the Economy* (Princeton, N.J.: Princeton University Press, 1978); and Campbell, et al., *The American Voter.* On the link between economic conditions and the 1964 election, see Kelley, *Interpreting Elections,* 194.

146. Stanley Karnow, *Vietnam: A History* (New York: Viking, 1983), 358.

147. Ibid., 362.

148. Ibid., 395.

149. James David Barber, *The Presidential Character* (Englewood Cliffs, N.J.: Prentice Hall, 1972), 34.

150. Karnow, *Vietnam,* 403.

151. Ibid., 479.

152. David Halberstam, *The Best and the Brightest* (New York: Random House, 1969).

153. Sundquist, *Dynamics of the Party System,* 384.

154. Ibid., 383.

155. The administration plank supported a bombing halt only when it "would not endanger the lives of our troops in the field," did not call for a reduction in search-and-destroy missions or a withdrawal of troops until the end of the war, and advocated a new government in Saigon only after the war had ended. The minority plank, drafted by McCarthy and McGovern, called for an immediate halt to the bombing, reduction of offensive operations in the South Vietnamese countryside, a negotiated troop withdrawal, and encouragement of the South Vietnamese government to negotiate with communist insurgents. After nearly three hours of debate, the minority plank was defeated, 1,567 and 3/4 to 1,041 and 1/4.

156. Theodore H. White, *The Making of the President 1968* (New York, Atheneum, 1969), 371.

157. Roseboom, *History of Presidential Elections,* 603.

158. See Russell Baker, *The Next President* (New York: Dell, 1968).

159. Theodore H. White, *The Making of the President 1972* (New York, New American Library, 1973), 129.

160. Ibid., 207.

161. On the politics of the period, see Sundquist, *Dynamics of the Party System,* 393–411; and Theodore H. White, *America in Search of Itself* (New York: Harper and Row, 1981). Good accounts of the Watergate scandal include those by Theodore H. White, *Breach of Faith* (New York: Atheneum, 1975); Jonathan Schell, *The Time of Illusion* (New York: Knopf, 1976); and Lewis Chester et al., *Watergate* (New York: Ballantine, 1973).

162. See Bruce Odes, ed., *From the President: Richard Nixon's Secret Files* (New York: Harper and Row, 1989).

163. Seymour Hersh, "The Pardon," *Atlantic,* August 1983, 55–78.

164. David J. Vogler, *The Politics of Congress* (Boston: Allyn and Bacon, 1977), 15–20, 25–26, 34, 147–155, 243–245.

165. For a good account of Carter's 1976 Iowa victory, see Hugh Winebrenner, *The Iowa Precinct Caucuses* (Ames: University of Iowa Press, 1987), 67–93.

166. Jules Witcover, *Marathon* (New York: Viking, 1977), 545–560.

167. Responding to a question during a debate, Ford said: "There is no Soviet domination of Eastern Europe, and there never will be under a Ford administration.... I don't believe ... that the Yugoslavians consider themselves dominated by the Soviet Union. I don't believe that the Romanians consider themselves dominated by the Soviet Union. I don't believe that the Poles consider themselves dominated by the Soviet Union." Ibid., 597, 598.

168. Richard Harwood, ed., *The Pursuit of the Presidency 1980* (New York: Berkeley, 1980), 305–307.

169. George Gilder, *Wealth and Poverty* (New York: Basic Books, 1980). Another prominent supply-side tract is that by Jude Wanniski, *The Way the World Works* (New York: Basic Books, 1978). A sympathetic summary of the whole movement can be found in Robert Craig Paul, *The Supply-Side Revolution* (Cambridge, Mass.: Harvard University Press, 1984).

170. Ferguson and Rogers, *Right Turn,* 86–88, n. 245.

171. Garry Wills, *Reagan's America: Innocents at Home* (Garden City, N.Y.: Doubleday, 1987), 387.

172. Ibid., 385.

173. Ferguson and Rogers, *Right Turn.*

174. Rep. Shirley Chisholm of Brooklyn, New York, was the first African American to seek a major party nomination. Her participation in the 1972 Democratic primaries won 151 delegates.

175. Geraldine Ferraro, with Linda Bird Francke, *Ferraro: My Story* (New York: Bantam, 1985), 164.

176. V.O. Key Jr., "A Theory of Critical Elections," *Journal of Politics* 17 (February 1955): 3–18.

177. Paul R. Abramson, John H. Aldrich, and David W. Rohde, *Change and Continuity in the 1984 Elections,* rev. ed. (Washington, D.C.: CQ Press, 1986), 286–287.

178. In the twelve days after Bush picked Quayle, ABC, CBS, and NBC aired ninety-three stories about him—more than Dukakis received during the whole primary season. Two-thirds of the stories were negative. See Taylor, *See How They Run,* 162.

179. Nelson W. Polsby and Aaron Wildavsky, *Presidential Elections: Contemporary Strategies of American Electoral Politics,* 8th ed. (New York: Basic Books, 1991), 248.

180. Michael Duffy and Dan Goodgame, *Marching in Place: The Status Quo Presidency of George Bush* (New York: Simon and Schuster, 1992), 267–268.

181. Quoted in Michael Nelson, "The Presidency: Clinton and the Cycle of Politics and Policy," in *The Elections of 1992,* ed. Michael Nelson (Washington, D.C.: CQ Press, 1993), 144.

182. Paul J. Quirk and Jon K. Dalager, "The Election: A 'New Democrat' and a New Kind of Presidential Campaign," in Nelson, *Elections of 1992,* 61.

183. The unofficial manifesto of this movement is that by George F. Will, *Restoration: Congress, Term Limits, and the Recovery of Deliberative Democracy* (New York: Free Press, 1993).

184. Perot's rescue of his employees from Tehran during the 1979 Iranian revolution, for example, resulted in a best-selling book—Ken Follett's *On Wings of Eagles* (New York: Morrow, 1983)—and a made-for-TV movie. Earlier, he had founded a national organization to support President Nixon's Vietnam policy. Later, his company's merger with General Motors provoked a public dispute that cast him as the problem solver and GM officials as entrenched bureaucrats.

185. Ryan J. Barilleaux and Randall E. Adkins, "The Nominations: Process and Patterns," in Nelson, *Elections of 1992,* 38–39.

186. See David Osborne and Ted Gaebler, *Reinventing Government: How the Entrepreneurial Spirit Is Transforming the Public Sector* (Reading, Mass.: Addison-Wesley, 1992), for a manifesto of Clinton's approach to government reform.

187 For an excellent treatment of the importance of the middle class and suburbanism on modern American politics, see Thomas Byrne Edsall and Mary D. Edsall, *Chain Reaction: The Impact of Race, Rights, and Taxes on American Politics* (New York: Norton, 1991).

188. Barilleaux and Adkins, "The Nominations," 48–49.

189. Duffy and Goodgame, *Marching in Place.*

190. Daniel Hellinger and Dennis R. Judd, *The Democratic Facade* (Belmont, Calif.: Wadsworth, 1994), 180.

191. Al Gore, *Earth in the Balance: Ecology and the Human Spirit* (Boston: Houghton Mifflin, 1992).

192. Ross K. Barker, "Sorting Out and Suiting Up: The Presidential Nominations," in *The Election of 1992,* ed. Gerald M. Pomper (Chatham, N.J.: Chatham House, 1993), 67.

193. See Mark J. Rozell and Clyde Wilcox, "It Isn't the Old Christian Right Anymore," *Los Angeles Times,* April 29, 1996, B5.

194. See Clyde Wilcox and Mark J. Rozell, "Dole's Delicate Balancing Act," *Christian Science Monitor,* June 4, 1996, 20.

195. Green Party candidate Ralph Nader polled 0.7 percent and Libertarian Harry Browne polled 0.5 percent. Rhodes Cook, "Even with Higher Vote, Clinton Remains Minority President," *Congressional Quarterly Weekly Report,* January 18, 1997, 185–188.

196. Howard Fineman, "Clinton's Big Win," *Newsweek,* November 18, 1996, 8–13; Rhodes Cook, "Clinton's Easy Second-Term Win Riddles GOP Electoral Map," *Congressional Quarterly Weekly Report,* November 9, 1996, 3189–3194.

197. Rhodes Cook, "The Nader Factor: Overrated?" *Rhodes Cook Letter,* January 2001, 7.

198. See Ken Ringle, "For Jan. 20, a Peaceful Precedent," *Washington Post,* January 10, 2001, C9.

199. John F. Harris, "Deficit Worries Threaten Bush Agenda," *Washington Post,* February 7, 2005, A5.

200. Federal Election Commission.

201. Del Quentin Wilber, "From Across U.S., 2,000 Police Officers Volunteer for Duty," *Washington Post,* January 18, 2005, B1.

202. Roxanne Roberts, "On Inaugural Night, ISO an After-Party with a Pulse," *Washington Post,* January 22, 2005, C1.

203. "Barack Obama's Inaugural Address." Transcript as transcribed by CQ Transcriptions. http://www.nytimes.com/2009/01/20/us/politics/20text-obama.htm.

chapter 3

Presidential Primaries

THE QUADRENNIAL PROCESS of electing a president has two distinct parts—the nominating process and the general election. In contrast to the stable character of the general election—a one-day nationwide vote on the first Tuesday after the first Monday in November—the nominating process has changed many times in the nation's history.

Modifications in the nominating process have been dramatic—beginning with congressional caucuses in the early nineteenth century, through the heyday of the national conventions over the next century and a half, to the present nominating system, where conventions merely ratify the choices made months earlier by Democratic and Republican primary and caucus voters.

While originating in the Progressive Era in the early twentieth century, primaries were few and far between until after the 1968 election. The Democrats' tumultuous convention in Chicago that year encouraged both parties, but the Democrats in particular, to look for ways to open the nominating process to broader participation. Primaries quickly mushroomed—from fifteen in 1968, to thirty-six in 1980, to forty-four (including those in the District of Columbia and Puerto Rico) in 2000, declining slightly to thirty-nine for both parties in 2008, including a primary and caucus in Puerto Rico.

Their significance increased as well. Gone were the days when candidates could win their party's nomination without entering the primaries. No nominee of either major party has done so since Democrat Hubert H. Humphrey in 1968. Gone too were the days when candidates could win their party's nomination without first proving broad-based popularity among millions of voters. Beginning with Democrat George McGovern in 1972 through 2004, every major party nominee has first been his party's highest vote-getter in the primaries. In 2008 Hillary Clinton actually won slightly more votes in the primaries than her fellow Democrat Barack Obama but fewer votes once caucus states were included. In the process, the once climactic conventions have become little more than giant pep rallies, ratifying the

choices of Democratic and Republican primary and caucus voters and providing the staging ground for the parties' general election campaigns.

The larger role of primary voters has also meant that the ability to mobilize voters has become more important than the bargaining skills of professional politicians. As a result, nominating campaigns now emphasize the skills of political consultants, the ability to use the Internet and influence the mass media, candidate-specific get-out-the vote and mobilization efforts, and the organizational clout of interest groups such as evangelical ministries and labor unions.

FRONT-LOADED PROCESS

As the number of primaries has grown, more and more states have moved their primaries forward to dates near the beginning of the election year in a bid to heighten their influence (a process that has become known as front-loading). As a result, with the notable exception of the Democrats in 2008, nominations have been settled earlier and earlier. In 1968 only New Hampshire's primary was held before the end of March. In 1980 ten states held primaries before the end of that month. By 1988 the number surpassed twenty. In 2008 the pace accelerated: exactly half the country (twenty-five) states held primaries by the end of February. These states included Florida and Michigan, which flouted Democratic Party rules by moving their contests to January to have a larger impact on the candidate selection. Only three states, under the party rule—New Hampshire and South Carolina—were allow to hold primaries before February. Indeed, including states choosing delegates by party caucuses, about two-thirds of the nation completed its actions by that early date.

The result has generally been an increasingly truncated nominating process that has followed a clear pattern. Early votes—caucuses in Iowa and a primary in New Hampshire—have winnowed the field to a handful of candidates. Then, after a short period of unpredictability, one candidate has scored a knockout in the glut of March primaries—a

TYPES OF PRIMARIES AND PROCEDURES

In many respects, the presidential nominating process is similar to a modern-day Alice in Wonderland. Its basic dynamics do not always appear logical. Primaries and caucuses are strewn across the calendar from January to June, culminating with party conventions in the summer. A nomination is won by a candidate attaining a majority of delegates, an honor that is formally bestowed at the conventions but for decades has been informally achieved much earlier during the primary season.

Size is less important in determining a state's importance in the nominating process than its tradition and place on the calendar (early is best). Hence the quadrennial starring role for Iowa and New Hampshire, and the bit parts frequently assigned to larger states, such as California or Texas.

States have different ground rules in the nominating process. Some have caucuses, many more have primaries. Almost all primaries currently allocate a state's delegates in line with the voters' presidential preference, but a few are nonbinding "beauty contests," with the delegates elected independently of the preference vote.

Rules on voter participation vary from state to state. Some states hold "closed" contests, which are open only to a party's registered voters. Some hold "semi-open" events, which allow independent voters to participate along with registered members of the party. About half the states have "open" primaries or caucuses, in which any registered voter can participate.

The parties themselves also have different playing fields. From 1980 to 2000, Democrats did not allow any states except Iowa, New Hampshire, and sometimes Maine to hold a primary or caucus before early March, but the party loosened these rules in 2004. They were loosened further for the 2008 campaign in an effort to strike regional, economic, and racial balance. After twelve states applied to hold early primaries and caucuses, the Democratic National Committee permitted Nevada to conduct a caucus between Iowa and New Hampshire and South Carolina to conduct a primary in late January, one week after New Hampshire. All other states were permitted to conduct primaries and caucuses beginning February 5. The rules stated that any states or candidates that violated these guidelines would face sanctions—the loss of all or at least half of their delegates votes.

That threat that took on new importance in the tight 2008 race after Florida and Michigan held primaries in January. While all the candidates adhered to their pledges not to campaign in these two states, Hillary Clinton bent the rules. She was the only candidate entered on the Michigan ballot, which she won, not surprisingly. In Florida, other candidates were listed on the ballot, but there was some unofficial campaigning for Clinton, unlike the other candidates, leading her to a popular majority. As the contest between Clinton and Barack Obama remained tight through the spring, the inclusion and counting of delegates from these states became an increasingly important issue. Republicans in 2008 took a less contentious position, in keeping with past practice. States that held Republican primaries outside the established window lost half their delegates.

Since 1984, Democrats have reserved between 10 and 20 percent of their delegate seats for high-level party and elected officials (such as Democratic governors, members of Congress, and members of the party's national committee). Often called "superdelegates," these automatic delegates do not have to declare a presidential preference, although they usually follow their state's primary vote. Given the close race between Obama and Clinton the battle for these superdelegates became heated. Although Clinton originally led among these members of the party "establishment," Obama's ability to eventually win them over (463–257) proved a crucial part of his victory. (Republicans did not have "superdelegates" until their 2004 convention, when they gave automatic representation to members of the Republican National Committee, a small group.)

victory ratified by a string of essentially meaningless primary votes over the spring months.

The Republican Party stuck to this script in 2008. Former Arkansas governor Mike Huckabee, a favorite of evangelicals, scored a surprise victory in the Iowa caucuses, a contest in which former governor Mitt Romney of Massachusetts finished second, and in which the eventual Republican nominee, Arizona Sen. John McCain, finished third even without active campaigning. McCain won in New Hampshire, consolidated his advantage over Huckabee with a victory in South Carolina the next day, and led Romney in a series of primaries in late January and early February. The race effectively ended after McCain emerged as the clear winner of the Super Tuesday primaries on February 5. Romney conceded February 7 and Huckabee retired from the field in early March.

The Democratic Party contest also quickly focused on two senators, Clinton of New York and Obama of Illinois. Obama won a surprising victory in the Iowa caucuses, a state with few minority voters. Clinton won her own surprising victory in the New Hampshire primary and the race became a tug of war for four more months.

Clinton began as the clear front-runner with the personal prestige she gained as first lady when her husband was president from 1993 to 2001, the support of the party establishment, her large financial resources, and her appeal as the first female candidate for the White House with a reasonable chance of winning. She expected to win a significant set of states on "Super Tuesday" February 5 that would all but prevent Obama from overtaking her. Clinton did score primary victories in such large states as California, New York, Massachusetts, and New Jersey that day, but Obama won his Illinois and Missouri, and he used his appeal to African Americans to help win Georgia and Alabama in the South. As he would throughout the nominating contest, Obama took advantage of an impressive ground organization to win nearly all of the caucuses, some by lopsided margins, thus netting substantially more delegates. Moreover, in those

Since they began party reform in the 1970s, Democrats have required states to distribute delegates among their candidates in proportion to their vote, statewide and in congressional districts. Since the 1992 conventions, the Democrats have set a 15 percent floor for candidates to share in the proportionate distribution at each level. This system proved helpful to Obama in 2008. Having organized early in most states, he was able to win delegates throughout the nation, and could reap a proportion of delegates even where he trailed in the statewide vote. An analysis indicates that if Democrats had employed a statewide winner-take-all system (in which the candidate winning the most votes statewide wins all the delegates), Obama probably would have lost the nomination to Clinton, largely because of her victories in larger states such as New York and California. In reality, although Obama trailed by eighty-four delegates in these two states, he neutralized his losses there by winning bigger margins in Illinois and Georgia, a net of eighty-six delegates. Overall, Clinton won twenty-one of the forty primaries, a net gain of forty-six delegates. Obama's victories in all but one of the seventeen smaller caucus constituencies netted him more, 141 delegates.

Republicans, in contrast, allow a variety of delegate allocation methods, including proportional representation, statewide winner-take-all congressional district and statewide winner-take-all (in which the high vote-getter in a district wins that district's delegates and the high vote-getter statewide wins all the at-large delegates), or some combination of the three. Still another method used by Republicans is the selection of individual delegates, often unpledged to any candidate, in a "loophole," or direct election primary.

How delegates are actually elected can vary from state to state. Most primary states hold presidential preference votes, in which voters choose among the candidates who have qualified for the ballot in their states. Although preference votes may be binding or nonbinding, in most states the vote does commit the delegates. For those primaries in which the preference vote is binding on delegates, state laws vary as to the number of ballots at the convention through which delegates must remain committed. Delegates may be bound for as few as one ballot or as many ballots as a candidate remains in the race. For the first time national Democratic rules in 1980 bound delegates for the first ballot unless released beforehand by the candidate they were elected to support. The rule became a flash point of controversy that year between the front-runner, President Jimmy Carter, and his major challenger, Sen. Edward M. Kennedy of Massachusetts. While Kennedy wanted the binding rule dropped, the Carter forces prevailed, keeping the rule in effect and enabling Carter to win the nomination on the first ballot. During the quadrennial review of party rules after the election, the binding rule was dropped, but presidential candidates retained the right to replace disloyal delegates with more faithful ones.

Until 1980 the Republicans had a rule requiring delegates bound to a specific candidate by state law in primary states to vote for that candidate at the convention regardless of their personal presidential preferences. That rule was repealed at the party's 1980 convention.

The final authority on delegate selection is the party itself, at its national convention. Regardless of state law or previous procedures, the convention can decide which delegates to seat to represent a state, and that decision is binding. Disputes on delegate credentials have sometimes been critical in party conventions, for example in the Republican nomination of Dwight Eisenhower in 1952 and the Democratic nomination of George McGovern in 1972. In 2008, despite Clinton's primary leads in Michigan and Florida, the Democratic National Committee first barred all delegates from those states, then softened to admit half. That decision proved to be the final nail in the coffin for Clinton's campaign. At the convention itself, in a gesture toward party unity, all of the delegates were seated for the ritual confirmation of Obama's nomination.

states where he ran behind in the primaries, Obama took advantage of Democratic rules that divided delegates in proportion to the candidates' votes to prevent Clinton from obtaining overwhelming delegate victories.

Obama also built on new forms of Internet fundraising and mobilization that party chairman Howard Dean had pioneered in 2004 to overcome Clinton's initial significant financial advantage. With the contest close, the loyalties of superdelegates—party officials and officeholders who were automatically allotted a slot at the convention—and the fate of contested delegates from Michigan and Florida became far more important. Superdelegates originally backed Clinton, but their allegiance shifted as Obama began winning in their states. Eventually he would lead by 463–257 among these officials. The race was effectively over after Obama won a decisive victory in North Carolina and nearly carried Indiana in May. But the final denouement came in the last weekend of the primary season when the Demoratic National Committee decided that it would seat at the convention only half of the delegates chosen in the Michigan and Florida primaries. Clinton emerged with only twenty-four additional delegates, an insignificant consolation prize.

The last time the Democrats had an extended contest for the presidential nomination was 1984, when former vice president Walter F. Mondale and Sen. Gary Hart of Colorado battled into the final week of Democratic primaries before Mondale won enough delegates to secure his nomination. Republicans had not had a competitive nominating contest at the time of its national convention since the 1976 Republican race between President Gerald R. Ford and former governor Ronald Reagan of California.

Front-loading has generally worked to the advantage of the most prominent candidates. In the contemporary system, only aspirants who already have popular recognition and campaign money can realistically compete in what is almost a nationwide primary. In nearly every contest since 1980 (with Obama in 2008 a notable exception), the eventual nominee has either led in opinion polls or raised the most money—and usually both—before, and often many months before, any voters have actually cast their primary ballots.

The need for early public recognition has resulted in the disappearance of the fabled "dark horse," a candidate of little prominence who develops strength over the course of the primary season. The large cost of widespread campaigning has further limited opportunities for surprises. As a result, candidates are withdrawing earlier in the nominating process, even before the first primary vote, as happened with Sen. Elizabeth Dole of North Carolina in the Republican 2000 race and Sen. Bob Graham of Florida in the Democratic 2004 race. The increasing cost of these campaigns has also undermined the system of public funding for presidential campaigns, with the most prominent candidates relying on private contributions rather than federal funds. These funds were first rejected by George W. Bush in 2000; following his precedent, the most prominent Democrats in 2008—Clinton and Obama—relied only on private contributions for their extensive war chests. McCain, a champion of public financing, proved an exception to this rule, turning to the public funding system for his campaign.

AN EVOLUTIONARY PROCESS

During the early years of the nation, presidential nominations were decided by party caucuses in Congress (derided by their critics as "King Caucus"). At the dawn of the Jacksonian era in the 1830s, though, the nominating role shifted to national conventions, a broader-based venue where party leaders from around the country held sway.

In the early twentieth century, presidential primaries appeared on the scene, adding a new element of grassroots democracy and voter input. But for the next half century, the primaries were relatively few in number and played a limited advisory role. Nominations continued to be settled in the party conventions.

After World War II, American society became more mobile and media-oriented, and once-powerful party organizations began to lose their clout. An increasing number of presidential aspirants saw the primaries as a way to generate popular support that might overcome the resistance of party leaders. Both Republican Dwight D. Eisenhower in 1952 and Democrat John F. Kennedy in 1960 won a string of primary victories that demonstrated their voter appeal and made their nominations possible. Yet conventions continued to be the most important part of the nominating process until 1968.

Legacy of the Progressive Era

Primaries may seem entrenched in the electoral process, but they are relatively recent replacements for the old smoke-filled rooms where party bosses once dictated the choice of presidential nominees. Presidential primaries originated as an outgrowth of the Progressive movement in the early twentieth century. Progressives, fighting state and municipal corruption, objected to the links between political bosses and big business and advocated returning the government to the people.

Part of this "return to the people" was a turn away from what were looked on as boss-dominated conventions. The primary idea in time spread from state and local elections to presidential contests. Because there was no provision for a nationwide primary, state primaries were initiated to choose delegates to the national party conventions (delegate-selection primaries) and to register voters' preferences on their parties' eventual presidential nominees (preference primaries).

Florida enacted the first presidential primary law in 1901. The law gave party officials an option of holding a party primary to choose any party candidate for public office, as well as delegates to the national conventions. However, there was no provision for placing names of presidential candidates on the ballot—either in the form of a preference vote or with information indicating the preference of the candidates for convention delegates.

Wisconsin's progressive Republican governor, Robert M. La Follette, gave a major boost to the presidential primary following the 1904 Republican National Convention. At that convention, the credentials of La Follette's progressive delegation were rejected and a regular Republican delegation from Wisconsin was seated instead. Angered by what he considered unfair treatment, La Follette returned to his home state and began pushing for a presidential primary law. The result was a 1905 Wisconsin law mandating the direct election of national convention delegates. The law, however, did not include a provision for indicating the delegates' presidential preference.

La Follette's sponsorship of the delegate-selection primary helped make the concept a part of the progressive political program. The growth of the progressive movement rapidly resulted in the enactment of presidential primary laws in other states.

The next step in presidential primaries—the preferential vote for president—took place in Oregon. There, in 1910, Sen. Jonathan Bourne, a progressive Republican colleague of La Follette (by then a senator), sponsored a referendum to establish a presidential preference primary, with delegates legally bound to support the primary winner. By 1912, with Oregon in the lead, a dozen states had enacted presidential primary laws that provided for either direct election of delegates, a preferential vote, or both. By 1916 the number had expanded to twenty-six states.

The first major test of the impact of presidential primary laws—in 1912—demonstrated that victories in the primaries did not ensure a candidate's nomination. Former president Theodore Roosevelt, campaigning in twelve

TABLE 3-1 **Votes Cast and Delegates Selected in Presidential Primaries, 1912–2008**

| Year | Democratic Party | | | Republican Party | | | Total | |
	Number of primaries	Votes cast	Delegates selected through primaries (%)	Number of primaries	Votes cast	Delegates selected through primaries (%)	Votes cast	Delegates selected through primaries (%)
1912	12	974,775	32.9	13	2,261,240	41.7	3,236,015	37.3
1916	20	1,187,691	53.5	20	1,923,374	58.9	3,111,065	56.2
1920	16	571,671	44.6	20	3,186,248	57.8	3,757,919	51.2
1924	14	763,858	35.5	17	3,525,185	45.3	4,289,043	40.4
1928	16	1,264,220	42.2	15	4,110,288	44.9	5,374,508	43.5
1932	16	2,952,933	40.0	14	2,346,996	37.7	5,299,929	38.8
1936	14	5,181,808	36.5	12	3,319,810	37.5	8,501,618	37.0
1940	13	4,468,631	35.8	13	3,227,875	38.8	7,696,506	37.3
1944	14	1,867,609	36.7	13	2,271,605	38.7	4,139,214	37.7
1948	14	2,151,865	36.3	12	2,653,255	36.0	4,805,120	36.1
1952	16	4,928,006	38.7	13	7,801,413	39.0	12,729,419	38.8
1956	19	5,832,592	42.7	19	5,828,272	44.8	11,660,864	43.7
1960	16	5,687,742	38.3	15	5,537,967	38.6	11,224,631	38.5
1964	16	6,247,435	45.7	16	5,935,339	45.6	12,182,774	45.6
1968	15	7,535,069	40.2	15	4,473,551	38.1	12,008,620	39.1
1972	21	15,993,965	65.3	20	6,188,281	56.8	22,182,246	61.0
1976	27	16,052,652	76.0	26	10,374,125	71.0	26,426,777	73.5
1980	34	18,747,825	71.8	34	12,690,451	76.0	31,438,276	73.7
1984	29	18,009,217	52.4	25	6,575,651	71.0	24,584,868	59.6
1988	36	22,961,936	66.6	36	12,165,115	76.9	35,127,051	70.2
1992	39	20,239,385	66.9	38	12,696,547	83.9	32,935,932	72.7
1996	35	10,996,395	65.3	42	14,233,939	84.6	25,230,334	69.2
2000	40	14,045,745	64.6	43	17,156,117	83.8	31,201,862	70.8
2004	37	16,182,439	67.5	27	7,940,331	55.5	24,122,770	63.1
2008	38	36,995,069[1]	68.9	39	20,840,681	79.8	57,686,569	72.8

NOTES: The number of primaries held include those in which delegates were elected and pledged to specific candidates. A few states also held "beauty contest" primaries that were nonbinding; in those states pledged delegates were selected in caucuses.

1. Figure includes 149,181 votes cast in a New Mexico contest in February. That contest was technically a caucus but had many characteristics of a regular primary.

SOURCE: Percentages of delegates selected are from Congressional Quarterly.

Republican primaries, won nine of them, including Ohio, the home state of incumbent Republican president William Howard Taft. Roosevelt lost to Taft by a narrow margin in Massachusetts and to La Follette in North Dakota and Wisconsin.

Despite this impressive string of primary victories, the convention rejected Roosevelt in favor of Taft. With primaries confined to a quarter of the states, Taft supporters kept control through the Republican National Committee (RNC), which ran the convention, and the convention's credentials committee, which ruled on contested delegates. Moreover, Taft was backed by many state organizations, especially in the South, where most delegates were chosen by caucuses or conventions dominated by party leaders.

On the Democratic side, the 1912 convention more closely reflected the primary results. Gov. Woodrow Wilson of New Jersey and Speaker of the House Champ Clark of Missouri were closely matched in total primary votes, with Wilson only 29,632 votes ahead of Clark. Wilson emerged with the nomination after a long convention struggle with Clark.

Decline and Revival of the Primaries

After the first wave of enthusiasm for presidential primaries, interest waned. By 1935, eight states had repealed their presidential primary laws. The diminution of reform zeal during the 1920s, the preoccupation of the country with the Great Depression in the 1930s, and war in the 1940s appeared to have been leading factors in this decline. Also, party leaders were not enthusiastic about primaries; the cost of conducting them was relatively high, both for the candidates and the states. Many presidential candidates ignored the primaries, and voter participation often was low.

But after World War II, interest picked up again. Some politicians with presidential ambitions, knowing the party leadership was not enthusiastic about their candidacies, entered the primaries to try to generate political momentum. In 1948 Harold Stassen, Republican governor of Minnesota from 1939 to 1943, entered presidential primaries in opposition to the Republican organization and made some headway before losing in Oregon to Gov. Thomas E. Dewey of New York. In 1952 Sen.

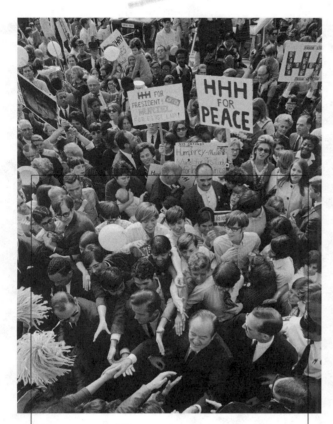

Democrat Hubert H. Humphrey in 1968 was the last candidate to win a major party's presidential nomination without entering the primaries.

Party domination of presidential nominations ended in 1968, amid the turmoil of the Vietnam War. Although the Republicans calmly chose Nixon, the nominating process tore the Democrats apart. Sens. Eugene McCarthy of Minnesota and Robert F. Kennedy of New York used the handful of Democratic primaries that spring to protest the war in Vietnam, together taking more than two-thirds of the party's primary vote and driving President Lyndon B. Johnson from the race.

History might have been different if Kennedy had not been assassinated after his victory in the California primary that June. But without Kennedy on the scene, the party's embattled leadership was able to maintain a tenuous control of the convention that August in Chicago, nominating Vice President Humphrey.

But Humphrey's nomination came at a price. Extensive street demonstrations in opposition to Humphrey and the war were met by brutal police force. On the floor of the convention, insurgent delegations were rebuffed, amid televised curses and fist fights. For the first time in several generations, the legitimacy of the convention itself was thrown into question. As an outgrowth, a series of Democratic rules review commissions began to overhaul the presidential nominating process to encourage much greater grassroots participation.

NOMINATIONS REFORM: REVERSAL OF FORTUNE

Democrats and Republicans have considered and enacted reforms of the nominating process frequently since the 1960s. Typically, the party that has lost the presidential election is more active, hoping to improve its chances in the next election, while the winners bask in complacency.

The initial thrust toward reform came from the Democrats, after their narrow defeat in the 1968 election. A commission originally headed by Sen. George McGovern of South Dakota established standards for broader and timely participation in the nominating process, which resulted in widespread adoption of primaries in place of party caucuses. Republicans followed suit, although more cautiously and more slowly.

Democrats Experiment with New Rules

Despite the growing importance of primaries, party leaders until 1968 maintained some control of the nominating process. With only a handful of the fifteen to twenty primaries regularly contested, candidates could count on a short primary season. The primaries began in New Hampshire in March, then candidates tested their appeal during the spring in Wisconsin, Nebraska, Oregon, and California before resuming their courtship of party leaders. In 1968— admittedly an unusual year, with incumbent Democratic

Estes Kefauver, D-Tenn., riding a wave of public recognition as head of the Senate Organized Crime Investigating Committee, challenged Democratic Party leaders by winning several primaries, including a New Hampshire upset of President Harry S. Truman, who announced three weeks later that he would not run for reelection. The struggle between Gen. Dwight D. Eisenhower and Sen. Robert A. Taft for the Republican Party nomination that year also stimulated interest in the primaries.

In 1960 Sen. John F. Kennedy of Massachusetts challenged Sen. Hubert Humphrey of Minnesota in two primaries: Wisconsin, which bordered on Humphrey's home state, and West Virginia, a labor state with few Catholic voters. (Kennedy was Roman Catholic, and some questioned whether voters would elect a Catholic president.) After Kennedy won both primaries, Humphrey withdrew from the race. The efforts of party leaders to draft an alternative to Kennedy came to be viewed as undemocratic by rank-and-file voters. Primaries now significantly challenged approval by party leaders as the preferred route to the nomination. Sen. Barry M. Goldwater, R-Ariz., in 1964 and former vice president Richard Nixon in 1968 also were able to use the primaries to show their vote-getting and organizational abilities on the way to becoming their party's presidential nominees.

president Lyndon B. Johnson suddenly withdrawing from his race for reelection, and the leading Democratic candidate (Sen. Robert F. Kennedy of New York) assassinated a few weeks before the convention—Vice President Hubert H. Humphrey was able to gain the party's nomination without entering a single primary.

But after 1968, the Democrats began altering their nominating rules, in an effort to reduce the alienation of liberals and minorities from the political system and to allow voters to choose their leaders. Republicans, who won in 1968 and four of the five presidential elections that followed, were slow to make any changes to their rules. The immediate result was a dramatic increase in presidential primaries that enhanced the chances of outsiders and produced Democratic presidential candidates such as McGovern, a liberal who lost in a landslide to Nixon in 1972, and Jimmy Carter, a former governor of Georgia who beat incumbent President Ford in 1976 but lost to Reagan in 1980.

In 1980 a then-record thirty-seven primaries (including those in the District of Columbia and Puerto Rico) provided more opportunity for mass participation in the nominating process than ever before. President Carter and Republican nominee Reagan were the clear winners of the long primary season. Although Carter received a bare majority of the cumulative Democratic primary vote, he was still more than 2.5 million votes ahead of his major rival, Sen. Edward M. Kennedy of Massachusetts. With no opposition in the late primary contests, Reagan emerged as a more one-sided choice of GOP primary voters. He finished nearly 4.8 million votes ahead of his closest competitor, George H.W. Bush.

Disheartened by Carter's massive defeat in 1980, the Democrats revised their nominating rules for the 1984 election. The party created a new bloc of so-called superdelegates—party leaders who were not formally committed to any presidential candidate. This reform had two main goals. First, Democratic leaders wanted to ensure that the party's elected officials would participate in the nomination decision at the convention. Second, they wanted to ensure that these uncommitted party leaders could play a major role in selecting the presidential nominee if no candidate was a clear front-runner.

While the reforms of the 1970s were designed to give more influence to grassroots activists and less to party regulars, this revision was intended to bring about a deliberative process in which experienced party leaders could help select a consensus Democratic nominee with a strong chance to win the presidency.

The Democrats' new rules had some expected, as well as unexpected, results. For the first time since 1968, the number of primaries declined and the number of caucuses increased. The Democrats held only thirty primaries in 1984 (including the District of Columbia and Puerto Rico). Yet, as did McGovern in 1972 and Carter in 1976, Colorado Sen. Gary Hart used the primaries to pull ahead (temporarily) of former vice president Walter F. Mondale, an early front-runner whose strongest ties were to the party leadership and its traditional core elements. (Still, Mondale wound up with more primary votes than Hart.) In 1984 the presence of superdelegates was important because about four out of five backed Mondale.

A few critics regarded the seating of superdelegates as undemocratic, and there were calls for reducing their numbers. Yet to those of most influence within the party, the superdelegates had served their purpose. In the following years, the Democratic National Committee (DNC) set aside additional seats for party leaders, increasing the number of superdelegates from 14 percent of the delegates in 1984 to 18 percent in 1996, edging close to 20 percent by 2008. All members of the DNC were guaranteed convention seats, as were all Democratic governors and members of Congress.

Moving the Windows

In the 1970s the primary calendar started slowly, giving little-known candidates the time to raise money and momentum after doing well in the early rounds. Most of the primaries then were held in May and June. But the schedule of the nominating process has been less favorable to dark horses since then. States began to move forward on the calendar in a bid to increase their influence, heightening the need for candidates to be well-organized and well-funded at the beginning of the primary season.

Democrats sought to put a brake on the calendar sprawl toward the beginning of the election year by instituting a "window," structuring the calendar to prohibit party primaries or caucuses before early March, with the exception of Iowa, New Hampshire, and, for a while, Maine.

Many states crept right up to this early March firewall, scheduling their primary in March—gradually at first, but then in tidal wave proportions in 1988, with the creation of a full-scale primary vote across the South on the second Tuesday in March that came to be known as "Super Tuesday." By doing so they hoped to steer the nomination toward a centrist son of the South, such as Sen. Albert "Al" Gore Jr. of Tennessee.

The Democratic "window" proved to be a confining brick wall for the Democrats in 2000. With no primaries scheduled for five weeks after New Hampshire, the party and its likely nominee, Gore—now vice president—disappeared from the news, while Republican George W. Bush continued to gain media attention. Attempting to recoup in 2004, Democrats allowed states to select delegates as early as a week after New Hampshire, and eighteen states—mostly small in population—took advantage of the opportunity to hold nine primaries and nine caucuses.

SELECTION BY CAUCUS

In the current primary-dominated era of presidential politics, which began three decades ago, caucuses have survived in the quiet backwater of the nominating process. The impact of caucuses decreased in the 1970s as the number of primaries grew dramatically. Previously, a candidate sought to run well in primary states mainly to have a bargaining chip with which to deal with powerful leaders in the caucus states. Republicans Barry Goldwater in 1964 and Richard Nixon in 1968 and Democrat Hubert H. Humphrey in 1968 all built up solid majorities among caucus state delegates that carried them to their parties' nominations. Humphrey did not compete in a single primary state in 1968.

After 1968, candidates placed their principal emphasis on primaries. First George McGovern in 1972—and then incumbent Republican president Gerald R. Ford and Democratic challenger Jimmy Carter in 1976—won nomination by securing large majorities of the primary state delegates. Neither McGovern nor Ford won a majority of the caucus state delegates. Carter was able to win a majority only after his opponents' campaigns collapsed.

More recently, there has been an increase in the number of states employing caucuses to choose convention delegates, mostly in smaller states. The increase was slight among Democrats, but more extensive among Republicans in 2004, when the party saw little reason to spend money or time in an uncontested renomination of President George W. Bush. The primaries continue to be the major prizes and to receive the most attention from the media and the candidates.

In 2008, however, the caucuses again became important, because they were critical in the nominating campaign of Democrat Barack Obama. The Illinois senator owed the margin of his victory over fellow senator Hillary Clinton to the delegates he accumulated in his well-designed efforts in the seventeen states and territories choosing delegates at caucuses.

COMPLEX METHOD

Compared with a primary, the caucus system is complicated. Instead of focusing on a single primary election ballot, the caucus presents a multitiered system that involves meetings scheduled over several weeks, sometimes even months. There is mass participation at the first level only, with meetings often lasting several hours and attracting only the most enthusiastic voters or dedicated party members.

Obama supporters cheer during January 2008 caucuses in Le Mars, Iowa.

The operation of the caucus varies from state to state, and each party has its own set of rules. Most begin with precinct caucuses or some other type of local mass meeting open to all who identify with the party, and even sometimes to all voters. In most states, there is at least one more step, sometimes two or three. Delegates in Iowa, for example, are elected at the precinct caucuses to county conventions, which are followed by congressional district conventions and the state convention, the two levels where the national convention delegates are chosen.

Participation, even at the first level of the caucus process, typically consists of local party activists. Many rank-and-file voters find a caucus complex, confusing, or intimidating. When a candidate arouses great popular enthusiasm, however, as Obama did in 2008, large numbers may come to the caucuses. In Washington State in 2008, more people—almost a quarter of a million—attended the caucuses than voted in the later (and less significant) primary.

In light of these characteristics, caucuses offer a opportunity particularly for candidates who arouse passionately dedicated supporters. That was evident as long ago as 1972, when a surprisingly strong showing in the Iowa precinct

Despite the diffusion of primaries over more weeks, Democrats remained dissatisfied with the concentration of selection at the beginning of the election year. There was too little time, critics said, for voters to consider alternatives and to test the campaign mettle of the declared candidates. After their defeat in the 2004 election, Democrats established a new reform group, the Commission on Presidential Nomination Timing and Scheduling.

The commission attempted to strike regional, economic, and racial balances, while allowing only one or two

"first-tier" caucuses and one or two "first-tier" primaries before February 5. After twelve states applied to hold early primaries and caucuses, the Democratic National Committee permitted Nevada to conduct a caucus between Iowa and New Hampshire and South Carolina to conduct a primary in late January, one week after New Hampshire. All other states were permitted to conduct primaries and caucuses beginning February 5. The rules stated that any states or candidates that violated these guidelines would face sanctions, including the loss of all or at least half of their delegates caucuses helped to propel Sen. George McGovern of South Dakota, an ardent foe of the Vietnam War, toward the Democratic nomination. In the same state in 2008, Democrats came out in record numbers for Obama and Mike Huckabee, Governor of Arkansas and an ordained minister, won the Republican caucuses due to the fervor of evangelical Christians.

Iowa has become the kick-off point for the quadrennial nominating process. It is not unusual for a politician, mulling a presidential run, to give a speech in Iowa as long as three or four years before an election. The state has become increasingly important and increasingly expensive for ambitious presidential candidates, as they must shell out money for everything from straw votes to radio and TV advertising. Sometimes, grassroots organization can overcome this need. Huckabee won the state in the face of large expenditures by Governor Mitt Romney. Obama did spend large sums in Iowa, but won many other caucus states with small spending.

Although the basic steps in the caucus process are the same for both parties, the rules that govern them are vastly different. Democratic rules have been revamped substantially since 1968, establishing national standards for grassroots participation. Democrats provide for proportional representation, dividing delegates to the next level of selection among candidates who receive support by at least 15 percent of caucus participants. Republican rules have remained largely unchanged, with the states given wide latitude in drawing up their delegate-selection plans.

CAUCUSES

For both the Republican and Democratic parties, the percentage of delegates elected from caucus states began a sharp decline throughout the 1970s, a trend that has continued. In 2008 primaries were held in thirty-six states, the District of Columbia, Puerto Rico, and among Democrats living abroad. Washington State held both a primary and caucuses, with Republican delegates chosen in the primary and Democratic delegates through caucuses. In Texas, Republicans chose candidates through the primary, while Democrats used both methods, two-thirds of the delegates chosen in the primary, one-third through separate caucuses held the same day. The Democrats elected 85.4 percent of their pledged national convention delegates in primaries, against only 14.6 percent in caucuses. (However, 19.3 percent of the total convention consisted of "superdelegates," unpledged

party and elected officials.) The Republicans in 2008 chose 84.5 percent of their pledged delegates in primaries and the rest by caucus or state committee; the convention also included 129 unpledged members of the Republican National Committee.

The caucus system is often criticized. Some have complained that they are easily dominated by party officials or organized interest groups such as church members, labor union members, and teachers, or open to capture by ideological extremists. The prominence of the Iowa caucus is sometimes seen as unrepresentative, especially among Democrats, because of the small proportion of minority group members in the state.

Yet in the elections of the twenty-first century, Iowa has again enjoyed center stage. In 2000, the campaigns of the eventual nominees—Gov. George W. Bush of Texas and Vice President Al Gore—were successfully launched in Iowa. In 2004 Iowa became an important turning point in the party's contest, when Sen. John Kerry overcame the initial enthusiasm for Gov. Howard Dean of Vermont. In 2008 Obama's surprise victory in Iowa became the foundation of his defeat of the Democratic front-runner, Senator Clinton. On the Republican side, Huckabee's win lifted him from obscurity to prominence and gave strong impetus to his campaign, which would eventually last longer than all the other major challenges to front-runner John McCain.

The major complaint about the caucus process is that it does not involve enough voters, and that the low turnouts are not as representative of voter sentiment as a higher-turnout primary. The combined turnout for both parties for the Iowa caucuses in 2000, for example, was roughly 150,000, less than half the number that turned out for the New Hampshire primary a week later. But this criticism is not always appropriate. In 2008 more than twice as many Democrats participated in the Iowa caucus than in the New Hampshire primary, and more Republicans attended the Iowa meetings than later voted in New Hampshire.

Staunch defenders believe a caucus has party-building attributes a primary cannot match. They note that several hours at a caucus can involve voters in a way that quickly casting a primary ballot does not. Following caucus meetings, the state party comes away with lists of thousands of voters who can be tapped to volunteer time or money, or even to run for local office. While the multitiered caucus process is often a chore for the state party to organize, a primary is substantially more expensive.

votes. The potential sanctions became an issue in 2008 when Florida and Michigan violated the rules by scheduling primaries in January. The rules also did little to discourage front-loading: sixteen primaries were held on "Super Tuesday," February 5. Nonetheless, the Democratic Party got its wish for a drawn-out contest that tested the mettle of its candidates and boosted party registration efforts. In primary voting in the states, including Michigan and Florida, just under 37 million votes were cast. When Puerto Rico's primary is added, the total was more than 37 million.

Republican Efforts

The Republican Party was slower to change its nominating procedures: it did not guarantee delegate seats to its leaders until the 2000 convention voted to make members of the RNC automatic superdelegates at the party's convention in 2004. Republicans had not acted before that in part because their rules permit less rigid pledging of delegates, which generally has led to substantial participation by Republican leaders, despite the absence of guarantees.

CHOOSING A RUNNING MATE: THE BALANCING ACT

In modern times, with presidential candidates wrapping up their party's nominations early in the primary season, the greatest suspense before a national convention had centered on the selection of a running mate. But this closely watched selection process is a recent development and it, too, has been passing out of the hands of the convention delegates.

During the country's first years, the runner-up for the presidency automatically took the second slot, although that system did not last long. In 1800 Thomas Jefferson and Aaron Burr found themselves in a tie for electoral votes, even though Jefferson was the Democratic-Republicans clear choice to be the top of the ticket. Burr's supporters, however, were unwilling to settle for the lesser office. The deadlock went to the House of Representatives, where Jefferson needed thirty-six ballots to clinch the presidency. It also led to the Twelfth Amendment to the U.S. Constitution, ratified in 1804, providing for separate electoral college balloting for president and vice president.

With the emergence of political parties after 1800, candidates ran as teams. Once party conventions began in 1831, delegates, with the guidance of party bosses, began to do the choosing. Sometimes the vice presidency was used as a bargaining chip, as when Franklin D. Roosevelt won the critical support of Texas by endorsing Rep. John Nance Garner for the second slot.

Only in 1940 did presidential nominees begin regularly hand-picking their running mates. That year, after failing to persuade Secretary of State Cordell Hull to accept the vice presidency, Franklin D. Roosevelt forced Henry A. Wallace on a reluctant Democratic convention by threatening to not run a third time if Wallace was rejected. Four years later, Roosevelt turned to Sen. Harry S. Truman to replace Wallace. The only exception to the practice that Roosevelt established came in 1956, when Democrat Adlai E. Stevenson left the choice up to the convention.

If the selection of a running mate often resembled an afterthought, it could be because the position itself was not especially coveted. John Adams, the first to hold the job, once complained, "My country has in its wisdom contrived for me the most insignificant office that ever the intention of man contrived or his imagination conceived."

The vice presidency has become a significant office in more recent times, both within government and politically. There is now a reasonable chance that whoever fills the position will get a chance to move up, either by succession or election. Almost every vice president elected since 1952 has later been nominated for president. In 1988 George H.W. Bush became the first vice president to be elected directly to the White House since Martin Van Buren in 1836. As of 2008, fourteen presidents had held the second-ranking post, seven in the twentieth century.

Also, since the mid-1970s the vice presidency has evolved from the somnolent office it once was; during this period five vice presidents enjoyed responsibility their predecessors did not. Nelson A. Rockefeller, who served under Gerald R. Ford, was given considerable authority in domestic policy coordination. Walter F. Mondale and George H.W. Bush helped to set policy for their respective presidents. Bill Clinton placed Albert "Al" Gore Jr. in charge of a "reinventing government" task force as well as environmental and high-tech initiatives. George W. Bush gave Richard B. Cheney wide influence throughout the government, particularly in foreign and defense policy. Many aspiring politicians now see the office as the premier base from which to campaign for the presidency.

Yet whoever is selected is often scrutinized for how well the choice balances (or unbalances) the ticket. One important factor is geography, which

Clinton of Arkansas used unconventionally in choosing Sen. Gore of Tennessee to form the first successful all-southern ticket in 164 years. Forty-six-year-old Clinton also chose someone in his own age group (Gore, forty-four) in another unbalancing act. Because George W. Bush and his vice-presidential choice, Cheney, both lived in Texas before their nominations, Cheney had to return to Wyoming to fulfill the constitutional requirement that the two executive officials come from different states. Other traditional factors weighed by nominees are religion and ethnicity. In modern national politics, however, those considerations seemed to be losing their place to race, gender, and age. In 1984 the Democrats chose Rep. Geraldine A. Ferraro of New York to be their vice-presidential candidate, the first woman to receive a major party nomination; Republicans followed up in 2008 with the nomination of Gov. Sarah Palin of Alaska.

Until Barack Obama's election in 2008, no African American had been selected by either party to fill any part of the ticket. In 1988 many Democrats thought that Jesse Jackson deserved second place on the ticket. Jackson had received 29 percent of the primary vote to 43 percent for Michael Dukakis. Instead, the fifty-four-year-old Dukakis chose Sen. Lloyd Bentsen of Texas, then sixty-seven, balancing the Democratic ticket by age as well as geographically and philosophically.

Age has become an important criterion with the rise of the "baby-boomer" generation. In 1988 George H.W. Bush surprised many by selecting Sen. James Danforth "Dan" Quayle of Indiana. Quayle was forty-one years old and had a relatively brief career in politics—two terms in the House of Representatives before his election to the Senate in 1980. Because of Quayle's youth and good looks, it was even suggested by some critics that Bush had selected him to appeal to young voters and women. Similar criticism was lobbed at McCain in the 2008 campaign, who at seventy-two was nearly three decades older than the forty-four-year-old Palin.

In 2000 Texas governor George W. Bush also took age into consideration, but in the opposite direction from his father, in choosing a running mate. The younger Bush chose Cheney, an experienced Washington hand, who was a former Wyoming representative and defense secretary in the elder Bush's administration. Obama in 2008 adopted a similar tack in 2008, picking the more senior Senate Foreign Relations Committee Chairman Joseph R. Biden Jr., a six-term senator, as his running mate.

When it was his turn atop the ticket in 2000, Gore too broke new ground. Rather than pick a southern baby-boomer as Clinton had, Gore chose Sen. Joseph I. Lieberman of Connecticut, the fifty-eight-year-old chair of the centrist Democratic Leadership Council and the first member of the Jewish faith to win a place on the national ticket of either major party. The Democrats' attention to age, as well as region, became evident again in 2004, when presidential candidate John F. Kerry chose a young southerner, Sen. John Edwards of North Carolina.

Recent presidential candidates, such as Gore and Kerry, and both Obama and McCain in 2008, have also developed a new practice, when they announced their choice of a vice-presidential candidate, after extensive investigations, even before the convention convened. In so doing, they demonstrated the final loss of independent power by the national convention. Delegates now had no function other than to be cheerleaders at the campaign launch of leaders who had been chosen without any deliberation by the party delegates.

When they were regularly winning the White House in the 1970s and 1980s, Republicans showed little interest in tinkering with the nominating process; they were happy to leave that as a concern of the Democrats. But once the GOP lost two presidential elections in the 1990s, many Republicans began to decry the front-loaded primary calendar that produced nominees within a few weeks of voting.

At their convention in San Diego in 1996, Republicans approved a rules change designed to help spread out the calendar. States were offered bonus delegates if they held their primary or caucus later, but the offer received few takers in 2000. Yet in the wake of that year's Bush-McCain contest, a party commission headed by former Tennessee senator and national GOP chairman Bill Brock recommended that the presidential primary calendar be dramatically overhauled, so that small states would vote first in 2004 and large states would vote last. That plan, called the "Delaware Plan," because of its state of origin, was shot down at the 2004 Republican national convention. The Republicans, like the Democrats, however chose to punish some states that held primaries before February 5. Under 2004 Republican National Committee (RNC) rules, no state was permitted to hold its primary before that date. In 2008 five states—Wyoming, New Hampshire, Michigan, South Carolina, and Florida—moved their primaries ahead and the RNC subsequently stripped them of one-half of their apportioned delegates. At their 2008 national convention, Republicans ensured that South Carolina and New Hampshire would not suffer a similar fate in the 2012 campaign, permitting them to hold primaries in January of that year.

Regional Primaries and Super Tuesdays

In addition to internal party concerns with the nominating process, other critics often found other problems of presidential primaries, including the length of the primary season (nearly twice as long as the general election campaign), the expense, the physical strain on the candidates, and the variations and complexities of state laws.

To deal with these problems, several states in 1974 and 1975 discussed the feasibility of creating regional primaries, in which individual states within a geographical region would hold their primaries on the same day. Supporters of the concept believed it would reduce candidate expenses and strain and would permit concentration on regional issues. The push toward regional primaries has generally been undermined by the more prominent development of front-loading.

The regional primary idea achieved some limited success in 1976 when three western states (Idaho, Nevada, and Oregon) and three southern states (Arkansas, Kentucky, and Tennessee) decided to organize regional primaries in each of their areas. Attempts also were made in New England to construct a regional primary. But New Hampshire would not participate because its law required the state to hold its primary at least one week before any other state. Only Vermont joined Massachusetts in holding a simultaneous presidential primary, on March 2.

In 1980 and 1984, limited regional primaries were held again in several areas of the country. Probably the most noteworthy was the trio of southern states (Alabama, Florida, and Georgia) that voted on the second Tuesday in March in both years. It became the basis for "Super Tuesday," which became a full-blown southern-oriented regional primary in 1988.

Sixteen states—a dozen from the South—held primaries on Super Tuesday, March 8, 1988. The long-held goal of many southern political leaders to hold an early regional primary was finally realized. Most of the GOP primaries were winner-take-all, and when Vice President George H.W. Bush swept every Republican primary on Super Tuesday, he effectively locked up the GOP nomination. For the Democrats, Gov. Michael S. Dukakis of Massachusetts also fared well on Super Tuesday. But despite Dukakis's victories, the Rev. Jesse Jackson—the first significant African American candidate for a major party presidential nomination—kept the contest going into June.

"March Madness"

By 1992 Super Tuesday had become part of a general rush among states to hold their primaries as early as possible. Dubbed "March Madness," after the college basketball tournament excitement at that time each year, the early clustering of primaries—seventeen states held primaries in February or March—was viewed with dismay by some political analysts. They said it could lead to nominees being locked in before most voters knew what was happening, resulting in less informed and deliberative voting in the general election.

In 1996 the process was even more heavily weighted in favor of early primaries, as more than two-thirds of them were held before the end of March. The idea of regional primaries also came the closest to fruition in 1996. "Junior Tuesday Week" (March 2–7) featured primary voting in ten states (five of which were in New England); Super Tuesday (March 12) had seven primaries (six of which were in the South); and "Big Ten" Tuesday (March 19) had four primaries in the industrial Midwest—Illinois, Michigan, Ohio, and Wisconsin. By the time California (which had moved its primary forward in the hope of increasing its sway on the nominating process) held its primary on March 26 (along with two other western states—Nevada and Washington), Sen. Robert J. "Bob" Dole of Kansas had all but clinched the Republican nomination.

In 2000 there were not only a glut of early primaries, but a large concentration on a single day—March 7. The clustering on this date—the first Tuesday of the month—was not

PRESIDENTS' REELECTION CHANCES

The record of U.S. presidential elections in the twentieth century and at the start of the twenty-first indicates that a smooth path to renomination is essential for incumbents seeking reelection. Every president who actively sought renomination during this period was successful. Those who were virtually unopposed within their party won another term. But all the presidents who faced significant opposition for renomination ended up losing in the general election.

The following chart shows the presidents who sought reelection to a second term since 1900, whether they had "clear sailing" or "tough sledding" for renomination and their fate in the general election.

Theodore Roosevelt did not seek renomination in 1908, after the completion of almost two full terms, even though he was eligible to run. However, four years later, he did seek another Republican nomination. Although he won most primaries, he was defeated at the Republican convention and then ran, unsuccessfully, as the Progressive Party candidate. Tellingly, President William H. Taft, who won the bitter fight against Roosevelt for the Republican nomination, lost in the general election to Democrat Woodrow Wilson.

Another two presidents—Harry S. Truman in 1952 and Lyndon B. Johnson in 1968—faced significant opposition at the end of their tenure and declined to run for another term. Truman was eligible for a third term because he was exempted from the Twentieth Amendment to the Constitution, which established the two-term limit. Johnson came to the presidency in 1963, completing John F. Kennedy's term, and was eligible for another four years.

A president with an asterisk (*) next to his name, such as George W. Bush in 2004, was completing his first full four-year term when he sought reelection. A dash (—) indicates there were no presidential preference primaries. The primary vote for President Johnson in 1964 included the vote cast for favorite sons and uncommitted delegate slates; Johnson was subsequently nominated by acclamation at the Democratic convention. George H.W. Bush in 1992 had to fight off a significant challenge by Patrick J. Buchanan in the Republican primaries before he went on to win 95 percent of the convention delegates.

	Incumbent's Percentage of:		
	Primary vote	Convention delegates	General election result
"Clear Sailing"			
William McKinley (1900)*	—	100%	Won
Theodore Roosevelt (1904)	—	100	Won
Woodrow Wilson (1916)*	99%	99	Won
Calvin Coolidge (1924)	68	96	Won
Franklin D. Roosevelt (1936)*	93	100	Won
Franklin D. Roosevelt (1940)	72	86	Won
Franklin D. Roosevelt (1944)	71	92	Won
Harry S. Truman (1948)	64	75	Won
Dwight D. Eisenhower (1956)*	86	100	Won
Lyndon B. Johnson (1964)	88	100	Won
Richard Nixon (1972)*	87	99	Won
Ronald Reagan (1984)*	99	100	Won
Bill Clinton (1996)*	88	100	Won
George W. Bush (2004)*	98	100	Won
"Tough Sledding"			
William H. Taft (1912)*	34%	52%	Lost
Herbert Hoover (1932)*	33	98	Lost
Gerald R. Ford (1976)	53	53	Lost
Jimmy Carter (1980)*	51	64	Lost
George H.W. Bush (1992)*	72	95	Lost

coincidental. It was the earliest date allowed by Democratic rules for states other than Iowa and New Hampshire to hold their primary or caucus. Eleven states scheduled primaries on March 7, 2000, creating a de facto national primary that became variously known as "Titanic Tuesday" or the new "Super Tuesday," although the large southern-oriented vote of the same name remained on the second Tuesday in March.

Political analysts predicted the huge volume of early primaries would result in both parties' nominations being decided by the ides of March, which is what occurred. George W. Bush and John McCain battled almost evenly through the seven states that held Republican primaries in February—Bush winning four, McCain, three. In March, Bush's well-financed campaign machine proved decisive as he dominated the vote March 7, and McCain withdrew soon afterwards. The result was the same on the Democratic side as it was on the Republican: an early knockout by the front-runner, Vice President Gore.

The regional primary effort then declined. In 2004, while the bulk of the New England states continued to vote on the first Tuesday in March, only a four-state remnant of the South remained grouped together on the second Tuesday, and there was no cohesion among either states in the Midwest or West.

The most notable change was the dramatic movement toward a broad-based, coast-to-coast vote on the first Tuesday in March. The day's primaries and caucuses involved states with a third of the nation's population, including three of the seven most populous states—California, New York, and Ohio. When Sen. John Kerry of Massachusetts won all but Vermont that day (and the Minnesota caucuses), his nomination was assured.

In 2008 this broad, virtually national primary took place a month earlier, on February 5, essentially ensuring both McCain's nomination and a drawn-out contest for the Democratic Party.

NOMINATIONS TODAY

During the past decades, the country has established a distinct process for presidential nominations. Many issues remain under debate, about that process itself and about its effects on the general election.

Current Process

Even though much of the primary calendar has changed dramatically since the 1960s, the accepted starting points have remained Iowa and New Hampshire. The two states illustrate the two different types of delegate-selection processes available to the states. Iowa is a caucus; New Hampshire is a primary. Primaries require voters only to cast a ballot, an exercise that usually takes just a few minutes. The deliberative nature of a neighborhood caucus, though, often requires the commitment of an afternoon or evening.

Both states have made their early events into cottage industries with the help of candidates and the media. More than ever, Iowa and New Hampshire are about the only states left where candidates have some personal role. They can woo voters one-on-one, whether in bowling alleys, coffee shops, or the frequent gatherings in neighborhood living rooms. Yet, as the importance of these contests has increased, they have also turned to extensive television advertisements to deliver their message more broadly. For if there is one thing that has become certain in recent years, once the New Hampshire primary is over and candidates must compete in several states simultaneously, there is a frenetic burst of

Presidential candidate Howard Dean's primal scream after losing the 2004 Iowa Caucuses—seen on television and in newspapers across the country—may have contributed to his demise as front-runner and John Kerry's rise to take the Democratic nomination.

VICE PRESIDENTS WHO HAVE BECOME PRESIDENT

Fourteen vice presidents have gone on to become president: John Adams, Thomas Jefferson, Martin Van Buren, John Tyler, Millard Fillmore, Andrew Johnson, Chester A. Arthur, Theodore Roosevelt, Calvin Coolidge, Harry S. Truman, Richard Nixon, Lyndon B. Johnson, Gerald R. Ford, and George H.W. Bush.

Of those, all but Adams, Jefferson, Van Buren, Nixon, and Bush first became president on the death or resignation of their predecessor. Only two—Van Buren in 1836 and Bush in 1988—have been elected president at a time of widespread suffrage while they held the office of vice-president.

Nine vice presidents since 1900 have run unsuccessfully for president:

- Thomas R. Marshall, Democratic vice president under Woodrow Wilson from 1913 to 1921, failed to win the nomination in 1920.
- Charles G. Dawes, Republican vice president under Coolidge from 1925 to 1929, unsuccessfully sought the nomination in 1928 and 1932.

- John Nance Garner, Democratic vice president under Franklin D. Roosevelt from 1933 to 1941, ran unsuccessfully (against Roosevelt) for the nomination in 1940.
- Henry A. Wallace, Democratic vice president under Roosevelt from 1941 to 1945, was Progressive Party nominee in 1948.
- Alben W. Barkley, Democratic vice president under Truman from 1949 to 1953, failed to win the 1952 nomination.
- Richard Nixon, Republican vice president under Dwight D. Eisenhower from 1953 to 1961, was the GOP nominee in 1960. (He won the nomination in 1968 and 1972.)
- Hubert H. Humphrey, Democratic vice president under Lyndon Johnson from 1965 to 1969, was the Democratic nominee in 1968.
- Walter F. Mondale, Democratic vice president under Jimmy Carter from 1977 to 1981, was the Democratic nominee in 1984.
- Al Gore, Democratic vice president under Bill Clinton from 1993 to 2001, was the Democratic nominee in 2000.

GROWTH OF PRESIDENTIAL PRIMARIES: MORE AND MORE, EARLIER AND EARLIER

The number of primaries has grown in recent decades along with states holding those primaries earlier in the presidential election year. The result is that a nominating system that once featured primaries sprinkled across the spring is now front-loaded with the bulk of the primaries held during the winter months of February and March. In 2004 for the first time New Hampshire held its first-in-the-nation primary in January.

In 2008 South Carolina also held party-sanctioned primaries in January. In addition, two states—Michigan and Florida—moved their primaries into January, in violation of party rules prohibiting any state other than New Hampshire and South Carolina from voting before February 1. Both states faced party sanctions that threaded to eliminate or reduce their delegate representations at the national conventions, although the controversy was resolved before the parties met.

One state, New Mexico, split its primary activity. Democrats held an event in February technically called a caucus but with characteristic that resembled a regular primary; it is included in the February total. New Mexico Republicans held a regular primary in June, which is included in the total for that month. However, the total, 41, counts the two New Mexico votes as a single vote.

Following is a list of primaries held in each month of every nominating season from 1968 through 2008. Primaries included are those in the fifty states and the District of Columbia in which at least one of the parties permitted a direct vote for presidential candidates, or there was an aggregated statewide vote for delegates. Primaries in the U.S. territories, such as Puerto Rico, are not included.

	1968	1972	1976	1980	1984	1988	1992	1996	2000	2004	2008
January	0	0	0	0	0	0	0	0	0	2	4
February	0	0	1	1	1	2	2	5	7	9	22[1]
March	1	3	5	9	8	20	15	24	20	14	5
April	3	3	2	4	3	3	5	1	2	1	1
May	7	11	13	13	11	7	10	8	9	7	7
June	4	4	6	9	7	5	7	4	5	5	3[2]
Total	15	21	27	36	30	37	39	42	43	38	41

1. Total includes a New Mexico Democratic presidential primary on February 5. This event was officially a caucus but had attributes of a regular primary. It was run by the Democratic Party in the state and was open exclusively to registered Democrats, who could vote by mail or in person at the more than 150 caucus sites between noon and 7 p.m. The results were used to assign pledged delegates to the candidates.

2. Total includes New Mexico Republicans who held a direct primary on June 3.

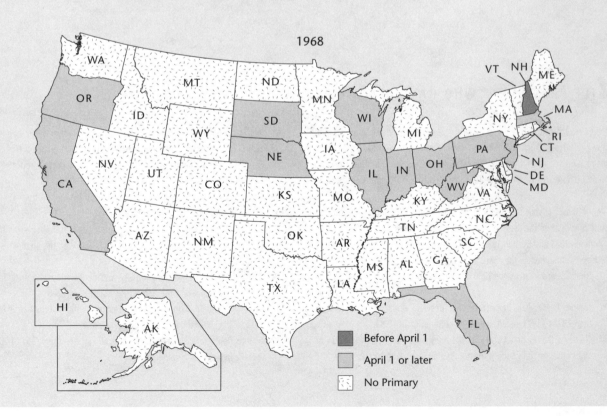

1968

Before April 1
April 1 or later
No Primary

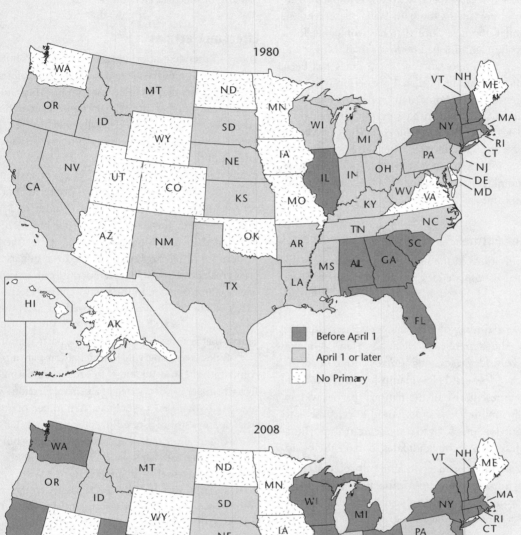

1980

Before April 1
April 1 or later
No Primary

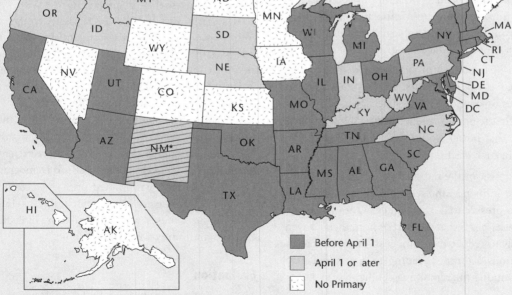

2008

Before April 1
April 1 or later
No Primary

* New Mexico's Democratic contest was held in February, while the Republican contest was held in June.

tarmac-to-tarmac campaigning heavily dependent on media advertising.

To be taken seriously, candidates are expected to win at least one of these two early states, with New Hampshire usually the more important of the pair. With one exception, every presidential nominee since 1976 has won either Iowa or New Hampshire and finished no lower than third in the other. However, the importance of these states has been questioned. Bill Clinton, in 1992, did not seriously contest Iowa in deference to the home-state appeal of Sen. Tom Harkin and finished second in New Hampshire behind a New Englander, former senator Paul E. Tsongas of Massachusetts. George W. Bush, in 2000, won the Iowa caucuses but lost to Sen. John McCain in New Hampshire. In 2008 the eventual nominees, McCain and Obama, both won only one of the two contests.

Change in the Future

The many innovations in the nominating process over the years continue to stimulate ideas for further change. These include:

■ Changes in timing of the state primaries, such as those of the Republican "Delaware Plan." A major motive behind these suggestions is to reduce the influence of Iowa and New Hampshire, often considered unrepresentative of the national parties' voters, especially among Democrats. Another purpose is to limit front-loading, so as to provide more opportunities for less prominent candidates to make their case.

■ A single national primary to allow all voters to have an equal impact on the presidential nomination. This change would require federal legislation, at least, and perhaps a constitutional amendment.

■ A system of regional primaries, whose order would be rotated every four years, recommended by the secretaries of state of all fifty states. This plan would give the first region to vote a considerable advantage, although that power would shift from one region to another in each election.

■ Revived power of the national convention to choose, or at least influence, the selection of the presidential and vice-presidential candidates. One suggestion along these lines is that the parties hold their conventions early to reduce the number of candidates to the most serious aspirants, leading to a national party primary among the remaining candidates.

Still, even without the Democrats or Republicans opting for bold changes, the nominating process is by nature evolutionary. Every four years at least a few states move their primary or caucus dates, creating a new calendar; and nearly every four years, at least one of the parties makes a change in its rules that proves significant. That effect will surely be evident for the 2012 elections as well.

Effect on Elections

Voters in presidential primaries are numerous but still represent a portion of the citizenry and may actually be unrepresentative of the national electorate. Voter turnout is usually much higher in a primary than a caucus, but even in primaries the turnout is generally much lower than in a general election. In New Hampshire, for instance, where interest in the presidential primary is probably greater than in any other state, nearly 400,000 voters turned out in February 2000 for the two presidential primaries, but that was still less than the general election turnout of 572,000. In 2004, when only the Democrats had a contest, 220,000 persons voted in the Democratic primary, but the total fall turnout was three times greater. The Iowa caucuses showed even greater differences—a Democratic caucus vote in 2004 of 124,000, compared to the party's general election vote of 742,000. The 2008 campaign proved an exception to this trend as the 239,000 that turned out for the Democratic caucus that year was nearly double the participation in 2004.

Rules governing voter participation play a role in the comparatively low turnouts for the nominating process. Every primary is not as open as a general election, where any registered voter can participate. A number of states limit participation to registered Democrats and Republicans. Some others allow independents to participate but list them on the voting rolls afterward as members of the party in which they cast their primary ballot.

Still, the vast majority of registered voters across the country can participate in a presidential primary or caucus if they want to do so. The fact that more do not has generated the conventional wisdom that the nominating process is dominated by ideological activists—liberals on the Democratic side, conservatives on the Republican.

That is debatable in the primaries, where the winners in recent years generally have been from the mainstreams of both parties. Candidates perceived as more extreme such as Republican Pat Robertson in 1988 or Democrat Howard Dean in 2004 have had limited primary success. An ideological bent is usually more evident in the low-turnout world of the caucuses, where a small cadre of dedicated voters can significantly affect the outcome.

Evaluation

The political community continues to debate whether the current primary-dominated nominating process is better than the old system in which party leaders controlled the selection process. But it is a fact that the increased number of primaries helps provide valuable clues about the voter appeal of candidates in the general election. Nominees that have exhibited broad-based appeal among the diverse array of primary voters in the winter and spring have gone on to be quite competitive in the fall, while those nominees who have struggled through the primaries showing limited appeal among one or two of their party's major constituency groups have usually been buried under landslides in November.

It is also true that the current system frequently results in quick decisions on the presidential candidates, which may come before their qualities are fully assessed by the voters, and that the process favors candidates who are already well-known and well-financed. The system of front-loading may also create, according to some critics, a "rush to judgment," which excludes a full evaluation of other talented aspirants. The diminished role of party politicians may mean that their expert skills and expert judgments are given too limited a role in choosing the next leaders of the nation. These questions are likely to induce continued changes in the American nominating process.

chapter 4

Popular Vote Returns for President

OPULAR VOTE RETURNS for all presidential elections from 1824 to 2008 are presented in this chapter. The presidential returns, except where indicated by a footnote, were obtained from three sources. The returns for 1824 to 1916 are from Inter-University Consortium for Political and Social Research (ICPSR) at the University of Michigan. The returns from 1920 to 1992 are from Richard M. Scammon and Alice V. McGillivray, *America at the Polls* (Washington, D.C.: CQ Press, 1994). The returns for 1996 and 2008 are from the *America Votes* series, compiled biennially by Rhodes Cook for CQ Press. This base source material has been supplemented with data from elections historian Michael J. Dubin. CQ Press editors believed the additional data was of scholarly merit and worthy of inclusion—much of it filling the gaps or correcting errors in previous editions of *Guide to U.S. Elections*. Dubin's original sources are also listed in the footnotes. This new information first appeared in the fourth edition and has been carried forward to this edition.

The 1824 starting date for the ICPSR collection was based on factors such as the pronounced trend by 1824 for the election of presidential electors by popular vote, as well as the availability, accessibility, and quality of the returns. The bulk of the ICPSR election data collection consists of returns at the county level in computer-readable form.

Table Organization

For each presidential election from 1824 to 2008, the following information is provided in the tables for the popular returns:

- Names and party affiliations of major candidates.
- Total state-by-state popular vote for president.
- State-by-state breakdown of the popular vote and the percentage of the vote received by each candidate.
- The aggregate vote and percentage of the total vote received in each state by minor party candidates, minor parties running unpledged electors, or unidentified votes. These figures appear in the column designated "Other"; a breakdown of these votes appears at the end of chapter 4.
- The plurality received by the candidate who carried each state, along with the candidate's party designation.
- The total national popular vote for president, the total national popular vote and percentage of the vote received by each candidate, and the nationwide plurality of the candidate who received the greatest number of votes.

The omission of popular vote returns for a state *after 1824* indicates an absence of popular voting for that election. The South Carolina legislature, for example, chose the state's presidential electors until 1860, and the state did not participate in the 1864 presidential election because of the Civil War. Thus, the first popular vote returns shown for South Carolina are for the 1868 election.

Party Designation

In many cases presidential candidates appeared on state ballots under different, even *multiple* party designations. Thus, in the returns for 1968, George C. Wallace ran for president under a variety of party designations in different states: Democratic, American, American Independent, Independent, George Wallace Party, Conservative, American Party of Missouri, Independent American, Courage, and George Wallace and Independent.

To provide one party designation for presidential candidates for the elections 1824 through 1916, CQ Press editors have aggregated under a single party designation the votes of candidates who are listed in the ICPSR data as receiving votes under more than one party designation. The source used for assigning party designation for these years is Svend Petersen, *A Statistical History of the American Presidential Elections* (Westport, Conn.: Greenwood Press, 1981). For the 1920 to 1992 elections, the source for party designation is Scammon and McGillivray, *America at the Polls.* For 1968 Scammon lists Wallace as an American Independent, and CQ Press follows this usage. For the 1996 to 2008 elections, the source for party designation is Cook, the *America Votes* series.

Vote Totals and Percentages

The total popular vote for each candidate in a given election was determined by adding the votes received by that candidate in each state (including write-in votes where available), even though the vote totals for some states may have come from sources other than ICPSR, Scammon, or Cook.

The percentages of the vote received in each state and nationally by any candidate or party has been calculated to two decimal places and rounded to one place; thus, 0.05 percent is listed as 0.1 percent. Due to rounding, state and national percentages do not always equal 100 percent.

Pluralities

The plurality column represents the differences between the vote received by the first- and second-place finishers in each state and in the nation. In most cases, most notably in 1912 and 1924, a losing major party candidate finished in third place in a state. In those few cases where votes from the "Other" column were needed to calculate the plurality, a footnote provides an explanation. For a breakdown of "Other" votes, see Popular Returns: Minor Candidates and Parties at the end of this chapter.

1824 Presidential Election

STATE	TOTAL VOTE	JOHN Q. ADAMS (Democratic-Republican)		ANDREW JACKSON (Democratic-Republican)		HENRY CLAY (Democratic-Republican)		WILLIAM H. CRAWFORD (Democratic-Republican)		OTHER[1]		PLURALITY[2]	
		Votes	%	Votes	%	Votes	%	Votes	%	Votes	%		
Alabama	13,603	2,422	17.8	9,429	69.3	96	0.7	1,656	12.2	—	0.0	7,007	AJ
Connecticut	10,647	7,494	70.4	—	0.0	—	0.0	1,965	18.5	1,188	11.2	5,529	JQA
Illinois	4,671	1,516	32.5	1,272	27.2	1,036	22.2	847	18.1	—	0.0	244	JQA
Indiana	15,838	3,071	19.4	7,444	47.0	5,316	33.6	—	0.0	7	0.0	2,128	AJ
Kentucky	23,338	—	0.0	6,356	27.2	16,982	72.8	—	0.0	—	0.0	10,626	HC
Maine[3]	12,625	10,289	81.5	—	0.0	—	0.0	2,336	18.5	—	0.0	7,953	JQA
Maryland[3]	33,214	14,632	44.1	14,523	43.7	695	2.1	3,364	10.1	—	0.0	109	JQA
Massachusetts	42,056	30,687	73.0	—	0.0	—	0.0	—	0.0	11,369	27.0	24,071	JQA[4]
Mississippi	4,894	1,654	33.8	3,121	63.8	—	0.0	119	2.4	—	0.0	1,467	AJ
Missouri	3,432	159	4.6	1,166	34.0	2,042	59.5	32	0.9	33	1.0	876	HC
New Hampshire[3]	10,032	9,389	93.6	—	0.0	—	0.0	643	6.4	—	0.0	8,746	JQA
New Jersey	19,837	8,309	41.9	10,332	52.1	—	0.0	1,196	6.0	—	0.0	2,023	AJ
North Carolina	36,109	—	0.0	20,231	56.0	—	0.0	15,622	43.3	256	0.7	4,609	AJ
Ohio[3]	50,024	12,280	24.5	18,489	37.0	19,255	38.5	—	0.0	—	0.0	766	HC
Pennsylvania	47,073	5,441	11.6	35,736	75.9	1,690	3.5	4,206	8.9	—	0.0	30,295	AJ
Rhode Island	2,344	2,144	91.5	—	0.0	—	0.0	—	0.0	200	8.5	1,944	JQA
Tennessee[3]	20,725	216	1.0	20,197	97.5	—	0.0	312	1.5	—	0.0	19,885	AJ
Virginia	15,371	3,419	22.2	2,975	19.4	419	2.7	8,558	55.7	—	0.0	5,139	WHC
Totals	365,833	113,122	30.9	151,271	41.3	47,531	13.0	40,856	11.2	13,053	3.6	38,149	AJ

1. For breakdown of "Other" vote, see minor candidate vote totals at the end of this chapter.

2. For the 1824 plurality winner the designations are JQA (John Quincy Adams), AJ (Andrew Jackson), WHC (William H. Crawford), and HC (Henry Clay). Adams was elected president by the House of Representatives.

3. Figures from Svend Petersen, *A Statistical History of the American Presidential Elections* (Westport, Conn.: Greenwood Press, 1981), 18.

4. Plurality of 24,071 votes is calculated on the basis of 6,616 for unpledged electors.

1828 Presidential Election

STATE	TOTAL VOTE	ANDREW JACKSON (Democratic-Republican)		JOHN Q. ADAMS (National Republican)		OTHER[1]		PLURALITY	
		Votes	%	Votes	%	Votes	%		
Alabama	18,618	16,736	89.9	1,878	10.1	4	0.0	14,858	DR
Connecticut	19,378	4,448	23.0	13,829	71.4	1,101	5.7	9,381	NR
Georgia[2]	20,004	19,362	96.8	642	3.2	—	0.0	18,720	DR
Illinois	14,222	9,560	67.2	4,662	32.8	—	0.0	4,898	DR
Indiana	39,210	22,201	56.6	17,009	43.4	—	0.0	5,192	DR
Kentucky	70,776	39,308	55.5	31,468	44.5	—	0.0	7,840	DR
Louisiana	8,687	4,605	53.0	4,082	47.0	—	0.0	523	DR
Maine	34,789	13,927	40.0	20,773	59.7	89	0.3	6,846	NR
Maryland	45,796	22,782	49.7	23,014	50.3	—	0.0	232	NR
Massachusetts	39,074	6,012	15.4	29,836	76.4	3,226	8.3	23,824	NR
Mississippi	8,344	6,763	81.1	1,581	18.9	—	0.0	5,182	DR
Missouri	11,654	8,232	70.6	3,422	29.4	—	0.0	4,810	DR
New Hampshire	44,035	20,212	45.9	23,823	54.1	—	0.0	3,611	NR
New Jersey	45,570	21,809	47.9	23,753	52.1	8	0.0	1,944	NR
New York	270,975	139,412	51.4	131,563	48.6	—	0.0	7,849	DR
North Carolina	51,747	37,814	73.1	13,918	26.9	15	0.0	23,896	DR
Ohio	131,049	67,596	51.6	63,453	48.4	—	0.0	4,143	DR
Pennsylvania	152,220	101,457	66.7	50,763	33.3	—	0.0	50,694	DR
Rhode Island	3,580	820	22.9	2,755	77.0	5	0.1	1,935	NR
Tennessee[2]	46,533	44,293	95.2	2,240	4.8	—	0.0	42,053	DR
Vermont	32,833	8,350	25.4	24,363	74.2	120	0.4	16,013	NR
Virginia	38,924	26,854	69.0	12,070	31.0	—	0.0	14,784	DR
Totals	1,148,018	642,553	56.0	500,897	43.6	4,568	0.4	141,656	DR

1. For breakdown of "Other" vote, see minor candidate vote totals at the end of this chapter.

2. Figures from Svend Petersen, *A Statistical History of the American Presidential Elections* (Westport, Conn.: Greenwood Press, 1981), 20.

1832 Presidential Election

STATE	TOTAL VOTE	ANDREW JACKSON (Democrat)		HENRY CLAY (National Republican)		WILLIAM WIRT (Anti-Mason)		OTHER[1]		PLURALITY	
		Votes	%	Votes	%	Votes	%	Votes	%		
Alabama	14,291	14,286	100.0	5	0.0	—	0.0	—	0.0	14,281	D
Connecticut	32,833	11,269	34.3	18,155	55.3	3,409	10.4	—	0.0	6,886	NR
Delaware	8,386	4,110	49.0	4,276	51.0	—	0.0	—	0.0	166	NR
Georgia[2]	20,750	20,750	100.0	—	0.0	—	0.0	—	0.0	20,750	D
Illinois	21,481	14,609	68.0	6,745	31.4	97	0.5	30	0.1	7,864	D
Indiana	57,152	31,652	55.4	25,473	44.6	27	0.0	—	0.0	6,179	D
Kentucky	79,741	36,292	45.5	43,449	54.5	—	0.0	—	0.0	7,157	NR
Louisiana	6,337	3,908	61.7	2,429	38.3	—	0.0	—	0.0	1,479	D
Maine	62,153	33,978	54.7	27,331	44.0	844	1.4	—	0.0	6,647	D
Maryland	38,316	19,156	50.0	19,160	50.0	—	0.0	—	0.0	4	NR
Massachusetts	67,619	13,933	20.6	31,963	47.3	14,692	21.7	7,031	10.4	17,271	NR
Mississippi	5,750	5,750	100.0	—	0.0	—	0.0	—	0.0	5,750	D
Missouri[2]	5,192	5,192	100.0	—	0.0	—	0.0	—	0.0	5,192	D
New Hampshire	43,793	24,855	56.8	18,938	43.2	—	0.0	—	0.0	5,917	D
New Jersey	47,760	23,826	49.9	23,466	49.1	468	1.0	—	0.0	360	D
New York	323,393	168,497	52.1	154,896	47.9	—	0.0	—	0.0	13,601	D
North Carolina	29,799	25,261	84.8	4,538	15.2	—	0.0	—	0.0	20,723	D
Ohio	158,350	81,246	51.3	76,566	48.4	538	0.3	—	0.0	4,680	D
Pennsylvania	157,679	90,973	57.7	—	0.0	66,706	42.3	—	0.0	24,267	D
Rhode Island	5,747	2,051	35.7	2,871	50.0	819	14.3	6	0.1	820	NR
Tennessee	29,425	28,078	95.4	1,347	4.6	—	0.0	—	0.0	26,731	D
Vermont	32,344	7,865	24.3	11,161	34.5	13,112	40.5	206	0.6	1,951	AM
Virginia	45,682	34,243	75.0	11,436	25.0	3	0.0	—	0.0	22,807	D
Totals	1,293,973	701,780	54.2	484,205	37.4	100,715	7.8	7,273	0.6	217,575	D

1. For breakdown of "Other" vote, see minor candidate vote totals at the end of this chapter.
2. Figures from Svend Petersen, *A Statistical History of the American Presidential Elections* (Westport, Conn.: Greenwood Press, 1981), 21.

1836 Presidential Election

STATE	TOTAL VOTE	MARTIN VAN BUREN (Democrat)		WILLIAM H. HARRISON (Whig)		HUGH L. WHITE (Whig)		DANIEL WEBSTER (Whig)		OTHER[1]		PLURALITY[2]	
		Votes	%	Votes	%	Votes	%	Votes	%	Votes	%		
Alabama	37,296	20,638	55.3	—	0.0	16,658	44.7	—	0.0	—	0.0	3,980	MBV
Arkansas	3,714	2,380	64.1	—	0.0	1,334	35.9	—	0.0	—	0.0	1,046	MBV
Connecticut	38,093	19,294	50.6	18,799	49.4	—	0.0	—	0.0	—	0.0	495	MBV
Delaware	8,895	4,154	46.7	4,736	53.2	—	0.0	—	0.0	5	0.1	582	WHH
Georgia	47,259	22,778	48.2	—	0.0	24,481	51.8	—	0.0	—	0.0	1,703	HLW
Illinois	33,589	18,369	54.7	15,220	45.3	—	0.0	—	0.0	—	0.0	3,149	MBV
Indiana	74,423	33,084	44.5	41,339	55.5	—	0.0	—	0.0	—	0.0	8,255	WHH
Kentucky	70,090	33,229	47.4	36,861	52.6	—	0.0	—	0.0	—	0.0	3,632	WHH
Louisiana	7,425	3,842	51.7	—	0.0	3,583	48.3	—	0.0	—	0.0	259	MBV
Maine	38,740	22,825	58.9	14,803	38.2	—	0.0	—	0.0	1,112	2.9	8,022	MBV
Maryland	48,119	22,267	46.3	25,852	53.7	—	0.0	—	0.0	—	0.0	3,585	WHH
Massachusetts	74,732	33,486	44.8	—	0.0	—	0.0	41,201	55.1	45	0.1	33,486	DW
Michigan	12,052	6,507	54.0	5,545	46.0	—	0.0	—	0.0	—	0.0	962	MBV
Mississippi	20,079	10,297	51.3	—	0.0	9,782	48.7	—	0.0	—	0.0	515	MBV
Missouri[3]	18,332	10,995	60.0	—	0.0	7,337	40.0	—	0.0	—	0.0	3,658	MBV
New Hampshire	24,925	18,697	75.0	6,228	25.0	—	0.0	—	0.0	—	0.0	12,469	MBV
New Jersey	51,729	25,592	49.5	26,137	50.5	—	0.0	—	0.0	—	0.0	545	WHH
New York	305,343	166,795	54.6	138,548	45.4	—	0.0	—	0.0	—	0.0	28,247	MBV
North Carolina	50,153	26,631	53.1	—	0.0	23,521	46.9	—	0.0	1	0.0	3,110	MBV
Ohio	202,931	97,122	47.9	105,809	52.1	—	0.0	—	0.0	—	0.0	8,687	WHH
Pennsylvania	178,701	91,466	51.2	87,235	48.8	—	0.0	—	0.0	—	0.0	4,231	MBV
Rhode Island	5,673	2,962	52.2	2,710	47.8	—	0.0	—	0.0	1	0.0	252	MBV
Tennessee	62,197	26,170	42.1	—	0.0	36,027	57.9	—	0.0	—	0.0	9,857	HLW
Vermont	35,099	14,040	40.0	20,994	59.8	—	0.0	—	0.0	65	0.2	6,954	WHH
Virginia	53,945	30,556	56.6	—	0.0	23,384	43.3	—	0.0	5	0.0	7,172	MBV
Totals	1,503,534	764,176	50.8	550,816	36.6	146,107	9.7	41,201	2.7	1,234	0.1	213,360	MBV

1. For breakdown of "Other" vote, see minor candidate vote totals at the end of this chapter.

2. For the 1836 plurality winner, the designations are MVB (Martin Van Buren), WHH (William Henry Harrison), HLW (Hugh L. White), and DW (Daniel Webster).

3. Figures from Svend Petersen, *A Statistical History of the American Presidential Elections* (Westport, Conn.: Greenwood Press, 1981), 22.

1840 Presidential Election

STATE	TOTAL VOTE	WILLIAM H. HARRISON (Whig)		MARTIN VAN BUREN (Democrat)		JAMES G. BIRNEY (Liberty)		OTHER[1]		PLURALITY	
		Votes	%	Votes	%	Votes	%	Votes	%		
Alabama	62,511	28,515	45.6	33,996	54.4	—	0.0	—	0.0	5,481	D
Arkansas	11,839	5,160	43.6	6,679	56.4	—	0.0	—	0.0	1,519	D
Connecticut	56,879	31,598	55.6	25,281	44.4	—	0.0	—	0.0	6,317	W
Delaware	10,852	5,967	55.0	4,872	44.9	—	0.0	13	0.1	1,095	W
Georgia	72,322	40,339	55.8	31,983	44.2	—	0.0	—	0.0	8,356	W
Illinois	93,175	45,574	48.9	47,441	50.9	160	0.2	—	0.0	1,867	D
Indiana	117,605	65,280	55.5	51,696	44.0	30	0.0	599	0.5	13,584	W
Kentucky	91,104	58,488	64.2	32,616	35.8	—	0.0	—	0.0	25,872	W
Louisiana	18,912	11,296	59.7	7,616	40.3	—	0.0	—	0.0	3,680	W
Maine	92,802	46,612	50.2	46,190	49.8	—	0.0	—	0.0	422	W
Maryland	62,280	33,528	53.8	28,752	46.2	—	0.0	—	0.0	4,776	W
Massachusetts	126,825	72,852	57.4	52,355	41.3	1,618	1.3	—	0.0	20,497	W
Michigan	44,029	22,933	52.1	21,096	47.9	—	0.0	—	0.0	1,837	W
Mississippi	36,525	19,515	53.4	17,010	46.6	—	0.0	—	0.0	2,505	W
Missouri	52,923	22,954	43.4	29,969	56.6	—	0.0	—	0.0	7,015	D
New Hampshire	59,956	26,310	43.9	32,774	54.7	872	1.5	—	0.0	6,464	D
New Jersey	64,454	33,351	51.7	31,034	48.1	69	0.1	—	0.0	2,317	W
New York	441,543	226,001	51.2	212,733	48.2	2,809	0.6	—	0.0	13,268	W
North Carolina	80,735	46,567	57.7	34,168	42.3	—	0.0	—	0.0	12,399	W
Ohio	272,890	148,043	54.3	123,944	45.4	903	0.3	—	0.0	24,099	W
Pennsylvania	287,695	144,023	50.1	143,672	49.9	—	0.0	—	0.0	351	W
Rhode Island	8,631	5,213	60.4	3,263	37.8	19	0.2	136	1.6	1,950	W
Tennessee	108,145	60,194	55.7	47,951	44.3	—	0.0	—	0.0	12,243	W
Vermont	50,782	32,440	63.9	18,006	35.5	317	0.6	19	0.0	14,434	W
Virginia	86,394	42,637	49.4	43,757	50.6	—	0.0	—	0.0	1,120	D
Totals	2,411,808	1,275,390	52.9	1,128,854	46.8	6,797	0.3	767	0.0	146,536	W

1. For breakdown of "Other" vote, see minor candidate vote totals at the end of this chapter.

1844 Presidential Election

STATE	TOTAL VOTE	JAMES K. POLK (Democrat)		HENRY CLAY (Whig)		JAMES G. BIRNEY (Liberty)		OTHER [1]		PLURALITY	
		Votes	%	Votes	%	Votes	%	Votes	%		
Alabama	63,403	37,401	59.0	26,002	41.0	—	0.0	—	0.0	11,399	D
Arkansas	15,150	9,546	63.0	5,604	37.0	—	0.0	—	0.0	3,942	D
Connecticut	64,616	29,841	46.2	32,832	50.8	1,943	3.0	—	0.0	2,991	W
Delaware	12,247	5,970	48.7	6,271	51.2	—	0.0	6	0.0	301	W
Georgia	86,247	44,147	51.2	42,100	48.8	—	0.0	—	0.0	2,047	D
Illinois	109,057	58,795	53.9	45,854	42.0	3,469	3.2	939	0.9	12,941	D
Indiana	140,157	70,183	50.1	67,866	48.4	2,108	1.5	—	0.0	2,317	D
Kentucky	113,237	51,988	45.9	61,249	54.1	—	0.0	—	0.0	9,261	W
Louisiana	26,865	13,782	51.3	13,083	48.7	—	0.0	—	0.0	699	D
Maine	84,933	45,719	53.8	34,378	40.5	4,836	5.7	—	0.0	11,341	D
Maryland	68,690	32,706	47.6	35,984	52.4	—	0.0	—	0.0	3,278	W
Massachusetts	132,037	53,039	40.2	67,062	50.8	10,830	8.2	1,106	0.8	14,023	W
Michigan	55,560	27,737	49.9	24,185	43.5	3,638	6.5	—	0.0	3,552	D
Mississippi	45,004	25,846	57.4	19,158	42.6	—	0.0	—	0.0	6,688	D
Missouri	72,522	41,322	57.0	31,200	43.0	—	0.0	—	0.0	10,122	D
New Hampshire	49,187	27,160	55.2	17,866	36.3	4,161	8.5	—	0.0	9,294	D
New Jersey	75,944	37,495	49.4	38,318	50.5	131	0.2	—	0.0	823	W
New York	485,882	237,588	48.9	232,482	47.8	15,812	3.3	—	0.0	5,106	D
North Carolina	82,521	39,287	47.6	43,232	52.4	—	0.0	2	0.0	3,945	W
Ohio	312,300	149,127	47.8	155,091	49.7	8,082	2.6	—	0.0	5,964	W
Pennsylvania	331,645	167,311	50.4	161,195	48.6	3,139	0.9	—	0.0	6,116	D
Rhode Island	12,194	4,867	39.9	7,322	60.0	—	0.0	5	0.0	2,455	W
Tennessee	119,957	59,917	49.9	60,040	50.1	—	0.0	—	0.0	123	W
Vermont	48,765	18,041	37.0	26,770	54.9	3,954	8.1	—	0.0	8,729	W
Virginia	95,539	50,679	53.0	44,860	47.0	—	0.0	—	0.0	5,819	D
Totals	2,703,659	1,339,494	49.5	1,300,004	48.1	62,103	2.3	2,058	0.1	39,490	D

1. For breakdown of "Other" vote, see minor candidate vote totals at the end of this chapter.

1848 Presidential Election

STATE	TOTAL VOTE	ZACHARY TAYLOR (Whig)		LEWIS CASS (Democrat)		MARTIN VAN BUREN (Free Soil)		OTHER[1]		PLURALITY	
		Votes	%	Votes	%	Votes	%	Votes	%		
Alabama	61,659	30,482	49.4	31,173	50.6	—	0.0	4	0.0	691	D
Arkansas	16,888	7,587	44.9	9,301	55.1	—	0.0	—	0.0	1,714	D
Connecticut	62,398	30,318	48.6	27,051	43.4	5,005	8.0	24	0.0	3,267	W
Delaware	12,432	6,440	51.8	5,910	47.5	82	0.7	—	0.0	530	W
Florida	7,203	4,120	57.2	3,083	42.8	—	0.0	—	0.0	1,037	W
Georgia	92,317	47,532	51.5	44,785	48.5	—	0.0	—	0.0	2,747	W
Illinois	124,596	52,853	42.4	55,952	44.9	15,702	12.6	89	0.1	3,099	D
Indiana	152,394	69,668	45.7	74,695	49.0	8,031	5.3	—	0.0	5,027	D
Iowa	22,271	9,930	44.6	11,238	50.5	1,103	5.0	—	0.0	1,308	D
Kentucky	116,865	67,145	57.5	49,720	42.5	—	0.0	—	0.0	17,425	W
Louisiana	33,866	18,487	54.6	15,379	45.4	—	0.0	—	0.0	3,108	W
Maine	87,625	35,273	40.3	40,195	45.9	12,157	13.9	—	0.0	4,922	D
Maryland	72,359	37,702	52.1	34,528	47.7	129	0.2	—	0.0	3,174	W
Massachusetts	134,748	61,072	45.3	35,281	26.2	38,333	28.4	62	0.0	22,739	W
Michigan	65,082	23,947	36.8	30,742	47.2	10,393	16.0	—	0.0	6,795	D
Mississippi	52,456	25,911	49.4	26,545	50.6	—	0.0	—	0.0	634	D
Missouri	72,748	32,671	44.9	40,077	55.1	—	0.0	—	0.0	7,406	D
New Hampshire	50,104	14,781	29.5	27,753	55.4	7,560	15.1	—	0.0	12,982	D
New Jersey	77,745	40,015	51.5	36,901	47.5	829	1.1	—	0.0	3,114	W
New York	455,944	218,583	47.9	114,319	25.1	120,497	26.4	2,545	0.6	98,086	W
North Carolina	79,826	44,054	55.2	35,772	44.8	—	0.0	—	0.0	8,282	W
Ohio	328,987	138,656	42.1	154,782	47.0	35,523	10.8	26	0.0	16,126	D
Pennsylvania	369,092	185,730	50.3	172,186	46.7	11,176	3.0	—	0.0	13,544	W
Rhode Island	11,049	6,705	60.7	3,613	32.7	726	6.6	5	0.0	3,092	W
Tennessee	122,463	64,321	52.5	58,142	47.5	—	0.0	—	0.0	6,179	W
Texas	17,000	5,281	31.1	11,644	68.5	—	0.0	75	0.4	6,363	D
Vermont	47,897	23,117	48.3	10,943	22.8	13,837	28.9	—	0.0	9,280	W
Virginia	92,004	45,265	49.2	46,739	50.8	—	0.0	—	0.0	1,474	D
Wisconsin	39,166	13,747	35.1	15,001	38.3	10,418	26.6	—	0.0	1,254	D
Totals	2,879,184	1,361,393	47.3	1,223,460	42.5	291,501	10.1	2,830	0.1	137,933	W

1. For breakdown of "Other" vote, see minor candidate vote totals at the end of this chapter.

1852 Presidential Election

STATE	TOTAL VOTE	FRANKLIN PIERCE (Democrat)		WINFIELD SCOTT (Whig)		JOHN P. HALE (Free Soil)		OTHER[1]		PLURALITY	
		Votes	%	Votes	%	Votes	%	Votes	%		
Alabama	44,147	26,881	60.9	15,061	34.1	—	0.0	2,205	5.0	11,820	D
Arkansas	19,577	12,173	62.2	7,404	37.8	—	0.0	—	0.0	4,769	D
California	76,810	40,721	53.0	35,972	46.8	61	0.1	56	0.1	4,749	D
Connecticut	66,781	33,249	49.8	30,359	45.5	3,161	4.7	12	0.0	2,890	D
Delaware	12,673	6,318	49.9	6,293	49.7	62	0.5	—	0.0	25	D
Florida	7,193	4,318	60.0	2,875	40.0	—	0.0	—	0.0	1,443	D
Georgia[2]	62,626	40,516	64.7	16,660	26.6	—	0.0	5,450	8.7	23,856	D
Illinois	154,974	80,378	51.9	64,733	41.8	9,863	6.4	—	0.0	15,645	D
Indiana	183,176	95,340	52.0	80,907	44.2	6,929	3.8	—	0.0	14,433	D
Iowa	35,364	17,763	50.2	15,856	44.8	1,606	4.5	139	0.4	1,907	D
Kentucky	111,643	53,949	48.3	57,428	51.4	266	0.2	—	0.0	3,479	W
Louisiana	35,902	18,647	51.9	17,255	48.1	—	0.0	—	0.0	1,392	D
Maine	82,182	41,609	50.6	32,543	39.6	8,030	9.8	—	0.0	9,066	D
Maryland	75,120	40,022	53.3	35,077	46.7	21	0.0	—	0.0	4,945	D
Massachusetts	127,103	44,569	35.1	52,683	41.4	28,023	22.0	1,828	1.4	8,114	W
Michigan	82,939	41,842	50.4	33,860	40.8	7,237	8.7	—	0.0	7,982	D
Mississippi	44,454	26,896	60.5	17,558	39.5	—	0.0	—	0.0	9,338	D
Missouri	68,801	38,817	56.4	29,984	43.6	—	0.0	—	0.0	8,833	D
New Hampshire	50,535	28,503	56.4	15,486	30.6	6,546	13.0	—	0.0	13,017	D
New Jersey	83,926	44,301	52.8	38,551	45.9	336	0.4	738	0.9	5,750	D
New York	522,294	262,083	50.2	234,882	45.0	25,329	4.8	—	0.0	27,201	D
North Carolina	78,891	39,788	50.4	39,043	49.5	—	0.0	60	0.1	745	D
Ohio	352,903	169,193	47.9	152,577	43.2	31,133	8.8	—	0.0	16,616	D
Pennsylvania	387,920	198,568	51.2	179,182	46.2	8,500	2.2	1,670	0.4	19,386	D
Rhode Island	17,005	8,735	51.4	7,626	44.8	644	3.8	—	0.0	1,109	D
Tennessee	115,486	56,900	49.3	58,586	50.7	—	0.0	—	0.0	1,686	W
Texas	20,223	14,857	73.5	5,356	26.5	—	0.0	10	0.0	9,501	D
Vermont	43,838	13,044	29.8	22,173	50.6	8,621	19.7	—	0.0	9,129	W
Virginia	132,604	73,872	55.7	58,732	44.3	—	0.0	—	0.0	15,140	D
Wisconsin	64,740	33,658	52.0	22,240	34.4	8,842	13.7	—	0.0	11,418	D
Totals	3,161,830	1,607,510	50.8	1,386,942	43.9	155,210	4.9	12,168	0.4	220,568	D

1. For breakdown of "Other" vote, see minor candidate vote totals at the end of this chapter.

2. Figures from Svend Petersen, *A Statistical History of the American Presidential Elections* (Westport, Conn.: Greenwood Press, 1981), 31.

1856 Presidential Election

STATE	TOTAL VOTE	JAMES BUCHANAN (Democrat)		JOHN C. FREMONT (Republican)		MILLARD FILLMORE (Whig-American)		OTHER [1]		PLURALITY	
		Votes	%	Votes	%	Votes	%	Votes	%		
Alabama	75,291	46,739	62.1	—	0.0	28,552	37.9	—	0.0	18,187	D
Arkansas	32,642	21,910	67.1	—	0.0	10,732	32.9	—	0.0	11,178	D
California	110,255	53,342	48.4	20,704	18.8	36,195	32.8	14	0.0	17,147	D
Connecticut	80,360	35,028	43.6	42,717	53.2	2,615	3.3	—	0.0	7,689	R
Delaware	14,598	8,004	54.8	310	2.1	6,275	43.0	9	0.1	1,729	D
Florida	11,191	6,358	56.8	—	0.0	4,833	43.2	—	0.0	1,525	D
Georgia	99,020	56,581	57.1	—	0.0	42,439	42.9	—	0.0	14,142	D
Illinois	239,334	105,528	44.1	96,275	40.2	37,531	15.7	—	0.0	9,253	D
Indiana	235,401	118,670	50.4	94,375	40.1	22,356	9.5	—	0.0	24,295	D
Iowa	92,310	37,568	40.7	45,073	48.8	9,669	10.5	—	0.0	7,505	R
Kentucky	142,058	74,642	52.5	—	0.0	67,416	47.5	—	0.0	7,226	D
Louisiana	42,873	22,164	51.7	—	0.0	20,709	48.3	—	0.0	1,455	D
Maine	109,689	39,140	35.7	67,279	61.3	3,270	3.0	—	0.0	28,139	R
Maryland	86,860	39,123	45.0	285	0.3	47,452	54.6	—	0.0	8,329	WA
Massachusetts	170,048	39,244	23.1	108,172	63.6	19,626	11.5	3,006	1.8	68,928	R
Michigan	125,558	52,136	41.5	71,762	57.2	1,660	1.3	—	0.0	19,626	R
Mississippi	59,647	35,456	59.4	—	0.0	24,191	40.6	—	0.0	11,265	D
Missouri	106,486	57,964	54.4	—	0.0	48,522	45.6	—	0.0	9,442	D
New Hampshire	69,774	31,891	45.7	37,473	53.7	410	0.6	—	0.0	5,582	R
New Jersey	99,396	46,943	47.2	28,338	28.5	24,115	24.3	—	0.0	18,605	D
New York	596,486	195,878	32.8	276,004	46.3	124,604	20.9	—	0.0	80,126	R
North Carolina	84,963	48,243	56.8	—	0.0	36,720	43.2	—	0.0	11,523	D
Ohio	386,640	170,874	44.2	187,497	48.5	28,121	7.3	148	0.0	16,623	R
Pennsylvania	460,937	230,772	50.1	147,963	32.1	82,202	17.8	—	0.0	82,809	D
Rhode Island	19,822	6,680	33.7	11,467	57.8	1,675	8.5	—	0.0	4,787	R
Tennessee	133,582	69,704	52.2	—	0.0	63,878	47.8	—	0.0	5,826	D
Texas	48,005	31,995	66.6	—	0.0	16,010	33.4	—	0.0	15,985	D
Vermont	50,675	10,569	20.9	39,561	78.1	545	1.1	—	0.0	28,992	R
Virginia	150,233	90,083	60.0	—	0.0	60,150	40.0	—	0.0	29,933	D
Wisconsin	120,513	52,843	43.8	67,090	55.7	580	0.5	—	0.0	14,247	R
Totals	4,054,647	1,836,072	45.3	1,342,345	33.1	373,053	21.5	3,177	0.1	493,727	D

1. For breakdown of "Other" vote, see minor candidate vote totals at the end of this chapter.

1860 Presidential Election

STATE	TOTAL VOTE	ABRAHAM LINCOLN (Republican)		STEPHEN A. DOUGLAS (Democrat)		JOHN C. BRECKINRIDGE (Southern Democrat)		JOHN BELL (Constitutional Union)		OTHER[1]		PLURALITY	
		Votes	%	Votes	%	Votes	%	Votes	%	Votes	%		
Alabama	90,122	—	0.0	13,618	15.1	48,669	54.0	27,835	30.9	—	0.0	20,834	SD
Arkansas	54,152	—	0.0	5,357	9.9	28,732	53.1	20,063	37.0	—	0.0	8,669	SD
California	119,827	38,733	32.3	37,999	31.7	33,969	28.3	9,111	7.6	15	0.0	734	R
Connecticut	74,819	43,488	58.1	15,431	20.6	14,372	19.2	1,528	2.0	—	0.0	28,057	R
Delaware	16,115	3,822	23.7	1,066	6.6	7,339	45.5	3,888	24.1	—	0.0	3,451	SD
Florida	13,301	—	0.0	223	1.7	8,277	62.2	4,801	36.1	—	0.0	3,476	SD
Georgia	106,717	—	0.0	11,581	10.9	52,176	48.9	42,960	40.3	—	0.0	9,216	SD
Illinois	339,666	172,171	50.7	160,215	47.2	2,331	0.7	4,914	1.4	35	0.0	11,956	R
Indiana	272,143	139,033	51.1	115,509	42.4	12,295	4.5	5,306	1.9	—	0.0	23,524	R
Iowa	128,739	70,302	54.6	55,639	43.2	1,035	0.8	1,763	1.4	—	0.0	14,663	R
Kentucky[2]	146,216	1,364	0.9	25,651	17.5	53,143	36.3	66,058	45.2	—	0.0	12,915	CU
Louisiana	50,510	—	0.0	7,625	15.1	22,681	44.9	20,204	40.0	—	0.0	2,477	SD
Maine	100,918	62,811	62.2	29,693	29.4	6,368	6.3	2,046	2.0	—	0.0	33,118	R
Maryland	92,502	2,294	2.5	5,966	6.4	42,482	45.9	41,760	45.1	—	0.0	722	SD
Massachusetts	169,876	106,684	62.8	34,370	20.2	6,163	3.6	22,331	13.1	328	0.2	72,314	R
Michigan	154,758	88,481	57.2	65,057	42.0	805	0.5	415	0.3	—	0.0	23,424	R
Minnesota	34,804	22,069	63.4	11,920	34.2	748	2.1	50	0.1	17	0.0	10,149	R
Mississippi	69,095	—	0.0	3,282	4.7	40,768	59.0	25,045	36.2	—	0.0	15,723	SD
Missouri	165,563	17,028	10.3	58,801	35.5	31,362	18.9	58,372	35.3	—	0.0	429	D
New Hampshire	65,943	37,519	56.9	25,887	39.3	2,125	3.2	412	0.6	—	0.0	11,632	R
New Jersey[2]	121,215	58,346	48.1	62,869	51.9	—	0.0	—	0.0	—	0.0	4,523	D
New York	675,156	362,646	53.7	312,510	46.3	—	0.0	—	0.0	—	0.0	50,136	R
North Carolina	96,712	—	0.0	2,737	2.8	48,846	50.5	45,129	46.7	—	0.0	3,717	SD
Ohio	442,866	231,709	52.3	187,421	42.3	11,406	2.6	12,194	2.8	136	0.0	44,288	R
Oregon	14,758	5,329	36.1	4,136	28.0	5,075	34.4	218	1.5	—	0.0	254	R
Pennsylvania	476,442	268,030	56.3	16,765	3.5	178,871	37.5	12,776	2.7	—	0.0	89,159	R
Rhode Island	19,951	12,244	61.4	7,707	38.6	—	0.0	—	0.0	—	0.0	4,537	R
Tennessee	146,106	—	0.0	11,281	7.7	65,097	44.6	69,728	47.7	—	0.0	4,631	CU
Texas	62,855	—	0.0	18	0.0	47,454	75.5	15,383	24.5	—	0.0	32,071	SD
Vermont	44,644	33,808	75.7	8,649	19.4	218	0.5	1,969	4.4	—	0.0	25,159	R
Virginia	166,891	1,887	1.1	16,198	9.7	74,325	44.5	74,481	44.6	—	0.0	156	CU
Wisconsin	152,179	86,110	56.6	65,021	42.7	887	0.6	161	0.1	—	0.0	21,089	R
Totals	4,685,561	1,865,908	39.9	1,380,202	29.5	848,019	18.1	590,901	12.6	531	0.0	485,706	R

1. For breakdown of "Other" vote, see minor candidate vote totals at the end of this chapter.

2. Figures from Svend Petersen, *A Statistical History of the American Presidential Elections* (Westport, Conn.: Greenwood Press, 1981), 37.

1864 Presidential Election

STATE[1]	TOTAL VOTE	ABRAHAM LINCOLN (Republican)		GEORGE B. McCLELLAN (Democrat)		OTHER[2]		PLURALITY	
		Votes	%	Votes	%	Votes	%		
California	105,890	62,053	58.6	43,837	41.4	—	0.0	18,216	R
Connecticut	86,958	44,673	51.4	42,235	48.6	—	0.0	2,388	R
Delaware	16,922	8,155	48.2	8,767	51.8	—	0.0	612	D
Illinois	348,236	189,512	54.4	158,724	45.6	—	0.0	30,788	R
Indiana	280,117	149,887	53.5	130,230	46.5	—	0.0	19,657	R
Iowa[3]	138,025	88,500	64.1	49,525	35.9	—	0.0	38,975	R
Kansas	21,580	17,089	79.2	3,836	17.8	655	3.0	13,253	R
Kentucky	92,088	27,787	30.2	64,301	69.8	—	0.0	36,514	D
Maine[4]	115,099	68,104	59.2	46,995	40.8	—	0.0	21,109	R
Maryland	72,892	40,153	55.1	32,739	44.9	—	0.0	7,414	R
Massachusetts	175,493	126,742	72.2	48,745	27.8	6	0.0	77,997	R
Michigan[5]	160,023	88,551	55.3	71,472	44.7	—	0.0	17,079	R
Minnesota	42,433	25,031	59.0	17,376	40.9	26	0.1	7,655	R
Missouri	104,346	72,750	69.7	31,596	30.3	—	0.0	41,154	R
Nevada	16,420	9,826	59.8	6,594	40.2	—	0.0	3,232	R
New Hampshire	69,630	36,596	52.6	33,034	47.4	—	0.0	3,562	R
New Jersey	128,744	60,724	47.2	68,020	52.8	—	0.0	7,296	D
New York	730,721	368,735	50.5	361,986	49.5	—	0.0	6,749	R
Ohio	471,283	265,674	56.4	205,609	43.6	—	0.0	60,065	R
Oregon	18,350	9,888	53.9	8,457	46.1	5	0.0	1,431	R
Pennsylvania[6]	572,707	296,391	51.7	276,316	48.3	—	0.0	20,075	R
Rhode Island	23,067	14,349	62.2	8,718	37.8	—	0.0	5,631	R
Vermont	55,740	42,419	76.1	13,321	23.9	—	0.0	29,098	R
West Virginia	34,877	23,799	68.2	11,073	31.8	—	0.0	12,721	R
Wisconsin	149,342	83,458	55.9	65,884	44.1	—	0.0	17,574	R
Totals	4,030,291	2,220,846	55.1	1,809,445	44.9	692	0.0	411,401	R

1. Eleven Confederate states did not participate in the election because of the Civil War.

2. For breakdown of "Other" vote, see minor candidate vote totals at the end of this chapter.

3. Figures from *Iowa Official Register, 1913–1914*.

4. Figures from Maine's Executive Council minutes.

5. Figures from *Michigan Manual 1913*, p. 689.

6. Figures from Pennsylvania's *Manual*, 1865.

1868 Presidential Election

STATE[1]	TOTAL VOTE	ULYSSES S. GRANT (Republican)		HORATIO SEYMOUR (Democrat)		OTHER[2]		PLURALITY	
		Votes	%	Votes	%	Votes	%		
Alabama	149,594	76,667	51.3	72,921	48.7	6	0.0	3,746	R
Arkansas	41,190	22,112	53.7	19,078	46.3	—	0.0	3,034	R
California	108,656	54,588	50.2	54,068	49.8	—	0.0	520	R
Connecticut	98,570	50,789	51.5	47,781	48.5	—	0.0	3,008	R
Delaware	18,571	7,614	41.0	10,957	59.0	—	0.0	3,343	D
Georgia	159,816	57,109	35.7	102,707	64.3	—	0.0	45,598	D
Illinois	449,420	250,304	55.7	199,116	44.3	—	0.0	51,188	R
Indiana	343,528	176,548	51.4	166,980	48.6	—	0.0	9,568	R
Iowa	194,439	120,399	61.9	74,040	38.1	—	0.0	46,359	R
Kansas	43,630	30,027	68.8	13,600	31.2	3	0.0	16,427	R
Kentucky	155,455	39,566	25.5	115,889	74.5	—	0.0	76,323	D
Louisiana	113,488	33,263	29.3	80,225	70.7	—	0.0	46,962	D
Maine	112,962	70,502	62.4	42,460	37.6	—	0.0	28,042	R
Maryland	92,795	30,438	32.8	62,357	67.2	—	0.0	31,919	D
Massachusetts	195,508	136,379	69.8	59,103	30.2	26	0.0	77,276	R
Michigan	225,632	128,563	57.0	97,069	43.0	—	0.0	31,494	R
Minnesota	71,620	43,545	60.8	28,075	39.2	—	0.0	15,470	R
Missouri	152,488	86,860	57.0	65,628	43.0	—	0.0	21,232	R
Nebraska	15,291	9,772	63.9	5,519	36.1	—	0.0	4,253	R
Nevada	11,689	6,474	55.4	5,215	44.6	—	0.0	1,259	R
New Hampshire	68,304	37,718	55.2	30,575	44.8	11	0.0	7,143	R
New Jersey	163,133	80,132	49.1	83,001	50.9	—	0.0	2,869	D
New York	849,771	419,888	49.4	429,883	50.6	—	0.0	9,995	D
North Carolina	181,498	96,939	53.4	84,559	46.6	—	0.0	12,380	R
Ohio	518,665	280,159	54.0	238,506	46.0	—	0.0	41,653	R
Oregon	22,086	10,961	49.6	11,125	50.4	—	0.0	164	D
Pennsylvania	655,662	342,280	52.2	313,382	47.8	—	0.0	28,898	R
Rhode Island	19,511	13,017	66.7	6,494	33.3	—	0.0	6,523	R
South Carolina	107,538	62,301	57.9	45,237	42.1	—	0.0	17,064	R
Tennessee	82,757	56,628	68.4	26,129	31.6	—	0.0	30,499	R
Vermont	56,224	44,173	78.6	12,051	21.4	—	0.0	32,122	R
West Virginia	49,321	29,015	58.8	20,306	41.2	—	0.0	8,709	R
Wisconsin	193,628	108,920	56.3	84,708	43.7	—	0.0	24,212	R
Totals	5,722,440	3,013,650	52.7	2,708,744	47.3	46		304,906	R

1. Mississippi, Texas, and Virginia did not participate in the election due to Reconstruction. In Florida the state legislature cast the electoral vote.

2. For breakdown of "Other" vote, see minor candidate vote totals at the end of this chapter.

1872 Presidential Election

STATE	TOTAL VOTE	ULYSSES S. GRANT (Republican)		HORACE GREELEY (Democrat, Liberal Republican)		CHARLES O'CONOR (Straight Out Democrat)		OTHER [1]		PLURALITY	
		Votes	%	Votes	%	Votes	%	Votes	%		
Alabama	169,716	90,272	53.2	79,444	46.8	—	0.0	—	0.0	10,828	R
Arkansas	79,300	41,373	52.2	37,927	47.8	—	0.0	—	0.0	3,446	R
California	95,785	54,007	56.4	40,717	42.5	1,061	1.1	—	0.0	13,290	R
Connecticut	95,992	50,307	52.4	45,685	47.6	—	0.0	—	0.0	4,622	R
Delaware	21,822	11,129	51.0	10,205	46.8	488	2.2	—	0.0	924	R
Florida	33,190	17,763	53.5	15,427	46.5	—	0.0	—	0.0	2,336	R
Georgia	138,906	62,550	45.0	76,356	55.0	—	0.0	—	0.0	13,806	D
Illinois	429,971	241,936	56.3	184,884	43.0	3,151	0.7	—	0.0	57,052	R
Indiana	349,779	186,147	53.2	163,632	46.8	—	0.0	—	0.0	22,515	R
Iowa	216,365	131,566	60.8	71,189	32.9	2,221	1.0	11,389	5.3	60,377	R
Kansas	100,512	66,805	66.5	32,970	32.8	156	0.2	581	0.6	33,835	R
Kentucky	191,552	88,970	45.5	100,208	54.5	2,374	1.2	—	0.0	11,238	D
Louisiana	128,692	71,663	55.7	57,029	44.3	—	0.0	—	0.0	14,634	R
Maine	90,523	61,426	67.9	29,097	32.1	—	0.0	—	0.0	32,329	R
Maryland	134,447	66,760	49.7	67,687	50.3	—	0.0	—	0.0	927	D
Massachusetts	192,650	133,455	69.3	59,195	30.7	—	0.0	—	0.0	74,260	R
Michigan	221,569	138,768	62.6	78,651	35.5	2,879	1.3	1,271	0.6	60,117	R
Minnesota	91,339	56,040	61.4	35,131	38.5	—	0.0	168	0.2	20,909	R
Mississippi	129,457	82,175	63.5	47,282	36.5	—	0.0	—	0.0	34,893	R
Missouri	273,059	119,196	43.7	151,434	55.5	2,429	0.9	—	0.0	32,238	D
Nebraska	25,932	18,329	70.7	7,603	29.3	—	0.0	—	0.0	10,726	R
Nevada	14,649	8,413	57.4	6,236	42.6	—	0.0	—	0.0	2,177	R
New Hampshire	68,906	37,168	53.9	31,425	45.6	—	0.0	313	0.5	5,743	R
New Jersey[2]	168,467	91,666	54.5	76,801	45.5	—	0.0	—	0.0	14,865	R
New York	829,692	440,758	53.1	387,279	46.7	1,454	0.2	201	0.0	53,479	R
North Carolina	165,163	94,772	57.4	70,130	42.5	261	0.2	—	0.0	24,642	R
Ohio	529,435	281,852	53.2	244,320	46.1	1,163	0.2	2,100	0.4	37,532	R
Oregon	20,107	11,818	58.8	7,742	38.5	547	2.7	—	0.0	4,076	R
Pennsylvania	561,629	349,589	62.2	212,040	37.8	—	0.0	—	0.0	137,549	R
Rhode Island	18,994	13,665	71.9	5,329	28.1	—	0.0	—	0.0	8,336	R
South Carolina	95,452	72,290	75.7	22,699	23.8	204	0.2	259	0.3	49,591	R
Tennessee	179,046	85,655	47.8	93,391	52.2	—	0.0	—	0.0	7,736	D
Texas	115,700	47,910	41.4	67,675	58.5	115	0.1	—	0.0	19,765	D
Vermont	52,961	41,480	78.3	10,926	20.6	553	1.0	—	0.0	30,554	R
Virginia	185,195	93,463	50.5	91,647	49.5	85	0.0	—	0.0	1,816	R
West Virginia	62,467	32,320	51.7	29,532	47.3	615	1.0	—	0.0	2,788	R
Wisconsin	192,255	105,012	54.6	86,390	44.9	853	0.4	—	0.0	18,622	R
Totals	6,470,674	3,598,468	55.6	2,835,315	43.8	20,609	0.3	16,282	0.3	763,153	R

1. For breakdown of "Other" vote, see minor candidate vote totals at the end of this chapter.
2. Figures from New Jersey's *Manual, 1873*.

1876 Presidential Election

STATE	TOTAL VOTE	RUTHERFORD B. HAYES [1] (Republican)		SAMUEL J. TILDEN [1] (Democrat)		PETER COOPER (Greenback)		OTHER [2]		PLURALITY	
		Votes	%	Votes	%	Votes	%	Votes	%		
Alabama	171,699	68,708	40.0	102,989	60.0	—	0.0	2	0.0	34,281	D
Arkansas	96,946	38,649	39.9	58,086	59.9	211	0.2	—	0.0	19,437	D
California	155,784	79,258	50.9	76,460	49.1	47	0.0	19	0.0	2,798	R
Connecticut	122,134	59,033	48.3	61,927	50.7	774	0.6	400	0.3	2,894	D
Delaware	24,133	10,752	44.6	13,381	55.4	—	0.0	—	0.0	2,629	D
Florida	46,776	23,849	51.0	22,927	49.0	—	0.0	—	0.0	922	R
Georgia	180,690	50,533	28.0	130,157	72.0	—	0.0	—	0.0	79,624	D
Illinois	554,368	278,232	50.2	258,611	46.6	17,207	3.1	318	0.1	19,621	R
Indiana	430,020	206,971	48.1	213,516	49.7	9,533	2.2	—	0.0	6,545	D
Iowa	293,398	171,326	58.4	112,121	38.2	9,431	3.2	520	0.2	59,205	R
Kansas	124,134	78,324	63.1	37,902	30.5	7,770	6.3	138	0.1	40,422	R
Kentucky	259,614	97,156	37.4	159,696	61.5	1,944	0.7	818	0.3	62,540	D
Louisiana	145,823	75,315	51.6	70,508	48.4	—	0.0	—	0.0	4,807	R
Maine[3]	117,045	66,300	56.6	49,917	42.6	662	0.6	166	0.1	16,383	R
Maryland	163,759	71,980	44.0	91,779	56.0	—	0.0	—	0.0	19,799	D
Massachusetts	259,619	150,063	57.8	108,777	41.9	—	0.0	779	0.3	41,286	R
Michigan	318,426	166,901	52.4	141,665	44.5	9,023	2.8	837	0.3	25,236	R
Minnesota[4]	124,119	72,982	58.8	48,816	39.3	2,321	1.9	—	0.0	24,166	R
Mississippi	164,776	52,603	31.9	112,173	68.1	—	0.0	—	0.0	59,570	D
Missouri	350,610	145,027	41.4	202,086	57.6	3,497	1.0	—	0.0	57,059	D
Nebraska	49,258	31,915	64.8	17,343	35.2	—	0.0	—	0.0	14,572	R
Nevada	19,691	10,383	52.7	9,308	47.3	—	0.0	—	0.0	1,075	R
New Hampshire	80,143	41,540	51.8	38,510	48.1	—	0.0	93	0.1	3,030	R
New Jersey	220,193	103,517	47.0	115,962	52.7	714	0.3	—	0.0	12,445	D
New York	1,015,503	489,207	48.2	521,949	51.4	1,978	0.2	2,369	0.2	32,742	D
North Carolina	233,911	108,484	46.4	125,427	53.6	—	0.0	—	0.0	16,943	D
Ohio	658,650	330,698	50.2	323,182	49.1	3,058	0.5	1,712	0.3	7,516	R
Oregon	29,873	15,207	50.9	14,157	47.4	509	1.7	—	0.0	1,050	R
Pennsylvania	758,973	384,157	50.6	366,204	48.2	7,209	0.9	1,403	0.2	17,953	R
Rhode Island	26,499	15,787	59.6	10,712	40.4	—	0.0	—	0.0	5,075	R
South Carolina	182,683	91,786	50.2	90,897	49.8	—	0.0	—	0.0	889	R
Tennessee	222,743	89,566	40.2	133,177	59.8	—	0.0	—	0.0	43,611	D
Texas	151,431	45,013	29.7	106,372	70.2	—	0.0	46	0.0	61,359	D
Vermont	64,460	44,092	68.4	20,254	31.4	—	0.0	114	0.2	23,838	R
Virginia	236,288	95,518	40.4	140,770	59.6	—	0.0	—	0.0	45,252	D
West Virginia	99,647	41,997	42.1	56,546	56.7	1,104	1.1	—	0.0	14,549	D
Wisconsin[5]	257,799	130,668	50.7	123,927	48.1	1,509	0.6	1,695	0.7	6,741	R
Totals	8,411,618	4,033,497	48.0	4,288,191	51.0	78,501	0.9	11,429	0.1	254,694	D

1. Hayes won the election. For resolution of disputed 1876 election, see pp. 196–198.

2. For breakdown of "Other" vote, see minor candidate vote totals at the end of this chapter.

3. Figures from *Maine Register, 1945*.

4. Figures from *Minnesota Votes*.

5. Figures from *Wisconsin Blue Book 1997*, p. 677.

1880 Presidential Election

STATE	TOTAL VOTE	JAMES A. GARFIELD (Republican)		WINFIELD S. HANCOCK (Democrat)		JAMES B. WEAVER (Greenback)		OTHER[1]		PLURALITY	
		Votes	%	Votes	%	Votes	%	Votes	%		
Alabama	151,902	56,350	37.1	91,130	60.0	4,422	2.9	—	0.0	34,780	D
Arkansas[2]	108,870	42,436	39.0	60,775	55.9	4,116	3.8	1,543	1.4	18,339	D
California	164,218	80,282	48.9	80,426	49.0	3,381	2.1	129	0.1	144	D
Colorado	53,546	27,450	51.3	24,647	46.0	1,435	2.7	14	0.0	2,803	R
Connecticut	132,798	67,071	50.5	64,411	48.5	868	0.7	448	0.3	2,660	R
Delaware	29,458	14,148	48.0	15,181	51.5	129	0.4	—	0.0	1,033	D
Florida	51,618	23,654	45.8	27,964	54.2	—	0.0	—	0.0	4,310	D
Georgia	157,451	54,470	34.6	102,981	65.4	—	0.0	—	0.0	48,511	D
Illinois	622,305	318,036	51.1	277,321	44.6	26,358	4.2	590	0.1	40,715	R
Indiana	470,758	232,169	49.3	225,523	47.9	13,066	2.8	—	0.0	6,646	R
Iowa	323,140	183,904	56.9	105,845	32.8	32,327	10.0	1,064	0.3	78,059	R
Kansas	201,054	121,520	60.4	59,789	29.7	19,710	9.8	35	0.0	61,731	R
Kentucky	266,884	106,059	39.7	149,068	55.9	11,499	4.3	258	0.1	43,009	D
Louisiana	104,462	38,978	37.3	65,047	62.3	437	0.4	—	0.0	26,069	D
Maine	143,903	74,052	51.5	65,211	45.3	4,409	3.1	231	0.2	8,841	R
Maryland	173,049	78,515	45.4	93,706	54.1	828	0.5	—	0.0	15,191	D
Massachusetts	282,505	165,198	58.5	111,960	39.6	4,548	1.6	799	0.3	53,238	R
Michigan	353,076	185,335	52.5	131,596	37.3	34,895	9.9	1,250	0.4	53,739	R
Minnesota	150,806	93,939	62.3	53,314	35.4	3,267	2.2	286	0.2	40,625	R
Mississippi	117,068	34,844	29.8	75,750	64.7	5,797	5.0	677	0.6	40,906	D
Missouri	397,289	153,647	38.7	208,600	52.5	35,042	8.8	—	0.0	54,953	D
Nebraska	87,355	54,979	62.9	28,523	32.7	3,853	4.4	—	0.0	26,456	R
Nevada	18,343	8,732	47.6	9,611	52.4	—	0.0	—	0.0	879	D
New Hampshire	86,361	44,856	51.9	40,797	47.2	528	0.6	180	0.2	4,059	R
New Jersey	245,928	120,555	49.0	122,565	49.8	2,617	1.1	191	0.1	2,010	D
New York	1,103,945	555,544	50.3	534,511	48.4	12,373	1.1	1,517	0.1	21,033	R
North Carolina	240,946	115,616	48.0	124,204	51.5	1,126	0.5	—	0.0	8,588	D
Ohio	724,984	375,048	51.7	340,867	47.0	6,456	0.9	2,613	0.4	34,181	R
Oregon	40,841	20,619	50.5	19,955	48.9	267	0.7	—	0.0	664	R
Pennsylvania	874,783	444,704	50.8	407,428	46.6	20,667	2.4	1,984	0.2	37,276	R
Rhode Island	29,235	18,195	62.2	10,779	36.9	236	0.8	25	0.1	7,416	R
South Carolina	169,793	57,954	34.1	111,236	65.5	567	0.3	36	0.0	53,282	D
Tennessee	243,263	107,677	44.3	129,569	53.3	6,017	2.5	—	0.0	21,892	D
Texas[2]	240,659	57,225	23.8	155,963	64.8	27,471	11.4	—	0.0	98,738	D
Vermont	65,098	45,567	70.0	18,316	28.1	1,215	1.9	—	0.0	27,251	R
Virginia[2]	212,660	83,634	39.3	128,647[3]	60.5	—	0.0	379	0.2	45,013	D
West Virginia	112,641	46,243	41.1	57,390	50.9	9,008	8.0	—	0.0	11,147	D
Wisconsin	267,202	144,406	54.0	114,650	42.9	7,986	3.0	160	0.1	29,756	R
Totals	9,220,197	4,453,611	48.3	4,445,256	48.2	306,921	3.3	14,409	0.2	8,355	R

1. For breakdown of "Other" vote, see minor candidate vote totals at the end of this chapter.

2. Figures from W. Dean Burnham, *Presidential Ballots 1836–1892* (New York: Arno Press, 1976).

3. According to Burnham there were two Democratic slates—regular with 96,594 votes and Readjuster Democrats with 32,053 votes—and he does not combine the two. They are combined here. It is not entirely clear if they ran the same set of electors.

1884 Presidential Election

STATE	TOTAL VOTE	GROVER CLEVELAND (Democrat)		JAMES G. BLAINE (Republican)		BENJAMIN F. BUTLER (Greenback)		JOHN P. ST. JOHN (Prohibition)		OTHER[1]		PLURALITY
		Votes	%	Votes	%	Votes	%	Votes	%	Votes	%	
Alabama	153,624	92,736	60.4	59,444	38.7	762	0.5	610	0.4	72	0.0	33,292 D
Arkansas	125,779	72,734	57.8	51,198	40.7	1,847	1.5	—	0.0	—	0.0	21,536 D
California	196,988	89,288	45.3	102,369	52.0	2,037	1.0	2,965	1.5	329	0.2	13,081 R
Colorado	66,519	27,723	41.7	36,084	54.2	1,956	2.9	756	1.1	—	0.0	8,361 R
Connecticut	137,221	67,167	48.9	65,879	48.0	1,682	1.2	2,493	1.8	—	0.0	1,288 D
Delaware	29,984	16,957	56.6	12,953	43.2	10	0.0	64	0.2	—	0.0	4,004 D
Florida	59,990	31,769	53.0	28,031	46.7	—	0.0	72	0.1	118	0.2	3,738 D
Georgia	143,610	94,667	65.9	48,603	33.8	145	0.1	195	0.1	—	0.0	46,064 D
Illinois	672,670	312,351	46.4	337,469	50.2	10,776	1.6	12,074	1.8	—	0.0	25,118 R
Indiana[2]	495,423	245,041	49.5	238,511	48.1	8,820	1.8	3,051	0.6	—	0.0	6,530 D
Iowa	393,542	177,316	45.1	197,089	50.1	16,341	4.2	1,499	0.4	1,297	0.3	19,773 R
Kansas	250,991	90,111	35.9	154,410	61.5	1,691	0.7	4,311	1.7	468	0.2	64,299 R
Kentucky	276,503	152,894	55.3	118,822	43.0	1,690	0.6	3,097	1.1	—	0.0	34,072 D
Louisiana	109,399	62,594	57.2	46,347	42.4	120	0.1	338	0.3	—	0.0	16,247 D
Maine[3]	130,489	52,153	40.0	72,217	55.3	3,953	3.0	2,160	1.7	6	0.0	20,064 R
Maryland	185,838	96,941	52.2	85,748	46.1	347	0.2	2,802	1.5	—	0.0	11,193 D
Massachusetts[4]	303,383	122,352	40.3	146,724	48.4	24,382	8.0	9,923	3.3	2	0.0	24,372 R
Michigan[5]	401,186	189,361	47.2	192,669	48.0	753	0.2	18,403	4.6	—	0.0	3,308 R
Minnesota[6]	190,236	70,135	36.7	111,819	58.8	3,583	1.9	4,696	2.5	—	0.0	41,684 R
Mississippi	120,688	77,653	64.3	43,035	35.7	—	0.0	—	0.0	—	0.0	34,618 D
Missouri	441,268	236,023	53.5	203,081	46.0	—	0.0	2,164	0.5	—	0.0	32,942 D
Nebraska	134,202	54,391	40.5	76,912	57.3	—	0.0	2,899	2.2	—	0.0	22,521 R
Nevada	12,779	5,577	43.6	7,176	56.2	26	0.2	—	0.0	—	0.0	1,599 R
New Hampshire	84,586	39,198	46.3	43,254	51.1	554	0.7	1,580	1.9	—	0.0	4,056 R
New Jersey	260,853	127,747	49.0	123,436	47.3	3,486	1.3	6,156	2.4	28	0.0	4,311 D
New York	1,167,003	563,048	48.2	562,001	48.2	16,955	1.5	24,999	2.1	—	0.0	1,047 D
North Carolina	268,356	142,905	53.3	125,021	46.6	—	0.0	430	0.2	—	0.0	17,884 D
Ohio	784,620	368,280	46.9	400,092	51.0	5,179	0.7	11,069	1.4	—	0.0	31,812 R
Oregon	52,683	24,598	46.7	26,845	51.0	726	1.4	479	0.9	35	0.1	2,247 R
Pennsylvania[7]	899,563	392,915	43.7	474,350	52.7	16,992	1.9	15,306	1.7	—	0.0	81,435 R
Rhode Island	32,771	12,391	37.8	19,030	58.1	422	1.3	928	2.8	—	0.0	6,639 R
South Carolina	92,812	69,845	75.3	21,730	23.4	—	0.0	—	0.0	1,237	1.3	48,115 D
Tennessee	259,978	133,770	51.5	124,101	47.7	957	0.4	1,150	0.4	—	0.0	9,669 D
Texas[2]	326,458	226,375	69.3	93,345	28.6	3,221	1.0	3,517	1.1	—	0.0	133,030 D
Vermont	59,409	17,331	29.2	39,514	66.5	785	1.3	1,752	2.9	27	0.0	22,183 R
Virginia	284,977	145,491	51.1	139,356	48.9	—	0.0	130	0.0	—	0.0	6,135 D
West Virginia	132,145	67,311	50.9	63,096	47.7	799	0.6	939	0.7	—	0.0	4,215 D
Wisconsin	319,847	146,447	45.8	161,155	50.4	4,594	1.4	7,651	2.4	—	0.0	14,708 R
Totals	10,058,373	4,915,586	48.9	4,852,916	48.2	135,594	1.3	150,658	1.5	3,619	0.0	62,670 D

1. For breakdown of "Other" vote, see minor candidate vote totals at the end of this chapter.

2. Figures from W. Dean Burnham, *Presidential Ballots 1836–1892* (New York: Arno Press, 1976).

3. Figures from Svend Petersen, *A Statistical History of the American Presidential Elections* (Westport, Conn.: Greenwood Press, 1981); *Maine Register, 1945*.

4. Figures from *Manual, 1885*.

5. Figures from *Michigan Manual, 1913*, p. 689. For Michigan's Democratic total, twelve out of thirteen electors ran on both the Democratic and Greenback ticket (a Fusion slate); the Fusion electors vote is used here. The vote listed under Greenback was solely for the "straight" Greenback slate.

6. Figures from *Minnesota Votes*.

7. Figures from Pennsylvania's *Manual, 1885*.

1888 Presidential Election

STATE	TOTAL VOTE	BENJAMIN HARRISON[1] (Republican)		GROVER CLEVELAND[1] (Democrat)		CLINTON B. FISK (Prohibition)		ALSON J. STREETER (Union Labor)		OTHER[2]		PLURALITY
		Votes	%	Votes	%	Votes	%	Votes	%	Votes	%	
Alabama	175,085	57,177	32.7	117,314	67.0	594	0.3	—	0.0	—	0.0	60,137 D
Arkansas	157,058	59,752	38.0	86,062	54.8	614	0.4	10,630	6.8	—	0.0	26,310 D
California	251,339	124,816	49.7	117,729	46.8	5,761	2.3	—	0.0	3,033	1.2	7,087 R
Colorado	91,946	50,772	55.2	37,549	40.8	2,182	2.4	1,266	1.4	177	0.2	13,223 R
Connecticut	153,978	74,584	48.4	74,920	48.7	4,234	2.7	240	0.2	—	0.0	336 D
Delaware	29,764	12,950	43.5	16,414	55.1	399	1.3	—	0.0	1	0.0	3,464 D
Florida	66,500	26,529	39.9	39,557	59.5	414	0.6	—	0.0	—	0.0	13,028 D
Georgia	142,936	40,499	28.3	100,493	70.3	1,808	1.3	136	0.1	—	0.0	59,994 D
Illinois	747,813	370,475	49.5	348,351	46.6	21,703	2.9	7,134	1.0	150	0.0	22,124 R
Indiana	536,988	263,366	49.0	260,990	48.6	9,939	1.9	2,693	0.5	—	0.0	2,376 R
Iowa	404,694	211,607	52.3	179,876	44.4	3,550	0.9	9,105	2.2	556	0.1	31,731 R
Kansas	331,133	182,845	55.2	102,739	31.0	6,774	2.0	37,838	11.4	937	0.3	80,106 R
Kentucky	344,868	155,138	45.0	183,830	53.3	5,223	1.5	677	0.2	—	0.0	28,692 D
Louisiana	115,891	30,660	26.5	85,032	73.4	150	0.1	39	0.0	—	0.0	54,372 D
Maine	128,253	73,730	57.5	50,472	39.4	2,691	2.1	1,344	1.0	16	0.0	23,258 R
Maryland	210,941	99,986	47.4	106,188	50.3	4,767	2.3	—	0.0	—	0.0	6,202 D
Massachusetts	344,243	183,892	53.4	151,590	44.0	8,701	2.5	—	0.0	60	0.0	32,302 R
Michigan	475,356	236,387	49.7	213,469	44.9	20,945	4.4	4,555	1.0	—	0.0	22,918 R
Minnesota	263,162	142,492	54.1	104,372	39.7	15,201	5.8	1,097	0.4	—	0.0	38,120 R
Mississippi	115,786	30,095	26.0	85,451	73.8	240	0.2	—	0.0	—	0.0	55,356 D
Missouri	521,359	236,252	45.3	261,943	50.2	4,539	0.9	18,625	3.6	—	0.0	25,691 D
Nebraska	202,630	108,417	53.5	80,552	39.8	9,435	4.7	4,226	2.1	—	0.0	27,865 R
Nevada	12,573	7,229	57.5	5,303	42.2	41	0.3	—	0.0	—	0.0	1,926 R
New Hampshire	90,770	45,734	50.4	43,382	47.8	1,596	1.8	—	0.0	58	0.1	2,352 R
New Jersey[3]	303,801	144,360	47.5	151,508	49.9	7,933	2.6	—	0.0	—	0.0	7,148 D
New York[4]	1,321,270	650,338	49.2	635,965	48.1	30,231	2.3	627	0.0	4,736	0.4	14,373 R
North Carolina[5]	285,946	134,784	47.1	148,336	51.9	2,789	1.0	—	0.0	37	0.0	13,552 D
Ohio	839,357	416,054	49.6	395,456	47.1	24,356	2.9	3,491	0.4	—	0.0	20,598 R
Oregon	61,889	33,291	53.8	26,518	42.8	1,676	2.7	—	0.0	404	0.7	6,773 R
Pennsylvania	997,568	526,091	52.7	446,633	44.8	20,947	2.1	3,873	0.4	24	0.0	79,458 R
Rhode Island	40,775	21,969	53.9	17,530	43.0	1,251	3.1	18	0.0	7	0.0	4,439 R
South Carolina	79,997	13,736	17.2	65,824	82.3	—	0.0	—	0.0	437	0.5	52,088 D
Tennessee[5]	304,313	139,511	45.8	158,779	52.2	5,975	2.0	48	0.0	—	0.0	19,268 D
Texas[6]	363,484	93,991	25.9	236,290	65.0	4,739	1.3	28,459	7.8	—	0.0	142,299 D
Vermont	63,476	45,193	71.2	16,788	26.4	1,460	2.3	—	0.0	35	0.1	28,405 R
Virginia	304,087	150,399	49.5	152,004	50.0	1,684	0.6	—	0.0	—	0.0	1,605 D
West Virginia	159,440	78,171	49.0	78,677	49.3	1,084	0.7	1,508	0.9	—	0.0	506 D
Wisconsin	354,614	176,553	49.8	155,232	43.8	14,277	4.0	8,552	2.4	—	0.0	21,321 R
Totals	11,395,705	5,449,825	47.8	5,539,118	48.6	249,492	2.2	146,602	1.3	10,668	0.1	89,293 D

1. Harrison won the election. See p. 231.

2. For breakdown of "Other" vote, see minor candidate vote totals at the end of this chapter.

3. Figures from *Manual, 1889*.

4. Figures from *New York Legislative Manual, 1889*.

5. Figures from Svend Petersen, *A Statistical History of the American Presidential Elections* (Westport, Conn.:Greenwood Press, 1981).

6. Figures from W. Dean Burnham, *Presidential Ballots 1836–1892* (New York: Arno Press, 1976).

1892 Presidential Election

STATE	TOTAL VOTE	GROVER CLEVELAND (Democrat)		BENJAMIN HARRISON (Republican)		JAMES B. WEAVER (Populist)		JOHN BIDWELL (Prohibition)		OTHER[1]		PLURALITY	
		Votes	%	Votes	%	Votes	%	Votes	%	Votes	%		
Alabama	232,543	138,135	59.4	9,184	3.9	84,984	36.5	240	0.1	—	0.0	53,151	D
Arkansas	148,117	87,834	59.3	47,072	31.8	11,831	8.0	113	0.1	1,267	0.9	40,762	D
California	269,585	118,151	43.8	118,027	43.8	25,311	9.4	8,096	3.0	—	0.0	124	D
Colorado	93,881	—	0.0	38,620	41.1	53,584	57.1	1,677	1.8	—	0.0	14,964	POP
Connecticut	164,593	82,395	50.1	77,030	46.8	809	0.5	4,026	2.4	333	0.2	5,365	D
Delaware	37,235	18,581	49.9	18,077	48.5	—	0.0	564	1.5	13	0.0	504	D
Florida[2]	35,567	30,154	84.8	—	0.0	4,843	13.6	570	1.6	—	0.0	25,311	D
Georgia[2]	223,961	129,386	57.8	48,305	21.6	42,937	19.2	988	0.4	2,345	1.0	81,081	D
Idaho	19,407	—	0.0	8,599	44.3	10,520	54.2	288	1.5	—	0.0	1,921	POP
Illinois	873,667	426,281	48.8	399,308	45.7	22,207	2.5	25,871	3.0	—	0.0	26,973	D
Indiana	553,613	262,740	47.5	255,615	46.2	22,208	4.0	13,050	2.4	—	0.0	7,125	D
Iowa	443,159	196,367	44.3	219,795	49.6	20,595	4.6	6,402	1.4	—	0.0	23,428	R
Kansas	323,591	—	0.0	156,134	48.3	162,888	50.3	4,569	1.4	—	0.0	6,754	POP
Kentucky	340,864	175,461	51.5	135,462	39.7	23,500	6.9	6,441	1.9	—	0.0	39,999	D
Louisiana[2]	118,287	87,922	74.3	27,903	23.6	2,462	2.1	—	0.0	—	0.0	60,023	D
Maine[3]	116,013	48,024	41.4	62,878	54.2	2,045	1.8	3,062	2.6	4	0.0	14,854	R
Maryland	213,275	113,866	53.4	92,736	43.5	796	0.4	5,877	2.8	—	0.0	21,130	D
Massachusetts	391,028	176,813	45.2	202,814	51.9	3,210	0.8	7,539	1.9	652	0.2	26,001	R
Michigan	466,917	202,396	43.3	222,708	47.7	20,031	4.3	20,857	4.5	925	0.2	20,312	R
Minnesota[4]	267,461	101,055	37.8	122,836	45.9	29,336	11.0	14,234	5.3	—	0.0	21,781	R
Mississippi	52,519	40,030	76.2	1,398	2.7	10,118	19.3	973	1.9	—	0.0	29,912	D
Missouri	541,583	268,400	49.6	227,646	42.0	41,204	7.6	4,333	0.8	—	0.0	40,754	D
Montana	44,461	17,690	39.8	18,871	42.4	7,338	16.5	562	1.3	—	0.0	1,181	R
Nebraska	200,205	24,956	12.5	87,213	43.6	83,134	41.5	4,902	2.4	—	0.0	4,079	R
Nevada	10,826	703	6.5	2,811	26.0	7,226	66.7	86	0.8	—	0.0	4,415	POP
New Hampshire	89,328	42,081	47.1	45,658	51.1	292	0.3	1,297	1.5	—	0.0	3,577	R
New Jersey	337,485	170,987	50.7	156,059	46.2	969	0.3	8,133	2.4	1,337	0.4	14,928	D
New York	1,336,793	654,868	49.0	609,350	45.6	16,429	1.2	38,190	2.9	17,956	1.3	45,518	D
North Carolina	280,270	132,951	47.4	100,346	35.8	44,336	15.8	2,637	0.9	—	0.0	32,605	D
North Dakota[2]	36,118	—	0.0	17,519	48.5	17,700	49.0	899	2.5	—	0.0	181	POP
Ohio	850,164	404,115	47.5	405,187	47.7	14,850	1.7	26,012	3.1	—	0.0	1,072	R
Oregon	78,378	14,243	18.2	35,002	44.7	26,875	34.3	2,258	2.9	—	0.0	8,127	R
Pennsylvania	1,003,000	452,264	45.1	516,011	51.4	8,714	0.9	25,123	2.5	888	0.1	63,747	R
Rhode Island	53,196	24,336	45.7	26,975	50.7	228	0.4	1,654	3.1	3	0.0	2,639	R
South Carolina	70,504	54,680	77.6	13,345	18.9	2,407	3.4	—	0.0	72	0.1	41,335	D
South Dakota	70,513	9,081	12.9	34,888	49.5	26,544	37.6	—	0.0	—	0.0	8,344	R
Tennessee	265,732	136,468	51.4	100,537	37.8	23,918	9.0	4,809	1.8	—	0.0	35,931	D
Texas[5]	422,447	239,148	56.6	77,478	18.3	99,688	23.6	2,165	0.5	3,968	1.0	161,670	D
Vermont	55,793	16,325	29.3	37,992	68.1	42	0.1	1,424	2.6	10	0.0	21,667	R
Virginia	292,238	164,136	56.2	113,098	38.7	12,275	4.2	2,729	0.9	—	0.0	51,038	D
Washington	87,968	29,802	33.9	36,459	41.4	19,165	21.8	2,542	2.9	—	0.0	6,657	R
West Virginia	171,079	84,467	49.4	80,292	46.9	4,167	2.4	2,153	1.3	—	0.0	4,175	D
Wisconsin	371,481	177,325	47.7	171,101	46.1	9,919	2.7	13,136	3.5	—	0.0	6,224	D
Wyoming	16,703	—	0.0	8,454	50.6	7,722	46.2	498	3.0	29	0.2	732	R
Totals	12,071,548	5,554,617	46.0	5,186,793	43.0	1,024,280	8.5	270,979	2.2	29,802	0.2	367,824	D

1. For breakdown of "Other" vote, see minor candidate vote totals at the end of this chapter.

2. Figures from Svend Petersen, *A Statistical History of the American Presidential Elections* (Westport, Conn.: Greenwood Press, 1981), p. 60.

3. Figures from *Maine Register, 1945*.

4. Figures from *Minnesota Votes*.

5. Figures from *The Texas Almanac's Political History of Texas*.

1896 Presidential Election

STATE	TOTAL VOTE	WILLIAM McKINLEY (Republican)		WILLIAM J. BRYAN (Democrat, Populist)[1]		JOHN M. PALMER (National Democrat)		JOSHUA LEVERING (Prohibition)		OTHER[2]		PLURALITY	
		Votes	%	Votes	%	Votes	%	Votes	%	Votes	%		
Alabama	194,580	55,673	28.6	130,298	67.0	6,375	3.3	2,234	1.1	—	0.0	74,625	D
Arkansas	149,396	37,512	25.1	110,103	73.7	—	0.0	889	0.6	892	0.6	72,591	D
California[3]	299,374	146,688	49.1	123,143	41.2	2,006	0.7	2,573	0.9	24,285	8.2	23,545	R
Colorado	189,539	26,271	13.9	161,005	84.9	1	0.0	1,717	0.9	545	0.3	134,734	D
Connecticut	174,394	110,285	63.2	56,740	32.5	4,336	2.5	1,806	1.0	1,227	0.7	53,545	R
Delaware[4]	31,538	16,883	53.5	13,425	42.6	877	2.8	355	1.1	—	0.0	3,458	R
Florida[3]	46,468	11,298	24.3	30,683	66.0	1,778	3.8	656	1.4	2,053	4.4	19,385	D
Georgia[5]	163,309	60,107	36.8	94,733	58.0	2,809	1.7	5,613	3.4	47	0.0	34,626	D
Idaho	29,631	6,324	21.3	23,135	78.1	—	0.0	172	0.6	—	0.0	16,811	D
Illinois	1,090,766	607,130	55.7	465,593	42.7	6,307	0.6	9,796	0.9	1,940	0.2	141,537	R
Indiana	637,089	323,754	50.8	305,538	48.0	2,145	0.3	3,061	0.5	2,591	0.4	18,216	R
Iowa	521,550	289,293	55.5	223,744	42.9	4,516	0.9	3,192	0.6	805	0.2	65,549	R
Kansas	336,085	159,484	47.5	173,049	51.5	1,209	0.4	1,723	0.5	620	0.2	13,565	D
Kentucky	445,928	218,171	48.9	217,894	48.9	5,084	1.1	4,779	1.1	—	0.0	277	R
Louisiana	101,046	22,037	21.8	77,175	76.4	1,834	1.8	—	0.0	—	0.0	55,138	D
Maine	118,419	80,403	67.9	34,587	29.2	1,867	1.6	1,562	1.3	—	0.0	45,816	R
Maryland	250,249	136,959	54.7	104,150	41.6	2,499	1.0	5,918	2.4	723	0.3	32,809	R
Massachusetts	401,269	278,976	69.5	105,414	26.3	11,749	2.9	2,998	0.7	2,132	0.5	173,562	R
Michigan	545,583	293,336	53.8	237,164	43.5	6,923	1.3	4,978	0.9	3,182	0.6	56,172	R
Minnesota	341,762	193,503	56.6	139,735	40.9	3,222	0.9	4,348	1.3	954	0.3	53,768	R
Mississippi	69,591	4,819	6.9	63,355	91.0	1,021	1.5	396	0.6	—	0.0	58,536	D
Missouri	674,032	304,940	45.2	363,667	54.0	2,365	0.4	2,169	0.3	891	0.1	58,727	D
Montana	53,330	10,509	19.7	42,628	79.9	—	0.0	193	0.4	—	0.0	32,119	D
Nebraska	223,181	103,064	46.2	115,007	51.5	2,885	1.3	1,242	0.6	983	0.4	11,943	D
Nevada[6]	10,314	1,938	18.8	7,802	75.6	—	0.0	—	0.0	574	5.6	5,864	D
New Hampshire[3]	83,670	57,444	68.7	21,271	25.4	3,520	4.2	779	0.9	656	0.8	36,173	R
New Jersey	371,014	221,367	59.7	133,675	36.0	6,373	1.7	—	0.0	9,599	2.6	87,692	R
New York	1,423,876	819,838	57.6	551,369	38.7	18,950	1.3	16,052	1.1	17,667	1.2	268,469	R
North Carolina	331,337	155,122	46.8	174,408	52.6	578	0.2	635	0.2	594	0.2	19,286	D
North Dakota	47,391	26,335	55.6	20,686	43.6	—	0.0	358	0.8	12	0.0	5,649	R
Ohio[3]	1,014,295	525,991	51.9	474,882	46.8	1,858	0.2	5,068	0.5	6,496	0.6	51,109	R
Oregon	97,335	48,700	50.0	46,739	48.0	977	1.0	919	0.9	—	0.0	1,961	R
Pennsylvania[7]	1,194,355	728,300	61.0	427,125	35.8	11,000	0.9	19,274	1.6	8,656	0.7	301,175	R
Rhode Island	54,785	37,437	68.3	14,459	26.4	1,166	2.1	1,160	2.1	563	1.0	22,978	R
South Carolina	68,938	9,313	13.5	58,801	85.3	824	1.2	—	0.0	—	0.0	49,488	D
South Dakota	82,937	41,040	49.5	41,225	49.7	—	0.0	672	0.8	—	0.0	185	D
Tennessee	320,903	148,683	46.3	167,168	52.1	1,953	0.6	3,099	1.0	—	0.0	18,485	D
Texas[8]	515,987	163,413	31.7	267,803	51.9	4,989	1.0	1,797	0.3	77,985	15.1	104,390	D
Utah	78,098	13,491	17.3	64,607	82.7	—	0.0	—	0.0	—	0.0	51,116	D
Vermont[9]	63831	51,127	80.1	10,179	15.9	1,331	2.1	733	1.1	461	0.7	40,948	R
Virginia	294,674	135,379	45.9	154,708	52.5	2,129	0.7	2,350	0.8	108	0.0	19,329	D
Washington[3]	93,583	39,153	41.8	51,646	55.2	—	0.0	968	1.0	1,668	1.8	12,493	D
West Virginia	201,757	105,379	52.2	94,480	46.8	678	0.3	1,220	0.6	—	0.0	10,899	R
Wisconsin	447,409	268,135	59.9	165,523	37.0	4,584	1.0	7,507	1.7	1,660	0.4	102,612	R
Wyoming[3]	21,093	10,072	47.8	10,376	49.3	—	0.0	159	0.8	486	2.3	304	D
Totals	13,905,691	7,105,144	51.1	6,370,897	45.8	132,718	1.0	125,118	0.9	171,814	1.2	734,247	R

1. Bryan was nominated by both the Democrats and the Populists but with different running mates. In several states different slates of electors were entered by each party. It is legally incorrect to combine the vote. The separate vote for Bryan usually under the Populist ticket is listed under "Other." In other states it appears that the two slates of electors were the same and it is correct to combine the vote.

2. For breakdown of "Other" vote, see minor candidate vote totals at the end of this chapter.

3. Figures from Edgar E. Robinson, *The Presidential Vote 1896–1932* (Stanford, Calif.: Stanford University Press, 1934).

4. The vote of Kent County was excluded from the official tally because two sets of returns were sent to the state. The vote of the county as reported would have made the vote: McKinley, 20,685; Bryan, 16,708; Palmer, 968; and Levering, 469.

5. Figures from Svend Petersen, *A Statistical History of the American Presidential Elections* (Westport, Conn. Greenwood Press, 1981).

6. Figures from *Political History of Nevada* (Secretary of State).

7. Figures from *Manual, 1897*.

8. There were two separate Bryan slates in Texas with various sources offering widely different totals. Figures here are from Robinson, *The Presidential Vote*, supplemented with manuscript returns supplied by the Texas secretary of state.

9. Figures from *Vermont Legislative Directory*.

1900 Presidential Election

STATE	TOTAL VOTE	WILLIAM McKINLEY (Republican)		WILLIAM J. BRYAN (Democrat)		JOHN G. WOOLEY (Prohibition)		EUGENE V. DEBS (Socialist)		OTHER[1]		PLURALITY	
		Votes	%	Votes	%	Votes	%	Votes	%	Votes	%		
Alabama[2]	160,477	55,634	34.7	96,368	60.1	3,796	2.4	928	0.6	3,751	2.3	40,734	D
Arkansas	127,966	44,800	35.0	81,242	63.5	584	0.5	—	0.0	1,340	1.0	36,442	D
California[3]	302,399	164,755	54.5	124,985	41.3	5,087	1.7	7,572	2.50	—	0.0	39,770	R
Colorado	220,895	92,701	42.0	122,705	55.5	3,790	1.7	686	0.3	1,013	0.5	30,004	D
Connecticut	180,195	102,572	56.9	74,014	41.1	1,617	0.9	1,029	0.6	963	0.5	28,558	R
Delaware	41,989	22,535	53.7	18,852	44.9	546	1.3	56	0.1	—	0.0	3,683	R
Florida[2]	39,777	7,463	18.8	28,273	71.1	2,244	5.7	654	1.6	1,143	2.9	20,810	D
Georgia	121,410	34,260	28.2	81,180	66.9	1,402	1.2	—	0.0	4,568	3.8	46,920	D
Idaho[2]	56,760	27,198	47.9	28,260	49.8	857	1.5	—	0.0	445	0.8	1,062	D
Illinois	1,131,898	597,985	52.8	503,061	44.4	17,626	1.6	9,687	0.9	3,539	0.3	94,924	R
Indiana	664,094	336,063	50.6	309,584	46.6	13,718	2.1	2,374	0.4	2,355	0.4	26,479	R
Iowa	530,345	307,799	58.0	209,261	39.5	9,502	1.8	2,743	0.5	1,040	0.2	98,538	R
Kansas[4]	353,766	185,955	52.6	162,601	46.0	3,605	1.0	1,605	0.5	—	0.0	23,354	R
Kentucky[5]	467,580	226,801	48.5	234,889	50.2	2,814	0.6	—	0.0	3,076	0.7	8,008	D
Louisiana	67,906	14,234	21.0	53,668	79.0	—	0.0	—	0.0	4	0.0	39,434	D
Maine[6]	107,698	66,413	61.7	37,822	35.1	2,585	2.4	878	0.8	—	0.0	28,591	R
Maryland	264,386	136,151	51.5	122,237	46.2	4,574	1.7	900	0.3	524	0.2	13,914	R
Massachusetts	414,804	238,866	57.6	156,997	37.8	6,202	1.5	9,607	2.3	3,132	0.8	81,869	R
Michigan	543,789	316,014	58.1	211,432	38.9	11,804	2.2	2,820	0.5	1,719	0.3	104,582	R
Minnesota	316,311	190,461	60.2	112,901	35.7	8,555	2.7	3,065	1.0	1,329	0.4	77,560	R
Mississippi	59,055	5,707	9.7	51,706	87.6	—	0.0	—	0.0	1,642	2.8	45,999	D
Missouri	683,658	314,092	45.9	351,922	51.5	5,965	0.9	6,139	0.9	5,540	0.8	37,830	D
Montana	63,856	25,409	39.8	37,311	58.4	306	0.5	711	1.1	119	0.2	11,902	D
Nebraska	241,430	121,835	50.5	114,013	47.2	3,655	1.5	823	0.3	1,104	0.5	7,822	R
Nevada	10,196	3,849	37.8	6,347	62.2	—	0.0	—	0.0	—	0.0	2,498	D
New Hampshire	92,364	54,799	59.3	35,489	38.4	1,270	1.4	790	0.9	16	0.0	19,310	R
New Jersey	401,050	221,707	55.3	164,808	41.1	7,183	1.8	4,609	1.1	2,743	0.7	56,899	R
New York	1,548,043	822,013	53.1	678,462	43.8	22,077	1.4	12,869	0.8	12,622	0.8	143,551	R
North Carolina	292,518	132,997	45.5	157,733	53.9	990	0.3	—	0.0	798	0.3	24,736	D
North Dakota	57,783	35,898	62.1	20,524	35.5	735	1.3	517	0.9	109	0.2	15,374	R
Ohio	1,040,073	543,918	52.3	474,882	45.7	10,203	1.0	4,847	0.5	6,223	0.6	69,036	R
Oregon[7]	84,216	46,526	55.2	33,385	39.6	2,536	3.1	1,494	1.8	275	0.3	13,141	R
Pennsylvania	1,173,210	712,665	60.7	424,232	36.2	27,908	2.4	4,831	0.4	3,574	0.3	288,433	R
Rhode Island	56,548	33,784	59.7	19,812	35.0	1,529	2.7	—	0.0	1,423	2.5	13,972	R
South Carolina	50,698	3,525	7.0	47,173	93.0	—	0.0	—	0.0	—	0.0	43,648	D
South Dakota	96,169	54,574	56.7	39,538	41.1	1,541	1.6	176	0.2	340	0.4	15,036	R
Tennessee	273,860	123,108	45.0	145,240	53.0	3,844	1.4	346	0.1	1,322	0.5	22,132	D
Texas	424,334	131,174	30.9	267,945	63.1	2,642	0.6	1,846	0.4	20,727	4.9	136,771	D
Utah	93,071	47,089	50.6	44,949	48.3	205	0.2	717	0.8	111	0.1	2,140	R
Vermont	56,212	42,569	75.7	12,849	22.9	383	0.7	39	0.1	372	0.7	29,720	R
Virginia	264,208	115,769	43.8	146,079	55.3	2,130	0.8	—	0.0	230	0.1	30,310	D
Washington	107,523	57,455	53.4	44,833	41.7	2,363	2.2	2,006	1.9	866	0.8	12,622	R
West Virginia	220,796	119,829	54.3	98,807	44.8	1,628	0.7	286	0.1	246	0.1	21,022	R
Wisconsin	442,501	265,760	60.1	159,163	36.0	10,027	2.3	7,048	1.6	503	0.1	106,597	R
Wyoming	24,708	14,482	58.6	10,164	41.1	—	0.0	21	0.1	41	0.2	4,318	R
Totals	13,972,525	7,219,193	51.7	6,357,698	45.5	210,028	1.5	94,719	0.7	90,887	0.7	861,495	R

1. For breakdown of "Other" vote, see minor candidate vote totals at the end of this chapter.

2. Figures from Edgar E. Robinson, *The Presidential Vote 1896–1932* (Stanford, Calif.: Stanford University Press, 1934).

3. Figures from Svend Petersen, *A Statistical History of the American Presidential Elections* (Westport, Conn.: Greenwood Press, 1981); *Blue Book, 1908,* p. 700.

4. Figures from Petersen, *A Statistical History,* p. 67.

5. Figures from *Official Manual, 1904,* pp. 118–121.

6. Figures from *Maine Register,* 1945.

7. Figures from Petersen, *A Statistical History*; Robinson, *The Presidential Vote.*

1904 Presidential Election

STATE	TOTAL VOTE	THEODORE ROOSEVELT (Republican)		ALTON B. PARKER (Democrat)		EUGENE V. DEBS (Socialist)		SILAS C. SWALLOW (Prohibition)		OTHER[1]		PLURALITY	
		Votes	%	Votes	%	Votes	%	Votes	%	Votes	%		
Alabama	108,785	22,472	20.7	79,797	73.4	853	0.8	612	0.6	5,051	4.6	57,325	D
Arkansas	116,328	46,760	40.2	64,434	55.4	1,816	1.6	992	0.9	2,326	2.0	17,674	D
California	331,768	205,226	61.9	89,294	26.9	29,535	8.9	7,380	2.2	333	0.1	115,932	R
Colorado	243,667	134,661	55.3	100,105	41.1	4,304	1.8	3,438	1.4	1,159	0.5	34,556	R
Connecticut	191,136	111,089	58.1	72,909	38.1	28	2.4	1,506	0.8	1,089	0.6	38,180	R
Delaware	43,856	23,705	54.1	19,347	44.1	146	0.3	607	1.4	51	0.1	4,358	R
Florida[2]	39,302	8,314	21.2	27,046	68.8	2,337	6.0	—	0.0	1,605	4.1	18,732	D
Georgia	130,986	24,004	18.3	83,466	63.7	196	0.1	685	0.5	22,635	17.3	59,462	D
Idaho	72,577	47,783	65.8	18,480	25.5	4,949	6.8	1,013	1.4	352	0.5	29,303	R
Illinois	1,076,495	632,645	58.8	327,606	30.4	69,225	6.4	34,770	3.2	12,249	1.1	305,039	R
Indiana	682,206	368,289	54.0	274,356	40.2	12,023	1.8	23,496	3.4	4,042	0.6	93,933	R
Iowa	485,703	307,907	63.4	149,141	30.7	14,847	3.1	11,601	2.4	2,207	0.5	158,766	R
Kansas	329,047	213,455	64.9	86,164	26.2	15,869	4.8	7,306	2.2	6,253	1.9	127,291	R
Kentucky	435,946	205,457	47.1	217,170	49.8	3,599	0.8	6,603	1.5	3,117	0.7	11,713	D
Louisiana	53,908	5,205	9.7	47,708	88.5	995	1.8	—	0.0	—	0.0	42,503	D
Maine[3]	96,036	64,438	67.1	27,648	28.8	2,103	2.2	1,510	1.6	337	0.3	36,790	R
Maryland	224,229	109,497	48.8	109,446	48.8	2,247	1.0	3,034	1.4	5	0.0	51	R
Massachusetts	445,100	257,813	57.9	165,746	37.2	13,604	3.1	4,279	1.0	3,658	0.8	92,067	R
Michigan	520,443	361,863	69.5	134,163	25.8	8,942	1.7	13,312	2.6	2,163	0.4	227,700	R
Minnesota	292,860	216,651	74.0	55,187	18.8	11,692	4.0	6,253	2.1	3,077	1.1	161,464	R
Mississippi	58,721	3,280	5.6	53,480	91.1	462	0.8	—	0.0	1,499	2.6	50,200	D
Missouri	643,861	321,449	49.9	296,312	46.0	13,009	2.0	7,191	1.1	5,900	0.9	25,137	R
Montana	63,568	33,994	53.5	21,816	34.3	5,675	8.9	339	0.5	1,744	2.7	12,178	R
Nebraska	225,732	138,558	61.4	52,921	23.4	7,412	3.3	6,323	2.8	20,518	9.1	85,637	R
Nevada	12,115	6,864	56.7	3,982	32.9	925	7.6	—	0.0	344	2.8	2,882	R
New Hampshire	90,151	54,157	60.1	34,071	37.8	1,090	1.2	750	0.8	83	0.1	20,086	R
New Jersey[4]	432,547	245,164	56.7	164,566	38.0	9,587	2.2	6,845	1.6	6,385	1.5	80,598	R
New York	1,617,765	859,533	53.1	683,981	42.3	36,883	2.3	20,787	1.3	16,581	1.0	175,552	R
North Carolina	207,818	82,442	39.7	124,091	59.7	124	0.1	342	0.2	819	0.4	41,649	D
North Dakota[2]	70,279	52,595	74.8	14,273	20.3	2,009	2.9	1,137	1.6	165	0.2	38,322	R
Ohio	1,004,395	600,095	59.7	344,674	34.3	36,260	3.6	19,339	1.9	4,027	0.4	255,421	R
Oregon	89,656	60,309	67.3	17,327	19.3	7,479	8.3	3,795	4.2	746	0.8	42,982	R
Pennsylvania	1,236,738	840,949	68.0	337,998	27.3	21,863	1.8	33,717	2.7	2,211	0.2	502,951	R
Rhode Island	68,656	41,605	60.6	24,839	36.2	956	1.4	768	1.1	488	0.7	16,766	R
South Carolina	55,890	2,570	4.6	53,320	95.4	—	0.0	—	0.0	—	0.0	50,750	D
South Dakota	101,395	72,083	71.1	21,969	21.7	3,138	3.1	2,965	2.9	1,240	1.2	50,114	R
Tennessee	242,750	105,363	43.4	131,653	54.2	1,354	0.6	1,889	0.8	2,491	1.0	26,290	D
Texas	233,609	51,307	22.0	167,088	71.5	2,788	1.2	3,933	1.7	8,493	3.6	115,781	D
Utah	101,626	62,446	61.4	33,413	32.9	5,767	5.7	—	0.0	—	0.0	29,033	R
Vermont	51,888	40,459	78.0	9,777	18.8	859	1.7	792	1.5	1	0.0	30,682	R
Virginia	130,410	48,180	36.9	80,649	61.8	202	0.2	1,379	1.1	—	0.0	32,469	D
Washington	145,151	101,540	70.0	28,098	19.4	10,023	6.9	3,229	2.2	2,261	1.6	73,442	R
West Virginia	239,986	132,620	55.3	100,855	42.0	1,573	0.7	4,599	1.9	339	0.1	31,765	R
Wisconsin	443,440	280,314	63.2	124,205	28.0	28,240	6.4	9,872	2.2	809	0.2	156,109	R
Wyoming	30,614	20,489	66.9	8,930	29.2	987	3.2	208	0.7	—	0.0	11,559	R
Totals	13,519,039	7,625,599	56.4	5,083,501	37.6	402,490	3.0	258,596	1.9	148,853	1.1	2,542,098	R

1. For breakdown of "Other" vote, see minor candidate vote totals at the end of this chapter.

2. Figures from Svend Petersen, *A Statistical History of the American Presidential Elections* (Westport, Conn.: Greenwood Press, 1981).

3. Figures from *Maine Register, 1945*.

4. Figures from *Manual, 1905*.

1908 Presidential Election

STATE	TOTAL VOTE	WILLIAM H. TAFT (Republican)		WILLIAM J. BRYAN (Democrat)		EUGENE V. DEBS (Socialist)		EUGENE W. CHAFIN (Prohibition)		OTHER[1]		PLURALITY	
		Votes	%	Votes	%	Votes	%	Votes	%	Votes	%		
Alabama	105,152	25,561	24.3	74,391	70.7	1,450	1.4	690	0.7	3,060	2.9	48,830	D
Arkansas	151,845	56,684	37.3	87,020	57.3	5,842	3.8	1,026	0.7	1,273	0.8	30,336	D
California	386,625	214,398	55.5	127,492	33.0	28,659	7.4	11,770	3.0	4,306	1.1	86,906	R
Colorado	263,858	123,693	46.9	126,644	48.0	7,960	3.0	5,559	2.1	2	0.0	2,951	D
Connecticut	189,903	112,815	59.4	68,255	35.9	5,113	2.7	2,380	1.3	1,340	0.7	44,560	R
Delaware	48,007	25,014	52.1	22,055	45.9	239	0.5	670	1.4	29	0.1	2,959	R
Florida	49,360	10,654	21.6	31,104	63.0	3,747	7.6	1,356	2.7	2,499	5.1	20,450	D
Georgia[2]	132,794	41,692	31.4	72,413	54.5	584	0.4	1,059	0.8	17,046	12.8	30,721	D
Idaho	97,293	52,621	54.1	36,162	37.2	6,400	6.6	1,986	2.0	124	0.1	16,459	R
Illinois	1,155,254	629,932	54.5	450,810	39.0	34,711	3.0	29,364	2.5	10,437	0.9	179,122	R
Indiana	721,117	348,993	48.4	338,262	46.9	13,476	1.9	18,036	2.5	2,350	0.3	10,731	R
Iowa	494,770	275,210	55.6	200,771	40.6	8,287	1.7	9,837	2.0	665	0.1	74,439	R
Kansas	376,043	197,316	52.5	161,209	42.9	12,420	3.3	5,030	1.3	68	0.0	36,107	R
Kentucky	490,719	235,711	48.0	244,092	49.7	4,093	0.8	5,885	1.2	938	0.2	8,381	D
Louisiana	75,117	8,958	11.9	63,568	84.6	2,514	3.3	—	0.0	77	0.1	54,610	D
Maine	106,335	66,987	63.0	35,403	33.3	1,758	1.7	1,487	1.4	700	0.7	31,584	R
Maryland	238,531	116,513	48.8	115,908	48.6	2,323	1.0	3,302	1.4	485	0.2	605	R
Massachusetts	456,905	265,966	58.2	155,533	34.0	10,778	2.4	4,373	1.0	20,255	4.4	110,433	R
Michigan	538,124	333,313	61.9	174,619	32.4	11,527	2.1	16,785	3.1	1,880	0.3	158,694	R
Minnesota[3]	331,328	195,846	59.1	109,411	33.0	14,528	4.4	11,114	3.4	429	0.1	86,435	R
Mississippi	66,904	4,363	6.5	60,287	90.1	978	1.5	—	0.0	1,276	1.9	55,924	D
Missouri	715,841	347,203	48.5	346,574	48.4	15,431	2.2	4,209	0.6	2,424	0.3	629	R
Montana	69,233	32,471	46.9	29,511	42.6	5,920	8.6	838	1.2	493	0.7	2,960	R
Nebraska	266,799	126,997	47.6	131,099	49.1	3,524	1.3	5,179	1.9	—	0.0	4,102	D
Nevada	24,526	10,775	43.9	11,212	45.7	2,103	8.6	—	0.0	436	1.8	437	D
New Hampshire	89,595	53,144	59.3	33,655	37.6	1,299	1.4	905	1.0	592	0.7	19,489	R
New Jersey	467,111	265,298	56.8	182,522	39.1	10,249	2.2	4,930	1.1	4,112	0.9	82,776	R
New York	1,638,350	870,070	53.1	667,468	40.7	38,451	2.3	22,667	1.4	39,694	2.4	202,602	R
North Carolina	252,554	114,887	45.5	136,928	54.2	372	0.1	354	0.1	13	0.0	22,041	D
North Dakota	94,524	57,680	61.0	32,884	34.8	2,421	2.6	1,496	1.6	43	0.0	24,796	R
Ohio	1,121,552	572,312	51.0	502,721	44.8	33,795	3.0	11,402	1.0	1,322	0.1	69,591	R
Oklahoma	254,260	110,473	43.4	122,362	48.1	21,425	8.4	—	0.0	—	0.0	11,889	D
Oregon	110,539	62,454	56.5	37,792	34.2	7,322	6.6	2,682	2.4	289	0.3	24,662	R
Pennsylvania	1,267,450	745,779	58.8	448,782	35.4	33,914	2.7	36,694	2.9	2,281	0.2	296,997	R
Rhode Island	72,317	43,942	60.8	24,706	34.2	1,365	1.9	1,016	1.4	1,288	1.8	19,236	R
South Carolina	66,379	3,945	5.9	62,288	93.8	100	0.2	—	0.0	46	0.1	58,343	D
South Dakota	114,775	67,536	58.8	40,266	35.1	2,846	2.5	4,039	3.5	88	0.1	27,270	R
Tennessee	257,180	117,977	45.9	135,608	52.7	1,870	0.7	301	0.1	1,424	0.6	17,631	D
Texas	292,913	65,605	22.4	216,662	74.0	7,779	2.7	1,626	0.6	1,241	0.4	151,057	D
Utah	108,757	61,165	56.2	42,610	39.2	4,890	4.5	—	0.0	92	0.1	18,555	R
Vermont	52,680	39,552	75.1	11,496	21.8	—	0.0	799	1.5	833	1.6	28,056	R
Virginia	137,065	52,572	38.4	82,946	60.5	255	0.2	1,111	0.8	181	0.1	30,374	D
Washington	183,570	106,062	57.8	58,383	31.8	14,177	7.7	4,700	2.6	248	0.1	47,679	R
West Virginia	258,098	137,869	53.4	111,410	43.2	3,679	1.4	5,140	2.0	—	0.0	26,459	R
Wisconsin	454,438	247,744	54.5	166,662	36.7	28,147	6.2	11,565	2.5	320	0.1	81,082	R
Wyoming	37,608	20,846	55.4	14,918	39.7	1,715	4.6	66	0.2	63	0.2	5,928	R
Totals	14,884,098	7,676,598	51.6	6,406,874	43.0	420,436	2.8	253,428	1.7	126,762	0.9	1,269,724	R

1. For breakdown of "Other" vote, see minor candidate vote totals at the end of this chapter.

2. Figures from Svend Petersen, *A Statistical History of the American Presidential Elections* (Westport, Conn.: Greenwood Press, 1981).

3. Figures from *Minnesota Votes*.

1912 Presidential Election

STATE	TOTAL VOTE	WOODROW WILSON (Democrat)		THEODORE ROOSEVELT (Progressive)		WILLIAM H. TAFT (Republican)		EUGENE V. DEBS (Socialist)		OTHER[1]		PLURALITY	
		Votes	%	Votes	%	Votes	%	Votes	%	Votes	%		
Alabama	117,959	82,438	69.9	22,680	19.2	9,807	8.3	3,029	2.6	5	0.0	59,758	D
Arizona	23,687	10,324	43.6	6,949	29.3	2,986	12.6	3,163	13.4	265	1.1	3,375	D
Arkansas	125,104	68,814	55.0	21,644	17.3	25,585	20.5	8,153	6.5	908	0.7	43,229	D
California	677,877	283,436	41.8	283,610	41.8	3,847	0.6	79,201	11.7	27,783	4.1	174	PR
Colorado	265,954	113,912	42.8	71,752	27.0	58,386	22.0	16,366	6.2	5,538	2.1	42,160	D
Connecticut	190,404	74,561	39.2	34,129	17.9	68,324	35.9	10,056	5.3	3,334	1.8	6,237	D
Delaware	48,690	22,631	46.5	8,886	18.3	15,997	32.9	556	1.1	620	1.3	6,634	D
Florida[2]	51,911	36,417	70.2	4,555	8.8	4,279	8.2	4,806	9.3	1,854	3.6	31,862	D
Georgia	121,470	93,087	76.6	21,985	18.1	5,191	4.3	1,058	0.9	149	0.1	71,102	D
Idaho	105,754	33,921	32.1	25,527	24.1	32,810	31.0	11,960	11.3	1,536	1.5	1,111	D
Illinois	1,146,173	405,048	35.3	386,478	33.7	253,593	22.1	81,278	7.1	19,776	1.7	18,570	D
Indiana	654,474	281,890	43.1	162,007	24.8	151,267	23.1	36,931	5.6	22,379	3.4	119,883	D
Iowa	492,353	185,322	37.6	161,819	32.9	119,805	24.3	16,967	3.4	8,440	1.7	23,503	D
Kansas	365,560	143,663	39.3	120,210	32.9	74,845	20.5	26,779	7.3	63	0.0	23,453	D
Kentucky[3]	453,707	219,585	48.4	102,766	22.7	115,520	25.5	11,647	2.6	4,189	0.9	104,065	D
Louisiana	79,248	60,871	76.8	9,283	11.7	3,833	4.8	5,261	6.6	—	0.0	51,588	D
Maine	129,641	51,113	39.4	48,495	37.4	26,545	20.5	2,541	2.0	947	0.7	2,618	D
Maryland	231,981	112,674	48.6	57,789	24.9	54,956	23.7	3,996	1.7	2,566	1.1	54,885	D
Massachusetts	488,056	173,408	35.5	142,228	29.1	155,948	32.0	12,616	2.6	3,856	0.8	17,460	D
Michigan	547,971	150,201	27.4	213,243	38.9	151,434	27.6	23,060	4.2	10,033	1.8	61,809	PR
Minnesota	334,219	106,426	31.8	125,856	37.7	64,334	19.2	27,505	8.2	10,098	3.0	19,430	PR
Mississippi	64,483	57,324	88.9	3,549	5.5	1,560	2.4	2,050	3.2	—	0.0	53,775	D
Missouri	698,566	330,746	47.3	124,375	17.8	207,821	29.7	28,466	4.1	7,158	1.0	122,925	D
Montana	80,256	28,129	35.0	22,709	28.3	18,575	23.1	10,811	13.5	32	0.0	5,420	D
Nebraska	249,483	109,008	43.7	72,681	29.1	54,226	21.7	10,185	4.1	3,383	1.4	36,327	D
Nevada	20,115	7,986	39.7	5,620	27.9	3,196	15.9	3,313	16.5	—	0.0	2,366	D
New Hampshire	87,961	34,724	39.5	17,794	20.2	32,927	37.4	1,981	2.3	535	0.6	1,797	D
New Jersey	433,663	178,638	41.2	145,679	33.6	89,066	20.5	15,948	3.7	4,332	1.0	32,959	D
New Mexico	48,807	20,437	41.9	8,347	17.1	17,164	35.2	2,859	5.9	—	0.0	3,273	D
New York	1,588,315	655,573	41.3	390,093	24.6	455,487	28.7	63,434	4.0	23,728	1.5	200,086	D
North Carolina	243,776	144,407	59.2	69,135	28.4	29,129	11.9	987	0.4	118	0.0	75,272	D
North Dakota	86,474	29,549	34.2	25,726	29.7	22,990	26.6	6,966	8.1	1,243	1.4	3,823	D
Ohio	1,037,114	424,834	41.0	229,807	22.2	278,168	26.8	90,164	8.7	14,141	1.4	146,666	D
Oklahoma	253,694	119,143	47.0	—	0.0	90,726	35.8	41,630	16.4	2,195	0.9	28,417	D
Oregon	137,040	47,064	34.3	37,600	27.4	34,673	25.3	13,343	9.7	4,360	3.2	9,464	D
Pennsylvania	1,217,736	395,637	32.5	444,894	36.5	273,360	22.4	83,614	6.9	20,231	1.7	49,257	PR
Rhode Island	77,894	30,412	39.0	16,878	21.7	27,703	35.6	2,049	2.6	852	1.1	2,709	D
South Carolina	50,403	48,355	95.9	1,293	2.6	536	1.1	164	0.3	55	0.1	47,062	D
South Dakota	116,327	48,942	42.1	58,811	50.6	—	0.0	4,664	4.0	3,910	3.4	9,869	PR
Tennessee	251,933	133,021	52.8	54,041	21.5	60,475	24.0	3,564	1.4	832	0.3	72,546	D
Texas	300,961	218,921	72.7	26,715	8.9	28,310	9.4	24,884	8.3	2,131	0.7	190,611	D
Utah	112,272	36,576	32.6	24,174	21.5	42,013	37.4	8,999	8.0	510	0.5	5,437	R
Vermont	62,804	15,350	24.4	22,129	35.2	23,303	37.1	928	1.5	1,094	1.7	1,174	R
Virginia	136,975	90,332	65.9	21,776	15.9	23,288	17.0	820	0.6	759	0.6	67,044	D
Washington	322,799	86,840	26.9	113,698	35.2	70,445	21.8	40,134	12.4	11,682	3.6	26,858	PR
West Virginia	268,728	113,097	42.1	79,112	29.4	56,754	21.1	15,248	5.7	4,517	1.7	33,985	D
Wisconsin	399,975	164,230	41.1	62,448	15.6	130,596	32.7	33,476	8.4	9,225	2.3	33,634	D
Wyoming	42,283	15,310	36.2	9,232	21.8	14,560	34.4	2,760	6.5	421	1.0	750	D
Totals	15,043,029	6,294,326	41.8	4,120,207	27.4	3,486,343	23.2	900,370	6.0	241,783	1.6	2,174,119	D

1. For breakdown of "Other" vote, see minor candidate vote totals at the end of this chapter.

2. Figures from Svend Petersen, *A Statistical History of the American Presidential Elections* (Westport, Conn.: Greenwood Press, 1981); Edgar E. Robinson, *The Presidential Vote 1896–1932* (Stanford, Calif.: Stanford University Press, 1934).

3. Figures from *Kentucky Directory 1916*, pp. 145–149.

1916 Presidential Election

STATE	TOTAL VOTE	WOODROW WILSON (Democrat) Votes	%	CHARLES E. HUGHES (Republican) Votes	%	ALLAN L. BENSON (Socialist) Votes	%	J. FRANK HANLY (Prohibition) Votes	%	OTHER[1] Votes	%	PLURALITY	
Alabama[2]	131,142	99,409	75.6	28,809	21.9	1,925	1.5	999	0.8	—	0.0	70,600	D
Arizona	58,019	33,170	57.2	20,522	35.4	3,174	5.5	1,153	2.0	—	0.0	12,648	D
Arkansas[3]	168,348	112,186	66.6	47,148	28.0	6,999	4.2	2,015	1.2	—	0.0	65,038	D
California	999,250	465,936	46.6	462,516	46.3	42,898	4.3	27,713	2.8	187	0.0	3,420	D
Colorado[3]	294,375	178,816	60.5	102,308	34.8	10,049	3.4	2,793	0.9	409	0.1	76,508	D
Connecticut	213,874	99,786	46.7	106,514	49.8	5,179	2.4	1,789	0.8	606	0.3	6,728	R
Delaware	51,810	24,753	47.8	26,011	50.2	480	0.9	566	1.1	—	0.0	1,258	R
Florida	80,734	55,984	69.3	14,611	18.1	5,353	6.6	4,786	5.9	—	0.0	41,373	D
Georgia[4]	158,690	125,845	79.3	11,225	7.1	967	0.6	—	0.0	20,653	12.9	105,192	D
Idaho	134,615	70,054	52.0	55,368	41.1	8,066	6.0	1,127	0.8	—	0.0	14,686	D
Illinois	2,192,707	950,229	43.3	1,152,549	52.6	61,394	2.8	26,047	1.2	2,488	0.1	202,320	R
Indiana	718,853	334,063	46.5	341,005	47.4	21,860	3.0	16,368	2.3	5,557	0.8	6,942	R
Iowa	518,738	221,699	42.7	280,439	54.1	10,976	2.1	3,371	0.6	2,253	0.4	58,740	R
Kansas	629,813	314,588	49.9	277,658	44.1	24,685	3.9	12,882	2.0	—	0.0	36,930	D
Kentucky	520,078	269,990	51.9	241,854	46.5	4,734	0.9	3,039	0.6	461	0.1	28,136	D
Louisiana	92,974	79,875	85.9	6,466	7.0	284	0.3	—	0.0	6,349	6.8	73,409	D
Maine	136,314	64,033	47.0	69,508	51.0	2,177	1.6	596	0.4	—	0.0	5,475	R
Maryland	262,039	138,359	52.8	117,347	44.8	2,674	1.0	2,903	1.1	756	0.3	21,012	D
Massachusetts	531,822	247,885	46.6	268,784	50.5	11,058	2.1	2,993	0.6	1,102	0.2	20,899	R
Michigan	646,873	283,993	43.9	337,952	52.2	16,012	2.5	8,085	1.2	831	0.1	53,959	R
Minnesota	387,367	179,155	46.2	179,544	46.3	20,117	5.2	7,793	2.0	758	0.2	389	R
Mississippi	86,679	80,422	92.8	4,253	4.9	1,484	1.7	—	0.0	520	0.6	76,169	D
Missouri	786,773	398,032	50.6	369,339	46.9	14,612	1.9	3,887	0.5	903	0.1	28,693	D
Montana	178,009	101,104	56.8	66,933	37.6	9,634	5.4	—	0.0	338	0.2	34,171	D
Nebraska	287,315	158,827	55.3	117,771	41.0	7,141	2.5	2,952	1.0	624	0.2	41,056	D
Nevada	33,314	17,776	53.4	12,127	36.4	3,065	9.2	346	1.0	—	0.0	5,649	D
New Hampshire	89,127	43,781	49.1	43,725	49.1	1,318	1.5	303	0.3	—	0.0	56	D
New Jersey	494,442	211,018	42.7	268,982	54.4	10,405	2.1	3,182	0.6	855	0.2	57,964	R
New Mexico	66,879	33,693	50.4	31,097	46.5	1,977	3.0	112	0.2	—	0.0	2,596	D
New York	1,706,305	759,426	44.5	879,238	51.5	45,944	2.7	19,031	1.1	2,666	0.2	119,812	R
North Carolina	289,837	168,383	58.1	120,890	41.7	509	0.2	55	0.0	—	0.0	47,493	D
North Dakota	115,390	55,206	47.8	53,471	46.3	5,716	5.0	997	0.9	—	0.0	1,735	D
Ohio	1,165,091	604,161	51.9	514,753	44.2	38,092	3.3	8,085	0.7	—	0.0	89,408	D
Oklahoma	292,327	148,123	50.7	97,233	33.3	45,091	15.4	1,646	0.6	234	0.1	50,890	D
Oregon	261,650	120,087	45.9	126,813	48.5	9,711	3.7	4,729	1.8	310	0.1	6,726	R
Pennsylvania	1,297,189	521,784	40.2	703,823	54.3	42,638	3.3	28,525	2.2	419	0.0	182,039	R
Rhode Island	87,816	40,394	46.0	44,858	51.1	1,914	2.2	470	0.5	180	0.2	4,464	R
South Carolina	63,950	61,845	96.7	1,550	2.4	135	0.2	—	0.0	420	0.7	60,295	D
South Dakota	128,942	59,191	45.9	64,217	49.8	3,760	2.9	1,774	1.4	—	0.0	5,026	R
Tennessee	272,190	153,280	56.3	116,223	42.7	2,542	0.9	145	0.1	—	0.0	37,057	D
Texas[5]	372,467	286,514	76.9	64,999	17.5	18,969	5.1	1,985	0.5	—	0.0	221,515	D
Utah	143,145	84,145	58.8	54,137	37.8	4,460	3.1	149	0.1	254	0.2	30,008	D
Vermont	64,475	22,708	35.2	40,250	62.4	798	1.2	709	1.1	10	0.0	17,542	R
Virginia[2]	153,993	102,825	66.8	49,358	32.1	1,060	0.7	683	0.4	67	0.0	53,467	D
Washington	380,994	183,388	48.1	167,208	43.9	22,800	6.0	6,868	1.8	730	0.2	16,180	D
West Virginia	289,671	140,403	48.5	143,124	49.4	6,144	2.1	—	0.0	—	0.0	2,721	R
Wisconsin	447,134	191,363	42.8	220,822	49.4	27,631	6.2	7,318	1.6	—	0.0	29,459	R
Wyoming	51,906	28,376	54.7	21,698	41.8	1,459	2.8	373	0.7	—	0.0	6,678	D
Totals	18,535,445	9,126,063	49.2	8,547,039	46.1	590,110	3.2	221,293	1.2	50,940	0.3	579,024	D

1. For breakdown of "Other" vote, see minor candidate vote totals at the end of this chapter.

2. Figures from Svend Petersen, *A Statistical History of the American Presidential Elections* (Westport, Conn.: Greenwood Press, 1981); Edgar E. Robinson, *The Presidential Vote 1896–1932* (Stanford, Calif.: Stanford University Press, 1934).

3. Figures from Petersen, *A Statistical History*.

4. Figures from Petersen, *A Statistical History*. Plurality of 105,192 votes is calculated on the basis of 20,653 votes cast for the Progressive Party.

5. Figures from Petersen, *A Statistical History*; *Texas Almanac*.

1920 Presidential Election

STATE	TOTAL VOTE	WARREN G. HARDING (Republican)		JAMES M. COX (Democrat)		EUGENE V. DEBS (Socialist)		PARLEY P. CHRISTENSEN (Farmer-Labor)		OTHER[1]		PLURALITY	
		Votes	%	Votes	%	Votes	%	Votes	%	Votes	%		
Alabama	233,951	74,719	31.9	156,064	66.7	2,402	1.0	—	0.0	766	0.3	81,345	D
Arizona	66,803	37,016	55.4	29,546	44.2	222	0.3	15	0.0	4	0.0	7,470	R
Arkansas[2]	183,637	71,117	38.7	107,409	58.5	5,11	2.8	—	0.0	—	0.0	36,292	D
California	943,463	624,992	66.2	229,191	24.3	64,076	6.8	—	0.0	25,204	2.7	395,801	R
Colorado	292,053	173,248	59.3	104,936	35.9	8,046	2.8	3,016	1.0	2,807	1.0	68,312	R
Connecticut	365,518	229,238	62.7	120,721	33.0	10,350	2.8	1,947	0.5	3,262	0.9	108,517	R
Delaware	94,875	52,858	55.7	39,911	42.1	988	1.0	93	0.1	1,025	1.1	12,947	R
Florida	145,684	44,853	30.8	90,515	62.1	5,189	3.6	—	0.0	5,127	3.5	45,662	D
Georgia	149,558	42,981	28.7	106,112	71.0	465	0.3	—	0.0	—	0.0	63,131	D
Idaho[2]	138,359	91,351	66.0	46,930	33.9	38	0.3	6	0.0	34	0.2	44,421	R
Illinois	2,094,714	1,420,480	67.8	534,395	25.5	74,747	3.6	49,630	2.4	15,462	0.7	886,085	R
Indiana	1,262,974	696,370	55.1	511,364	40.5	24,713	2.0	16,499	1.3	14,028	1.1	185,006	R
Iowa	894,959	634,674	70.9	227,804	25.5	16,981	1.9	10,321	1.2	5,179	0.6	406,870	R
Kansas	570,243	369,268	64.8	185,464	32.5	15,511	2.7	—	0.0	—	0.0	183,804	R
Kentucky	918,636	452,480	49.3	456,497	49.7	6,409	0.7	—	0.0	3,250	0.4	4,017	D
Louisiana	126,397	38,539	30.5	87,519	69.2	—	0.0	—	0.0	339	0.3	48,980	D
Maine	197,840	136,355	68.9	58,961	29.8	2,214	1.1	—	0.0	310	0.2	77,394	R
Maryland	428,443	236,117	55.1	180,626	42.2	8,876	2.1	1,645	0.4	1,179	0.3	55,491	R
Massachusetts	993,718	681,153	68.5	276,691	27.8	32,267	3.2	—	0.0	3,607	0.4	404,462	R
Michigan	1,048,411	762,865	72.8	233,450	22.3	28,947	2.8	10,480	1.0	12,669	1.2	529,415	R
Minnesota	735,838	519,421	70.6	142,994	19.4	56,106	7.6	—	0.0	17,317	2.4	376,427	R
Mississippi	82,351	11,576	14.1	69,136	84.0	1,639	2.0	—	0.0	—	0.0	57,560	D
Missouri	1,332,140	727,252	54.6	574,699	43.1	20,342	1.5	3,108	0.2	6,739	0.5	152,553	R
Montana	179,006	109,430	61.1	57,372	32.1	—	0.0	12,204	6.8	—	0.0	52,058	R
Nebraska	382,743	247,498	64.7	119,608	31.3	9,600	2.5	—	0.0	6,037	1.6	127,890	R
Nevada	27,194	15,479	56.9	9,851	36.2	1,864	6.9	—	0.0	—	0.0	5,628	R
New Hampshire	159,092	95,196	59.8	62,662	39.4	1,234	0.8	—	0.0	—	0.0	32,534	R
New Jersey	910,251	615,333	67.6	258,761	28.4	27,385	3.0	2,264	0.2	6,508	0.7	356,572	R
New Mexico	105,412	57,634	54.7	46,668	44.3	2	0.0	1,104	1.0	4	0.0	10,966	R
New York	2,898,513	1,871,167	64.6	781,238	27.0	203,201	7.0	18,413	0.6	24,494	0.8	1,089,929	R
North Carolina	538,649	232,819	43.2	305,367	56.7	446	0.1	—	0.0	17	0.0	72,548	D
North Dakota	205,786	160,082	77.8	37,422	18.2	8,282	4.0	—	0.0	—	0.0	122,660	R
Ohio	2,021,653	1,182,022	58.5	780,037	38.6	57,147	2.8	—	0.0	2,447	0.1	401,985	R
Oklahoma	485,678	243,840	50.2	216,122	44.5	25,716	5.3	—	0.0	—	0.0	27,718	R
Oregon	238,522	143,592	60.2	80,019	33.5	9,801	4.1	—	0.0	5,110	2.1	63,573	R
Pennsylvania	1,851,248	1,218,215	65.8	503,202	27.2	70,021	3.8	15,642	0.8	44,168	2.4	715,013	R
Rhode Island	167,981	107,463	64.0	55,062	32.8	4,351	2.6	—	0.0	1,105	0.7	52,401	R
South Carolina[3]	66,808	2,610	3.9	64,170	96.1	28	0.0	—	0.0	—	0.0	61,560	D
South Dakota	182,237	110,692	60.7	35,938	19.7	—	0.0	34,707	19.0	900	0.5	74,754	R
Tennessee	428,036	219,229	51.2	206,558	48.3	2,249	0.5	—	0.0	—	0.0	12,671	R
Texas	486,109	114,658	23.6	287,920	59.2	8,124	1.7	—	0.0	75,407	15.5	173,262	D
Utah	145,828	81,555	55.9	56,639	38.8	3,159	2.2	4,475	3.1	—	0.0	24,916	R
Vermont	89,961	68,212	75.8	20,919	23.3	—	0.0	—	0.0	830	0.9	47,293	R
Virginia	231,000	87,456	37.9	141,670	61.3	808	0.3	240	0.1	826	0.4	54,214	D
Washington	398,715	223,137	56.0	84,298	21.1	8,913	2.2	77,246	19.4	5,121	1.3	138,839	R
West Virginia	509,936	282,007	55.3	220,785	43.3	5,618	1.1	—	0.0	1,526	0.3	61,222	R
Wisconsin	701,281	498,576	71.1	113,422	16.2	80,635	11.5	—	0.0	8,648	1.2	385,154	R
Wyoming	56,253	35,091	62.4	17,429	31.0	1,288	2.3	2,180	3.9	265	0.5	17,662	R
Totals	26,768,457	16,151,916	60.3	9,134,074	34.1	915,511	3.4	265,235	1.0	301,721	1.1	7,017,842	R

1. For breakdown of "Other" vote, see minor candidate vote totals at the end of this chapter.

2. Figures from Svend Petersen, *A Statistical History of the American Presidential Elections* (Westport, Conn.: Greenwood Press, 1981); *America at the Polls 1920-1956* (Washington, D.C.: CQ Press, 1994).

3. Two sets of Harding electors are combined here: Republican, 2,244; Insurgent Referendum, 366.

1924 Presidential Election

STATE	TOTAL VOTE	CALVIN COOLIDGE (Republican)		JOHN W. DAVIS (Democrat)		ROBERT M. LA FOLLETTE (Progressive)		HERMAN P. FARIS (Prohibition)		OTHER[1]		PLURALITY	
		Votes	%	Votes	%	Votes	%	Votes	%	Votes	%		
Alabama[2]	166,593	45,005	27.0	112,966	67.8	8,084	4.9	538	0.3	—	0.0	67,961	D
Arizona	73,961	30,516	41.3	26,235	35.5	17,210	23.3	—	0.0	—	0.0	4,281	R
Arkansas	138,540	40,583	29.3	84,790	61.2	13,167	9.5	—	0.0	—	0.0	44,207	D
California	1,281,778	733,250	57.2	105,514	8.2	424,649	33.1	18,365	1.4	—	0.0	308,601	R
Colorado[3]	342,261	195,171	57.0	75,238	22.0	69,945	20.4	966	0.3	940	0.3	119,933	R
Connecticut	400,396	246,322	61.5	110,184	27.5	42,416	10.6	—	0.0	1,474	0.4	136,138	R
Delaware	90,885	52,441	57.7	33,445	36.8	4,979	5.5	—	0.0	20	0.0	18,996	R
Florida	109,158	30,633	28.1	62,083	56.9	8,625	7.9	5,498	5.0	2,319	2.1	31,450	D
Georgia	166,635	30,300	18.2	123,262	74.0	12,687	7.6	231	0.1	155	0.1	92,962	D
Idaho	147,690	69,791	47.3	23,951	16.2	53,948	36.5	—	0.0	—	0.0	15,843	R
Illinois	2,470,067	1,453,321	58.8	576,975	23.4	432,027	17.5	2,367	0.1	5,377	0.2	876,346	R
Indiana	1,272,390	703,042	55.3	492,245	38.7	71,700	5.6	4,416	0.3	987	0.1	210,797	R
Iowa	976,770	537,458	55.0	160,382	16.4	274,448	28.1	—	0.0	4,482	0.5	263,010	R
Kansas	662,456	407,671	61.5	156,320	23.6	98,461	14.9	—	0.0	4	0.0	251,351	R
Kentucky[4]	816,070	398,966	48.9	375,593	46.0	38,465	4.7	—	0.0	3,046	0.4	23,373	R
Louisiana	121,951	24,670	20.2	93,218	76.4	—	0.0	—	0.0	4,063	3.3	68,548	D
Maine	192,192	138,440	72.0	41,964	21.8	11,382	5.9	—	0.0	406	0.2	96,476	R
Maryland	358,630	162,414	45.3	148,072	41.3	47,157	13.1	—	0.0	987	0.3	14,342	R
Massachusetts	1,129,837	703,476	62.3	280,831	24.9	141,225	12.5	—	0.0	4,305	0.4	422,645	R
Michigan	1,160,419	874,631	75.4	152,359	13.1	122,014	10.5	6,085	0.5	5,330	0.5	722,272	R
Minnesota	822,146	420,759	51.2	55,913	6.8	339,192	41.3	—	0.0	6,282	0.8	81,567	R
Mississippi	112,442	8,494	7.6	100,474	89.4	3,474	3.1	—	0.0	—	0.0	91,980	D
Missouri[5]	1,310,095	648,488	49.5	574,962	43.9	83,986	6.4	1,418	0.1	1,231	0.1	73,526	R
Montana[6]	174,425	74,138	42.5	33,805	19.4	65,876	37.9	—	0.0	358	0.2	8,014	R
Nebraska	463,559	218,985	47.2	137,299	29.6	105,681	22.8	1,594	0.3	—	0.0	81,686	R
Nevada	26,921	11,243	41.8	5,909	21.9	9,769	36.3	—	0.0	—	0.0	1,474	R
New Hampshire	164,769	98,575	59.8	57,201	34.7	8,993	5.5	—	0.0	—	0.0	41,374	R
New Jersey	1,088,054	676,277	62.2	298,043	27.4	109,028	10.0	1,660	0.2	3,046	0.3	378,234	R
New Mexico	112,830	54,745	48.5	48,542	43.0	9,543	8.5	—	0.0	—	0.0	6,203	R
New York[7]	3,263,939	1,820,058	55.8	950,796	29.1	474,913	14.6	—	0.0	18,172	0.6	869,262	R
North Carolina	481,608	190,754	39.6	284,190	59.0	6,651	1.4	13	0.0	—	0.0	93,436	D
North Dakota	199,081	94,931	47.7	13,858	7.0	89,922	45.2	—	0.0	370	0.2	5,009	R
Ohio	2,016,296	1,176,130	58.3	477,887	23.7	358,008	17.8	—	0.0	4,271	0.2	698,243	R
Oklahoma[8]	527,928	225,755	42.8	255,798	48.4	41,141	7.8	—	0.0	5,234	1.0	30,043	D
Oregon	279,488	142,579	51.0	67,589	24.2	68,403	24.5	—	0.0	917	0.3	74,176	R
Pennsylvania[9]	2,144,850	1,401,481	65.3	409,192	19.1	307,567	14.3	9,779	0.5	16,831	0.8	992,289	R
Rhode Island	210,115	125,286	59.6	76,606	36.5	7,628	3.6	—	0.0	595	0.3	48,680	R
South Carolina	50,755	1,123	2.2	49,008	96.6	623	1.2	—	0.0	1	0.0	47,885	D
South Dakota	203,868	101,299	49.7	27,214	13.3	75,355	37.0	—	0.0	—	0.0	25,944	R
Tennessee	301,030	130,831	43.5	159,339	52.9	10,666	3.5	94	0.0	100	0.0	28,508	D
Texas	657,054	130,794	19.9	483,381	73.6	42,879	6.5	—	0.0	—	0.0	352,587	D
Utah	156,990	77,327	49.3	47,001	29.9	32,662	20.8	—	0.0	—	0.0	30,326	R
Vermont	102,917	80,498	78.2	16,124	15.7	5,964	5.8	326	0.3	5	0.0	64,374	R
Virginia	223,603	73,328	32.8	139,717	62.5	10,369	4.6	—	0.0	189	0.1	66,389	D
Washington	421,549	220,224	52.2	42,842	10.2	150,727	35.8	—	0.0	7,756	1.8	69,497	R
West Virginia[10]	583,662	288,635	49.5	257,232	44.1	36,723	6.3	—	0.0	1,072	0.2	31,403	R
Wisconsin	840,827	311,614	37.1	68,115	8.1	453,678	54.0	2,918	0.3	4,502	0.5	142,064	P
Wyoming	79,900	41,858	52.4	12,868	16.1	25,174	31.5	—	0.0	—	0.0	16,684	R
Totals	29,099,380	15,724,310	54.0	8,386,532	28.8	4,827,184	16.6	56,268	0.2	104,827	0.4	7,337,778	R

1. For breakdown of "Other" vote, see minor candidate vote totals at the end of this chapter.

2. Figures from Svend Petersen, *A Statistical History of the American Presidential Elections* (Westport, Conn.: Greenwood Press, 1981); Clerk of the House of Representatives, *Statistics of the Congressional and Presidential Election* (Washington, D.C.: U.S. Government Printing Office, 1924).

3. Two sets of La Follette electors are combined here: Colorado Independent Progressive, 57,368; Farmer-Labor, 12,577.

4. Figures from Petersen, *A Statistical History*; Clerk of the House, *Congressional and Presidential Election*; *Kentucky Directory 1925*, p. 142.

5. Two sets of La Follette electors are combined here: Missouri Socialist, 56,723; Liberal, 27,263.

6. Two sets of La Follette electors are combined here: Montana Independent Progressive, 61,105; Farmer-Labor, 4,771.

7. Two sets of La Follette electors are combined here: New York Socialist, 268,518; Progressive, 206,395.

8. There were two separate slates of electors pledged to La Follette in Oklahoma that could not legally be combined. State Election Board *Directory of Oklahoma 1973*, p. 343.

9. Two sets of La Follette electors are combined here: Pennsylvania Socialist, 93,441; Labor, 214,126.

10. Two sets of La Follette electors are combined here: West Virginia Socialist, 14,903; Farmer-Labor, 21,820.

1928 Presidential Election

STATE	TOTAL VOTE	HERBERT C. HOOVER (Republican)		ALFRED E. SMITH (Democrat)		NORMAN M. THOMAS (Socialist)		WILLIAM Z. FOSTER (Communist)		OTHER[1]		PLURALITY	
		Votes	%	Votes	%	Votes	%	Votes	%	Votes	%		
Alabama	248,981	120,725	48.5	127,796	51.3	460	0.2	—	0.0	—	0.0	7,071	D
Arizona	91,254	52,533	57.6	38,537	42.2	—	0.0	184	0.2	—	0.0	13,996	R
Arkansas	197,726	77,784	39.3	119,196	60.3	429	0.2	317	0.2	—	0.0	41,412	D
California	1,796,656	1,162,323	64.7	614,365	34.2	19,595	1.1	—	0.0	373	0.0	547,958	R
Colorado	392,242	253,872	64.7	133,131	33.9	3,472	0.9	675	0.2	1,092	0.3	120,741	R
Connecticut	553,118	296,641	53.6	252,085	45.6	3,029	0.5	738	0.1	625	0.1	44,556	R
Delaware	104,602	68,860	65.8	35,354	33.8	329	0.3	59	0.1	—	0.0	33,506	R
Florida[2]	253,672	144,168	56.8	101,764	40.1	4,036	1.6	3,704	1.5	—	0.0	42,404	R
Georgia[3]	231,592	101,800	44.0	129,604	56.0	124	0.1	64	0.0	—	0.0	27,804	D
Idaho[4]	154,230	99,848	64.7	53,074	34.4	1,308	0.8	—	0.0	—	0.0	46,774	R
Illinois	3,107,489	1,769,141	56.9	1,313,817	42.3	19,138	0.6	3,581	0.1	1,812	0.1	455,324	R
Indiana	1,421,314	848,290	59.7	562,691	39.6	3,871	0.3	321	0.0	6,141	0.4	285,599	R
Iowa	1,009,189	623,570	61.8	379,011	37.6	2,960	0.3	328	0.0	3,320	0.3	244,559	R
Kansas	713,200	513,672	72.0	193,003	27.1	6,205	0.9	320	0.0	—	0.0	320,669	R
Kentucky	940,521	558,064	59.3	381,070	40.5	783	0.1	288	0.0	316	0.0	176,994	R
Louisiana	215,833	51,160	23.7	164,655	76.3	—	0.0	—	0.0	18	0.0	113,495	D
Maine	262,170	179,923	68.6	81,179	31.0	1,063	0.4	—	0.0	—	0.0	98,744	R
Maryland	528,348	301,479	57.1	223,626	42.3	1,701	0.3	636	0.1	906	0.2	77,853	R
Massachusetts	1,577,823	775,566	49.2	792,758	50.2	6,262	0.4	2,461	0.2	776	0.0	17,192	D
Michigan	1,372,082	965,396	70.4	396,762	28.9	3,516	0.3	2,881	0.2	3,527	0.3	568,634	R
Minnesota	970,976	560,977	57.8	396,451	40.8	6,774	0.7	4,853	0.5	1,921	0.2	164,526	R
Mississippi[5]	151,568	27,030	17.8	124,538	82.2	—	0.0	—	0.0	—	0.0	97,508	D
Missouri	1,500,845	834,080	55.6	662,684	44.2	3,739	0.2	—	0.0	342	0.0	171,396	R
Montana	194,108	113,300	58.4	78,578	40.5	1,667	0.9	563	0.3	—	0.0	34,722	R
Nebraska	547,128	345,745	63.2	197,950	36.2	3,433	0.6	—	0.0	—	0.0	147,795	R
Nevada	32,417	18,327	56.5	14,090	43.5	—	0.0	—	0.0	—	0.0	4,237	R
New Hampshire	196,757	115,404	58.7	80,715	41.0	465	0.2	173	0.1	—	0.0	34,689	R
New Jersey	1,549,381	926,050	59.8	616,517	39.8	4,897	0.3	1,257	0.1	660	0.0	309,533	R
New Mexico	118,077	69,708	59.0	48,211	40.8	—	0.0	158	0.1	—	0.0	21,497	R
New York	4,405,626	2,193,344	49.8	2,089,863	47.4	107,332	2.4	10,876	0.2	4,211	0.1	103,481	R
North Carolina	635,150	348,923	54.9	286,227	45.1	—	0.0	—	0.0	—	0.0	62,696	R
North Dakota	239,845	131,419	54.8	106,648	44.5	936	0.4	842	0.4	—	0.0	24,771	R
Ohio	2,508,346	1,627,546	64.9	864,210	34.5	8,683	0.3	2,836	0.1	5,071	0.2	763,336	R
Oklahoma	618,427	394,046	63.7	219,174	35.4	3,924	0.6	—	0.0	1,283	0.2	174,872	R
Oregon	319,942	205,341	64.2	109,223	34.1	2,720	0.9	1,094	0.3	1,564	0.5	96,118	R
Pennsylvania	3,150,612	2,055,382	65.2	1,067,586	33.9	18,647	0.6	4,726	0.2	4,271	0.1	987,796	R
Rhode Island	237,194	117,522	49.5	118,973	50.2	—	0.0	283	0.1	416	0.2	1,451	D
South Carolina[6]	68,605	5,858	8.5	62,700	91.4	47	0.1	—	0.0	—	0.0	56,842	D
South Dakota	261,857	157,603	60.2	102,660	39.2	443	0.2	224	0.1	927	0.4	54,943	R
Tennessee	353,192	195,388	55.3	157,143	44.5	567	0.2	94	0.0	—	0.0	38,245	R
Texas[7]	708,999	367,036	51.8	341,032	48.1	722	0.1	209	0.0	—	0.0	26,004	R
Utah	176,603	94,618	53.6	80,985	45.9	954	0.5	46	0.0	—	0.0	13,633	R
Vermont	135,191	90,404	66.9	44,440	32.9	—	0.0	—	0.0	347	0.3	45,964	R
Virginia	305,364	164,609	53.9	140,146	45.9	249	0.1	179	0.1	181	0.1	24,463	R
Washington	500,840	335,844	67.1	156,772	31.3	2,615	0.5	1,541	0.3	4,068	0.8	179,072	R
West Virginia	642,752	375,551	58.4	263,784	41.0	1,313	0.2	401	0.1	1,703	0.3	111,767	R
Wisconsin	1,016,831	544,205	53.5	450,259	44.3	18,213	1.8	1,528	0.2	2,626	0.3	93,946	R
Wyoming	82,835	52,748	63.7	29,299	35.4	788	1.0	—	0.0	—	0.0	23,449	R
Totals	36,801,510	21,432,823	58.2	15,004,336	40.8	267,414	0.7	48,440	0.1	48,497	0.1	6,428,487	R

1. For breakdown of "Other" vote, see minor candidate vote totals at the end of this chapter.

2. Figures from Clerk of the House of Representatives, *Statistics of the Congressional and Presidential Election* (Washington, D.C.: U.S. Government Printing Office, 1928).

3. Two sets of Hoover electors are combined here: Republican, 65,423; Anti-Smith, 36,377.

4. Figures from Clerk of the House, *Congressional and Presidential Election*.

5. Three sets of Hoover electors are combined here: Republican, 26,222; Ligon electors, 544; Rogers electors, 264.

6. Two sets of Hoover electors are combined here: Republican, 3,188; Anti-Smith, 2,670.

7. Figures from Svend Petersen, *A Statistical History of the American Presidential Elections* (Westport, Conn.: Greenwood Press, 1981); Clerk of the House, *Congressional and Presidential Election; Texas Almanac.*

1932 Presidential Election

STATE	TOTAL VOTE	FRANKLIN D. ROOSEVELT (Democrat)		HERBERT C. HOOVER (Republican)		NORMAN M. THOMAS (Socialist)		WILLIAM Z. FOSTER (Communist)		OTHER[1]		PLURALITY	
		Votes	%	Votes	%	Votes	%	Votes	%	Votes	%		
Alabama	245,303	207,910	84.8	34,675	14.1	2,030	0.8	675	0.3	13	0.0	173,235	D
Arizona	118,251	79,264	67.0	36,104	30.5	2,618	2.2	256	0.2	9	0.0	43,160	D
Arkansas	216,569	186,829	86.3	27,465	12.7	1,166	0.5	157	0.1	952	0.4	159,364	D
California	2,266,972	1,324,157	58.4	847,902	37.4	63,299	2.8	1,023	0.0	30,591	1.3	476,255	D
Colorado	457,696	250,877	54.8	189,617	41.4	13,591	3.0	787	0.2	2,824	0.6	61,260	D
Connecticut	594,183	281,632	47.4	288,420	48.5	20,480	3.4	1,364	0.2	2,287	0.4	6,788	R
Delaware	112,901	54,319	48.1	57,073	50.6	1,376	1.2	133	0.1	—	0.0	2,754	R
Florida	276,943	206,307	74.5	69,170	25.0	775	0.3	—	0.0	691	0.2	137,137	D
Georgia	255,590	234,118	91.6	19,863	7.8	461	0.2	23	0.0	1,125	0.4	214,255	D
Idaho	186,520	109,479	58.7	71,312	38.2	526	0.3	491	0.3	4,712	2.5	38,167	D
Illinois	3,407,926	1,882,304	55.2	1,432,756	42.0	67,258	2.0	15,582	0.5	10,026	0.3	449,548	D
Indiana	1,576,927	862,054	54.7	677,184	42.9	21,388	1.4	2,187	0.1	14,114	0.9	184,870	D
Iowa	1,036,687	598,019	57.7	414,433	40.0	20,467	2.0	559	0.1	3,209	0.3	183,586	D
Kansas	791,978	424,204	53.6	349,498	44.1	18,276	2.3	—	0.0	—	0.0	74,706	D
Kentucky	983,059	580,574	59.1	394,716	40.2	3,853	0.4	271	0.0	3,645	0.4	185,858	D
Louisiana	268,804	249,418	92.8	18,853	7.0	—	0.0	—	0.0	533	0.2	230,565	D
Maine	298,444	128,907	43.2	166,631	55.8	2,489	0.8	162	0.1	255	0.1	37,724	R
Maryland	511,054	314,314	61.5	184,184	36.0	10,489	2.1	1,031	0.2	1,036	0.2	130,130	D
Massachusetts	1,580,114	800,148	50.6	736,959	46.6	34,305	2.2	4,821	0.3	3,881	0.2	63,189	D
Michigan	1,664,765	871,700	52.4	739,894	44.4	39,205	2.4	9,318	0.6	4,648	0.3	131,806	D
Minnesota	1,002,843	600,806	59.9	363,959	36.3	25,476	2.5	6,101	0.6	6,501	0.6	236,847	D
Mississippi[2]	146,034	140,168	96.0	5,180	3.5	686	0.5	—	0.0	—	0.0	134,988	D
Missouri	1,609,894	1,025,406	63.7	564,713	35.1	16,374	1.0	568	0.0	2,833	0.2	460,693	D
Montana	216,479	127,286	58.8	78,078	36.1	7,891	3.6	1,775	0.8	1,449	0.7	49,208	D
Nebraska	570,135	359,082	63.0	201,177	35.3	9,876	1.7	—	0.0	—	0.0	157,905	D
Nevada	41,430	28,756	69.4	12,674	30.6	—	0.0	—	0.0	—	0.0	16,082	D
New Hampshire	205,520	100,680	49.0	103,629	50.4	947	0.5	264	0.1	—	0.0	2,949	R
New Jersey	1,630,063	806,630	49.5	775,684	47.6	42,998	2.6	2,915	0.2	1,836	0.1	30,946	D
New Mexico	151,606	95,089	62.7	54,217	35.8	1,776	1.2	135	0.1	389	0.3	40,872	D
New York	4,688,614	2,534,959	54.1	1,937,963	41.3	177,397	3.8	27,956	0.6	10,339	0.2	596,996	D
North Carolina	711,498	497,566	69.9	208,344	29.3	5,588	0.8	—	0.0	—	0.0	289,222	D
North Dakota	256,290	178,350	69.6	71,772	28.0	3,521	1.4	830	0.3	1,817	0.7	106,578	D
Ohio	2,609,728	1,301,695	49.9	1,227,319	47.0	64,094	2.5	7,231	0.3	9,389	0.4	74,376	D
Oklahoma	704,633	516,468	73.3	188,165	26.7	—	0.0	—	0.0	—	0.0	328,303	D
Oregon	368,751	213,871	58.0	136,019	36.9	15,450	4.2	1,681	0.5	1,730	0.5	77,852	D
Pennsylvania	2,859,021	1,295,948	45.3	1,453,540	50.8	91,119	3.2	5,658	0.2	12,756	0.4	157,592	R
Rhode Island	266,170	146,604	55.1	115,266	43.3	3,138	1.2	546	0.2	616	0.2	31,338	D
South Carolina	104,407	102,347	98.0	1,978	1.9	82	0.1	—	0.0	—	0.0	100,369	D
South Dakota	288,438	183,515	63.6	99,212	34.4	1,551	0.5	364	0.1	3,796	1.3	84,303	D
Tennessee	390,273	259,473	66.5	126,752	32.5	1,796	0.5	254	0.1	1,998	0.5	132,721	D
Texas[3]	863,406	760,348	88.1	97,959	11.3	4,450	0.5	207	0.0	442	0.0	662,389	D
Utah	206,578	116,750	56.5	84,795	41.0	4,087	2.0	946	0.5	—	0.0	31,955	D
Vermont	136,980	56,266	41.1	78,984	57.7	1,533	1.1	195	0.1	2	0.0	22,718	R
Virginia	297,942	203,979	68.5	89,637	30.1	2,382	0.8	86	0.0	1,858	0.6	114,342	D
Washington	614,814	353,260	57.5	208,645	33.9	17,080	2.8	2,972	0.5	32,857	5.3	144,615	D
West Virginia	743,774	405,124	54.5	330,731	44.5	5,133	0.7	444	0.1	2,342	0.3	74,393	D
Wisconsin	1,114,814	707,410	63.5	347,741	31.2	53,379	4.8	3,105	0.3	3,179	0.3	359,669	D
Wyoming	96,962	54,370	56.1	39,583	40.8	2,829	2.9	180	0.2	—	0.0	14,787	D
Totals	39,747,783	22,818,740	57.4	15,760,425	39.6	884,685	2.2	103,253	0.3	180,680	0.5	7,058,315	D

1. For breakdown of "Other" vote, see minor candidate vote totals at the end of this chapter.

2. Two sets of Hoover electors are combined here: Lily White, 3,210; Black and Tan, 1,970.

3. Figures from Svend Petersen, *A Statistical History of the American Presidential Elections* (Westport, Conn.: Greenwood Press, 1981); Clerk of the House of Representatives, *Statistics of the Congressional and Presidential Election* (Washington, D.C.: U.S. Government Printing Office, 1932); *Texas Almanac*.

1936 Presidential Election

STATE	TOTAL VOTE	FRANKLIN D. ROOSEVELT (Democrat)		ALFRED M. LANDON (Republican)		WILLIAM LEMKE (Union)		NORMAN M. THOMAS (Socialist)		OTHER[1]		PLURALITY	
		Votes	%	Votes	%	Votes	%	Votes	%	Votes	%		
Alabama	275,744	238,196	86.4	35,358	12.8	551	0.2	242	0.1	1,397	0.5	202,838	D
Arizona	124,163	86,722	69.8	33,433	26.9	3,307	2.7	317	0.3	384	0.3	53,289	D
Arkansas	179,431	146,765	81.8	32,049	17.9	4	0.0	446	0.2	167	0.1	114,716	D
California	2,638,882	1,766,836	67.0	836,431	31.7	—	0.0	11,331	0.4	24,284	0.9	930,405	D
Colorado	488,685	295,021	60.4	181,267	37.1	9,962	2.0	1,594	0.3	841	0.2	113,754	D
Connecticut	690,723	382,129	55.3	278,685	40.3	21,805	3.2	5,683	0.8	2,421	0.4	103,444	D
Delaware[2]	127,603	69,702	54.6	54,014	42.3	442	0.3	172	0.1	3,273	2.6	15,688	D
Florida	327,436	249,117	76.1	78,248	23.9	—	0.0	—	0.0	71	0.0	170,869	D
Georgia	293,170	255,363	87.1	36,943	12.6	136	0.0	68	0.0	660	0.2	218,420	D
Idaho	199,617	125,683	63.0	66,256	33.2	7,678	3.8	—	0.0	—	0.0	59,427	D
Illinois	3,956,522	2,282,999	57.7	1,570,393	39.7	89,439	2.3	7,530	0.2	6,161	0.2	712,606	D
Indiana	1,650,897	934,974	56.6	691,570	41.9	19,407	1.2	3,856	0.2	1,090	0.1	243,404	D
Iowa	1,142,737	621,756	54.4	487,977	42.7	29,687	2.6	1,373	0.1	1,944	0.2	133,779	D
Kansas	865,507	464,520	53.7	397,727	46.0	494	0.1	2,766	0.3	—	0.0	66,793	D
Kentucky	926,214	541,944	58.5	369,702	39.9	12,501	1.3	627	0.1	1,440	0.2	172,242	D
Louisiana	329,778	292,894	88.8	36,791	11.2	—	0.0	—	0.0	93	0.0	256,103	D
Maine	304,240	126,333	41.5	168,823	55.5	7,581	2.5	783	0.3	720	0.2	42,490	R
Maryland	624,896	389,612	62.3	231,435	37.0	—	0.0	1,629	0.3	2,220	0.4	158,177	D
Massachusetts	1,840,357	942,716	51.2	768,613	41.8	118,639	6.4	5,111	0.3	5,278	0.3	174,103	D
Michigan	1,805,098	1,016,794	56.3	699,733	38.8	75,795	4.2	8,208	0.5	4,568	0.3	317,061	D
Minnesota	1,129,975	698,811	61.8	350,461	31.0	74,296	6.6	2,872	0.3	3,535	0.3	348,350	D
Mississippi	162,142	157,333	97.0	4,467	2.8	—	0.0	342	0.2	—	0.0	152,866	D
Missouri	1,828,635	1,111,043	60.8	697,891	38.2	14,630	0.8	3,454	0.2	1,617	0.1	413,152	D
Montana	230,502	159,690	69.3	63,598	27.6	5,539	2.4	1,066	0.5	609	0.3	96,092	D
Nebraska	608,023	347,445	57.1	247,731	40.7	12,847	2.1	—	0.0	—	0.0	99,714	D
Nevada	43,848	31,925	72.8	11,923	27.2	—	0.0	—	0.0	—	0.0	20,002	D
New Hampshire	218,114	108,460	49.7	104,642	48.0	4,819	2.2	—	0.0	193	0.1	3,818	D
New Jersey	1,820,437	1,083,850	59.5	720,322	39.6	9,407	0.5	3,931	0.2	2,927	0.2	363,528	D
New Mexico	169,135	106,037	62.7	61,727	36.5	924	0.5	343	0.2	104	0.1	44,310	D
New York	5,596,398	3,293,222	58.8	2,180,670	39.0	—	0.0	86,897	1.6	35,609	0.6	1,112,552	D
North Carolina	839,475	616,141	73.4	223,294	26.6	2	0.0	21	0.0	17	0.0	392,847	D
North Dakota	273,716	163,148	59.6	72,751	26.6	36,708	13.4	552	0.2	557	0.2	90,397	D
Ohio	3,012,660	1,747,140	58.0	1,127,855	37.4	132,212	4.4	167	0.0	5,286	0.2	619,285	D
Oklahoma	749,740	501,069	66.8	245,122	32.7	—	0.0	2,221	0.3	1,328	0.2	255,947	D
Oregon	414,021	266,733	64.4	122,706	29.6	21,831	5.3	2,143	0.5	608	0.1	144,027	D
Pennsylvania	4,138,105	2,353,788	56.9	1,690,300	40.8	67,467	1.6	14,375	0.3	12,175	0.3	663,488	D
Rhode Island	310,278	164,338	53.0	125,031	40.3	19,569	6.3	—	0.0	1,340	0.4	39,307	D
South Carolina	115,437	113,791	98.6	1,646	1.4	—	0.0	—	0.0	—	0.0	112,145	D
South Dakota	296,452	160,137	54.0	125,977	42.5	10,338	3.5	—	0.0	—	0.0	34,160	D
Tennessee[3]	475,533	327,083	68.8	146,516	30.8	296	0.1	687	0.1	951	0.2	180,567	D
Texas[4]	843,482	734,485	87.1	103,874	12.3	3,281	0.4	1,075	0.1	767	0.1	630,611	D
Utah	216,679	150,248	69.3	64,555	29.8	1,121	0.5	432	0.2	323	0.1	85,693	D
Vermont	143,689	62,124	43.2	81,023	56.4	—	0.0	—	0.0	542	0.4	18,899	R
Virginia	334,590	234,980	70.2	98,336	29.4	233	0.1	313	0.1	728	0.2	136,644	D
Washington	692,338	459,579	66.4	206,892	29.9	17,463	2.5	3,496	0.5	4,908	0.7	252,687	D
West Virginia	829,945	502,582	60.6	325,358	39.2	—	0.0	832	0.1	1,173	0.1	177,224	D
Wisconsin	1,258,560	802,984	63.8	380,828	30.3	60,297	4.8	10,626	0.8	3,825	0.3	422,156	D
Wyoming	103,382	62,624	60.6	38,739	37.5	1,653	1.6	200	0.2	166	0.2	23,885	D
Totals	45,656,991	27,750,866	60.8	16,679,683	36.5	892,361	2.0	187,781	0.4	136,300	0.3	11,071,183	D

1. For breakdown of "Other" vote, see minor candidate vote totals at the end of this chapter.

2. Figures from Clerk of the House of Representatives, *Statistics of the Congressional and Presidential Election* (Washington. D.C.: U.S. Government Printing Office, 1936). Two sets of Landon electors—Republican and Independent Republican—are combined here.

3. Figures from Svend Petersen, *A Statistical History of the American Presidential Elections* (Westport, Conn.: Greenwood Press, 1981); Clerk of the House, *Congressional and Presidential Election.*

4. Figures from Petersen, *A Statistical History*; Clerk of the House, *Congressional and Presidential Election*; *Texas Almanac.*

1940 Presidential Election

STATES	TOTAL VOTE	FRANKLIN D. ROOSEVELT (Democrat)		WENDELL WILLKIE (Republican)		NORMAN M. THOMAS (Socialist)		ROGER W. BABSON (Prohibition)		OTHER [1]		PLURALITY	
		Votes	%	Votes	%	Votes	%	Votes	%	Votes	%		
Alabama	294,219	250,726	85.2	42,184	14.3	100	0.0	700	0.2	509	0.2	208,542	D
Arizona	150,039	95,267	63.5	54,030	36.0	—	0.0	742	0.5	—	0.0	41,237	D
Arkansas	200,429	157,213	78.4	42,122	21.0	301	0.2	793	0.4	—	0.0	115,091	D
California	3,268,791	1,877,618	57.4	1,351,419	41.3	16,506	0.5	9,400	0.3	13,848	0.4	526,199	D
Colorado	549,004	265,554	48.4	279,576	50.9	1,899	0.3	1,597	0.3	378	0.1	14,022	R
Connecticut	781,502	417,621	53.4	361,819	46.3	—	0.0	—	0.0	2,062	0.3	55,802	D
Delaware	136,374	74,599	54.7	61,440	45.1	115	0.1	220	0.2	—	0.0	13,159	D
Florida	485,640	359,334	74.0	126,158	26.0	—	0.0	—	0.0	148	0.0	233,176	D
Georgia[2]	312,686	265,194	84.8	46,495	14.9	—	0.0	983	0.3	14	0.0	218,699	D
Idaho	235,168	127,842	54.4	106,553	45.3	497	0.2	—	0.0	276	0.1	21,289	D
Illinois	4,217,935	2,149,934	51.0	2,047,240	48.5	10,914	0.3	9,190	0.2	657	0.0	102,694	D
Indiana	1,782,747	874,063	49.0	899,466	50.5	2,075	0.1	6,437	0.4	706	0.0	25,403	R
Iowa	1,215,432	578,802	47.6	632,370	52.0	—	0.0	2,284	0.2	1,976	0.2	53,568	R
Kansas	860,297	364,725	42.4	489,169	56.9	2,347	0.3	4,056	0.5	—	0.0	124,444	R
Kentucky	970,163	557,322	57.4	410,384	42.3	1,014	0.1	1,443	0.1	—	0.0	146,938	D
Louisiana	372,305	319,751	85.9	52,446	14.1	—	0.0	—	0.0	108	0.0	267,305	D
Maine	320,840	156,478	48.8	163,951	51.1	—	0.0	—	0.0	411	0.1	7,473	R
Maryland	660,104	384,546	58.3	269,534	40.8	4,093	0.6	—	0.0	1,931	0.3	115,012	D
Massachusetts	2,026,993	1,076,522	53.1	939,700	46.4	4,091	0.2	1,370	0.1	5,310	0.3	136,822	D
Michigan	2,085,929	1,032,991	49.5	1,039,917	49.9	7,593	0.4	1,795	0.1	3,633	0.2	6,926	R
Minnesota	1,251,188	644,196	51.5	596,274	47.7	5,454	0.4	—	0.0	5,264	0.4	47,922	D
Mississippi	175,824	168,267	95.7	7,364	4.2	193	0.1	—	0.0	—	0.0	160,903	D
Missouri	1,833,729	958,476	52.3	871,009	47.5	2,226	0.1	1,809	0.1	209	0.0	87,467	D
Montana	247,873	145,698	58.8	99,579	40.2	1,443	0.6	664	0.3	489	0.2	46,119	D
Nebraska	615,878	263,677	42.8	352,201	57.2	—	0.0	—	0.0	—	0.0	88,524	R
Nevada	53,174	31,945	60.1	21,229	39.9	—	0.0	—	0.0	—	0.0	10,716	D
New Hampshire	235,419	125,292	53.2	110,127	46.8	—	0.0	—	0.0	—	0.0	15,165	D
New Jersey	1,972,552	1,016,808	51.5	945,475	47.9	2,433	0.1	873	0.0	6,963	0.4	71,333	D
New Mexico	183,258	103,699	56.6	79,315	43.3	144	0.1	100	0.1	—	0.0	24,384	D
New York	6,301,596	3,251,918	51.6	3,027,478	48.0	18,950	0.3	3,250	0.1	—	0.0	224,440	D
North Carolina	822,648	609,015	74.0	213,633	26.0	—	0.0	—	0.0	—	0.0	395,382	D
North Dakota	280,775	124,036	44.2	154,590	55.1	1,279	0.5	325	0.1	545	0.2	30,554	R
Ohio	3,319,912	1,733,139	52.2	1,586,773	47.8	—	0.0	—	0.0	—	0.0	146,366	D
Oklahoma	826,212	474,313	57.4	348,872	42.2	—	0.0	3,027	0.4	—	0.0	125,441	D
Oregon	481,240	258,415	53.7	219,555	45.6	398	0.1	154	0.0	2,718	0.6	38,860	D
Pennsylvania	4,078,714	2,171,035	53.2	1,889,848	46.3	10,967	0.3	—	0.0	6,864	0.2	281,187	D
Rhode Island	321,152	182,181	56.7	138,654	43.2	—	0.0	74	0.0	243	0.1	43,527	D
South Carolina	99,830	95,470	95.6	4,360	4.4	—	0.0	—	0.0	—	0.0	91,110	D
South Dakota	308,427	131,362	42.6	177,065	57.4	—	0.0	—	0.0	—	0.0	45,703	R
Tennessee	522,823	351,601	67.3	169,153	32.4	463	0.1	1,606	0.3	—	0.0	182,448	D
Texas[3]	1,041,168	840,151	80.7	199,152	19.1	728	0.1	925	0.1	212	0.0	640,999	D
Utah	247,819	154,277	62.3	93,151	37.6	200	0.1	—	0.0	191	0.1	61,126	D
Vermont	143,062	64,269	44.9	78,371	54.8	—	0.0	—	0.0	422	0.3	14,102	R
Virginia	346,608	235,961	68.1	109,363	31.6	282	0.1	882	0.3	120	0.0	126,598	D
Washington	793,833	462,145	58.2	322,123	40.6	4,586	0.6	1,686	0.2	3,293	0.4	140,022	D
West Virginia	868,076	495,662	57.1	372,414	42.9	—	0.0	—	0.0	—	0.0	123,248	D
Wisconsin	1,405,522	704,821	50.1	679,206	48.3	15,071	1.1	2,148	0.2	4,276	0.3	25,615	D
Wyoming	112,240	59,287	52.8	52,633	46.9	148	0.1	172	0.2	—	0.0	6,654	D
Totals	49,817,149	27,343,218	54.7	22,334,940	44.8	116,510	0.2	58,705	0.1	63,776	0.1	5,008,278	D

1. For breakdown of "Other" vote, see minor candidate vote totals at the end of this chapter.

2. Two sets of Willkie electors are combined here: Republican, 23,934; Independent Democrat, 22,561.

3. Figures from Svend Petersen, *A Statistical History of the American Presidential Elections* (Westport, Conn.: Greenwood Press, 1981); Clerk of the House of Representatives, *Statistical of the Congressional and Presidential Election* (Washington, D.C.: U.S. Government Printing Office, 1940); *Texas Almanac.*

1944 Presidential Election

STATE	TOTAL VOTE	FRANKLIN D. ROOSEVELT (Democrat)		THOMAS E. DEWEY (Republican)		NORMAN THOMAS (Socialist)		CLAUDE A. WATSON (Prohibition)		OTHER [1]		PLURALITY	
		Votes	%	Votes	%	Votes	%	Votes	%	Votes	%		
Alabama	244,743	198,918	81.3	44,540	18.2	190	0.1	1,095	0.4	—	0.0	154,378	D
Arizona	137,634	80,926	58.8	56,287	40.9	—	0.0	421	0.3	—	0.0	24,639	D
Arkansas	212,954	148,965	70.0	63,551	29.8	438	0.2	—	0.0	—	0.0	85,414	D
California	3,520,875	1,988,564	56.5	1,512,965	43.0	2,515	0.1	14,770	0.4	2,061	0.1	475,599	D
Colorado	505,039	234,331	46.4	268,731	53.2	1,977	0.4	—	0.0	—	0.0	34,400	R
Connecticut	831,990	435,146	52.3	390,527	46.9	5,097	0.6	—	0.0	1,220	0.1	44,619	D
Delaware	125,361	68,166	54.4	56,747	45.3	154	0.1	294	0.2	—	0.0	11,419	D
Florida	482,803	339,377	70.3	143,215	29.7	—	0.0	—	0.0	211	0.0	196,162	D
Georgia[2]	328,129	268,187	81.7	56,506	17.2	6	0.0	36	0.0	3,373	1.0	211,681	D
Idaho	208,321	107,399	51.6	100,137	48.1	282	0.1	503	0.2	—	0.0	7,262	D
Illinois	4,036,061	2,079,479	51.5	1,939,314	48.0	180	0.0	7,411	0.2	9,677	0.2	140,165	D
Indiana	1,672,091	781,403	46.7	875,891	52.4	2,223	0.1	12,574	0.8	—	0.0	94,488	R
Iowa	1,052,599	499,876	47.5	547,267	52.0	1,511	0.1	3,752	0.4	193	0.0	47,391	R
Kansas	733,776	287,458	39.2	442,096	60.2	1,613	0.2	2,609	0.4	—	0.0	154,638	R
Kentucky	867,924	472,589	54.5	392,448	45.2	535	0.1	2,023	0.2	329	0.0	80,141	D
Louisiana	349,383	281,564	80.6	67,750	19.4	—	0.0	—	0.0	69	0.0	213,814	D
Maine	296,400	140,631	47.4	155,434	52.4	—	0.0	—	0.0	335	0.1	14,803	R
Maryland	608,439	315,490	51.9	292,949	48.1	—	0.0	—	0.0	—	0.0	22,541	D
Massachusetts	1,960,665	1,035,296	52.8	921,350	47.0	—	0.0	973	0.0	3,046	0.2	113,946	D
Michigan	2,205,223	1,106,899	50.2	1,084,423	49.2	4,598	0.2	6,503	0.3	2,800	0.1	22,476	D
Minnesota	1,125,504	589,864	52.4	527,416	46.9	5,048	0.4	—	0.0	3,176	0.3	62,448	D
Mississippi	180,234	168,621	93.6	11,613	6.4	—	0.0	—	0.0	—	0.0	157,008	D
Missouri	1,571,697	807,356	51.4	761,175	48.4	1,751	0.1	1,195	0.1	220	0.0	46,181	D
Montana	207,355	112,556	54.3	93,163	44.9	1,296	0.6	340	0.2	—	0.0	19,393	D
Nebraska	563,126	233,246	41.4	329,880	58.6	—	0.0	—	0.0	—	0.0	96,634	R
Nevada	54,234	29,623	54.6	24,611	45.4	—	0.0	—	0.0	—	0.0	5,012	D
New Hampshire	229,625	119,663	52.1	109,916	47.9	46	0.0	—	0.0	—	0.0	9,747	D
New Jersey	1,963,761	987,874	50.3	961,335	49.0	3,358	0.2	4,255	0.2	6,939	0.4	26,539	D
New Mexico	152,225	81,389	53.5	70,688	46.4	—	0.0	148	0.1	—	0.0	10,701	D
New York	6,316,790	3,304,238	52.3	2,987,647	47.3	10,553	0.2	—	0.0	14,352	0.2	316,591	D
North Carolina	790,554	527,399	66.7	263,155	33.3	—	0.0	—	0.0	—	0.0	264,244	D
North Dakota	220,182	100,144	45.5	118,535	53.8	954	0.4	549	0.2	—	0.0	18,391	R
Ohio	3,153,056	1,570,763	49.8	1,582,293	50.2	—	0.0	—	0.0	—	0.0	11,530	R
Oklahoma	722,636	401,549	55.6	319,424	44.2	—	0.0	1,663	0.2	—	0.0	82,125	D
Oregon	480,147	248,635	51.8	225,365	46.9	3,785	0.8	2,362	0.5	—	0.0	23,270	D
Pennsylvania	3,794,793	1,940,479	51.1	1,835,054	48.4	11,721	0.3	5,750	0.2	1,789	0.0	105,425	D
Rhode Island	299,276	175,356	58.6	123,487	41.3	—	0.0	433	0.1	—	0.0	51,869	D
South Carolina[3]	103,382	90,601	87.6	4,554	4.4	—	0.0	365	0.4	7,862	7.6	82,802	D
South Dakota	232,076	96,711	41.7	135,365	58.3	—	0.0	—	0.0	—	0.0	38,654	R
Tennessee	510,692	308,707	60.4	200,311	39.2	792	0.2	882	0.2	—	0.0	108,396	D
Texas	1,150,334	821,605	71.4	191,423	16.6	594	0.1	1,018	0.1	135,694	11.8	630,182	D
Utah	248,319	150,088	60.4	97,891	39.4	340	0.1	—	0.0	—	0.0	52,197	D
Vermont	125,361	53,820	42.9	71,527	57.1	—	0.0	—	0.0	14	0.0	17,707	R
Virginia	388,485	242,276	62.4	145,243	37.4	417	0.1	459	0.1	90	0.0	97,033	D
Washington	856,328	486,774	56.8	361,689	42.2	3,824	0.4	2,396	0.3	1,645	0.2	125,085	D
West Virginia	715,596	392,777	54.9	322,819	45.1	—	0.0	—	0.0	—	0.0	69,958	D
Wisconsin	1,339,152	650,413	48.6	674,532	50.4	13,205	1.0	—	0.0	1,002	0.1	24,119	R
Wyoming	101,340	49,419	48.8	51,921	51.2	—	0.0	—	0.0	—	0.0	2,502	R
Totals	47,976,670	25,612,610	53.4	22,021,053	45.9	79,003	0.2	74,779	0.2	196,097	0.4	3,591,557	D

1. For breakdown of "Other" vote, see minor candidate vote totals at the end of this chapter.

2. Clerk of the House of Representatives, *Statistics of the Congressional and Presidential Election* (Washington, D.C.: U.S. Government Printing Office, 1944). There were two separate slates of electors pledged to Dewey in Georgia that could not legally be combined: Republican, 56,606; Independent Democrat, 3,373.

3. Clerk of the House, *Congressional and Presidential Election*. There were two separate slates of electors pledged to Dewey in South Carolina that could not legally be combined: Republican, 4,554; Tobert Faction, 63. Plurality of 82,802 votes is calculated on the basis of 7,799 votes cast for the Southern Democrats Party.

1948 Presidential Election

STATE	TOTAL VOTE	HARRY S. TRUMAN (Democrat)		THOMAS E. DEWEY (Republican)		J. STROM THURMOND (States' Rights Democrat)		HENRY A. WALLACE (Progressive)		OTHER[1]		PLURALITY
		Votes	%	Votes	%	Votes	%	Votes	%	Votes	%	
Alabama	214,980	—	0.0	40,930	19.0	171,443	79.7	1,522	0.7	1,085	0.5	130,513 SR
Arizona	177,065	95,251	53.8	77,597	43.8	—	0.0	3,310	1.9	907	0.5	17,654 D
Arkansas	242,475	149,659	61.7	50,959	21.0	40,068	16.5	751	0.3	1,038	0.4	98,700 D
California	4,021,538	1,913,134	47.6	1,895,269	47.1	1,228	0.0	190,381	4.7	21,526	0.5	17,865 D
Colorado	515,237	267,288	51.9	239,714	46.5	—	0.0	6,115	1.2	2,120	0.4	27,574 D
Connecticut	883,518	423,297	47.9	437,754	49.5	—	0.0	13,713	1.6	8,754	1.0	14,457 R
Delaware	139,073	67,813	48.8	69,588	50.0	—	0.0	1,050	0.8	622	0.4	1,775 R
Florida	577,643	281,988	48.8	194,280	33.6	89,755	15.5	11,620	2.0	—	0.0	87,708 D
Georgia	418,844	254,646	60.8	76,691	18.3	85,135	20.3	1,636	0.4	736	0.2	169,511 D
Idaho	214,816	107,370	50.0	101,514	47.3	—	0.0	4,972	2.3	960	0.4	5,856 D
Illinois	3,984,046	1,994,715	50.1	1,961,103	49.2	—	0.0	—	0.0	28,228	0.7	33,612 D
Indiana	1,656,212	807,831	48.8	821,079	49.6	—	0.0	9,649	0.6	17,653	1.1	13,248 R
Iowa	1,038,264	522,380	50.3	494,018	47.6	—	0.0	12,125	1.2	9,741	0.9	28,362 D
Kansas	788,819	351,902	44.6	423,039	53.6	—	0.0	4,603	0.6	9,275	1.2	71,137 R
Kentucky	822,658	466,756	56.7	341,210	41.5	10,411	1.3	1,567	0.2	2,714	0.3	125,546 D
Louisiana	416,336	136,344	32.7	72,657	17.5	204,290	49.1	3,035	0.7	10	0.0	67,946 SR
Maine	264,787	111,916	42.3	150,234	56.7	—	0.0	1,884	0.7	753	0.3	38,318 R
Maryland	596,748	286,521	48.0	294,814	49.4	2,489	0.4	9,983	1.7	2,941	0.5	8,293 R
Massachusetts	2,107,146	1,151,788	54.7	909,370	43.2	—	0.0	38,157	1.8	7,831	0.4	242,418 D
Michigan	2,109,609	1,003,448	47.6	1,038,595	49.2	—	0.0	46,515	2.2	21,051	1.0	35,147 R
Minnesota	1,212,226	692,966	57.2	483,617	39.9	—	0.0	27,866	2.3	7,777	0.6	209,349 D
Mississippi	192,190	19,384	10.1	5,043	2.6	167,538	87.2	225	0.1	—	0.0	148,154 SR
Missouri	1,578,628	917,315	58.1	655,039	41.5	—	0.0	3,998	0.3	2,276	0.1	262,276 D
Montana	224,278	119,071	53.1	96,770	43.1	—	0.0	7,313	3.3	1,124	0.5	22,301 D
Nebraska	488,940	224,165	45.8	264,774	54.2	—	0.0	—	0.0	1	0.0	40,609 R
Nevada	62,117	31,291	50.4	29,357	47.3	—	0.0	1,469	2.4	—	0.0	1,934 D
New Hampshire	231,440	107,995	46.7	121,299	52.4	7	0.0	1,970	0.9	169	0.1	13,304 R
New Jersey	1,949,555	895,455	45.9	981,124	50.3	—	0.0	42,683	2.2	30,293	1.6	85,669 R
New Mexico	187,063	105,464	56.4	80,303	42.9	—	0.0	1,037	0.6	259	0.1	25,161 D
New York	6,177,337	2,780,204	45.0	2,841,163	46.0	—	0.0	509,559	8.2	46,411	0.8	60,959 R
North Carolina	791,209	459,070	58.0	258,572	32.7	69,652	8.8	3,915	0.5	—	0.0	200,498 D
North Dakota	220,716	95,812	43.4	115,139	52.2	374	0.2	8,391	3.8	1,000	0.5	19,327 R
Ohio	2,936,071	1,452,791	49.5	1,445,684	49.2	—	0.0	37,596	1.3	—	0.0	7,107 D
Oklahoma	721,599	452,782	62.7	268,817	37.3	—	0.0	—	0.0	—	0.0	183,965 D
Oregon	524,080	243,147	46.4	260,904	49.8	—	0.0	14,978	2.9	5,051	1.0	17,757 R
Pennsylvania	3,735,348	1,752,426	46.9	1,902,197	50.9	—	0.0	55,161	1.5	25,564	0.7	149,771 R
Rhode Island	327,702	188,736	57.6	135,787	41.4	—	0.0	2,619	0.8	560	0.2	52,949 D
South Carolina	142,571	34,423	24.1	5,386	3.8	102,607	72.0	154	0.1	1	0.0	68,184 SR
South Dakota	250,105	117,653	47.0	129,651	51.8	—	0.0	2,801	1.1	—	0.0	11,998 R
Tennessee	550,283	270,402	49.1	202,914	36.9	73,815	13.4	1,864	0.3	1,288	0.2	67,488 D
Texas[2]	1,147,245	750,700	65.4	282,240	24.6	106,909	9.3	3,764	0.3	3,632	0.3	468,460 D
Utah	276,306	149,151	54.0	124,402	45.0	—	0.0	2,679	1.0	74	0.0	24,749 D
Vermont	123,382	45,557	36.9	75,926	61.5	—	0.0	1,279	1.0	620	0.5	30,369 R
Virginia	419,256	200,786	47.9	172,070	41.0	43,393	10.4	2,047	0.5	960	0.2	28,716 D
Washington	905,058	476,165	52.6	386,314	42.7	—	0.0	31,692	3.5	10,887	1.2	89,851 D
West Virginia	748,750	429,188	57.3	316,251	42.2	—	0.0	3,311	0.4	—	0.0	112,937 D
Wisconsin	1,276,800	647,310	50.7	590,959	46.3	—	0.0	25,282	2.0	13,249	1.0	56,351 D
Wyoming	101,425	52,354	51.6	47,947	47.3	—	0.0	931	0.9	193	0.2	4,407 D
Totals	48,691,494	24,105,810	49.5	21,970,064	45.1	1,169,114	2.4	1,157,172	2.4	289,334	0.6	2,135,746 D

1. For breakdown of "Other" vote, see minor candidate vote totals at the end of this chapter.

2. Figures from Svend Petersen, *A Statistical History of the American Presidential Elections* (Westport, Conn.: Greenwood Press, 1981); Clerk of the House of Representatives, *Statistics of the Congressional and Presidential Election* (Washington, D.C.: U.S. Government Printing Office, 1948); *Texas Almanac*. Totals do not include the vote in thirty-five counties that were excluded from the official returns. Had these counties been counted, the vote in Texas would have been as follows: Total, 1,249,577; Truman, 824,235; Dewey, 303,467; Thurmond, 113,920; Wallace, 3,918; Other, 4,037; Plurality, 520,768 D. The totals for the nation would have been as follows: Total, 48,793,826; Truman, 24,179,345; Dewey, 21,991,291; Thurmond, 1,176,125; Wallace, 1,157,326; Other, 289,739; Plurality, 2,188,054 D.

1952 Presidential Election

STATE	TOTAL VOTE	DWIGHT D. EISENHOWER (Republican)		ADLAI E. STEVENSON (Democrat)		VINCENT HALLINAN (Progressive)		STUART HAMBLEN (Prohibition)		OTHER[1]		PLURALITY	
		Votes	%	Votes	%	Votes	%	Votes	%	Votes	%		
Alabama	426,120	149,231	35.0	275,075	64.6	—	0.0	1,814	0.4	—	0.0	125,844	D
Arizona	260,570	152,042	58.3	108,528	41.7	—	0.0	—	0.0	—	0.0	43,514	R
Arkansas	404,800	177,155	43.8	226,300	55.9	—	0.0	886	0.2	459	0.1	49,145	D
California	5,141,849	2,897,310	56.3	2,197,548	42.7	24,106	0.5	15,653	0.3	7,232	0.1	699,762	R
Colorado	630,103	379,782	60.3	245,504	39.0	1,919	0.3	—	0.0	2,898	0.5	134,278	R
Connecticut	1,096,911	611,012	55.7	481,649	43.9	1,466	0.1	—	0.0	2,784	0.3	129,363	R
Delaware	174,025	90,059	51.8	83,315	47.9	155	0.1	234	0.1	262	0.2	6,744	R
Florida	989,337	544,036	55.0	444,950	45.0	—	0.0	—	0.0	351	0.0	99,086	R
Georgia	655,785	198,961	30.3	456,823	69.7	—	0.0	—	0.0	1	0.0	257,862	D
Idaho	276,254	180,707	65.4	95,081	34.4	443	0.2	—	0.0	23	0.0	85,626	R
Illinois	4,481,058	2,457,327	54.8	2,013,920	44.9	—	0.0	—	0.0	9,811	0.2	443,407	R
Indiana	1,955,049	1,136,259	58.1	801,530	41.0	1,085	0.1	15,335	0.8	840	0.0	334,729	R
Iowa	1,268,773	808,906	63.8	451,513	35.6	5,085	0.4	2,882	0.2	387	0.0	357,393	R
Kansas	896,166	616,302	68.8	273,296	30.5	—	0.0	6,038	0.7	530	0.1	343,006	R
Kentucky	993,148	495,029	49.8	495,729	49.9	336	0.0	1,161	0.1	893	0.1	700	D
Louisiana	651,952	306,925	47.1	345,027	52.9	—	0.0	—	0.0	—	0.0	38,102	D
Maine	351,786	232,353	66.0	118,806	33.8	332	0.1	—	0.0	295	0.1	113,547	R
Maryland	902,074	499,424	55.4	395,337	43.8	7,313	0.8	—	0.0	—	0.0	104,087	R
Massachusetts	2,383,398	1,292,325	54.2	1,083,525	45.5	4,636	0.2	886	0.0	2,026	0.1	208,800	R
Michigan	2,798,592	1,551,529	55.4	1,230,657	44.0	3,922	0.1	10,331	0.4	2,153	0.1	320,872	R
Minnesota	1,379,483	763,211	55.3	608,458	44.1	2,666	0.2	2,147	0.2	3,001	0.2	154,753	R
Mississippi	285,532	112,966	39.6	172,566	60.4	—	0.0	—	0.0	—	0.0	59,600	D
Missouri	1,892,062	959,429	50.7	929,830	49.1	987	0.1	885	0.0	931	0.0	29,599	R
Montana	265,037	157,394	59.4	106,213	40.1	723	0.3	548	0.2	159	0.1	51,181	R
Nebraska	609,660	421,603	69.2	188,057	30.8	—	0.0	—	0.0	—	0.0	233,546	R
Nevada	82,190	50,502	61.4	31,688	38.6	—	0.0	—	0.0	—	0.0	18,814	R
New Hampshire	272,950	166,287	60.9	106,663	39.1	—	0.0	—	0.0	—	0.0	59,624	R
New Jersey	2,418,554	1,373,613	56.8	1,015,902	42.0	5,589	0.2	989	0.0	22,461	0.9	357,711	R
New Mexico	238,608	132,170	55.4	105,661	44.3	225	0.1	297	0.1	255	0.1	26,509	R
New York	7,128,239	3,952,813	55.5	3,104,601	43.6	64,211	0.9	—	0.0	6,614	0.1	848,212	R
North Carolina	1,210,910	558,107	46.1	652,803	53.9	—	0.0	—	0.0	—	0.0	94,696	D
North Dakota	270,127	191,712	71.0	76,694	28.4	344	0.1	302	0.1	1,075	0.4	115,018	R
Ohio	3,700,758	2,100,391	56.8	1,600,367	43.2	—	0.0	—	0.0	—	0.0	500,024	R
Oklahoma	948,984	518,045	54.6	430,939	45.4	—	0.0	—	0.0	—	0.0	87,106	R
Oregon	695,059	420,815	60.5	270,579	38.9	3,665	0.5	—	0.0	—	0.0	150,236	R
Pennsylvania	4,580,969	2,415,789	52.7	2,146,269	46.9	4,222	0.1	8,951	0.2	5,738	0.1	269,520	R
Rhode Island	414,498	210,935	50.9	203,293	49.0	187	0.0	—	0.0	83	0.0	7,642	R
South Carolina[2]	341,087	9,793	2.9	173,004	50.7	—	0.0	1	0.0	158,289	46.4	4,922	D
South Dakota	294,283	203,857	69.3	90,426	30.7	—	0.0	—	0.0	—	0.0	113,431	R
Tennessee	892,553	446,147	50.0	443,710	49.7	885	0.1	1,432	0.2	379	0.0	2,437	R
Texas	2,075,946	1,102,878	53.1	969,228	46.7	294	0.0	1,983	0.1	1,563	0.1	133,650	R
Utah	329,554	194,190	58.9	135,364	41.1	—	0.0	—	0.0	—	0.0	58,826	R
Vermont	153,557	109,717	71.5	43,355	28.2	282	0.2	—	0.0	203	0.1	66,362	R
Virginia	619,689	349,037	56.3	268,677	43.4	311	0.1	—	0.0	1,664	0.3	80,360	R
Washington	1,102,708	599,107	54.3	492,845	44.7	2,460	0.2	—	0.0	8,296	0.8	106,262	R
West Virginia	873,548	419,970	48.1	453,578	51.9	—	0.0	—	0.0	—	0.0	33,608	D
Wisconsin	1,607,370	979,744	61.0	622,175	38.7	2,174	0.1	—	0.0	3,277	0.2	357,569	R
Wyoming	129,253	81,049	62.7	47,934	37.1	—	0.0	194	0.2	76	0.1	33,115	R
Totals	61,550,918	33,777,945	54.9	27,314,992	44.4	140,023	0.2	72,949	0.1	245,009	0.4	6,462,953	R

1. For breakdown of "Other" vote, see minor candidate vote totals at the end of this chapter.

2. There were two separate slates of electors pledged to Eisenhower in South Carolina that could not legally be combined: Republican, 9,793; Independent slate, 158,289. Had these two been combined Eisenhower would have totaled 168,082 in the state and 33,936,234 nationally.

1956 Presidential Election

STATE	TOTAL VOTE	DWIGHT D. EISENHOWER (Republican)		ADLAI E. STEVENSON (Democrat)		T. COLEMAN ANDREWS (Constitution)		ERIC HASS (Socialist Labor)		OTHER[1]		PLURALITY	
		Votes	%	Votes	%	Votes	%	Votes	%	Votes	%		
Alabama	496,861	195,694	39.4	280,844	56.5	—	0.0	—	0.0	20,323	4.1	885,150	D
Arizona	290,173	176,990	61.0	112,880	38.9	303	0.1	—	0.0	—	0.0	64,110	R
Arkansas	406,572	186,287	45.8	213,277	52.5	7,008	1.7	—	0.0	—	0.0	26,990	D
California	5,466,355	3,027,668	55.4	2,420,135	44.3	6,087	0.1	300	0.0	12,165	0.2	607,533	R
Colorado	657,074	394,479	60.0	257,997	39.3	759	0.1	3,308	0.5	531	0.1	136,482	R
Connecticut	1,117,121	711,837	63.7	405,079	36.3	—	0.0	—	0.0	205	0.0	306,758	R
Delaware	177,988	98,057	55.1	79,421	44.6	—	0.0	110	0.1	400	0.2	18,636	R
Florida	1,125,762	643,849	57.2	480,371	42.7	—	0.0	—	0.0	1,542	0.1	163,478	R
Georgia	669,655	222,778	33.3	444,688	66.4	2,096	0.3	—	0.0	93	0.0	221,910	D
Idaho	272,989	166,979	61.2	105,868	38.8	126	0.0	—	0.0	16	0.0	61,111	R
Illinois	4,407,407	2,623,327	59.5	1,775,682	40.3	—	0.0	8,342	0.2	56	0.0	847,645	R
Indiana	1,974,607	1,182,811	59.9	783,908	39.7	—	0.0	1,334	0.1	6,554	0.3	398,903	R
Iowa	1,234,564	729,187	59.1	501,858	40.7	3,202	0.3	125	0.0	192	0.0	227,329	R
Kansas	866,243	566,878	65.4	296,317	34.2	—	0.0	—	0.0	3,048	0.4	270,561	R
Kentucky	1,053,805	572,192	54.3	476,453	45.2	—	0.0	358	0.0	4,802	0.5	95,739	R
Louisiana	617,544	329,047	53.3	243,977	39.5	—	0.0	—	0.0	44,520	7.2	85,070	R
Maine	351,706	249,238	70.9	102,468	29.1	—	0.0	—	0.0	—	0.0	146,770	R
Maryland	932,827	559,738	60.0	372,613	39.9	—	0.0	—	0.0	476	0.1	187,125	R
Massachusetts	2,348,506	1,393,197	59.3	948,190	40.4	—	0.0	5,573	0.2	1,546	0.1	445,007	R
Michigan	3,080,468	1,713,647	55.6	1,359,898	44.1	—	0.0	—	0.0	6,923	0.2	353,749	R
Minnesota	1,340,005	719,302	53.7	617,525	46.1	—	0.0	2,080	0.2	1,098	0.1	101,777	R
Mississippi	248,104	60,685	24.5	144,453	58.2	—	0.0	—	0.0	42,966	17.3	83,768	D
Missouri	1,832,562	914,289	49.9	918,273	50.1	—	0.0	—	0.0	—	0.0	3,984	D
Montana	271,171	154,933	57.1	116,238	42.9	—	0.0	—	0.0	—	0.0	38,695	R
Nebraska	577,137	378,108	65.5	199,029	34.5	—	0.0	—	0.0	—	0.0	179,079	R
Nevada	96,689	56,049	58.0	40,640	42.0	—	0.0	—	0.0	—	0.0	15,409	R
New Hampshire	266,994	176,519	66.1	90,364	33.8	111	0.0	—	0.0	—	0.0	86,155	R
New Jersey	2,484,312	1,606,942	64.7	850,337	34.2	5,317	0.2	6,736	0.3	14,980	0.6	756,605	R
New Mexico	253,926	146,788	57.8	106,098	41.8	364	0.1	69	0.0	607	0.2	40,690	R
New York	7,095,971	4,345,506	61.2	2,747,944	38.7	1,027	0.0	150	0.0	1,344	0.0	1,597,562	R
North Carolina	1,165,592	575,062	49.3	590,530	50.7	—	0.0	—	0.0	—	0.0	15,468	D
North Dakota	253,991	156,766	61.7	96,742	38.1	483	0.2	—	0.0	—	0.0	60,024	R
Ohio	3,702,265	2,262,610	61.1	1,439,655	38.9	—	0.0	—	0.0	—	0.0	822,955	R
Oklahoma	859,350	473,769	55.1	385,581	44.9	—	0.0	—	0.0	—	0.0	88,188	R
Oregon	736,132	406,393	55.2	329,204	44.7	—	0.0	—	0.0	535	0.1	77,189	R
Pennsylvania	4,576,503	2,585,252	56.5	1,981,769	43.3	—	0.0	7,447	0.2	2,035	0.0	603,483	R
Rhode Island	387,609	225,819	58.3	161,790	41.7	—	0.0	—	0.0	—	0.0	64,029	R
South Carolina[2]	300,583	75,700	25.2	136,372	45.4	2	0.0	—	0.0	88,509	29.4	47,863	D
South Dakota	293,857	171,569	58.4	122,288	41.6	—	0.0	—	0.0	—	0.0	49,281	R
Tennessee	939,404	462,288	49.2	456,507	48.6	19,820	2.1	—	0.0	789	0.1	5,781	R
Texas	1,955,168	1,080,619	55.3	859,958	44.0	14,591	0.7	—	0.0	—	0.0	220,661	R
Utah	333,995	215,631	64.6	118,364	35.4	—	0.0	—	0.0	—	0.0	97,267	R
Vermont	152,978	110,390	72.2	42,549	27.8	—	0.0	—	0.0	39	0.0	67,841	R
Virginia	697,978	386,459	55.4	267,760	38.4	42,964	6.2	351	0.1	444	0.1	118,699	R
Washington	1,150,889	620,430	53.9	523,002	45.4	—	0.0	7,457	0.6	—	0.0	97,428	R
West Virginia	830,831	449,297	54.1	381,534	45.9	—	0.0	—	0.0	—	0.0	67,763	R
Wisconsin	1,550,558	954,844	61.6	586,768	37.8	6,918	0.4	710	0.0	1,318	0.1	368,076	R
Wyoming	124,127	74,573	60.1	49,554	39.9	—	0.0	—	0.0	—	0.0	25,019	R
Totals	62,026,908	35,590,472	57.4	26,022,752	42.0	111,178	0.2	44,450	0.1	258,056	0.4	9,567,720	R

1. For breakdown of "Other" vote, see minor candidate vote totals at the end of this chapter.

2. Plurality of 47,863 votes is calculated on the basis of Stevenson's vote and the 88,509 votes cast for unpledged electors.

1960 Presidential Election

STATE	TOTAL VOTE	JOHN F. KENNEDY (Democrat) Votes	%	RICHARD M. NIXON (Republican) Votes	%	ERIC HASS (Socialist Labor) Votes	%	(UNPLEDGED) Votes	%	OTHER[1] Votes	%	PLURALITY	
Alabama	570,225	324,050	56.8	237,981	41.7	—	0.0	—	0.0	8,194	1.4	86,069	D
Alaska	60,762	29,809	49.1	30,953	50.9	—	0.0	—	0.0	—	0.0	1,144	R
Arizona	398,491	176,781	44.4	221,241	55.5	469	0.1	—	0.0	—	0.0	44,460	R
Arkansas	428,509	215,049	50.2	184,508	43.1	—	0.0	—	0.0	28,952	6.8	30,541	D
California	6,506,578	3,224,099	49.6	3,259,722	50.1	1,051	0.0	—	0.0	21,706	0.3	35,623	R
Colorado	736,236	330,629	44.9	402,242	54.6	2,803	0.4	—	0.0	562	0.1	71,613	R
Connecticut	1,222,883	657,055	53.7	565,813	46.3	—	0.0	—	0.0	15	0.0	91,242	D
Delaware	196,683	99,590	50.6	96,373	49.0	82	0.0	—	0.0	638	0.3	3,217	D
Florida	1,544,176	748,700	48.5	795,476	51.5	—	0.0	—	0.0	—	0.0	46,776	R
Georgia	733,349	458,638	62.5	274,472	37.4	—	0.0	—	0.0	239	0.0	184,166	D
Hawaii	184,705	92,410	50.0	92,295	50.0	—	0.0	—	0.0	—	0.0	115	D
Idaho	300,450	138,853	46.2	161,597	53.8	—	0.0	—	0.0	—	0.0	22,744	R
Illinois	4,757,409	2,377,846	50.0	2,368,988	49.8	10,560	0.2	—	0.0	15	0.0	8,858	D
Indiana	2,135,360	952,358	44.6	1,175,120	55.0	1,136	0.1	—	0.0	6,746	0.3	222,762	R
Iowa	1,273,810	550,565	43.2	722,381	56.7	230	0.0	—	0.0	634	0.0	171,816	R
Kansas	928,825	363,213	39.1	561,474	60.4	—	0.0	—	0.0	4,138	0.4	198,261	R
Kentucky	1,124,462	521,855	46.4	602,607	53.6	—	0.0	—	0.0	—	0.0	80,752	R
Louisiana	807,891	407,339	50.4	230,980	28.6	—	0.0	—	0.0	169,572	21.0	176,359	D
Maine	421,767	181,159	43.0	240,608	57.0	—	0.0	—	0.0	—	0.0	59,449	R
Maryland	1,055,349	565,808	53.6	489,538	46.4	—	0.0	—	0.0	3	0.0	76,270	D
Massachusetts	2,469,480	1,487,174	60.2	976,750	39.6	3,892	0.2	—	0.0	1,664	0.1	510,424	D
Michigan	3,318,097	1,687,269	50.9	1,620,428	48.8	1,718	0.1	—	0.0	8,682	0.3	66,841	D
Minnesota	1,541,887	779,933	50.6	757,915	49.2	962	0.1	—	0.0	3,077	0.2	22,018	D
Mississippi[2]	298,171	108,362	36.3	73,561	24.7	—	0.0	116,248	39.0	—	0.0	7,886	U
Missouri	1,934,422	972,201	50.3	962,221	49.7	—	0.0	—	0.0	—	0.0	9,980	D
Montana	277,579	134,891	48.6	141,841	51.1	—	0.0	—	0.0	847	0.3	6,950	R
Nebraska	613,095	232,542	37.9	380,553	62.1	—	0.0	—	0.0	—	0.0	148,011	R
Nevada	107,267	54,880	51.2	52,387	48.8	—	0.0	—	0.0	—	0.0	2,493	D
New Hampshire	295,761	137,772	46.6	157,989	53.4	—	0.0	—	0.0	—	0.0	20,217	R
New Jersey	2,773,111	1,385,415	50.0	1,363,324	49.2	4,262	0.2	—	0.0	20,110	0.7	22,091	D
New Mexico	311,107	156,027	50.2	153,733	49.4	570	0.2	—	0.0	777	0.2	2,294	D
New York	7,291,079	3,830,085	52.5	3,446,419	47.3	—	0.0	—	0.0	14,575	0.2	383,666	D
North Carolina	1,368,556	713,136	52.1	655,420	47.9	—	0.0	—	0.0	—	0.0	57,716	D
North Dakota	278,431	123,963	44.5	154,310	55.4	—	0.0	—	0.0	158	0.1	30,347	R
Ohio	4,161,859	1,944,248	46.7	2,217,611	53.3	—	0.0	—	0.0	—	0.0	273,363	R
Oklahoma	903,150	370,111	41.0	533,039	59.0	—	0.0	—	0.0	—	0.0	162,928	R
Oregon	776,421	367,402	47.3	408,060	52.6	—	0.0	—	0.0	959	0.1	40,658	R
Pennsylvania	5,006,541	2,556,282	51.1	2,439,956	48.7	7,185	0.1	—	0.0	3,118	0.1	116,326	D
Rhode Island	405,535	258,032	63.6	147,502	36.4	—	0.0	—	0.0	1	0.0	110,530	D
South Carolina	386,688	198,129	51.2	188,558	48.8	—	0.0	—	0.0	1	0.0	9,571	D
South Dakota	306,487	128,070	41.8	178,417	58.2	—	0.0	—	0.0	—	0.0	50,347	R
Tennessee	1,051,792	481,453	45.8	556,577	52.9	—	0.0	—	0.0	13,762	1.3	75,124	R
Texas	2,311,084	1,167,567	50.5	1,121,310	48.5	—	0.0	—	0.0	22,207	1.0	46,257	D
Utah	374,709	169,248	45.2	205,361	54.8	—	0.0	—	0.0	100	0.0	36,113	R
Vermont	167,324	69,186	41.3	98,131	58.6	—	0.0	—	0.0	7	0.0	28,945	R
Virginia	771,449	362,327	47.0	404,521	52.4	397	0.1	—	0.0	4,204	0.5	42,194	R
Washington	1,241,572	599,298	48.3	629,273	50.7	10,895	0.9	—	0.0	2,106	0.2	29,975	R
West Virginia	837,781	441,786	52.7	395,995	47.3	—	0.0	—	0.0	—	0.0	45,791	D
Wisconsin	1,729,082	830,805	48.0	895,175	51.8	1,310	0.1	—	0.0	1,792	0.1	64,370	R
Wyoming	140,782	63,331	45.0	77,451	55.0	—	0.0	—	0.0	—	0.0	14,120	R
Totals	68,838,219	34,226,731	49.7	34,108,157	49.5	47,522	0.1	116,248	0.2	339,561	0.5	118,574	D

1. For breakdown of "Other" vote, see minor candidate vote totals at the end of this chapter.

2. Votes for unpledged electors who carried the state and cast electoral votes for Harry F. Eyrd (D-Va.).

1964 Presidential Election

STATE	TOTAL VOTE	LYNDON B. JOHNSON (Democrat)		BARRY M. GOLDWATER (Republican)		ERIC HASS (Socialist Labor)		CLIFTON DeBERRY (Socialist Workers)		OTHER[1]		PLURALITY	
		Votes	%	Votes	%	Votes	%	Votes	%	Votes	%		
Alabama[2]	689,818	—	0.0	479,085	69.5	—	0.0	—	0.0	210,732	30.5	268,353	R
Alaska	67,259	44,329	65.9	22,930	34.1	—	0.0	—	0.0	—	0.0	21,399	D
Arizona	480,770	237,753	49.5	242,535	50.4	482	0.1	—	0.0	—	0.0	4,782	R
Arkansas	560,426	314,197	56.1	243,264	43.4	—	0.0	—	0.0	2,965	0.5	70,933	D
California	7,057,586	4,171,877	59.1	2,879,108	40.8	489	0.0	378	0.0	5,734	0.1	1,292,769	D
Colorado	776,986	476,024	61.3	296,767	38.2	302	0.0	2,537	0.3	1,356	0.2	179,257	D
Connecticut	1,218,578	826,269	67.8	390,996	32.1	—	0.0	—	0.0	1,313	0.1	435,273	D
Delaware	201,320	122,704	60.9	78,078	38.8	113	0.1	—	0.0	425	0.2	44,626	D
Florida	1,854,481	948,540	51.1	905,941	48.9	—	0.0	—	0.0	—	0.0	42,599	D
Georgia	1,139,335	522,556	45.9	616,584	54.1	—	0.0	—	0.0	195	0.0	94,028	R
Hawaii	207,271	163,249	78.8	44,022	21.2	—	0.0	—	0.0	—	0.0	119,227	D
Idaho	292,477	148,920	50.9	143,557	49.1	—	0.0	—	0.0	—	0.0	5,363	D
Illinois	4,702,841	2,796,833	59.5	1,905,946	40.5	—	0.0	—	0.0	62	0.0	890,887	D
Indiana	2,091,606	1,170,848	56.0	911,118	43.6	1,374	0.1	—	0.0	8,266	0.4	259,730	D
Iowa	1,184,539	733,030	61.9	449,148	37.9	182	0.0	159	0.0	2,020	0.2	283,882	D
Kansas	857,901	464,028	54.1	386,579	45.1	1,901	0.2	—	0.0	5,393	0.6	77,449	D
Kentucky	1,046,105	669,659	64.0	372,977	35.7	—	0.0	—	0.0	3,469	0.3	296,682	D
Louisiana	896,293	387,068	43.2	509,225	56.8	—	0.0	—	0.0	—	0.0	122,157	R
Maine	380,965	262,264	68.8	118,701	31.2	—	0.0	—	0.0	—	0.0	143,563	D
Maryland	1,116,457	730,912	65.5	385,495	34.5	—	0.0	—	0.0	50	0.0	345,417	D
Massachusetts	2,344,798	1,786,422	76.2	549,727	23.4	4,755	0.2	—	0.0	3,894	0.2	1,236,695	D
Michigan	3,203,102	2,136,615	66.7	1,060,152	33.1	1,704	0.1	3,817	0.1	814	0.0	1,076,463	D
Minnesota	1,554,462	991,117	63.8	559,624	36.0	2,544	0.2	1,177	0.1	—	0.0	431,493	D
Mississippi	409,146	52,618	12.9	356,528	87.1	—	0.0	—	0.0	—	0.0	303,910	R
Missouri	1,817,879	1,164,344	64.0	653,535	36.0	—	0.0	—	0.0	—	0.0	510,809	D
Montana	278,628	164,246	58.9	113,032	40.6	—	0.0	332	0.1	1,018	0.4	51,214	D
Nebraska	584,154	307,307	52.6	276,847	47.4	—	0.0	—	0.0	—	0.0	30,460	D
Nevada	135,433	79,339	58.6	56,094	41.4	—	0.0	—	0.0	—	0.0	23,245	D
New Hampshire	288,093	184,064	63.9	104,029	36.1	—	0.0	—	0.0	—	0.0	80,035	D
New Jersey	2,847,663	1,868,231	65.6	964,174	33.9	7,075	0.2	8,183	0.3	—	0.0	904,057	D
New Mexico	328,645	194,015	59.0	132,838	40.4	1,217	0.4	—	0.0	575	0.2	61,177	D
New York	7,166,275	4,913,102	68.6	2,243,559	31.3	6,118	0.1	3,228	0.0	268	0.0	2,669,543	D
North Carolina	1,424,983	800,139	56.2	624,844	43.8	—	0.0	—	0.0	—	0.0	175,295	D
North Dakota	258,389	149,784	58.0	108,207	41.9	—	0.0	224	0.1	174	0.1	41,577	D
Ohio	3,969,196	2,498,331	62.9	1,470,865	37.1	—	0.0	—	0.0	—	0.0	1,027,466	D
Oklahoma	932,499	519,834	55.7	412,665	44.3	—	0.0	—	0.0	—	0.0	107,169	D
Oregon	786,305	501,017	63.7	282,779	36.0	—	0.0	—	0.0	2,509	0.3	218,238	D
Pennsylvania	4,822,690	3,130,954	64.9	1,673,657	34.7	5,092	0.1	10,456	0.2	2,531	0.1	1,457,297	D
Rhode Island	390,091	315,463	80.9	74,615	19.1	—	0.0	—	0.0	13	0.0	240,848	D
South Carolina	524,779	215,723	41.1	309,048	58.9	—	0.0	—	0.0	8	0.0	93,325	R
South Dakota	293,118	163,010	55.6	130,108	44.4	—	0.0	—	0.0	—	0.0	32,902	D
Tennessee	1,143,946	634,947	55.5	508,965	44.5	—	0.0	—	0.0	34	0.0	125,982	D
Texas	2,626,811	1,663,185	63.3	958,566	36.5	—	0.0	—	0.0	5,060	0.2	704,619	D
Utah	401,413	219,628	54.7	181,785	45.3	—	0.0	—	0.0	—	0.0	37,843	D
Vermont	163,089	108,127	66.3	54,942	33.7	—	0.0	—	0.0	20	0.0	53,185	D
Virginia	1,042,267	558,038	53.5	481,334	46.2	2,895	0.3	—	0.0	—	0.0	76,704	D
Washington	1,258,556	779,881	62.0	470,366	37.4	7,772	0.6	537	0.0	—	0.0	309,515	D
West Virginia	792,040	538,087	67.9	253,953	32.1	—	0.0	—	0.0	—	0.0	284,134	D
Wisconsin	1,691,815	1,050,424	62.1	638,495	37.7	1,204	0.1	1,692	0.1	—	0.0	411,929	D
Wyoming	142,716	80,718	56.6	61,998	43.4	—	0.0	—	0.0	—	0.0	18,720	D
Dist. of Col.	198,597	169,796	85.5	28,801	14.5	—	0.0	—	0.0	—	0.0	140,995	D
Totals	70,644,592	43,129,566	61.1	27,178,188	38.5	45,219	0.1	32,720	0.0	258,899	0.4	15,951,378	D

1. For breakdown of "Other" vote, see minor candidate vote totals at the end of this chapter.
2. Plurality of 268,353 votes is calculated on the basis of Goldwater's vote and the 210,732 votes cast for the unpledged Democratic elector ticket.

1968 Presidential Election

STATE	TOTAL VOTE	RICHARD M. NIXON (Republican)		HUBERT H. HUMPHREY (Democrat)		GEORGE C. WALLACE (American Independent)		HENNING A. BLOMEN (Socialist Labor)		OTHER[1]		PLURALITY	
		Votes	%	Votes	%	Votes	%	Votes	%	Votes	%		
Alabama	1,049,922	146,923	14.0	196,579	18.7	691,425	65.9	—	0.0	14,995	1.4	494,846	A
Alaska	83,035	37,600	45.3	35,411	42.6	10,024	12.1	—	0.0	—	0.0	2,189	R
Arizona	486,936	266,721	54.8	170,514	35.0	46,573	9.6	75	0.0	3,053	0.6	96,207	R
Arkansas	619,969	190,759	30.8	188,228	30.4	240,982	38.9	—	0.0	—	0.0	50,223	A
California	7,251,587	3,467,664	47.8	3,244,318	44.7	487,270	6.7	341	0.0	51,994	0.7	223,346	R
Colorado	811,199	409,345	50.5	335,174	41.3	60,813	7.5	3,016	0.4	2,851	0.4	74,171	R
Connecticut	1,256,232	556,721	44.3	621,561	49.5	76,650	6.1	—	0.0	1,300	0.1	64,840	D
Delaware	214,367	96,714	45.1	89,194	41.6	28,459	13.3	—	0.0	—	0.0	7,520	R
Florida	2,187,805	886,804	40.5	676,794	30.9	624,207	28.5	—	0.0	—	0.0	210,010	R
Georgia	1,250,266	380,111	30.4	334,440	26.7	535,550	42.8	—	0.0	165	0.0	155,439	A
Hawaii	236,218	91,425	38.7	141,324	59.8	3,469	1.5	—	0.0	—	0.0	49,899	D
Idaho	291,183	165,369	56.8	89,273	30.7	36,541	12.5	—	0.0	—	0.0	76,096	R
Illinois	4,619,749	2,174,774	47.1	2,039,814	44.2	390,958	8.5	13,878	0.3	325	0.0	134,960	R
Indiana	2,123,597	1,067,885	50.3	806,659	38.0	243,108	11.4	—	0.0	5,945	0.3	261,226	R
Iowa	1,167,931	619,106	53.0	476,699	40.8	66,422	5.7	241	0.0	5,463	0.5	142,407	R
Kansas	872,783	478,674	54.8	302,996	34.7	88,921	10.2	—	0.0	2,192	0.3	175,678	R
Kentucky	1,055,893	462,411	43.8	397,541	37.6	193,098	18.3	—	0.0	2,843	0.3	64,870	R
Louisiana	1,097,450	257,535	23.5	309,615	28.2	530,300	48.3	—	0.0	—	0.0	220,685	A
Maine	392,936	169,254	43.1	217,312	55.3	6,370	1.6	—	0.0	—	0.0	48,058	D
Maryland	1,235,039	517,995	41.9	538,310	43.6	178,734	14.5	—	0.0	—	0.0	20,315	D
Massachusetts	2,331,752	766,844	32.9	1,469,218	63.0	87,088	3.7	6,180	0.3	2,422	0.1	702,374	D
Michigan	3,306,250	1,370,665	41.5	1,593,082	48.2	331,968	10.0	1,762	0.1	8,773	0.3	222,417	D
Minnesota	1,588,506	658,643	41.5	857,738	54.0	68,931	4.3	285	0.0	2,909	0.2	199,095	D
Mississippi	654,509	88,516	13.5	150,644	23.0	415,349	63.5	—	0.0	—	0.0	264,705	A
Missouri	1,809,502	811,932	44.9	791,444	43.7	206,126	11.4	—	0.0	—	0.0	20,488	R
Montana	274,404	138,835	50.6	114,117	41.6	20,015	7.3	—	0.0	1,437	0.5	24,718	R
Nebraska	536,851	321,163	59.8	170,784	31.8	44,904	8.4	—	0.0	—	0.0	150,379	R
Nevada	154,218	73,188	47.5	60,598	39.3	20,432	13.2	—	0.0	—	0.0	12,590	R
New Hampshire	297,298	154,903	52.1	130,589	43.9	11,173	3.8	—	0.0	633	0.2	24,314	R
New Jersey	2,875,395	1,325,467	46.1	1,264,206	44.0	262,187	9.1	6,784	0.2	16,751	0.6	61,261	R
New Mexico	327,350	169,692	51.8	130,081	39.7	25,737	7.9	—	0.0	1,840	0.6	39,611	R
New York	6,791,688	3,007,932	44.3	3,378,470	49.7	358,864	5.3	8,432	0.1	37,990	0.6	370,538	D
North Carolina	1,587,493	627,192	39.5	464,113	29.2	496,188	31.3	—	0.0	—	0.0	131,004	R
North Dakota	247,882	138,669	55.9	94,769	38.2	14,244	5.7	—	0.0	200	0.1	43,900	R
Ohio	3,959,698	1,791,014	45.2	1,700,586	42.9	467,495	11.8	120	0.0	483	0.0	90,428	R
Oklahoma	943,086	449,697	47.7	301,658	32.0	191,731	20.3	—	0.0	—	0.0	148,039	R
Oregon	819,622	408,433	49.8	358,866	43.8	49,683	6.1	—	0.0	2,640	0.3	49,567	R
Pennsylvania	4,747,928	2,090,017	44.0	2,259,405	47.6	378,582	8.0	4,977	0.1	14,947	0.3	169,388	D
Rhode Island	385,000	122,359	31.8	246,518	64.0	15,678	4.1	—	0.0	445	0.1	124,159	D
South Carolina	666,978	254,062	38.1	197,486	29.6	215,430	32.3	—	0.0	—	0.0	38,632	R
South Dakota	281,264	149,841	53.3	118,023	42.0	13,400	4.8	—	0.0	—	0.0	31,818	R
Tennessee	1,248,617	472,592	37.8	351,233	28.1	424,792	34.0	—	0.0	—	0.0	47,800	R
Texas	3,079,216	1,227,844	39.9	1,266,804	41.1	584,269	19.0	—	0.0	299	0.0	38,960	D
Utah	422,568	238,728	56.5	156,665	37.1	26,906	6.4	—	0.0	269	0.1	82,063	R
Vermont	161,404	85,142	52.8	70,255	43.5	5,104	3.2	—	0.0	903	0.6	14,887	R
Virginia	1,361,491	590,319	43.4	442,387	32.5	321,833	23.6	4,671	0.3	2,281	0.2	147,932	R
Washington	1,304,281	588,510	45.1	616,037	47.2	96,990	7.4	488	0.0	2,256	0.2	27,527	D
West Virginia	754,206	307,555	40.8	374,091	49.6	72,560	9.6	—	0.0	—	0.0	66,536	D
Wisconsin	1,691,538	809,997	47.9	748,804	44.3	127,835	7.6	1,338	0.1	3,564	0.2	61,193	R
Wyoming	127,205	70,927	55.8	45,173	35.5	11,105	8.7	—	0.0	—	0.0	25,754	R
Dist. of Col.	170,578	31,012	18.2	139,566	81.8	—	0.0	—	0.0	—	0.0	108,554	D
Totals	73,211,875	31,785,480	43.4	31,275,166	42.7	9,906,473	13.5	52,588	0.1	192,168	0.3	510,314	R

1. For breakdown of "Other" vote, see minor candidate vote totals at the end of this chapter.

1972 Presidential Election

STATE	TOTAL VOTE	RICHARD M. NIXON (Republican)		GEORGE S. McGOVERN (Democrat)		JOHN G. SCHMITZ (American)		BENJAMIN SPOCK (People's)		OTHER [1]		PLURALITY	
		Votes	%	Votes	%	Votes	%	Votes	%	Votes	%		
Alabama	1,006,111	728,701	72.4	256,923	25.5	11,928	1.2	—	0.0	8,559	0.9	471,778	R
Alaska	95,219	55,349	58.1	32,967	34.6	6,903	7.2	—	0.0	—	0.0	22,382	R
Arizona	622,926	402,812	64.7	198,540	31.9	21,208	3.4	—	0.0	366	0.1	204,272	R
Arkansas	651,320	448,541	68.9	199,892	30.7	2,887	0.4	—	0.0	—	0.0	248,649	R
California	8,367,862	4,602,096	55.0	3,475,847	41.5	232,554	2.8	55,167	0.7	2,198	0.0	1,126,249	R
Colorado	953,884	597,189	62.6	329,980	34.6	17,269	1.8	2,403	0.3	7,043	0.7	267,209	R
Connecticut	1,384,277	810,763	58.6	555,498	40.1	17,239	1.2	—	0.0	777	0.1	255,265	R
Delaware	235,516	140,357	59.6	92,283	39.2	2,638	1.1	—	0.0	238	0.1	48,074	R
Florida	2,583,283	1,857,759	71.9	718,117	27.8	—	0.0	—	0.0	7,407	0.3	1,139,642	R
Georgia	1,174,772	881,496	75.0	289,529	24.6	812	0.1	—	0.0	2,935	0.2	591,967	R
Hawaii	270,274	168,865	62.5	101,409	37.5	—	0.0	—	0.0	—	0.0	67,456	R
Idaho	310,379	199,384	64.2	80,826	26.0	28,869	9.3	903	0.3	397	0.1	118,558	R
Illinois	4,723,236	2,788,179	59.0	1,913,472	40.5	2,471	0.1	—	0.0	19,114	0.4	874,707	R
Indiana	2,125,529	1,405,154	66.1	708,568	33.3	—	0.0	4,544	0.2	7,263	0.3	696,586	R
Iowa	1,225,944	706,207	57.6	496,206	40.5	22,056	1.8	—	0.0	1,475	0.1	210,001	R
Kansas	916,095	619,812	67.7	270,287	29.5	21,808	2.4	—	0.0	4,188	0.5	349,525	R
Kentucky	1,067,499	676,446	63.4	371,159	34.8	17,627	1.7	1,118	0.1	1,149	0.1	305,287	R
Louisiana	1,051,491	686,852	65.3	298,142	28.4	52,099	5.0	—	0.0	14,398	1.4	388,710	R
Maine	417,042	256,458	61.5	160,584	38.5	—	0.0	—	0.0	—	0.0	95,874	R
Maryland	1,353,812	829,305	61.3	505,781	37.4	18,726	1.4	—	0.0	—	0.0	323,524	R
Massachusetts	2,458,756	1,112,078	45.2	1,332,540	54.2	2,877	0.1	101	0.0	11,160	0.5	220,462	D
Michigan	3,489,727	1,961,721	56.2	1,459,435	41.8	63,321	1.8	—	0.0	5,250	0.2	502,286	R
Minnesota	1,741,652	898,269	51.6	802,346	46.1	31,407	1.8	2,805	0.2	6,825	0.4	95,923	R
Mississippi	645,963	505,125	78.2	126,782	19.6	11,598	1.8	—	0.0	2,458	0.4	378,343	R
Missouri	1,855,803	1,153,852	62.2	697,147	37.6	—	0.0	—	0.0	4,804	0.3	456,705	R
Montana	317,603	183,976	57.9	120,197	37.8	13,430	4.2	—	0.0	—	0.0	63,779	R
Nebraska	576,289	406,298	70.5	169,991	29.5	—	0.0	—	0.0	—	0.0	236,307	R
Nevada	181,766	115,750	63.7	66,016	36.3	—	0.0	—	0.0	—	0.0	49,734	R
New Hampshire	334,055	213,724	64.0	116,435	34.9	3,386	1.0	—	0.0	510	0.2	97,289	R
New Jersey	2,997,229	1,845,502	61.6	1,102,211	36.8	34,378	1.1	5,355	0.2	9,783	0.3	743,291	R
New Mexico	386,241	235,606	61.0	141,084	36.5	8,767	2.3	—	0.0	784	0.2	94,522	R
New York	7,165,919	4,192,778	58.5	2,951,084	41.2	—	0.0	—	0.0	22,057	0.3	1,241,694	R
North Carolina	1,518,612	1,054,889	69.5	438,705	28.9	25,018	1.6	—	0.0	—	0.0	616,184	R
North Dakota	280,514	174,109	62.1	100,384	35.8	5,646	2.0	—	0.0	375	0.1	73,725	R
Ohio	4,094,787	2,441,827	59.6	1,558,889	38.1	80,067	2.0	—	0.0	14,004	0.3	882,938	R
Oklahoma	1,029,900	759,025	73.7	247,147	24.0	23,728	2.3	—	0.0	—	0.0	511,878	R
Oregon	927,946	486,686	52.4	392,760	42.3	46,211	5.0	—	0.0	2,289	0.2	93,926	R
Pennsylvania	4,592,106	2,714,521	59.1	1,796,951	39.1	70,593	1.5	—	0.0	10,041	0.2	917,570	R
Rhode Island	415,808	220,383	53.0	194,645	46.8	25	0.0	5	0.0	750	0.2	25,738	R
South Carolina	673,960	477,044	70.8	186,824	27.7	10,075	1.5	—	0.0	17	0.0	290,220	R
South Dakota	307,415	166,476	54.2	139,945	45.5	—	0.0	—	0.0	994	0.3	26,531	R
Tennessee	1,201,182	813,147	67.7	357,293	29.7	30,373	2.5	—	0.0	369	0.0	455,854	R
Texas	3,471,281	2,298,896	66.2	1,154,289	33.3	6,039	0.2	—	0.0	12,057	0.3	1,144,607	R
Utah	478,476	323,643	67.6	126,284	26.4	28,549	6.0	—	0.0	—	0.0	197,359	R
Vermont	186,947	117,149	62.7	68,174	36.5	—	0.0	1,010	0.5	614	0.3	48,975	R
Virginia	1,457,019	988,493	67.8	438,887	30.1	19,721	1.4	—	0.0	9,918	0.7	549,606	R
Washington	1,470,847	837,135	56.9	568,334	38.6	58,906	4.0	2,644	0.2	3,828	0.3	268,801	R
West Virginia	762,399	484,964	63.6	277,435	36.4	—	0.0	—	0.0	—	0.0	207,529	R
Wisconsin	1,852,890	989,430	53.4	810,174	43.7	47,525	2.6	2,701	0.1	3,060	0.2	179,256	R
Wyoming	145,570	100,464	69.0	44,358	30.5	748	0.5	—	0.0	—	0.0	56,106	R
Dist. of Col.	163,421	35,226	21.6	127,627	78.1	—	0.0	—	0.0	568	0.3	92,401	D
Totals	77,718,554	47,169,911	60.7	29,170,383	37.5	1,099,482	1.4	78,756	0.1	200,022	0.3	17,999,528	R

1. For breakdown of "Other" vote, see minor candidate vote totals at the end of this chapter.

1976 Presidential Election

STATE	TOTAL VOTE	JIMMY CARTER (Democrat)		GERALD R. FORD (Republican)		EUGENE J. McCARTHY (Independent)		ROGER MacBRIDE (Libertarian)		OTHER[1]		PLURALITY	
		Votes	%	Votes	%	Votes	%	Votes	%	Votes	%		
Alabama	1,182,850	659,170	55.7	504,070	42.6	99	0.0	1,481	0.1	18,030	1.5	155,100	D
Alaska	123,574	44,058	35.7	71,555	57.9	—	0.0	6,785	5.5	1,176	1.0	27,497	R
Arizona	742,719	295,602	39.8	418,642	56.4	19,229	2.6	7,647	1.0	1,599	0.2	123,040	R
Arkansas	767,535	498,604	65.0	267,903	34.9	639	0.1	—	0.0	389	0.1	230,701	D
California	7,867,117	3,742,284	47.6	3,882,244	49.3	58,412	0.7	56,388	0.7	127,789	1.6	139,960	R
Colorado	1,081,554	460,353	42.6	584,367	54.0	26,107	2.4	5,330	0.5	5,397	0.5	124,014	R
Connecticut	1,381,526	647,895	46.9	719,261	52.1	3,759	0.3	209	0.0	10,402	0.8	71,366	R
Delaware	235,834	122,596	52.0	109,831	46.6	2,437	1.0	—	0.0	970	0.4	12,765	D
Florida	3,150,631	1,636,000	51.9	1,469,531	46.6	23,643	0.8	103	0.0	21,354	0.7	166,469	D
Georgia	1,467,458	979,409	66.7	483,743	33.0	991	0.1	175	0.0	3,140	0.2	495,666	D
Hawaii	291,301	147,375	50.6	140,003	48.1	—	0.0	3,923	1.3	—	0.0	7,372	D
Idaho	344,071	126,549	36.8	204,151	59.3	1,194	0.3	3,558	1.0	8,619	2.5	77,602	R
Illinois	4,718,914	2,271,295	48.1	2,364,269	50.1	55,939	1.2	8,057	0.2	19,354	0.4	92,974	R
Indiana	2,220,362	1,014,714	45.7	1,183,958	53.3	—	0.0	—	0.0	21,690	1.0	169,244	R
Iowa	1,279,306	619,931	48.5	632,863	49.5	20,051	1.6	1,452	0.1	5,009	0.4	12,932	R
Kansas	957,845	430,421	44.9	502,752	52.5	13,185	1.4	3,242	0.3	8,245	0.9	72,331	R
Kentucky	1,167,142	615,717	52.8	531,852	45.6	6,837	0.6	814	0.1	11,922	1.0	83,865	D
Louisiana	1,278,439	661,365	51.7	587,446	46.0	6,588	0.5	3,325	0.3	19,715	1.5	73,919	D
Maine	483,216	232,279	48.1	236,320	48.9	10,874	2.3	11	0.0	3,732	0.8	4,041	R
Maryland	1,439,897	759,612	52.8	672,661	46.7	4,541	0.3	255	0.0	2,828	0.2	86,951	D
Massachusetts	2,547,558	1,429,475	56.1	1,030,276	40.4	65,637	2.6	135	0.0	22,035	0.9	399,199	D
Michigan	3,653,749	1,696,714	46.4	1,893,742	51.8	47,905	1.3	5,406	0.1	9,982	0.3	197,028	R
Minnesota	1,949,931	1,070,440	54.9	819,395	42.0	35,490	1.8	3,529	0.2	21,077	1.1	251,045	D
Mississippi	769,361	381,309	49.6	366,846	47.7	4,074	0.5	2,788	0.4	14,344	1.9	14,463	D
Missouri	1,953,600	998,387	51.1	927,443	47.5	24,029	1.2	—	0.0	3,741	0.2	70,944	D
Montana	328,734	149,259	45.4	173,703	52.8	—	0.0	—	0.0	5,772	1.8	24,444	R
Nebraska	607,668	233,692	38.5	359,705	59.2	9,409	1.5	1,482	0.2	3,380	0.6	126,013	R
Nevada	201,876	92,479	45.8	101,273	50.2	—	0.0	1,519	0.8	6,605	3.3	8,794	R
New Hampshire	339,618	147,635	43.5	185,935	54.7	4,095	1.2	936	0.3	1,017	0.3	38,300	R
New Jersey	3,014,472	1,444,653	47.9	1,509,688	50.1	32,717	1.1	9,449	0.3	17,965	0.6	65,035	R
New Mexico	418,409	201,148	48.1	211,419	50.5	1,161	0.3	1,110	0.3	3,571	0.9	10,271	R
New York	6,534,170	3,389,558	51.9	3,100,791	47.5	4,303	0.1	12,197	0.2	27,321	0.4	288,767	D
North Carolina	1,678,914	927,365	55.2	741,960	44.2	780	0.0	2,219	0.1	6,590	0.4	185,405	D
North Dakota	297,188	136,078	45.8	153,470	51.6	2,952	1.0	253	0.1	4,435	1.5	17,392	R
Ohio	4,111,873	2,011,621	48.9	2,000,505	48.7	58,258	1.4	8,961	0.2	32,528	0.8	11,116	D
Oklahoma	1,092,251	532,442	48.7	545,708	50.0	14,101	1.3	—	0.0	—	0.0	13,266	R
Oregon	1,029,876	490,407	47.6	492,120	47.8	40,207	3.9	—	0.0	7,142	0.7	1,713	R
Pennsylvania	4,620,787	2,328,677	50.4	2,205,604	47.7	50,584	1.1	—	0.0	35,922	0.8	123,073	D
Rhode Island	411,170	227,636	55.4	181,249	44.1	479	0.1	715	0.2	1,091	0.3	46,387	D
South Carolina	802,583	450,807	56.2	346,149	43.1	289	0.0	53	0.0	5,285	0.7	104,658	D
South Dakota	300,678	147,068	48.9	151,505	50.4	—	0.0	1,619	0.5	486	0.2	4,437	R
Tennessee	1,476,345	825,879	55.9	633,969	42.9	5,004	0.3	1,375	0.1	10,118	0.7	191,910	D
Texas	4,071,884	2,082,319	51.1	1,953,300	48.0	20,118	0.5	189	0.0	15,958	0.4	129,019	D
Utah	541,198	182,110	33.6	337,908	62.4	3,907	0.7	2,438	0.5	14,835	2.7	155,798	R
Vermont	187,765	80,954	43.1	102,085	54.4	4,001	2.1	—	0.0	725	0.4	21,131	R
Virginia	1,697,094	813,896	48.0	836,554	49.3	—	0.0	4,648	0.3	41,996	2.5	22,658	R
Washington	1,555,534	717,323	46.1	777,732	50.0	36,986	2.4	5,042	0.3	18,451	1.2	60,409	R
West Virginia	750,964	435,914	58.0	314,760	41.9	113	0.0	16	0.0	161	0.0	121,154	D
Wisconsin	2,104,175	1,040,232	49.4	1,004,987	47.8	34,943	1.7	3,814	0.2	20,199	1.0	35,245	D
Wyoming	156,343	62,239	39.8	92,717	59.3	624	0.4	89	0.1	674	0.4	30,478	R
Dist. of Col.	168,830	137,818	81.6	27,873	16.5	—	0.0	274	0.2	2,865	1.7	109,945	D
Totals	81,555,889	40,830,763	50.1	39,147,793	48.0	756,691	0.9	173,011	0.2	647,631	0.8	1,682,970	D

1. For breakdown of "Other" vote, see minor candidate vote totals at the end of this chapter.

1980 Presidential Election

STATE	TOTAL VOTE	RONALD REAGAN (Republican)		JIMMY CARTER (Democrat)		JOHN B. ANDERSON (Independent)		ED CLARK (Libertarian)		OTHER[1]		PLURALITY	
		Votes	%	Votes	%	Votes	%	Votes	%	Votes	%		
Alabama	1,341,929	654,192	48.8	636,730	47.4	16,481	1.2	13,318	1.0	21,208	1.6	17,462	R
Alaska	158,445	86,112	54.3	41,842	26.4	11,155	7.0	18,479	11.7	857	0.5	44,270	R
Arizona	873,945	529,688	60.6	246,843	28.2	76,952	8.8	18,784	2.1	1,678	0.2	282,845	R
Arkansas	837,582	403,164	48.1	398,041	47.5	22,468	2.7	8,970	1.1	4,939	0.6	5,123	R
California	8,587,063	4,524,858	52.7	3,083,661	35.9	739,833	8.6	148,434	1.7	90,277	1.1	1,441,197	R
Colorado	1,184,415	652,264	55.1	367,973	31.1	130,633	11.0	25,744	2.2	7,801	0.7	284,291	R
Connecticut	1,406,285	677,210	48.2	541,732	38.5	171,807	12.2	8,570	0.6	6,966	0.5	135,478	R
Delaware	235,900	111,252	47.2	105,754	44.8	16,288	6.9	1,974	0.8	632	0.3	5,498	R
Florida	3,686,930	2,046,951	55.5	1,419,475	38.5	189,692	5.1	30,524	0.8	288	0.0	627,476	R
Georgia	1,596,695	654,168	41.0	890,733	55.8	36,055	2.3	15,627	1.0	112	0.0	236,565	D
Hawaii	303,287	130,112	42.9	135,879	44.8	32,021	10.6	3,269	1.1	2,006	0.7	5,767	D
Idaho	437,431	290,699	66.5	110,192	25.2	27,058	6.2	8,425	1.9	1,057	0.2	180,507	R
Illinois	4,749,721	2,358,049	49.6	1,981,413	41.7	346,754	7.3	38,939	0.8	24,566	0.5	376,636	R
Indiana	2,242,033	1,255,656	56.0	844,197	37.7	111,639	5.0	19,627	0.9	10,914	0.5	411,459	R
Iowa	1,317,661	676,026	51.3	508,672	38.6	115,633	8.8	13,123	1.0	4,207	0.3	167,354	R
Kansas	979,795	566,812	57.9	326,150	33.3	68,231	7.0	14,470	1.5	4,132	0.4	240,662	R
Kentucky	1,294,627	635,274	49.1	616,417	47.6	31,127	2.4	5,531	0.4	6,278	0.5	18,857	R
Louisiana	1,548,591	792,853	51.2	708,453	45.7	26,345	1.7	8,240	0.5	12,700	0.8	84,400	R
Maine	523,011	238,522	45.6	220,974	42.3	53,327	10.2	5,119	1.0	5,069	1.0	17,548	R
Maryland	1,540,496	680,606	44.2	726,161	47.1	119,537	7.8	14,192	0.9	—	0.0	45,555	D
Massachusetts[2]	2,522,890	1,057,631	41.9	1,053,802	41.7	382,539	15.2	22,038	0.9	6,880	0.3	3,829	R
Michigan	3,909,725	1,915,225	49.0	1,661,532	42.5	275,223	7.0	41,597	1.1	16,148	0.4	253,693	R
Minnesota	2,051,980	873,268	42.6	954,174	46.5	174,990	8.5	31,592	1.5	17,956	0.9	80,906	D
Mississippi	892,620	441,089	49.4	429,281	48.1	12,036	1.3	5,465	0.6	4,749	0.5	11,808	R
Missouri	2,099,824	1,074,181	51.2	931,182	44.3	77,920	3.7	14,422	0.7	2,119	0.1	142,999	R
Montana	363,952	206,814	56.8	118,032	32.4	29,281	8.0	9,825	2.7	—	0.0	88,782	R
Nebraska	640,854	419,937	65.5	166,851	26.0	44,993	7.0	9,073	1.4	—	0.0	253,086	R
Nevada	247,885	155,017	62.5	66,666	26.9	17,651	7.1	4,358	1.8	4,193	1.7	88,351	R
New Hampshire	383,990	221,705	57.7	108,864	28.4	49,693	12.9	2,064	0.5	1,664	0.4	112,841	R
New Jersey	2,975,684	1,546,557	52.0	1,147,364	38.6	234,632	7.9	20,652	0.7	26,479	0.9	399,193	R
New Mexico	456,971	250,779	54.9	167,826	36.7	29,459	6.4	4,365	1.0	4,542	1.0	82,953	R
New York	6,201,959	2,893,831	46.7	2,728,372	44.0	467,801	7.5	52,648	0.8	59,307	1.0	165,459	R
North Carolina	1,855,833	915,018	49.3	875,635	47.2	52,800	2.8	9,677	0.5	2,703	0.1	39,383	R
North Dakota	301,545	193,695	64.2	79,189	26.3	23,640	7.8	3,743	1.2	1,278	0.4	114,506	R
Ohio	4,283,603	2,206,545	51.5	1,752,414	40.9	254,472	5.9	49,033	1.1	21,139	0.5	454,131	R
Oklahoma	1,149,708	695,570	60.5	402,026	35.0	38,284	3.3	13,828	1.2	—	0.0	293,544	R
Oregon	1,181,516	571,044	48.3	456,890	38.7	112,389	9.5	25,838	2.2	15,355	1.3	114,154	R
Pennsylvania	4,561,501	2,261,872	49.6	1,937,540	42.5	292,921	6.4	33,263	0.7	35,905	0.8	324,332	R
Rhode Island	416,072	154,793	37.2	198,342	47.7	59,819	14.4	2,458	0.6	660	0.2	43,549	D
South Carolina	894,071	441,841	49.4	430,385	48.1	14,153	1.6	5,139	0.6	2,553	0.3	11,456	R
South Dakota	327,703	198,343	60.5	103,855	31.7	21,431	6.5	3,824	1.2	250	0.1	94,488	R
Tennessee	1,617,616	787,761	48.7	783,051	48.4	35,991	2.2	7,116	0.4	3,697	0.2	4,710	R
Texas	4,541,636	2,510,705	55.3	1,881,147	41.4	111,613	2.5	37,643	0.8	528	0.0	629,558	R
Utah	604,222	439,687	72.8	124,266	20.6	30,284	5.0	7,226	1.2	2,759	0.5	315,421	R
Vermont	213,299	94,628	44.4	81,952	38.4	31,761	14.9	1,900	0.9	3,058	1.4	12,676	R
Virginia	1,866,032	989,609	53.0	752,174	40.3	95,418	5.1	12,821	0.7	16,010	0.9	237,435	R
Washington	1,742,394	865,244	49.7	650,193	37.3	185,073	10.6	29,213	1.7	12,671	0.7	215,051	R
West Virginia	737,715	334,206	45.3	367,462	49.8	31,691	4.3	4,356	0.6	—	0.0	33,256	D
Wisconsin	2,273,221	1,088,845	47.9	981,584	43.2	160,657	7.1	29,135	1.3	13,000	0.6	107,261	R
Wyoming	176,713	110,700	62.6	49,427	28.0	12,072	6.8	4,514	2.6	—	0.0	61,273	R
Dist. of Col.	175,237	23,545	13.4	131,113	74.8	16,337	9.3	1,114	0.6	3,128	1.8	107,568	D
Totals	86,513,813	43,904,153	50.7	35,483,883	41.0	5,720,060	6.6	921,299	1.1	484,418	0.6	8,420,270	R

1. For breakdown of "Other" vote, see minor candidate vote totals at the end of this chapter.

2. Figures from Clerk of the House of Representatives, *Statistics of the Congressional and Presidential Election* (Washington, D.C.: U.S. Government Printing Office, 1980); *Massachusetts Election Statistics, 1980.*

1984 Presidential Election

STATE	TOTAL VOTE	RONALD REAGAN (Republican) Votes	%	WALTER F. MONDALE (Democrat) Votes	%	DAVID BERGLAND (Libertarian) Votes	%	LYNDON H. LaROUCHE JR. (Independent) Votes	%	OTHER[1] Votes	%	PLURALITY	
Alabama	1,441,713	872,849	60.5	551,899	38.3	9,504	0.7	—	0.0	7,461	0.5	320,950	R
Alaska	207,605	138,377	66.7	62,007	29.9	6,378	3.1	—	0.0	843	0.4	76,370	R
Arizona	1,025,897	681,416	66.4	333,854	32.5	10,585	1.0	—	0.0	42	0.0	347,562	R
Arkansas	884,406	534,774	60.5	338,646	38.3	2,221	0.3	1,890	0.2	6,875	0.8	196,128	R
California	9,505,423	5,467,009	57.5	3,922,519	41.3	49,951	0.5	—	0.0	65,944	0.7	1,544,490	R
Colorado	1,295,380	821,817	63.4	454,975	35.1	11,257	0.9	4,662	0.4	2,669	0.2	366,842	R
Connecticut	1,466,900	890,877	60.7	569,597	38.8	204	0.0	—	0.0	6,222	0.4	321,280	R
Delaware	254,572	152,190	59.8	101,656	39.9	268	0.1	—	0.0	458	0.2	50,534	R
Florida	4,180,051	2,730,350	65.3	1,448,816	34.7	754	0.0	—	0.0	131	0.0	1,281,534	R
Georgia	1,776,120	1,068,722	60.2	706,628	39.8	152	0.0	34	0.0	584	0.0	362,094	R
Hawaii	335,846	185,050	55.1	147,154	43.8	2,167	0.6	654	0.2	821	0.2	37,896	R
Idaho	411,144	297,523	72.4	108,510	26.4	2,823	0.7	—	0.0	2,288	0.6	189,013	R
Illinois	4,819,088	2,707,103	56.2	2,086,499	43.3	10,086	0.2	—	0.0	15,400	0.3	620,604	R
Indiana	2,233,069	1,377,230	61.7	841,481	37.7	6,741	0.3	—	0.0	7,617	0.3	535,749	R
Iowa	1,319,805	703,088	53.3	605,620	45.9	1,844	0.1	6,248	0.5	3,005	0.2	97,468	R
Kansas	1,021,991	677,296	66.3	333,149	32.6	3,329	0.3	—	0.0	8,217	0.8	344,147	R
Kentucky	1,369,345	821,702	60.0	539,539	39.4	—	0.0	1,776	0.1	6,328	0.5	282,163	R
Louisiana	1,706,822	1,037,299	60.8	651,586	38.2	1,876	0.1	3,552	0.2	12,509	0.7	385,713	R
Maine	553,144	336,500	60.8	214,515	38.8	—	0.0	—	0.0	2,129	0.4	121,985	R
Maryland	1,675,873	879,918	52.5	787,935	47.0	5,721	0.3	—	0.0	2,299	0.1	91,983	R
Massachusetts	2,559,453	1,310,936	51.2	1,239,606	48.4	—	0.0	—	0.0	8,911	0.3	71,330	R
Michigan	3,801,658	2,251,571	59.2	1,529,638	40.2	10,055	0.3	3,862	0.1	6,532	0.2	721,933	R
Minnesota	2,084,449	1,032,603	49.5	1,036,364	49.7	2,996	0.1	3,865	0.2	8,621	0.4	3,761	D
Mississippi	941,104	582,377	61.9	352,192	37.4	2,336	0.2	1,001	0.1	3,198	0.3	230,185	R
Missouri	2,122,783	1,274,188	60.0	848,583	40.0	—	0.0	—	0.0	12	0.0	425,605	R
Montana	384,377	232,450	60.5	146,742	38.2	5,185	1.3	—	0.0	—	0.0	85,708	R
Nebraska	652,090	460,054	70.6	187,866	28.8	2,079	0.3	—	0.0	2,091	0.3	272,188	R
Nevada	286,667	188,770	65.8	91,655	32.0	2,292	0.8	—	0.0	3,950	1.4	97,115	R
New Hampshire	389,066	267,051	68.6	120,395	30.9	735	0.2	467	0.1	418	0.1	146,656	R
New Jersey	3,217,862	1,933,630	60.1	1,261,323	39.2	6,416	0.2	—	0.0	16,493	0.5	672,307	R
New Mexico	514,370	307,101	59.7	201,769	39.2	4,459	0.9	—	0.0	1,041	0.2	105,332	R
New York	6,806,810	3,664,763	53.8	3,119,609	45.8	11,949	0.2	—	0.0	10,489	0.2	545,154	R
North Carolina	2,175,361	1,346,481	61.9	824,287	37.9	3,794	0.2	—	0.0	799	0.0	522,194	R
North Dakota	308,971	200,336	64.8	104,429	33.8	703	0.2	1,278	0.4	2,225	0.7	95,907	R
Ohio	4,547,619	2,678,560	58.9	1,825,440	40.1	5,886	0.1	10,693	0.2	27,040	0.6	853,120	R
Oklahoma	1,255,676	861,530	68.6	385,080	30.7	9,066	0.7	—	0.0	—	0.0	476,450	R
Oregon	1,226,527	685,700	55.9	536,479	43.7	—	0.0	—	0.0	4,348	0.4	149,221	R
Pennsylvania	4,844,903	2,584,323	53.3	2,228,131	46.0	6,982	0.1	—	0.0	25,467	0.5	356,192	R
Rhode Island	410,492	212,080	51.7	197,106	48.0	277	0.1	—	0.0	1,029	0.3	14,974	R
South Carolina	968,529	615,539	63.6	344,459	35.6	4,359	0.5	—	0.0	4,172	0.4	271,080	R
South Dakota	317,867	200,267	63.0	116,113	36.5	—	0.0	—	0.0	1,487	0.5	84,154	R
Tennessee	1,711,994	990,212	57.8	711,714	41.6	3,072	0.2	1,852	0.1	5,144	0.3	278,498	R
Texas	5,397,571	3,433,428	63.6	1,949,276	36.1	—	0.0	14,613	0.3	254	0.0	1,484,152	R
Utah	629,656	469,105	74.5	155,369	24.7	2,447	0.4	—	0.0	2,735	0.4	313,736	R
Vermont	234,561	135,865	57.9	95,730	40.8	1,002	0.4	423	0.2	1,541	0.7	40,135	R
Virginia	2,146,635	1,337,078	62.3	796,250	37.1	—	0.0	13,307	0.6	—	0.0	540,828	R
Washington	1,883,910	1,051,670	55.8	807,352	42.9	8,844	0.5	4,712	0.3	11,332	0.6	244,318	R
West Virginia	735,742	405,483	55.1	328,125	44.6	—	0.0	—	0.0	2,134	0.3	77,358	R
Wisconsin	2,211,689	1,198,584	54.2	995,740	45.0	4,883	0.2	3,791	0.2	8,691	0.4	202,844	R
Wyoming	188,968	133,241	70.5	53,370	28.2	2,357	1.2	—	0.0	—	0.0	79,871	R
Dist. of Col.	211,288	29,009	13.7	180,408	85.4	279	0.1	127	0.1	1,465	0.7	151,399	D
Totals	92,652,842	54,455,075	58.8	37,577,185	40.6	228,314	0.2	78,807	0.1	313,461	0.3	16,877,890	R

1. For breakdown of "Other" vote, see minor candidate vote totals at the end of this chapter.

1988 Presidential Election

STATE	TOTAL VOTE	GEORGE H. W. BUSH (Republican)		MICHAEL S. DUKAKIS (Democrat)		RON PAUL (Libertarian)		LENORA B. FULANI (New Alliance)		OTHER[1]		PLURALITY	
		Votes	%	Votes	%	Votes	%	Votes	%	Votes	%		
Alabama	1,378,476	815,576	59.2	549,506	39.9	8,460	0.6	3,311	0.2	1,623	0.1	266,070	R
Alaska	200,116	119,251	59.6	72,584	36.3	5,484	2.7	1,024	0.5	1,773	0.9	46,667	R
Arizona	1,171,873	702,541	60.0	454,029	38.7	13,351	1.1	1,662	0.1	290	0.0	248,512	R
Arkansas	827,738	466,578	56.4	349,237	42.2	3,297	0.4	2,161	0.3	6,465	0.8	117,341	R
California	9,887,065	5,054,917	51.1	4,702,233	47.6	70,105	0.7	31,181	0.3	28,629	0.3	352,684	R
Colorado	1,372,394	728,177	53.1	621,453	45.3	15,482	1.1	2,539	0.2	4,743	0.3	106,724	R
Connecticut	1,443,394	750,241	52.0	676,584	46.9	14,071	1.0	2,491	0.2	7	0.0	73,657	R
Delaware	249,891	139,639	55.9	108,647	43.5	1,162	0.5	443	0.2	—	0.0	30,992	R
Florida	4,302,313	2,618,885	60.9	1,656,701	38.5	19,796	0.5	6,655	0.2	276	0.0	962,184	R
Georgia	1,809,672	1,081,331	59.8	714,792	39.5	8,435	0.5	5,099	0.3	15	0.0	366,539	R
Hawaii	354,461	158,625	44.8	192,364	54.3	1,999	0.6	1,003	0.3	470	0.1	33,739	D
Idaho	408,968	253,881	62.1	147,272	36.0	5,313	1.3	2,502	0.6	—	0.0	106,609	R
Illinois	4,559,120	2,310,939	50.7	2,215,940	48.6	14,944	0.3	10,276	0.2	7,021	0.2	94,999	R
Indiana	2,168,621	1,297,763	59.8	860,643	39.7	—	0.0	10,215	0.5	—	0.0	437,120	R
Iowa	1,225,614	545,355	44.5	670,557	54.7	2,494	0.2	540	0.0	6,668	0.5	125,202	D
Kansas	993,044	554,049	55.8	422,636	42.6	12,553	1.3	3,806	0.4	—	0.0	131,413	R
Kentucky	1,322,517	734,281	55.5	580,368	43.9	2,118	0.2	1,256	0.1	4,494	0.3	153,913	R
Louisiana	1,628,202	883,702	54.3	717,460	44.1	4,115	0.3	2,355	0.1	20,570	1.3	166,242	R
Maine	555,035	307,131	55.3	243,569	43.9	2,700	0.5	1,405	0.3	230	0.0	63,562	R
Maryland	1,714,358	876,167	51.1	826,304	48.2	6,748	0.4	5,115	0.3	24	0.0	49,863	R
Massachusetts	2,632,805	1,194,635	45.4	1,401,415	53.2	24,251	0.9	9,561	0.4	2,943	0.1	206,780	D
Michigan	3,669,163	1,965,486	53.6	1,675,783	45.7	18,336	0.5	2,513	0.1	7,045	0.2	289,703	R
Minnesota	2,096,790	962,337	45.9	1,109,471	52.9	5,109	0.2	1,734	0.1	18,139	0.9	147,134	D
Mississippi	931,527	557,890	59.9	363,921	39.1	3,329	0.4	2,155	0.2	4,232	0.5	193,969	R
Missouri	2,093,713	1,084,953	51.8	1,001,619	47.8	434	0.0	6,656	0.3	51	0.0	83,334	R
Montana	365,674	190,412	52.1	168,936	46.2	5,047	1.4	1,279	0.3	—	0.0	21,476	R
Nebraska	661,465	397,956	60.2	259,235	39.2	2,534	0.4	1,740	0.3	—	0.0	138,721	R
Nevada	350,067	206,040	58.9	132,738	37.9	3,520	1.0	835	0.2	6,934	2.0	73,302	R
New Hampshire	451,074	281,537	62.4	163,696	36.3	4,502	1.0	790	0.2	549	0.1	117,841	R
New Jersey	3,099,553	1,743,192	56.2	1,320,352	42.6	8,421	0.3	5,139	0.2	22,449	0.7	422,840	R
New Mexico	521,287	270,341	51.9	244,497	46.9	3,268	0.6	2,237	0.4	944	0.2	25,844	R
New York	6,485,683	3,081,871	47.5	3,347,882	51.6	12,109	0.2	15,845	0.2	27,976	0.4	266,011	D
North Carolina	2,134,370	1,237,258	58.0	890,167	41.7	1,263	0.1	5,682	0.3	—	0.0	347,091	R
North Dakota	297,261	166,559	56.0	127,739	43.0	1,315	0.4	396	0.1	1,252	0.4	38,820	R
Ohio	4,393,699	2,416,549	55.0	1,939,629	44.1	11,989	0.3	12,017	0.3	13,515	0.3	476,920	R
Oklahoma	1,171,036	678,367	57.9	483,423	41.3	6,261	0.5	2,985	0.3	—	0.0	194,944	R
Oregon	1,201,694	560,126	46.6	616,206	51.3	14,811	1.2	6,487	0.5	4,064	0.3	56,080	D
Pennsylvania	4,536,251	2,300,087	50.7	2,194,944	48.4	12,051	0.3	4,379	0.1	24,790	0.5	105,143	R
Rhode Island	404,620	177,761	43.9	225,123	55.6	825	0.2	280	0.1	631	0.2	47,362	D
South Carolina	986,009	606,443	61.5	370,554	37.6	4,935	0.5	4,077	0.4	—	0.0	235,889	R
South Dakota	312,991	165,415	52.8	145,560	46.5	1,060	0.3	730	0.2	226	0.1	19,855	R
Tennessee	1,636,250	947,233	57.9	679,794	41.5	2,041	0.1	1,334	0.1	5,848	0.4	267,439	R
Texas	5,427,410	3,036,829	56.0	2,352,748	43.3	30,355	0.6	7,208	0.1	270	0.0	684,081	R
Utah	647,008	428,442	66.2	207,343	32.0	7,473	1.2	455	0.1	3,295	0.5	221,099	R
Vermont	243,328	124,331	51.1	115,775	47.6	1,000	0.4	205	0.1	2,017	0.8	8,556	R
Virginia	2,191,609	1,309,162	59.7	859,799	39.2	8,336	0.4	14,312	0.7	—	0.0	449,363	R
Washington	1,865,253	903,835	48.5	933,516	50.0	17,240	0.9	3,520	0.2	7,142	0.4	29,681	D
West Virginia	653,311	310,065	47.5	341,016	52.2	—	0.0	2,230	0.3	—	0.0	30,951	D
Wisconsin	2,191,608	1,047,499	47.8	1,126,794	51.4	5,157	0.2	1,953	0.1	10,205	0.5	79,295	D
Wyoming	176,551	106,867	60.5	67,113	38.0	2,026	1.1	545	0.3	—	0.0	39,754	R
Dist. of Col.	192,877	27,590	14.3	159,407	82.6	554	0.3	2,901	1.5	2,425	1.3	131,817	D
Totals	91,594,809	48,886,097	53.4	41,809,074	45.6	432,179	0.5	217,219	0.2	250,240	0.3	7,077,023	R

1. For breakdown of "Other" vote, see minor candidate vote totals at the end of this chapter.

1992 Presidential Election

STATE	TOTAL VOTE	BILL CLINTON (Democrat) Votes	%	GEORGE H. W. BUSH (Republican) Votes	%	ROSS PEROT (Independent) Votes	%	ANDRE V. MARROU (Libertarian) Votes	%	OTHER[1] Votes	%	PLURALITY	
Alabama	1,688,060	690,080	40.9	804,283	47.6	183,109	10.8	5,737	0.3	4,851	0.3	114,203	R
Alaska	258,506	78,294	30.3	102,000	39.5	73,481	28.4	1,378	0.5	3,353	1.3	23,706	R
Arizona	1,486,975	543,050	36.5	572,086	38.5	353,741	23.8	6,759	0.5	11,339	0.8	29,036	R
Arkansas	950,653	505,823	53.2	337,324	35.5	99,132	10.4	1,261	0.1	7,113	0.7	168,499	D
California	11,131,721	5,121,325	46.0	3,630,574	32.6	2,296,006	20.6	48,139	0.4	35,677	0.3	1,490,751	D
Colorado	1,569,180	629,681	40.1	562,850	35.9	366,010	23.3	8,669	0.6	1,970	0.1	66,831	D
Connecticut	1,616,332	682,318	42.2	578,313	35.8	348,771	21.6	5,391	0.3	1,539	0.1	104,005	D
Delaware	289,735	126,054	43.5	102,313	35.3	59,213	20.4	935	0.3	1,220	0.4	23,741	D
Florida	5,314,392	2,072,698	39.0	2,173,310	40.9	1,053,067	19.8	15,079	0.3	238		100,612	R
Georgia	2,321,125	1,008,966	43.5	995,252	42.9	309,657	13.3	7,110	0.3	140		13,714	D
Hawaii	372,842	179,310	48.1	136,822	36.7	53,003	14.2	1,119	0.3	2,588	0.7	42,488	D
Idaho	482,142	137,013	28.4	202,645	42.0	130,395	27.0	1,167	0.2	10,922	2.3	65,632	R
Illinois	5,050,157	2,453,350	48.6	1,734,096	34.3	840,515	16.6	9,218	0.2	12,978	0.3	719,254	D
Indiana	2,305,871	848,420	36.8	989,375	42.9	455,934	19.8	7,936	0.3	4,206	0.2	140,955	R
Iowa	1,354,607	586,353	43.3	504,891	37.3	253,468	18.7	1,076	0.1	8,819	0.7	81,462	D
Kansas	1,157,335	390,434	33.7	449,951	38.9	312,358	27.0	4,314	0.4	278		59,517	R
Kentucky	1,492,900	665,104	44.6	617,178	41.3	203,944	13.7	4,513	0.3	2,161	0.1	47,926	D
Louisiana	1,790,017	815,971	45.6	733,386	41.0	211,478	11.8	3,155	0.2	26,027	1.5	82,585	D
Maine	679,499	263,420	38.8	206,504	30.4	206,820	30.4	1,681	0.2	1,074	0.2	56,600	D
Maryland	1,985,046	988,571	49.8	707,094	35.6	281,414	14.2	4,715	0.2	3,252	0.2	281,477	D
Massachusetts	2,773,700	1,318,662	47.5	805,049	29.0	630,731	22.7	9,024	0.3	10,234	0.4	513,613	D
Michigan	4,274,673	1,871,182	43.8	1,554,940	36.4	824,813	19.3	10,175	0.2	13,563	0.3	316,242	D
Minnesota	2,347,948	1,020,997	43.5	747,841	31.9	562,506	24.0	3,374	0.1	13,230	0.6	273,156	D
Mississippi	981,793	400,258	40.8	487,793	49.7	85,626	8.7	2,154	0.2	5,962	0.6	87,535	R
Missouri	2,391,565	1,053,873	44.1	811,159	33.9	518,741	21.7	7,497	0.3	295		242,714	D
Montana	410,611	154,507	37.6	144,207	35.1	107,225	26.1	986	0.2	3,686	0.9	10,300	D
Nebraska	737,546	216,864	29.4	343,678	46.6	174,104	23.6	1,340	0.2	1,560	0.2	126,814	R
Nevada	506,318	189,148	37.4	175,828	34.7	132,580	26.2	1,835	0.4	6,927	1.4	13,320	D
New Hampshire	537,943	209,040	38.9	202,484	37.6	121,337	22.6	3,548	0.7	1,534	0.3	6,556	D
New Jersey	3,343,594	1,436,206	43.0	1,356,865	40.6	521,829	15.6	6,822	0.2	21,872	0.7	79,341	D
New Mexico	569,986	261,617	45.9	212,824	37.3	91,895	16.1	1,615	0.3	2,035	0.4	48,793	D
New York	6,926,925	3,444,450	49.7	2,346,649	33.9	1,090,721	15.7	13,451	0.2	31,654	0.5	1,097,801	D
North Carolina	2,611,850	1,114,042	42.7	1,134,661	43.4	357,864	13.7	5,171	0.2	112		20,619	R
North Dakota	308,133	99,168	32.2	136,244	44.2	71,084	23.1	416	0.1	1,221	0.4	37,076	R
Ohio	4,939,967	1,984,942	40.2	1,894,310	38.3	1,036,426	21.0	7,252	0.1	17,037	0.3	90,632	D
Oklahoma	1,390,359	473,066	34.0	592,929	42.6	319,878	23.0	4,486	0.3	—		119,863	R
Oregon	1,462,643	621,314	42.5	475,757	32.5	354,091	24.2	4,277	0.3	7,204	0.5	145,557	D
Pennsylvania	4,959,810	2,239,164	45.1	1,791,841	36.1	902,667	18.2	21,477	0.4	4,661	0.1	447,323	D
Rhode Island	453,477	213,299	47.0	131,601	29.0	105,045	23.2	571	0.1	2,961	0.7	81,698	D
South Carolina	1,202,527	479,514	39.9	577,507	48.0	138,872	11.5	2,719	0.2	3,915	0.3	97,993	R
South Dakota	336,254	124,888	37.1	136,718	40.7	73,295	21.8	814	0.2	539	0.2	11,830	R
Tennessee	1,982,638	933,521	47.1	841,300	42.4	199,968	10.1	1,847	0.1	6,002	0.3	92,221	D
Texas	6,154,018	2,281,815	37.1	2,496,071	40.6	1,354,781	22.0	19,699	0.3	1,652		214,256	R
Utah	743,999	183,429	24.7	322,632	43.4	203,400	27.3	1,900	0.3	32,638	4.4	119,232	R
Vermont	289,701	133,592	46.1	88,122	30.4	65,991	22.8	501	0.2	1,495	0.5	45,470	D
Virginia	2,558,665	1,038,650	40.6	1,150,517	45.0	348,639	13.6	5,730	0.2	15,129	0.6	111,867	R
Washington	2,288,230	993,037	43.4	731,234	32.0	541,780	23.7	7,533	0.3	14,646	0.6	261,803	D
West Virginia	683,762	331,001	48.4	241,974	35.4	108,829	15.9	1,873	0.3	85		89,027	D
Wisconsin	2,531,114	1,041,066	41.1	930,855	36.8	544,479	21.5	2,877	0.1	11,837	0.5	110,211	D
Wyoming	200,598	68,160	34.0	79,347	39.6	51,263	25.6	844	0.4	984	0.5	11,187	R
Dist. of Col.	227,572	192,619	84.6	20,698	9.1	9,681	4.3	467	0.2	4,107	1.8	171,921	D
Totals	104,425,014	44,909,326	43.0	39,103,882	37.4	19,741,657	18.9	291,627	0.3	378,522	0.4	5,805,444	D

1. For breakdown of "Other" vote, see minor candidate vote totals at the end of this chapter.

1996 Presidential Election

STATE	TOTAL VOTE	BILL CLINTON (Democrat) Votes	%	BOB DOLE (Republican) Votes	%	ROSS PEROT (Reform) Votes	%	RALPH NADER (Green) Votes	%	OTHER[1] Votes	%	PLURALITY	
Alabama	1,534,349	662,165	43.2	769,044	50.1	92,149	6.0	—		10,991	0.7	106,879	R
Alaska	241,620	80,380	33.3	122,746	50.8	26,333	10.9	7,597	3.1	4,564	1.9	42,366	R
Arizona	1,404,405	653,288	46.5	622,073	44.3	112,072	8.0	2,062	0.1	14,910	1.1	31,215	D
Arkansas	884,262	475,171	53.7	325,416	36.8	69,884	7.9	3,649	0.4	10,142	1.1	149,755	D
California	10,019,484	5,119,835	51.1	3,828,380	38.2	697,847	7.0	237,016	2.4	136,406	1.4	1,291,455	D
Colorado	1,510,704	671,152	44.4	691,848	45.8	99,629	6.6	25,070	1.7	23,005	1.5	20,696	R
Connecticut	1,392,614	735,740	52.8	483,109	34.7	139,523	10.0	24,321	1.7	9,921	0.7	252,631	D
Delaware	270,845	140,355	51.8	99,062	36.6	28,719	10.6	18		2,691	1.0	41,293	D
Florida	5,303,794	2,546,870	48.0	2,244,536	42.3	483,870	9.1	4,101	0.1	24,417	0.5	302,334	D
Georgia	2,299,071	1,053,849	45.8	1,080,843	47.0	146,337	6.4	—		18,042	0.8	26,994	R
Hawaii	360,120	205,012	56.9	113,943	31.6	27,358	7.6	10,386	2.9	3,421	0.9	91,069	D
Idaho	491,719	165,443	33.6	256,595	52.2	62,518	12.7	—		7,163	1.5	91,152	R
Illinois	4,311,391	2,341,744	54.3	1,587,021	36.8	346,408	8.0	1,447		34,771	0.8	754,723	D
Indiana	2,135,431	887,424	41.6	1,006,693	47.1	224,299	10.5	895		16,120	0.8	119,269	R
Iowa	1,234,075	620,258	50.3	492,644	39.9	105,159	8.5	6,550	0.5	9,464	0.8	127,614	D
Kansas	1,074,300	387,659	36.1	583,245	54.3	92,639	8.6	914	0.1	9,843	0.9	195,586	R
Kentucky	1,388,708	636,614	45.8	623,283	44.9	120,396	8.7	701	0.1	7,714	0.6	13,331	D
Louisiana	1,783,959	927,837	52.0	712,586	39.9	123,293	6.9	4,719	0.3	15,524	0.9	215,251	D
Maine	605,897	312,788	51.6	186,378	30.8	85,970	14.2	15,279	2.5	5,482	0.9	126,410	D
Maryland	1,780,870	966,207	54.3	681,530	38.3	115,812	6.5	2,606	0.1	14,715	0.8	284,677	D
Massachusetts	2,556,786	1,571,763	61.5	718,107	28.1	227,217	8.9	4,565	0.2	35,134	1.4	853,656	D
Michigan	3,848,844	1,989,653	51.7	1,481,212	38.5	336,670	8.7	2,322	0.1	38,987	1.0	508,441	D
Minnesota	2,192,640	1,120,438	51.1	766,476	35.0	257,704	11.8	24,908	1.1	23,114	1.1	353,962	D
Mississippi	893,857	394,022	44.1	439,838	49.2	52,222	5.8	—		7,775	0.9	45,816	R
Missouri	2,158,065	1,025,935	47.5	890,016	41.2	217,188	10.1	534		24,392	1.1	135,919	D
Montana	407,261	167,922	41.3	179,652	44.1	55,229	13.6	—		4,458	1.1	11,730	R
Nebraska	677,415	236,761	35.0	363,467	53.7	71,278	10.5	—		5,909	0.9	126,706	R
Nevada	464,279	203,974	43.9	199,244	42.9	43,986	9.5	4,730	1.0	12,345	2.7	4,730	D
New Hampshire	499,175	246,214	49.3	196,532	39.4	48,390	9.7	—		8,039	1.6	49,682	D
New Jersey	3,075,807	1,652,329	53.7	1,103,078	35.9	262,134	8.5	32,465	1.1	25,801	0.8	549,251	D
New Mexico	556,074	273,495	49.2	232,751	41.9	32,257	5.8	13,218	2.4	4,353	0.8	40,744	D
New York	6,316,129	3,756,177	59.5	1,933,492	30.6	503,458	8.0	75,956	1.2	47,046	0.7	1,822,685	D
North Carolina	2,515,807	1,107,849	44.0	1,225,938	48.7	168,059	6.7	2,108	0.1	11,853	0.4	118,089	R
North Dakota	266,411	106,905	40.1	125,050	46.9	32,515	12.2	—		1,941	0.7	18,145	R
Ohio	4,534,434	2,148,222	47.4	1,859,883	41.0	483,207	10.7	2,962	0.1	40,160	0.9	288,339	D
Oklahoma	1,206,713	488,105	40.4	582,315	48.3	130,788	10.8	—		5,505	0.5	94,210	R
Oregon	1,377,760	649,641	47.2	538,152	39.1	121,221	8.8	49,415	3.6	19,331	1.4	111,489	D
Pennsylvania	4,506,118	2,215,819	49.2	1,801,169	40.0	430,984	9.6	3,086	0.1	55,060	1.2	414,650	D
Rhode Island	390,284	233,050	59.7	104,683	26.8	43,723	11.2	6,040	1.5	2,788	0.7	128,367	D
South Carolina	1,151,689	506,283	44.0	573,458	49.8	64,386	5.6	—		7,562	0.7	67,175	R
South Dakota	323,826	139,333	43.0	150,543	46.5	31,250	9.7	—		2,700	0.8	11,210	R
Tennessee	1,894,105	909,146	48.0	863,530	45.6	105,918	5.6	6,427	0.3	9,084	0.4	45,616	D
Texas	5,611,644	2,459,683	43.8	2,736,167	48.8	378,537	6.7	4,810	0.1	32,447	0.6	276,484	R
Utah	665,629	221,633	33.3	361,911	54.4	66,461	10.0	4,615	0.7	11,009	1.7	140,278	R
Vermont	258,449	137,894	53.4	80,352	31.1	31,024	12.0	5,585	2.2	3,594	1.4	57,542	D
Virginia	2,416,642	1,091,060	45.1	1,138,350	47.1	159,861	6.6	—		27,371	1.1	47,290	R
Washington	2,253,837	1,123,323	49.8	840,712	37.3	201,003	8.9	60,322	2.7	28,477	1.3	282,611	D
West Virginia	636,459	327,812	51.5	233,946	36.8	71,639	11.3	—		3,062	0.5	93,866	D
Wisconsin	2,196,169	1,071,971	48.8	845,029	38.5	227,339	10.4	28,723	1.3	23,107	1.1	226,942	D
Wyoming	211,571	77,934	36.8	105,388	49.8	25,928	12.3	—		2,321	1.1	27,454	R
Dist. of Col.	185,726	158,220	85.2	17,339	9.3	3,611	1.9	4,780	2.6	1,776	1.0	140,881	D
Totals	96,277,223	47,402,357	49.2	39,198,755	40.7	8,085,402	8.4	684,902	0.7	905,807	0.9	8,203,602	D

1. For breakdown of "Other" vote, see minor candidate vote totals at the end of this chapter.

2000 Presidential Election

STATE	TOTAL VOTE	GEORGE W. BUSH (Republican) Votes	%	AL GORE (Democrat) Votes	%	RALPH NADER (Green) Votes	%	PATRICK J. BUCHANAN (Reform) Votes	%	OTHER[1] Votes	%	PLURALITY	
Alabama	1,666,272	941,173	56.5	692,611	41.6	18,323	1.1	6,351	0.4	7,814	0.5	248,562	R
Alaska	285,560	167,398	58.6	79,004	27.7	28,747	10.1	5,192	1.8	5,219	1.8	88,394	R
Arizona	1,532,016	781,652	51.0	685,341	44.7	45,645	3.0	12,373	0.8	7,005	0.5	96,311	R
Arkansas	921,781	472,940	51.3	422,768	45.9	13,421	1.5	7,358	0.8	5,294	0.6	50,172	R
California	10,965,856	4,567,429	41.7	5,861,203	53.4	418,707	3.8	44,987	0.4	75,530	0.7	1,293,774	D
Colorado	1,741,368	883,748	50.8	738,227	42.4	91,434	5.3	10,465	0.6	17,494	1.0	145,521	R
Connecticut	1,459,525	561,094	38.4	816,015	55.9	64,452	4.4	4,731	0.3	13,233	0.9	254,921	D
Delaware	327,622	137,288	41.9	180,068	55.0	8,307	2.5	777	0.2	1,182	0.4	42,780	D
Florida	5,963,110	2,912,790	48.8	2,912,253	48.8	97,488	1.6	17,484	0.3	23,095	0.4	537	R
Georgia	2,596,645	1,419,720	54.7	1,116,230	43.0	13,273	0.5	10,926	0.4	36,496	1.4	303,490	R
Hawaii	367,951	137,845	37.5	205,286	55.8	21,623	5.9	1,071	0.3	2,126	0.6	67,441	D
Idaho	501,621	336,937	67.2	138,637	27.6	12,292	2.5	7,615	1.5	6,140	1.2	198,300	R
Illinois	4,742,123	2,019,421	42.6	2,589,026	54.6	103,759	2.2	16,106	0.3	13,811	0.3	569,605	D
Indiana	2,199,302	1,245,836	56.6	901,980	41.0	18,531	0.8	16,959	0.8	15,996	0.7	343,856	R
Iowa	1,315,563	634,373	48.2	638,517	48.5	29,374	2.2	5,731	0.4	7,568	0.6	4,144	D
Kansas	1,072,218	622,332	58.0	399,276	37.2	36,086	3.4	7,370	0.7	7,154	0.7	223,056	R
Kentucky	1,544,187	872,492	56.5	638,898	41.4	23,192	1.5	4,173	0.3	5,432	0.4	233,594	R
Louisiana	1,765,656	927,871	52.6	792,344	44.9	20,473	1.2	14,356	0.8	10,612	0.6	135,527	R
Maine	651,817	286,616	44.0	319,951	49.1	37,127	5.7	4,443	0.7	3,680	0.6	33,335	D
Maryland	2,020,480	813,797	40.3	1,140,782	56.5	53,768	2.7	4,248	0.2	7,885	0.4	326,985	D
Massachusetts	2,702,984	878,502	32.5	1,616,487	59.8	173,564	6.4	11,149	0.4	23,282	0.9	737,985	D
Michigan	4,232,711	1,953,139	46.1	2,170,418	51.3	84,165	2.0	2,061	0.0	22,928	0.5	217,279	D
Minnesota	2,438,685	1,109,659	45.5	1,168,266	47.9	126,696	5.2	22,166	0.9	11,898	0.5	58,607	D
Mississippi	994,184	572,844	57.6	404,614	40.7	8,122	0.8	2,265	0.2	6,339	0.6	168,230	R
Missouri	2,359,892	1,189,924	50.4	1,111,138	47.1	38,515	1.6	9,818	0.4	10,497	0.4	78,786	R
Montana	410,997	240,178	58.4	137,126	33.4	24,437	5.9	5,697	1.4	3,559	0.9	103,052	R
Nebraska	697,019	433,862	62.2	231,780	33.3	24,540	3.5	3,646	0.5	3,191	0.5	202,082	R
Nevada	608,970	301,575	49.5	279,978	46.0	15,008	2.5	4,747	0.8	7,662	1.3	21,597	R
New Hampshire	569,081	273,559	48.1	266,348	46.8	22,198	3.9	2,615	0.5	4,361	0.8	7,211	R
New Jersey	3,187,226	1,284,173	40.3	1,788,850	56.1	94,554	3.0	6,989	0.2	12,660	0.4	504,677	D
New Mexico	598,605	286,417	47.8	286,783	47.9	21,251	3.6	1,392	0.2	2,762	0.5	366	D
New York	6,821,999	2,403,374	35.2	4,107,697	60.2	244,030	3.6	31,599	0.5	35,299	0.5	1,704,323	D
North Carolina	2,911,262	1,631,163	56.0	1,257,692	43.2	—	0.0	8,874	0.3	13,533	0.5	373,471	R
North Dakota	288,256	174,852	60.7	95,284	33.1	9,486	3.3	7,288	2.5	1,346	0.5	79,568	R
Ohio	4,701,998	2,350,363	50.0	2,183,628	46.4	117,799	2.5	26,721	0.6	23,484	0.5	166,735	R
Oklahoma	1,234,229	744,337	60.3	474,276	38.4	—	0.0	9,014	0.7	6,602	0.5	270,061	R
Oregon	1,533,968	713,577	46.5	720,342	47.0	77,357	5.0	7,063	0.5	15,629	1.0	6,765	D
Pennsylvania	4,913,119	2,281,127	46.4	2,485,967	50.6	103,392	2.1	16,023	0.3	26,610	0.5	204,840	D
Rhode Island	409,047	130,555	31.9	249,508	61.0	25,052	6.1	2,273	0.6	1,659	0.4	118,953	D
South Carolina	1,382,717	785,937	56.8	565,561	40.9	20,200	1.5	3,519	0.3	7,500	0.5	220,376	R
South Dakota	316,269	190,700	60.3	118,804	37.6	—	0.0	3,322	1.1	3,443	1.1	71,896	R
Tennessee	2,076,181	1,061,949	51.1	981,720	47.3	19,781	1.0	4,250	0.2	8,481	0.4	80,229	R
Texas	6,407,637	3,799,639	59.3	2,433,746	38.0	137,994	2.2	12,394	0.2	23,864	0.4	1,365,893	R
Utah	770,754	515,096	66.8	203,053	26.3	35,850	4.7	9,319	1.2	7,436	1.0	312,043	R
Vermont	294,308	119,775	40.7	149,022	50.6	20,374	6.9	2,192	0.7	2,945	1.0	29,247	D
Virginia	2,739,447	1,437,490	52.5	1,217,290	44.4	59,398	2.2	5,455	0.2	19,814	0.7	220,200	R
Washington	2,487,433	1,108,864	44.6	1,247,652	50.2	103,002	4.1	7,171	0.3	20,744	0.8	138,788	D
West Virginia	648,124	336,475	51.9	295,497	45.6	10,680	1.6	3,169	0.5	2,303	0.4	40,978	R
Wisconsin	2,598,607	1,237,279	47.6	1,242,987	47.8	94,070	3.6	11,446	0.4	12,825	0.5	5,708	D
Wyoming	218,351	147,947	67.8	60,481	27.7	4,625	2.1	2,724	1.2	2,574	1.2	87,466	R
Dist. of Col.	201,894	18,073	9.0	171,923	85.2	10,576	5.2	—	0.0	1,322	0.7	153,850	D
Totals	105,396,627	50,455,156	47.9	50,992,335	48.4	2,882,738	2.7	449,077	0.4	617,321	0.6	537,179	D

1. For breakdown of "Other" vote, see minor candidate vote totals at the end of this chapter.

2004 Presidential Election

STATE	TOTAL VOTE	GEORGE W. BUSH (Republican)		JOHN KERRY (Democrat)		OTHER[1]		PLURALITY	
		Votes	%	Votes	%	Votes	%		
Alabama	1,883,449	1,176,394	62.5	693,933	36.8	13,122	0.7	482,461	R
Alaska	312,598	190,889	61.1	111,025	35.5	10,684	3.4	79,864	R
Arizona	2,012,585	1,104,294	54.9	893,524	44.4	14,767	0.7	210,770	R
Arkansas	1,054,945	572,898	54.3	469,953	44.5	12,094	1.2	102,945	R
California	12,421,852	5,509,826	44.4	6,745,485	54.3	166,541	1.3	1,235,659	D
Colorado	2,130,330	1,101,255	51.7	1,001,732	47.0	27,343	1.3	99,523	R
Connecticut	1,578,769	693,826	43.9	857,488	54.3	27,455	1.8	163,662	D
Delaware	375,190	171,660	45.8	200,152	53.3	3,378	0.9	28,492	D
Florida	7,609,810	3,964,522	52.1	3,583,544	47.1	61,744	0.8	380,978	R
Georgia	3,301,875	1,914,254	58.0	1,366,149	41.4	21,472	0.6	548,105	R
Hawaii	429,013	194,191	45.3	231,708	54.0	3,114	0.7	37,517	D
Idaho	598,447	409,235	68.4	181,098	30.3	8,114	1.3	228,137	R
Illinois	5,274,322	2,345,946	44.5	2,891,550	54.8	36,826	0.7	545,604	D
Indiana	2,468,002	1,479,438	59.9	969,011	39.3	19,553	0.8	510,427	R
Iowa	1,506,908	751,957	49.9	741,898	49.2	13,053	0.9	10,059	R
Kansas	1,187,756	736,456	62.0	434,993	36.6	16,307	1.4	301,463	R
Kentucky	1,795,860	1,069,439	59.6	712,733	39.7	13,688	0.7	356,706	R
Louisiana	1,943,106	1,102,169	56.7	820,299	42.2	20,638	1.1	281,870	R
Maine	740,752	330,201	44.6	396,842	53.6	13,709	1.8	66,641	D
Maryland	2,386,678	1,024,703	42.9	1,334,493	55.9	27,482	1.2	309,790	D
Massachusetts	2,912,388	1,071,109	36.8	1,803,800	61.9	37,479	1.3	732,691	D
Michigan	4,839,252	2,313,746	47.8	2,479,183	51.2	46,323	1.0	165,437	D
Minnesota	2,828,387	1,346,695	47.6	1,445,014	51.1	36,678	1.3	98,319	D
Mississippi	1,152,145	684,981	59.5	458,094	39.8	9,070	0.7	226,887	R
Missouri	2,731,364	1,455,713	53.3	1,259,171	46.1	16,480	0.6	196,542	R
Montana	450,445	266,063	59.1	173,710	38.6	10,672	2.3	92,353	R
Nebraska	778,186	512,814	65.9	254,328	32.7	11,044	1.4	258,486	R
Nevada	829,587	418,690	50.5	397,190	47.9	13,707	1.6	21,500	R
New Hampshire	677,738	331,237	48.9	340,511	50.2	5,990	0.9	9,274	D
New Jersey	3,611,691	1,670,003	46.2	1,911,430	52.9	30,258	0.9	241,427	D
New Mexico	756,304	376,930	49.8	370,942	49.0	8,432	1.2	5,988	R
New York	7,391,036	2,962,567	40.1	4,314,280	58.4	114,189	1.5	1,351,713	D
North Carolina	3,501,007	1,961,166	56.0	1,525,849	43.6	13,992	0.4	435,317	R
North Dakota	312,833	196,651	62.9	111,052	35.5	5,130	1.6	85,599	R
Ohio	5,627,903	2,859,764	50.8	2,741,165	48.7	26,974	0.5	118,599	R
Oklahoma	1,463,758	959,792	65.6	503,966	34.4	—	0.0	455,826	R
Oregon	1,836,782	866,831	47.2	943,163	51.3	26,788	1.5	76,332	D
Pennsylvania	5,769,590	2,793,847	48.4	2,938,095	50.9	37,648	0.7	144,248	D
Rhode Island	437,134	169,046	38.7	259,760	59.4	8,328	1.9	90,714	D
South Carolina	1,617,730	937,974	58.0	661,699	40.9	18,057	1.1	276,275	R
South Dakota	388,215	232,584	59.9	149,244	38.4	6,387	1.7	83,340	R
Tennessee	2,437,319	1,384,375	56.8	1,036,477	42.5	16,467	0.7	347,898	R
Texas	7,410,765	4,526,917	61.1	2,832,704	38.2	51,144	0.7	1,694,213	R
Utah	927,844	663,742	71.5	241,199	26.0	22,903	2.5	422,543	R
Vermont	312,309	121,180	38.8	184,067	58.9	7,062	2.3	62,887	D
Virginia	3,198,367	1,716,959	53.7	1,454,742	45.5	26,666	0.8	262,217	R
Washington	2,859,084	1,304,894	45.6	1,510,201	52.8	43,989	1.6	205,307	D
West Virginia	755,887	423,778	56.1	326,541	43.2	5,568	0.7	97,237	R
Wisconsin	2,997,007	1,478,120	49.3	1,489,504	49.7	29,383	1.0	11,384	D
Wyoming	243,428	167,629	68.9	70,776	29.1	5,023	2.0	96,853	R
District of Columbia	227,586	21,256	9.3	202,970	89.2	3,360	1.5	181,714	D
Totals	122,295,345	62,040,610	50.7	59,028,439	48.3	1,226,296	1.0	3,012,171	R

1. For breakdown of "Other" vote, see minor candidate vote totals at the end of this chapter.

2008 Presidential Election

STATE	TOTAL VOTE	BARACK OBAMA (Democrat)		JOHN McCAIN (Republican)		OTHER[1]		PLURALITY	
		Votes	%	Votes	%	Votes	%		
Alabama	2,099,819	813,479	38.7	1,266,546	60.3	19,794	0.9	453,067	R
Alaska	326,197	123,594	37.9	193,841	59.4	8,762	2.7	70,247	R
Arizona	2,293,475	1,034,707	45.1	1,230,111	53.6	28,657	1.2	195,404	R
Arkansas	1,086,617	422,310	38.9	638,017	58.7	26,290	2.4	215,707	R
California	13,561,900	8,274,473	61.0	5,011,781	37.0	275,646	2.0	3,262,692	D
Colorado	2,401,462	1,288,633	53.7	1,073,629	44.7	39,200	1.6	215,004	D
Connecticut	1,646,792	997,772	60.6	629,428	38.2	19,592	1.1	368,344	D
Delaware	412,412	255,459	61.9	152,374	36.9	4,579	1.1	103,085	D
Florida	8,390,744	4,282,074	51.0	4,045,624	48.2	63,046	0.8	236,450	D
Georgia	3,924,486	1,844,123	47.0	2,048,759	52.2	31,604	0.8	204,636	R
Hawaii	453,568	325,871	71.8	120,566	26.6	7,131	1.6	205,305	D
Idaho	655,032	236,440	36.1	403,012	61.5	15,580	2.4	166,572	R
Illinois	5,522,371	3,419,348	61.9	2,031,179	36.8	71,844	1.3	1,388,169	D
Indiana	2,751,054	1,374,039	49.9	1,345,648	48.9	31,367	1.1	28,391	D
Iowa	1,537,123	828,940	53.9	682,379	44.4	25,804	1.7	146,561	D
Kansas	1,235,872	514,765	41.7	699,655	56.6	21,452	1.7	184,890	R
Kentucky	1,826,620	751,985	41.2	1,048,462	57.4	26,173	1.4	296,477	R
Louisiana	1,960,761	782,989	39.9	1,148,275	58.6	29,497	1.5	365,286	R
Maine	731,163	421,923	57.7	295,273	40.4	13,967	1.9	126,650	D
Maryland	2,631,596	1,629,467	61.9	959,862	36.5	42,267	1.6	669,605	D
Massachusetts	3,080,985	1,904,097	61.8	1,108,854	36.0	68,034	2.2	795,243	D
Michigan	5,001,766	2,872,579	57.4	2,048,639	41.0	80,548	1.6	823,940	D
Minnesota	2,910,369	1,573,354	54.1	1,275,409	43.8	61,606	2.1	297,945	D
Mississippi	1,289,865	554,662	43.0	724,597	56.2	10,606	0.8	169,935	R
Missouri	2,925,205	1,441,911	49.3	1,445,814	49.4	37,480	1.3	3,903	R
Montana	490,302	231,667	47.2	242,763	49.5	15,872	3.2	11,096	R
Nebraska	801,281	333,319	41.6	452,979	56.5	14,983	1.9	119,660	R
Nevada	967,848	533,736	55.1	412,827	42.7	21,285	2.2	120,909	D
New Hampshire	710,970	384,826	54.1	316,534	44.5	9,610	1.4	68,292	D
New Jersey	3,868,237	2,215,422	57.3	1,613,207	41.7	39,608	1.0	602,215	D
New Mexico	830,158	472,422	56.9	346,832	41.8	10,904	1.3	125,590	D
New York	7,640,931	4,804,945	62.9	2,752,771	36.0	83,215	1.1	2,052,174	D
North Carolina	4,310,789	2,142,651	49.7	2,128,474	49.4	39,664	0.9	14,177	D
North Dakota	316,621	141,278	44.6	168,601	53.3	6,742	2.1	27,323	R
Ohio	5,708,350	2,940,044	51.5	2,677,820	46.9	90,486	1.6	262,224	D
Oklahoma	1,462,661	502,496	34.4	960,165	65.6	–	0.0	457,669	R
Oregon	1,827,864	1,037,291	56.7	738,475	40.4	52,098	2.9	298,816	D
Pennsylvania	6,013,272	3,276,363	54.5	2,655,885	44.2	81,024	1.0	620,478	D
Rhode Island	471,766	296,571	62.9	165,391	35.1	9,804	1.7	131,180	D
South Carolina	1,920,969	862,449	44.9	1,034,896	53.9	23,624	1.2	172,447	R
South Dakota	381,975	170,924	44.7	203,054	53.2	7,997	2.1	32,130	R
Tennessee	2,599,749	1,087,437	41.8	1,479,178	56.9	33,134	1.3	391,741	R
Texas	8,077,795	3,528,633	43.7	4,479,328	55.5	69,834	0.9	950,695	R
Utah	952,370	327,670	34.4	596,030	62.6	28,670	3.0	268,360	R
Vermont	325,046	219,262	67.5	98,974	30.4	6,810	2.1	120,288	D
Virginia	3,723,260	1,959,532	52.6	1,725,005	46.3	38,723	1.0	234,527	D
Washington	3,036,878	1,750,848	57.7	1,229,216	40.5	56,814	1.9	521,632	D
West Virginia	713,451	303,857	42.6	397,466	55.7	12,128	1.7	93,609	R
Wisconsin	2,983,417	1,677,211	56.2	1,262,393	42.3	43,813	1.5	414,818	D
Wyoming	254,658	82,868	32.5	164,958	64.8	6,832	2.7	82,090	R
District of Columbia	265,853	245,800	92.5	17,367	6.5	2,686	1.0	228,433	D
Totals	131,313,725	69,498,516	52.9	59,948,323	45.7	1,866,886	1.4	9,550,193	D

1. For breakdown of "Other" vote, see minor candidate totals at the end of this chapter.

Presidential Popular Vote Returns: Minor Candidates and Parties, 1824–2008

This section contains popular vote returns for minor candidates and parties that were aggregated in the columns labeled "Other" in the presidential election returns in this chapter. The source for these data for 1824–1916, except where indicated by a footnote, is the Inter-University Consortium for Political and Social Research (ICPSR). For the 1920 to 1992 elections, the source is Richard M. Scammon and Alice V. McGillivray, *America at the Polls* (Washington, D.C.: CQ Press, 1994). For the 1996 to 2008 elections, the source is the *America Votes* series, compiled biennially by Rhodes Cook for CQ Press in Washington, D.C.

CQ Press editors have supplemented the base source material with additional research provided by elections historian Michael J. Dubin. This additional material first appeared in the fourth edition of the *Guide* and is carried forward in this edition. For the state returns marked with an asterisk (*), the sources for the revised data are found in the footnotes to the same states in the corresponding presidential election table found earlier in this chapter.

The material in this section is presented in the following order:

- Year of presidential election.

- Name of candidate and party, if available from the ICPSR, Scammon, and Cook data, or from other sources considered reliable. "Scattered write-ins" is used where votes were recorded but neither the candidate nor a party was known. In most cases, these figures were the total write-in vote.

- State name and number of votes. Percentages may be calculated by using the state vote totals from the presidential election tables found in this chapter.

- Nationwide vote totals. Percentages may be calculated by using the national vote total from the presidential election tables.

In the ICPSR data, the distinct party designations appearing in the original sources are preserved. Thus, in the ICPSR returns for 1880, John W. Phelps received votes under the following four party designations: "Anti-Masonic"—California, 5 votes, Illinois, 150 votes, and Pennsylvania, 44 votes; "Anti-Secret"—Kansas, 25 votes; "National American"—Michigan, 312 votes; and "American"—Rhode Island, 4 votes, and Wisconsin, 91 votes.

To provide one party designation for each minor candidate for the elections 1824 to 1916, CQ Press has aggregated under a single party designation the votes of minor candidates who are listed in the ICPSR data as receiving votes under more than one party designation. The source used for assigning party designations for these years is Svend Petersen, *A Statistical History of the American Presidential Elections* (Westport, Conn.: Greenwood Press, 1981) where Petersen gives a party designation. In the 1880 election cited above, Peterson lists John W. Phelps as an American Party candidate. Where Petersen lists no party designation, CQ Press selected the party designation for a candidate that appeared most frequently in the ICPSR returns. For the 1920 to 1992 elections, the source for party designations is Scammon and McGillivray, *America at the Polls*. For the 1996 to 2008 elections, the source is Cook, *America Votes*.

1824 Election

Unpledged Republican
Massachusetts, 6,616 votes.
Scattered write-ins
Connecticut, 1,188 votes; Indiana, 7; Massachusetts, 4,753; Missouri, 33; North Carolina, 256; Rhode Island, 200.
　Total: 6,437

1828 Election

Scattered write-ins
Alabama, 4 votes; Connecticut, 1,101; Maine, 89; Massachusetts, 3,226; New Jersey, 8; North Carolina, 15; Rhode Island, 5; Vermont, 120.
　Total: 4,568

1832 Election

Scattered write-ins
Illinois, 30 votes; Massachusetts, 7,031; Rhode Island, 6; Vermont, 206.
　Total: 7,273

1836 Election

Scattered write-ins
Delaware, 5 votes; Maine, 1,112; Massachusetts, 45; North Carolina, 1; Rhode Island, 1; Vermont, 65; Virginia, 5.
　Total: 1,234

1840 Election

Scattered write-ins

Delaware, 13 votes; Indiana, 599; Rhode Island, 136; Vermont, 19.
Total: 767

1844 Election

Scattered write-ins

Delaware, 6 votes; Illinois, 939; Massachusetts, 1,106; North Carolina, 2; Rhode Island, 5.
Total: 2,058

1848 Election

Gerrit Smith (Liberty)

New York, 2,545 votes.

Henry Clay (Clay Whig)

Illinois, 89 votes.

Scattered write-ins

Alabama, 4 votes; Connecticut, 24; Massachusetts, 62; North Carolina, 26; Rhode Island, 5; Texas, 75.
Total: 196

1852 Election

Daniel Webster (Whig)[1]

Georgia, 5,324 votes; Massachusetts, 1,670.
Total: 6,994

—Broome (Native American)

Massachusetts, 158 votes; New Jersey, 738; Pennsylvania, 1,670.
Total: 2,566

George Michael Troup (Southern Rights)[2]

Alabama, 2,205 votes; Georgia, 126.
Total: 2,331

Scattered write-ins

California, 56 votes; Connecticut, 12; Iowa, 139; North Carolina, 60; Texas, 10.
Total: 272

1856 Election

Scattered write-ins

California, 14 votes; Delaware, 9; Massachusetts, 3,006; Ohio, 148.
Total: 3,177

1860 Election

Gerrit Smith (Union)

Illinois, 35 votes; Ohio, 136.

Scattered write-ins

California, 15 votes; Massachusetts, 328; Minnesota, 17.
Total: 360

1864 Election

E. Cheeseborough

Kansas, 543 votes.
Kansas, 112 votes; Massachusetts, 6; Minnesota, 26; Oregon, 5.
Total: 149

1868 Election

Scattered write-ins

Alabama, 6 votes; Kansas, 3; Massachusetts, 26; New Hampshire, 11.
Total: 46

1872 Election

James Black (Prohibition)

Michigan, 1,271 votes; New York, 201*; Ohio, 2,100.
Total: 3,572

Liberal Republican Elector

Iowa, 10,447 votes.

Scattered write-ins

Iowa, 942 votes; Kansas, 581; Minnesota, 168; New Hampshire, 313; South Carolina, 259.
Total: 2,263

1876 Election

Green Clay Smith (Prohibition)

Connecticut, 374 votes; Illinois, 141; Kansas, 110; Kentucky, 818*; Michigan, 766; New York, 2,369; Ohio, 1,636; Pennsylvania, 1,320; Wisconsin, 27.
Total: 7,561

James B. Walker (American)

Illinois, 177 votes; Kansas, 23; Michigan, 71; Ohio, 76; Pennsylvania, 83; Wisconsin, 29.
Total: 459

Communist

Wisconsin, 32 votes.

Scattered write-ins

Alabama, 2 votes; California, 19; Connecticut, 26; Iowa, 520; Kansas, 5; Maine, 165*; Massachusetts, 779; New Hampshire, 93; Texas, 46; Vermont, 114; Wisconsin, 1,607.
Total: 3,377

1880 Election

Neal Dow (Prohibition)

California, 54 votes; Connecticut, 409; Illinois, 440; Kansas, 10; Kentucky, 258*; Maine, 92; Massachusetts, 682; Michigan, 938; Minnesota, 286; New Hampshire, 180; New Jersey, 191; New York, 1,517; Ohio, 2,613; Pennsylvania, 1,940; Rhode Island, 20; Wisconsin, 69.
Total: 9,699

John W. Phelps (American)

California, 5 votes; Illinois, 150; Kansas, 25; Michigan, 312; Pennsylvania, 44; Rhode Island, 4; Wisconsin, 91.
Total: 631

A.C. Brewer (Independent Democrat)

Arkansas, 322 votes.

Scattered write-ins

Arkansas, 1,221 votes; California, 70; Colorado, 14; Connecticut, 39; Iowa, 1,064; Maine, 139; Massachusetts, 117; Mississippi, 677; Rhode Island, 1; South Carolina, 36; Virginia, 379*.
Total: 3,757

1884 Election

Scattered write-ins

Alabama, 72 votes; California, 329; Florida, 118; Iowa, 1,297; Kansas, 468; Maine, 6; Massachusetts, 2; New Jersey, 28; Oregon, 35; South Carolina, 1,237; Vermont, 27.
Total: 3,619

1888 Election

Robert H. Cowdrey (United Labor)

Illinois, 150 votes; New York, 2,668*; Oregon, 351.
Total: 3,169

Socialist Labor

New York, 2,068 votes.

James Langdon Curtis (American)

California, 1,591 votes; Pennsylvania, 24.
Total: 1,615

Scattered write-ins

California, 1,442 votes; Colorado, 177; Delaware, 1; Iowa, 556; Kansas, 937; Maine, 16; Massachusetts, 60; New Hampshire, 58; North Carolina, 37; Oregon, 53; Rhode Island, 7; South Carolina, 437; Vermont, 35.
Total: 3,816

1892 Election

Simon Wing (Socialist Labor)

Connecticut, 333 votes; Massachusetts, 649; New Jersey, 1,337; New York, 17,956; Pennsylvania, 888.
Total: 21,163

Scattered write-ins

Arkansas, 1,267 votes; Delaware, 13; Georgia, 2,345; Maine, 4; Massachusetts, 3; Michigan, 925; Rhode Island, 3; South Carolina, 72; Texas, 3,968*; Vermont, 10; Wyoming, 29.
Total: 8,639

1896 Election

William Jennings Bryan (Populist)

California, 21,734* votes; Florida, 2,053*; Nevada, 574*; New Hampshire, 379*; Ohio, 2,615*; Pennsylvania, 6,103*; Texas, 77,985*; Vermont, 461*; Washington, 1,668*, Wyoming, 486*.
Total: 114,558

Charles Horatio Matchett (Socialist Labor)

California, 1,611 votes; Colorado, 159; Connecticut, 1,223; Illinois, 1,147; Indiana, 324; Iowa, 453; Maryland, 587; Massachusetts, 2,112; Michigan, 293; Minnesota, 954; Missouri, 599; Nebraska, 186; New Hampshire, 228; New Jersey, 3,985; New York, 17,667; Ohio, 1,165; Pennsylvania, 1,683; Rhode Island, 558; Virginia, 108; Wisconsin, 1,314
Total: 36,356

Charles Eugene Bentley (National Prohibition)

Arkansas, 892 votes; California, 1,047; Colorado, 386; Illinois, 793; Indiana, 2,267; Iowa, 352; Kansas, 620; Maryland, 136; Michigan, 1,816; Missouri, 292; Nebraska, 797; New Hampshire, 49; New Jersey, 5,614; North Carolina, 222; Ohio, 2,716; Pennsylvania, 870; Washington, 148; Wisconsin, 346.
Total: 19,363

Scattered write-ins

California, 4 votes; Connecticut, 4; Georgia, 47; Massachusetts, 20; Michigan, 1,073; North Carolina, 372; North Dakota, 12; Rhode Island, 5.
Total: 1,537

1900 Election

Wharton Barker (Populist)

Alabama, 3,751* votes; Arkansas, 972; Colorado, 333; Florida, 1,143; Georgia, 4,568; Idaho, 445; Illinois, 1,141; Indiana, 1,438; Iowa, 615; Kentucky, 1,961; Michigan, 889; Mississippi, 1,642; Missouri, 4,244; Nebraska, 1,104; New Jersey, 669; North Carolina, 798; North Dakota,

109; Ohio, 251; Oregon, 275*; Pennsylvania, 638; South Dakota, 340; Tennessee, 1,322; Texas, 20,981*; Vermont, 367; Virginia, 63; West Virginia, 246; Wyoming, 20.
Total: 50,329

Joseph P. Malloney (Socialist Labor)

Colorado, 654 votes; Connecticut, 908; Illinois, 1,374; Indiana, 663; Iowa, 259; Kentucky, 390; Maryland, 382; Massachusetts, 2,599; Michigan, 830; Minnesota, 1,329; Missouri, 1,296; Montana, 119; New Jersey, 2,074; New York, 12,622; Ohio, 1,688; Pennsylvania, 2,936; Rhode Island, 1,423; Texas, 162; Utah, 102; Virginia, 167; Washington, 866; Wisconsin, 503.
Total: 33,346

Seth Hockett Ellis (Union Reform)

Arkansas, 341 votes; Illinois, 672; Indiana, 254; Maryland, 142; Ohio, 4,284.
Total: 5,693

Alexander Hirschberg (Social Democrat)

Kentucky, 770* votes.

Jonah Fitz Randolph Leonard (United Christian)

Illinois, 352 votes; Iowa, 166.
Total: 518

Anti-Imperialist

Connecticut, 45 votes.

Scattered write-ins

Arkansas, 27 votes; Colorado, 26; Connecticut, 10; Louisiana, 4; Massachusetts, 533, New Hampshire, 16; Utah, 9; Vermont, 5; Wyoming, 21.
Total: 651

1904 Election

Thomas E. Watson (Populist)

Alabama, 5,051 votes; Arkansas, 2,326; Colorado, 824; Connecticut, 495; Delaware, 51; Florida, 1,605; Georgia, 22,635; Idaho, 352; Illinois, 6,725; Indiana, 2,444; Iowa, 2,207; Kansas, 6,253; Kentucky, 2,521; Maine, 337; Maryland, 1; Massachusetts, 1,294; Michigan, 1,145; Minnesota, 2,103; Mississippi, 1,499; Missouri, 4,226; Montana, 1,531; Nebraska, 20,518; Nevada, 344; New Hampshire, 82; New Jersey, 3,705; New York, 7,459; North Carolina, 819; North Dakota, 165*; Ohio, 1,392; Oregon, 746; South Dakota, 1,240; Tennessee, 2,491; Texas, 8,062; Washington, 669; West Virginia, 339; Wisconsin, 560.
Total: 114,216

Charles Hunter Corregan (Socialist Labor)

Colorado, 335 votes; Connecticut, 583; Illinois, 4,698; Indiana, 1,598; Kentucky, 596; Massachusetts, 2,359; Michigan, 1,018; Minnesota, 974; Missouri, 1,674; Montana, 213; New Jersey, 2,680*; New York, 9,122; Ohio, 2,635; Pennsylvania, 2,211; Rhode Island, 488; Texas, 431; Washington, 1,592; Wisconsin, 249.
Total: 33,456

Austin Holcomb (Continental)

Illinois, 826 votes.

Scattered write-ins

California, 333 votes; Connecticut, 11; Maryland, 4; Massachusetts, 5; New Hampshire, 1; Vermont, 1.
Total: 355

1908 Election

Thomas L. Hisgen (Independence)

Alabama, 497 votes; Arkansas, 286; California, 4,278; Connecticut, 728; Delaware, 29; Florida, 553; Georgia, 77*; Idaho, 124; Illinois, 7,724; Indiana, 514; Iowa, 404; Kansas, 68; Kentucky, 200; Louisiana, 77; Maine, 700; Maryland, 485; Massachusetts, 19,235; Michigan, 734;

Minnesota, 429*; Missouri, 392; Montana, 493; Nevada, 436; New Hampshire, 584; New Jersey, 2,916; New York, 35,817; North Dakota, 43; Ohio, 439; Oregon, 289; Pennsylvania, 1,057; Rhode Island, 1,105; South Carolina, 46; South Dakota, 88; Tennessee, 332; Texas, 106; Utah, 92; Vermont, 804; Virginia, 51; Washington, 248; Wyoming, 63.

Total: 82,543

Thomas E. Watson (Populist)

Alabama, 1,576 votes; Arkansas, 987; Florida, 1,946; Georgia, 16,969*; Illinois, 633; Indiana, 1,193; Iowa, 261; Kentucky, 333; Mississippi, 1,276; Missouri, 1,165; Ohio, 162; Tennessee, 1,092; Texas, 960; Virginia, 105.

Total: 28,658

August Gillhaus (Socialist Labor)

Connecticut, 608 votes; Illinois, 1,680; Indiana, 643; Kentucky, 405; Massachusetts, 1,011; Michigan, 1,085; Missouri, 867; New Jersey, 1,196; New York, 3,877; Ohio, 721; Pennsylvania, 1,224; Rhode Island, 183; Texas, 175; Virginia, 25; Wisconsin, 318.

Total: 14,018

Daniel Braxton Turney (United Christian)

Illinois, 400 votes; Michigan, 61.

Republican (Davidson Faction)

Alabama, 987 votes.

Scattered write-ins

California, 28 votes; Colorado, 2; Connecticut, 4; Massachusetts, 9; New Hampshire, 8; North Carolina, 13; Vermont, 29; Wisconsin, 2.

Total: 95

1912 Election

Eugene W. Chafin (Prohibition)

Arizona, 265 votes; Arkansas, 908; California, 23,366; Colorado, 5,063; Connecticut, 2,068; Delaware, 620; Florida, 1,854; Georgia, 149; Idaho, 1,536; Illinois, 15,710; Indiana, 19,249; Iowa, 8,440; Kentucky, 3,233*; Maine, 947; Maryland, 2,244; Massachusetts, 2,753; Michigan, 8,794; Minnesota, 7,886; Missouri, 5,380; Montana, 32; Nebraska, 3,383; New Hampshire, 535; New Jersey, 2,936; New York, 19,455; North Carolina, 118; North Dakota, 1,243; Ohio, 11,511; Oklahoma, 2,195; Oregon, 4,360; Pennsylvania, 19,525; Rhode Island, 616; South Dakota, 3,910; Tennessee, 832; Texas, 1,701; Vermont, 1,094; Virginia, 709; Washington, 9,810; West Virginia, 4,517; Wisconsin, 8,584; Wyoming, 421.

Total: 207,952

Arthur E. Reimer (Socialist Labor)

Colorado, 475 votes; Connecticut, 1,260; Illinois, 4,066; Indiana, 3,130; Kentucky, 956*; Maryland, 322; Massachusetts, 1,102; Michigan, 1,239; Minnesota, 2,212; Missouri, 1,778; New Jersey, 1,396; New York, 4,273; Ohio, 2,630; Pennsylvania, 706; Rhode Island, 236; Texas, 430; Utah, 510; Virginia, 50; Washington, 1,872; Wisconsin, 632.

Total: 29,275

Scattered write-ins

Alabama, 5 votes; California, 4,417; Connecticut, 6; Kansas, 63; Massachusetts, 1; South Carolina, 55; Wisconsin, 9.

Total: 4,556

1916 Election

Arthur E. Reimer (Socialist Labor)

Connecticut, 606 votes; Illinois, 2,488; Indiana, 1,659; Iowa, 460; Kentucky, 332; Maryland, 756; Massachusetts, 1,096; Michigan, 831; Minnesota, 468; Missouri, 903; Nebraska, 624; New Jersey, 855; New York, 2,666; Pennsylvania, 419; Rhode Island, 180; Utah, 144; Virginia, 67; Washington, 730.

Total: 15,284

Progressive[3]

Colorado, 409 votes; Georgia, 20,653*; Indiana, 3,898; Iowa, 1,793; Kentucky, 129; Louisiana, 6,349; Minnesota, 290; Mississippi, 520; Montana, 338; Oklahoma, 234; Oregon, 310; South Carolina, 162; Utah, 110.

Total: 35,195

Scattered write-ins

California, 187 votes; Massachusetts, 6; South Carolina, 258; Vermont, 10.

Total: 461

1920 Election

Aaron Sherman Watkins (Prohibition)

Alabama, 766 votes; Arizona, 4; California, 25,204; Colorado, 2,807; Connecticut, 1,771; Delaware, 986; Florida, 5,127; Idaho, 34*; Illinois, 11,216; Indiana, 13,462; Iowa, 4,197; Kentucky, 3,250; Michigan, 9,646; Minnesota, 11,489; Missouri, 5,152; Nebraska, 5,947; New Jersey, 4,895; New York, 19,653; North Carolina, 17; Ohio, 294; Oregon, 3,595; Pennsylvania, 42,612; Rhode Island, 510; South Dakota, 900; Vermont, 774; Virginia, 826; Washington, 3,800; West Virginia, 1,526; Wisconsin, 8,648; Wyoming, 265.

Total: 189,373

James Edward Ferguson (American)

Texas, 48,098 votes.

William W. Cox (Socialist Labor)

Connecticut, 1,491 votes; Illinois, 3,471; Iowa, 982; Maryland, 1,178; Massachusetts, 3,583; Michigan, 2,539; Minnesota, 5,828; Missouri, 1,587; New Jersey, 1,010; New York, 4,841; Oregon, 1,515; Pennsylvania, 753; Rhode Island, 495; Washington, 1,321.

Total: 30,594

Robert Colvin Macauley (Single Tax)

Delaware, 39 votes; Illinois, 775; Indiana, 566; Maine, 310; Michigan, 484; New Jersey, 603; Ohio, 2,153; Pennsylvania, 803; Rhode Island, 100.

Total: 5,833

Black and Tan Republican

Texas, 27,309 votes.

Scattered write-ins

Louisiana, 339 votes; Maryland, 1; Massachusetts, 24; Nebraska, 90; New Mexico, 4; Vermont, 56.

Total: 514

1924 Election

Frank T. Johns (Socialist Labor)

Colorado, 378 votes; Connecticut, 1,373; Illinois, 2,334; Kentucky, 1,499*; Maine, 406; Maryland, 987; Massachusetts, 1,668; Michigan, 5,330; Minnesota, 1,855; Missouri, 1,066; New Jersey, 853; New York, 9,928; Ohio, 3,025; Oregon, 917; Pennsylvania, 634; Rhode Island, 268; Virginia, 189; Washington, 1,004; Wisconsin, 458.

Total: 34,172

William Z. Foster (Communist)

Colorado, 562 votes; Illinois, 2,622; Indiana, 987; Iowa, 4,037; Massachusetts, 2,635; Minnesota, 4,427; Montana, 358; New Jersey, 1,560; New York, 8,244; North Dakota, 370; Pennsylvania, 2,735; Rhode Island, 289; Washington, 761; Wisconsin, 3,773.

Total: 33,360

Gilbert Owen Nations (American)

Florida, 2,319 votes; Georgia, 155; Kentucky, 1,299*; New Jersey, 368; Pennsylvania, 15,035; Tennessee, 100; Washington, 5,991; West Virginia, 1,072.

Total: 24,339

Robert M. La Follette (Socialist)

Oklahoma, 5,234* votes.

William J. Wallace (Commonwealth Land)

Delaware, 20 votes; Illinois, 421; Kentucky, 248*; Missouri, 165; New Jersey, 265; Ohio, 1,246, Pennsylvania, 296; Rhode Island, 38; Wisconsin, 271.

Total: 2,970

Scattered write-ins

Connecticut, 101 votes; Iowa, 445; Kansas, 4; Louisiana, 4,063; Pennsylvania, 131; South Carolina, 1; Vermont, 5.

Total: 4,752

1928 Election

Verne L. Reynolds (Socialist Labor)

Connecticut, 625 votes; Illinois, 1,812; Indiana, 645; Iowa, 230; Kentucky, 316; Maryland, 906; Massachusetts, 772; Michigan, 799; Minnesota, 1,921; Missouri, 342; New Jersey, 500; New York, 4,211; Ohio, 1,515; Oregon, 1,564; Pennsylvania, 382; Rhode Island, 416; Virginia, 181; Washington, 4,068; Wisconsin, 381.

Total: 21,586

William Frederick Varney (Prohibition)

Indiana, 5,496 votes; Michigan, 2,728; New Jersey, 160; Ohio, 3,556; Pennsylvania, 3,875; Vermont, 338; West Virginia, 1,703; Wisconsin, 2,245.

Total: 20,101

Frank Elbridge Webb (Farmer Labor)

Colorado, 1,092 votes; Iowa, 3,088; Oklahoma, 1,283; South Dakota, 927.

Total: 6,390

Scattered write-ins

California, 373 votes; Iowa, 2; Massachusetts, 4; Pennsylvania, 14; Vermont, 9.

Total: 420

1932 Election

William David Upshaw (Prohibition)

Alabama, 13 votes; California, 20,637; Colorado, 1,928; Georgia, 1,125; Illinois, 6,388; Indiana, 10,399; Iowa, 2,111; Kentucky, 2,252; Massachusetts, 1,142; Michigan, 2,893; Missouri, 2,429; New Jersey, 774; Ohio, 7,421; Pennsylvania, 11,319; Rhode Island, 183; South Dakota, 463; Tennessee, 1,998; Virginia, 1,843; Washington, 1,540; West Virginia, 2,342; Wisconsin, 2,672.

Total: 81,872

William Hope Harvey (Liberty)

Arkansas, 952 votes; California, 9,827; Idaho, 4,712; Michigan, 217; Montana, 1,449; New Mexico, 389; North Dakota, 1,817; South Dakota, 3,333; Texas, 324*; Washington, 30,308.

Total: 53,328

Verne L. Reynolds (Socialist Labor)

Colorado, 427 votes; Connecticut, 2,287; Illinois, 3,638; Indiana, 2,070; Kentucky, 1,393; Maine, 255; Maryland, 1,036; Massachusetts, 2,668; Michigan, 1,401; Minnesota, 770; Missouri, 404; New Jersey, 1,062; New York, 10,339; Ohio, 1,968; Oregon, 1,730; Pennsylvania, 659; Rhode Island, 433; Washington, 1,009; Wisconsin, 494.

Total: 34,043

Jacob S. Coxey (Farmer Labor)

Colorado, 469 votes; Iowa, 1,094; Michigan, 137; Minnesota, 5,731.

Total: 7,431

John Zahnd (National)

Indiana, 1,645 votes.

James R. Cox (Jobless)

Pennsylvania, 725 votes; Virginia, 15.

Total: 740.

Jacksonian

Texas, 104* votes.

Arizona Progressive Democrat

Arizona, 9 votes.

Scattered write-ins

California, 127 votes; Florida, 691; Iowa, 4; Louisiana, 533; Massachusetts, 71; Pennsylvania, 53; Texas, 34; Vermont, 2; Wisconsin, 13.

Total: 1,528

1936 Election

Earl Browder (Communist)

Alabama, 678 votes; Arkansas, 167; California, 10,877; Colorado, 497; Connecticut, 1,193; Delaware, 51; Illinois, 801; Indiana, 1,090; Iowa, 506; Kentucky, 207; Maine, 257; Maryland, 915; Massachusetts, 2,930; Michigan, 3,384; Minnesota, 2,574; Missouri, 417; Montana, 385; New Hampshire, 193; New Jersey, 1,639; New Mexico, 43; New York, 35,609; North Carolina, 11; North Dakota, 360; Ohio, 5,251; Oregon, 104; Pennsylvania, 4,060; Rhode Island, 411; Tennessee, 319*; Texas, 253*; Utah, 280; Vermont, 405; Virginia, 98; Washington, 1,907; Wisconsin, 2,197; Wyoming, 91.

Total: 80,160

D. Leigh Colvin (Prohibition)

Alabama, 719 votes; Arizona, 384; California, 12,917; Georgia, 660; Illinois, 3,439; Iowa, 1,182; Kentucky, 939; Maine, 334; Massachusetts, 1,032; Michigan, 579; Missouri, 908; Montana, 224; New Jersey, 926; New Mexico, 61; North Dakota, 197; Oklahoma, 1,328; Oregon, 4; Pennsylvania, 6,691; Tennessee, 632*; Texas, 514*; Utah, 43; Virginia, 594; Washington, 1,041; West Virginia, 1,173; Wisconsin, 1,071; Wyoming, 75.

Total: 37,667

John W. Aiken (Socialist Labor)

Colorado, 344 votes; Connecticut, 1,228; Illinois, 1,921; Iowa, 252; Kentucky, 294; Maine, 129; Maryland, 1,305; Massachusetts, 1,305; Michigan, 600; Minnesota, 961; Missouri, 292; New Jersey, 362; Ohio, 28; Oregon, 500; Pennsylvania, 1,424; Rhode Island, 929; Virginia, 36; Washington, 362; Wisconsin, 557.

Total: 12,829

Independent Republicans

Delaware, 3,222* votes.

William Dudley Pelley (Christian)

Washington, 1,598 votes.

Scattered write-ins

California, 490 votes; Florida, 71; Iowa, 4; Louisiana, 93; Massachusetts, 11; Michigan, 5; North Carolina, 6; Ohio, 7; Oregon, 108; Vermont, 137.

Total: 824

1940 Election

Earl Browder (Communist)

Alabama, 509 votes; California, 13,586; Colorado, 378; Connecticut, 1,091; Idaho, 276; Iowa, 1,524; Maine, 411; Maryland, 1,274; Massachusetts, 3,806; Michigan, 2,834; Minnesota, 2,711; Montana, 489; New Jersey, 6,508; Oregon, 191; Pennsylvania, 4,519; Rhode Island, 243; Texas, 212*; Utah, 191; Vermont, 411; Virginia, 72; Washington, 2,626; Wisconsin, 2,394.

Total: 46,256

John W. Aiken (Socialist Labor)

Connecticut, 971 votes; Indiana, 706; Iowa, 452; Maryland, 657; Massachusetts, 1,492; Michigan, 795; Minnesota, 2,553; Missouri, 209; New Jersey, 455; Oregon, 2,487; Pennsylvania, 1,518; Virginia, 48; Washington, 667; Wisconsin, 1,882.

Total: 14,892

Alfred Knutson (Independent)

North Dakota, 545 votes.

Scattered write-ins

California, 262 votes; Florida, 148; Georgia, 14; Illinois, 657; Louisiana, 108; Massachusetts, 12; Michigan, 4; Oregon, 40: Pennsylvania, 827; Vermont, 11.

Total: 2,083

1944 Election

Edward A. Teichert (Socialist Labor)

California, 180 votes; Connecticut, 1,220; Illinois, 9,677; Iowa, 193; Kentucky, 329; Maine, 335; Massachusetts, 2,780; Michigan, 1,264; Minnesota, 3,176; Missouri, 220; New Jersey, 6,939; New York, 14,352; Pennsylvania, 1,789; Virginia, 90; Washington, 1,645; Wisconsin, 1,002.

Total: 45,191

Gerald L. K. Smith (America First)

Michigan, 1,530 votes; Texas, 250.

Total: 1,780

Texas Regulars

Texas, 135,444 votes.

Southern Democrat

South Carolina, 7,799 votes.

Independent Democrat

Georgia, 3,373* votes.

Republican (Tobert faction)

South Carolina, 63* votes.

Scattered write-ins

California, 1,881 votes; Florida, 211; Louisiana, 69; Massachusetts, 266; Michigan, 6; Vermont, 14.

Total: 2,447

1948 Election

Norman M. Thomas (Socialist)

Arkansas, 1,037 votes; California, 3,459; Colorado, 1,678; Connecticut, 6,964; Delaware, 250; Georgia, 3; Idaho, 332; Illinois, 11,522; Indiana, 2,179; Iowa, 1,829; Kansas, 2,807; Kentucky, 1,284; Maine, 547; Maryland, 2,941; Michigan, 6,063; Minnesota, 4,646; Missouri, 2,222; Montana, 695; New Hampshire, 86; New Jersey, 10,521; New Mexico, 83; New York, 40,879; North Dakota; 1,000; Oregon, 5,051; Pennsylvania, 11,325; Rhode Island, 429; South Carolina, 1; Tennessee, 1,288; Texas, 874*; Vermont, 585; Virginia, 726; Washington, 3,534; Wisconsin, 12,547; Wyoming, 137.

Total: 139,524

Claude A. Watson (Prohibition)

Alabama, 1,085 votes; Arizona, 786; Arkansas, 1; California, 16,926; Delaware, 343; Georgia, 732; Idaho, 628; Illinois, 11,959; Indiana, 14,711; Iowa, 3,382; Kansas, 6,468; Kentucky, 1,245; Massachusetts, 1,663; Michigan, 13,052; Montana, 429; New Jersey, 10,593; New Mexico, 127; Pennsylvania, 10,538; Texas, 2,758*; Washington, 6,117.

Total: 103,543

Edward A. Teichert (Socialist Labor)

Arizona, 121 votes; California, 195; Colorado, 214; Connecticut, 1,184; Delaware, 29; Illinois, 3,118; Indiana, 763; Iowa, 4,274; Kentucky, 185; Maine, 206; Massachusetts, 5,535; Michigan, 1,263; Minnesota,

2,525; New Hampshire, 83; New Jersey, 3,354; New Mexico, 49; New York, 2,729; Pennsylvania, 1,461; Rhode Island, 131; Virginia, 234; Washington, 1,133; Wisconsin, 399; Wyoming, 56.

Total: 29,241

Farrell Dobbs (Socialist Workers)

California, 133 votes; Colorado, 228; Connecticut, 606; Iowa, 256; Michigan, 672; Minnesota, 606; New Jersey, 5,825; New York, 2,675; Pennsylvania, 2,133; Utah, 74; Washington, 103; Wisconsin, 303.

Total: 13,614

Scattered write-ins

California, 313 votes; Georgia, 1; Illinois, 1,629; Louisiana, 10; Massachusetts, 633; Michigan, 1; Missouri, 54; Nebraska, 1; New York, 128; Pennsylvania, 107; Vermont, 35.

Total: 3,412

1952 Election

Eric Hass (Socialist Labor)

Arkansas, 1 vote; California, 273; Colorado, 352; Connecticut, 535; Delaware, 242; Illinois, 9,363; Indiana, 840; Iowa, 139; Kentucky, 893; Maine, 156; Massachusetts, 1,957; Michigan, 1,495; Minnesota, 2,383; Missouri, 169; New Jersey, 5,815; New Mexico, 35; New York, 1,560; Pennsylvania, 1,377; Rhode Island, 83; Virginia, 1,160; Washington, 633; Wisconsin, 770; Wyoming, 36.

Total: 30,267

Darlington Hoopes (Socialist)

California, 206 votes; Colorado, 365; Connecticut, 2,244; Delaware, 20; Iowa, 219; Kansas, 530; Maine, 138; Missouri, 227; Montana, 159; New Jersey, 8,593; New York, 2,664; Pennsylvania, 2,698; Vermont, 185; Virginia, 504; Washington, 254; Wisconsin, 1,157; Wyoming, 40.

Total: 20,203

Douglas MacArthur (Constitution)[4]

Arkansas, 453 votes; California, 3,504; Colorado, 2,181; Missouri, 535; New Mexico; 220; North Dakota, 1,075; Tennessee, 379; Texas, 1,563; Washington, 7,290.

Total: 17,205

Farrell Dobbs (Socialist Workers)

Michigan, 655 votes; Minnesota, 618; New Jersey, 3,850; New York, 2,212; Pennsylvania, 1,508; Washington, 119; Wisconsin, 1,350.

Total: 10,312

Henry Krajewski (Poor Man's)

New Jersey, 4,203 votes.

Independent Republican

South Carolina, 158,289* votes.

Scattered write-ins

California, 3,249 votes; Connecticut, 5; Florida, 351; Georgia, 1; Idaho, 23; Illinois, 443; Iowa, 29; Maine, 1; Massachusetts, 69; Michigan, 3; New York, 178; Pennsylvania, 155; Vermont, 18.

Total: 4,530

1956 Election

Enoch A. Holtwick (Prohibition)

California, 11,119 votes; Delaware, 400; Indiana, 6,554; Kansas, 3,048; Kentucky, 2,145; Massachusetts, 1,205; Michigan, 6,923; New Jersey, 9,147; New Mexico, 607; Tennessee, 789.

Total: 41,937

Farrell Dobbs (Socialist Workers)

California, 96 votes; Minnesota, 1,098; New Jersey, 4,004; Pennsylvania, 2,035; Wisconsin, 564.

Total: 7,797

Harry F. Byrd (States' Rights)

Kentucky, 2,657 votes.

Darlington Hoopes (Socialist)

California, 123 votes; Colorado, 531; Iowa, 192; New York, 82; Virginia, 444; Wisconsin, 754.

Total: 2,126

Henry Krajewski (American Third Party)

New Jersey, 1,829 votes.

Gerald L.K. Smith (Christian Nationalist)

California, 8 votes.

Independent Electors

Alabama, 20,323 votes; Louisiana, 44,520; Mississippi, 42,966; South Carolina, 88,509.

Total: 196,318

Scattered write-ins

California, 819 votes; Connecticut, 205; Florida, 1,542; Georgia, 93; Idaho, 16; Illinois, 56; Maryland, 476; Massachusetts, 341; New York, 1,262; Oregon, 535; Vermont, 39.

Total: 5,384

1960 Election

Rutherford L. Decker (Prohibition)

Alabama, 2,106 votes; California, 21,706; Delaware, 284; Indiana, 6,746; Kansas, 4,138; Massachusetts, 1,633; Michigan, 2,029; Montana, 456; New Mexico, 777; Tennessee, 2,458; Texas, 3,870.

Total: 46,203

Orval E. Faubus (National States' Rights)

Alabama, 4,367 votes; Arkansas, 28,952; Delaware, 354; Tennessee, 11,296.

Total: 44,977

Farrell Dobbs (Socialist Workers)

Colorado, 562 votes; Iowa, 634; Michigan, 4,347; Minnesota, 3,077; Montana, 391; New Jersey, 11,402; New York, 14,319; North Dakota, 158; Pennsylvania, 2,678; Utah, 100; Washington, 705; Wisconsin, 1,792.

Total: 40,165

Charles L. Sullivan (Constitutional)

Texas, 18,162 votes.

J. Bracken Lee (Conservative)

New Jersey, 8,708 votes.

C. Benton Coiner (Virginia Conservative)

Virginia, 4,204 votes.

Lar Daly (Tax Cut)

Michigan, 1,767 votes.

Clennon King (Independent Afro-American Unity)

Alabama, 1,485 votes.

Merritt B. Curtis (Constitution)

Washington, 1,401 votes.

Independent Electors

Louisiana, 169,572 votes; Michigan, 539.

Total: 170,111

Scattered write-ins

Alabama, 236 votes; Connecticut, 15; Georgia, 239; Illinois, 15; Maryland, 3; Massachusetts, 31; Oregon, 959; Pennsylvania, 440; South Carolina, 1; Texas, 175; Vermont, 7.

Total: 2,378

1964 Election

E. Harold Munn (Prohibition)

California, 305 votes; Colorado, 1,356; Delaware, 425; Indiana, 8,266; Iowa, 1,902; Kansas, 5,393; Massachusetts, 3,735; Michigan, 669; Montana, 499; New Mexico, 543; North Dakota, 174.

Total: 23,267

John Kasper (National States' Rights)

Arkansas, 2,965 votes; Kentucky, 3,469; Montana, 519.

Total: 6,953

Joseph B. Lightburn (Constitution)

Texas, 5,060 votes.

James Hensley (Universal Party)

California, 19 votes.

Unpledged Democrat

Alabama, 210,732 votes.

Scattered write-ins

Alabama, 1 vote; California, 5,410; Connecticut, 1,313; Georgia, 195; Illinois, 62; Iowa, 118; Maryland, 50; Massachusetts, 159; Michigan, 145; New York, 268; Oregon, 2,509; Pennsylvania, 2,531; Rhode Island, 13; South Carolina, 8; Tennessee, 34; Vermont, 20.

Total: 12,868

1968 Election

Dick Gregory (Freedom and Peace)

California, 3,230 votes; Colorado, 1,393; Indiana, 36; New Jersey, 8,084; New York, 24,517; Ohio, 372; Pennsylvania, 7,821; Virginia, 1,680.

Total: 47,133

Fred Halstead (Socialist Workers)

Arizona, 85 votes; Colorado, 235; Indiana, 1,293; Iowa, 3,377; Kentucky, 2,843; Michigan, 4,099; Minnesota, 807; Montana, 457; New Hampshire, 104; New Jersey, 8,667; New Mexico, 252; New York, 11,851; North Dakota, 128; Ohio, 69; Pennsylvania, 4,862; Rhode Island, 383; Utah, 89; Vermont, 295; Washington, 270; Wisconsin, 1,222.

Total: 41,388

Eldridge Cleaver (Peace and Freedom)

Arizona, 217 votes; California, 27,707; Iowa, 1,332; Michigan, 4,585; Minnesota, 933; Utah, 180; Washington, 1,609.

Total: 36,563

Eugene J. McCarthy

Arizona, 2,751 votes; California, 20,721; Minnesota, 584; Oregon, 1,496.

Total: 25,552

E. Harold Munn (Prohibition)

Alabama, 4,022 votes; California, 59; Colorado, 275; Indiana, 4,616; Iowa, 362; Kansas, 2,192; Massachusetts, 2,369; Michigan, 60; Montana, 510; North Dakota, 38; Ohio, 19; Virginia, 601.

Total: 15,123

Ventura Chavez (People's Constitution)

New Mexico, 1,519 votes.

Charlene Mitchell (Communist)

California, 260 votes; Minnesota, 415; Ohio, 23; Washington, 377.

Total: 1,075

James Hensley (Universal)

Iowa, 142 votes.

Richard K. Troxell (Constitution)

North Dakota, 34 votes.

Kent M. Soeters (Berkeley Defense Group)

California, 17 votes.

American Independent Democrat

Alabama, 10,960 votes.

New Party

New Hampshire, 421 votes; Vermont, 579.

Total: 1,000

New Reform

Montana, 470 votes.

Scattered write-ins

Alabama, 13 votes; Colorado, 948; Connecticut, 1,300; Georgia, 165; Illinois, 325; Iowa, 250; Massachusetts, 53; Michigan, 29; Minnesota, 170; New Hampshire, 108; New Mexico, 69; New York, 1,622; Oregon, 1,144; Pennsylvania, 2,264; Rhode Island, 62; Texas, 299; Vermont, 29; Wisconsin, 2,342.

Total: 11,192

1972 Election

Louis Fisher (Socialist Labor)

California, 197 votes; Colorado, 4,361; Georgia, 3; Illinois, 12,344; Indiana, 1,688; Iowa, 195; Massachusetts, 129; Michigan, 2,437; Minnesota, 4,261; New Jersey, 4,544; New York, 4,530; Ohio, 7,107; Virginia, 9,918; Washington, 1,102; Wisconsin, 998.

Total: 53,814

Linda Jenness (Socialist Workers)

Arizona, 366 votes; California, 574; Colorado, 666; District of Columbia, 316; Idaho, 397; Iowa, 488; Kentucky, 685; Louisiana, 14,398; Massachusetts, 10,600; Michigan, 1,603; Minnesota, 940; Mississippi, 2,458; New Hampshire, 368; New Jersey, 2,233; New Mexico, 474; North Dakota, 288; Pennsylvania, 4,639; Rhode Island, 729; South Dakota, 994; Texas, 8,664; Vermont, 296; Washington, 623.

Total: 52,799

Gus Hall (Communist)

California, 373 votes; Colorado, 432; District of Columbia, 252; Illinois, 4,541; Iowa, 272; Kentucky, 464; Massachusetts, 46; Michigan, 1,210; Minnesota, 662; New Jersey, 1,263; New York, 5,641; North Dakota, 87; Ohio, 6,437; Pennsylvania, 2,686; Washington, 566; Wisconsin, 663.

Total: 25,595

Evelyn Reed (Socialist Workers)

Indiana, 5,575 votes; New York, 7,797; Wisconsin, 506.

Total: 13,878

E. Harold Munn (Prohibition)

Alabama, 8,559 votes; California, 53; Colorado, 467; Delaware, 238; Kansas, 4,188.

Total: 13,505

John Hospers (Libertarian)

California, 980 votes; Colorado, 1,111; Massachusetts, 43; Rhode Island, 2; Washington, 1,537.

Total: 3,673

John V. Mahalchik (America First)

New Jersey, 1,743 votes.

Gabriel Green (Universal)

California, 21 votes; Iowa, 199.

Total: 220

Scattered write-ins

Colorado, 6 votes; Connecticut, 777; Florida, 7,407; Georgia, 2,932; Illinois, 2,229; Iowa, 321; Massachusetts, 342; Minnesota, 962; Missouri, 4,804; New Hampshire, 142; New Mexico, 310; New York, 4,089; Ohio, 460; Oregon, 2,289; Pennsylvania, 2,716; Rhode Island, 19; South Carolina, 17; Tennessee, 369; Texas, 3,393; Vermont, 318; Wisconsin, 893.

Total: 34,795

1976 Election

Lester Maddox (American Independent)

Alabama, 9,198 votes; Arizona, 85; California, 51,098; Connecticut, 7,101; Georgia, 1,071; Idaho, 5,935; Kansas, 2,118; Kentucky, 2,328; Louisiana, 10,058; Maine, 8; Maryland, 171; Mississippi, 4,861; Nebraska,

3,380; Nevada, 1,497; New Jersey, 7,716; New Mexico, 31; New York, 97; North Dakota, 269; Ohio, 15,529; Pennsylvania, 25,344; Rhode Island, 1; South Carolina, 1,950; Tennessee, 2,303; Texas, 41; Utah, 1,162; Washington, 8,585; West Virginia, 12; Wisconsin, 8,552; Wyoming, 30.

Total: 170,531

Thomas J. Anderson (American)

Alabama, 70 votes; Arizona, 564; Arkansas, 389; California, 4,565; Colorado, 397; Connecticut, 155; Delaware, 645; Florida, 21,325; Georgia, 1,168; Idaho, 493; Illinois, 387; Indiana, 14,048; Iowa, 3,040; Kansas, 4,724; Kentucky, 8,308; Maine, 28; Maryland, 321; Massachusetts, 7,555; Minnesota, 13,592; Mississippi, 6,678; Montana, 5,772; New Mexico, 106; New York, 451; North Carolina, 5,607; North Dakota, 3,796; Oregon, 1,035; Rhode Island, 24; South Carolina, 2,996; Tennessee, 5,769; Texas, 11,442; Utah, 13,284; Virginia, 16,686; Washington, 5,046; West Virginia, 17; Wyoming, 290.

Total: 160,773

Peter Camejo (Socialist Workers)

Alabama, 1 vote; Arizona, 928; California, 17,259; Colorado, 1,126; Connecticut, 42; District of Columbia, 545; Georgia, 43; Idaho, 14; Illinois, 3,615; Indiana, 5,695; Iowa, 267; Kentucky, 350; Louisiana, 2,240; Maine, 1; Maryland, 261; Massachusetts, 8,138; Michigan, 1,804; Minnesota, 4,149; Mississippi, 2,805; New Hampshire, 161; New Jersey, 1,184; New Mexico, 2,462; New York, 6,996; North Dakota, 43; Ohio, 4,717; Pennsylvania, 3,009; Rhode Island, 462; South Carolina, 8; South Dakota, 168; Texas, 1,723; Utah, 268; Vermont, 430; Virginia, 17,802; Washington, 905; West Virginia, 2; Wisconsin, 1,691.

Total: 91,314

Gus Hall (Communist)

Alabama, 1,954 votes; California, 12,766; Colorado, 403; Connecticut, 186; District of Columbia, 219; Georgia, 3; Idaho, 5; Illinois, 9,250; Iowa, 554; Kentucky, 426; Louisiana, 7,417; Maine, 14; Maryland, 68; Minnesota, 1,092; New Jersey, 1,662; New Mexico, 19; New York, 10,270; North Dakota, 84; Ohio, 7,817; Pennsylvania, 1,891; Rhode Island, 334; South Carolina, 1; South Dakota, 318; Tennessee, 547; Utah, 121; Washington, 817; West Virginia, 5; Wisconsin, 749.

Total: 58,992

Margaret Wright (People's Party)

California, 41,731 votes; Connecticut, 1; Idaho, 1; Maryland, 8; Massachusetts, 33; Michigan, 3,504; Minnesota, 635; New Jersey, 1,044; Washington, 1,124; Wisconsin, 943.

Total: 49,024

Lyndon H. LaRouche Jr. (U.S. Labor)

Alabama, 1 vote; Colorado, 567; Connecticut, 1,789; Delaware, 136; District of Columbia, 157; Georgia, 1; Idaho, 739; Illinois, 2,018; Indiana, 1,947; Iowa, 241; Kentucky, 510; Maryland, 21; Massachusetts, 4,922; Michigan, 1,366; Minnesota, 543; New Hampshire, 186; New Jersey, 1,650; New Mexico, 1; New York, 5,413; North Carolina, 755; North Dakota, 142; Ohio, 4,335; Pennsylvania, 2,744; South Carolina, 2; Tennessee, 512; Vermont, 196; Virginia, 7,508; Washington, 903; Wisconsin, 738.

Total: 40,043

Benjamin C. Bubar (Prohibition)

Alabama, 6,669 votes; California, 34; Colorado, 2,882; Delaware, 103; Kansas, 1,403; Maine, 3,495; Maryland, 2; Massachusetts, 14; New Jersey, 554; New Mexico, 211; North Dakota, 63; Ohio, 62; Tennessee, 442.

Total: 15,934

Jules Levin (Socialist Labor)

California, 221 votes; Colorado, 14; Connecticut, 1; Delaware, 86; Florida, 19; Georgia, 2; Illinois, 2,422; Iowa, 167; Maine, 1; Maryland, 7; Massachusetts, 19; Michigan, 1,148; Minnesota, 370; New Hampshire, 66; New Jersey, 3,686; New York, 28; Ohio, 68; Rhode Island, 188; Washington, 713; Wisconsin, 389.

Total: 9,616

Frank P. Zeidler (Socialist)

Connecticut, 5 votes; Florida, 8; Georgia, 2; Idaho, 2; Iowa, 234; Maryland, 16; Minnesota, 354; New Jersey, 469; New Mexico, 240; New York, 14; North Dakota, 38; Washington, 358; Wisconsin, 4,298.

Total: 6,038

Ernest L. Miller (Restoration)

California, 26 votes; Colorado, 6; Florida, 2; Georgia, 3; Maryland, 8; Tennessee, 316.

Total: 361

Frank Taylor (United American)

Arizona, 22 votes; California, 14.

Total: 36

Scattered write-ins

Alabama, 137 votes; Alaska, 1,176; California, 74; Colorado, 2; Connecticut, 1,122; District of Columbia, 1,944, 1.2; Georgia, 847; Idaho, 1,430; Illinois, 1,662; Iowa, 506; Maine, 185; Maryland, 1,945; Massachusetts, 1,354; Michigan, 2,160; Minnesota, 342; Missouri, 3,741; Nevada, 5,108 (none of the above), 2.5; New Hampshire, 604; New Mexico, 501; New York, 4,052; North Carolina, 228; Oregon, 6,107; Pennsylvania, 2,934; Rhode Island, 82; South Carolina, 328; Tennessee, 229; Texas, 2,752; Vermont, 99; West Virginia, 125; Wisconsin, 2,839; Wyoming, 354.

Total: 44,969

1980 Election

Barry Commoner (Citizens)

Alabama, 517 votes; Arizona, 551; Arkansas, 2,345; California, 61,063; Colorado, 5,614; Connecticut, 6,130; Delaware, 103; District of Columbia, 1,840; Georgia, 104; Hawaii, 1,548; Illinois, 10,692; Indiana, 4,852; Iowa, 2,273; Kentucky, 1,304; Louisiana, 1,584; Maine, 4,394; Massachusetts, 2,056; Michigan, 11,930; Minnesota, 8,407; Missouri, 573; New Hampshire, 1,320; New Jersey, 8,203; New Mexico, 2,202; New York, 23,186; North Carolina, 2,287; North Dakota, 429; Ohio, 8,564; Oregon, 13,642; Pennsylvania, 10,430; Rhode Island, 67; Tennessee, 1,112; Texas, 453; Utah, 1,009; Vermont, 2,316; Virginia, 14,024; Washington, 9,403; Wisconsin, 7,767.

Total: 234,294

Gus Hall (Communist)

Alabama, 1,629 votes; Arizona, 25; Arkansas, 1,244; California, 847; Colorado, 487; Delaware, 13; District of Columbia, 371; Florida, 123; Hawaii, 458; Illinois, 9,711; Indiana, 702; Iowa, 298; Kansas, 967; Kentucky, 348; Maine, 591; Michigan, 3,262; Minnesota, 1,184; Missouri, 26; New Hampshire, 129; New Jersey, 2,555; New York, 7,414; North Dakota, 93; Pennsylvania, 5,184; Rhode Island, 218; Tennessee, 503; Texas, 49; Utah, 139; Vermont, 118; Washington, 834; Wisconsin, 772.

Total: 45,023

John R. Rarick (American Independent)

Alabama, 15,010 votes; California, 9,856; Idaho, 1,057; Kansas, 789; Louisiana, 10,333; Michigan, 5; South Carolina, 2,177; Utah, 522; Wisconsin, 1,519.

Total: 41,268

Clifton DeBerry (Socialist Workers)

Alabama, 1,303 votes; Arizona, 1,100; District of Columbia, 173; Florida, 41; Illinois, 1,302; Indiana, 610; Iowa, 244; Louisiana, 783; Massachusetts, 3,735*; Minnesota, 711; Missouri, 1,515; New Hampshire, 71; New York, 2,068; North Carolina, 416; North Dakota, 89; Pennsylvania, 20,291; Rhode Island, 90; Tennessee, 490; Utah, 124; Vermont, 75; Virginia, 1,986; Washington, 1,137.

Total: 37,329

Ellen McCormack (Right to Life)

Delaware, 3 votes; Kentucky, 4,233; Missouri, 5; New Jersey, 3,927; New York, 24,159; Rhode Island, 1.

Total: 32,327

Maureen Smith (Peace and Freedom)

California, 18,116 votes.

Deirdre Griswold (Workers World)

California, 15 votes; Delaware, 3; District of Columbia, 52; Florida, 8; Georgia, 1; Illinois, 2,257; Massachusetts, 19; Michigan, 30; Minnesota, 698; Mississippi, 2,402; New Hampshire, 76; New Jersey, 1,288; Ohio, 3,790; Rhode Island, 77; Tennessee, 400; Texas, 11; Washington, 341; Wisconsin, 414.

Total: 13,300

Benjamin C. Bubar (Statesman)

Alabama, 1,743 votes; Arkansas, 1,350; California, 36; Colorado, 1,180; Delaware, 6; Iowa, 150; Kansas, 821; Massachusetts, 34; Michigan, 9; New Mexico, 1,281; North Dakota, 54; Ohio, 27; Tennessee, 521.

Total: 7,212

David McReynolds (Socialist)

Alabama, 1,006 votes; Florida, 116; Iowa, 534; Massachusetts, 62; Minnesota, 536; New Jersey, 1,973; North Dakota, 82; Rhode Island, 170; Tennessee, 519; Vermont, 136; Washington, 956; Wisconsin, 808.

Total: 6,898

Percy L. Greaves (American)

California, 87 votes, Delaware, 400; Indiana, 4,750; Iowa, 189; Michigan, 21; North Dakota, 235; Utah, 965.

Total: 6,647

Andrew Pulley (Socialist Workers)

California, 231 votes; Colorado, 520; Delaware, 4; Georgia, 4; Kentucky, 393; Mississippi, 2,347; New Jersey, 2,198; New Mexico, 325; South Dakota, 250.

Total: 6,272

Richard Congress (Socialist Workers)

Ohio, 4,029 votes.

Kurt Lynen (Middle Class)

New Jersey, 3,694 votes.

Bill Gahres (Down With Lawyers)

New Jersey, 1,718 votes.

Frank W. Shelton (American)

Kansas, 1,555 votes.

Martin E. Wendelken (Independent)

New Jersey, 923 votes.

Harley McLain (Natural Peoples League)

North Dakota, 296 votes.

Scattered write-ins

Alaska, 857 votes; California, 1,242; Connecticut, 836; Delaware, 101; District of Columbia, 690; Georgia, 112; Illinois, 604; Iowa, 519; Maine, 84; Massachusetts, 2,382; Michigan, 891; Minnesota, 6,139 (American Party, with no candidate specified); Missouri, 604; Nevada, 4,193 (none of the above); New Hampshire, 68; New Mexico, 734; New York, 1,064; Oregon, 1,713; Rhode Island, 37; South Carolina, 376; Tennessee, 152; Vermont, 413; Wisconsin, 1,337.

Total: 23,517

1984 Election

Sonia Johnson (Citizens)

Arizona, 18 votes; Arkansas, 960; California, 26,297; Colorado, 23; Connecticut, 14; Delaware, 121; Florida, 58; Georgia, 4; Illinois, 2,716; Kentucky, 599; Louisiana, 9,502; Massachusetts, 18; Michigan, 1,191; Minnesota, 1,219; Missouri, 2; New Jersey, 1,247; New Mexico, 455; North Dakota, 368; Pennsylvania, 21,628; Rhode Island, 240; Tennessee, 978; Texas, 87; Utah, 844; Vermont, 264; Washington, 1,891; Wisconsin, 1,456.

Total: 72,200

Bob Richards (Populist)

Alabama, 1,401 votes; Arkansas, 1,461; California, 39,265; Georgia, 95; Idaho, 2,288; Kansas, 3,564; Louisiana, 1,310; Minnesota, 2,377; Mississippi, 641; North Dakota, 1,077; Rhode Island, 10; Tennessee, 1,763; Washington, 5,724; West Virginia, 996; Wisconsin, 3,864.

Total: 66,336

Dennis L. Serrette (Independent Alliance)

Alabama, 659 votes; Arkansas, 1,291; California, 16; Colorado, 978; Connecticut, 1,374; Delaware, 68; District of Columbia, 165; Georgia, 2; Illinois, 2,386; Iowa, 463; Kansas, 2,544; Kentucky, 365; Louisiana, 533; Maine, 755; Maryland, 656; Massachusetts, 7,998; Michigan, 665; Minnesota, 232; Mississippi, 356; Nebraska, 1,025; New Hampshire, 305; New Jersey, 2,293; New Mexico, 155; New York, 3,200; North Dakota, 152; Ohio, 12,090; Rhode Island, 49; South Carolina, 682; South Dakota, 1,150; Tennessee, 524; Texas, 41;

Utah, 220; Vermont, 323; Washington, 1,654; West Virginia, 493; Wisconsin, 1,006.

Total: 46,868

Gus Hall (Communist)

Alabama, 4,671 votes; Arkansas, 1,499; Connecticut, 4,826; District of Columbia, 257; Georgia, 1; Hawaii, 821; Illinois, 4,672; Iowa, 286; Kentucky, 328; Maine, 1,292; Maryland, 898; Michigan, 1,048; Minnesota, 630; New Jersey, 1,564; New York, 4,226; North Dakota, 169; Ohio, 4,438; Pennsylvania, 1,780; Rhode Island, 75; Tennessee, 1,036; Texas, 126; Utah, 184; Vermont, 115; Washington, 814; Wisconsin, 596.

Total: 36,386

Mel Mason (Socialist Workers)

Alabama, 730 votes; Colorado, 810; District of Columbia, 127; Florida, 7; Georgia, 10; Illinois, 2,132; Iowa, 313; Kentucky, 3,129; Louisiana, 1,164; Michigan, 1,049; Minnesota, 3,180; Mississippi, 1,032; Missouri, 8; Nebraska, 1,066; New Jersey, 1,264; New Mexico, 224; North Carolina, 799; North Dakota, 239; Ohio, 4,344; Rhode Island, 61; South Dakota, 337; Tennessee, 715; Utah, 142; Vermont, 127; Washington, 608; West Virginia, 645; Wisconsin, 444.

Total: 24,706

Larry Holmes (Workers World)

District of Columbia, 107 votes; Georgia, 2; Maryland, 745; Michigan, 1,416; Mississippi, 1,169; New Jersey, 8,404; New York, 2,226; Washington, 641; Wisconsin, 619.

Total: 15,329

Delmar Dennis (American)

Delaware, 269 votes; Georgia, 4; Indiana, 7,617; Kentucky, 428; Missouri, 1; South Carolina, 3,490; Tennessee, 7; Utah, 1,345.

Total: 13,161

Ed Winn (Workers League)

Arizona, 3 votes; Illinois, 2,632; Michigan, 561; Minnesota, 260; New Jersey, 1,721; Ohio, 3,565; Pennsylvania, 2,059.

Total: 10,801

Earl F. Dodge (Prohibition)

Arkansas, 842 votes; Colorado, 858; Kansas, 2,109; Massachusetts, 3; New Mexico, 206; North Dakota, 220; Ohio, 4.

Total: 4,242

Gavrielle Holmes (Workers World)

Ohio, 2,565 votes; Rhode Island, 91.

Total: 2,656

John B. Anderson (National Unity Party of Kentucky)

Georgia, 3 votes; Kentucky, 1,479; Tennessee, 4.

Total: 1,486

Gerald Baker (Big Deal)

Iowa, 892 votes.

Arthur J. Lowery (United Sovereign Citizens)

Arkansas, 822 votes; Georgia, 3.

Total: 825

Scattered write-ins

Alaska, 843 votes; Arizona, 21; California, 366; Connecticut, 8; District of Columbia, 809; Florida, 32; Georgia, 460; Illinois, 862; Iowa, 1,051; Maine, 82; Massachusetts, 892; Michigan, 602; Minnesota, 723; Montana, 1; Nevada, 3,950 (none of the above); New Hampshire, 113; New Mexico, 1; New York, 837; Ohio, 34; Oregon, 4,348; Rhode Island, 3; Tennessee, 117 Vermont, 712; Wisconsin, 706.

Total: 17,573

1988 Election

David E. Duke (Populist)

Arizona, 113 votes; Arkansas, 5,146; California, 483; Colorado, 139; Florida, 249; Iowa, 755; Kentucky, 4,494; Louisiana, 18,612; Michigan, 60; Minnesota, 1,529; Mississippi, 4,232; Missouri, 44; New Jersey, 2,446; Oregon, 90; Pennsylvania, 3,444; Rhode Island, 159; Tennessee, 1,807; Vermont, 189; Wisconsin, 3,056.

Total: 47,047

Eugene J. McCarthy (Consumer)

Arizona, 159 votes; California, 234; Michigan, 2,497; Minnesota, 5,403; New Jersey, 3,454; Pennsylvania, 19,158.

Total: 30,905

James C. Griffin (American Independent)

California, 27,818 votes.

Lyndon H. LaRouche Jr. (National Economic Recovery)

Alaska, 816 votes; Hawaii, 470; Iowa, 3,526; Louisiana, 1,958; Minnesota, 1,702; North Dakota, 905; Ohio, 7,733; Tennessee, 873; Utah, 427; Vermont, 275; Washington, 4,412; Wisconsin, 2,302; District of Columbia, 163.

Total: 25,562

William A. Marra (Right to Life)

Connecticut, 7 votes; New York, 20,497.

Total: 20,504

Ed Winn (Workers League)

Alabama, 46 votes; Illinois, 7,021; Iowa, 235; Michigan, 1,958; Minnesota, 489; New Jersey, 691; New York, 10; Ohio, 5,432; Pennsylvania, 2,188; District of Columbia, 208.

Total: 18,693

James Warren (Socialist Workers)

Alabama, 655 votes; Iowa, 205; Michigan, 819; Minnesota, 2,155; New Jersey, 2,298; New Mexico, 344; New York, 3,287 0.1; North Dakota, 347; Rhode Island, 130; South Dakota, 226; Tennessee, 718; Texas, 110; Utah, 209; Vermont, 113; Washington, 1,290; Wisconsin, 2,574; District of Columbia, 123.

Total: 15,604

Herbert Lewin (Peace and Freedom)

California, 58 votes; New Jersey, 9,953; Rhode Island, 195; Vermont, 164.

Total: 10,370

Earl F. Dodge (Prohibition)

Arkansas, 1,319 votes; Colorado, 4,604; Massachusetts, 18; Michigan, 5; New Mexico, 249; Tennessee, 1,807.

Total: 8.002

Larry Holmes (Workers World)

California, 11 votes; Michigan, 804; New Jersey, 1,020; New Mexico, 258; New York, 4,179; Ohio, 134; Washington, 1,440.

Total: 7,846

Willa Kenoyer (Socialist)

Florida, 14 votes; Iowa, 334; Massachusetts, 15; New Jersey, 2,587; New York, 3; Rhode Island, 96; Tennessee, 358; Texas, 62; Utah, 129; Vermont, 142; District of Columbia, 142.

Total: 3,382

Delmar Dennis (American)

Arizona, 18 votes; Minnesota, 1,298; Missouri, 1; Utah, 2,158.

Total: 3,475

Jack E. Herer (Grassroots)

Minnesota, 1,949 votes.

Louie G. Youngkeit (Independent)

Utah, 372 votes.

John G. Martin (Third World Assembly)

District of Columbia, 236 votes.

Scattered write-ins

Alabama, 506 votes; Alaska, 957; California, 25; Florida, 13; Georgia, 15; Iowa, 1,613; Maine, 230; Maryland, 24; Massachusetts, 2,910; Michigan, 902; Minnesota, 3,614; Missouri, 6; Nevada, 6,934 (none of the above); New Hampshire, 549; New Mexico, 93; Ohio, 216; Oregon, 3,974; Rhode Island, 51; Tennessee, 285; Texas, 98; Vermont, 1,134; Wisconsin, 2,273; District of Columbia, 1,553.

Total: 27,975

1992 Election

James "Bo" Gritz (Populist)

Alaska, 1,379 votes; Arizona, 8,141; Arkansas, 819; California, 3,077; Colorado, 274; Connecticut, 72; Delaware, 9; Georgia, 78; Hawaii, 1,452; Idaho, 10,281; Illinois, 3,577; Indiana, 1,467; Iowa, 1,177; Kansas, 79; Kentucky, 47; Louisiana, 18,545; Maryland, 41; Michigan, 168; Minnesota, 3,363; Mississippi, 545; Missouri, 180; Montana, 3,658; Nevada, 2,892; New Jersey, 1,867; New York, 23; Ohio, 4,699; Oregon, 1,470; Rhode Island, 3; Tennessee, 756; Texas, 505; Utah, 28,602, 3.8; Washington, 4,854; West Virginia, 34; Wisconsin, 2,311; Wyoming, 569.

Total: 107,014

Lenora B. Fulani (New Alliance)

Alabama, 2,161 votes; Alaska, 330; Arizona, 923; Arkansas, 1,022; Colorado, 1,608; Connecticut, 1,363; Delaware, 1,105; District of Columbia, 1,459; Georgia, 44; Hawaii, 720; Idaho, 613; Illinois, 5,267; Indiana, 2,583; Iowa, 197; Kansas, 10; Kentucky, 430; Louisiana, 1,434; Maine, 519; Maryland, 2,786; Massachusetts, 3,172; Michigan, 21; Minnesota, 958; Mississippi, 2,625; Missouri, 17; Montana, 8; Nebraska, 846; Nevada, 483; New Hampshire, 512; New Jersey, 3,513; New Mexico, 369; New York, 11,318; North Carolina, 59; North Dakota, 143; Ohio, 6,413; Oregon, 3,030; Pennsylvania, 4,661; Rhode Island, 1,878; South Carolina, 1,235; South Dakota, 110; Tennessee, 727; Texas, 301; Utah, 414; Vermont, 429; Virginia, 3,192; Washington, 1,776; West Virginia, 6; Wisconsin, 654; Wyoming, 270.

Total: 73,714

Howard Phillips (U.S. Taxpayers)

Alaska, 377 votes; Arkansas, 1,437; California, 12,711; Connecticut, 20; Delaware, 2; Georgia, 7; Iowa, 480; Kansas, 55; Kentucky, 989; Louisiana, 1,552; Maine, 464; Maryland, 22; Massachusetts, 2,218; Michigan, 8,263; Minnesota, 733; Mississippi, 1,652; Nevada, 677; New Jersey, 2,670; New Mexico, 620; Rhode Island, 215; South Carolina, 2,680; Tennessee, 579; Texas, 359; Utah, 393; Vermont, 124; Washington, 2,354; West Virginia, 2; Wisconsin, 1,772; Wyoming, 7.

Total: 43,434

John Hagelin (Natural Law)

Alabama, 495 votes; Alaska, 433; Arizona, 2,267; Arkansas, 764; California, 836; Colorado, 47; Connecticut, 75; Delaware, 6; District of Columbia, 230; Florida, 214; Hawaii, 416; Idaho, 24; Illinois, 2,751; Indiana, 126; Iowa, 3,079; Kansas, 77; Kentucky, 695; Louisiana, 889; Maryland, 191; Massachusetts, 1,812; Michigan, 2,954; Minnesota, 1,406; Mississippi, 1,140; Missouri, 64; Montana, 20; Nebraska, 714; Nevada, 338; New Hampshire, 292; New Jersey, 1,353; New Mexico, 562; New York, 4,420; North Carolina, 41; North Dakota, 240; Ohio, 3,437; Oregon, 91; Rhode Island, 262; South Dakota, 429; Tennessee, 599; Texas,

217; Utah, 1,319; Vermont, 315; Washington, 2,456; West Virginia, 2; Wisconsin, 1,070; Wyoming, 11.

Total: 39,179

Ron Daniels (Peace and Freedom)

California, 18,597 votes; District of Columbia, 1,186; Iowa, 212; Louisiana, 1,663; Maryland, 167; Missouri, 12; New Jersey, 1,996; New York, 385; Rhode Island, 1; Tennessee, 511; Utah, 177; Washington, 1,171; Wisconsin, 1,883.

Total: 27,961

Lyndon H. LaRouche Jr. (Economic Recovery)

Alabama, 641 votes; Alaska, 469; Arizona, 8; Arkansas, 762; California, 180; Colorado, 20; Connecticut, 4; Delaware, 9; District of Columbia, 260; Idaho, 1; Indiana, 14; Iowa, 238; Louisiana, 1,136; Maryland, 18; Massachusetts, 1,027; Michigan, 14; Minnesota, 622; Missouri, 13; New Jersey, 2,095; New York, 20; North Dakota, 642; Ohio, 2,446; Rhode Island, 494; Tennessee, 460; Texas, 169; Utah, 1,089; Vermont, 57; Virginia, 11,937; Washington, 855; Wisconsin, 633.

Total: 26,333

James Warren (Socialist Workers)

Alabama, 831 votes; California, 115; Connecticut, 5; Delaware, 3; District of Columbia, 105; Georgia, 9; Illinois, 1,361; Iowa, 273; Maryland, 25; Minnesota, 990; Missouri, 6; New Jersey, 2,011; New Mexico, 183; New York, 15,472; North Carolina, 12; North Dakota, 193; Ohio, 32; Tennessee, 277; Utah, 200; Vermont, 82; Washington, 515; West Virginia, 6; Wisconsin, 390.

Total: 23,096

Drew Bradford (Independent)

New Jersey, 4,749 votes.

Jack E. Herer (Grassroots)

Iowa, 669 votes; Minnesota, 2,659; Wisconsin, 547.

Total: 3,875

J. Quinn Brisben (Socialist)

District of Columbia, 191 votes; Florida, 16; Idaho, 3; Indiana, 16; Massachusetts, 13; New York, 16; Oregon, 4; Rhode Island, 2; Tennessee, 1,356; Texas, 78; Utah, 151; Wisconsin, 1,211.

Total: 3,057

Helen Halyard (Workers League)

Michigan, 1,432 votes; New Jersey, 1,618.

Total: 3,050

John Yiamouyiannas (Take Back America)

Arkansas, 554 votes; Iowa, 604; Louisiana, 808; Tennessee, 233.

Total: 2,199

Delbert L. Ehlers (Independent)

Iowa, 1,149 votes.

Earl F. Dodge (Prohibition)

Arkansas, 472 votes; Colorado, 21; Massachusetts, 2; New Mexico, 120; North Dakota, 3; Tennessee, 343.

Total: 961

Jim Boren (Apathy)

Arkansas, 956 votes.

Eugene A. Hem (Third)

Wisconsin, 405 votes.

Isabell Masters (Looking Back)

Arkansas, 327 votes; California, 12.

Total: 339

Robert J. Smith (American)

Utah, 292 votes.

Gloria La Riva (Workers World)

New Mexico, 181 votes.

Scattered write-ins

Alabama, 723 votes; Alaska, 365; California, 149; Delaware, 86; District of Columbia, 676; Florida, 8; Georgia, 2; Illinois, 22; Iowa, 741; Kansas, 57; Maine, 91; Maryland, 2; Massachusetts, 1,990; Michigan,

711; Minnesota, 2,499; Missouri, 3; Nevada (None of these candidates), 2,537; New Hampshire, 730; Ohio, 10; Oregon, 2,609; Rhode Island, 106; Tennessee, 161; Texas, 23; Utah, 1; Vermont, 488; Washington, 665; West Virginia, 35; Wisconsin, 961; Wyoming, 127.

Total: 16,578

1996 Election

Harry Browne (Libertarian)

Alabama, 5,290 votes; Alaska, 2,276; Arizona, 14,358; Arkansas, 3,076; California, 73,600; Colorado, 12,392; Connecticut, 5,788; Delaware, 2,052; District of Columbia, 588; Florida, 23,965; Georgia, 17,870; Hawaii, 2,493; Idaho, 3,325; Illinois, 22,548; Indiana, 15,632; Iowa, 2,315; Kansas, 4,557; Kentucky, 4,009; Louisiana, 7,499; Maine, 2,996; Maryland, 8,765; Massachusetts, 20,426; Michigan, 27,670; Minnesota, 8,271; Mississippi, 2,809; Missouri, 10,522; Montana, 2,526; Nebraska, 2,792; Nevada, 4,460; New Hampshire, 4,237; New Jersey, 14,763; New Mexico, 2,996; New York, 12,220; North Carolina, 8,740; North Dakota, 847; Ohio, 12,851; Oklahoma, 5,505; Oregon, 8,903; Pennsylvania, 28,000; Rhode Island, 1,109; South Carolina, 4,271; South Dakota, 1,472; Tennessee, 5,020; Texas, 20,256; Utah, 4,129; Vermont, 1,183; Virginia, 9,174; Washington, 12,522; West Virginia, 3,062; Wisconsin, 7,929; Wyoming, 1,739.

Total: 485,798

Howard Phillips (U.S. Taxpayers)

Alabama, 2,365 votes; Alaska, 925; Arizona, 347; Arkansas, 2,065; California, 21,202; Colorado, 2,813; Connecticut, 2,425; Delaware, 348; Georgia, 145; Hawaii, 358; Idaho, 2,230; Illinois, 7,606; Indiana, 291; Iowa, 2,229; Kansas, 3,519; Kentucky, 2,204; Louisiana, 3,366; Maine, 1,517; Maryland, 3,402; Michigan, 539; Minnesota, 3,416; Mississippi, 2,314; Missouri, 11,521; Montana, 152; Nebraska, 1,928; Nevada, 1,732; New Hampshire, 1,346; New Jersey, 3,440; New Mexico, 713; New York, 23,580; North Carolina, 258; North Dakota, 745; Ohio, 7,361; Oregon, 3,379; Pennsylvania, 19,552; Rhode Island, 1,021; South Carolina, 2,043; South Dakota, 912; Tennessee, 1,818; Texas, 7,472; Utah, 2,601; Vermont, 382; Virginia, 13,687; Washington, 4,578; Wisconsin, 8,811.

Total: 184,658

John Hagelin (Natural Law)

Alabama, 1,697 votes; Alaska, 729; Arizona, 153; Arkansas, 729; California, 15,403; Colorado, 2,547; Connecticut, 1,703; Delaware, 274; District of Columbia, 283; Florida, 418; Hawaii, 570; Idaho, 1,600; Illinois, 4,606; Indiana, 118; Iowa, 3,349; Kansas, 1,655; Kentucky, 1,493; Louisiana, 2,981; Maine, 825; Maryland, 2,517; Massachusetts, 5,184; Michigan, 4,254; Minnesota, 1,808; Mississippi, 1,447; Missouri, 2,287; Montana, 1,754; Nebraska, 1,189; Nevada, 545; New Jersey, 3,887; New Mexico, 644; New York, 5,011; North Carolina, 2,771; North Dakota, 349; Ohio, 9,120; Oregon, 2,798; Pennsylvania, 5,783; Rhode Island, 435; South Carolina, 1,248; South Dakota, 316; Tennessee, 636; Texas, 4,422; Utah, 1,085; Vermont, 498; Virginia, 4,510; Washington, 6,076; Wisconsin, 1,379; Wyoming, 582.

Total: 113,668

Monica Moorehead (Workers World)

Arkansas, 747 votes; Colorado, 599; Louisiana, 1,678; Massachusetts, 3,277; Michigan, 3,153; New Jersey, 1,337; New York, 3,473; Ohio, 10,813; Rhode Island, 186; Utah, 298; Washington, 2,189; Wisconsin, 1,333.

Total: 29,083

Marsha Feinland (Peace and Freedom)

California, 25,332 votes.

Charles E. Collins (Independent)

Arizona, 36 votes; Arkansas, 823; California, 765; Colorado, 2,809; Georgia, 15; Idaho, 7; Indiana, 11; Kansas, 112; Maryland, 6;

Mississippi, 1,205; Missouri, 62; Montana, 20; Tennessee, 688; Utah, 8; Washington, 2,374.

Total: 8,941

James E. Harris (Socialist Workers)

Alabama, 516 votes; California, 77; Colorado, 244; Connecticut, 4; District of Columbia, 257; Florida, 13; Georgia, 12; Iowa, 331; Minnesota, 684; New Jersey, 1,837; New York, 2,762; North Carolina, 84; Utah, 235; Vermont, 199; Washington, 738; Wisconsin, 483.

Total: 8,476

"None of These Candidates"

Nevada, 5,608 votes.

Dennis Peron (Grassroots)

Minnesota, 4,898 votes; Vermont 480.

Total: 5,378

Mary Cal Hollis (Socialist)

Arkansas, 538 votes; Colorado, 669; Florida, 21; Indiana, 59; Maryland, 4; Massachusetts, 61; Montana, 1; Oregon, 1,922; Texas, 297; Utah, 53; Vermont, 292; Wisconsin, 848.

Total: 4,765

Jerome White (Socialist Equality)

Michigan, 1,554 votes; Minnesota, 347, New Jersey, 537.

Total: 2,438

Diane Beall Templin (American)

Colorado, 557 votes; Utah, 1,290.

Total: 1,847

Earl F. Dodge (Prohibition)

Arkansas, 483 votes; Colorado, 375; Illinois, 1; Massachusetts, 4; Tennessee, 324; Utah, 111.

Total: 1,298

A. Peter Crane (Independent Party of Utah)

Utah, 1,101 votes.

Ralph Forbes (America First)

Arkansas, 932 votes.

John Birrenbach (Independent Grassroots)

Minnesota, 787 votes.

Isabell Masters (Looking Back)

Arkansas, 749 votes; California, 2; Maryland 1.

Total: 752

Steve Michael (Independent)

Tennessee, 408 votes.

Scattered write-ins

Alabama, 1,123 votes; Alaska, 634; Arizona, 16; California, 25; Connecticut, 1; Delaware, 17; District of Columbia 648; Idaho, 1; Illinois, 10; Indiana, 9; Iowa, 1,240; Kentucky, 8; Maine, 144; Maryland, 20; Massachusetts, 6,182; Michigan, 1,817; Minnesota, 2,903; Montana, 5; New Hampshire, 2,456; Ohio, 15; Oregon, 2,329; Pennsylvania, 1,725; Rhode Island, 37; Tennessee, 190; Utah, 98; Vermont, 560; Wisconsin, 2,324.

Total: 24,537

2000 Election

Harry Browne (Libertarian)

Alabama, 5,893 votes; Alaska, 2,636; Arkansas, 2,781; California, 45,520; Colorado, 12,799; Connecticut, 3,484; Delaware, 774; District of Columbia, 669; Florida, 16,415; Georgia, 36,332; Hawaii, 1,477; Idaho, 3,488; Illinois, 11,623; Indiana, 15,530; Iowa, 3,209; Kansas, 4,525; Kentucky, 2,896 Louisiana, 2,951; Maine, 3,074; Maryland, 5,310; Massachusetts, 16,366; Michigan, 16,711; Minnesota, 5,282; Mississippi, 2,009; Missouri, 7,436; Montana, 1,718; Nebraska, 2,245; Nevada, 3,311; New Hampshire, 2,757; New Jersey, 6,312; New Mexico, 2,058; New York, 7,649; North Carolina, 12,307; North Dakota, 660; Ohio, 13,473; Oklahoma, 6,602; Oregon, 7,447; Pennsylvania, 11,248; Rhode

Island, 742; South Carolina, 4,876; South Dakota, 1,662; Tennessee, 4,284; Texas, 23,160; Utah, 3,616; Vermont, 784; Virginia, 15,198; Washington, 13,135; West Virginia, 1,912; Wisconsin, 6,640; Wyoming, 1,443.

Total: 384,429

Howard Phillips (Constitution)

Alabama, 775 votes; Alaska, 596; Arizona, 110; Arkansas, 1,415; California, 17,042; Colorado, 1,319; Connecticut, 9,695; Delaware, 208; Florida, 1,371; Georgia, 140; Hawaii, 343; Idaho, 1,469; Illinois, 57; Indiana, 200; Iowa, 613; Kansas, 1,254; Kentucky, 923; Louisiana, 5,483; Maine, 579; Maryland, 919; Michigan, 3,791; Minnesota, 3,272; Mississippi, 3,267; Missouri, 1,957; Montana, 1,155; Nebraska, 468; Nevada, 621; New Hampshire, 328; New Jersey, 1,409; New Mexico, 343; New York, 1,498; North Dakota, 373; Ohio, 3,823; Oregon, 2,189; Pennsylvania, 14,428; Rhode Island, 97; South Carolina, 1,682; South Dakota, 1,781; Tennessee, 1,015; Texas, 567; Utah, 2,709; Vermont, 153; Virginia, 1,809; Washington, 1,989; West Virginia, 23; Wisconsin, 2,042; Wyoming, 720.

Total: 98,020

John Hagelin (Natural Law)

Alabama, 447 votes; Alaska, 919; Arizona, 1,120; Arkansas, 1,098; California, 10,934; Colorado, 2,240; Connecticut, 40; Delaware, 107; Florida, 2,281; Hawaii, 306; Idaho, 1,177; Illinois, 2,127; Indiana, 167; Iowa, 2,281; Kansas, 1,375; Kentucky, 1,533; Louisiana, 1,075; Maryland, 176; Massachusetts, 2,884; Michigan, 2,426; Minnesota, 2,294; Mississippi, 450; Missouri, 1,104; Montana, 675; Nebraska, 478; Nevada, 415; New Jersey, 2,215; New Mexico, 361; New York, 24,361; North Dakota, 313; Ohio, 6,181; Oregon, 2,574; Rhode Island, 271; South Carolina, 942; Tennessee, 613; Utah, 763; Vermont, 219; Washington, 2,927; West Virginia, 367; Wisconsin, 878; Wyoming, 411.

Total: 83,525

James E. Harris Jr. (Socialist Workers)

Colorado, 216 votes; Connecticut, 4; District of Columbia, 114; Florida, 562; Georgia, 11; Iowa, 190; Louisiana, 1,103; Minnesota, 1,022; Mississippi, 613; New Jersey, 844; New York, 1,789; Ohio, 10; Rhode Island, 34; Utah, 186; Vermont, 70; Washington, 304; Wisconsin, 306.

Total: 7,378

L. Neil Smith (Arizona Libertarian)[5]

Arizona, 5,775.

David McReynolds (Socialist)

California, 28 votes; Colorado, 712; Florida, 622; Illinois, 4; Indiana, 43; Iowa, 107; Massachusetts, 42; New Jersey, 1,880; New York, 2; North Carolina, 1,226; Rhode Island, 52; Texas, 63; Vermont, 161; Washington, 660.

Total: 5,602

Monica Moorehead (Workers World)

Florida, 1,804 votes; Rhode Island, 199; Washington, 1,729; Wisconsin, 1,063.

Total: 4,795

"None of These Candidates"

Nevada, 3,315 votes.

Cathy Gordon Brown (Independent)

Tennessee, 1,606 votes.

Denny Lane (Vermont Grassroots)

Vermont, 1,044 votes.

Randall Venson (Independent)

Tennessee, 535 votes.

Earl F. Dodge (Prohibition)

Colorado, 208 votes.

Louie G. Youngkeit (Independent)

Utah, 161 votes.

Scattered write-ins

Alabama, 699 votes; Alaska, 1,068; California, 6; Connecticut, 10; Delaware, 93; District of Columbia, 539; Florida, 40; Georgia, 13; Idaho,

6; Indiana, 56; Iowa, 1,168; Kentucky, 80; Maine, 27; Maryland, 1,480; Massachusetts, 3,990; Minnesota, 28; Montana, 11; New Hampshire, 1,221; Oregon, 3,419; Pennsylvania, 934; Rhode Island, 329; Tennessee, 428; Texas, 74; Utah, 1; Vermont, 514; Virginia, 2,807; West Virginia, 1; Wisconsin, 1,896.

Total: 20,938

2004 Election

Ralph Nader (Independent)

Alabama, 6,701 votes; Alaska, 5,069; Arizona, 2,773; California, 21,213; Colorado, 12,718; Connecticut, 12,969; Delaware, 2,153; District of Columbia, 1,485; Florida, 32,971; Georgia, 2,231; Idaho, 1,115; Illinois, 3,571; Indiana, 1,328; Iowa, 5,973; Kansas, 9,348; Kentucky, 8,856; Louisiana, 7,032; Maine, 8,069; Maryland, 11,854; Massachusetts, 4,806; Michigan, 24,035; Minnesota, 18,683; Mississippi, 3,177; Missouri, 1,294; Montana, 6,168; Nebraska, 5,698; Nevada, 4,838; New Hampshire, 4,479; New Jersey, 19,418; New Mexico, 4,053; New York, 99,873; North Carolina, 1,805; North Dakota, 3,756; Pennsylvania, 2,656; Rhode Island, 4,651; South Carolina, 5,520; South Dakota, 4,320; Tennessee, 8,992; Texas, 9,159; Utah, 11,305; Vermont, 4,494; Virginia, 2,393; Washington, 23,283; West Virginia, 4,063; Wisconsin, 16,390; Wyoming, 2,741.

Total 465,650

Michael Badnarik (Libertarian)

Alabama, 3,529 votes; Alaska, 1,675; Arizona, 11,856; California, 50,165; Colorado, 7,664; Connecticut, 3,367; Delaware, 586; District of Columbia, 502; Florida, 11,996; Georgia, 18,387; Hawaii, 1,377; Idaho, 3,844; Illinois, 32,442; Indiana, 18,058; Iowa, 2,992; Kansas, 4,013; Kentucky, 2,619; Louisiana, 2,781; Maine, 1,965; Maryland, 6,094; Massachusetts, 15,022; Michigan, 10,552; Minnesota, 4,639; Mississippi, 1,793; Missouri, 9,831; Montana, 1,733; Nebraska, 2,041; Nevada, 3,176; New Hampshire, 372; New Jersey, 4,514; New Mexico, 2,382; New York, 11,607; North Carolina, 11,731; North Dakota, 851; Ohio, 14,676; Oregon, 7,260; Pennsylvania, 21,185; Rhode Island, 907; South Carolina, 3,608; South Dakota, 964; Tennessee, 4,866; Texas, 38,787; Utah, 3,375; Vermont, 1,102; Virginia, 11,032; Washington, 11,955; West Virginia, 1,405; Wisconsin, 6,464; Wyoming, 1,171.

Total 397,265

Michael Peroutka (Constitution)

Alabama, 1,994 votes; Alaska, 2,092; California, 26,645; Colorado, 2,562; Connecticut, 1,543; Delaware, 289; Florida, 6,626; Georgia, 580; Idaho, 3,084; Illinois, 440; Iowa, 1,304; Kansas, 2,899; Kentucky, 2,213; Louisiana, 5,203; Maine, 735; Maryland, 3,421; Michigan, 4,980; Minnesota, 3,074; Mississippi, 1,759; Missouri, 5,355; Montana, 1,764; Nebraska, 1,314; Nevada, 1,152; New Hampshire, 161; New Jersey, 2,750; New Mexico, 771; New York, 207; North Dakota, 514; Ohio, 11,940; Oregon, 5,257; Pennsylvania, 6,318; Rhode Island, 339; South Carolina, 5,317; South Dakota, 1,103; Tennessee, 2,570; Texas, 1,636; Utah, 6,841; Virginia, 10,161; Washington, 3,922; West Virginia, 82; Wyoming, 631.

Total 143,630

David Cobb (Green)

Alaska, 1,058 votes; Arizona, 138; California, 40,771; Colorado, 1,591; Connecticut, 9,564; Delaware, 250; District of Columbia, 737; Florida, 3,917; Georgia, 228; Hawaii, 1,737; Idaho, 58; Illinois, 241; Indiana, 102; Iowa, 1,141; Kansas, 33; Louisiana, 1,276; Maine, 2,936; Maryland, 3,632; Massachusetts, 10,623; Michigan, 5,325; Minnesota, 4,408; Mississippi, 1,073; Montana, 996; Nebraska, 978; Nevada, 853; New Jersey, 1,807; New Mexico, 1,226; New York, 87; North Carolina, 108; Ohio, 192; Oregon, 5,315; Pennsylvania, 6,319; Rhode Island, 1,333; South Carolina, 1,488; Tennessee, 33; Texas, 1,014; Utah, 39; Virginia, 104; Washington, 2,974; West Virginia, 5; Wisconsin, 2,661.

Total 119,859

Leonard Peltier (Peace and Freedom)

California, 27,607 votes.

Walter F. Brown (Socialist)

Colorado, 216 votes; Delaware, 100; Florida, 3,502; Idaho, 3; Indiana, 22; Kansas, 4; Louisiana, 1,795; Michigan, 1,431; Minnesota, 2; Montana, 2; New Jersey, 664; North Carolina, 348; South Carolina, 2,124; Tennessee, 6; Texas, 111; Virginia, 23; Wisconsin, 471.

Total 10,837

James Harris (Socialist Workers)

Colorado, 241 votes; District of Columbia, 130; Florida, 2,732; Iowa, 373; Louisiana, 985; Mississippi, 1,268; Ohio, 22; Utah, 393; Washington, 547; Wisconsin, 411.

Total 7,102

Roger Calero (Socialist Workers)

Connecticut, 12 votes; Minnesota, 416; Nebraska, 82; New Jersey, 530; 2,405; Vermont, 244.

Total 3,689

Thomas J. Harens (Christian Freedom)

Minnesota, 2,387 votes.

Gene Amondson (Concerns of People)

Colorado, 378 votes; Louisiana, 1,566.

Total 1,944

Bill Van Auken (Socialist Equality)

Colorado, 329 votes; Iowa, 176; Kansas, Minnesota, 539; New Jersey, 575; New York, 2; Washington, 231.

Total 1,861

John Parker (Workers World)

Ohio, 2 votes; Rhode Island, 253; Vermont, 265; Washington, 1,077.

Total 1,646

Charles Jay (Personal Choice)

Utah, 946 votes.

Stanford E. "Andy" Andress (Unaffiliated)

Colorado, 804 votes.

Earl F. Dodge (Prohibition)

Colorado, 140 votes.

"None of These Candidates"

Nevada, 3,688 votes.

Scattered write-ins

Alabama, 898 votes; Alaska, 790; California, 140; Colorado, 700; District of Columbia, 506; Georgia, 46; Idaho, 10; Illinois, 132; Indiana 43; Iowa, 1,094; Maine, 4; Maryland, 2481; Massachusetts, 7,028; Minnesota, 2530; Montana, 9; Nebraska, 931; New Hampshire, 980; North Dakota, 9; Ohio, 142; Oregon, 8,956; Pennsylvania, 1,170; Rhode Island, 845; Texas, 437; Utah, 4; Vermont, 957; Virginia, 2953; West Virginia, 13; Wisconsin, 2,986; Wyoming, 480.

Total: 37,241

2008 Election

Ralph Nader (Independent)

Alabama, 6,788 votes; Alaska, 3,783; Arizona, 11,301; Arkansas, 12,882; California, 108,381; Colorado, 13,350; Connecticut, 18,410; Delaware, 2,401; District of Columbia, 958; Florida, 28,124; Georgia, 1,120; Hawaii, 3,825; Idaho, 7,175; Illinois, 30,952; Indiana, 909; Iowa, 8,014; Kansas, 10,527; Kentucky, 15,378; Louisiana, 6,997; Maine, 10,636; Maryland, 14,710; Massachusetts, 28,841; Michigan, 33,085; Minnesota, 30,152; Mississippi, 4,011; Missouri, 17,813; Montana, 3,686; Nebraska, 5,406; Nevada, 6,150; New Hampshire, 3,503; New Jersey, 21,298; New Mexico, 5,327; New York, 41,086; North Carolina, 1,448; North Dakota, 4,189; Ohio, 42,288; Oregon, 18,614; Pennsylvania, 42,977; Rhode Island, 4,829; South Carolina, 5,053; South Dakota,

4,267; Tennessee, 11,560; Texas, 5,214; Utah, 8,416; Vermont, 3,339; Virginia, 11,483; Washington, 29,489; West Virginia, 7,230; Wisconsin, 17,605; Wyoming, 2,525.

Total 737,505

Bob Barr (Libertarian)

Alabama, 4,991 votes; Alaska, 1,589; Arizona, 12,555; Arkansas, 4,776; California 67,582; Colorado, 10,897; Delaware, 1,109; Florida, 17,218; Georgia, 28,812; Hawaii, 1,314; Idaho, 3,658; Illinois, 19,645; Indiana, 29,257; Iowa, 4,590; Kansas, 6,706; Kentucky, 5,989; Maryland, 9,839; Massachusetts, 13,189; Michigan, 23,716; Minnesota, 9,174; Mississippi, 2,529; Missouri, 11,386; Montana, 1,355; Nebraska, 2,740; Nevada, 4,263; New Hampshire, 2,217; New Jersey, 8,441; New Mexico, 2,428; New York, 19,513; North Carolina, 25,722; North Dakota, 1,354; Ohio, 19,888; Oregon, 7,635; Pennsylvania, 19,912; Rhode Island, 1,382; South Carolina, 7,283; South Dakota, 1,835; Tennessee, 8,547; Texas, 56,116; Utah, 6,966; Vermont, 1,067; Virginia, 11,067; Washington, 12,728; Wisconsin, 8,858; Wyoming, 1,594.

Total 523,432

Charles O. "Chuck" Baldwin (Constitution)

Alabama, 4,310 votes; Alaska, 1,660; Arizona, 1,371; Arkansas, 4,023; California, 3,145; Colorado, 6,234; Connecticut, 199; Delaware, 626; Florida, 7,915; Georgia, 1,314; Hawaii, 1,013; Idaho, 4,747; Illinois, 8,256; Indiana, 1,024; Iowa, 4,445; Kansas, 4,148; Kentucky, 4,694; Louisiana, 2,581; Maryland, 3,759; Massachusetts, 4,971; Michigan, 14,685; Minnesota, 6,787; Mississippi, 2,551; Missouri, 8,201; Nebraska, 2,972; Nevada, 3,194; New Hampshire, 226; New Jersey, 3,956; New Mexico, 1,597; New York, 614; North Dakota, 1,199; Ohio, 12,550; Oregon, 7,693; Rhode Island, 675; South Carolina, 6,827; South Dakota, 1,895; Tennessee, 8,191; Texas, 5,052; Utah, 12,012; Vermont, 500; Virginia, 7,474; Washington, 9,432; West Virginia, 2,471; Wisconsin, 5,072; Wyoming, 1,192.

Total 197,453

Cynthia A. McKinney (Green)

Arizona, 3,406 votes; Arkansas, 3,470; California, 38,774; Colorado, 2,822; Connecticut, 49; Delaware, 385; District of Columbia, 590; Florida, 2,887; Georgia, 250; Hawaii, 979; Illinois, 11,838; Indiana, 87; Iowa, 1,423; Kansas, 35; Louisiana, 9,187; Maine, 2,900; Maryland, 4,745; Massachusetts, 6,550; Michigan, 8,892; Minnesota, 5,174; Mississippi, 1,034; Missouri, 80; Nebraska, 1,028; Nevada, 1,411; New Hampshire, 40; New Jersey, 3,636; New Mexico, 1,552; New York, 12,729; North Carolina, 158; Ohio, 8,513; Oregon, 4,543; Rhode Island, 797; South Carolina, 4,461; Tennessee, 2,499; Texas, 671; Utah, 982; Virginia, 2,344; Washington, 3,819; West Virginia, 2,357; Wisconsin, 4,216.

Total 161,313

Alan L. Keyes (America's Independent)

California, 40,673 votes; Colorado, 3,051; Florida, 2,550; Kansas, 31; Maryland, 103; Michigan, 129; Minnesota, 22; New York, 35; Ohio, 160; Texas, 895; Utah, 25.

Total 47,674

Ron Paul (Taxpayers and Constitution)

California, 17,006 votes; Illinois, 1; Louisiana, 9,368; Montana, 10,638; New Hampshire, 1,092.

Total 38,105

Brian P. Moore (Socialist)

Colorado, 226 votes; Connecticut, 15; Florida, 405; Illinois, 3; Indiana, 14; Iowa, 182; Maryland, 10; Michigan, 41; Minnesota, 7; New Jersey, 699; New York, 10; North Carolina, 38; Ohio, 2,731; Tennessee, 1,326; Texas, 910; Utah, 3; Vermont, 141; Wisconsin, 540.

Total 7,301

Gloria E. LaRiva (Socialism and Liberation)

Arkansas, 1,139 votes; Colorado, 158; Florida, 1,516; Iowa, 121; Louisiana, 354; New Jersey, 416; New York, 1,629; Rhode Island, 122; Utah, 262; Vermont, 149; Washington, 705; Wisconsin, 237.

Total 6,808

Roger Calero (Socialist Workers)

Connecticut, 20 votes; Delaware, 58; Minnesota, 790; New Jersey, 523; New York, 3,596; Vermont, 150.

Total 5,137

Richard Duncan (Independent)

Ohio, 3,902 votes.

Charles Jay (Boston Tea)

Arizona, 16 votes; Colorado, 598; Florida, 795; Illinois, 4; Tennessee, 1,011; Utah, 1.

Total 2,426

James E. Harris (Socialist Workers)

California, 49 votes; Colorado, 154; Florida, 533; Georgia, 20; Iowa, 292; Louisiana, 735; Washington, 641.

Total 2,424

John J. Polachek (New)

Illinois, 1,149 votes.

Thaddaus Hill (Write-in)

Texas, 876 votes.

Frank E. McEnulty (New American Independent)

Colorado, 828 votes.

Jeffrey Wambolt (We the People)

Wisconsin, 764 votes.

Thomas R. Stevens (Objectivist)

Colorado, 336 votes; Florida, 419.

Total 755

Gene C. Amondson (Prohibition)

Colorado, 85 votes; Florida, 293; Louisiana, 275.

Total 653

Jeffrey Boss (Vote Here)

New Hampshire, 639 votes.

George Phillies (Libertarian)

New Hampshire, 531 votes.

Jonathan E. Allen (HeartQuake)

Arizona, 8 votes; Colorado, 348; Georgia, 8; Illinois, 3; Kansas, 2; Maryland, 17; New York, 1; Ohio, 2; Texas, 100; Utah, 2.

Total 491

Ted Weill (Reform)

Mississippi, 481 votes.

Gary Nettles (Write-in)

Florida, 391 votes.

Bradford Lyttle (Pacifist)

Colorado, 110 votes.

None of these candidates

Nevada, 6,267 votes.

Scattered write-ins

Alabama, 3,705 votes; Alaska, 1,730; District of Columbia, 1,138; Georgia, 35; Indiana, 2; Iowa, 6,737; Kansas, 3; Maine, 431; Maryland, 9,074; Massachusetts, 14,483; Minnesota, 9,499; Nebraska, 2,837; New Hampshire, 2,001; New York, 3,602; North Carolina, 12,298; Ohio, 347; Oregon, 13,613; Vermont, 1,464; Virginia, 6,355; Wisconsin, 6,521; Wyoming, 1,521.

Total 97,396

★

NOTES

1. Georgia figures for Webster obtained from Svend Petersen, A *Statistical History of the American Presidential Elections* (Westport, Conn.: Greenwood Press, 1981), 31.

2. Troup figures obtained from Petersen, *A Statistical History,* 31.

3. Iowa and Mississippi figures from Petersen, *A Statistical History,* 81. Petersen lists these votes, as well as Progressive votes in all other states, for Theodore Roosevelt. In the ICPSR data for 1916, votes are listed for Progressive electors; Roosevelt's name does not appear. Since Roosevelt declined to be a candidate, CQ Press followed ICPSR in listing these votes as Progressive.

4. MacArthur ran under a variety of party designations: Christian Nationalist in Arkansas, New Mexico, Tennessee, North Dakota, and Washington; Christian Nationalist—Constitution in California and Texas; Constitution in Colorado; and Christian Nationalist—America First in Missouri.

5. L. Neil Smith ran as the Libertarian Party's presidential candidate in Arizona only. Harry Browne ran as the party's candidate in the other forty-nine states.

chapter 5

The Electoral College

OR MORE THAN TWO CENTURIES, Americans have been electing their presidents through the electoral college. Created by the Framers of the Constitution as a compromise between selection by Congress and election by direct popular vote, the system has continued to function even though the United States has undergone radical transformation from an agricultural seaboard nation to a world power.

But despite its durability, the electoral college is perhaps the least cherished of the nation's venerable political institutions. Thomas Jefferson called it "the most dangerous blot on our Constitution," and people have been calling for its abolition or reform ever since.

Under the electoral college system, each state is entitled to electoral votes equal in number to its congressional delegation—that is, the number of representatives from the state, plus two for the state's two senators. (The District of Columbia has three electoral votes, the number it would have if it were a state, making the total electoral college membership 538.) As it works today, the electoral college is largely a "winner-take-all" system. The party that receives a plurality of a state's popular vote is virtually assured of receiving all of that state's electoral votes. Exceptions are Maine and Nebraska, where two electoral votes are awarded to the statewide winner and the others are allocated by presidential election districts that match the states' congressional districts (two in Maine and three in Nebraska). Before 2008 neither state ever split its vote. But in the 2008 presidential election, while Republican John McCain swept most of Nebraska, Democrat Barack Obama won the majority in the congressional district around Omaha, which gave him one of the state's five electoral votes. In the past there were even more variations of today's procedure, including choosing electors by congressional district, voting statewide for each individual elector, and selection of electors by state legislatures. There also have been several cases of a so-called faithless elector, who cast his or her electoral vote for a candidate other than the one who won the popular vote in the elector's state. (See box, Splitting of States' Electoral Votes, p. 188.)

Critics call the electoral college anachronistic and anti-democratic. Many believe that direct election is fairer and more likely to express the will of the people. Public opinion polls consistently show that most Americans favor switching to direct popular vote. Supporters, however, view the college as a bulwark of federalism and the two-party system. They note that most of the time it works flawlessly. They maintain that the system forces a winning candidate to build a national coalition covering many states, which usually enables the president to govern from a wide base even if the popular vote margin of victory is close. Only four times has the popular vote winner not won the presidency.

CONSTITUTIONAL BACKGROUND

The method of selecting a president was the subject of long debate at the Constitutional Convention of 1787. Several plans were proposed and rejected before a compromise solution, which was modified only slightly in later years, was adopted (Article II, Section I, Clause 2).

Facing the convention when it opened May 25 was the question of whether the chief executive should be chosen by direct popular election, by the Congress, by state legislatures, or by intermediate electors. Direct election was opposed because it was felt generally that the people lacked sufficient knowledge of the character and qualifications of possible candidates to make an intelligent choice. Many delegates also feared that the people of the various states would be unlikely to agree on a single person, usually casting their votes for favorite-son candidates well known to them.

The possibility of giving Congress the power to choose the president also received consideration. This plan was rejected, however, largely because of fear that it would jeopardize the principle of executive independence. Similarly, a plan favored by many delegates, to let state legislatures choose the president, was turned down because the delegates thought the president might feel so indebted to the states as to allow them to encroach on federal authority.

Unable to agree on a plan, the convention appointed a "Committee of Eleven" on August 31 to solve the problem.

SPLITTING OF STATES' ELECTORAL VOTES: FACTIONALISM AND "FAITHLESS ELECTORS"

Throughout the history of presidential elections, there have been numerous instances when the U.S. electoral votes from an individual state have been divided among two or more candidates. These cases of split electoral votes occurred for a variety of reasons.

ELECTORAL VOTE SPLITS, 1789–1836

Splits of a state's electoral votes cast for president before 1836 occurred for these reasons:

■ For the first four presidential elections (1789–1800) held under Article II, Section 1 of the Constitution, each elector cast two votes without designating which vote was for president and which for vice president. As a result, electoral votes for each state were often scattered among several candidates. The Twelfth Amendment, ratified in 1804, required electors to vote separately for president and vice president.

■ The district system of choosing electors, in which different candidates each could carry several districts, is the explanation for the split electoral votes in Maryland in 1804, 1808, 1812, 1824, 1828, and 1832; North Carolina in 1808; Illinois in 1824; Maine in 1828; and New York in 1828.

■ The selection of electors by the legislatures of some states sometimes led to party factionalism or political deals that resulted in the choice of electors loyal to more than one presidential candidate. This was the cause for the division of electoral votes in New York in 1808 and 1824; Delaware in 1824; and Louisiana in 1824.

■ The vote of an individual elector for someone other than his party's candidate occured in New Hampshire in 1820, when one Democratic-Republican elector voted for John Quincy Adams instead of the party nominee, James Monroe, to preserve George Washington's distinction as the only unanimously elected president. Three other electors did not vote in 1820.

VOTING FOR INDIVIDUAL ELECTORS

By 1836 all states except South Carolina, which selected its electors by the state legislature until after the Civil War, had established a system of statewide popular election of electors. The new system limited the frequency of electoral vote splits.

Nevertheless, a few states on occasion still divided their electoral votes among different presidential candidates. This occurred because of the practice of listing on the ballot the names of all electors and allowing voters to cross off the names of any particular electors they did not like, or, alternatively, requiring voters to vote for each individual elector. In a close election, electors of different parties sometimes were chosen. An example occurred in California in 1880 when one of the state's electoral votes went to Republican James A. Garfield, although the Democrat Winfield S. Hancock won the state's popular vote by 144 votes. One Democratic elector on the California ballot ran behind a Republican, as shown in this tally of electors:

Winning votes	Elector's party	Losing votes	Elector's party
80,443	Democratic	80,282	Republican
80,443	Democratic	80,282	Republican
80,426	Democratic	80,252	Republican
80,420	Democratic	80,242	Republican
80,413	Democratic	80,228	Republican
80,348	Republican	79,885	Democratic

■ *New Jersey, 1860.* Four Republican and three Douglas Democratic electors won.

■ *California, 1892.* Eight Democratic electors and one Republican won.

■ *North Dakota, 1892.* Two Fusionists (Democrats and Populists) and one Republican won. One of the Fusion electors voted for Democrat Grover Cleveland, and the other voted for Populist James B. Weaver, while the Republican elector voted for Benjamin Harrison, thus splitting the state's electoral vote three ways.

■ *Ohio, 1892.* Twenty-two Republicans and one Democratic elector won.

■ *Oregon, 1892.* Three Republicans and one Populist with Democratic support won.

■ *California, 1896.* Eight Republicans and one Democratic elector won.

■ *Kentucky, 1896.* Twelve Republicans and one Democratic elector won.

On September 4 it suggested a compromise under which each state would appoint presidential electors equal to the total number of its representatives and senators. The electors, chosen in a manner set forth by each state legislature, would meet in their respective states and each cast votes for two persons. The votes would be counted in Congress, with the candidate receiving a majority elected president and the second-highest candidate becoming vice president.

No distinction was made between ballots for president and vice president. Moreover, the development of national political parties, which was not anticipated at that time, and

the nomination of tickets for president and vice president created further confusion in the electoral system. All the electors of one party tended to cast ballots for their two party nominees. But with no distinction between the presidential and vice-presidential nominees, the danger arose of a tie vote between the two. That actually happened in 1800, leading to a change in the original electoral system with ratification of the Twelfth Amendment in 1804.

The committee's compromise plan constituted a great concession to the less populous states, because it ensured them a minimum of three votes (two for their two senators

- *Maryland, 1904.* Seven Democratic electors and one Republican won.

- *Maryland, 1908.* Six Democratic and two Republican electors won.

- *California, 1912.* Eleven Progressive and two Democratic electors won.

- *West Virginia, 1916.* Seven Republicans and one Democratic elector won.

The increasing use of voting machines and straight-ticket voting—where the pull of a lever or the marking of an "X" results in automatically casting a vote for every elector—led to the decline in split electoral votes.

"FAITHLESS ELECTORS"

Yet another cause for occasional splits in a state's electoral vote is the so-called faithless elector. By 2008, according to the Congressional Research Service, twenty-seven states including the District of Columbia had laws requiring electors to vote for the state's popular vote winner. These states were Alabama, Alaska, California, Colorado, Connecticut, District of Columbia, Florida, Hawaii, Maine, Maryland, Massachusetts, Michigan, Mississippi, Montana, Nebraska, Nevada, New Mexico, North Carolina, Ohio, Oklahoma, Oregon, South Carolina, Vermont, Virginia, Washington, Wisconsin, and Wyoming.

In Michigan and North Carolina a "faithless elector" was not to be counted, with the remaining electors filling the vacancy. New Mexico, North Carolina, Oklahoma, South Carolina, and Washington provided criminal penalties or fines for violations. However, no faithless elector has ever been punished and experts doubt that it would be constitutionally possible to do so.

In reality, electors are almost always faithful to the candidate of the party with which they are affiliated, law or no law. But at times in U.S. political history, electors have broken ranks to vote for candidates not supported by their parties. In 1796 a Pennsylvania Federalist elector voted for Democratic-Republican Thomas Jefferson instead of Federalist John Adams. Some historians and political scientists claim that three Democratic-Republican electors voted for Adams. However, the fluidity of political party lines at that early date and the well-known personal friendship between Adams and at least one of the electors make the claim of their being faithless electors one of continuing controversy. In 1820 a New Hampshire Democratic-Republican elector voted for John Quincy Adams instead of the party nominee, James Monroe.

There was no further occurrence until 1948, when Preston Parks, a Truman elector in Tennessee, voted for Gov. J. Strom Thurmond of South Carolina, the States Rights Democratic Party (Dixiecrat) presidential nominee. Since then, there have been the following instances:

- In 1956 W. F. Turner, a Stevenson elector in Alabama, voted for a local judge, Walter B. Jones.

- In 1960 Henry D. Irwin, a Nixon elector in Oklahoma, voted for Sen. Harry F. Byrd, a Virginia Democrat.

- In 1968 Lloyd W. Bailey, a Nixon elector in North Carolina, voted for George C. Wallace, the American Independent Party candidate.

- In 1972 Roger L. MacBride, a Nixon elector in Virginia, voted for John Hospers, the Libertarian Party candidate.

- In 1976 Mike Padden, a Ford elector in the state of Washington, voted for former governor Ronald Reagan of California.

- In 1988 Margaret Leach, a Dukakis elector in West Virginia, voted for Dukakis's running mate, Sen. Lloyd Bentsen of Texas.

- In 2000 Barbara Lett-Simmons, a Gore elector in Washington, D.C., withheld her vote from Gore.

- In 2004 an anonymous Kerry elector in Minnesota voted for Kerry's running mate, Sen. John Edwards of North Carolina.

VOTES FROM CONGRESSIONAL DISTRICTS

In 2008 Nebraska split its five electoral votes, with four going to Sen. John McCain and one to Sen. Barack Obama. Nebraska is one of two states (Maine is the other) that splits its electoral vote between congressional districts. The winner of each district receives that district's vote. The statewide winner receives the state's other two electoral votes. Nebraska has used this system since 1996 and Maine since 1972. The 2008 election was the first time that a split electoral vote occurred in either state. All other states use the winner-take-all method in which the candidate who wins the statewide vote gets all the state's electoral votes.

and at least one for their representative), however small their populations might be. The plan also left important powers with the states by giving complete discretion to state legislatures to determine the method of choosing electors.

The only part of the committee's plan that aroused serious opposition was a provision giving the Senate the right to decide presidential elections in which no candidate received a majority of electoral votes. Some delegates feared that the Senate, which already had been given treaty ratification powers and the responsibility to "advise and consent" on all important executive appointments, might become too

powerful. A proposal was made and accepted to let the House of Representatives decide the winner in instances when the electors failed to give a majority of their votes to a single candidate. The interests of the small states were preserved by giving each state's delegation only one vote in the House on roll calls to elect a president.

The system adopted by the Constitutional Convention was a compromise born out of problems involved in diverse state voting requirements, the slavery problem, big-state versus small-state rivalries, and the complexities of the balance of power among different branches of the government.

Moreover, it was probably as close to a direct popular election as the men who wrote the Constitution thought possible and appropriate at the time.

The term *electoral college* itself does not appear in the Constitution. It was first used unofficially in the early 1800s and became the official designation for the electoral body in 1845.

The Twelfth Amendment

Only once since ratification of the Constitution has an amendment been adopted that substantially altered the method of electing the president. In the 1800 presidential election, the Democratic-Republican electors inadvertently caused a tie in the electoral college by casting equal numbers of votes for Thomas Jefferson, whom they wished to be elected president, and Aaron Burr, whom they wished to elect vice president. The election was thrown into the House, and thirty-six ballots were required before Jefferson was finally elected president. The Twelfth Amendment, ratified in 1804, sought to prevent a recurrence of this incident by providing that the electors should vote separately for president and vice president.

Other changes in the system evolved over the years. The authors of the Constitution, for example, had intended that each state should choose its most distinguished citizens as electors and that they would deliberate and vote as individuals in electing the president. But as strong political parties began to appear, the electors came to be chosen merely as representatives of the parties; independent voting by electors disappeared almost entirely.

METHODS OF CHOOSING ELECTORS

In the early years of the Republic, states used a variety of methods to select presidential electors. For the first presidential election, in 1789, four states held direct popular elections to choose their electors: Pennsylvania and Maryland (at large) as well as Virginia and Delaware (by district). In five states—Connecticut, Georgia, New Jersey, New York, and South Carolina—the state legislatures were to make the choice.

New Hampshire and Massachusetts adopted a combination of the legislative and popular methods. New Hampshire held a statewide popular vote for presidential electors with the stipulation that any elector would have to win a majority of the popular vote to be elected; otherwise, the legislature would choose. In Massachusetts the arrangement was for the voters in each congressional district to vote for the two persons they wanted to be presidential electors. From the two individuals in each district receiving the highest number of votes, the legislature, by joint ballot of both houses, was to choose one. In addition, the legislature was to choose two electors at large.

Because of a dispute between the two chambers, the New York Legislature failed to choose electors. The state Senate insisted on full equality with the Assembly (lower house); that is, the Senate wanted each house to take a separate ballot and to resolve any differences between them by agreement rather than by having one house impose its will on the other. The Assembly, on the other hand, wanted a joint ballot, on which the lower house's larger numbers would prevail, or it was willing to divide the electors with the Senate. The failure to compromise cost the state its vote in the first presidential election.

The twelfth and thirteenth states—North Carolina and Rhode Island—had not ratified the Constitution by the time the electors were chosen, so they did not participate in the 1789 election.

Generally similar arrangements prevailed for the election of 1792. Massachusetts, while continuing to choose electors by district, changed the system somewhat to provide for automatic election of any candidate for elector who received a majority of the popular vote. New Hampshire continued the system of popular election at large, but substituted a popular runoff election in place of legislative choice, if no candidate received a majority of the popular vote.

Besides Massachusetts and New Hampshire, electors were chosen in 1792 by popular vote in Maryland and Pennsylvania (at large) and Virginia and Kentucky (by district). State legislatures chose electors in Connecticut, Delaware, Georgia, New Jersey, New York, North Carolina, Rhode Island, South Carolina, and Vermont.

By 1796 several changes had occurred. New Hampshire switched back to legislative choice for those electors who failed to receive a majority of the popular vote. Tennessee entered the Union (1796) with a unique system for choosing presidential electors: the state legislature appointed three persons in each county, who in turn chose the presidential electors. Massachusetts retained the system used in 1792. Other states chose their electors as follows: at-large popular vote: Georgia and Pennsylvania; district popular vote: Kentucky, Maryland, North Carolina, and Virginia; state legislature: Connecticut, Delaware, New Jersey, New York, Rhode Island, South Carolina, and Vermont.

Political Parties and Electors: 1800

As political parties gained power, manipulation of the system of choosing electors became increasingly widespread. For example, in 1800 Massachusetts switched from popular voting to legislative selection of electors because of recent successes by the Democratic-Republican Party in that state. The Federalists, still in firm control of the legislature, sought to secure the state's entire electoral vote for its presidential candidate, native son John Adams. New Hampshire did likewise.

The rival Democratic-Republicans were not innocent of this kind of political maneuver. In Virginia, where that party was in control, the legislature changed the system for choosing electors from districts to a statewide at-large ballot. That way, the expected statewide Democratic-Republican majority could overcome Federalist control in some districts and garner a unanimous vote for Jefferson, the Democratic-Republican presidential candidate.

In Pennsylvania the two houses of the state legislature could not agree on legislation providing for popular ballots, the system used in the first three elections, so the legislature itself chose the electors, dividing them between the parties.

In other changes in 1800, Rhode Island switched to popular election and Georgia reverted to legislative elections. The sixteen states used the following methods of choosing presidential electors in 1800:

■ By popular vote: Kentucky, Maryland, North Carolina (by district); Rhode Island, and Virginia (at large).

■ By the legislature: Connecticut, Delaware, Georgia, Massachusetts, New Hampshire, New Jersey, New York, Pennsylvania, South Carolina, Tennessee (indirectly, as in 1796), and Vermont.

Trend to Winner-Take-All System

For the next third of a century, the states moved gradually toward a standard system of choosing presidential electors—the statewide, winner-take-all popular ballot. The development of political parties resulted in the adoption of slates of electors pledged to vote for the parties' presidential candidates. Each party organization saw a statewide ballot as being in its best interest, with the hope of sweeping in all its electors and preventing the opposition group from capitalizing on local areas of strength (which could result in winning only part of the electoral vote under the districting system).

From 1804 to 1832 the states used three basic methods of choosing presidential electors—at-large popular vote, district popular vote, and election by the state legislature. The following list shows the changing methods of choosing presidential electors for each state from 1804 to 1832:

1804

Popular vote, at large: New Hampshire, New Jersey, Ohio, Pennsylvania, Rhode Island, and Virginia.

Popular vote, by district: Kentucky, Maryland, Massachusetts, North Carolina, and Tennessee.

State legislature: Connecticut, Delaware, Georgia, New York, South Carolina, and Vermont.

1808

Popular vote, at large: New Hampshire, New Jersey, Ohio, Pennsylvania, Rhode Island, and Virginia.

Popular vote, by district: Kentucky, Maryland, North Carolina, and Tennessee.

State legislature: Connecticut, Delaware, Georgia, Massachusetts, New York, South Carolina, and Vermont.

1812

Popular vote, at large: New Hampshire, Ohio, Pennsylvania, Rhode Island, and Virginia.

Popular vote, by district: Kentucky, Maryland, Massachusetts, and Tennessee.

State legislature: Connecticut, Delaware, Georgia, Louisiana, New Jersey, New York, North Carolina, South Carolina, and Vermont.

1816

Popular vote, at large: New Hampshire, New Jersey, North Carolina, Ohio, Pennsylvania, Rhode Island, and Virginia.

Popular vote, by district: Kentucky, Maryland, and Tennessee.

State legislature: Connecticut, Delaware, Georgia, Indiana, Louisiana, Massachusetts, New York, South Carolina, and Vermont.

1820

Popular vote, at large: Connecticut, Mississippi, New Hampshire, New Jersey, North Carolina, Ohio, Pennsylvania, Rhode Island, and Virginia.

Popular vote, by district: Illinois, Kentucky, Maine, Maryland, Massachusetts, and Tennessee.

State legislature: Alabama, Delaware, Georgia, Indiana, Louisiana, Missouri, New York, South Carolina, and Vermont.

1824

Popular vote, at large: Alabama, Connecticut, Indiana, Massachusetts, Mississippi, New Hampshire, New Jersey, North Carolina, Ohio, Pennsylvania, Rhode Island, and Virginia.

Popular vote, by district: Illinois, Kentucky, Maine, Maryland, Missouri, and Tennessee.

State legislature: Delaware, Georgia, Louisiana, New York, South Carolina, and Vermont.

1828

Popular vote, at large: Alabama, Connecticut, Georgia, Illinois, Indiana, Kentucky, Louisiana, Massachusetts, Mississippi, Missouri, New Hampshire, New Jersey, North Carolina, Ohio, Pennsylvania, Rhode Island, Vermont, and Virginia.

Popular vote, by district: Maine, Maryland, New York, and Tennessee.

State legislature: Delaware, and South Carolina.

1832

Popular vote, at large: All states except Maryland and South Carolina.

Popular vote, by district: Maryland.

State legislature: South Carolina.

By 1836 Maryland switched to the system of choosing its electors by statewide popular vote. This left only South Carolina selecting its electors through the state legislature. The state continued this practice through the election of 1860. Only after the Civil War was popular voting for presidential electors instituted in South Carolina.

Since 1836 the statewide, winner-take-all popular vote for electors has been the almost universal practice. Exceptions include the following:

■ *Massachusetts, 1848.* Three slates of electors ran—Whig, Democratic, and Free Soil—none of which received a majority of the popular vote. Under the law then in force, the state legislature was to choose in such a case. It chose the Whig electors.

■ *Florida, 1868.* The state legislature chose the electors.

■ *Colorado, 1876.* The state legislature chose the electors because the state had just been admitted to the Union, had held state elections in August, and did not want to go to the trouble and expense of holding a popular vote for the presidential election so soon thereafter.

■ *Michigan, 1892.* Republicans had been predominant in the state since the 1850s. However, in 1890 the Democrats gained control of the legislature and the governorship and enacted a districting system of choosing presidential electors in the expectation that the Democrats could carry some districts and thus some electoral votes in 1892. They were correct; the Republicans won nine and the Democrats five electoral votes that year. But the Republicans soon regained control of the state and reenacted the at-large system for the 1896 election.

■ *Maine, 1972.* In 1969 the Maine legislature enacted a district system for choosing presidential electors. Two of the state's four electors were selected on the basis of the statewide vote, and the other two were determined according to which party carried each of the state's two congressional districts. The system is still in force. Although the district system allowed splitting electoral votes, from its inception through 2008 the system had not produced a split vote in Maine.

■ *Nebraska, 1992.* Nebraska, with five electoral votes, adopted an allocation system similar to Maine's. Like Maine, Nebraska did not split its electoral votes under the new system through the 2004 presidential election. In 2008, however, one district and therefore one electoral vote went to Obama with the remaining four to McCain.

■ *Florida, 2000.* The Republican-controlled legislature met in special session to choose the state's twenty-five electors. The action ensured that Florida's electoral votes would not be disqualified if the winner of the state's popular vote had not been determined by the federal date for counting electoral votes. Florida is one of twenty-seven states that bind electors to the popular vote winner, but the constitutionality of such laws has not been tested.

■ *Colorado, 2004.* Voters soundly defeated a ballot measure that would have allocated the state's nine electoral votes to presidential candidates in proportion to their share of the total votes cast for president in the state. The Republican administration of Gov. Bill Owens opposed the amendment.

HISTORICAL ANOMALIES

The complicated and indirect system of electing the president has led to anomalies from time to time. In 1836, for example, the Whigs sought to take advantage of the electoral system by running different presidential candidates in different parts of the country. William Henry Harrison ran in most of New England, the mid-Atlantic states, and the Midwest; Daniel Webster ran in Massachusetts; and Hugh White of Tennessee ran in the South.

The theory was that each candidate could capture electoral votes for the Whig Party in the region where he was strongest. Then the Whig electors could combine on one candidate or, alternatively, throw the election into the House, whichever seemed to their advantage. However, the scheme did not work because Martin Van Buren, the Democratic nominee, captured a majority of the electoral vote.

Another quirk in the system surfaced in 1872. The losing Democratic presidential nominee, Horace Greeley, died between the time of the popular vote and the meeting of the presidential electors. The Democratic electors had no party nominee to vote for, and they were left to their own judgment. Forty-two of the sixty-six Democratic electors chose to vote for the Democratic governor-elect of Indiana, Thomas Hendricks. The rest of the electors split their votes among three other politicians: eighteen for B. Gratz Brown of Missouri, the Democratic vice-presidential nominee; two for Charles J. Jenkins of Georgia; and one for David Davis of Illinois. Three Georgia electors insisted on casting their votes for Greeley, but Congress refused to count them. Counting Republican Ulysses S. Grant, who won, five candidates received electoral votes in 1872, tied for the largest number in U.S. history (five candidates also received electoral votes in 1800 and 1836).

In four elections the electoral college has chosen presidents who ran behind their opponents in the popular vote. In two of these instances—Republican Rutherford B. Hayes in 1876 and Republican Benjamin Harrison in 1888—the winning candidate carried a number of key states by close margins, while losing other states by wide margins. In the third instance—Democratic-Republican John Quincy Adams in 1824—the House chose the new

ELECTORAL COLLEGE CHRONOLOGY

1787. The U.S. Constitution establishes the electoral college system for electing the president: a majority vote of state-appointed "electors" elects the president; each state is free to determine method of choosing electors; the plan calls for second-place finisher to become vice president and for House of Representatives to elect president if no candidate has majority.

1800s. Electoral college is tested in three contentious elections but survives with one significant modification, effective 1804; states gradually move to winner-take-all system, giving electoral votes to winner of the state's popular vote for president.

1800. Presidential election is thrown into House, which takes thirty-six ballots to elect Thomas Jefferson over Aaron Burr.

1804. The Twelfth Amendment provides for separate election of vice president.

1824–1825. John Quincy Adams trails in popular vote and electoral vote behind Andrew Jackson but is elected president after one House ballot.

1830s. Most states adopt popular election of presidential electors; by 1860 only South Carolina lets state legislature choose.

1845. Congress adopts uniform national election day: first Tuesday after first Monday in November in even-numbered years.

1876–1877. Rutherford B. Hayes is elected president with one-vote electoral college majority, 185–184, after a fifteen-member commission splits along party lines in awarding him disputed votes from three southern states.

1887. Electoral Vote Count Act specifies states' authority to determine legality of their choices for electors.

1900s. Proposals to abolish electoral college surface periodically, but no constitutional amendment emerges from Congress.

1950. Senate approves "proportional vote" plan to divide state electors on basis of popular vote; House kills measure.

1960. John F. Kennedy wins electoral college majority over Richard Nixon, 303–219; Kennedy's popular vote margin is closest in twentieth century. Fourteen unpledged electors and one "faithless" Republican elector vote for Sen. Harry F. Byrd, Virginia Democrat.

1968. Nixon wins electoral college majority over Democrat Hubert H. Humphrey and third-party candidate George Wallace (301–191–46); both Nixon and Humphrey had vowed not to negotiate with Wallace if election were thrown into House.

1969. House approves constitutional amendment to shift to direct popular election of president; measure dies after Senate filibuster in 1970. Maine, in 1969, replaces winner-take-all with district-by-district system.

1980–1988. Electoral college issue fades as Republican candidates win three successive elections with decisive popular votes and electoral majorities. One Democratic elector in 1988 votes for vice-presidential nominee Lloyd Bentsen to protest system.

1992. Strong third-party bid by H. Ross Perot stirs fears of throwing election to House, but Bill Clinton wins electoral college majority as Perot fails to carry any state. Nebraska adopts district voting for electors.

2000–2001. Democrat Al Gore surpasses Republican George W. Bush in popular vote, but electoral college outcome turns on close count in Florida; Gore and Bush vie in state and federal courts over recount. U.S. Supreme Court halts count, settling election contest in Bush's favor. Final electoral vote tally is Bush 271 (one more than needed to win) and Gore 266 (one fewer than he was entitled to because a District of Columbia elector withheld her vote to protest the District's lack of congressional representation). When Congress meets to count the electoral votes, several minority and women House members object to Florida's votes. Gore, presiding as vice president, rules each objection out of order because it was not also signed by a senator, as the 1887 law requires.

2004. Colorado voters defeat a ballot measure, Amendment 36, that would have dropped the "winner-take-all" system and allocated the state's electoral votes proportionally among the presidential candidates who received the most votes in the state. The measure loses with 65.2 percent against and 34.8 percent in favor. As the winning candidate President George W. Bush receives all nine Colorado electoral votes. Had the measure become law in 2004, Bush would have received only five of Colorado's electoral votes.

2004–2005. In contrast to 2001, a Democratic senator, Barbara Boxer of California, joins a House petition objecting to Ohio's electoral votes because of numerous irregularities reported there. Boxer's action triggers provisions of the 1887 law calling for debates in each chamber on whether to count the Ohio votes. *(See box, Law for Counting Electoral Votes in Congress, p. 199).* After two hours of debate, the Senate votes 74–1 against Boxer, and the House objection led by Democrat Stephanie Tubbs Jones of Ohio is defeated 267–31. Several of the objectors, including Tubbs Jones, are African Americans and none are Republicans. Bush receives Ohio's twenty electoral votes and his election is certified.

2009. On January 8 Congress meets in joint session to count the electoral votes from the 2008 presidential election. The process is purely routine. Barack Obama of Illinois, the Democratic candidate for president, and his running mate, Joseph R. Biden Jr. of Delaware, each receive 365 votes to 173 votes each for Republicans John McCain of Arizona and his running mate, Sarah Palin of Alaska.

president after no candidate had achieved a majority in the electoral college. In the fourth instance, the 2000 election hinged on Florida's twenty-five electoral votes, which went to Republican George W. Bush when the U.S. Supreme Court rejected the challenge of the state's vote count by Democrat Albert "Al" Gore Jr. *(See Chapter 2, Chronology of Presidential Elections.)*

ELECTION BY CONGRESS

Under the Constitution, Congress has two major responsibilities relating to the election of the president and vice president. First, it is directed to receive and, in joint session, count the electoral votes certified by the states. Second, if no candidate has a majority of the electoral vote, the House of

Representatives must elect the president and the Senate the vice president.

Although many of the Framers of the Constitution apparently thought that most elections would be decided by Congress, the House actually has chosen a president only twice, in 1801 and 1825. But a number of campaigns have been deliberately designed to throw elections into the House, where each state has one vote and a majority of states is needed to elect.

In modern times the formal counting of electoral votes has been largely a ceremonial function, but the congressional role can be decisive when votes are contested. The pre-eminent example is the Hayes-Tilden contest of 1876, when congressional decisions on disputed electoral votes from four states gave the election to Republican Hayes despite the fact that Democrat Samuel J. Tilden had a majority of the popular vote. (See "Hayes-Tilden Contest," p. 196.)

From the beginning, the constitutional provisions governing the selection of the president have had few defenders, and many efforts at electoral college reform have been undertaken. Although prospects for reform seemed favorable after the close 1968 presidential election, the Ninety-first Congress (1969–1971) did not take final action on a proposed constitutional amendment that would have provided for direct popular election of the president and eliminated the existing provision for contingent election by the House. Reform legislation was reintroduced in the Senate during the Ninety-fourth Congress (1975–1977) and Ninety-fifth Congress (1977–1979). In the 107th Congress (2001–2003), more talk of reforming or replacing the electoral college system followed the fiercely fought 2000 election, but once again Congress did not act.

In addition to its role in electing the president, Congress bears responsibility in the related areas of presidential succession and disability. The Twelfth Amendment empowers Congress to decide what to do if the president-elect and the vice president-elect both fail to qualify by the date prescribed for commencement of their terms; it also gives Congress authority to settle problems arising from the death of candidates in cases where the election devolves upon Congress. Under the Twenty-fifth Amendment, Congress has ultimate responsibility for resolving disputes over presidential disability. It also must confirm presidential nominations to fill a vacancy in the vice presidency.

Jefferson-Burr Deadlock

The election of 1800 was the first in which the Constitution's contingent election procedures were put to the test and the House elected the president. The Federalists, a declining but still potent political force, nominated John Adams for a second term and chose Charles Cotesworth Pinckney as his running mate. A Democratic-Republican congressional caucus chose Vice President Jefferson for president and Burr, who had been instrumental in winning the New York legislature for the Democratic-Republicans earlier in 1800, for vice president.

The electors met in each state on December 4, with the following results: Jefferson and Burr, seventy-three electoral votes each; Adams, sixty-five; Pinckney, sixty-four; and John Jay, one. The Federalists had lost, but because the Democratic-Republicans had neglected to withhold one electoral vote from Burr, their presidential and vice-presidential candidates were tied, and the election was thrown into the House.

The lame-duck Congress, with a partisan Federalist majority, was still in office for the electoral count, and the possibilities for intrigue were only too apparent. After toying with and rejecting a proposal to block any election until March 4, when Adams's term expired, the Federalists decided to support Burr and thereby elect a relatively pliant politician over a man they considered a "dangerous radical." Alexander Hamilton opposed this move. "I trust the Federalists will not finally be so mad as to vote for Burr," he wrote. "I speak with intimate and accurate knowledge of his character. His elevation can only promote the purposes of the desperate and the profligate. If there be a man in the world I ought to hate, it is Jefferson. With Burr I have always been personally well. But the public good must be paramount to every private consideration."

On February 11, 1801, Congress met in joint session—with Jefferson, the outgoing vice president, in the chair—to count the electoral vote. This ritual ended, the House retired to its own chamber to elect a president. When the House met, it became apparent that Hamilton's advice had been rejected; a majority of Federalists insisted on backing Burr over Jefferson, the man they despised more. Indeed, if Burr had given clear assurances that he would run the country as a Federalist, he might have been elected. But Burr was unwilling to make those assurances; and, as one chronicler put it, "No one knows whether it was honor or a wretched indecision which gagged Burr's lips."

In all, there were 106 members of the House at the time, fifty-eight Federalists and forty-eight Democratic-Republicans. If the ballots had been cast per capita Burr would have been elected, but the Constitution provided that each state should cast a single vote and that a majority of states was necessary for election.

On the first ballot Jefferson received the votes of eight states, one short of a majority of the sixteen states then in the Union. Six states backed Burr. The representatives of Vermont and Maryland were equally divided and, therefore, could not cast their states' votes. By midnight of the first day of voting, nineteen ballots had been taken, and the deadlock remained.

In all, thirty-six ballots were taken before the House came to a decision on February 17. Predictably, there were men who sought to exploit the situation for personal gain. Jefferson wrote: "Many attempts have been made to obtain terms and promises from me. I have declared to them unequivocally that I would not receive the Government on capitulation; that I would not go in with my hands tied."

The impasse was broken finally when Vermont and Maryland switched to support Jefferson. Delaware and South Carolina also withdrew their support from Burr by casting blank ballots. The final vote: ten states for Jefferson, four (all in New England) for Burr. Jefferson became president, and Burr, under the Constitution as it then stood, automatically became vice president.

Federalist James A. Bayard of Delaware, who had played an important role in breaking the deadlock, wrote to Hamilton: "The means existed of electing Burr, but this required his cooperation. By deceiving one man (a great blockhead) and tempting two (not incorruptible), he might have secured a majority of the states. He will never have another chance of being president of the United States; and the little use he has made of the one which has occurred gives me but an humble opinion of the talents of an unprincipled man."

The Jefferson-Burr contest clearly illustrated the dangers of the double-balloting system established by the original Constitution, and pressure began to build for an amendment requiring separate votes for president and vice president. Congress approved the Twelfth Amendment in December 1803, and the states—acting with unexpected speed—ratified it in time for the 1804 election.

John Quincy Adams Election

The only other time the House of Representatives elected a president was in 1825. There were many contenders in the 1824 election, but four predominated: John Quincy Adams, Henry Clay, William H. Crawford, and Andrew Jackson. Crawford, secretary of the Treasury under President James Monroe, was the early front-runner, but his candidacy faltered after he suffered an incapacitating illness in 1823.

When the electoral votes were counted, Jackson had ninety-nine, Adams eighty-four, Crawford forty-one, and Clay thirty-seven. With eighteen of the twenty-four states choosing their electors by popular vote, Jackson also led in the popular voting, although the significance of the popular vote was open to challenge. Under the Twelfth Amendment, the names of the three top contenders—Jackson, Adams, and the ailing Crawford—were placed before the House. Clay's support was vital to either of the two front-runners.

From the start, Clay apparently intended to support Adams as the lesser of two evils. But before the House voted, a great scandal erupted. A Philadelphia newspaper published an anonymous letter alleging that Clay had agreed to support Adams in return for being made secretary of state. The letter alleged also that Clay would have been willing to make the same deal with Jackson. Clay immediately denied the charge and pronounced the writer of the letter "a base and infamous character, a dastard and a liar."

When the House met to vote, Adams was supported by the six New England states and New York and, in large part through Clay's backing, by Maryland, Ohio, Kentucky, Illinois, Missouri, and Louisiana. A majority of thirteen delegations voted for him—the bare minimum he needed for election, because there were twenty-four states in the Union at the time. The election was accomplished on the first ballot, but Adams took office under a cloud from which his administration never emerged.

Jackson had believed the charges and found his suspicions vindicated when Adams, after the election, appointed Clay as secretary of state. "Was there ever witnessed such a bare-faced corruption in any country before?" Jackson wrote to a friend. Jackson's successful 1828 campaign made much of his contention that the House of Representatives had thwarted the will of the people by denying him the presidency in 1825, even though he had been the leader in the popular and electoral votes.

Other Anomalies

The Senate has chosen the vice president only once. That was in 1837, when Van Buren was elected president with 170 of the 294 electoral votes while his vice-presidential running mate, Richard M. Johnson, received only 147 electoral votes—one less than a majority. This discrepancy occurred because Van Buren electors from Virginia boycotted Johnson, reportedly in protest against his social behavior. The Senate elected Johnson, 33–16, over Francis Granger of New York, the runner-up in the electoral vote for vice president.

In 1912 President William Howard Taft's vice president, James S. Sherman, died in October after he and Taft won renomination by the Republican Party. Taft and his substitute running mate, Nicholas Murray Butler, lost the election to Democrats Woodrow Wilson and Thomas R. Marshall. But because it had been too late to change the GOP state ballots, Butler received Sherman's eight electoral votes.

Although only two presidential elections actually have been decided by the House, a number of others—including those of 1836, 1856, 1860, 1892, 1948, 1960, and 1968—could have been thrown into the House by only a small shift in the popular vote.

The threat of House election was most clearly evident in 1968, when Democrat George C. Wallace of Alabama ran as a strong third-party candidate. Wallace frequently asserted that he could win an outright majority in the electoral college by the addition of key Midwestern and Mountain states to his hoped-for base in the South and border states. In reality, the Wallace campaign had a narrower goal: to win the balance of power in electoral college voting, thereby depriving either major party of the clear electoral majority required for election. Wallace made it clear that he then would expect one of the major party candidates to make concessions in return for enough votes from Wallace electors to win the election. Wallace indicated that he expected the election to be settled in the electoral college and not in the House of Representatives. At the end of the campaign it was disclosed that Wallace had obtained written affidavits from all of his electors in which they promised to vote for Wallace "or whomsoever he may direct" in the electoral college.

In response to the Wallace challenge, both major party candidates, Republican Richard Nixon and Democrat Hubert H. Humphrey, maintained that they would refuse to bargain with Wallace for his electoral votes. Nixon asserted that the House, if the decision rested there, should elect the popular-vote winner. Humphrey said the representatives should select "the president they believe would be best for the country." Bipartisan efforts to obtain advance agreements from House candidates to vote for the national popular-vote winner if the election should go to the House ended in failure. Neither Nixon nor Humphrey replied to suggestions that they pledge before the election to swing enough electoral votes to the popular-vote winner to ensure his election without help from Wallace.

In the end Wallace received only 13.5 percent of the popular vote and forty-six electoral votes (including the vote of one Republican defector), all from southern states. He failed to win the balance of power in the electoral college, which he had hoped to use to wring policy concessions from one of the major party candidates. If Wallace had won a few border states, or if a few thousand more Democratic votes had been cast in northern states barely carried by Nixon, reducing Nixon's electoral vote below 270, Wallace would have been in a position to bargain off his electoral votes or to throw the election into the House for final settlement. Wallace later told journalist Neal R. Peirce that he would have tried to instruct his electors to vote for Nixon rather than have the election go to the House.

COUNTING THE ELECTORAL VOTE

Over the years Congress has mandated a variety of dates for the casting of popular votes, the meeting of the electors to cast ballots in the various states, and the official counting of the electoral votes before both houses of Congress.

The Continental Congress made the provisions for the first election. On September 13, 1788, it directed that each state choose its electors on the first Wednesday in January 1789. It further directed these electors to cast their ballots on the first Wednesday in February 1789.

In 1792 the Second Congress passed legislation setting up a permanent calendar for choosing electors. Allowing some flexibility in dates, the law directed that states choose their electors within the thirty-four days preceding the first Wednesday in December of each presidential election year. Then the electors would meet in their various states and cast their ballots on the first Wednesday in December. On the second Wednesday of the following February, the votes were to be opened and counted before a joint session of Congress. Provision also was made for a special presidential election in case of the removal, death, resignation, or disability of both the president and vice president.

Under that system, states chose presidential electors at various times. For instance, in 1840 the popular balloting for electors began in Pennsylvania and Ohio on October 30 and ended in North Carolina on November 12. South Carolina, the only state still choosing presidential electors through its state legislature, appointed its electors on November 26.

Congress modified the system in 1845, providing that each state choose its electors on the same day—the Tuesday next after the first Monday in November—a provision that still remains in force. Otherwise, the days for casting and counting the electoral votes remained the same.

The next change occurred in 1887, when Congress provided that electors were to meet and cast their ballots on the second Monday in January instead of the first Wednesday in December. Congress also dropped the provision for a special presidential election.

In 1934 Congress again revised the law. The new arrangements, still in force, directed the electors to meet on the first Monday after the second Wednesday in December. The ballots are opened and counted before Congress on January 6 (the next day if January 6 falls on a Sunday).

The Constitution states: "The President of the Senate shall, in the presence of the Senate and House of Representatives, open all the certificates, and the votes shall then be counted." It gives no guidance on disputed ballots. Early objections to electoral votes usually arose from disputes about whether a state had fully qualified for statehood. After the Civil War, some southern votes were contested on grounds that the states were still considered in "insurrection" against the United Sates.

Before counting the electoral votes in 1865, Congress adopted the Twenty-second Joint Rule, which provided that no electoral votes objected to in joint session could be counted except by the concurrent votes of both the Senate and House. The rule was pushed by congressional Republicans to ensure rejection of the electoral votes from the newly reconstructed states of Louisiana and Tennessee. Under this rule, Congress in 1873 also threw out the electoral votes of Louisiana and Arkansas and three from Georgia.

The rule lapsed at the beginning of 1876, however, when the Senate refused to readopt it because the House was under Democratic control. As a consequence, Congress had no rules to guide it following the 1876 Hayes-Tilden election, when it became apparent that for the first time the outcome of an election would be determined by decisions on disputed electoral votes.

Hayes-Tilden Contest

The 1876 campaign pitted Republican Hayes against Democrat Tilden. Early returns indicated that Tilden had been elected. He had won the swing states of Indiana, New York, Connecticut, and New Jersey. Those states plus his expected southern support would give Tilden the election. However,

PRESIDENTIAL ELECTION BY THE HOUSE

The following rules, reprinted from Hinds's *Precedents of the House of Representatives*, were adopted by the House in 1825 for use in deciding the presidential election of 1824. They would provide a precedent for any future House election of a president, although the House could change them.

1. In the event of its appearing, on opening all the certificates, and counting the votes given by the electors of the several States for President, that no person has a majority of the votes of the whole number of electors appointed, the same shall be entered on the Journals of this House.

2. The roll of the House shall then be called by States; and, on its appearing that a Member or Members from two-thirds of the States are present, the House shall immediately proceed, by ballot, to choose a President from the persons having the highest numbers, not exceeding three, on the list of those voted for as President; and, in case neither of those persons shall receive the votes of a majority of all the states on the first ballot, the House shall continue to ballot for a President, without interruption by other business, until a President be chosen.

3. The doors of the Hall shall be closed during the balloting, except against the Members of the Senate, stenographers, and the officers of the House.

4. From the commencement of the balloting until an election is made no proposition to adjourn shall be received, unless on the motion of one State, seconded by another State, and the question shall be decided by States. The same rule shall be observed in regard to any motion to change the usual hour for the meeting of the House.

5. In balloting the following mode shall be observed, to wit:

The Representatives of each State shall be arranged and seated together, beginning with the seats at the right hand of the Speaker's chair, with the Members from the State of Maine; thence, proceeding with the Members from the States, in the order the States are usually named for receiving petitions[1] around the Hall of the House, until all are seated.

A ballot box shall be provided for each State.

The Representatives of each State shall, in the first instance, ballot among themselves, in order to ascertain the vote of their State; and they may, if necessary, appoint tellers of their ballots.

After the vote of each State is ascertained, duplicates thereof shall be made out; and in case any one of the persons from whom the choice is to be made shall receive a majority of the votes given, on any one balloting by the Representatives of a State, the name of that person shall be written on each of the duplicates; and in case the votes so given shall be divided so that neither of said persons shall have a majority of the whole number of votes given by such State, on any one balloting, then the word "divided" shall be written on each duplicate.

After the delegation from each State shall have ascertained the vote of their State, the Clerk shall name the States in the order they are usually named for receiving petitions; and as the name of each is called the Sergeant-at-Arms shall present to the delegation of each two ballot boxes, in each of which shall be deposited, by some Representative of the State, one of the duplicates made as aforesaid of the vote of said State, in the presence and subject to the examination of all the Members from said State then present; and where there is more than one Representative from a State, the duplicates shall not both be deposited by the same person.

When the votes of the States are thus all taken in, the Sergeant-at-Arms shall carry one of said ballot boxes to one table and the other to a separate and distinct table.

One person from each State represented in the balloting shall be appointed by the Representatives to tell off said ballots; but, in case the Representatives fail to appoint a teller, the Speaker shall appoint.

The said tellers shall divide themselves into two sets, as nearly equal in number as can be, and one of the said sets of tellers shall proceed to count the votes in one of said boxes, and the other set the votes in the other box.

When the votes are counted by the different sets of tellers, the result shall be reported to the House; and if the reports agree, the same shall be accepted as the true votes of the States; but if the reports disagree, the States shall proceed, in the same manner as before, to a new ballot.

6. All questions arising after the balloting commences, requiring the decision of the House, which shall be decided by the House, voting per capita, to be incidental to the power of choosing a President, shall be decided by States without debate; and in case of an equal division of the votes of States, the question shall be lost.

7. When either of the persons from whom the choice is to be made shall have received a majority of all the States, the Speaker shall declare the same, and that that person is elected President of the United States.

8. The result shall be immediately communicated to the Senate by message, and a committee of three persons shall be appointed to inform the President of the United States and the President-elect of said election.

On February 9, 1825, the election of John Quincy Adams took place in accordance with these rules.

---

1. *Petitions are no longer introduced in this way. This old procedure of calling the states beginning with Maine proceeded through the original thirteen states and then through the remaining states in the order of their admission to the Union.*

by the following morning it became apparent that if the Republicans could hold South Carolina, Florida, and Louisiana, Hayes would be elected with 185 electoral votes to 184 for Tilden. But if a single elector in any of these states voted for Tilden, he would throw the election to the Democrats. Tilden led in the popular-vote count by more than a quarter million votes.

The situation was much the same in each of the three contested states. Historian Eugene H. Roseboom described it as follows:

The Republicans controlled the state governments and the election machinery, had relied upon the Negro masses for votes, and had practiced frauds as in the past. The Democrats used threats, intimidation, and even violence when necessary, to keep Negroes from the polls; and where they were in a position to do so they resorted to fraud also. The firm determination of the whites to overthrow carpetbag rule contributed to make a full and fair vote impossible; carpetbag hold on the state governments made a fair count impossible. Radical reconstruction was reaping its final harvest.

Both parties pursued the votes of the three states with a fine disregard for propriety or legality, and in the end double sets of elector returns were sent to Congress from all three. Oregon also sent two sets of returns. Although Hayes carried that state, the Democratic governor discovered that one of the Hayes electors was a postmaster and therefore ineligible under the Constitution, so he certified the election of the top-polling Democratic elector. However, the Republican electors met, received the resignation of their ineligible colleague, then reappointed him to the vacancy because he had in the meantime resigned his postmastership.

Had the Twenty-second Joint Rule remained in effect, the Democratic House of Representatives could have objected to any of Hayes's disputed votes. But because the rule had lapsed, Congress had to find a new method of resolving electoral disputes. A joint committee was created to work out a plan, and the resulting Electoral Commission Law was approved by large majorities and signed into law January 29, 1877—only days before the date scheduled for counting the electoral votes.

The law, which applied only to the 1876 electoral vote count, established a fifteen-member commission that was to have final authority over disputed electoral votes, unless both houses of Congress agreed to overrule it. The commission was to consist of five senators, five representatives, and five Supreme Court justices. Each chamber was to appoint its own members of the commission, with the understanding that the majority party would have three members and the minority two. Four justices, two from each party, were named in the bill, and these four were to select the fifth. It was expected that they would choose Justice David Davis, who was considered a political independent, but he disqualified himself when the Illinois legislature named him to a seat in the Senate. Justice Joseph P. Bradley, a Republican, then was named to the fifteenth seat. The Democrats supported his selection because they considered him the most independent of the remaining justices, all of whom were Republicans. However, he was to vote with the Republicans on every dispute and thus ensure the victory of Hayes.

The electoral count began in Congress February 1 (moved up from the second Wednesday in February for this one election), and the proceedings continued until March 2. States were called in alphabetical order, and as each disputed state was reached objections were raised to both the Hayes and Tilden electors. The question was then referred to the electoral commission, which in every case voted 8–7 for Hayes. In each case, the Democratic House rejected the commission's decision, but the Republican Senate upheld it, so the decision stood.

As the count went on, Democrats in the House threatened to launch a filibuster to block resumption of joint sessions so that the count could not be completed before Inauguration Day. The threat was never carried out because of an agreement reached between the Hayes forces and southern conservatives. The southerners agreed to let the electoral count continue without obstruction. In return Hayes agreed that, as president, he would withdraw federal troops from the South, end Reconstruction, and make other concessions. The southerners, for their part, pledged to respect African American rights, a pledge they did not carry out.

Consequently, at 4 a.m. March 2, 1877, the president of the Senate was able to announce that Hayes had been elected president with 185 electoral votes, as against 184 for Tilden. Later that day Hayes arrived in Washington. The next evening he took the oath of office privately at the White House, because March 4 fell on a Sunday. His formal inauguration followed on Monday. The country acquiesced. So ended a crisis that could have resulted in renewed civil war.

Not until 1887 did Congress enact permanent legislation on the handling of disputed electoral votes. The Electoral Count Act of that year gave each state final authority in determining the legality of its choice of electors and required a concurrent majority of both the Senate and House to reject any electoral votes. It also established procedures for counting electoral votes in Congress. (*See box, Law for Counting Electoral Votes in Congress, p. 199.*)

Application of the 1887 Law in 1969

The procedures relating to disputed electoral votes were used for the first time after the election of 1968. When Congress met in joint session January 6, 1969, to count the electoral votes, Sen. Edmund S. Muskie of Maine and Rep. James G. O'Hara of Michigan, both Democrats, joined by six other senators and thirty-seven other representatives, filed a written objection to the vote cast by a North Carolina elector, Lloyd W. Bailey of Rocky Mount. He had been elected as a Republican but chose to vote for George Wallace and Curtis LeMay, the candidates of the American Independent Party, instead of Republican Nixon and his running mate, Spiro T. Agnew.

Acting under the 1887 law, Muskie and O'Hara objected to Bailey's vote on the grounds that it was "not properly given" because a plurality of the popular votes in North Carolina were cast for Nixon-Agnew and the state's voters had chosen electors to vote for Nixon and Agnew only. Muskie and O'Hara asked that Bailey's vote not be counted at all by Congress.

The 1887 statute stipulated that "no electoral vote or votes from any State which shall have been regularly given by electors whose appointment has been lawfully certified … from which but one return has been received shall be rejected, but the two Houses concurrently may reject the vote or votes when they agree that such vote or votes have not been so regularly given by electors whose appointment has been so certified." The statute did not define the term "regularly given," although at the time of its adoption the chief concern centered on problems of dual sets of electoral vote returns from a state, votes cast on an improper day, or

Law for Counting Electoral Votes in Congress

Following is the complete text of Title 3, section 15 of the U.S. Code, enacted originally in 1887, governing the counting of electoral votes in Congress:

Congress shall be in session on the sixth day of January succeeding every meeting of the electors. The Senate and House of Representatives shall meet in the Hall of the House of Representatives at the hour of 1 o'clock in the afternoon on that day, and the President of the Senate shall be their presiding officer. Two tellers shall be previously appointed on the part of the Senate and two on the part of the House of Representatives, to whom shall be handed, as they are opened by the President of the Senate, all the certificates and papers purporting to be certificates of the electoral votes, which certificates and papers shall be opened, presented, and acted upon in the alphabetical order of the States, beginning with the letter A; and said tellers, having then read the same in the presence and hearing of the two Houses, shall make a list of the votes as they shall appear from the said certificates; and the votes having been ascertained and counted according to the rules in this subchapter provided, the result of the same shall be delivered to the President of the Senate, who shall thereupon announce the state of the vote, which announcement shall be deemed a sufficient declaration of the persons, if any, elected President and Vice President of the United States, and, together with a list of votes, be entered on the Journals of the two Houses. Upon such reading of any such certificate or paper, the President of the Senate shall call for objections, if any. Every objection shall be made in writing, and shall state clearly and concisely, and without argument, the ground thereof, and shall be signed by at least one Senator and one Member of the House of Representatives before the same shall be received. When all objections so made to any vote or paper from a State shall have been received and read, the Senate shall thereupon withdraw, and such objections shall be submitted to the Senate for its decision; and the Speaker of the House of Representatives shall, in like manner, submit such objections to the House of Representatives for its decision; and no electoral vote or votes from any State which shall have been regularly given by electors whose appointment has been lawfully certified to according to section 6[1] of this title from which but one return has been received shall be rejected, but the two Houses concurrently may reject the vote or votes when they agree that such vote or votes have not been so regularly given by electors whose appointment has been so certified. If more than one return or paper purporting to be a return from a State shall have been received by the President of the Senate, those votes, and those only, shall be counted which shall have been regularly given by the electors who are shown by the determination mentioned in section 5[2] of this title to have been appointed, if the determination in said section provided for shall have been made, or by such successors or substitutes, in case of a vacancy in the board of electors so ascertained, as have been appointed to fill such vacancy in the mode provided by the laws of the State; but in case there shall arise the question which of two or more of such State authorities determining what electors have been appointed, as mentioned in section 5 of this title, is the lawful tribunal of such State, the votes regularly given of those electors, and those only, of such State shall be counted whose title as electors the two Houses, acting separately, shall concurrently decide is supported by the decision of such State so authorized by its law; and in such case of more than one return or paper purporting to be a return from a State, if there shall have been no such determination of the question in the State aforesaid, then those votes, and those only, shall be counted which the two Houses shall concurrently decide were cast by lawful electors appointed in accordance with the laws of the State, unless the two Houses, acting separately, shall concurrently decide such votes not to be the lawful votes of the legally appointed electors of such State. But if the two Houses shall disagree in respect of the counting of such votes, then, and in that case, the votes of the electors whose appointment shall have been certified by the executive of the State, under the seal thereof, shall be counted. When the two Houses have voted, they shall immediately again meet, and the presiding officer shall then announce the decision of the questions submitted. No votes or papers from any other State shall be acted upon until the objections previously made to the votes or papers from any State shall have been finally disposed of.

---

1. Section 6 provides for certification of votes by electors by state governors.

2. Section 5 provides that if state law specifies a method for resolving disputes concerning the vote for presidential electors, Congress must respect any determination so made by a state.

votes disputed because of uncertainty about whether a state lawfully was in the Union when the vote was cast.

The 1887 statute provided that if written objection to any state's vote was received from at least one member of both the Senate and House, the two legislative bodies were to retire immediately to separate sessions, debate for two hours with a five-minute limitation on speeches, and each decide the issue by vote before resuming the joint session. The statute made clear that both the Senate and House had to reject a challenged electoral vote (or votes) for such action to prevail.

At the January 6 joint session, with President Pro Tempore Richard B. Russell, Georgia Democrat, presiding, the counting of the electoral vote proceeded smoothly through the alphabetical order of states until the North Carolina result was announced, at which time O'Hara rose to announce filing of the complaint. The two houses then reassembled in joint session, at which the results of the separate deliberations were announced and the count of the electoral vote by state proceeded without event. At the conclusion, Russell announced the vote and declared Nixon and Agnew elected.

Application of the 1887 Law in 2001

The U.S. Supreme Court's peremptory 5–4 ruling in *Bush v. Gore* that ended the recount of Florida's extremely close presidential vote left many Americans angry and embittered. Vice President Albert "Al" Gore Jr., the Democratic nominee, had bested Republican governor George W. Bush of Texas by more than a half-million votes in the popular election and also led in the electoral vote, pending determination of the Florida winner. African Americans were particularly dissatisfied with the result. They had overwhelmingly supported Gore nationally, and in Florida their votes made up a disproportionately large share of the ballots not counted because of problems with the obsolete punch-card voting system used in many counties. These voters and many others felt that the majority had been disfranchised and that Gore might have won had the Court not stopped the recount.

But the Court's ruling left no recourse through the judicial system. Only one step remained before the 2000 election became official: the formal counting of the 538 electoral votes by both chambers of Congress. When that day came, on January 6, 2001, twenty Democratic House members, mostly members of the Congressional Black Caucus, made a last-ditch effort to deny Florida's twenty-five electoral votes to Bush. With Gore, as the outgoing vice president, presiding over the session, each House member submitted a written objection to the counting of Florida's votes. Gore asked each representative if the objection were also signed by a senator, as the 1887 law required. When each responded no, Gore ruled the objection out of order. At one point he thanked Rep. Jesse L. Jackson Jr. of Illinois for his remarks and said, "But, hey," and spread his arms in a gesture of futility.

It was the first time since the 1969 faithless elector incident that there had been any objections to the counting of electoral votes. In the 2001 counting there was one abstention, by a District of Columbia elector for Gore, resulting in a total of 537 electoral votes being cast.

Application of the 1887 Law in 2005

The partisan bitterness that characterized the 2000 presidential election remained virulent in 2004. Many states had changed their voting systems in the preceding four years, but the changes did not always build confidence that every vote would be counted. There were widespread complaints about the new electronic systems, most of which left no "paper trail" of ballot receipts that could be counted in case of a disputed outcome. Breakdowns of the computerized machines and unfamiliarity with their operation led to unusually long waits for voters. Some gave up and left without voting. Some who voted feared that their vote had not been recorded. In Ohio and other states, those who felt disfranchised were disproportionately minority voters. President George W. Bush carried Ohio by 118,000 votes.

On December 30, 2004, Democratic representative John Conyers of Michigan wrote to all senators asking for their support in challenging Ohio's twenty electoral votes because of "numerous unexplained irregularities" in the state's presidential vote. In contrast to 2001, when no senator provided the necessary signature for a challenge to Florida's vote, Democratic senator Barbara Boxer of

California signed the House petition for a debate on Ohio's vote. On January 6, 2005, when Congress met in joint session to count the electoral votes, presiding officer Vice President Richard B. Cheney, in accordance with the 1887 law, directed the House and Senate to their respective chambers for a two-hour debate on the Ohio vote question. In the House, several white members joined Conyers and other African Americans, including Democrat Stephanie Tubbs Jones of Ohio, in objecting to the Ohio votes. The vote in the House was 267–31 against Tubbs Jones's objection. The Senate voted 74–1 against Boxer's position.

In the electoral college, Democratic presidential nominee John F. Kerry was denied one of Minnesota's ten electoral votes when an elector voted for Kerry's running mate, John Edwards, for president. Because the voting was secret, the name of the defector was never identified. Kerry was to have received 252 electoral votes, including all ten of Minnesota's votes, but the defection reduced Kerry's total to 251. The unknown defector, however, also voted for Edwards for vice president, making his national total 252 votes.

REFORM PROPOSALS

Since January 6, 1797, when Rep. William L. Smith, a South Carolina Federalist, introduced in Congress the first proposed constitutional amendment for reform of the electoral college system, hardly a session of Congress has passed without the introduction of one or more resolutions of this nature. In all, more than seven hundred such proposals have been submitted. But only one—the Twelfth Amendment, ratified in 1804—ever has been approved.

In recent years, public interest in a change in the electoral college system was spurred by the close 1960, 1968, and 2000 elections, by a series of Supreme Court rulings relating to apportionment and redistricting, and by the introduction of unpledged elector systems in the southern states.

House Approval of Amendment

Early in 1969 President Nixon asked Congress to take prompt action on electoral college reform. He said he would support any plan that would eliminate individual electors and distribute among the presidential candidates the electoral vote of every state and the District of Columbia in a manner more closely approximating the popular vote.

Later that year the House approved, 338–70, a resolution proposing a constitutional amendment to eliminate the electoral college and to provide instead for direct popular election of the president and vice president. The measure set a minimum of 40 percent of the popular vote as sufficient for election and provided for a runoff election between the two top candidates for the presidency if no candidate received 40 percent. Under this plan the House of Representatives would no longer be called on to select a president.

The proposed amendment also authorized Congress to provide a method of filling vacancies caused by the death, resignation, or disability of presidential nominees before the election and a method of filling postelection vacancies caused by the death of the president-elect or vice president-elect.

Nixon, who previously had favored a proportional plan of allocating each state's electoral votes, endorsed the House resolution and urged the Senate to adopt it. To become effective, the proposed amendment had to be approved by a two-thirds majority in both the Senate and House and be ratified by the legislatures of three-fourths of the states. When the proposal reached the Senate floor in September 1970, senators from small states and the South succeeded in blocking final action. The resolution was laid aside October 5, after two unsuccessful efforts to cut off debate by invoking cloture.

Carter Endorsement of Plan

Another major effort to eliminate the electoral college occurred in 1977, when President Jimmy Carter included such a proposal in his election reform package, unveiled March 22. Carter endorsed the amendment approved by the House in 1969 to replace the electoral college with direct popular election of the president and vice president, and provide for a runoff if no candidate received at least 40 percent of the vote. Because the Senate again was seen as the major stumbling block, the House waited to see what the Senate would do before beginning any deliberation of its own.

After several months of deadlock, the Senate Judiciary Committee approved September 15 the direct presidential election plan by a 9–8 vote. But Senate opponents threatened a filibuster, and the Senate leadership decided it could not spare the time or effort to try to break it. The measure was never brought to the floor and died when the Ninety-fifth Congress adjourned in 1978.

On January 15, 1979, the opening day of the Ninety-sixth Congress, Sen. Birch Bayh, Indiana Democrat, began another effort to abolish the electoral college through a constitutional amendment. In putting off action in the previous Congress, Senate leaders had agreed to try for early action in the Ninety-sixth.

A proposed constitutional amendment to abolish the electoral college and elect the president by popular vote did reach the Senate floor in July 1979. The Senate voted in favor of the measure, 51 to 48, fifteen votes short of the required two-thirds majority of those present and voting needed to approve a constitutional amendment.

Supporters of the resolution blamed defections by several northern liberals for the margin of defeat. Major Jewish and black groups extensively lobbied the northern senators, arguing that the voting strength of black and Jewish voters is maximized under the electoral college system because both groups are concentrated in urban areas of the large electoral vote states.

Alternative Plans

Besides direct election of the president and vice president, two other major proposals to replace the electoral college have gained considerable support. One is the district plan, similar to the Maine and Nebraska systems, that would award an electoral vote to the candidate who carried a congressional district and two to the candidate who carried the state as a whole. The other is the proportional plan that would distribute a state's electoral votes on the basis of the proportion of the vote each candidate received.

Had any of the three plans been in effect since 1960, the outcome of several close elections would have been different, according to Stephen J. Wayne, professor of American Government at Georgetown University. In his book *The Road to the White House, 2000,* Wayne calculates that the district plan would have elected Richard Nixon in 1960 over John F. Kennedy, and that in 1976 it would have resulted in an electoral college tie between Gerald R. Ford and Jimmy Carter. The proportional plan would have thrown the 1960, 1968, 1992, and 1996 elections to the House of Representatives, because none of the candidates would have received an electoral vote majority.

Wayne advocated direct election, which he said would require a national system of voting and tabulating of the results. The United States had neither at the beginning of the twenty-first century. Of the eleven presidential elections since 1960, only the 2000 election would have had a different result under direct election. As the popular vote winner, Gore would have been elected over George W. Bush. Although the 1960 popular vote was even closer, Kennedy won both the popular and electoral college votes.

As in the 1969 plan, most of the direct election proposals call for a minimum plurality, usually 40 percent, with a runoff election to be held if no candidate receives the minimum percentage.

PRESIDENTIAL DISABILITY

A decade of congressional concern over the question of presidential disability was eased in 1967 by ratification of the Twenty-fifth Amendment to the Constitution. The amendment for the first time provided for continuity in carrying out the functions of the presidency in the event of presidential disability and for filling a vacancy in the vice presidency. The amendment was approved by the Senate and House in 1965 and took effect February 10, 1967, after ratification by thirty-eight states. Congressional consideration of the problem of presidential disability had been prompted by

President Ford and Vice President Rockefeller confer in the Oval Office in 1974. For the first time in American history, the two highest executive positions were held by men appointed, not elected, to their posts.

President Dwight D. Eisenhower's heart attack in 1955. The ambiguity of the language of the disability clause (Article II, Section 1, Clause 5) of the Constitution had provoked occasional debate ever since the Constitutional Convention of 1787. But it never had been decided how far the term *disability* extended or who would be the judge of it.

Clause 5 provided that Congress should decide who was to succeed to the presidency if both the president and the vice president died, resigned, or became disabled. Congress enacted succession laws three times. By the Act of March 1, 1792, it provided for succession (after the vice president) of the president pro tempore of the Senate, then of the House Speaker; if those offices were vacant, states were to send electors to Washington to choose a new president.

That law stood until passage of the Presidential Succession Act of January 19, 1886, which changed the line of succession to run from the vice president to the secretary of state, secretary of the Treasury, and so on through the cabinet in order of rank. Sixty-one years later the Presidential Succession Act of July 18, 1947 (still in force), placed the Speaker of the House and the president pro tempore of the Senate ahead of cabinet officers in succession after the vice president.

Before ratification of the Twenty-fifth Amendment, no procedures had been laid down to govern situations arising in the event of presidential incapacity or of a vacancy in the office of vice president. Two presidents had had serious disabilities: James A. Garfield was shot in 1881 and confined to his bed until he died two and a half months later, and Woodrow Wilson suffered a stroke in 1919. In each case the vice president did not assume any duties of the presidency for fear he would appear to be usurping the powers of that office.

Ratification of the Twenty-fifth Amendment established procedures that clarified these areas of uncertainty in the Constitution. The amendment provided that the vice president should become acting president under either one of two circumstances: (1) if the president informed Congress of inability to perform duties, the vice president would become acting president until the president could resume normal responsibilities; (2) if the vice president and a majority of the cabinet, or another body designated by Congress, found the president to be incapacitated, the vice president would become acting president until the president informed Congress that the disability had ended. Congress was given twenty-one days to resolve any dispute over the president's disability; a two-thirds vote of both chambers was required to overrule the president's declaration of being no longer incapacitated.

Vacancy in the Vice Presidency

The Twenty-fifth Amendment also specified what to do when a vacancy occurred in the office of the vice president, by death, succession to the presidency, or resignation. Through July 2005 the United States has been without a vice president eighteen times for a total of forty years, but since the amendment went into effect such vacancies have been brief. Under the amendment, the president nominates a replacement vice president, with the nomination subject to confirmation by a majority vote of both chambers of Congress. Within only eight years after ratification, two presidents used the power to appoint a new vice president.

In October 1973 when Vice President Agnew resigned, President Nixon nominated Gerald R. Ford as the new vice president. Ford was confirmed by both houses of Congress and sworn in December 6, 1973. On Nixon's resignation August 9, 1974, Ford succeeded to the presidency, becoming the first president in American history who was elected neither to the presidency nor to the vice presidency. President Ford chose as his new vice president Nelson A. Rockefeller, former governor of New York, who was sworn in December 19, 1974.

With both the president and vice president holding office through appointment rather than election, members of Congress and the public expressed concern about the power of a president to appoint, in effect, his or her own successor. Accordingly, Sen. John O. Pastore, Rhode Island Democrat, introduced a proposed constitutional amendment February 3, 1975, to provide for a special national election for president when more than one year remained in a presidential term. Hearings were held before the Senate Judiciary Subcommittee on Constitutional Amendments, but no action was taken.

Invoking the Twenty-Fifth Amendment

In the aftermath of the attempted assassination of President Ronald Reagan in March 1981, there was no need to invoke the presidential disability provisions of the Twenty-fifth Amendment. However, some of the public statements made by administration officials immediately after the president was shot by John W. Hinckley Jr. reflected continuing confusion over the issue of who is in charge when the president temporarily is unable to function. Soon after news of the shooting became known, the members of the Reagan cabinet gathered in the White House, ready to invoke the amendment's procedures, if necessary. Vice President George H.W. Bush was on an Air Force jet returning to Washington from Texas.

At a televised press briefing later that afternoon, Secretary of State Alexander M. Haig Jr. confirmed that Reagan was in surgery and under anesthesia. It was clear that he temporarily was unable to make presidential decisions should the occasion—such as a foreign attack or other national emergency—require them. Attempting to reassure the country, Haig stated that he was in control in the White House pending the return of Vice President Bush, with whom he was in contact.

This assertion was followed by a question from the press about who was making administration decisions. Haig responded, "Constitutionally, gentlemen, you have the president, the vice president, and the secretary of state in that order, and should the president decide he wants to transfer the helm to the vice president, he will do so. He has not done that. As of now, I am in control here, in the White House, pending the return of the vice president and in close touch with him. If something came up, I would check with him, of course." Actually, the Constitution is silent on the order of succession beyond the vice president. Haig was referring to succession under laws superseded by the 1947 act, which specifies that the line of succession is the vice president, the Speaker of the House, the president pro tempore of the Senate, and then the cabinet officials in order of rank.

Criticism of the administration's failure to act after Reagan was shot shaped its response to the second instance of presidential disability, Reagan's cancer surgery on July 13, 1985. This time Reagan did relinquish his powers and duties to Vice President George H. W. Bush before undergoing anesthesia. Curiously, however, he did not explicitly invoke the Twenty-fifth Amendment, saying instead that he was not convinced that the amendment was meant to apply to "such brief and temporary periods of incapacity." Still, a precedent was established that the Twenty-fifth Amendment would work as intended in future administrations. This precedent was followed in May 1991 when President George H. W. Bush said he would turn power over to Vice President Dan Quayle if his irregular heartbeat required electroshock therapy. It did not.

George W. Bush invoked the amendment when he underwent a colonoscopy that required anesthesia on June 29, 2002. In a letter citing his upcoming procedure, he temporarily transferred his powers to Vice President Richard B. Cheney: "In view of present circumstances, I have determined to transfer temporarily my Constitutional powers and duties to the Vice President during the brief period of the procedure and recovery." Two hours after the procedure, he transmitted a second letter announcing the resumption of the powers and duties of his office: "In accordance with the provisions of Section 3 of the Twenty-Fifth Amendment to the United States Constitution, this letter shall constitute my written declaration that I am presently able to resume the discharge of the Constitutional powers and duties of the office of President of the United States."

chapter 6

Electoral Votes for President, 1789–2008

E LECTORAL MAPS and vote charts for all presidential elections from 1789 to 2008 are presented in this chapter. The sources for electoral votes cast for presidential candidates are the *Senate Manual* (Washington, D.C., U.S. Government Printing Office, 1997) and *CQ Weekly Report.*

Article II, Section 1 of the Constitution gives each state a number of electors equal to the number of senators and representatives to which it is entitled. Total electoral votes for each state through the 2000 election were compiled from a chart of each apportionment of the House of Representatives, published in Kenneth C. Martis and Gregory A. Elmes, *The Historical Atlas of State Power in Congress, 1790–1990* (Washington, D.C., CQ Press, 1993), pp. 6–7.

Under the Constitution (Article II, Section 1) each presidential elector was originally given two votes and was required to cast each vote for a different person. The person receiving the highest number of votes from a majority of electors was elected president; the person receiving the second highest total became vice president. For the first presidential election in 1789, there were sixty-nine electors, and George Washington's sixty-nine votes constituted a unanimous election. After ratification of the Twelfth Amendment in 1804, electors were required to designate which of their two votes was for president and which was for vice president. The electoral college charts on pages 206–209 show *all* electoral votes cast in the elections of 1789, 1792, 1796, and 1800; the charts for 1804 and thereafter show electoral votes cast only for president.

For electoral votes cast for vice–presidential candidates, see pages 262–263 at the end of this chapter.

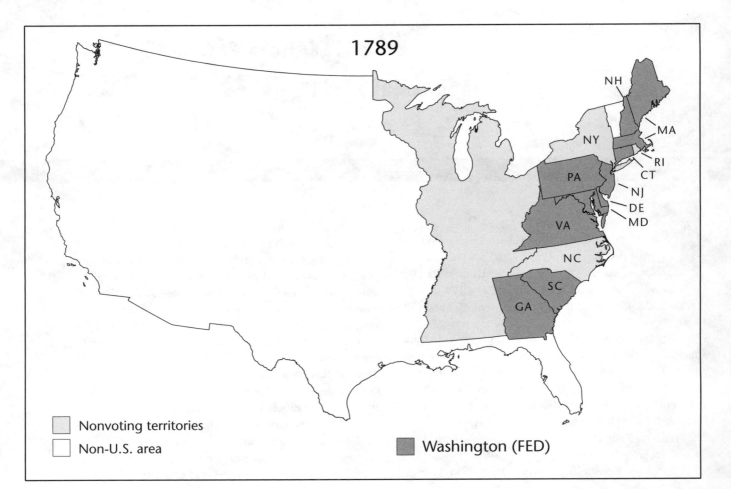

Key: FED—Federalist

States	Electoral votes[1]	Washington	Adams	Jay	Harrison	Rutledge	Hancock	Clinton	Huntington	Milton	Armstrong	Lincoln	Telfair
Connecticut[2]	(14)	7	5	—	—	—	—	—	2	—	—	—	—
Delaware	(6)	3	—	3	—	—	—	—	—	—	—	—	—
Georgia[2]	(10)	5	—	—	—	—	—	—	—	2	1	1	1
Maryland[3]	(16)	6	—	—	6	—	—	—	—	—	—	—	—
Massachusetts	(20)	10	10	—	—	—	—	—	—	—	—	—	—
New Hampshire	(10)	5	5	—	—	—	—	—	—	—	—	—	—
New Jersey[2]	(12)	6	1	5	—	—	—	—	—	—	—	—	—
New York[4]	(16)	—	—	—	—	—	—	—	—	—	—	—	—
North Carolina[5]	(14)	—	—	—	—	—	—	—	—	—	—	—	—
Pennsylvania[2]	(20)	10	8	—	—	—	2	—	—	—	—	—	—
Rhode Island[5]	(6)	—	—	—	—	—	—	—	—	—	—	—	—
South Carolina[2]	(14)	7	—	—	—	6	1	—	—	—	—	—	—
Virginia[6]	(24)	10	5	1	—	—	1	3	—	—	—	—	—
Totals	(182)	69	34	9	6	6	4	3	2	2	1	1	1

1. Two votes for each elector; see explanation, p. 205.

2. For explanation of split electoral votes, see p. 188.

3. Two Maryland electors did not vote.

4. Not voting. Because of a dispute between its two chambers, the New York legislature failed to choose electors.

5. Not voting because had not yet ratified the Constitution.

6. Two Virginia electors did not vote. For explanation of split electoral votes, see p. 188.

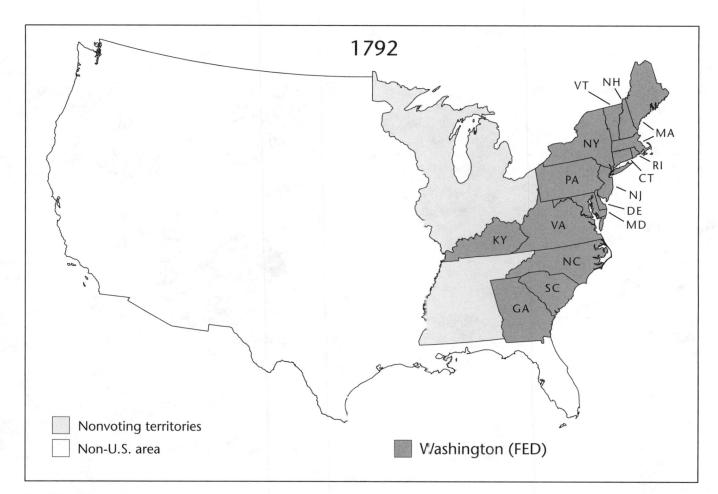

1792

Nonvoting territories

Non-U.S. area

Washington (FED)

Key: FED—Federalist

States	Electoral votes[1]	Washington	Adams	Clinton	Jefferson	Burr
Connecticut	(18)	9	9	—	—	—
Delaware	(6)	3	3	—	—	—
Georgia	(8)	4	—	4	—	—
Kentucky	(8)	4	—	—	4	—
Maryland[2]	(20)	8	8	—	—	—
Massachusetts	(32)	16	16	—	—	—
New Hampshire	(12)	6	6	—	—	—
New Jersey	(14)	7	7	—	—	—
New York	(24)	12	—	12	—	—
North Carolina	(24)	12	—	12	—	—
Pennsylvania[3]	(30)	15	14	1	—	—
Rhode Island	(8)	4	4	—	—	—
South Carolina[3]	(16)	8	7	—	—	1
Vermont[2]	(8)	3	3	—	—	—
Virginia	(42)	21	—	21	—	—
Totals	(270)	132	77	50	4	1

1. Two votes for each elector; see explanation, p. 205.

2. Two Maryland electors and one Vermont elector did not vote.

3. For explanation of split electoral votes, see p. 188.

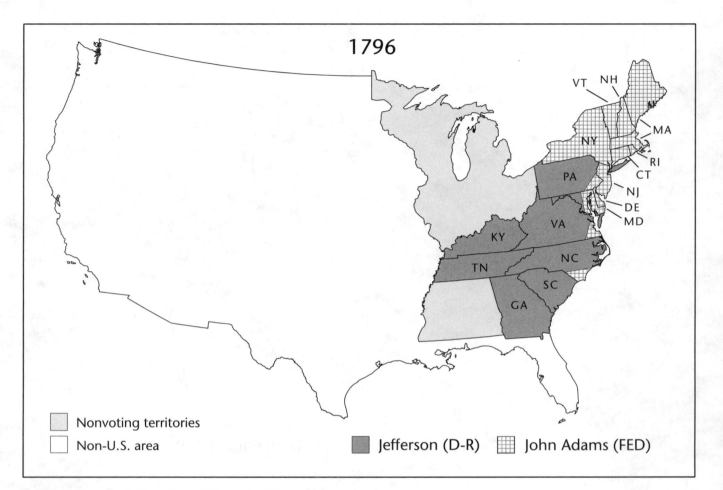

1796

Nonvoting territories
Non-U.S. area
Jefferson (D-R)   John Adams (FED)

Key: D-R—Democratic-Republican; FED—Federalist

States	Electoral votes[1]	J. Adams	Jefferson	T. Pinckney	Burr	S. Adams	Ellsworth	Clinton	Jay	Iredell	Henry	Johnston	Washington	C. Pinckney
Connecticut[2]	(18)	9	—	4	—	—	—	—	5	—	—	—	—	—
Delaware	(6)	3	—	3	—	—	—	—	—	—	—	—	—	—
Georgia	(8)	—	4	—	—	—	—	4	—	—	—	—	—	—
Kentucky	(8)	—	4	—	4	—	—	—	—	—	—	—	—	—
Maryland[2]	(20)	7	4	4	3	—	—	—	—	—	2	—	—	—
Massachusetts[2]	(32)	16	—	13	—	—	1	—	—	—	—	2	—	—
New Hampshire	(12)	6	—	—	—	—	6	—	—	—	—	—	—	—
New Jersey	(14)	7	—	7	—	—	—	—	—	—	—	—	—	—
New York	(24)	12	—	12	—	—	—	—	—	—	—	—	—	—
North Carolina[2]	(24)	1	11	1	6	—	—	—	—	3	—	—	1	1
Pennsylvania[2]	(30)	1	14	2	13	—	—	—	—	—	—	—	—	—
Rhode Island	(8)	4	—	—	—	—	4	—	—	—	—	—	—	—
South Carolina	(16)	—	8	8	—	—	—	—	—	—	—	—	—	—
Tennessee	(6)	—	3	—	3	—	—	—	—	—	—	—	—	—
Vermont	(8)	4	—	4	—	—	—	—	—	—	—	—	—	—
Virginia[2]	(42)	1	20	1	1	15	—	3	—	—	—	—	1	—
Totals	(276)	71	68	59	30	15	11	7	5	3	2	2	2	1

1. Two votes for each elector; see explanation, p. 205.

2. For explanation of split electoral votes, see p. 188.

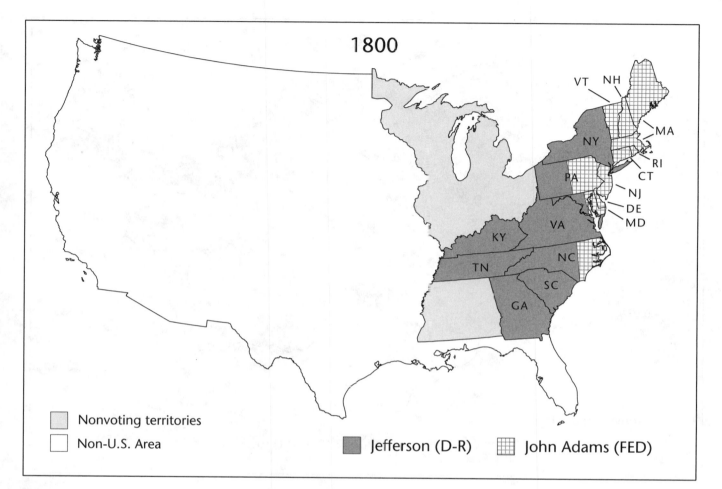

1800

Nonvoting territories

Non-U.S. Area

◼ Jefferson (D-R)   ▦ John Adams (FED)

Key: D-R—Democratic-Republican; FED—Federalist

States	Electoral Votes[1]	Jefferson[2]	Burr[2]	Adams	Pinckney	Jay	States	Electoral votes[1]	Jefferson[2]	Burr[2]	Adams	Pinckney	Jay
Connecticut	(18)	—	—	9	9	—	North Carolina[3]	(24)	8	8	4	4	—
Delaware	(6)	—	—	3	3	—	Pennsylvania[3]	(30)	8	8	7	7	—
Georgia	(8)	4	4	—	—	—	Rhode Island[3]	(8)	—	—	4	3	1
Kentucky	(8)	4	4	—	—	—	South Carolina	(16)	8	8	—	—	—
Maryland[3]	(20)	5	5	5	5	—	Tennessee	(6)	3	3	—	—	—
Massachusetts	(32)	—	—	16	16	—	Vermont	(8)	—	—	4	4	—
New Hampshire	(12)	—	—	6	6	—	Virginia	(42)	21	21	—	—	—
New Jersey	(14)	—	—	7	7	—							
New York	(24)	12	12	—	—	—	Totals	(276)	73	73	65	64	1

1. Two votes for each elector; see explanation, p. 205.

2. Since Jefferson and Burr tied in the electoral college, the election was decided (in Jefferson's favor) by the House of Representatives. See "Jefferson's Revenge: 1800," p. 20.

3. For explanation of split electoral votes, see p. 188.

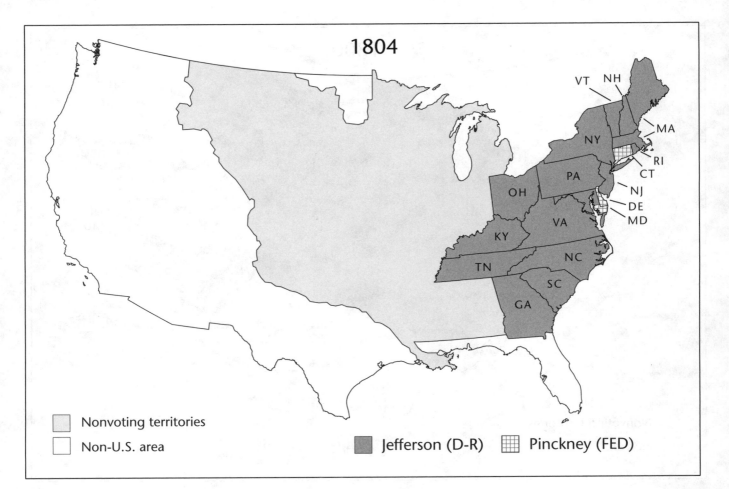

1804

Nonvoting territories

Non-U.S. area

Jefferson (D-R) Pinckney (FED)

Key: D-R—Democratic-Republican; FED—Federalist

States	Electoral votes	Jefferson	Pinckney	States	Electoral votes	Jefferson	Pinckney
Connecticut	(9)	—	9	Ohio	(3)	3	—
Delaware	(3)	—	3	Pennsylvania	(20)	20	—
Georgia	(6)	6	—	Rhode Island	(4)	4	—
Kentucky	(8)	8	—	South Carolina	(10)	10	—
Maryland[1]	(11)	9	2	Tennessee	(5)	5	—
Massachusetts	(19)	19	—	Vermont	(6)	6	—
New Hampshire	(7)	7	—	Virginia	(24)	24	—
New Jersey	(8)	8	—				
New York	(19)	19	—	Totals	(176)	162	14
North Carolina	(14)	14	—				

1. For explanation of split electoral votes, see p. 188.

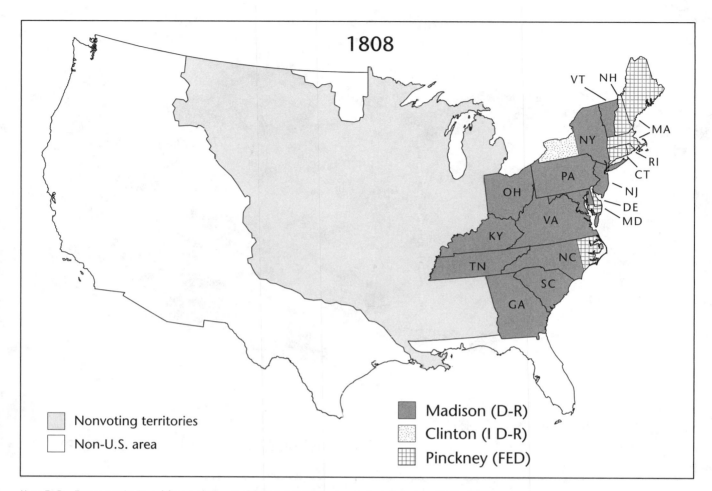

1808

Nonvoting territories

Non-U.S. area

Madison (D-R)

Clinton (I D-R)

Pinckney (FED)

Key: D-R—Democratic-Republican; FED—Federalist; I D-R—Independent Democratic-Republican

States	Electoral votes	Madison	Pinckney	Clinton	States	Electoral votes	Madison	Pinckney	Clinton
Connecticut	(9)	—	9	—	Ohio	(3)	3	—	—
Delaware	(3)	—	3	—	Pennsylvania	(20)	20	—	—
Georgia	(6)	6	—	—	Rhode Island	(4)	—	4	—
Kentucky[1]	(8)	7	—	—	South Carolina	(10)	10	—	—
Maryland[2]	(11)	9	2	—	Tennessee	(5)	5	—	—
Massachusetts	(19)	—	19	—	Vermont	(6)	6	—	—
New Hampshire	(7)	—	7	—	Virginia	(24)	24	—	—
New Jersey	(8)	8	—	—					
New York[2]	(19)	13	—	6	Totals	(176)	122	47	6
North Carolina[2]	(14)	11	3	—					

1. One Kentucky elector did not vote.

2. For explanation of split electoral votes, see p. 183.

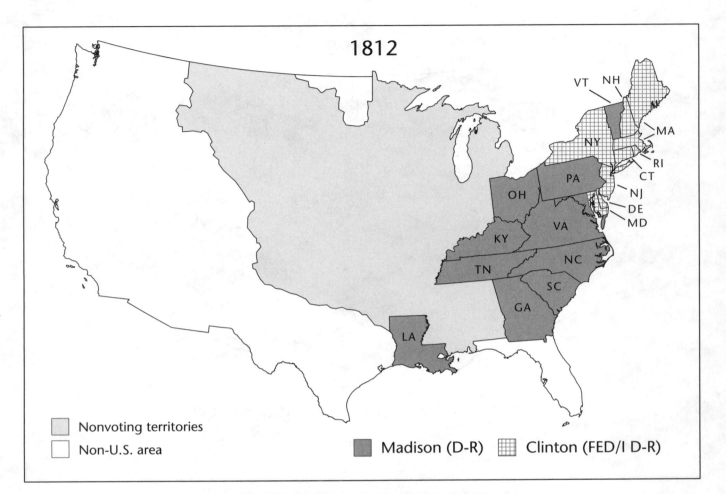

1812

Nonvoting territories

Non-U.S. area

Madison (D-R)   Clinton (FED/I D-R)

Key: D-R—Democratic-Republican; FED/I D-R—Federalist/Independent Democratic-Republican

States	Electoral votes	Madison	Clinton	States	Electoral votes	Madison	Clinton
Connecticut	(9)	—	9	North Carolina	(15)	15	—
Delaware	(4)	—	4	Ohio[2]	(8)	7	—
Georgia	(8)	8	—	Pennsylvania	(25)	25	—
Kentucky	(12)	12	—	Rhode Island	(4)	—	4
Louisiana	(3)	3	—	South Carolina	(11)	11	—
Maryland[1]	(11)	6	5	Tennessee	(8)	8	—
Massachusetts	(22)	—	22	Vermont	(8)	8	—
New Hampshire	(8)	—	8	Virginia	(25)	25	—
New Jersey	(8)	—	8				
New York	(29)	—	29	Totals	(218)	128	89

1. For explanation of split electoral votes, see p. 188.

2. One Ohio elector did not vote.

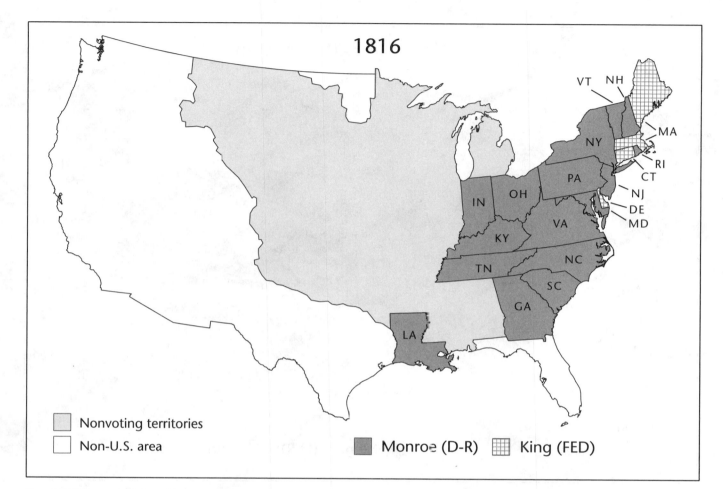

1816

Nonvoting territories

Non-U.S. area

Monroe (D-R)   King (FED)

Key: D-R—Democratic-Republican; FED—Federalist

States	Electoral votes	Monroe	King	States	Electoral votes	Monroe	King
Connecticut	(9)	—	9	North Carolina	(15)	15	—
Delaware[1]	(4)	—	3	Ohio	(8)	8	—
Georgia	(8)	8	—	Pennsylvania	(25)	25	—
Indiana	(3)	3	—	Rhode Island	(4)	4	—
Kentucky	(12)	12	—	South Carolina	(11)	11	—
Louisiana	(3)	3	—	Tennessee	(8)	8	—
Maryland[1]	(11)	8	—	Vermont	(8)	8	—
Massachusetts	(22)	—	22	Virginia	(25)	25	—
New Hampshire	(8)	8	—				
New Jersey	(8)	8	—	Totals	(221)	183	34
New York	(29)	29	—				

1. One Delaware and three Maryland electors did not vote.

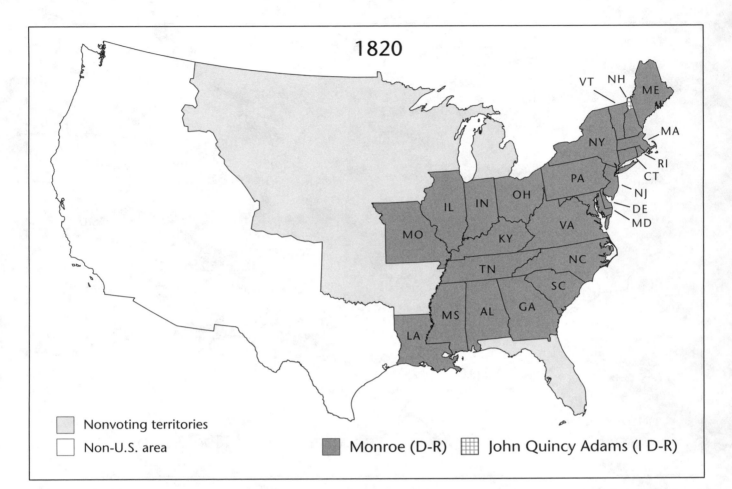

Key: D-R—Democratic-Republican; I D-R—Independent Democratic-Republican

States	Electoral votes	Monroe	Adams	States	Electoral votes	Monroe	Adams
Alabama	(3)	3	—	New Hampshire[2]	(8)	7	1
Connecticut	(9)	9	—	New Jersey	(8)	8	—
Delaware	(4)	4	—	New York	(29)	29	—
Georgia	(8)	8	—	North Carolina	(15)	15	—
Illinois	(3)	3	—	Ohio	(8)	8	—
Indiana	(3)	3	—	Pennsylvania[1]	(25)	24	—
Kentucky	(12)	12	—	Rhode Island	(4)	4	—
Louisiana	(3)	3	—	South Carolina	(11)	11	—
Maine	(9)	9	—	Tennessee[1]	(8)	7	—
Maryland	(11)	11	—	Vermont	(8)	8	—
Massachusetts	(15)	15	—	Virginia	(25)	25	—
Mississippi[1]	(3)	2	—				
Missouri	(3)	3	—	Totals	(235)	231	1

1. One elector each from Mississippi, Pennsylvania, and Tennessee did not vote.

2. For explanation of split electoral votes, see p. 188.

1824

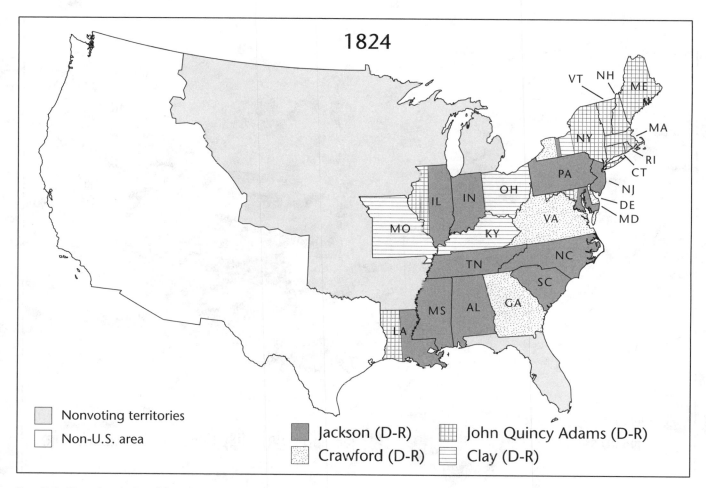

Nonvoting territories

Non-U.S. area

Jackson (D-R)   John Quincy Adams (D-R)

Crawford (D-R)   Clay (D-R)

Key: D-R—Democratic-Republican

States	Electoral votes	Jackson	Adams	Crawford	Clay	States	Electoral votes	Jackson	Adams	Crawford	Clay
Alabama	(5)	5	—	—	—	New Hampshire	(8)	—	8	—	—
Connecticut	(8)	—	8	—	—	New Jersey	(8)	8	—	—	—
Delaware[1]	(3)	—	1	2	—	New York[1]	(36)	1	26	5	4
Georgia	(9)	—	—	9	—	North Carolina	(15)	15	—	—	—
Illinois[1]	(3)	2	1	—	—	Ohio	(16)	—	—	—	16
Indiana	(5)	5	—	—	—	Pennsylvania	(28)	28	—	—	—
Kentucky	(14)	—	—	—	14	Rhode Island	(4)	—	4	—	—
Louisiana[1]	(5)	3	2	—	—	South Carolina	(11)	11	—	—	—
Maine	(9)	—	9	—	—	Tennessee	(11)	11	—	—	—
Maryland[1]	(11)	7	3	1	—	Vermont	(7)	—	7	—	—
Massachusetts	(15)	—	15	—	—	Virginia	(24)	—	—	24	—
Mississippi	(3)	3	—	—	—						
Missouri	(3)	—	—	—	3	Totals	(261)	99[2]	84	41	37

1. For explanation of split electoral votes, see p. 188.

2. As no candidate received a majority of the electoral votes, the election was decided (in Adams's favor) by the House of Representatives.

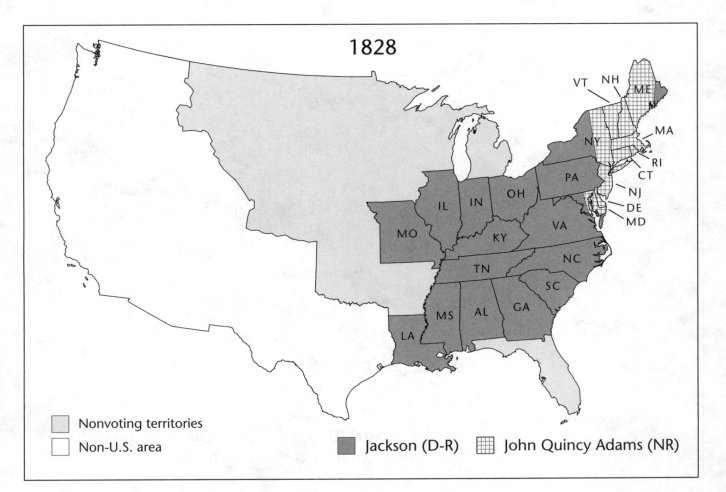

1828

Key: D-R—Democratic-Republican; NR—National Republican

States	Electoral votes	Jackson	Adams	States	Electoral votes	Jackson	Adams
Alabama	(5)	5	—	New Hampshire	(8)	—	8
Connecticut	(8)	—	8	New Jersey	(8)	—	8
Delaware	(3)	—	3	New York[1]	(36)	20	16
Georgia	(9)	9	—	North Carolina	(15)	15	—
Illinois	(3)	3	—	Ohio	(16)	16	—
Indiana	(5)	5	—	Pennsylvania	(28)	28	—
Kentucky	(14)	14	—	Rhode Island	(4)	—	4
Louisiana	(5)	5	—	South Carolina	(11)	11	—
Maine[1]	(9)	1	8	Tennessee	(11)	11	—
Maryland[1]	(11)	5	6	Vermont	(7)	—	7
Massachusetts	(15)	—	15	Virginia	(24)	24	—
Mississippi	(3)	3	—				
Missouri	(3)	3	—	Totals	(261)	178	83

1. For explanation of split electoral votes, see p. 188.

1832

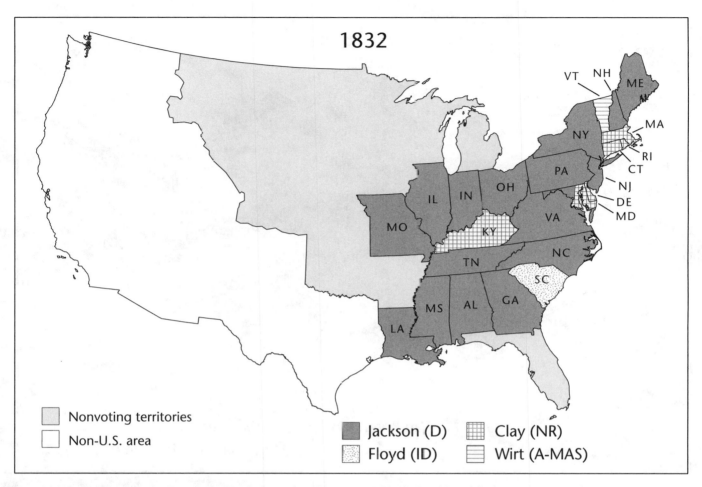

Nonvoting territories

Non-U.S. area

Jackson (D)   Clay (NR)

Floyd (ID)   Wirt (A-MAS)

Key: A-MAS—Anti-Mason; D—Democrat; ID—Independent Democrat; NR—National Republican

States	Electoral votes	Jackson	Clay	Floyd	Wirt	States	Electoral votes	Jackson	Clay	Floyd	Wirt
Alabama	(7)	7	—	—	—	New Hampshire	(7)	7	—	—	—
Connecticut	(8)	—	8	—	—	New Jersey	(8)	8	—	—	—
Delaware	(3)	—	3	—	—	New York	(42)	42	—	—	—
Georgia	(11)	11	—	—	—	North Carolina	(15)	15	—	—	—
Illinois	(5)	5	—	—	—	Ohio	(21)	21	—	—	—
Indiana	(9)	9	—	—	—	Pennsylvania	(30)	30	—	—	—
Kentucky	(15)	—	15	—	—	Rhode Island	(4)	—	4	—	—
Louisiana	(5)	5	—	—	—	South Carolina	(11)	—	—	11	—
Maine	(10)	10	—	—	—	Tennessee	(15)	15	—	—	—
Maryland[1]	(10)	3	5	—	—	Vermont	(7)	—	—	—	7
Massachusetts	(14)	—	14	—	—	Virginia	(23)	23	—	—	—
Mississippi	(4)	4	—	—	—						
Missouri	(4)	4	—	—	—	Totals	(288)	219	49	11	7

1. Two Maryland electors did not vote. For explanation of split electoral votes, see p. 188.

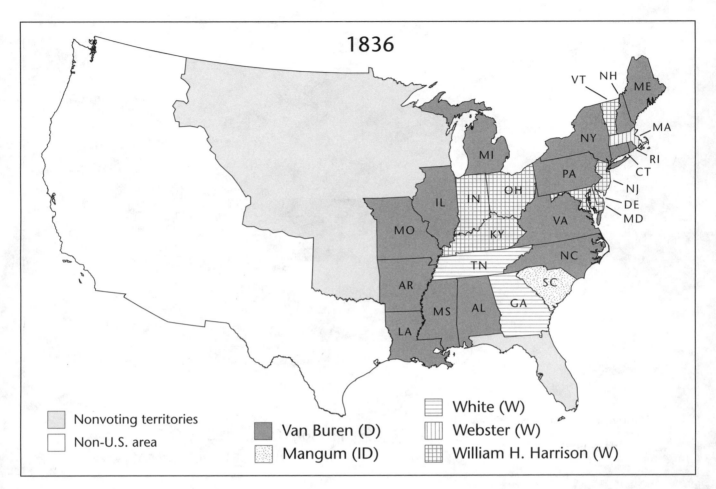

1836

Key: D—Democrat; ID—Independent Democrat; W—Whig

States	Electoral votes	Van Buren	Harrison[1]	White[1]	Webster[1]	Mangum
Alabama	(7)	7	—	—	—	—
Arkansas	(3)	3	—	—	—	—
Connecticut	(8)	8	—	—	—	—
Delaware	(3)	—	3	—	—	—
Georgia	(11)	—	—	11	—	—
Illinois	(5)	5	—	—	—	—
Indiana	(9)	—	9	—	—	—
Kentucky	(15)	—	15	—	—	—
Louisiana	(5)	5	—	—	—	—
Maine	(10)	10	—	—	—	—
Maryland	(10)	—	10	—	—	—
Massachusetts	(14)	—	—	—	14	—
Michigan	(3)	3	—	—	—	—
Mississippi	(4)	4	—	—	—	—
Missouri	(4)	4	—	—	—	—
New Hampshire	(7)	7	—	—	—	—
New Jersey	(8)	—	8	—	—	—
New York	(42)	42	—	—	—	—
North Carolina	(15)	15	—	—	—	—
Ohio	(21)	—	21	—	—	—
Pennsylvania	(30)	30	—	—	—	—
Rhode Island	(4)	4	—	—	—	—
South Carolina	(11)	—	—	—	—	11
Tennessee	(15)	—	—	15	—	—
Vermont	(7)	—	7	—	—	—
Virginia	(23)	23	—	—	—	—
Totals	(294)	170	73	26	14	11

1. For an explanation of the Whigs' strategy in running several candidates, see "Van Buren's Win: 1836," p. 28.

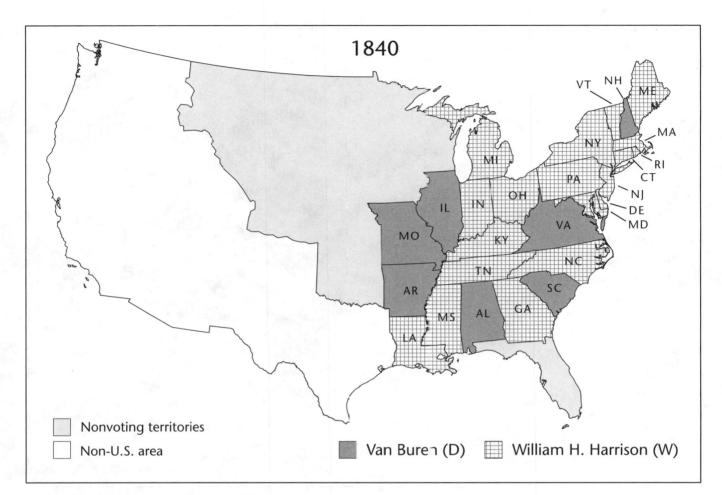

1840

Nonvoting territories

Non-U.S. area

Van Buren (D)   William H. Harrison (W)

Key: D—Democrat; W—Whig

States	Electoral votes	Harrison	Van Buren	States	Electoral votes	Harrison	Van Buren
Alabama	(7)	—	7	Missouri	(4)	—	4
Arkansas	(3)	—	3	New Hampshire	(7)	—	7
Connecticut	(8)	8	—	New Jersey	(8)	8	—
Delaware	(3)	3	—	New York	(42)	42	—
Georgia	(11)	11	—	North Carolina	(15)	15	—
Illinois	(5)	—	5	Ohio	(21)	21	—
Indiana	(9)	9	—	Pennsylvania	(30)	30	—
Kentucky	(15)	15	—	Rhode Island	(4)	4	—
Louisiana	(5)	5	—	South Carolina	(11)	—	11
Maine	(10)	10	—	Tennessee	(15)	15	—
Maryland	(10)	10	—	Vermont	(7)	7	—
Massachusetts	(14)	14	—	Virginia	(23)	—	23
Michigan	(3)	3	—				
Mississippi	(4)	4	—	Totals	(294)	234	60

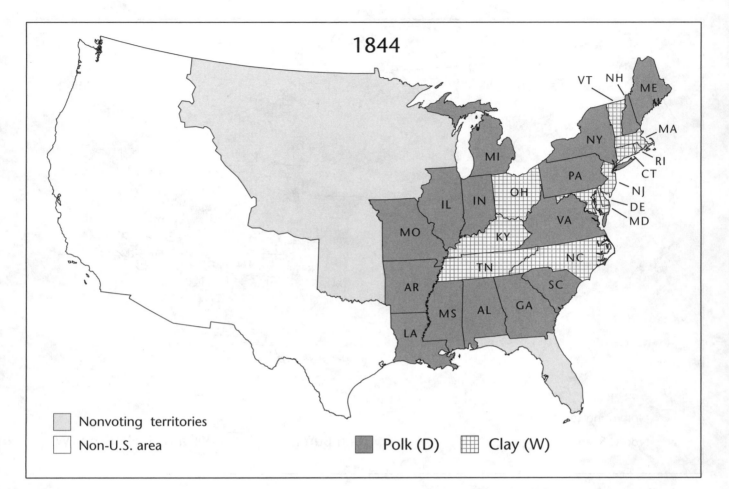

Key: D—Democrat; W—Whig

States	Electoral votes	Polk	Clay	States	Electoral votes	Polk	Clay
Alabama	(9)	9	—	Missouri	(7)	7	—
Arkansas	(3)	3	—	New Hampshire	(6)	6	—
Connecticut	(6)	—	6	New Jersey	(7)	—	7
Delaware	(3)	—	3	New York	(36)	36	—
Georgia	(10)	10	—	North Carolina	(11)	—	11
Illinois	(9)	9	—	Ohio	(23)	—	23
Indiana	(12)	12	—	Pennsylvania	(26)	26	—
Kentucky	(12)	—	12	Rhode Island	(4)	—	4
Louisiana	(6)	6	—	South Carolina	(9)	9	—
Maine	(9)	9	—	Tennessee	(13)	—	13
Maryland	(8)	—	8	Vermont	(6)	—	6
Massachusetts	(12)	—	12	Virginia	(17)	17	—
Michigan	(5)	5	—				
Mississippi	(6)	6	—	Totals	(275)	170	105

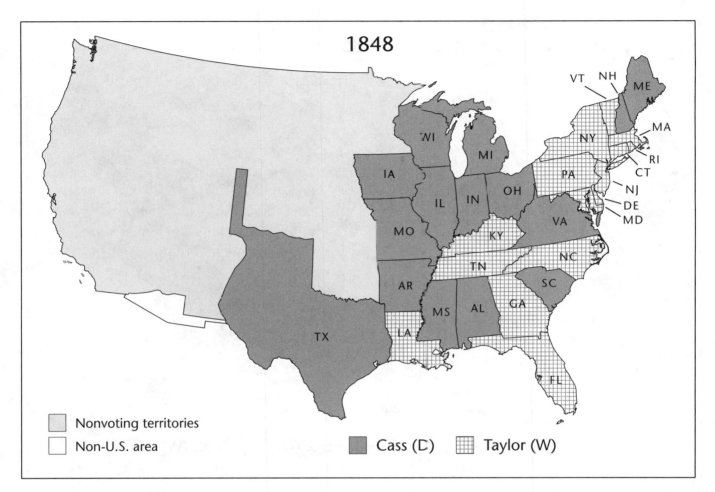

1848

Nonvoting territories

Non-U.S. area

Cass (D)   Taylor (W)

Key: D—Democrat; W—Whig

States	Electoral votes	Taylor	Cass	States	Electoral votes	Taylor	Cass
Alabama	(9)	—	9	Missouri	(7)	—	7
Arkansas	(3)	—	3	New Hampshire	(6)	—	6
Connecticut	(6)	6	—	New Jersey	(7)	7	—
Delaware	(3)	3	—	New York	(36)	36	—
Florida	(3)	3	—	North Carolina	(11)	11	—
Georgia	(10)	10	—	Ohio	(23)	—	23
Illinois	(9)	—	9	Pennsylvania	(26)	26	—
Indiana	(12)	—	12	Rhode Island	(4)	4	—
Iowa	(4)	—	4	South Carolina	(9)	—	9
Kentucky	(12)	12	—	Tennessee	(13)	13	—
Louisiana	(6)	6	—	Texas	(4)	—	4
Maine	(9)	—	9	Vermont	(6)	6	—
Maryland	(8)	8	—	Virginia	(17)	—	17
Massachusetts	(12)	12	—	Wisconsin	(4)	—	4
Michigan	(5)	—	5				
Mississippi	(6)	—	6	Totals	(290)	163	127

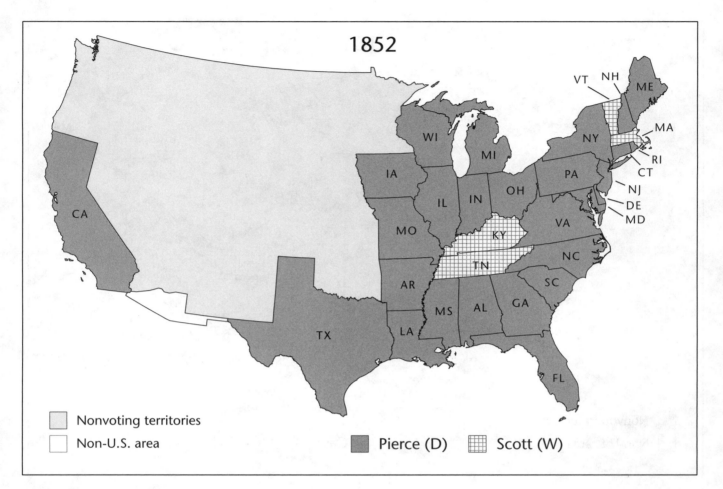

1852

Nonvoting territories
Non-U.S. area
Pierce (D) Scott (W)

Key: D—Democrat; W—Whig

States	Electoral votes	Pierce	Scott	States	Electoral votes	Pierce	Scott
Alabama	(9)	9	—	Missouri	(9)	9	—
Arkansas	(4)	4	—	New Hampshire	(5)	5	—
California	(4)	4	—	New Jersey	(7)	7	—
Connecticut	(6)	6	—	New York	(35)	35	—
Delaware	(3)	3	—	North Carolina	(10)	10	—
Florida	(3)	3	—	Ohio	(23)	23	—
Georgia	(10)	10	—	Pennsylvania	(27)	27	—
Illinois	(11)	11	—	Rhode Island	(4)	4	—
Indiana	(13)	13	—	South Carolina	(8)	8	—
Iowa	(4)	4	—	Tennessee	(12)	—	12
Kentucky	(12)	—	12	Texas	(4)	4	—
Louisiana	(6)	6	—	Vermont	(5)	—	5
Maine	(8)	8	—	Virginia	(15)	15	—
Maryland	(8)	8	—	Wisconsin	(5)	5	—
Massachusetts	(13)	—	13				
Michigan	(6)	6	—	Totals	(296)	254	42
Mississippi	(7)	7	—				

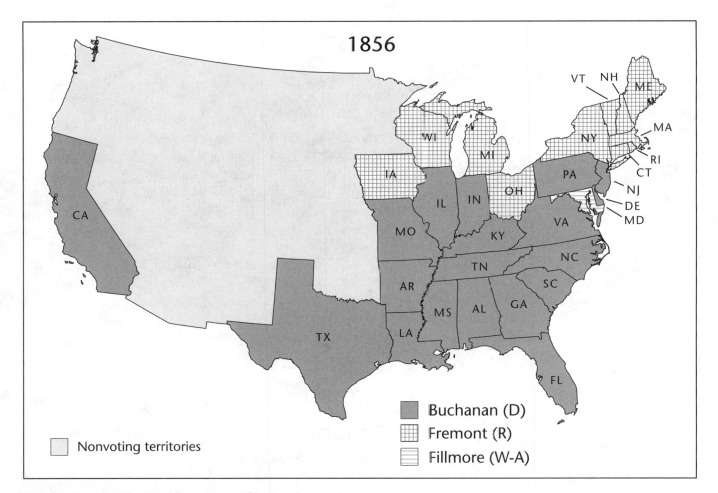

1856

Buchanan (D)
Fremont (R)
Fillmore (W-A)

Nonvoting territories

Key: D—Democrat; R—Republican; W-A—Whig-American

States	Electoral votes	Buchanan	Fremont	Fillmore	States	Electoral votes	Buchanan	Fremont	Fillmore
Alabama	(9)	9	—	—	Missouri	(9)	9	—	—
Arkansas	(4)	4	—	—	New Hampshire	(5)	—	5	—
California	(4)	4	—	—	New Jersey	(7)	7	—	—
Connecticut	(6)	—	6	—	New York	(35)	—	35	—
Delaware	(3)	3	—	—	North Carolina	(10)	10	—	—
Florida	(3)	3	—	—	Ohio	(23)	—	23	—
Georgia	(10)	10	—	—	Pennsylvania	(27)	27	—	—
Illinois	(11)	11	—	—	Rhode Island	(4)	—	4	—
Indiana	(13)	13	—	—	South Carolina	(8)	8	—	—
Iowa	(4)	—	4	—	Tennessee	(12)	12	—	—
Kentucky	(12)	12	—	—	Texas	(4)	4	—	—
Louisiana	(6)	6	—	—	Vermont	(5)	—	5	—
Maine	(8)	—	8	—	Virginia	(15)	15	—	—
Maryland	(8)	—	—	8	Wisconsin	(5)	—	5	—
Massachusetts	(13)	—	13	—					
Michigan	(6)	—	6	—	Totals	(296)	174	114	8
Mississippi	(7)	7	—	—					

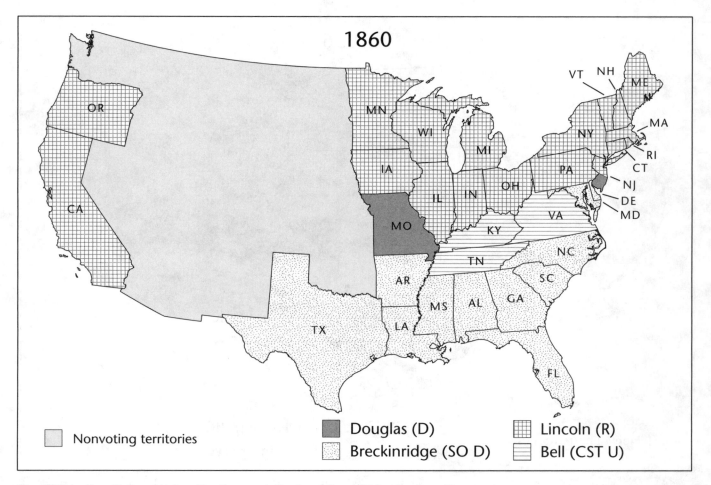

1860

Key: CST U—Constitutional Union; D—Democrat; R—Republican; SO D—Southern Democrat

Legend:
- Nonvoting territories
- Douglas (D)
- Breckinridge (SO D)
- Lincoln (R)
- Bell (CST U)

States	Electoral votes	Lincoln	Breckinridge	Bell	Douglas	States	Electoral votes	Lincoln	Breckinridge	Bell	Douglas
Alabama	(9)	—	9	—	—	Missouri	(9)	—	—	—	9
Arkansas	(4)	—	4	—	—	New Hampshire	(5)	5	—	—	—
California	(4)	4	—	—	—	New Jersey[1]	(7)	4	—	—	3
Connecticut	(6)	6	—	—	—	New York	(35)	35	—	—	—
Delaware	(3)	—	3	—	—	North Carolina	(10)	—	10	—	—
Florida	(3)	—	3	—	—	Ohio	(23)	23	—	—	—
Georgia	(10)	—	10	—	—	Oregon	(3)	3	—	—	—
Illinois	(11)	11	—	—	—	Pennsylvania	(27)	27	—	—	—
Indiana	(13)	13	—	—	—	Rhode Island	(4)	4	—	—	—
Iowa	(4)	4	—	—	—	South Carolina	(8)	—	8	—	—
Kentucky	(12)	—	—	12	—	Tennessee	(12)	—	—	12	—
Louisiana	(6)	—	6	—	—	Texas	(4)	—	4	—	—
Maine	(8)	8	—	—	—	Vermont	(5)	5	—	—	—
Maryland	(8)	—	8	—	—	Virginia	(15)	—	—	15	—
Massachusetts	(13)	13	—	—	—	Wisconsin	(5)	5	—	—	—
Michigan	(6)	6	—	—	—						
Minnesota	(4)	4	—	—	—	Totals	(303)	180	72	39	12
Mississippi	(7)	—	7	—	—						

1. For explanation of split electoral votes, see p. 188.

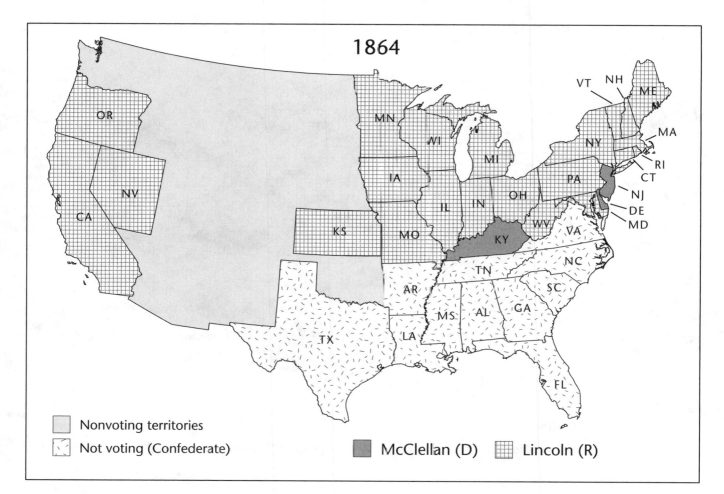

1864

Nonvoting territories

Not voting (Confederate)

McClellan (D)   **Lincoln (R)**

Key: D—Democrat; R—Republican

States[1]	Electoral votes	Lincoln	McClellan	States[1]	Electoral votes	Lincoln	McClellan
California	(5)	5	—	Nevada[2]	(3)	2	—
Connecticut	(6)	6	—	New Hampshire	(5)	5	—
Delaware	(3)	—	3	New Jersey	(7)	—	7
Illinois	(16)	16	—	New York	(33)	33	—
Indiana	(13)	13	—	Ohio	(21)	21	—
Iowa	(8)	8	—	Oregon	(3)	3	—
Kansas	(3)	3	—	Pennsylvania	(26)	26	—
Kentucky	(11)	—	11	Rhode Island	(4)	4	—
Maine	(7)	7	—	Vermont	(5)	5	—
Maryland	(7)	7	—	West Virginia	(5)	5	—
Massachusetts	(12)	12	—	Wisconsin	(8)	8	—
Michigan	(8)	8	—				
Minnesota	(4)	4	—	Totals	(234)	212	21
Missouri	(11)	11	—				

1. Eleven southern states—Alabama, Arkansas, Florida, Georgia, Louisiana, Mississippi, North Carolina, South Carolina, Tennessee, Texas, and Virginia—had seceded from the Union and did not vote.

2. One Nevada elector did not vote.

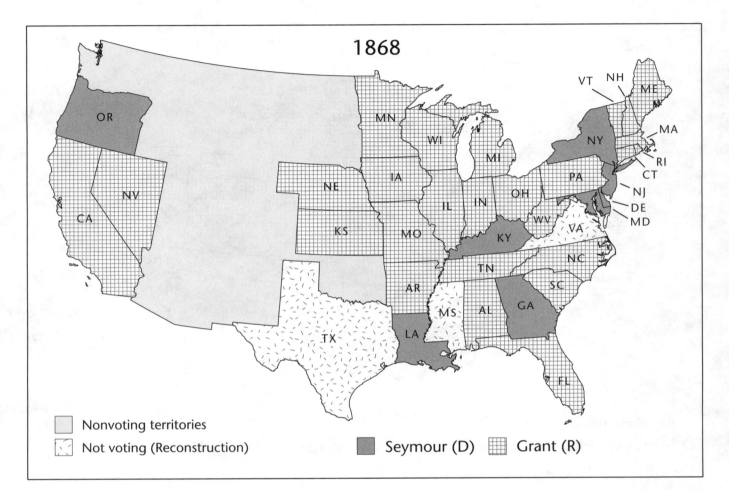

Key: D—Democrat; R—Republican

States[1]	Electoral votes	Grant	Seymour	States[1]	Electoral votes	Grant	Seymour
Alabama	(8)	8	—	Missouri	(11)	11	—
Arkansas	(5)	5	—	Nebraska	(3)	3	—
California	(5)	5	—	Nevada	(3)	3	—
Connecticut	(6)	6	—	New Hampshire	(5)	5	—
Delaware	(3)	—	3	New Jersey	(7)	—	7
Florida	(3)	3	—	New York	(33)	—	33
Georgia	(9)	—	9	North Carolina	(9)	9	—
Illinois	(16)	16	—	Ohio	(21)	21	—
Indiana	(13)	13	—	Oregon	(3)	—	3
Iowa	(8)	8	—	Pennsylvania	(26)	26	—
Kansas	(3)	3	—	Rhode Island	(4)	4	—
Kentucky	(11)	—	11	South Carolina	(6)	6	—
Louisiana	(7)	—	7	Tennessee	(10)	10	—
Maine	(7)	7	—	Vermont	(5)	5	—
Maryland	(7)	—	7	West Virginia	(5)	5	—
Massachusetts	(12)	12	—	Wisconsin	(8)	8	—
Michigan	(8)	8	—				
Minnesota	(4)	4	—	Totals	(294)	214	80

1. Mississippi, Texas, and Virginia were not yet readmitted to the Union and did not participate in the election.

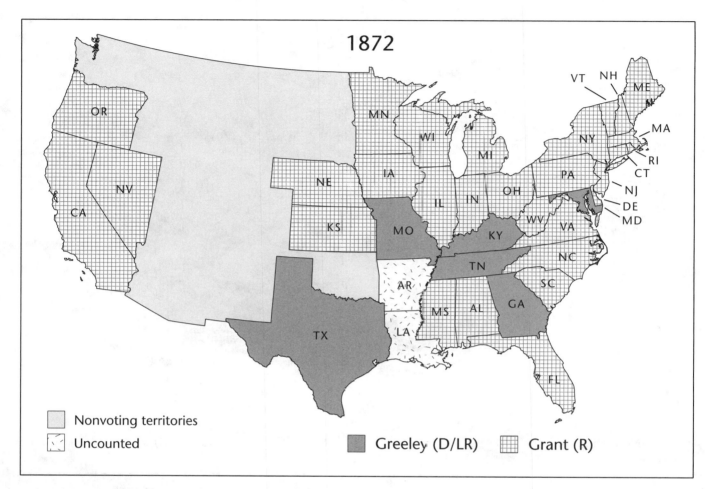

1872

Nonvoting territories

Uncounted

Greeley (D/LR)   Grant (R)

Key: D/LR—Democrat/Liberal Republican; R—Republican

States	Electoral votes	Grant	Hendricks[1]	Brown[1]	Jenkins[1]	Davis[1]	States	Electoral votes	Grant	Hendricks[1]	Brown[1]	Jenkins[1]	Davis[1]
Alabama	(10)	10	—	—	—	—	Nebraska	(3)	3	—	—	—	—
Arkansas[2]	(6)	—	—	—	—	—	Nevada	(3)	3	—	—	—	—
California	(6)	6	—	—	—	—	New Hampshire	(5)	5	—	—	—	—
Connecticut	(6)	6	—	—	—	—	New Jersey	(9)	9	—	—	—	—
Delaware	(3)	3	—	—	—	—	New York	(35)	35	—	—	—	—
Florida	(4)	4	—	—	—	—	North Carolina	(10)	10	—	—	—	—
Georgia[3]	(11)	—	—	6	2	—	Ohio	(22)	22	—	—	—	—
Illinois	(21)	21	—	—	—	—	Oregon	(3)	3	—	—	—	—
Indiana	(15)	15	—	—	—	—	Pennsylvania	(29)	29	—	—	—	—
Iowa	(11)	11	—	—	—	—	Rhode Island	(4)	4	—	—	—	—
Kansas	(5)	5	—	—	—	—	South Carolina	(7)	7	—	—	—	—
Kentucky	(12)	—	8	4	—	—	Tennessee	(12)	—	12	—	—	—
Louisiana[2]	(8)	—	—	—	—	—	Texas	(8)	—	8	—	—	—
Maine	(7)	7	—	—	—	—	Vermont	(5)	5	—	—	—	—
Maryland	(8)	—	8	—	—	—	Virginia	(11)	11	—	—	—	—
Massachusetts	(13)	13	—	—	—	—	West Virginia	(5)	5	—	—	—	—
Michigan	(11)	11	—	—	—	—	Wisconsin	(10)	10	—	—	—	—
Minnesota	(5)	5	—	—	—								
Mississippi	(8)	8	—	—	—	—	Totals	(366)	286	42	18	2	1
Missouri	(15)	—	6	8	—	1							

1. Liberal Republican and Democratic presidential candidate Horace Greeley died November 29, 1872 In the electoral college, the electors who had been pledged to Greeley split their presidential electoral votes among four candidates, including 18 for Benjamin Gratz Brown, Greeley's running mate.

2. Congress refused to accept the electoral votes of Arkansas and Louisiana because of disruptive conditions during Reconstruction.

3. Three Georgia electoral votes cast for Greeley were not counted.

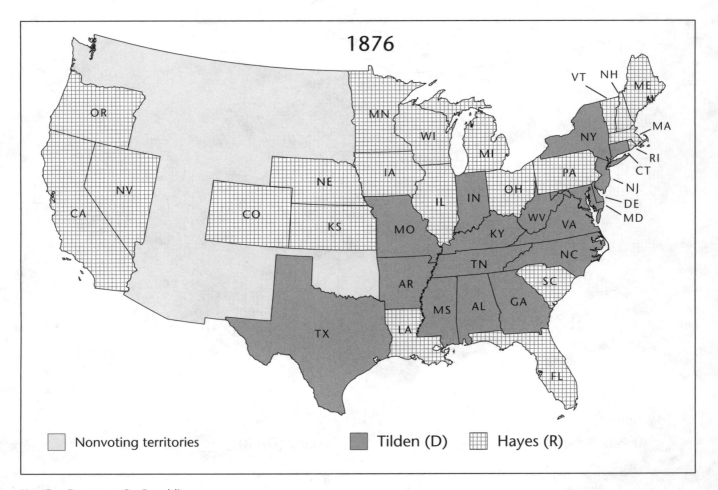

1876

Nonvoting territories   Tilden (D)   Hayes (R)

Key: D—Democrat; R—Republican

States	Electoral votes	Hayes	Tilden	States	Electoral votes	Hayes	Tilden
Alabama	(10)	—	10	Missouri	(15)	—	15
Arkansas	(6)	—	6	Nebraska	(3)	3	—
California	(6)	6	—	Nevada	(3)	3	—
Colorado	(3)	3	—	New Hampshire	(5)	5	—
Connecticut	(6)	—	6	New Jersey	(9)	—	9
Delaware	(3)	—	3	New York	(35)	—	35
Florida[1]	(4)	4	—	North Carolina	(10)	—	10
Georgia	(11)	—	11	Ohio	(22)	22	—
Illinois	(21)	21	—	Oregon[1]	(3)	3	—
Indiana	(15)	—	15	Pennsylvania	(29)	29	—
Iowa	(11)	11	—	Rhode Island	(4)	4	—
Kansas	(5)	5	—	South Carolina[1]	(7)	7	—
Kentucky	(12)	—	12	Tennessee	(12)	—	12
Louisiana[1]	(8)	8	—	Texas	(8)	—	8
Maine	(7)	7	—	Vermont	(5)	5	—
Maryland	(8)	—	8	Virginia	(11)	—	11
Massachusetts	(13)	13	—	West Virginia	(5)	—	5
Michigan	(11)	11	—	Wisconsin	(10)	10	—
Minnesota	(5)	5	—				
Mississippi	(8)	—	8	Totals	(369)	185	184

1. The electoral votes of Florida, Louisiana, Oregon, and South Carolina were disputed. See "Compromise: 1876" p. 42.

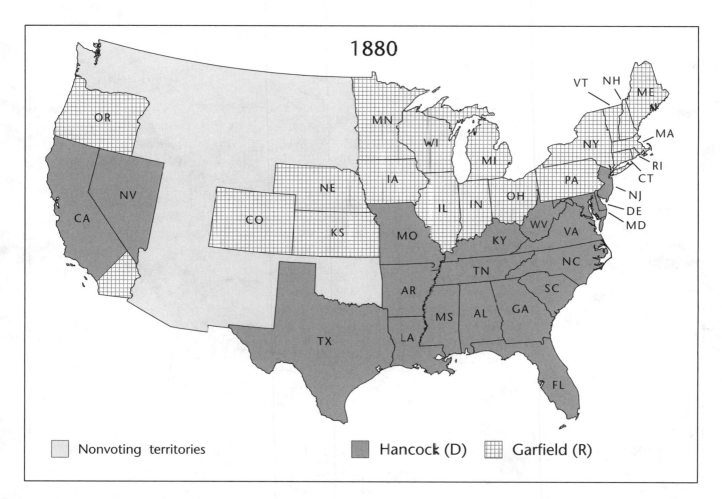

1880

Nonvoting territories   Hancock (D)   Garfield (R)

Key: D—Democrat; R—Republican

States	Electoral votes	Garfield	Hancock	States	Electoral votes	Garfield	Hancock
Alabama	(10)	—	10	Missouri	(15)	—	15
Arkansas	(6)	—	6	Nebraska	(3)	3	—
California[1]	(6)	1	5	Nevada	(3)	—	3
Colorado	(3)	3	—	New Hampshire	(5)	5	—
Connecticut	(6)	6	—	New Jersey	(9)	—	9
Delaware	(3)	—	3	New York	(35)	35	—
Florida	(4)	—	4	North Carolina	(10)	—	10
Georgia	(11)	—	11	Ohio	(22)	22	—
Illinois	(21)	21	—	Oregon	(3)	3	—
Indiana	(15)	15	—	Pennsylvania	(29)	29	—
Iowa	(11)	11	—	Rhode Island	(4)	4	—
Kansas	(5)	5	—	South Carolina	(7)	—	7
Kentucky	(12)	—	12	Tennessee	(12)	—	12
Louisiana	(8)	—	8	Texas	(8)	—	8
Maine	(7)	7	—	Vermont	(5)	5	—
Maryland	(8)	—	8	Virginia	(11)	—	11
Massachusetts	(13)	13	—	West Virginia	(5)	—	5
Michigan	(11)	11	—	Wisconsin	(10)	10	—
Minnesota	(5)	5	—				
Mississippi	(8)	—	8	Totals	(369)	214	155

1. For explanation of split electoral votes, see p. 188.

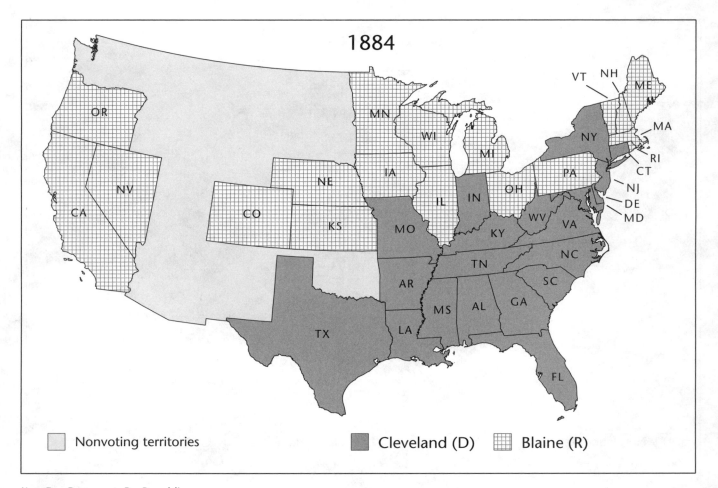

1884

Key: D—Democrat; R—Republican

States	Electoral votes	Cleveland	Blaine	States	Electoral votes	Cleveland	Blaine
Alabama	(10)	10	—	Missouri	(16)	16	—
Arkansas	(7)	7	—	Nebraska	(5)	—	5
California	(8)	—	8	Nevada	(3)	—	3
Colorado	(3)	—	3	New Hampshire	(4)	—	4
Connecticut	(6)	6	—	New Jersey	(9)	9	—
Delaware	(3)	3	—	New York	(36)	36	—
Florida	(4)	4	—	North Carolina	(11)	11	—
Georgia	(12)	12	—	Ohio	(23)	—	23
Illinois	(22)	—	22	Oregon	(3)	—	3
Indiana	(15)	15	—	Pennsylvania	(30)	—	30
Iowa	(13)	—	13	Rhode Island	(4)	—	4
Kansas	(9)	—	9	South Carolina	(9)	9	—
Kentucky	(13)	13	—	Tennessee	(12)	12	—
Louisiana	(8)	8	—	Texas	(13)	13	—
Maine	(6)	—	6	Vermont	(4)	—	4
Maryland	(8)	8	—	Virginia	(12)	12	—
Massachusetts	(14)	—	14	West Virginia	(6)	6	—
Michigan	(13)	—	13	Wisconsin	(11)	—	11
Minnesota	(7)	—	7				
Mississippi	(9)	9	—	Totals	(401)	219	182

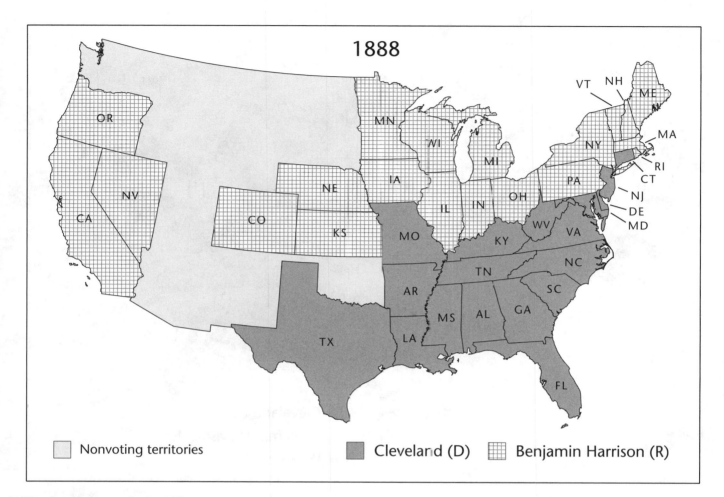

1888

Nonvoting territories   Cleveland (D)   Benjamin Harrison (R)

Key: D—Democrat; R—Republican

States	Electoral votes	Harrison	Cleveland	States	Electoral votes	Harrison	Cleveland
Alabama	(10)	—	10	Missouri	(16)	—	16
Arkansas	(7)	—	7	Nebraska	(5)	5	—
California	(8)	8	—	Nevada	(3)	3	—
Colorado	(3)	3	—	New Hampshire	(4)	4	—
Connecticut	(6)	—	6	New Jersey	(9)	—	9
Delaware	(3)	—	3	New York	(36)	36	—
Florida	(4)	—	4	North Carolina	(11)	—	11
Georgia	(12)	—	12	Ohio	(23)	23	—
Illinois	(22)	22	—	Oregon	(3)	3	—
Indiana	(15)	15	—	Pennsylvania	(30)	30	—
Iowa	(13)	13	—	Rhode Island	(4)	4	—
Kansas	(9)	9	—	South Carolina	(9)	—	9
Kentucky	(13)	—	13	Tennessee	(12)	—	12
Louisiana	(8)	—	8	Texas	(13)	—	13
Maine	(6)	6	—	Vermont	(4)	4	—
Maryland	(8)	—	8	Virginia	(12)	—	12
Massachusetts	(14)	14	—	West Virginia	(6)	—	6
Michigan	(13)	13	—	Wisconsin	(11)	11	—
Minnesota	(7)	7	—				
Mississippi	(9)	—	9	Totals	(401)	233	168

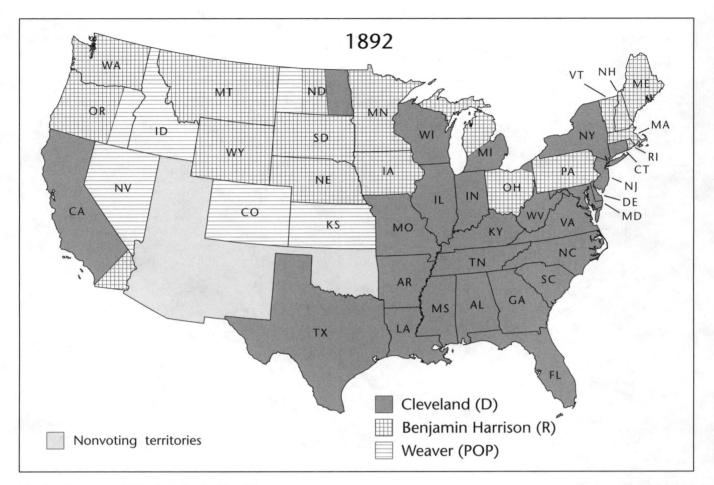

1892

Cleveland (D)
Benjamin Harrison (R)
Weaver (POP)

Nonvoting territories

Key: D—Democrat; POP—Populist; R—Republican

States	Electoral votes	Cleveland	Harrison	Weaver	States	Electoral votes	Cleveland	Harrison	Weaver
Alabama	(11)	11	—	—	Nebraska	(8)	—	8	—
Arkansas	(8)	8	—	—	Nevada	(3)	—	—	3
California[1]	(9)	8	1	—	New Hampshire	(4)	—	4	—
Colorado	(4)	—	—	4	New Jersey	(10)	10	—	—
Connecticut	(6)	6	—	—	New York	(36)	36	—	—
Delaware	(3)	3	—	—	North Carolina	(11)	11	—	—
Florida	(4)	4	—	—	North Dakota[1]	(3)	1	1	1
Georgia	(13)	13	—	—	Ohio[1]	(23)	1	22	—
Idaho	(3)	—	—	3	Oregon[1]	(4)	—	3	1
Illinois	(24)	24	—	—	Pennsylvania	(32)	—	32	—
Indiana	(15)	15	—	—	Rhode Island	(4)	—	4	—
Iowa	(13)	—	13	—	South Carolina	(9)	9	—	—
Kansas	(10)	—	—	10	South Dakota	(4)	—	4	—
Kentucky	(13)	13	—	—	Tennessee	(12)	12	—	—
Louisiana	(8)	8	—	—	Texas	(15)	15	—	—
Maine	(6)	—	6	—	Vermont	(4)	—	4	—
Maryland	(8)	8	—	—	Virginia	(12)	12	—	—
Massachusetts	(15)	—	15	—	Washington	(4)	—	4	—
Michigan[1]	(14)	5	9	—	West Virginia	(6)	6	—	—
Minnesota	(9)	—	9	—	Wisconsin	(12)	12	—	—
Mississippi	(9)	9	—	—	Wyoming	(3)	—	3	—
Missouri	(17)	17	—	—					
Montana	(3)	—	3	—	Totals	(444)	277	145	22

1. For explanation of split electoral votes, see p. 188.

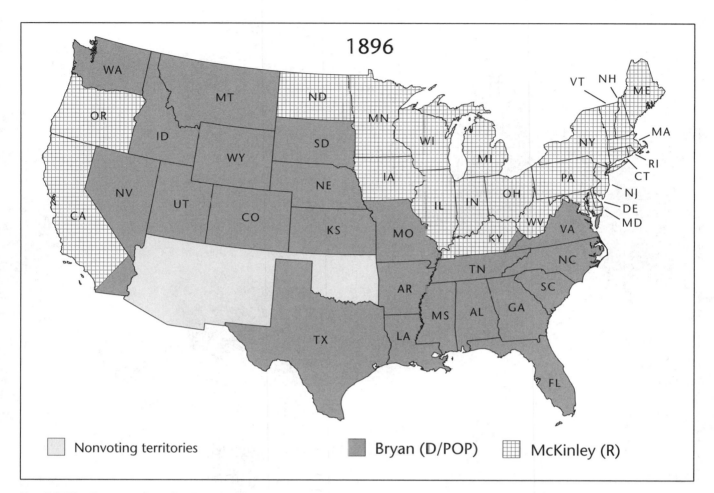

1896

Nonvoting territories   Bryan (D/POP)   McKinley (R)

Key: D/POP—Democrat/Populist; R—Republican

States	Electoral votes	McKinley	Bryan	States	Electoral votes	McKinley	Bryan
Alabama	(11)	—	11	Nevada	(3)	—	3
Arkansas	(8)	—	8	New Hampshire	(4)	4	—
California[1]	(9)	8	1	New Jersey	(10)	10	—
Colorado	(4)	—	4	New York	(36)	36	—
Connecticut	(6)	6	—	North Carolina	(11)	—	11
Delaware	(3)	3	—	North Dakota	(3)	3	—
Florida	(4)	—	4	Ohio	(23)	23	—
Georgia	(13)	—	13	Oregon	(4)	4	—
Idaho	(3)	—	3	Pennsylvania	(32)	32	—
Illinois	(24)	24	—	Rhode Island	(4)	4	—
Indiana	(15)	15	—	South Carolina	(9)	—	9
Iowa	(13)	13	—	South Dakota	(4)	—	4
Kansas	(10)	—	10	Tennessee	(12)	—	12
Kentucky[1]	(13)	12	1	Texas	(15)	—	15
Louisiana	(8)	—	8	Utah	(3)	—	3
Maine	(6)	6	—	Vermont	(4)	4	—
Maryland	(8)	8	—	Virginia	(12)	—	12
Massachusetts	(15)	15	—	Washington	(4)	—	4
Michigan	(14)	14	—	West Virginia	(6)	6	—
Minnesota	(9)	9	—	Wisconsin	(12)	12	—
Mississippi	(9)	—	9	Wyoming	(3)	—	3
Missouri	(17)	—	17				
Montana	(3)	—	3	Totals	(447)	271	176
Nebraska	(8)	—	8				

1. For explanation of split electoral votes, see p. 188.

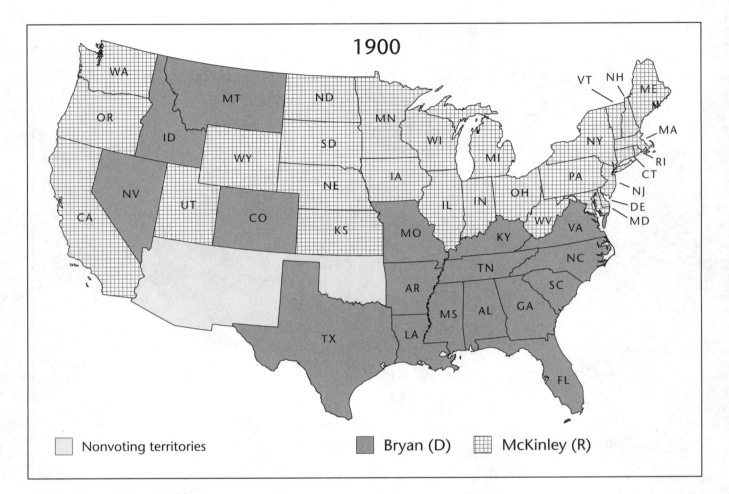

1900

Nonvoting territories   Bryan (D)   McKinley (R)

Key: D—Democrat; R—Republican

States	Electoral votes	McKinley	Bryan	States	Electoral votes	McKinley	Bryan
Alabama	(11)	—	11	Nevada	(3)	—	3
Arkansas	(8)	—	8	New Hampshire	(4)	4	—
California	(9)	9	—	New Jersey	(10)	10	—
Colorado	(4)	—	4	New York	(36)	36	—
Connecticut	(6)	6	—	North Carolina	(11)	—	11
Delaware	(3)	3	—	North Dakota	(3)	3	—
Florida	(4)	—	4	Ohio	(23)	23	—
Georgia	(13)	—	13	Oregon	(4)	4	—
Idaho	(3)	—	3	Pennsylvania	(32)	32	—
Illinois	(24)	24	—	Rhode Island	(4)	4	—
Indiana	(15)	15	—	South Carolina	(9)	—	9
Iowa	(13)	13	—	South Dakota	(4)	4	—
Kansas	(10)	10	—	Tennessee	(12)	—	12
Kentucky	(13)	—	13	Texas	(15)	—	15
Louisiana	(8)	—	8	Utah	(3)	3	—
Maine	(6)	6	—	Vermont	(4)	4	—
Maryland	(8)	8	—	Virginia	(12)	—	12
Massachusetts	(15)	15	—	Washington	(4)	4	—
Michigan	(14)	14	—	West Virginia	(6)	6	—
Minnesota	(9)	9	—	Wisconsin	(12)	12	—
Mississippi	(9)	—	9	Wyoming	(3)	3	—
Missouri	(17)	—	17				
Montana	(3)	—	3	Totals	(447)	292	155
Nebraska	(8)	8	—				

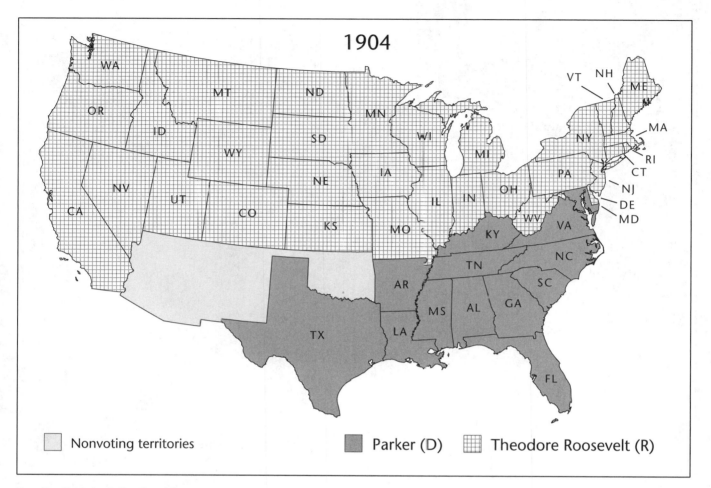

1904

Nonvoting territories   Parker (D)   Theodore Roosevelt (R)

Key: D—Democrat; R—Republican

States	Electoral votes	Roosevelt	Parker	States	Electoral votes	Roosevelt	Parker
Alabama	(11)	—	11	Nevada	(3)	3	—
Arkansas	(9)	—	9	New Hampshire	(4)	4	—
California	(10)	10	—	New Jersey	(12)	12	—
Colorado	(5)	5	—	New York	(39)	39	—
Connecticut	(7)	7	—	North Carolina	(12)	—	12
Delaware	(3)	3	—	North Dakota	(4)	4	—
Florida	(5)	—	5	Ohio	(23)	23	—
Georgia	(13)	—	13	Oregon	(4)	4	—
Idaho	(3)	3	—	Pennsylvania	(34)	34	—
Illinois	(27)	27	—	Rhode Island	(4)	4	—
Indiana	(15)	15	—	South Carolina	(9)	—	9
Iowa	(13)	13	—	South Dakota	(4)	4	—
Kansas	(10)	10	—	Tennessee	(12)	—	12
Kentucky	(13)	—	13	Texas	(18)	—	18
Louisiana	(9)	—	9	Utah	(3)	3	—
Maine	(6)	6	—	Vermont	(4)	4	—
Maryland[1]	(8)	1	7	Virginia	(12)	—	12
Massachusetts	(16)	16	—	Washington	(5)	5	—
Michigan	(14)	14	—	West Virginia	(7)	7	—
Minnesota	(11)	11	—	Wisconsin	(13)	13	—
Mississippi	(10)	—	10	Wyoming	(3)	3	—
Missouri	(18)	18	—				
Montana	(3)	3	—	Totals	(476)	336	140
Nebraska	(8)	8	—				

1. For explanation of split electoral votes, see p. 188.

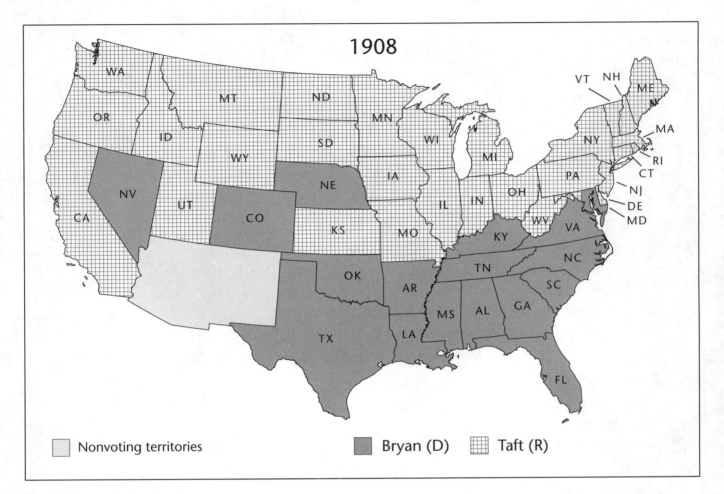

1908

Nonvoting territories　　Bryan (D)　　Taft (R)

Key: D—Democrat; R—Republican

States	Electoral votes	Taft	Bryan	States	Electoral votes	Taft	Bryan
Alabama	(11)	—	11	Nevada	(3)	—	3
Arkansas	(9)	—	9	New Hampshire	(4)	4	—
California	(10)	10	—	New Jersey	(12)	12	—
Colorado	(5)	—	5	New York	(39)	39	—
Connecticut	(7)	7	—	North Carolina	(12)	—	12
Delaware	(3)	3	—	North Dakota	(4)	4	—
Florida	(5)	—	5	Ohio	(23)	23	—
Georgia	(13)	—	13	Oklahoma	(7)	—	7
Idaho	(3)	3	—	Oregon	(4)	4	—
Illinois	(27)	27	—	Pennsylvania	(34)	34	—
Indiana	(15)	15	—	Rhode Island	(4)	4	—
Iowa	(13)	13	—	South Carolina	(9)	—	9
Kansas	(10)	10	—	South Dakota	(4)	4	—
Kentucky	(13)	—	13	Tennessee	(12)	—	12
Louisiana	(9)	—	9	Texas	(18)	—	18
Maine	(6)	6	—	Utah	(3)	3	—
Maryland[1]	(8)	2	6	Vermont	(4)	4	—
Massachusetts	(16)	16	—	Virginia	(12)	—	12
Michigan	(14)	14	—	Washington	(5)	5	—
Minnesota	(11)	11	—	West Virginia	(7)	7	—
Mississippi	(10)	—	10	Wisconsin	(13)	13	—
Missouri	(18)	18	—	Wyoming	(3)	3	—
Montana	(3)	3	—				
Nebraska	(8)	—	8	Totals	(483)	321	162

1. For explanation of split electoral votes, see p. 188.

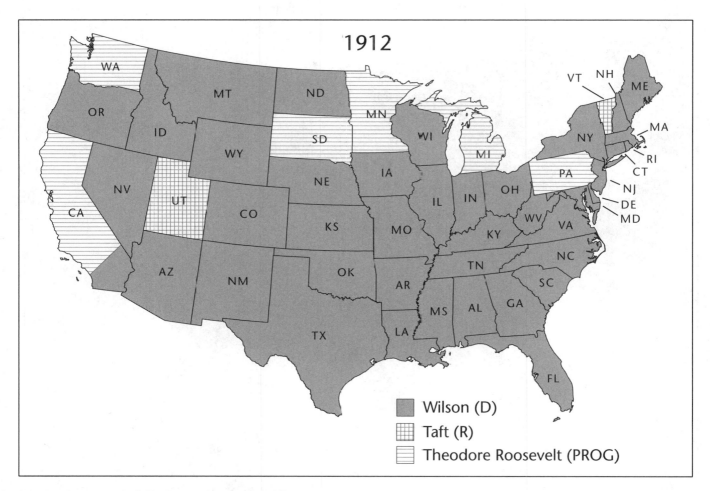

Key: D—Democrat; PROG—Progressive; R—Republican

States	Electoral votes	Wilson	Roosevelt	Taft	States	Electoral votes	Wilson	Roosevelt	Taft
Alabama	(12)	12	—	—	Nevada	(3)	3	—	—
Arizona	(3)	3	—	—	New Hampshire	(4)	4	—	—
Arkansas	(9)	9	—	—	New Jersey	(14)	14	—	—
California[1]	(13)	2	11	—	New Mexico	(3)	3	—	—
Colorado	(6)	6	—	—	New York	(45)	45	—	—
Connecticut	(7)	7	—	—	North Carolina	(12)	12	—	—
Delaware	(3)	3	—	—	North Dakota	(5)	5	—	—
Florida	(6)	6	—	—	Ohio	(24)	24	—	—
Georgia	(14)	14	—	—	Oklahoma	(10)	10	—	—
Idaho	(4)	4	—	—	Oregon	(5)	5	—	—
Illinois	(29)	29	—	—	Pennsylvania	(38)	—	38	—
Indiana	(15)	15	—	—	Rhode Island	(5)	5	—	—
Iowa	(13)	13	—	—	South Carolina	(9)	9	—	—
Kansas	(10)	10	—	—	South Dakota	(5)	—	5	—
Kentucky	(13)	13	—	—	Tennessee	(12)	12	—	—
Louisiana	(10)	10	—	—	Texas	(20)	20	—	—
Maine	(6)	6	—	—	Utah	(4)	—	—	4
Maryland	(8)	8	—	—	Vermont	(4)	—	—	4
Massachusetts	(18)	18	—	—	Virginia	(12)	12	—	—
Michigan	(15)	—	15	—	Washington	(7)	—	7	—
Minnesota	(12)	—	12	—	West Virginia	(8)	8	—	—
Mississippi	(10)	10	—	—	Wisconsin	(13)	13	—	—
Missouri	(18)	18	—	—	Wyoming	(3)	3	—	—
Montana	(4)	4	—	—					
Nebraska	(8)	8	—	—	Totals	(531)	435	88	8

1. For explanation of split electoral votes, see p. 188.

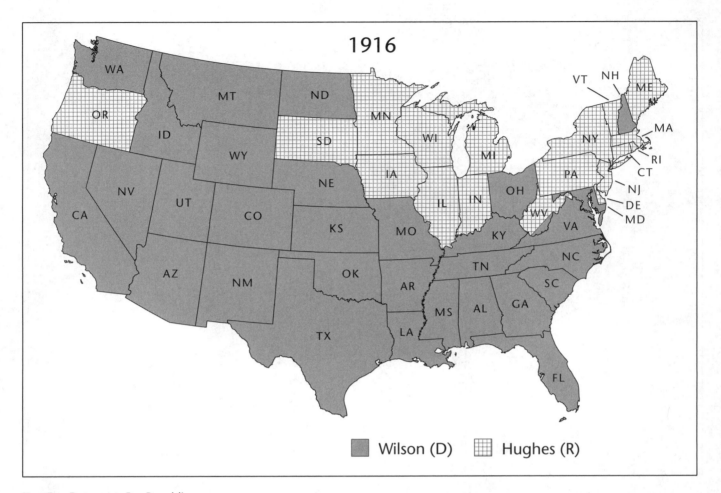

1916

Wilson (D)   Hughes (R)

Key: D—Democrat; R—Republican

States	Electoral votes	Wilson	Hughes	States	Electoral votes	Wilson	Hughes
Alabama	(12)	12	—	Nevada	(3)	3	—
Arizona	(3)	3	—	New Hampshire	(4)	4	—
Arkansas	(9)	9	—	New Jersey	(14)	—	14
California	(13)	13	—	New Mexico	(3)	3	—
Colorado	(6)	6	—	New York	(45)	—	45
Connecticut	(7)	—	7	North Carolina	(12)	12	—
Delaware	(3)	—	3	North Dakota	(5)	5	—
Florida	(6)	6	—	Ohio	(24)	24	—
Georgia	(14)	14	—	Oklahoma	(10)	10	—
Idaho	(4)	4	—	Oregon	(5)	—	5
Illinois	(29)	—	29	Pennsylvania	(38)	—	38
Indiana	(15)	—	15	Rhode Island	(5)	—	5
Iowa	(13)	—	13	South Carolina	(9)	9	—
Kansas	(10)	10	—	South Dakota	(5)	—	5
Kentucky	(13)	13	—	Tennessee	(12)	12	—
Louisiana	(10)	10	—	Texas	(20)	20	—
Maine	(6)	—	6	Utah	(4)	4	—
Maryland	(8)	8	—	Vermont	(4)	—	4
Massachusetts	(18)	—	18	Virginia	(12)	12	—
Michigan	(15)	—	15	Washington	(7)	7	—
Minnesota	(12)	—	12	West Virginia[1]	(8)	1	7
Mississippi	(10)	10	—	Wisconsin	(13)	—	13
Missouri	(18)	18	—	Wyoming	(3)	3	—
Montana	(4)	4	—				
Nebraska	(8)	8	—	Totals	(531)	277	254

1. For explanation of split electoral votes, see p. 188.

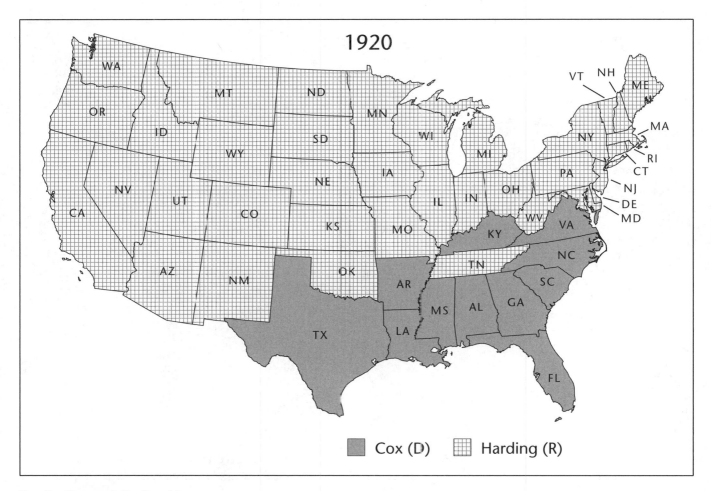

Key: D—Democrat; R—Republican

States	Electoral votes	Harding	Cox	States	Electoral votes	Harding	Cox
Alabama	(12)	—	12	Nevada	(3)	3	—
Arizona	(3)	3	—	New Hampshire	(4)	4	—
Arkansas	(9)	—	9	New Jersey	(14)	14	—
California	(13)	13	—	New Mexico	(3)	3	—
Colorado	(6)	6	—	New York	(45)	45	—
Connecticut	(7)	7	—	North Carolina	(12)	—	12
Delaware	(3)	3	—	North Dakota	(5)	5	—
Florida	(6)	—	6	Ohio	(24)	24	—
Georgia	(14)	—	14	Oklahoma	(10)	10	—
Idaho	(4)	4	—	Oregon	(5)	5	—
Illinois	(29)	29	—	Pennsylvania	(38)	38	—
Indiana	(15)	15	—	Rhode Island	(5)	5	—
Iowa	(13)	13	—	South Carolina	(9)	—	9
Kansas	(10)	10	—	South Dakota	(5)	5	—
Kentucky	(13)	—	13	Tennessee	(12)	12	—
Louisiana	(10)	—	10	Texas	(20)	—	20
Maine	(6)	6	—	Utah	(4)	4	—
Maryland	(8)	8	—	Vermont	(4)	4	—
Massachusetts	(18)	18	—	Virginia	(12)	—	12
Michigan	(15)	15	—	Washington	(7)	7	—
Minnesota	(12)	12	—	West Virginia	(8)	8	—
Mississippi	(10)	—	10	Wisconsin	(13)	13	—
Missouri	(18)	18	—	Wyoming	(3)	3	—
Montana	(4)	4	—				
Nebraska	(8)	8	—	Totals	(531)	404	127

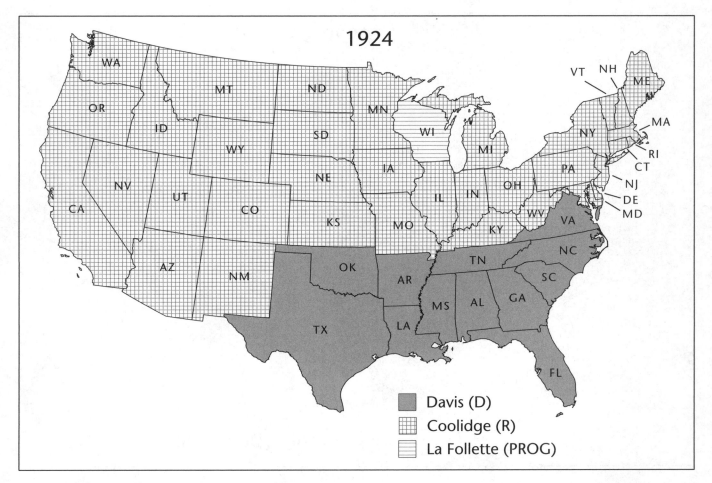

1924

Davis (D)
Coolidge (R)
La Follette (PROG)

Key: D—Democrat; PROG—Progressive; R—Republican

States	Electoral votes	Coolidge	Davis	La Follette	States	Electoral votes	Coolidge	Davis	La Follette
Alabama	(12)	—	12	—	Nevada	(3)	3	—	—
Arizona	(3)	3	—	—	New Hampshire	(4)	4	—	—
Arkansas	(9)	—	9	—	New Jersey	(14)	14	—	—
California	(13)	13	—	—	New Mexico	(3)	3	—	—
Colorado	(6)	6	—	—	New York	(45)	45	—	—
Connecticut	(7)	7	—	—	North Carolina	(12)	—	12	—
Delaware	(3)	3	—	—	North Dakota	(5)	5	—	—
Florida	(6)	—	6	—	Ohio	(24)	24	—	—
Georgia	(14)	—	14	—	Oklahoma	(10)	—	10	—
Idaho	(4)	4	—	—	Oregon	(5)	5	—	—
Illinois	(29)	29	—	—	Pennsylvania	(38)	38	—	—
Indiana	(15)	15	—	—	Rhode Island	(5)	5	—	—
Iowa	(13)	13	—	—	South Carolina	(9)	—	9	—
Kansas	(10)	10	—	—	South Dakota	(5)	5	—	—
Kentucky	(13)	13	—	—	Tennessee	(12)	—	12	—
Louisiana	(10)	—	10	—	Texas	(20)	—	20	—
Maine	(6)	6	—	—	Utah	(4)	4	—	—
Maryland	(8)	8	—	—	Vermont	(4)	4	—	—
Massachusetts	(18)	18	—	—	Virginia	(12)	—	12	—
Michigan	(15)	15	—	—	Washington	(7)	7	—	—
Minnesota	(12)	12	—	—	West Virginia	(8)	8	—	—
Mississippi	(10)	—	10	—	Wisconsin	(13)	—	—	13
Missouri	(18)	18	—	—	Wyoming	(3)	3	—	—
Montana	(4)	4	—	—					
Nebraska	(8)	8	—	—	Totals	(531)	382	136	13

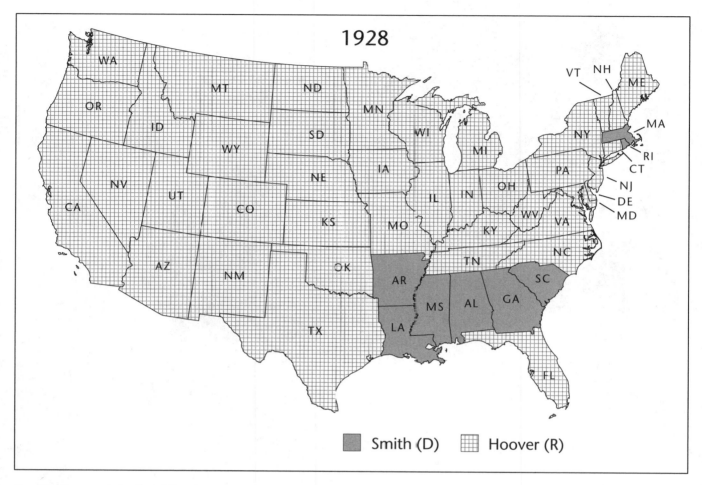

Key: D—Democrat; R—Republican

States	Electoral votes	Hoover	Smith	States	Electoral votes	Hoover	Smith
Alabama	(12)	—	12	Nevada	(3)	3	—
Arizona	(3)	3	—	New Hampshire	(4)	4	—
Arkansas	(9)	—	9	New Jersey	(14)	14	—
California	(13)	13	—	New Mexico	(3)	3	—
Colorado	(6)	6	—	New York	(45)	45	—
Connecticut	(7)	7	—	North Carolina	(12)	12	—
Delaware	(3)	3	—	North Dakota	(5)	5	—
Florida	(6)	6	—	Ohio	(24)	24	—
Georgia	(14)	—	14	Oklahoma	(10)	10	—
Idaho	(4)	4	—	Oregon	(5)	5	—
Illinois	(29)	29	—	Pennsylvania	(38)	38	—
Indiana	(15)	15	—	Rhode Island	(5)	—	5
Iowa	(13)	13	—	South Carolina	(9)	—	9
Kansas	(10)	10	—	South Dakota	(5)	5	—
Kentucky	(13)	13	—	Tennessee	(12)	12	—
Louisiana	(10)	—	10	Texas	(20)	20	—
Maine	(6)	6	—	Utah	(4)	4	—
Maryland	(8)	8	—	Vermont	(4)	4	—
Massachusetts	(18)	—	18	Virginia	(12)	12	—
Michigan	(15)	15	—	Washington	(7)	7	—
Minnesota	(12)	12	—	West Virginia	(8)	8	—
Mississippi	(10)	—	10	Wisconsin	(13)	13	—
Missouri	(18)	18	—	Wyoming	(3)	3	—
Montana	(4)	4	—				
Nebraska	(8)	8	—	Totals	(531)	444	87

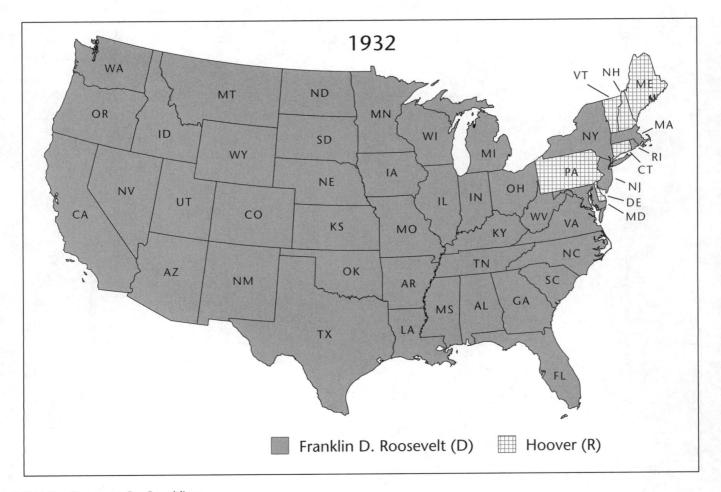

1932

Franklin D. Roosevelt (D)   Hoover (R)

Key: D—Democrat; R—Republican

States	Electoral votes	Roosevelt	Hoover	States	Electoral votes	Roosevelt	Hoover
Alabama	(11)	11	—	Nevada	(3)	3	—
Arizona	(3)	3	—	New Hampshire	(4)	—	4
Arkansas	(9)	9	—	New Jersey	(16)	16	—
California	(22)	22	—	New Mexico	(3)	3	—
Colorado	(6)	6	—	New York	(47)	47	—
Connecticut	(8)	—	8	North Carolina	(13)	13	—
Delaware	(3)	—	3	North Dakota	(4)	4	—
Florida	(7)	7	—	Ohio	(26)	26	—
Georgia	(12)	12	—	Oklahoma	(11)	11	—
Idaho	(4)	4	—	Oregon	(5)	5	—
Illinois	(29)	29	—	Pennsylvania	(36)	—	36
Indiana	(14)	14	—	Rhode Island	(4)	4	—
Iowa	(11)	11	—	South Carolina	(8)	8	—
Kansas	(9)	9	—	South Dakota	(4)	4	—
Kentucky	(11)	11	—	Tennessee	(11)	11	—
Louisiana	(10)	10	—	Texas	(23)	23	—
Maine	(5)	—	5	Utah	(4)	4	—
Maryland	(8)	8	—	Vermont	(3)	—	3
Massachusetts	(17)	17	—	Virginia	(11)	11	—
Michigan	(19)	19	—	Washington	(8)	8	—
Minnesota	(11)	11	—	West Virginia	(8)	8	—
Mississippi	(9)	9	—	Wisconsin	(12)	12	—
Missouri	(15)	15	—	Wyoming	(3)	3	—
Montana	(4)	4	—				
Nebraska	(7)	7	—	Totals	(531)	472	59

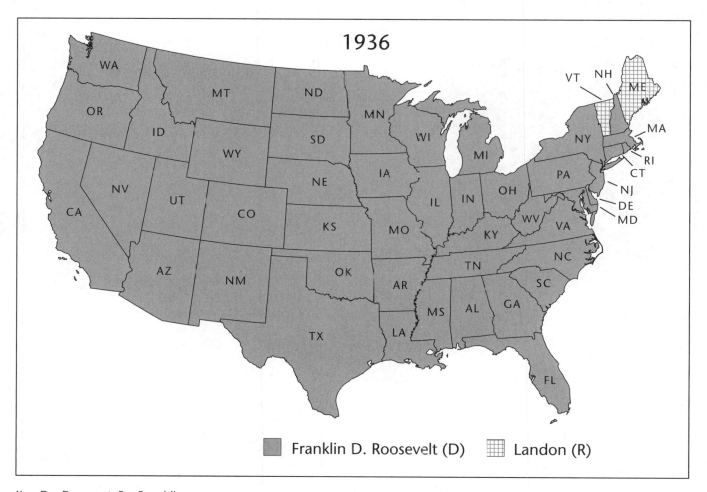

1936

Franklin D. Roosevelt (D)   Landon (R)

Key: D—Democrat; R—Republican

States	Electoral votes	Roosevelt	Landon	States	Electoral votes	Roosevelt	Landon
Alabama	(11)	11	—	Nevada	(3)	3	—
Arizona	(3)	3	—	New Hampshire	(4)	4	—
Arkansas	(9)	9	—	New Jersey	(16)	16	—
California	(22)	22	—	New Mexico	(3)	3	—
Colorado	(6)	6	—	New York	(47)	47	—
Connecticut	(8)	8	—	North Carolina	(13)	13	—
Delaware	(3)	3	—	North Dakota	(4)	4	—
Florida	(7)	7	—	Ohio	(26)	26	—
Georgia	(12)	12	—	Oklahoma	(11)	11	—
Idaho	(4)	4	—	Oregon	(5)	5	—
Illinois	(29)	29	—	Pennsylvania	(36)	36	—
Indiana	(14)	14	—	Rhode Island	(4)	4	—
Iowa	(11)	11	—	South Carolina	(8)	8	—
Kansas	(9)	9	—	South Dakota	(4)	4	—
Kentucky	(11)	11	—	Tennessee	(11)	11	—
Louisiana	(10)	10	—	Texas	(23)	23	—
Maine	(5)	—	5	Utah	(4)	4	—
Maryland	(8)	8	—	Vermont	(3)	—	3
Massachusetts	(17)	17	—	Virginia	(11)	11	—
Michigan	(19)	19	—	Washington	(8)	8	—
Minnesota	(11)	11	—	West Virginia	(8)	8	—
Mississippi	(9)	9	—	Wisconsin	(12)	12	—
Missouri	(15)	15	—	Wyoming	(3)	3	—
Montana	(4)	4	—				
Nebraska	(7)	7	—	Totals	(531)	523	8

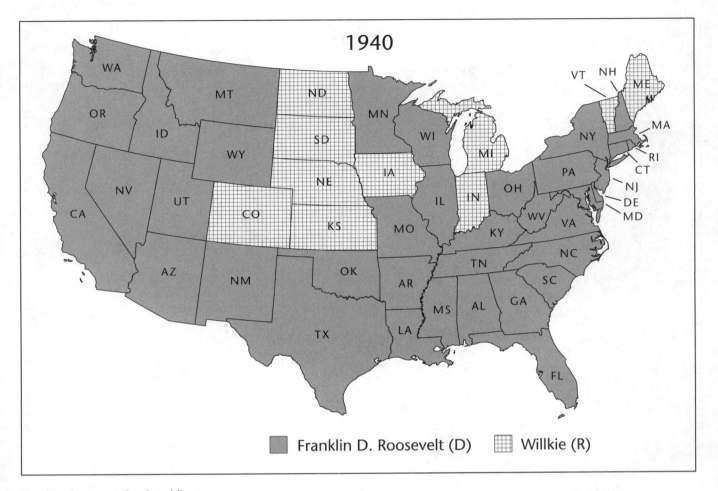

1940

■ Franklin D. Roosevelt (D)   ▦ Willkie (R)

Key: D—Democrat; R—Republican

States	Electoral votes	Roosevelt	Willkie	States	Electoral votes	Roosevelt	Willkie
Alabama	(11)	11	—	Nevada	(3)	3	—
Arizona	(3)	3	—	New Hampshire	(4)	4	—
Arkansas	(9)	9	—	New Jersey	(16)	16	—
California	(22)	22	—	New Mexico	(3)	3	—
Colorado	(6)	—	6	New York	(47)	47	—
Connecticut	(8)	8	—	North Carolina	(13)	13	—
Delaware	(3)	3	—	North Dakota	(4)	—	4
Florida	(7)	7	—	Ohio	(26)	26	—
Georgia	(12)	12	—	Oklahoma	(11)	11	—
Idaho	(4)	4	—	Oregon	(5)	5	—
Illinois	(29)	29	—	Pennsylvania	(36)	36	—
Indiana	(14)	—	14	Rhode Island	(4)	4	—
Iowa	(11)	—	11	South Carolina	(8)	8	—
Kansas	(9)	—	9	South Dakota	(4)	—	4
Kentucky	(11)	11	—	Tennessee	(11)	11	—
Louisiana	(10)	10	—	Texas	(23)	23	—
Maine	(5)	—	5	Utah	(4)	4	—
Maryland	(8)	8	—	Vermont	(3)	—	3
Massachusetts	(17)	17	—	Virginia	(11)	11	—
Michigan	(19)	—	19	Washington	(8)	8	—
Minnesota	(11)	11	—	West Virginia	(8)	8	—
Mississippi	(9)	9	—	Wisconsin	(12)	12	—
Missouri	(15)	15	—	Wyoming	(3)	3	—
Montana	(4)	4	—				
Nebraska	(7)	—	7	Totals	(531)	449	82

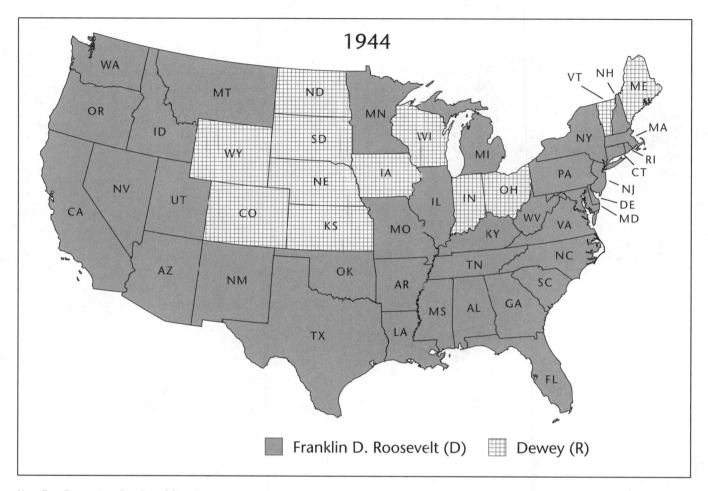

1944

Franklin D. Roosevelt (D)   Dewey (R)

Key: D—Democrat; R—Republican

States	Electoral votes	Roosevelt	Dewey	States	Electoral votes	Roosevelt	Dewey
Alabama	(11)	11	—	Nevada	(3)	3	—
Arizona	(4)	4	—	New Hampshire	(4)	4	—
Arkansas	(9)	9	—	New Jersey	(16)	16	—
California	(25)	25	—	New Mexico	(4)	4	—
Colorado	(6)	—	6	New York	(47)	47	—
Connecticut	(8)	8	—	North Carolina	(14)	14	—
Delaware	(3)	3	—	North Dakota	(4)	—	4
Florida	(8)	8	—	Ohio	(25)	—	25
Georgia	(12)	12	—	Oklahoma	(10)	10	—
Idaho	(4)	4	—	Oregon	(6)	6	—
Illinois	(28)	28	—	Pennsylvania	(35)	35	—
Indiana	(13)	—	13	Rhode Island	(4)	4	—
Iowa	(10)	—	10	South Carolina	(8)	8	—
Kansas	(8)	—	8	South Dakota	(4)	—	4
Kentucky	(11)	11	—	Tennessee	(12)	12	—
Louisiana	(10)	10	—	Texas	(23)	23	—
Maine	(5)	—	5	Utah	(4)	4	—
Maryland	(8)	8	—	Vermont	(3)	—	3
Massachusetts	(16)	16	—	Virginia	(11)	11	—
Michigan	(19)	19	—	Washington	(8)	8	—
Minnesota	(11)	11	—	West Virginia	(8)	8	—
Mississippi	(9)	9	—	Wisconsin	(12)	—	12
Missouri	(15)	15	—	Wyoming	(3)	—	3
Montana	(4)	4	—				
Nebraska	(6)	—	6	Totals	(531)	432	99

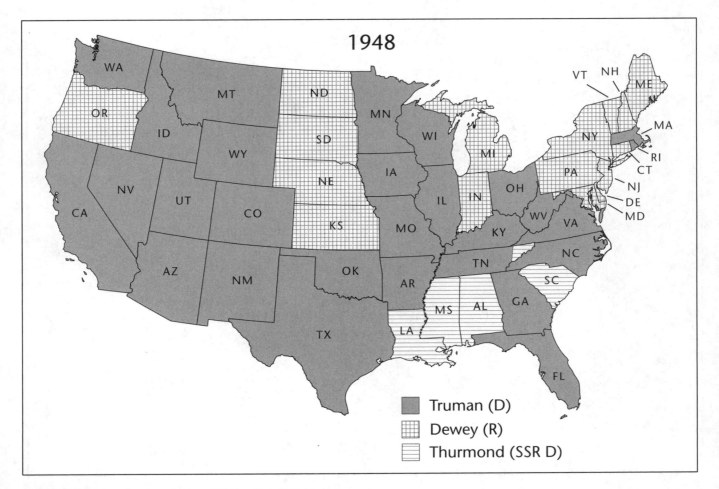

1948

Truman (D)

Dewey (R)

Thurmond (SSR D)

Key: D—Democrat; R—Republican; SSR D—States' Rights Democrat

States	Electoral votes	Truman	Dewey	Thurmond	States	Electoral votes	Truman	Dewey	Thurmond
Alabama	(11)	—	—	11	Nevada	(3)	3	—	—
Arizona	(4)	4	—	—	New Hampshire	(4)	—	4	—
Arkansas	(9)	9	—	—	New Jersey	(16)	—	16	—
California	(25)	25	—	—	New Mexico	(4)	4	—	—
Colorado	(6)	6	—	—	New York	(47)	—	47	—
Connecticut	(8)	—	8	—	North Carolina	(14)	14	—	—
Delaware	(3)	—	3	—	North Dakota	(4)	—	4	—
Florida	(8)	8	—	—	Ohio	(25)	25	—	—
Georgia	(12)	12	—	—	Oklahoma	(10)	10	—	—
Idaho	(4)	4	—	—	Oregon	(6)	—	6	—
Illinois	(28)	28	—	—	Pennsylvania	(35)	—	35	—
Indiana	(13)	—	13	—	Rhode Island	(4)	4	—	—
Iowa	(10)	10	—	—	South Carolina	(8)	—	—	8
Kansas	(8)	—	8	—	South Dakota	(4)	—	4	—
Kentucky	(11)	11	—	—	Tennessee[1]	(12)	11	—	1
Louisiana	(10)	—	—	10	Texas	(23)	23	—	—
Maine	(5)	—	5	—	Utah	(4)	4	—	—
Maryland	(8)	—	8	—	Vermont	(3)	—	3	—
Massachusetts	(16)	16	—	—	Virginia	(11)	11	—	—
Michigan	(19)	—	19	—	Washington	(8)	8	—	—
Minnesota	(11)	11	—	—	West Virginia	(8)	8	—	—
Mississippi	(9)	—	—	9	Wisconsin	(12)	12	—	—
Missouri	(15)	15	—	—	Wyoming	(3)	3	—	—
Montana	(4)	4	—	—					
Nebraska	(6)	—	6	—	Totals	(531)	303	189	39

1. For explanation of split electoral votes, see p. 188.

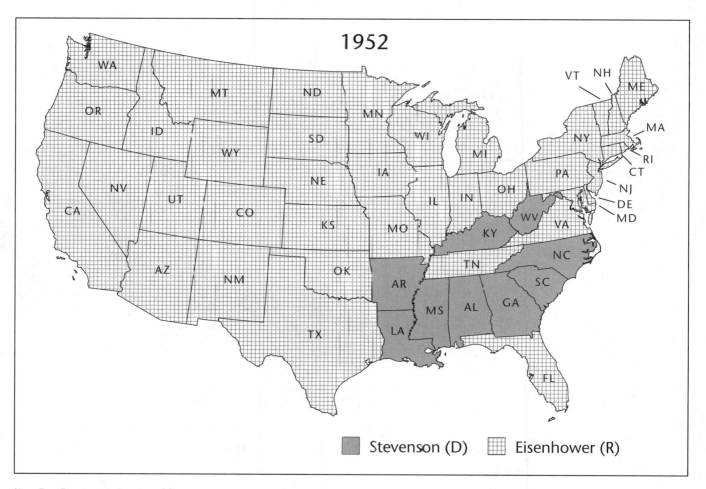

1952

Key: D—Democrat; R—Republican

States	Electoral votes	Eisenhower	Stevenson	States	Electoral votes	Eisenhower	Stevenson
Alabama	(11)	—	11	Nevada	(3)	3	—
Arizona	(4)	4	—	New Hampshire	(4)	4	—
Arkansas	(8)	—	8	New Jersey	(16)	16	—
California	(32)	32	—	New Mexico	(4)	4	—
Colorado	(6)	6	—	New York	(45)	45	—
Connecticut	(8)	8	—	North Carolina	(14)	—	14
Delaware	(3)	3	—	North Dakota	(4)	4	—
Florida	(10)	10	—	Ohio	(25)	25	—
Georgia	(12)	—	12	Oklahoma	(8)	8	—
Idaho	(4)	4	—	Oregon	(6)	6	—
Illinois	(27)	27	—	Pennsylvania	(32)	32	—
Indiana	(13)	13	—	Rhode Island	(4)	4	—
Iowa	(10)	10	—	South Carolina	(8)	—	8
Kansas	(8)	8	—	South Dakota	(4)	4	—
Kentucky	(10)	—	10	Tennessee	(11)	11	—
Louisiana	(10)	—	10	Texas	(24)	24	—
Maine	(5)	5	—	Utah	(4)	4	—
Maryland	(9)	9	—	Vermont	(3)	3	—
Massachusetts	(16)	16	—	Virginia	(12)	12	—
Michigan	(20)	20	—	Washington	(9)	9	—
Minnesota	(11)	11	—	West Virginia	(8)	—	8
Mississippi	(8)	—	8	Wisconsin	(12)	12	—
Missouri	(13)	13	—	Wyoming	(3)	3	—
Montana	(4)	4	—				
Nebraska	(6)	6	—	Totals	(531)	442	89

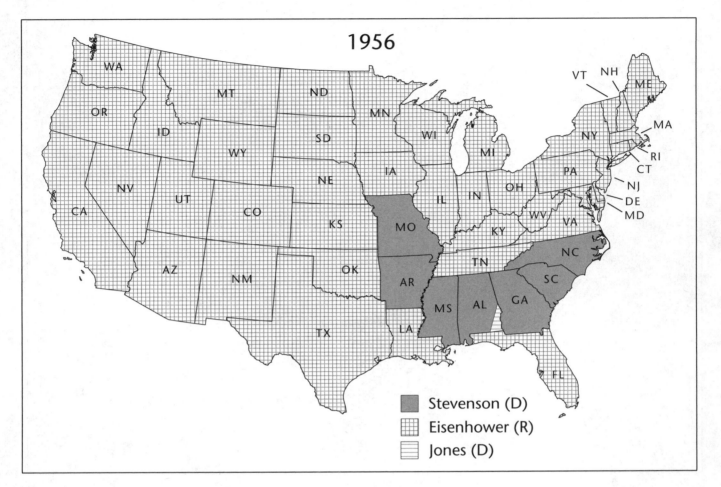

1956

Stevenson (D)
Eisenhower (R)
Jones (D)

Key: D—Democrat; R—Republican

States	Electoral votes	Eisenhower	Stevenson	Jones	States	Electoral votes	Eisenhower	Stevenson	Jones
Alabama[1]	(11)	—	10	1	Nevada	(3)	3	—	—
Arizona	(4)	4	—	—	New Hampshire	(4)	4	—	—
Arkansas	(8)	—	8	—	New Jersey	(16)	16	—	—
California	(32)	32	—	—	New Mexico	(4)	4	—	—
Colorado	(6)	6	—	—	New York	(45)	45	—	—
Connecticut	(8)	8	—	—	North Carolina	(14)	—	14	—
Delaware	(3)	3	—	—	North Dakota	(4)	4	—	—
Florida	(10)	10	—	—	Ohio	(25)	25	—	—
Georgia	(12)	—	12	—	Oklahoma	(8)	8	—	—
Idaho	(4)	4	—	—	Oregon	(6)	6	—	—
Illinois	(27)	27	—	—	Pennsylvania	(32)	32	—	—
Indiana	(13)	13	—	—	Rhode Island	(4)	4	—	—
Iowa	(10)	10	—	—	South Carolina	(8)	—	8	—
Kansas	(8)	8	—	—	South Dakota	(4)	4	—	—
Kentucky	(10)	10	—	—	Tennessee	(11)	11	—	—
Louisiana	(10)	10	—	—	Texas	(24)	24	—	—
Maine	(5)	5	—	—	Utah	(4)	4	—	—
Maryland	(9)	9	—	—	Vermont	(3)	3	—	—
Massachusetts	(16)	16	—	—	Virginia	(12)	12	—	—
Michigan	(20)	20	—	—	Washington	(9)	9	—	—
Minnesota	(11)	11	—	—	West Virginia	(8)	8	—	—
Mississippi	(8)	—	8	—	Wisconsin	(12)	12	—	—
Missouri	(13)	—	13	—	Wyoming	(3)	3	—	—
Montana	(4)	4	—	—					
Nebraska	(6)	6	—	—	Totals	(531)	457	73	1

1. For explanation of split electoral votes, see p. 188.

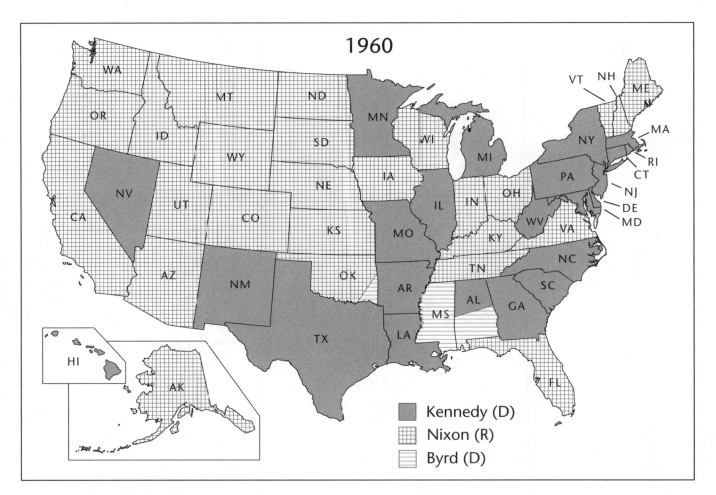

Key: D—Democrat; R—Republican

States	Electoral votes	Kennedy	Nixon	Byrd	States	Electoral votes	Kennedy	Nixon	Byrd
Alabama[1]	(11)	5	—	6	Nebraska	(6)	—	6	—
Alaska	(3)	—	3	—	Nevada	(3)	3	—	—
Arizona	(4)	—	4	—	New Hampshire	(4)	—	4	—
Arkansas	(8)	8	—	—	New Jersey	(16)	16	—	—
California	(32)	—	32	—	New Mexico	(4)	4	—	—
Colorado	(6)	—	6	—	New York	(45)	45	—	—
Connecticut	(8)	8	—	—	North Carolina	(14)	14	—	—
Delaware	(3)	3	—	—	North Dakota	(4)	—	4	—
Florida	(10)	—	10	—	Ohio	(25)	—	25	—
Georgia	(12)	12	—	—	Oklahoma[2]	(8)	—	7	1
Hawaii	(3)	3	—	—	Oregon	(6)	—	6	—
Idaho	(4)	—	4	—	Pennsylvania	(32)	32	—	—
Illinois	(27)	27	—	—	Rhode Island	(4)	4	—	—
Indiana	(13)	—	13	—	South Carolina	(8)	8	—	—
Iowa	(10)	—	10	—	South Dakota	(4)	—	4	—
Kansas	(8)	—	8	—	Tennessee	(11)	—	11	—
Kentucky	(10)	—	10	—	Texas	(24)	24	—	—
Louisiana	(10)	10	—	—	Utah	(4)	—	4	—
Maine	(5)	—	5	—	Vermont	(3)	—	3	—
Maryland	(9)	9	—	—	Virginia	(12)	—	12	—
Massachusetts	(16)	16	—	—	Washington	(9)	—	9	—
Michigan	(20)	20	—	—	West Virginia	(8)	8	—	—
Minnesota	(11)	11	—	—	Wisconsin	(12)	—	12	—
Mississippi[1]	(8)	—	—	8	Wyoming	(3)	—	3	—
Missouri	(13)	13	—	—	**Totals**	(537)	303	219	15
Montana	(4)	—	4	—					

1. Six Alabama electors and all eight Mississippi electors, elected as "unpledged Democrats," cast their votes for Byrd.

2. For explanation of split electoral votes, see p. 188.

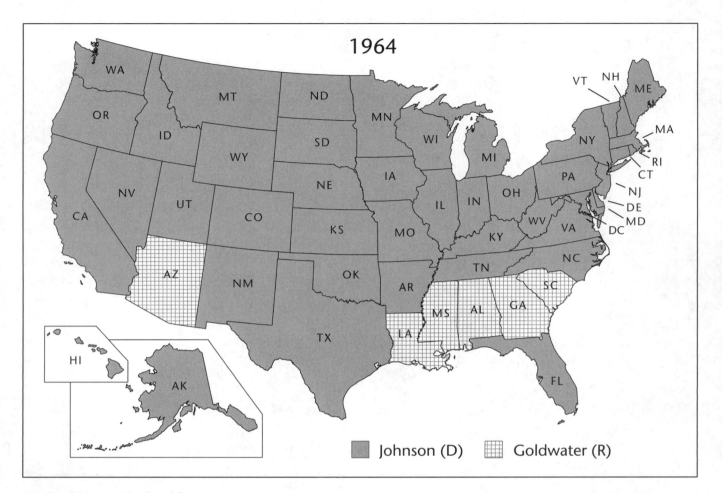

Key: D—Democrat; R—Republican

States	Electoral votes	Johnson	Goldwater	States	Electoral votes	Johnson	Goldwater
Alabama	(10)	—	10	Nebraska	(5)	5	—
Alaska	(3)	3	—	Nevada	(3)	3	—
Arizona	(5)	—	5	New Hampshire	(4)	4	—
Arkansas	(6)	6	—	New Jersey	(17)	17	—
California	(40)	40	—	New Mexico	(4)	4	—
Colorado	(6)	6	—	New York	(43)	43	—
Connecticut	(8)	8	—	North Carolina	(13)	13	—
Delaware	(3)	3	—	North Dakota	(4)	4	—
District of Columbia	(3)	3	—	Ohio	(26)	26	—
Florida	(14)	14	—	Oklahoma	(8)	8	—
Georgia	(12)	—	12	Oregon	(6)	6	—
Hawaii	(4)	4	—	Pennsylvania	(29)	29	—
Idaho	(4)	4	—	Rhode Island	(4)	4	—
Illinois	(26)	26	—	South Carolina	(8)	—	8
Indiana	(13)	13	—	South Dakota	(4)	4	—
Iowa	(9)	9	—	Tennessee	(11)	11	—
Kansas	(7)	7	—	Texas	(25)	25	—
Kentucky	(9)	9	—	Utah	(4)	4	—
Louisiana	(10)	—	10	Vermont	(3)	3	—
Maine	(4)	4	—	Virginia	(12)	12	—
Maryland	(10)	10	—	Washington	(9)	9	—
Massachusetts	(14)	14	—	West Virginia	(7)	7	—
Michigan	(21)	21	—	Wisconsin	(12)	12	—
Minnesota	(10)	10	—	Wyoming	(3)	3	—
Mississippi	(7)	—	7				
Missouri	(12)	12	—	Totals	(538)	486	52
Montana	(4)	4	—				

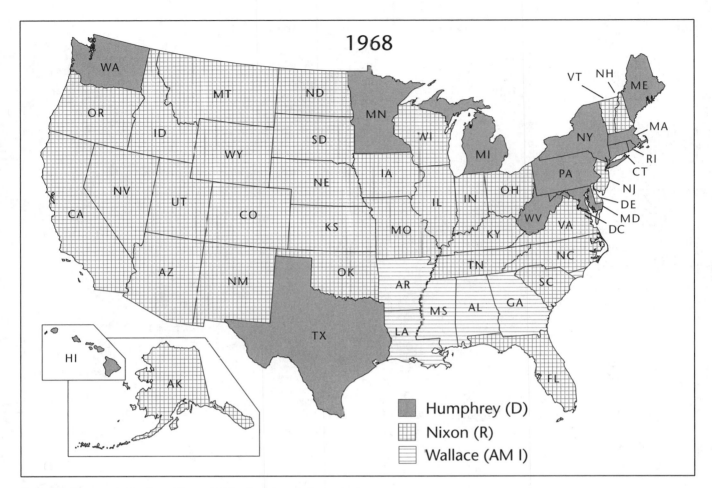

1968

Humphrey (D)
Nixon (R)
Wallace (AM I)

Key: D—Democrat; R—Republican; AM I—American Independent

States	Electoral votes	Nixon	Humphrey	Wallace	States	Electoral votes	Nixon	Humphrey	Wallace
Alabama	(10)	—	—	10	Nebraska	(5)	5	—	—
Alaska	(3)	3	—	—	Nevada	(3)	3	—	—
Arizona	(5)	5	—	—	New Hampshire	(4)	4	—	—
Arkansas	(6)	—	—	6	New Jersey	(17)	17	—	—
California	(40)	40	—	—	New Mexico	(4)	4	—	—
Colorado	(6)	6	—	—	New York	(43)	—	43	—
Connecticut	(8)	—	8	—	North Carolina[1]	(13)	12	—	1
Delaware	(3)	3	—	—	North Dakota	(4)	4	—	—
District of Columbia	(3)	—	3	—	Ohio	(26)	26	—	—
Florida	(14)	14	—	—	Oklahoma	(8)	8	—	—
Georgia	(12)	—	—	12	Oregon	(6)	6	—	—
Hawaii	(4)	—	4	—	Pennsylvania	(29)	—	29	—
Idaho	(4)	4	—	—	Rhode Island	(4)	—	4	—
Illinois	(26)	26	—	—	South Carolina	(8)	8	—	—
Indiana	(13)	13	—	—	South Dakota	(4)	4	—	—
Iowa	(9)	9	—	—	Tennessee	(11)	11	—	—
Kansas	(7)	7	—	—	Texas	(25)	—	25	—
Kentucky	(9)	9	—	—	Utah	(4)	4	—	—
Louisiana	(10)	—	—	10	Vermont	(3)	3	—	—
Maine	(4)	—	4	—	Virginia	(12)	12	—	—
Maryland	(10)	—	10	—	Washington	(9)	—	9	—
Massachusetts	(14)	—	14	—	West Virginia	(7)	—	7	—
Michigan	(21)	—	21	—	Wisconsin	(12)	12	—	—
Minnesota	(10)	—	10	—	Wyoming	(3)	3	—	—
Mississippi	(7)	—	—	7					
Missouri	(12)	12	—	—	Totals	(538)	301	191	46
Montana	(4)	4	—	—					

1. For explanation of split electoral votes, see p. 188.

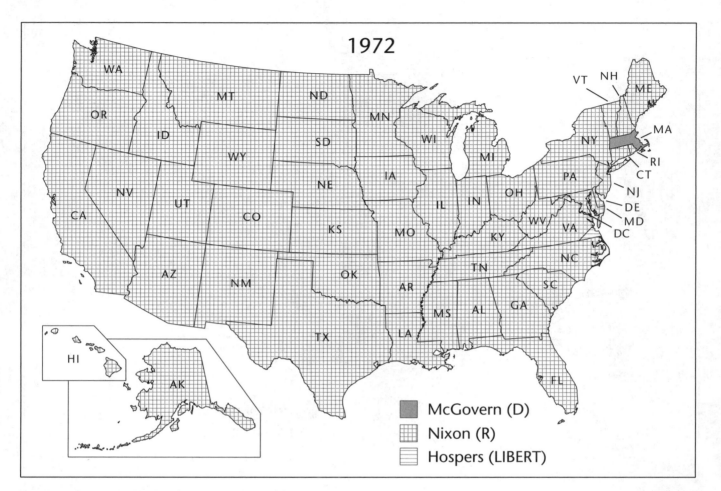

1972

■ McGovern (D)
▦ Nixon (R)
▤ Hospers (LIBERT)

Key: D—Democrat; LIBERT—Libertarian; R—Republican

States	Electoral votes	Nixon	McGovern	Hospers	States	Electoral votes	Nixon	McGovern	Hospers
Alabama	(9)	9	—	—	Nebraska	(5)	5	—	—
Alaska	(3)	3	—	—	Nevada	(3)	3	—	—
Arizona	(6)	6	—	—	New Hampshire	(4)	4	—	—
Arkansas	(6)	6	—	—	New Jersey	(17)	17	—	—
California	(45)	45	—	—	New Mexico	(4)	4	—	—
Colorado	(7)	7	—	—	New York	(41)	41	—	—
Connecticut	(8)	8	—	—	North Carolina	(13)	13	—	—
Delaware	(3)	3	—	—	North Dakota	(3)	3	—	—
District of Columbia	(3)	—	3	—	Ohio	(25)	25	—	—
Florida	(17)	17	—	—	Oklahoma	(8)	8	—	—
Georgia	(12)	12	—	—	Oregon	(6)	6	—	—
Hawaii	(4)	4	—	—	Pennsylvania	(27)	27	—	—
Idaho	(4)	4	—	—	Rhode Island	(4)	4	—	—
Illinois	(26)	26	—	—	South Carolina	(8)	8	—	—
Indiana	(13)	13	—	—	South Dakota	(4)	4	—	—
Iowa	(8)	8	—	—	Tennessee	(10)	10	—	—
Kansas	(7)	7	—	—	Texas	(26)	26	—	—
Kentucky	(9)	9	—	—	Utah	(4)	4	—	—
Louisiana	(10)	10	—	—	Vermont	(3)	3	—	—
Maine	(4)	4	—	—	Virginia[1]	(12)	11	—	1
Maryland	(10)	10	—	—	Washington	(9)	9	—	—
Massachusetts	(14)	—	14	—	West Virginia	(6)	6	—	—
Michigan	(21)	21	—	—	Wisconsin	(11)	11	—	—
Minnesota	(10)	10	—	—	Wyoming	(3)	3	—	—
Mississippi	(7)	7	—	—					
Missouri	(12)	12	—	—	Totals	(538)	520	17	1
Montana	(4)	4	—	—					

1. For explanation of split electoral votes, see p. 188.

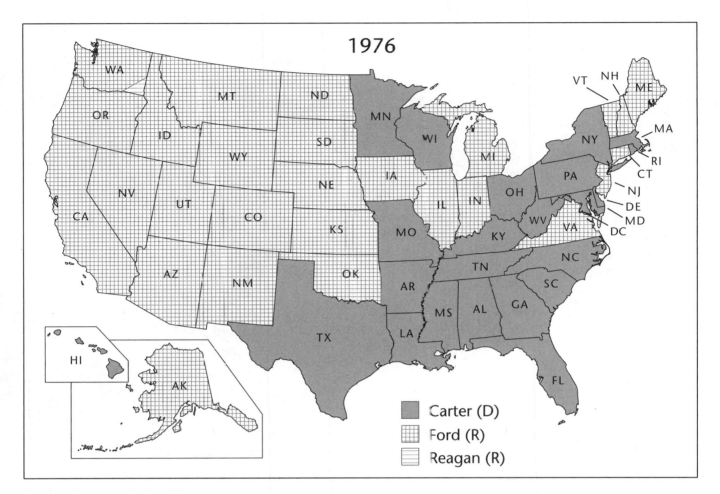

1976

Carter (D)
Ford (R)
Reagan (R)

Key: D—Democrat; R—Republican

States	Electoral votes	Carter	Ford	Reagan	States	Electoral votes	Carter	Ford	Reagan
Alabama	(9)	9	—	—	Nebraska	(5)	—	5	—
Alaska	(3)	—	3	—	Nevada	(3)	—	3	—
Arizona	(6)	—	6	—	New Hampshire	(4)	—	4	—
Arkansas	(6)	6	—	—	New Jersey	(17)	—	17	—
California	(45)	—	45	—	New Mexico	(4)	—	4	—
Colorado	(7)	—	7	—	New York	(41)	41	—	—
Connecticut	(8)	—	8	—	North Carolina	(13)	13	—	—
Delaware	(3)	3	—	—	North Dakota	(3)	—	3	—
District of Columbia	(3)	3	—	—	Ohio	(25)	25	—	—
Florida	(17)	17	—	—	Oklahoma	(8)	—	8	—
Georgia	(12)	12	—	—	Oregon	(6)	—	6	—
Hawaii	(4)	4	—	—	Pennsylvania	(27)	27	—	—
Idaho	(4)	—	4	—	Rhode Island	(4)	4	—	—
Illinois	(26)	—	26	—	South Carolina	(8)	8	—	—
Indiana	(13)	—	13	—	South Dakota	(4)	—	4	—
Iowa	(8)	—	8	—	Tennessee	(10)	10	—	—
Kansas	(7)	—	7	—	Texas	(26)	26	—	—
Kentucky	(9)	9	—	—	Utah	(4)	—	4	—
Louisiana	(10)	10	—	—	Vermont	(3)	—	3	—
Maine	(4)	—	4	—	Virginia	(12)	—	12	—
Maryland	(10)	10	—	—	Washington[1]	(9)	—	8	1
Massachusetts	(14)	14	—	—	West Virginia	(6)	6	—	—
Michigan	(21)	—	21	—	Wisconsin	(11)	11	—	—
Minnesota	(10)	10	—	—	Wyoming	(3)	—	3	—
Mississippi	(7)	7	—	—					
Missouri	(12)	12	—	—	Totals	(538)	297	240	1
Montana	(4)	—	4	—					

1. For explanation of split electoral votes, see p. 188.

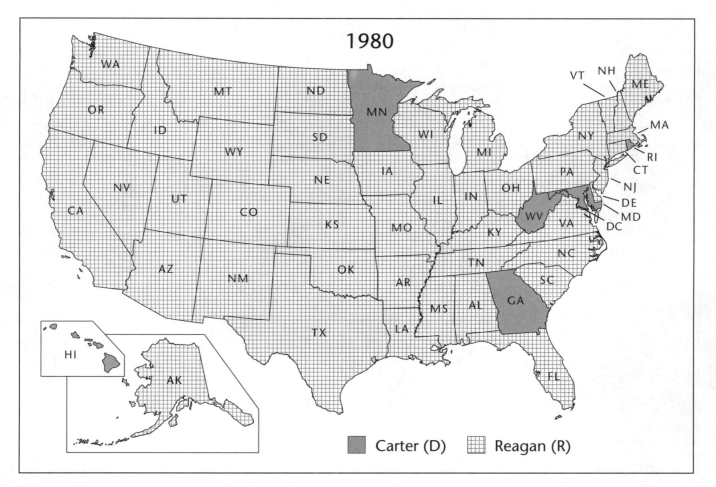

1980

Carter (D)   Reagan (R)

Key: D—Democrat; R—Republican

States	Electoral votes	Reagan	Carter	States	Electoral votes	Reagan	Carter
Alabama	(9)	9	—	Nebraska	(5)	5	—
Alaska	(3)	3	—	Nevada	(3)	3	—
Arizona	(6)	6	—	New Hampshire	(4)	4	—
Arkansas	(6)	6	—	New Jersey	(17)	17	—
California	(45)	45	—	New Mexico	(4)	4	—
Colorado	(7)	7	—	New York	(41)	41	—
Connecticut	(8)	8	—	North Carolina	(13)	13	—
Delaware	(3)	3	—	North Dakota	(3)	3	—
District of Columbia	(3)	—	3	Ohio	(25)	25	—
Florida	(17)	17	—	Oklahoma	(8)	8	—
Georgia	(12)	—	12	Oregon	(6)	6	—
Hawaii	(4)	—	4	Pennsylvania	(27)	27	—
Idaho	(4)	4	—	Rhode Island	(4)	—	4
Illinois	(26)	26	—	South Carolina	(8)	8	—
Indiana	(13)	13	—	South Dakota	(4)	4	—
Iowa	(8)	8	—	Tennessee	(10)	10	—
Kansas	(7)	7	—	Texas	(26)	26	—
Kentucky	(9)	9	—	Utah	(4)	4	—
Louisiana	(10)	10	—	Vermont	(3)	3	—
Maine	(4)	4	—	Virginia	(12)	12	—
Maryland	(10)	—	10	Washington	(9)	9	—
Massachusetts	(14)	14	—	West Virginia	(6)	—	6
Michigan	(21)	21	—	Wisconsin	(11)	11	—
Minnesota	(10)	—	10	Wyoming	(3)	3	—
Mississippi	(7)	7	—				
Missouri	(12)	12	—	Totals	(538)	489	49
Montana	(4)	4	—				

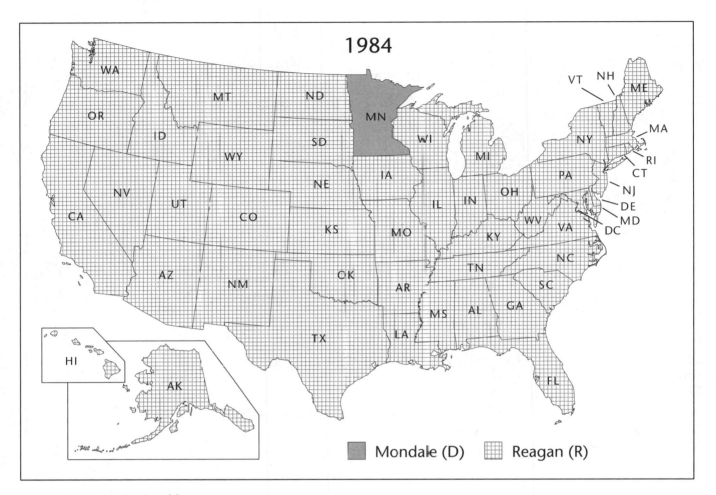

1984

Mondale (D)   Reagan (R)

Key: D—Democrat; R—Republican

States	Electoral votes	Reagan	Mondale	States	Electoral votes	Reagan	Mondale
Alabama	(9)	9	—	Nebraska	(5)	5	—
Alaska	(3)	3	—	Nevada	(4)	4	—
Arizona	(7)	7	—	New Hampshire	(4)	4	—
Arkansas	(6)	6	—	New Jersey	(16)	16	—
California	(47)	47	—	New Mexico	(5)	5	—
Colorado	(8)	8	—	New York	(36)	36	—
Connecticut	(8)	8	—	North Carolina	(13)	13	—
Delaware	(3)	3	—	North Dakota	(3)	3	—
District of Columbia	(3)	—	3	Ohio	(23)	23	—
Florida	(21)	21	—	Oklahoma	(8)	8	—
Georgia	(12)	12	—	Oregon	(7)	7	—
Hawaii	(4)	4	—	Pennsylvania	(25)	25	—
Idaho	(4)	4	—	Rhode Island	(4)	4	—
Illinois	(24)	24	—	South Carolina	(8)	8	—
Indiana	(12)	12	—	South Dakota	(3)	3	—
Iowa	(8)	8	—	Tennessee	(11)	11	—
Kansas	(7)	7	—	Texas	(29)	29	—
Kentucky	(9)	9	—	Utah	(5)	5	—
Louisiana	(10)	10	—	Vermont	(3)	3	—
Maine	(4)	4	—	Virginia	(12)	12	—
Maryland	(10)	10	—	Washington	(10)	10	—
Massachusetts	(13)	13	—	West Virginia	(6)	6	—
Michigan	(20)	20	—	Wisconsin	(11)	11	—
Minnesota	(10)	—	10	Wyoming	(3)	3	—
Mississippi	(7)	7	—				
Missouri	(11)	11	—	Totals	(538)	525	13
Montana	(4)	4	—				

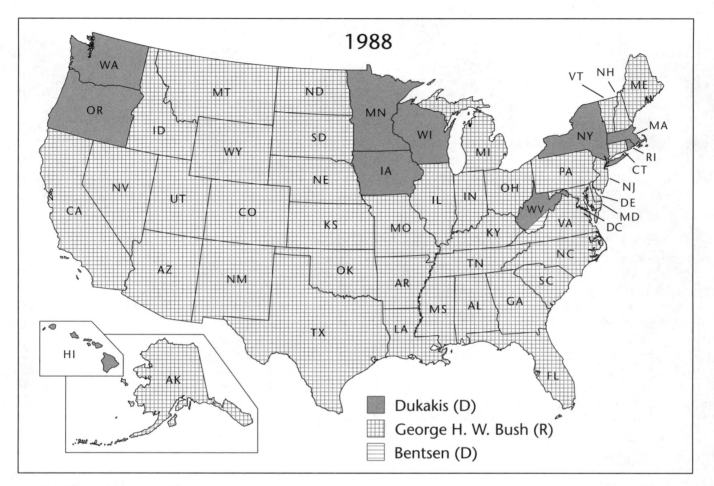

Key: D—Democrat; R—Republican

States	Electoral votes	Bush	Dukakis	Bentsen	States	Electoral votes	Bush	Dukakis	Bentsen
Alabama	(9)	9	—	—	Nebraska	(5)	5	—	—
Alaska	(3)	3	—	—	Nevada	(4)	4	—	—
Arizona	(7)	7	—	—	New Hampshire	(4)	4	—	—
Arkansas	(6)	6	—	—	New Jersey	(16)	16	—	—
California	(47)	47	—	—	New Mexico	(5)	5	—	—
Colorado	(8)	8	—	—	New York	(36)	—	36	—
Connecticut	(8)	8	—	—	North Carolina	(13)	13	—	—
Delaware	(3)	3	—	—	North Dakota	(3)	3	—	—
District of Columbia	(3)	—	3	—	Ohio	(23)	23	—	—
Florida	(21)	21	—	—	Oklahoma	(8)	8	—	—
Georgia	(12)	12	—	—	Oregon	(7)	—	7	—
Hawaii	(4)	—	4	—	Pennsylvania	(25)	25	—	—
Idaho	(4)	4	—	—	Rhode Island	(4)	—	4	—
Illinois	(24)	24	—	—	South Carolina	(8)	8	—	—
Indiana	(12)	12	—	—	South Dakota	(3)	3	—	—
Iowa	(8)	—	8	—	Tennessee	(11)	11	—	—
Kansas	(7)	7	—	—	Texas	(29)	29	—	—
Kentucky	(9)	9	—	—	Utah	(5)	5	—	—
Louisiana	(10)	10	—	—	Vermont	(3)	3	—	—
Maine	(4)	4	—	—	Virginia	(12)	12	—	—
Maryland	(10)	10	—	—	Washington	(10)	—	10	—
Massachusetts	(13)	—	13	—	West Virginia[1]	(6)	—	5	1
Michigan	(20)	20	—	—	Wisconsin	(11)	—	11	—
Minnesota	(10)	—	10	—	Wyoming	(3)	3	—	—
Mississippi	(7)	7	—	—					
Missouri	(11)	11	—	—	Totals	(538)	426	111	1
Montana	(4)	4	—	—					

1. For explanation of split electoral vote, see p. 188.

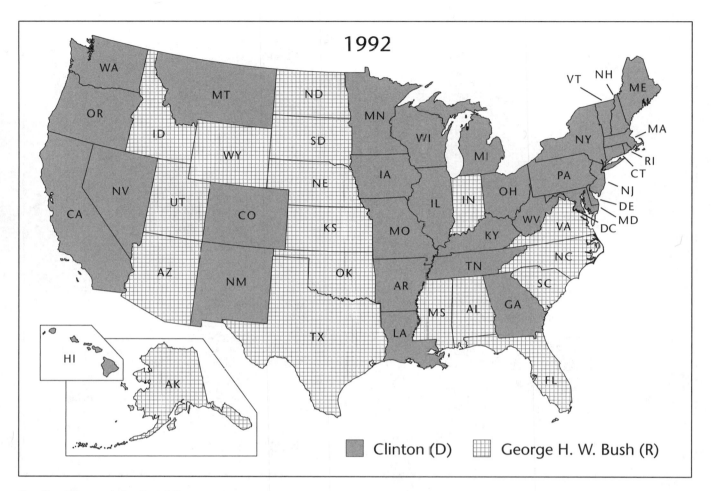

1992

Clinton (D)   George H. W. Bush (R)

Key: D—Democrat; R—Republican

States	Electoral votes	Clinton	Bush	States	Electoral votes	Clinton	Bush
Alabama	(9)	—	9	Nebraska	(5)	—	5
Alaska	(3)	—	3	Nevada	(4)	4	—
Arizona	(8)	—	8	New Hampshire	(4)	4	—
Arkansas	(6)	6	—	New Jersey	(15)	15	—
California	(54)	54	—	New Mexico	(5)	5	—
Colorado	(8)	8	—	New York	(33)	33	—
Connecticut	(8)	8	—	North Carolina	(14)	—	14
Delaware	(3)	3	—	North Dakota	(3)	—	3
District of Columbia	(3)	3	—	Ohio	(21)	21	—
Florida	(25)	—	25	Oklahoma	(8)	—	8
Georgia	(13)	13	—	Oregon	(7)	7	—
Hawaii	(4)	4	—	Pennsylvania	(23)	23	—
Idaho	(4)	—	4	Rhode Island	(4)	4	—
Illinois	(22)	22	—	South Carolina	(8)	—	8
Indiana	(12)	—	12	South Dakota	(3)	—	3
Iowa	(7)	7	—	Tennessee	(11)	11	—
Kansas	(6)	—	6	Texas	(32)	—	32
Kentucky	(8)	8	—	Utah	(5)	—	5
Louisiana	(9)	9	—	Vermont	(3)	3	—
Maine	(4)	4	—	Virginia	(13)	—	13
Maryland	(10)	10	—	Washington	(11)	11	—
Massachusetts	(12)	12	—	West Virginia	(5)	5	—
Michigan	(18)	18	—	Wisconsin	(11)	11	—
Minnesota	(10)	10	—	Wyoming	(3)	—	3
Mississippi	(7)	—	7				
Missouri	(11)	11	—	Totals	(538)	370	168
Montana	(3)	3	—				

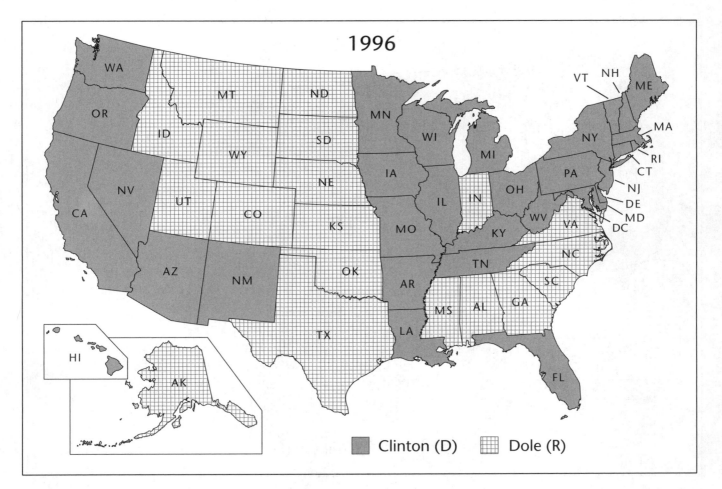

1996

Clinton (D) ▢ Dole (R)

Key: D—Democrat; R—Republican

States	Electoral votes	Clinton	Dole	States	Electoral votes	Clinton	Dole
Alabama	(9)	—	9	Nebraska	(5)	—	5
Alaska	(3)	—	3	Nevada	(4)	4	—
Arizona	(8)	8	—	New Hampshire	(4)	4	—
Arkansas	(6)	6	—	New Jersey	(15)	15	—
California	(54)	54	—	New Mexico	(5)	5	—
Colorado	(8)	—	8	New York	(33)	33	—
Connecticut	(8)	8	—	North Carolina	(14)	—	14
Delaware	(3)	3	—	North Dakota	(3)	—	3
District of Columbia	(3)	3	—	Ohio	(21)	21	—
Florida	(25)	25	—	Oklahoma	(8)	—	8
Georgia	(13)	—	13	Oregon	(7)	7	—
Hawaii	(4)	4	—	Pennsylvania	(23)	23	—
Idaho	(4)	—	4	Rhode Island	(4)	4	—
Illinois	(22)	22	—	South Carolina	(8)	—	8
Indiana	(12)	—	12	South Dakota	(3)	—	3
Iowa	(7)	7	—	Tennessee	(11)	11	—
Kansas	(6)	—	6	Texas	(32)	—	32
Kentucky	(8)	8	—	Utah	(5)	—	5
Louisiana	(9)	9	—	Vermont	(3)	3	—
Maine	(4)	4	—	Virginia	(13)	—	13
Maryland	(10)	10	—	Washington	(11)	11	—
Massachusetts	(12)	12	—	West Virginia	(5)	5	—
Michigan	(18)	18	—	Wisconsin	(11)	11	—
Minnesota	(10)	10	—	Wyoming	(3)	—	3
Mississippi	(7)	—	7				
Missouri	(11)	11	—	Totals	(538)	379	159
Montana	(3)	—	3				

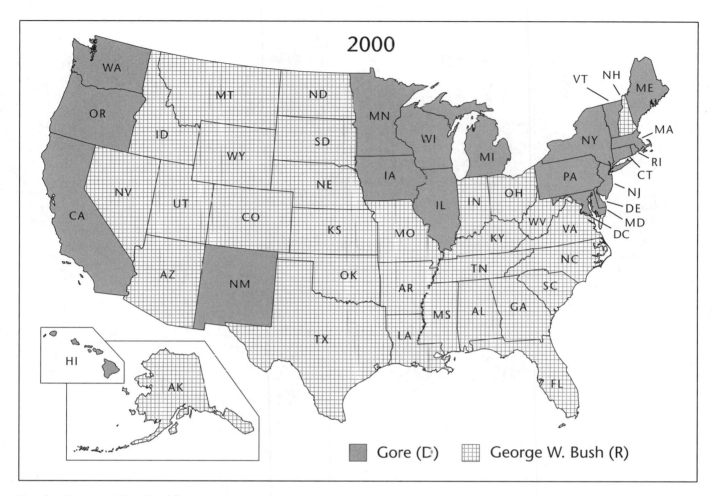

Key: D—Democrat; R—Republican

States	Electoral votes	Bush	Gore	States	Electoral votes	Bush	Gore
Alabama	(9)	9	—	Nebraska	(5)	5	—
Alaska	(3)	3	—	Nevada	(4)	4	—
Arizona	(8)	8	—	New Hampshire	(4)	4	—
Arkansas	(6)	6	—	New Jersey	(15)	—	15
California	(54)	—	54	New Mexico	(5)	—	5
Colorado	(8)	8	—	New York	(33)	—	33
Connecticut	(8)	—	8	North Carolina	(14)	14	—
Delaware	(3)	—	3	North Dakota	(3)	3	—
District of Columbia[1]	(3)	—	2	Ohio	(21)	21	—
Florida	(25)	25	—	Oklahoma	(8)	8	—
Georgia	(13)	13	—	Oregon	(7)	—	7
Hawaii	(4)	—	4	Pennsylvania	(23)	—	23
Idaho	(4)	4	—	Rhode Island	(4)	—	4
Illinois	(22)	—	22	South Carolina	(8)	8	—
Indiana	(12)	12	—	South Dakota	(3)	3	—
Iowa	(7)	—	7	Tennessee	(11)	11	—
Kansas	(6)	6	—	Texas	(32)	32	—
Kentucky	(8)	8	—	Utah	(5)	5	—
Louisiana	(9)	9	—	Vermont	(3)	—	3
Maine	(4)	—	4	Virginia	(13)	13	—
Maryland	(10)	—	10	Washington	(11)	—	11
Massachusetts	(12)	—	12	West Virginia	(5)	5	—
Michigan	(18)	—	18	Wisconsin	(11)	—	11
Minnesota	(10)	—	10	Wyoming	(3)	3	—
Mississippi	(7)	7	—				
Missouri	(11)	11	—	Totals	(538)	271	266
Montana	(3)	3	—				

1. For explanation of split electoral votes, see p. 188.

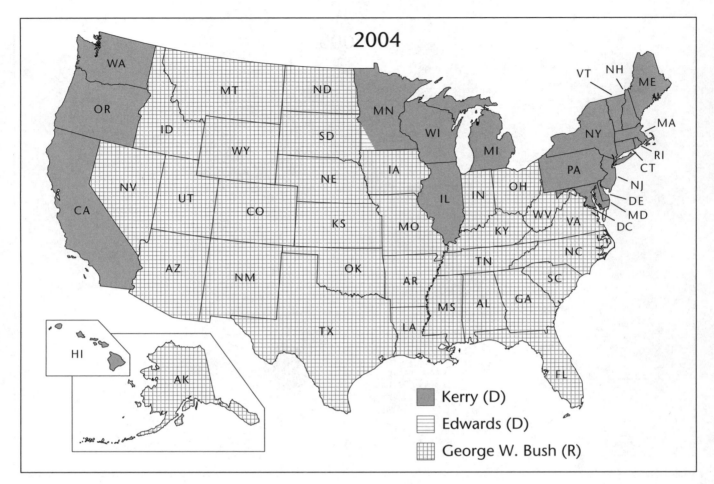

Key: D—Democrat; R—Republican

States	Electoral votes	Bush	Kerry	Edwards	States	Electoral votes	Bush	Kerry	Edwards
Alabama	(9)	9	—	—	Nebraska	(5)	5	—	—
Alaska	(3)	3	—	—	Nevada	(5)	5	—	—
Arizona	(10)	10	—	—	New Hampshire	(4)	—	4	—
Arkansas	(6)	6	—	—	New Jersey	(15)	—	15	—
California	(55)	—	55	—	New Mexico	(5)	5	—	—
Colorado	(9)	9	—	—	New York	(31)	—	31	—
Connecticut	(7)	—	7	—	North Carolina	(15)	15	—	—
Delaware	(3)	—	3	—	North Dakota	(3)	3	—	—
District of Columbia	(3)	—	3	—	Ohio	(20)	20	—	—
Florida	(27)	27	—	—	Oklahoma	(7)	7	—	—
Georgia	(15)	15	—	—	Oregon	(7)	—	7	—
Hawaii	(4)	—	4	—	Pennsylvania	(21)	—	21	—
Idaho	(4)	4	—	—	Rhode Island	(4)	—	4	—
Illinois	(21)	—	21	—	South Carolina	(8)	8	—	—
Indiana	(11)	11	—	—	South Dakota	(3)	3	—	—
Iowa	(7)	7	—	—	Tennessee	(11)	11	—	—
Kansas	(6)	6	—	—	Texas	(34)	34	—	—
Kentucky	(8)	8	—	—	Utah	(5)	5	—	—
Louisiana	(9)	9	—	—	Vermont	(3)	—	3	—
Maine	(4)	—	4	—	Virginia	(13)	13	—	—
Maryland	(10)	—	10	—	Washington	(11)	—	11	—
Massachusetts	(12)	—	12	—	West Virginia	(5)	5	—	—
Michigan	(17)	—	17	—	Wisconsin	(10)	—	10	—
Minnesota[1]	(10)	—	9	1	Wyoming	(3)	3	—	—
Mississippi	(6)	6	—	—					
Missouri	(11)	11	—	—	Totals	(538)	286	251	1
Montana	(3)	3	—	—					

1. For explanation of split electoral vote, see p. 188.

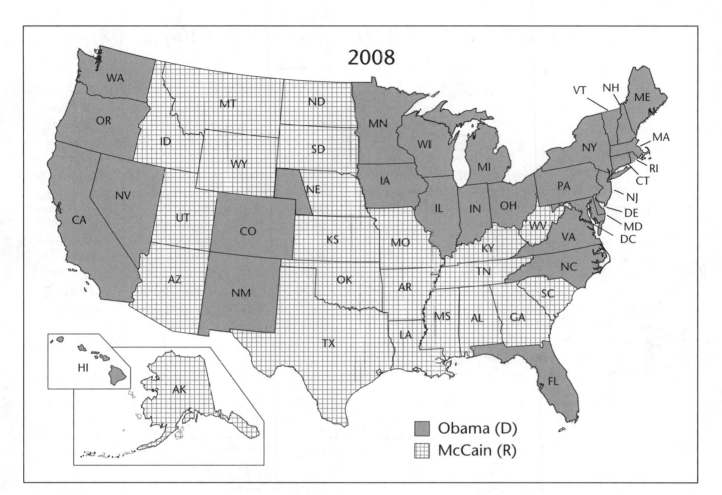

Key: D—Democrat; R—Republican

States	Electoral votes	Obama	McCain	States	Electoral votes	Obama	McCain
Alabama	(9)	—	9	Nebraska[1]	(5)	1	4
Alaska	(3)	—	3	Nevada	(5)	5	—
Arizona	(10)	—	10	New Hampshire	(4)	4	—
Arkansas	(6)	—	6	New Jersey	(15)	15	—
California	(55)	55	—	New Mexico	(5)	5	—
Colorado	(9)	9	—	New York	(31)	31	—
Connecticut	(7)	7	—	North Carolina	(15)	15	—
Delaware	(3)	3	—	North Dakota	(3)	—	3
District of Columbia	(3)	3	—	Ohio	(20)	20	—
Florida	(27)	27	—	Oklahoma	(7)	—	7
Georgia	(15)	—	15	Oregon	(7)	7	—
Hawaii	(4)	4	—	Pennsylvania	(21)	21	—
Idaho	(4)	—	4	Rhode Island	(4)	4	—
Illinois	(21)	21	—	South Carolina	(8)	—	8
Indiana	(11)	11	—	South Dakota	(3)	—	3
Iowa	(7)	7	—	Tennessee	(11)	—	11
Kansas	(6)	—	6	Texas	(34)	—	34
Kentucky	(8)	—	8	Utah	(5)	—	5
Louisiana	(9)	—	9	Vermont	(3)	3	—
Maine	(4)	4	—	Virginia	(13)	13	—
Maryland	(10)	10	—	Washington	(11)	11	—
Massachusetts	(12)	12	—	West Virginia	(5)	—	5
Michigan	(17)	17	—	Wisconsin	(10)	10	—
Minnesota	(10)	10	—	Wyoming	(3)	—	3
Mississippi	(6)	—	6				
Missouri	(11)	—	11	Totals	(538)	365	173
Montana	(3)	—	3				

1. For explanation of split electoral votes, see p. 183.

Electoral Votes for Vice President, 1804–2008

The following list gives the electoral votes for vice president from 1804 to 2008. Unless indicated by a note, the state-by-state breakdown of electoral votes for each party's vice-presidential candidate was the same as for that party's presidential candidate.

Prior to 1804, under Article II, Section 1 of the Constitution, each elector cast two votes—each vote for a different person. The electors did not distinguish between votes for president and vice president. The candidate receiving the second highest total became vice president. The Twelfth Amendment, ratified in 1804, required electors to vote separately for president and vice president.

In some cases, persons had received electoral votes although they had never been formally nominated. The word *candidate* is used in this section to designate persons receiving electoral votes.

The *Senate Manual* (Washington, D.C.: Government Printing Office, 1997) was the source used for

vice-presidential electoral votes for all elections up to 1996. The source for 2000, 2004, and 2008 was Rhodes Cook, *American Votes 28* (Washington, D.C.: CQ Press, 2009).

For political party designation, the basic source was Svend Petersen, *A Statistical History of the American Presidential Elections* (Westport, Conn.: Greenwood Press, 1981). Petersen gives the party designation of *presidential candidates only*. CQ Press adopted Petersen's party designations for the running mates of presidential candidates.

To supplement Petersen, CQ Press editors consulted the *Biographical Directory of the American Congress, 1774–1996* (Washington, D.C.: CQ Staff Directories, 1997); the *Dictionary of American Biography* (New York: Charles Scribner's Sons, 1928–1936); the *Encyclopedia of American Biography* (New York: Harper and Row, 1974); and *Who Was Who in America, 1607–1968* (Chicago: Marquis Co., 1943–1968).

Year	Candidate	Electoral Votes	Year	Candidate	Electoral Votes
1804	George Clinton (Democratic-Republican)	162	1836	Richard M. Johnson (Democrat)[8]	147
	Rufus King (Federalist)	14		William Smith (Independent Democrat)	23
1808	George Clinton (Democratic-Republican)[1]	113		Francis Granger (Whig)	77
	John Langdon (Democratic-Republican)	9		John Tyler (Whig)	47
	James Madison (Democratic-Republican)	3	1840	John Tyler (Whig)	234
	James Monroe (Democratic-Republican)	3		Richard M. Johnson (Democrat)[9]	48
	Rufus King (Federalist)	47		L. W. Tazewell (Democrat)	11
1812	Elbridge Gerry (Democratic-Republican)[2]	131		James K. Polk (Democrat)	1
	Jared Ingersoll (Federalist)	86	1844	George M. Dallas (Democrat)	170
1816	Daniel D. Tompkins (Democratic-Republican)	183		Theodore Frelinghuysen (Whig)	105
	John E. Howard (Federalist)[3]	22	1848	Millard Fillmore (Whig)	163
	James Ross (Federalist)	5		William Orlando Butler (Democrat)	127
	John Marshall (Federalist)	4	1852	William R. King (Democrat)	254
	Robert G. Harper (Federalist)	3		William Alexander Graham (Whig)	42
1820	Daniel D. Tompkins (Democratic-Republican)[4]	218	1856	John C. Breckinridge (Democrat)	174
	Richard Rush (Democratic-Republican)	1		William L. Dayton (Republican)	114
	Richard Stockton (Federalist)	8		Andrew Jackson Donelson (Whig-American)	8
	Daniel Rodney (Federalist)	4	1860	Hannibal Hamlin (Republican)	180
	Robert G. Harper (Federalist)	1		Joseph Lane (Southern Democrat)	72
1824	John C. Calhoun (Democratic-Republican)[5]	182		Edward Everett (Constitutional Union)	39
	Nathan Sanford (Democratic-Republican)	30		Herschel V. Johnson (Democrat)	12
	Nathaniel Macon (Democratic-Republican)	24	1864	Andrew Johnson (Republican)	212
	Andrew Jackson (Democratic-Republican)	13		George H. Pendleton (Democrat)	21
	Martin Van Buren (Democratic-Republican)	9	1868	Schuyler Colfax (Republican)	214
	Henry Clay (Democratic-Republican)	2		Francis P. Blair (Democrat)	80
1828	John C. Calhoun (Democratic-Republican)[6]	171	1872	Henry Wilson (Republican)	286
	William Smith (Independent Democratic-Republican)	7		Benjamin Gratz Brown (Democrat)[10]	47
	Richard Rush (National Republican)	83		Alfred H. Colquitt (Democrat)	5
1832	Martin Van Buren (Democrat)[7]	189		John M. Palmer (Democrat)	3
	William Wilkins (Democrat)	30		Thomas E. Bramlette (Democrat)	3
	Henry Lee (Independent Democrat)	11		William S. Groesbeck (Democrat)	1
	John Sergeant (National Republican)	49		Willis B. Machen (Democrat)	1
	Amos Ellmaker (Anti-Mason)	7		George W. Julian (Liberal Republican)	5
				Nathaniel P. Banks (Liberal Republican)	1

Year	Candidate	Electoral Votes	Year	Candidate	Electoral Votes
1876	William A. Wheeler (Republican)	185	1948	Alben W. Barkley (Democrat)	303
	Thomas A. Hendricks (Democrat)	184		Earl Warren (Republican)	189
1880	Chester A. Arthur (Republican)	214		Fielding L. Wright (States' Rights Democrat)	39
	William H. English (Democrat)	155	1952	Richard Nixon (Republican)	442
1884	Thomas A. Hendricks (Democrat)	219		John J. Sparkman (Democrat)	89
	John A. Logan (Republican)	182	1956	Richard Nixon (Republican)	457
1888	Levi P. Morton (Republican)	233		Estes Kefauver (Democrat)	73
	Allen G. Thurman (Democrat)	168		Herman Talmadge (Democrat)	1
1892	Adlai E. Stevenson (Democrat)	277	1960	Lyndon B. Johnson (Democrat)	303
	Whitelaw Reid (Republican)	145		Strom Thurmond (Democrat)[13]	14
	James G. Field (Populist)	22		Henry Cabot Lodge Jr. (Republican)	219
1896	Garret A. Hobart (Republican)	271		Barry Goldwater (Republican)	1
	Arthur Sewall (Democrat)[11]	149	1964	Hubert H. Humphrey (Democrat)	486
	Thomas E. Watson (Populist)	27		William E. Miller (Republican)	52
1900	Theodore Roosevelt (Republican)	292	1968	Spiro T. Agnew (Republican)	301
	Adlai E. Stevenson (Democrat)	155		Edmund S. Muskie (Democrat)	191
1904	Charles W. Fairbanks (Republican)	336		Curtis E. LeMay (American Independent)	46
	Henry G. Davis (Democrat)	140	1972	Spiro T. Agnew (Republican)	520
1908	James S. Sherman (Republican)	321		R. Sargent Shriver (Democrat)	17
	John W. Kern (Democrat)	162		Theodora Nathan (Libertarian)	1
1912	Thomas R. Marshall (Democrat)	435	1976	Walter F. Mondale (Democrat)	297
	Hiram W. Johnson (Progressive)	88		Robert J. Dole (Republican)[14]	241
	Nicholas Murray Butler (Republican)[12]	8	1980	George H. W. Bush (Republican)	489
1916	Thomas R. Marshall (Democrat)	277		Walter F. Mondale (Democrat)	49
	Charles W. Fairbanks (Republican)	254	1984	George H. W. Bush (Republican)	525
1920	Calvin Coolidge (Republican)	404		Geraldine A. Ferraro (Democrat)	13
	Franklin D. Roosevelt (Democrat)	127	1988	Dan Quayle (Republican)	426
1924	Charles G. Dawes (Republican)	382		Lloyd Bentsen (Democrat)[15]	111
	Charles W. Bryan (Democrat)	136		Michael S. Dukakis (Democrat)	1
	Burton K. Wheeler (Progressive)	13	1992	Al Gore (Democrat)	370
1928	Charles Curtis (Republican)	444		Dan Quayle (Republican)	168
	Joseph T. Robinson (Democrat)	87	1996	Al Gore (Democrat)	379
1932	John N. Garner (Democrat)	472		Jack Kemp (Republican)	159
	Charles Curtis (Republican)	59	2000	Richard B. Cheney (Republican)	271
1936	John N. Garner (Democrat)	523		Joseph Lieberman (Democrat)[16]	266
	Frank Knox (Republican)	8	2004	Richard B. Cheney (Republican)	286
1940	Henry A. Wallace (Democrat)	449		John Edwards (Democrat)[17]	252
	Charles L. McNary (Republican)	82	2008	Joseph R. Biden (Democrat)	365
1944	Harry S. Truman (Democrat)	432		Sarah Palin (Republican)	173
	John W. Bricker (Republican)	99			

1. New York cast 13 presidential electoral votes for Democratic-Republican James Madison and 6 votes for Clinton; for vice president, New York cast 13 votes for Clinton, 3 votes for Madison, and 3 votes for Monroe. Langdon received Ohio's 3 votes and Vermont's 6 votes.

2. The state-by-state vote for Gerry was the same as for Democratic-Republican presidential candidate Madison, except for Massachusetts and New Hampshire. Massachusetts cast 2 votes for Gerry and 20 votes for Ingersoll; New Hampshire cast 1 vote for Gerry and 7 votes for Ingersoll.

3. Four Federalists received vice-presidential electoral votes: Howard—Massachusetts, 22 votes; Ross—Connecticut, 5 votes; Marshall—Connecticut, 4 votes; Harper—Delaware, 3 votes.

4. The state-by-state vote for Tompkins was the same as for Democratic-Republican presidential candidate Monroe, except for Delaware, Maryland, and Massachusetts. Delaware cast 4 votes for Rodney; Maryland cast 10 votes for Tompkins and 1 for Harper; Massachusetts cast 7 votes for Tompkins and 8 for Stockton.

New Hampshire, which cast 7 presidential electoral votes for Monroe and 1 vote for John Quincy Adams, cast 7 vice-presidential electoral votes for Tompkins and 1 vote for Rush.

5. The state-by-state vice-presidential electoral vote was as follows:

Calhoun—Alabama, 5 votes; Delaware, 1 vote; Illinois, 3 votes; Indiana, 5 votes; Kentucky, 7 votes; Louisiana, 5 votes; Maine, 9 votes; Maryland, 10 votes; Massachusetts, 15 votes; Mississippi, 3 votes; New Hampshire, 7 votes; New Jersey, 8 votes; New York, 29 votes; North Carolina, 15 votes; Pennsylvania, 28 votes; Rhode Island, 3 votes; South Carolina, 11 votes; Tennessee, 11 votes; Vermont, 7 votes.

Sanford—Kentucky, 7 votes; New York, 7 votes; Ohio, 16 votes.
Macon—Virginia, 24 votes.
Jackson—Connecticut, 8 votes; Maryland, 1 vote; Missouri, 3 votes; New Hampshire, 1 vote.
Van Buren—Georgia, 9 votes.
Clay—Delaware, 2 votes.

6. The state-by-state vote for Calhoun was the same as for Democratic-Republican presidential candidate Jackson, except for Georgia, which cast 2 votes for Calhoun and 7 votes for Smith.

7. The state-by-state vote for Van Buren was the same as for Democratic-Republican presidential candidate Jackson, except for Pennsylvania, which cast 30 votes for Wilkins.

South Carolina cast 11 presidential electoral votes for Independent Democratic presidential candidate Floyd and 11 votes for Independent Democratic vice-presidential candidate Lee.

Vermont cast 7 presidential electoral votes for Anti-Masonic candidate Wirt and 7 vice-presidential electoral votes for Wirt's running mate, Ellmaker.

8. The state-by-state vote for Johnson was the same as for Democratic presidential candidate Van Buren, except for Virginia, which cast 23 votes for Smith.

Granger's state-by-state vote was the same as for Whig presidential candidate Harrison, except for Maryland and Massachusetts. Maryland cast 10 presidential electoral votes for Harrison and 10 vice-presidential votes for Tyler; Massachusetts cast 14 presidential electoral votes for Whig candidate Webster and 14 vice-presidential votes for Granger.

Tyler received 11 votes from Georgia, 10 from Maryland, 11 from South Carolina, and 15 from Tennessee.

No vice-presidential candidate received a majority of the electoral vote. As a result the Senate, for the only time in history, selected the vice president under the provisions of the Twelfth Amendment. Johnson was elected vice president by a vote of 33 to 16 over Granger.

9. The Democratic Party did not nominate a vice-presidential candidate in 1840. Johnson's state-by-state vote was the same as for presidential candidate Van Buren, except for South Carolina and Virginia. South Carolina cast 11 votes for Tazewell. Virginia cast 23 presidential electoral votes for Van Buren, 22 vice-presidential votes for Johnson, and 1 vice-presidential vote for Polk.

10. Liberal Republican and Democratic presidential candidate Horace Greeley died November 29, 1872. As a result eighteen electors pledged to Greeley cast their presidential electoral votes for Brown, Greeley's running mate.

The vice-presidential vote was as follows:

Brown—Georgia, 5 votes; Kentucky, 8 votes; Maryland, 8 votes; Missouri, 6 votes; Tennessee, 12 votes; Texas, 8 votes.

Colquitt—Georgia, 5 votes.
Palmer—Missouri, 3 votes.
Bramlette—Kentucky, 3 votes.
Groesbeck—Missouri, 1 vote.
Machen—Kentucky, 1 vote.
Julian—Missouri, 5 votes.
Banks—Georgia, 1 vote.

11. The state-by-state vote for Sewall was the same as for Democratic-Populist candidate William Jennings Bryan, except for the following states, which cast electoral votes for Watson: Arkansas, 3 votes; Louisiana, 4;

Missouri, 4; Montana, 1; Nebraska, 4; North Carolina, 5; South Dakota, 2; Utah, 1; Washington, 2; Wyoming, 1.

12. Butler received the 8 electoral votes of Vice President James Sherman, who died Oct. 30, 1912, after being renominated on the Republican ticket. Butler was named as the substitute candidate.

13. Democratic electors carried Alabama's 11 electoral votes. Five of the electors were pledged to the national Democratic ticket of Kennedy and Johnson. Six electors ran unpledged and voted for Harry F. Byrd for president and Strom Thurmond for vice president.

Mississippi's eight electors voted for Byrd and Thurmond.

In Oklahoma the Republican ticket of Nixon and Lodge carried the state, but Henry D. Irwin, one of the state's eight electors voted for Byrd for president and Goldwater for vice president.

14. Mike Padden, a Republican elector from the state of Washington cast his presidential electoral vote for Reagan instead of the Republican nominee, Ford. But he voted for Dole, Ford's running mate, for vice president. Dole thus received one more electoral vote than Ford.

15. Margaret Leach, a Democratic elector from West Virginia, cast her vice-presidential electoral vote for Dukakis, the Democratic nominee for president, and her presidential vote for his running mate, Bentsen.

16. Barbara Lett-Simmons, a Democratic elector from the District of Columbia, withheld her vice-presidential electoral vote for Lieberman (and presidential electoral vote for Gore).

17. Edwards received one more electoral vote for vice president than Democratic candidate John Kerry received for president due to an annonymous Minnesota elector who cast both presidential and vice-presidential votes for Edwards.

chapter 7

Biographical Directory of Presidential and Vice-Presidential Candidates

HE NAMES in the directory include all persons who have received electoral votes for president or vice president since 1789. Also included are prominent third-party candidates who received popular votes but no electoral votes, and Nelson A. Rockefeller, appointed vice president by Gerald R. Ford, who became president following the resignation of Richard Nixon.

The material is organized as follows: name, state of residence in the year(s) the individual received electoral votes, party or parties with which the individual identified when he or she received electoral votes, date of birth, date of death (where applicable), major offices held, and the year(s) of candidacy.

For the elections of 1789 through 1800, presidential electors did not vote separately for president or vice president. It was, therefore, difficult in many cases to determine if an individual receiving electoral votes in these elections was a candidate for the office of president or vice president. Where no determination could be made from the sources consulted by CQ Press, the year in which the individual received electoral votes is given with no specification as to whether the individual was a candidate for president or vice president.

The following sources were used: *American Political Leaders, 1789–2000*, (Washington, D.C.: CQ Press, 2000);

Biographical Directory of the United States Congress, 1774–1989, (Washington, D.C.: Government Printing Office, 1989); *Dictionary of American Biography*, (New York: Scribner's, 1928–36); John A. Garraty, ed., *Encyclopedia of American Biography*, (New York: Harper and Row, 1974); Jaques Cattell Press, ed., *Who's Who in American Politics, 1977–78*, 6th ed. (New York: R. R. Bowker, 1977); *Who Was Who in America, 1607–1968*, (Chicago: Marquis, 1943–68); Svend Petersen, *A Statistical History of the American Presidential Elections*, (Westport, Conn.: Greenwood Press, 1981); Richard M. Scammon, *America Votes 10* (Washington, D.C.: CQ Press, 1973); Richard M. Scammon and Alice V. McGillivray, *America Votes 12* (Washington, D.C.: CQ Press, 1977); *America Votes 14* (Washington, D.C.: CQ Press, 1979, *America Votes 18* (Washington, D.C.: CQ Press, 1983, *America Votes 20* (Washington, D.C.: CQ Press, 1993); Rhodes Cook, *America Votes 22* (Washington, D.C.: CQ Press, 1997); Rhodes Cook, *America Votes 24* (Washington, D.C.: CQ Press, 2001); Rhodes Cook, *America Votes 25* (Washington, D.C.: CQ Press, 2003); Rhodes Cook, *America Votes 26* (Washington, D.C.: CQ Press, 2005); Rhodes Cook, *America Votes 27* (Washington, D.C.: CQ Press, 2007); Rhodes Cook, *America Votes 28* (Washington, D.C.: CQ Press, 2009).

Adams, Charles Francis - Mass. (Free Soil) Aug. 18, 1807–Nov. 21, 1886; House, 1859–1861; minister to Great Britain, 1861–1868. Candidacy: VP - 1848.

Adams, John - Mass. (Federalist) Oct. 30, 1735–July 4, 1826; Continental Congress, 1774; signer of Declaration of Independence, 1776; minister to Great Britain, 1785; U.S. vice president, 1789–1797; U.S. president, 1797–1801. Candidacies: VP - 1789, 1792; P - 1796, 1800.

Adams, John Quincy - Mass. (Democratic-Republican, National Republican) July 11, 1767–Feb. 23, 1848; Senate, 1803–1808; minister to Russia, 1809–1814; minister to Great Britain, 1815–1817; secretary of state, 1817–1825; U.S. president, 1825–1829; House, 1831–1848. Candidacies: P - 1820, 1824, 1828.

Adams, Samuel - Mass. (Federalist) Sept. 27, 1722–Oct. 2, 1803; Continental Congress, 1774–1781; signer of Declaration of Independence; governor, 1793–1797. Candidacy: 1796.

Agnew, Spiro Theodore - Md. (Republican) Nov. 9, 1918–Sept. 17, 1996; governor, 1967–1969; U.S. vice president, 1969–1973 (resigned Oct. 10, 1973). Candidacies: VP - 1968, 1972.

Anderson, John B. - Ill. (Republican, Independent) Feb. 15, 1922– ; state's attorney, 1956–1960; House, 1961–1981. Candidacy: P - 1980.

Armstrong, James - Pa. (Federalist) Aug. 29, 1748–May 6, 1828; House, 1793–1795. Candidacy: 1789.

Arthur, Chester Alan - N.Y. (Republican) Oct. 5, 1830–Nov. 18, 1886; collector, Port of N.Y., 1871–1878; U.S. vice president, 1881; U.S. president, 1881–1885. Candidacy: VP - 1880.

Banks, Nathaniel Prentice - Mass. (Liberal Republican) Jan. 30, 1816–Sept. 1, 1894; House, 1853–1857, 1865–1873, 1875–1879, 1889–1891; governor, 1858–1861. Candidacy: VP - 1872.

Barkley, Alben William - Ky. (Democratic) Nov. 24, 1877–April 30, 1956; House, 1913–1927; Senate, 1927–1949, 1955–1956; Senate majority leader, 1937–1947; Senate minority leader, 1947–1949; U.S. vice president, 1949–1953. Candidacy: VP - 1948.

Bell, John - Tenn. (Constitutional Union) Feb. 15, 1797–Sept. 10, 1869; House, 1827–1841; Speaker of the House, 1834–1835; secretary of war, 1841; Senate, 1847–1859. Candidacy: P - 1860.

Benson, Allan Louis - N.Y. (Socialist) Nov. 6, 1871–Aug. 19, 1940; writer, editor; founder of *Reconstruction Magazine,* 1918. Candidacy: P - 1916.

Bentsen, Lloyd Millard Jr. - Texas (Democratic) Feb. 11, 1921–May 26, 2006; House 1948–1955; Senate 1971–1993; secretary of Treasury, 1993–1994. Candidacy: VP - 1988.

Biden, Joseph R. Jr. - Del. (Democratic) Nov. 20, 1942– ; Senate 1973–Jan. 15, 2009. Candidacy: VP - 2008.

Bidwell, John - Calif. (Prohibition) Aug. 5, 1819–April 4, 1900; California pioneer; major in Mexican War; House, 1865–1867. Candidacy: P - 1892.

Birney, James Gillespie - N.Y. (Liberty) Feb. 4, 1792–Nov. 25, 1857; Kentucky Legislature, 1816–1817; Alabama Legislature, 1819–1820. Candidacies: P - 1840, 1844.

Blaine, James Gillespie - Maine (Republican) Jan. 31, 1830–Jan. 27, 1893; House, 1863–1876; Speaker of the House, 1869–1875; Senate, 1876–1881; secretary of state, 1881, 1889–1892; president, first Pan American Congress, 1889. Candidacy: P - 1884.

Blair, Francis Preston Jr. - Mo. (Democratic) Feb. 19, 1821–July 8, 1875; House, 1857–1859, 1860, 1861–1862, 1863–1864; Senate, 1871–1873. Candidacy: VP - 1868.

Bramlette, Thomas E. - Ky. (Democratic) Jan. 3, 1817–Jan. 12, 1875; governor, 1863–1867. Candidacy: VP - 1872.

Breckinridge, John Cabell - Ky. (Democratic, Southern Democratic) Jan. 21, 1821–May 17, 1875; House, 1851–1855; U.S. vice president, 1857–1861; Senate, 1861; major general, Confederacy, 1861–1865; secretary of war, Confederacy, 1865. Candidacies: VP - 1856; P - 1860.

Bricker, John William - Ohio (Republican) Sept. 6, 1893–March 22, 1986; attorney general of Ohio, 1933–1937; governor, 1939–1945; Senate, 1947–1959. Candidacy: VP - 1944.

Brown, Benjamin Gratz - Mo. (Democratic) May 28, 1826–Dec. 13, 1885; Senate, 1863–1867; governor, 1871–1873. Candidacy: VP - 1872.

Bryan, Charles Wayland - Neb. (Democratic) Feb. 10, 1867–March 4, 1945; governor, 1923–1925, 1931–1935; Candidacy: VP - 1924.

Bryan, William Jennings - Neb. (Democratic, Populist) March 19, 1860–July 26, 1925; House, 1891–1895; secretary of state, 1913–1915. Candidacies: P - 1896, 1900, 1908.

Buchanan, James - Pa. (Democratic) April 23, 1791–June 1, 1868; House, 1821–1831; minister to Russia, 1832–1834; Senate, 1834–1845; secretary of state, 1845–1849; minister to Great Britain, 1853–1856; U.S. president, 1857–1861. Candidacy: P - 1856.

Burr, Aaron - N.Y. (Democratic-Republican) Feb. 6, 1756–Sept. 14, 1836; attorney general of N.Y., 1789–1790; Senate, 1791–1797; U.S. vice president, 1801–1805. Candidacies: 1792, 1796, 1800.

Bush, George H.W. - Texas (Republican) June 12, 1924– ; House, 1967–1970; ambassador to the United Nations, 1971–1973; chairman of the Republican National Committee, 1973–1974; head of the U.S. liaison office in Peking, 1974–1975; director of the Central Intelligence Agency, 1976–1977; U.S. vice president, 1981–1989; U.S. president, 1989–1993. Candidacies: VP - 1980, 1984; P - 1988, 1992.

Bush, George W. - Texas (Republican) July, 6, 1946– ; governor, 1995–2000; U.S. president, 2001–2009. Candidacies: P - 2000, 2004.

Butler, Benjamin Franklin - Mass. (Greenback, Anti-Monopoly) Nov. 5, 1818–Jan. 11, 1893; House, 1867–1875, 1877–1879; governor, 1883–1884. Candidacy: P - 1884.

Butler, Nicholas Murray - N.Y. (Republican) April 2, 1862–Dec. 7, 1947; president, Columbia University, 1901–1945; president, Carnegie Endowment for International Peace, 1925–1945. Candidacy: VP - 1912. (Substituted as candidate after Oct. 30 death of nominee James S. Sherman.)

Butler, William Orlando - Ky. (Democratic) April 19, 1791–Aug. 6, 1880; House, 1939–1943. Candidacy: VP - 1848.

Byrd, Harry Flood - Va. (States' Rights Democratic, Independent Democratic) June 10, 1887–Oct. 20, 1966; governor, 1926–1930; Senate, 1933–1965. Candidacies: P - 1956, 1960.

Calhoun, John Caldwell - S.C. (Democratic-Republican, Democratic) March 18, 1782–March 31, 1850; House, 1811–1817; secretary of war, 1817–1825; U.S. vice president, 1825–1832; Senate, 1832–1843, 1845–1850; secretary of state, 1844–1845. Candidacies: VP - 1824, 1828.

Carter, James Earl Jr. - Ga. (Democratic) Oct. 1, 1924– ; Georgia Legislature, 1963–1967; governor, 1971–1975; U.S. president, 1977–1981. Candidacies: P - 1976, 1980.

Cass, Lewis - Mich. (Democratic) Oct. 9, 1782–June 17, 1866; military and civil governor of Michigan Territory, 1813–1831; secretary of war, 1831–1836; minister to France, 1836–1842; Senate, 1845–1848, 1849–1857; secretary of state, 1857–1860. Candidacy: P - 1848.

Cheney, Richard B. - Wyo. (Republican) Jan. 30, 1941– ; House 1979–1989; secretary of defense, 1989–1993; U.S. vice president, 2001–2009. Candidacies: VP - 2000, 2004.

Clay, Henry - Ky. (Democratic-Republican, National Republican, Whig) April 12, 1777–June 29, 1852; Senate, 1806–1807, 1810–1811, 1831–1842, 1849–1852; House, 1811–1814, 1815–1821, 1823–1825; Speaker of the House, 1811–1814, 1815–1820, 1823–1825; secretary of state, 1825–1829. Candidacies: P - 1824, 1832, 1844.

Cleveland, Stephen Grover - N.Y. (Democratic) March 18, 1837–June 24, 1908; mayor of Buffalo, 1882; governor, 1883–1885; U.S. president, 1885–1889, 1893–1897. Candidacies: P - 1884, 1888, 1892.

Clinton, Bill - Ark. (Democrat) Aug. 19, 1946– ; attorney general of Arkansas, 1977–1979; governor, 1979–1981, 1983–1992; U.S. president, 1993–2001. Candidacies: P - 1992, 1996.

Clinton, De Witt - N.Y. (Independent Democratic-Republican, Federalist) March 2, 1769–Feb. 11, 1828; Senate, 1802–1803; mayor of New York, 1803–1807, 1810, 1811, 1813, 1814; governor, 1817–1823, 1825–1828. Candidacy: P - 1812.

Clinton, George - N.Y. (Democratic-Republican) July 26, 1739–April 20, 1812; Continental Congress, 1775–1776; governor, 1777–1795, 1801–1804; U.S. vice president, 1805–1812. Candidacies: VP - 1789, 1792, 1796, 1804, 1808.

Colfax, Schuyler - Ind. (Republican) March 23, 1823–Jan. 13, 1885; House, 1855–1869; Speaker of the House, 1863–1869; U.S. vice president, 1869–1873. Candidacy: VP - 1868.

Colquitt, Alfred Holt - Ga. (Democratic) April 20, 1824–March 26, 1894; House, 1853–1855; governor, 1877–1882; Senate, 1883–1894. Candidacy: VP - 1872.

Coolidge, Calvin - Mass. (Republican) July 4, 1872–Jan. 5, 1933; governor, 1919–1921; U.S. vice president, 1921–1923; U.S. president, 1923–1929. Candidacies: VP - 1920; P - 1924.

Cox, James Middleton - Ohio (Democratic) March 31, 1870–July 15, 1957; House, 1909–1913; governor, 1913–1915, 1917–1921. Candidacy: P - 1920.

Crawford, William Harris - Ga. (Democratic-Republican) Feb. 24, 1772–Sept. 15, 1834; Senate, 1807–1813; president pro tempore of the Senate, 1812–1813; secretary of war, 1815–1816; secretary of the Treasury, 1816–1825. Candidacy: P - 1824.

Curtis, Charles - Kan. (Republican) Jan. 25, 1860–Feb. 8, 1936; House, 1893–1907; Senate, 1907–1913, 1915–1929; president pro tempore of the Senate, 1911; Senate majority leader, 1925–1929; U.S. vice president, 1929–1933. Candidacies: VP - 1928, 1932.

Dallas, George Mifflin - Pa. (Democratic) July 10, 1792–Dec. 31, 1864; Senate, 1831–1833; minister to Russia, 1837–1839; U.S. vice president, 1845–1849; minister to Great Britain, 1856–1861. Candidacy: VP - 1844.

Davis, David - Ill. (Democratic) March 9, 1815–June 26, 1886; associate justice of U.S. Supreme Court, 1862–1877; Senate, 1877–1883; president pro tempore of the Senate, 1881. Candidacy: P - 1872.

Davis, Henry Gassaway - W.Va. (Democratic) Nov. 16, 1823–March 11, 1916; Senate, 1871–1883; chair of Pan American Railway Committee, 1901–1916. Candidacy: VP - 1904.

Davis, John William - W.Va., N.Y. (Democratic) April 13, 1873–March 24, 1955; House, 1911–1913; solicitor general, 1913–1918; ambassador to Great Britain, 1918–1921. Candidacy: P - 1924.

Dawes, Charles Gates - Ill. (Republican) Aug. 27, 1865–April 3, 1951; U.S. comptroller of the currency, 1898–1901; first director of Bureau of the Budget, 1921–1922; U.S. vice president, 1925–1929; ambassador to Great Britain, 1929–1932. Candidacy: VP - 1924.

Dayton, William Lewis - N.J. (Republican) Feb. 17, 1807–Dec. 1, 1864; Senate, 1842–1851; minister to France, 1861–1864. Candidacy: VP - 1856.

Debs, Eugene Victor - Ind. (Socialist) Nov. 5, 1855–Oct. 20, 1926; Indiana Legislature, 1885; president, American Railway Union, 1893–1897. Candidacies: P - 1900, 1904, 1908, 1912, 1920.

Dewey, Thomas Edmund - N.Y. (Republican) March 24, 1902–March 16, 1971; district attorney, New York County, 1937–1941; governor, 1943–1955. Candidacies: P - 1944, 1948.

Dole, Robert Joseph - Kan. (Republican) July 22, 1923– ; House, 1961–1969; Senate, 1969–1996; Senate majority leader, 1985–1987, 1995–1996; Senate minority leader, 1987–1995; chair of the Republican National Committee, 1971–1973. Candidacies: VP - 1976; P - 1996.

Donelson, Andrew Jackson - Tenn. (American "Know-Nothing") Aug. 25, 1799–June 26, 1871; minister to Prussia, 1846–1848; minister to Germany, 1848–1849. Candidacy: VP - 1856.

Douglas, Stephen Arnold - Ill. (Democratic) April 23, 1813–June 3, 1861; House, 1843–1847; Senate, 1847–1861. Candidacy: P - 1860.

Dukakis, Michael Stanley - Mass. (Democratic) Nov. 3, 1933– ; governor, 1975–1979, 1983–1991. Candidacy: P - 1988.

Eagleton, Thomas Francis - Mo. (Democratic) Sept. 4, 1929–March 4, 2007; attorney general of Missouri, 1961–1965; lieutenant governor, 1965–1968; Senate, 1968–1987. Candidacy: VP - 1972. (Resigned from Democratic ticket July 31; replaced by R. Sargent Shriver Jr.)

Edwards, John - N.C. (Democrat) June 10, 1953– ; Senate 1999–2005; Candidacy: VP - 2004.

Eisenhower, Dwight David - N.Y., Pa. (Republican) Oct. 14, 1890–March 28, 1969; general of U.S. Army, 1942–1948; Army chief of staff, 1945–1948; president of Columbia University, 1948–1951; commander of North Atlantic Treaty Organization, 1951–1952; U.S. president, 1953–1961. Candidacies: P - 1952, 1956.

Ellmaker, Amos - Pa. (Anti-Masonic) Feb. 2, 1787–Nov. 28, 1851; elected to the House for the term beginning in 1815 but did not qualify; attorney general of Pennsylvania, 1816–1819, 1828–1829. Candidacy: VP - 1832.

Ellsworth, Oliver - Conn. (Federalist) April 29, 1745–Nov. 26, 1807; Continental Congress, 1778–1783; Senate, 1789–1796; chief justice of the United States, 1796–1800; minister to France, 1799. Candidacy: 1796.

English, William Hayden - Ind. (Democratic) Aug. 27, 1822–Feb. 7, 1896; House, 1853–1861. Candidacy: VP - 1880.

Everett, Edward - Mass. (Constitutional Union) April 11, 1794–Jan. 15, 1865; House, 1825–1835; governor, 1836–1840; minister to Great Britain, 1841–1845; president of Harvard University, 1846–1849; secretary of state, 1852–1853; Senate, 1853–1854. Candidacy: VP - 1860.

Fairbanks, Charles Warren - Ind. (Republican) May 11, 1852–June 4, 1918; Senate, 1897–1905; U.S. vice president, 1905–1909. Candidacies: VP - 1904, 1916.

Ferraro, Geraldine Anne - N.Y. (Democratic) Aug. 26, 1935– ; assistant district attorney, Queens County, 1974–1978; House, 1979–1985. Candidacy: VP - 1984.

Field, James Gaven - Va. (Populist) Feb. 24, 1826–Oct. 12, 1901; major in the Confederate Army, 1861–1865; attorney general of Virginia, 1877–1882. Candidacy: VP - 1892.

Fillmore, Millard - N.Y. (Whig, American "Know-Nothing") Jan. 7, 1800–March 8, 1874; House, 1833–1835, 1837–1843; N.Y. comptroller, 1847–1849; U.S. vice president, 1849–1850; U.S. president, 1850–1853. Candidacies: VP - 1848; P - 1856.

Fisk, Clinton Bowen - N.J. (Prohibition) Dec. 8, 1828–July 9, 1890; Civil War brevet major general; founder of Fisk University, 1866; member, Board of Indian Commissioners, 1874, president, 1881–1890. Candidacy: P - 1888.

Floyd, John - Va. (Independent Democratic) April 24, 1783–Aug. 17, 1837; House, 1817–1829; governor, 1830–1834. Candidacy: P - 1832.

Ford, Gerald Rudolph Jr. - Mich. (Republican) July 14, 1913–Dec. 26, 2006; House, 1949–1973; House minority leader, 1965–1973; U.S. vice president, 1973–1974; U.S. president, 1974–1977. Candidacy: P - 1976.

Frelinghuysen, Theodore - N.J. (Whig) March 28, 1787–April 12, 1862; attorney general of New Jersey, 1817–1829; Senate, 1829–1835; president of Rutgers College, 1850–1862. Candidacy: VP - 1844.

Fremont, John Charles - Calif. (Republican) Jan. 21, 1813–July 13, 1890; explorer and Army officer in West before 1847; Senate, 1850–1851; governor of Arizona Territory, 1878–1881. Candidacy: P - 1856.

Garfield, James Abram - Ohio (Republican) Nov. 19, 1831–Sept. 19, 1881; major general in Union Army during Civil War; House, 1863–1880; U.S. president, 1881. Candidacy: P - 1880.

Garner, John Nance - Texas (Democratic) Nov. 22, 1868–Nov. 7, 1967; House, 1903–1933; House minority leader, 1929–1931; Speaker of the House, 1931–1933; U.S. vice president, 1933–1941. Candidacies: VP - 1932, 1936.

Gerry, Elbridge - Mass. (Democratic-Republican) July 17, 1744–Nov. 23, 1814; Continental Congress, 1776–1780, 1783–1785; signer of Declaration of Independence; Constitutional Convention, 1787; House, 1789–1793; governor, 1810–1812; U.S. vice president, 1813–1814. Candidacy: VP - 1812.

Goldwater, Barry Morris - Ariz. (Republican) Jan. 1, 1909–May 29, 1998; Senate, 1953–1965, 1969–1987. Candidacies: VP - 1960; P - 1964.

Gore, Albert Jr. - Tenn. (Democratic) March 31, 1948–; House, 1977–1985; Senate, 1985–1993; U.S. vice president, 1993–2001. Candidacies: VP - 1992, 1996; P - 2000.

Graham, William Alexander - N.C. (Whig) Sept. 5, 1804–Aug. 11, 1875; Senate, 1840–1843; governor, 1845–1849; secretary of the Navy, 1850–1852; Confederate Senate, 1864. Candidacy: VP - 1852.

Granger, Francis - N.Y. (Whig) Dec. 1, 1792–Aug. 31, 1868; House, 1835–1837, 1839–1841, 1841–1843; postmaster general, 1841. Candidacy: VP - 1836.

Grant, Ulysses Simpson - Ill. (Republican) April 27, 1822–July 23, 1885; commander-in-chief, Union Army during Civil War; U.S. president, 1869–1877. Candidacies: P - 1868, 1872.

Greeley, Horace - N.Y. (Liberal Republican, Democratic) Feb. 3, 1811–Nov. 29, 1872; founder and editor, *New York Tribune*, 1841–1872; House, 1848–1849. Candidacy: P - 1872.

Griffin, S. Marvin - Ga. (American Independent) Sept. 4, 1907–June 13, 1982; governor, 1955–1959. Candidacy: VP - 1968. (Substituted as candidate until permanent candidate Curtis LeMay was chosen.)

Groesbeck, William Slocum - Ohio (Democratic) July 24, 1815–July 7, 1897; House, 1857–1859; delegate to International Monetary Conference in Paris, 1878. Candidacy: VP - 1872.

Hale, John Parker - N.H. (Free Soil) March 31, 1806–Nov. 19, 1873; House, 1843–1845; Senate, 1847–1853, 1855–1865; minister to Spain, 1865–1869. Candidacy: P - 1852.

Hamlin, Hannibal - Maine (Republican) Aug. 27, 1809–July 4, 1891; House, 1843–1847; Senate, 1848–1857, 1857–1861, 1869–1881; governor, 1857; U.S. vice president, 1861–1865. Candidacy: VP - 1860.

Hancock, John - Mass. (Federalist) Jan. 23, 1737–Oct. 8, 1793; Continental Congress, 1775–1778, 1785–1786; president of Continental Congress, 1775–1777; governor, 1780–1785, 1787–1793. Candidacy: 1789.

Hancock, Winfield Scott - Pa. (Democratic) Feb. 14, 1824 - Feb. 9, 1886; brigadier general, commander of II Army Corps, Civil War. Candidacy: P - 1880.

Harding, Warren Gamaliel - Ohio (Republican) Nov. 2, 1865–Aug. 2, 1923; lieutenant governor, 1904–1905; Senate, 1915–1921; U.S. president, 1921–1923. Candidacy: P - 1920.

Harper, Robert Goodloe - Md. (Federalist) January 1765–Jan. 14, 1825; House, 1795–1801; Senate, 1816. Candidacies: VP - 1816, 1820.

Harrison, Benjamin - Ind. (Republican) Aug. 20, 1833–March 13, 1901; Union officer in Civil War; Senate, 1881–1887; U.S. president, 1889–1893. Candidacies: P - 1888, 1892.

Harrison, Robert H. - Md. 1745–April 2, 1790; chief justice, General Court of Maryland, 1781. Candidacy: 1789.

Harrison, William Henry - Ohio (Whig) Feb. 9, 1773–April 4, 1841; delegate to Congress from the Northwest Territory, 1799–1800; territorial governor of Indiana, 1801–1813; House, 1816–1819; Senate, 1825–1828; U.S. president, 1841. Candidacies: P - 1836, 1840.

Hayes, Rutherford Birchard - Ohio (Republican) Oct. 4, 1822–Jan. 17, 1893; major general in Union Army during Civil War; House, 1865–1867; governor, 1868–1872, 1876–1877; U.S. president, 1877–1881. Candidacy: P - 1876.

Hendricks, Thomas Andrews - Ind. (Democratic) Sept. 7, 1819–Nov. 25, 1885; House, 1851–1855; Senate, 1863–1869; governor, 1873–1877; U.S. vice president, 1885. Candidacies: P - 1872; VP - 1876, 1884.

Henry, John - Md. (Democratic-Republican) Nov. 1750–Dec. 16, 1798; Continental Congress, 1778–1780, 1785–1786; Senate, 1789–1797; governor, 1797–1798. Candidacy: 1796.

Hobart, Garret Augustus - N.J. (Republican) June 3, 1844–Nov. 21, 1899; New Jersey Senate, 1876–1882; president of New Jersey Senate, 1881–1882; Republican National Committee, 1884–1896; U.S. vice president, 1897–1899. Candidacy: VP - 1896.

Hoover, Herbert Clark - Calif. (Republican) Aug. 10, 1874–Oct. 20, 1964; U.S. food administrator, 1917–1919; secretary of commerce, 1921–1928; U.S. president, 1929–1933; chair, Commission on Organization of the Executive Branch of Government, 1947–1949, 1953–1955. Candidacies: P - 1928, 1932.

Hospers, John - Calif. (Libertarian) June 9, 1918– ; director of school of philosophy at University of Southern California. Candidacy: P - 1972.

Howard, John Eager - Md. (Federalist) June 4, 1752–Oct. 12, 1827; Continental Congress, 1788; governor, 1788–1791; Senate, 1796–1803. Candidacy: VP - 1816.

Hughes, Charles Evans - N.Y. (Republican) April 11, 1862–Aug. 27, 1948; governor, 1907–1910; associate justice of U.S. Supreme Court, 1910–1916; secretary of state, 1921–1925; chief justice of United States, 1930–1941. Candidacy: P - 1916.

Humphrey, Hubert Horatio Jr. - Minn. (Democratic) May 27, 1911–Jan. 13, 1978; mayor of Minneapolis, 1945–1948; Senate, 1949–1964, 1971–1978; U.S. vice president, 1965–1969. Candidacies: VP - 1964; P - 1968.

Huntington, Samuel - Conn., July 3, 1731–Jan. 5, 1796; Continental Congress, 1776, 1778–1781, 1783; president of the Continental Congress, 1779–1781; governor, 1786–1796. Candidacy: 1789.

Ingersoll, Jared - Pa. (Federalist) Oct. 24, 1749–Oct. 31, 1822; Continental Congress, 1780–1781; Constitutional Convention, 1787. Candidacy: VP - 1812.

Iredell, James - N.C. (Federalist) Oct. 5, 1751–Oct. 20, 1799; associate justice of U.S. Supreme Court, 1790–1799. Candidacy: 1796.

Jackson, Andrew - Tenn. (Democratic-Republican, Democratic) March 15, 1767–June 8, 1845; House, 1796–1797; Senate, 1797–1798, 1823–1825; territorial governor of Florida, 1821; U.S. president, 1829–1837. Candidacies: P - 1824, 1828, 1832.

Jay, John - N.Y. (Federalist) Dec. 12, 1745–May 17, 1829; Continental Congress, 1774–1776, 1778–1779; president of Continental Congress, 1778–1779; minister to Spain, 1779; chief justice of United States, 1789–1795; governor, 1795–1801. Candidacies: - 1789, 1796, 1800.

Jefferson, Thomas - Va. (Democratic-Republican) April 13, 1743–July 4, 1826; Continental Congress, 1775–1776, 1783–1784; author and signer of Declaration of Independence, 1776; governor, 1779–1781; minister to France, 1784–1789; secretary of state, 1790–1793; U.S. vice president, 1797–1801; U.S. president, 1801–1809. Candidacies: VP - 1792; P - 1796, 1800, 1804.

Jenkins, Charles Jones - Ga. (Democratic) Jan. 6, 1805–June 14, 1883; governor, 1865–1868. Candidacy: P - 1872.

Johnson, Andrew - Tenn. (Republican) Dec. 29, 1808–July 31, 1875; House, 1843–1853; governor, 1853–1857; Senate, 1857–1862, 1875; U.S. vice president, 1865; U.S. president, 1865–1869. Candidacy: VP - 1864.

Johnson, Herschel Vespasian - Ga. (Democratic) Sept. 18, 1812–Aug. 16, 1880; Senate, 1848–1849; governor, 1853–1857; senator, Confederate Congress, 1862–1865. Candidacy: VP - 1860.

Johnson, Hiram Warren - Calif. (Progressive) Sept. 2, 1866–Aug. 6, 1945; governor, 1911–1917; Senate, 1917–1945. Candidacy: VP - 1912.

Johnson, Lyndon Baines - Texas (Democratic) Aug. 27, 1908–Jan. 22, 1973; House, 1937–1949; Senate, 1949–1961; Senate minority leader, 1953–1955; Senate majority leader, 1955–1961; U.S. vice president, 1961–1963; U.S. president, 1963–1969. Candidacies: VP - 1960; P - 1964.

Johnson, Richard Mentor - Ky. (Democratic) Oct. 17, 1780–Nov. 19, 1850; House, 1807–1819, 1829–1837; Senate, 1819–1829; U.S. vice president, 1837–1841. Candidacies: VP - 1836, 1840.

Johnston, Samuel - N.C. (Federalist) Dec. 15, 1733–Aug. 17, 1816; Continental Congress, 1780–1781; governor, 1787–1789; Senate, 1789–1793. Candidacy: 1796.

Jones, Walter Burgwyn - Ala. (Independent Democratic) Oct. 16, 1888–Aug. 1, 1963; Alabama Legislature, 1919–1920; Alabama circuit court judge, 1920–1935; presiding judge, 1935–1963. Candidacy: P - 1956.

Julian, George Washington - Ind. (Free Soil, Liberal Republican) May 5, 1817–July 7, 1899; House, 1849–1851, 1861–1871. Candidacies: VP - 1852, 1872.

Kefauver, Estes - Tenn. (Democratic) July 26, 1903–Aug. 10, 1963; House, 1939–1949; Senate, 1949–1963. Candidacy: VP - 1956.

Kemp, Jack F. - N.Y. (Republican) July 13, 1935–May 2, 2009; House, 1971–1989; secretary of housing and urban development, 1989–1993. Candidacy: VP - 1996.

Kennedy, John Fitzgerald - Mass. (Democratic) May 29, 1917–Nov. 22, 1963; House, 1947–1953; Senate, 1953–1960; U.S. president, 1961–1963. Candidacy: P - 1960.

Kern, John Worth - Ind. (Democratic) Dec. 20, 1849–Aug. 17, 1917; Senate, 1911–1917; Senate majority leader, 1913–1917. Candidacy: VP - 1908.

Kerry, John F. - Mass. (Democrat) December 11, 1943– ; lieutenant governor of Massachusetts 1982–1984; Senate 1985– ; Candidacy: P - 2004.

King, Rufus - N.Y. (Federalist) March 24, 1755–April 29, 1827; Continental Congress, 1784–1787; Constitutional Convention, 1787; Senate, 1789–1796, 1813–1825; minister to Great Britain, 1796–1803, 1825–1826. Candidacies: VP - 1804, 1808; P - 1816.

King, William Rufus de Vane - Ala. (Democratic) April 7, 1786–April 18, 1853; House, 1811–1816; Senate, 1819–1844, 1848–1852; president pro tempore of the Senate, 1836, 1837, 1838, 1839, 1840, 1841, 1850; minister to France, 1844–1846; U.S. vice president, 1853. Candidacy: VP - 1852.

Knox, Franklin - Ill. (Republican) Jan. 1, 1874–April 28, 1944; secretary of the Navy, 1940–1944. Candidacy: VP - 1936.

La Follette, Robert Marion - Wis. (Progressive) June 14, 1855–June 18, 1925; House, 1885–1891; governor, 1901–1906; Senate, 1906–1925. Candidacy: P - 1924.

Landon, Alfred Mossman - Kan. (Republican) Sept. 9, 1887–Oct. 12, 1987; governor, 1933–1937. Candidacy: P - 1936.

Lane, Joseph - Ore. (Southern Democratic) Dec. 14, 1801–April 19, 1881; governor of Oregon Territory,

1849–1850, 1853; House (territorial delegate), 1851–1859; Senate, 1859–1861. Candidacy: VP - 1860.

Langdon, John - N.H. (Democratic-Republican) June 26, 1741–Sept. 18, 1819; Continental Congress, 1775–1776, 1787; governor, 1805–1809, 1810–1812; Senate, 1789–1801; first president pro tempore of the Senate, 1789. Candidacy: VP - 1808.

Lee, Henry - Mass. (Independent Democratic) Feb. 4, 1782–Feb. 6, 1867; merchant and publicist. Candidacy: VP - 1832.

LeMay, Curtis Emerson - Ohio (American Independent) Nov. 15, 1906–Oct. 1, 1990; Air Force chief of staff, 1961–1965. Candidacy: VP - 1968.

Lemke, William - N.D. (Union) Aug. 13, 1878–May 30, 1950; House, 1933–1941, 1943–1950. Candidacy: P - 1936.

Lieberman, Joseph I. - Conn. (Independent) Feb. 24, 1942– ; Connecticut Legislature, 1971–1981; attorney general of Connecticut, 1983–1989; Senate 1989– . Candidacy: VP - 2000 (A Democratic candidate in 2000, he later changed parties.)

Lincoln, Abraham - Ill. (Republican) Feb. 12, 1809–April 15, 1865; House, 1847–1849; U.S. president, 1861–1865. Candidacies: P - 1860, 1864.

Lincoln, Benjamin - Mass. (Federalist) Jan. 24, 1733–May 9, 1810; major general in Continental Army, 1777–1781. Candidacy: - 1789.

Lodge, Henry Cabot Jr. - Mass. (Republican) July 5, 1902–Feb. 27, 1985; Senate, 1937–1944, 1947–1953; ambassador to United Nations, 1953–1960; ambassador to Republic of Vietnam, 1963–1964, 1965–1967. Candidacy: VP - 1960.

Logan, John Alexander - Ill. (Republican) Feb. 9, 1826–Dec. 26, 1886; House, 1859–1862, 1867–1871; Senate, 1871–1877, 1879–1886. Candidacy: VP - 1884.

Machen, Willis Benson - Ky. (Democratic) April 10, 1810–Sept. 29, 1893; Confederate Congress, 1861–1865; Senate, 1872–1873. Candidacy: VP - 1872.

Macon, Nathaniel - N.C. (Democratic-Republican) Dec. 17, 1757–June 29, 1837; House, 1791–1815; Speaker of the House, 1801–1807; Senate, 1815–1828; president pro tempore of the Senate, 1826, 1827. Candidacy: VP - 1824.

Madison, James - Va. (Democratic-Republican) March 16, 1751–June 28, 1836; Continental Congress, 1780–1783, 1787–1788; Constitutional Convention, 1787; House, 1789–1797; secretary of state, 1801–1809; U.S. president, 1809–1817. Candidacies: P - 1808, 1812.

Mangum, Willie Person - N.C. (Independent Democratic) May 10, 1792–Sept. 7, 1861; House, 1823–1826; Senate, 1831–1836, 1840–1853. Candidacy: P - 1836.

Marshall, John - Va. (Federalist) Sept. 24, 1755–July 6, 1835; House, 1799–1800; secretary of state, 1800–1801; chief justice of United States, 1801–1835. Candidacy: VP - 1816.

Marshall, Thomas Riley - Ind. (Democratic) March 14, 1854–June 1, 1925; governor, 1909–1913; U.S. vice president, 1913–1921. Candidacies: VP - 1912, 1916.

McCarthy, Eugene Joseph - Minn. (Independent) March 29, 1916–Dec. 10, 2005; House, 1949–1959; Senate, 1959–1971. Candidacy: P - 1976.

McCain, John - Ariz. (Republican) Aug. 29, 1936– ; House 1983–1987; Senate 1987– . Candidacy: P - 2008.

McClellan, George Brinton - N.J. (Democratic) Dec. 3, 1826–Oct. 29, 1885; general-in-chief of Army of the Potomac, 1861; governor, 1878–1881. Candidacy: P - 1864.

McGovern, George Stanley - S.D. (Democratic) July 19, 1922– ; House, 1957–1961; Senate, 1963–1981. Candidacy: P - 1972.

McKinley, William Jr. - Ohio (Republican) Jan. 29, 1843–Sept. 14, 1901; House, 1877, 1885–1891; governor, 1892–1896; U.S. president, 1897–1901. Candidacies: P - 1896, 1900.

McNary, Charles Linza - Ore. (Republican) June 12, 1874–Feb. 25, 1944; state Supreme Court judge, 1913–1915; Senate, 1917–1918, 1918–1944; Senate minority leader, 1933–1944. Candidacy: VP - 1940.

Miller, William Edward - N.Y. (Republican) March 22, 1914–June 24, 1983; House, 1951–1965; chair of Republican National Committee, 1960–1964. Candidacy: VP - 1964.

Milton, John - Ga. circa 1740–circa 1804; secretary of state, Georgia, circa 1778, 1781, 1783. Candidacy: 1789.

Mondale, Walter Frederick - Minn. (Democratic) Jan. 5, 1928– ; Senate, 1964–1976; U.S. vice president, 1977–1981; ambassador to Japan, 1993–1996. Candidacies: VP - 1976, 1980; P - 1984.

Monroe, James - Va. (Democratic-Republican) April 28, 1758–July 4, 1831; Continental Congress, 1783–1786; Senate, 1790–1794; minister to France, 1794–1796, 1803; minister to England, 1803–1807; governor, 1799–1802, 1811; secretary of state, 1811–1814, 1815–1817; U.S. president, 1817–1825. Candidacies: VP - 1808; P - 1816, 1820.

Morton, Levi Parsons - N.Y. (Republican) May 16, 1824–May 16, 1920; House, 1879–1881; minister to France, 1881–1885; U.S. vice president, 1889–1893; governor, 1895–1897. Candidacy: VP - 1888.

Muskie, Edmund Sixtus - Maine (Democratic) March 28, 1914–March 26, 1996; governor, 1955–1959; Senate,

1959–1980; secretary of state, 1980–1981. Candidacy: VP - 1968.

Nader, Ralph - Conn. (Green, Reform, Independent) Nov. 27, 1934– . Candidacy: P - 2000, 2004, 2008.

Nathan, Theodora Nathalia - Ore. (Libertarian) Feb. 9, 1923– ; broadcast journalist; National Judiciary Committee, Libertarian Party, 1972–1975; vice chair, Oregon Libertarian Party, 1974–1975. Candidacy: VP - 1972.

Nixon, Richard Milhous - Calif., N.Y. (Republican) Jan. 9, 1913–April 22, 1994; House, 1947–1950; Senate, 1950–1953; U.S. vice president, 1953–1961; U.S. president, 1969–1974. Candidacies: VP - 1952, 1956; P - 1960, 1968, 1972.

Obama, Barack H. - Ill. (Democratic) Aug. 4, 1961– ; Senate, 2005–2008; U.S. president, 2009– . Candidacy: P - 2008.

Palin, Sarah - Alaska (Republican) Feb. 11, 1964– ; governor 2006–2009. Candidacy: VP - 2008.

Palmer, John McAuley - Ill. (Democratic, National Democratic) Sept. 13, 1817–Sept. 25, 1900; governor, 1869–1873; Senate, 1891–1897. Candidacies: VP - 1872; P - 1896.

Parker, Alton Brooks - N.Y. (Democratic) May 14, 1852–May 10, 1926; chief justice of N.Y. Court of Appeals, 1898–1904. Candidacy: P - 1904.

Pendleton, George Hunt - Ohio (Democratic) July 19, 1825–Nov. 24, 1889; House, 1857–1865; Senate, 1879–1885; minister to Germany, 1885–1889. Candidacy: VP - 1864.

Perot, H. Ross - Texas (Independent, Reform) June 27, 1930– ; business executive. Candidacies: P - 1992, 1996.

Pierce, Franklin - N.H. (Democratic) Nov. 23, 1804–Oct. 8, 1869; House, 1833–1837; Senate, 1837–1842; U.S. president, 1853–1857. Candidacy: P - 1852.

Pinckney, Charles Cotesworth - S.C. (Federalist) Feb. 25, 1746–Aug. 16, 1825; president, state senate, 1779; minister to France, 1796. Candidacies: VP - 1800; P - 1804, 1808.

Pinckney, Thomas - S.C. (Federalist) Oct. 23, 1750–Nov. 2, 1828; governor, 1787–1789; minister to Great Britain, 1792–1796; envoy to Spain, 1794–1795; House, 1797–1801. Candidacy: 1796.

Polk, James Knox - Tenn. (Democratic) Nov. 2, 1795–June 15, 1849; House, 1825–1839; speaker of the house, 1835–1839; governor, 1839–1841; U.S. president, 1845–1849. Candidacies: VP - 1840; P - 1844.

Quayle, Dan - Ind. (Republican) Feb. 4, 1947– ; House, 1977–1981; Senate, 1981–1989; U.S. vice president, 1989–1993. Candidacies; VP - 1988, 1992.

Reagan, Ronald Wilson - Calif. (Republican) Feb. 6, 1911–June 5, 2004; governor, 1967–1975; U.S. president, 1981–1989. Candidacies: P - 1980, 1984.

Reid, Whitelaw - N.Y. (Republican) Oct. 27, 1837–Dec. 15, 1912; minister to France, 1889–1892; editor-in-chief, *New York Tribune,* 1872–1905. Candidacy: VP - 1892.

Robinson, Joseph Taylor - Ark. (Democratic) Aug. 26, 1872–July 14, 1937; House, 1903–1913; governor, 1913; Senate, 1913–1937; Senate minority leader, 1923–1933; Senate majority leader, 1933–1937. Candidacy: VP - 1928.

Rockefeller, Nelson Aldrich - N.Y. (Republican) July 8, 1908–Jan. 26, 1979; governor, 1959–1973; U.S. vice president, 1974–1977 (nominated under the provisions of the 25th Amendment).

Rodney, Daniel - Del. (Federalist) Sept. 10, 1764–Sept. 2, 1846; governor, 1814–1817; House, 1822–1823; Senate, 1826–1827. Candidacy: VP - 1820.

Roosevelt, Franklin Delano - N.Y. (Democratic) Jan. 30, 1882–April 12, 1945; assistant secretary of the Navy, 1913–1920; governor, 1929–1933; U.S. president, 1933–1945. Candidacies: VP - 1920; P - 1932, 1936, 1940, 1944.

Roosevelt, Theodore - N.Y. (Republican, Progressive) Oct. 27, 1858–Jan. 6, 1919; assistant secretary of the Navy, 1897–1898; governor, 1899–1901; U.S. vice president, 1901; U.S. president, 1901–1909. Candidacies: VP - 1900; P - 1904, 1912.

Ross, James - Pa. (Federalist) July 12, 1762–Nov. 27, 1847; Senate, 1794–1803. Candidacy: VP - 1816.

Rush, Richard - Pa. (Democratic-Republican, National-Republican) Aug. 29, 1780–July 30, 1859; attorney general, 1814–1817; minister to Great Britain, 1817–1824; secretary of Treasury, 1825–1829. Candidacies: VP - 1820, 1828.

Rutledge, John - S.C. (Federalist) Sept. 1739–July 23, 1800; Continental Congress, 1774–1775, 1782–1783; governor, 1779–1782; Constitutional Convention, 1787; associate justice of U.S. Supreme Court, 1789–1791; chief justice of United States, 1795. Candidacy: 1789.

Sanford, Nathan - N.Y. (Democratic-Republican) Nov. 5, 1777–Oct. 17, 1838; Senate, 1815–1821, 1826–1831. Candidacy: VP - 1824.

Schmitz, John George - Calif. (American Independent) Aug. 12, 1930–Jan. 10, 2001; House, 1970–1973. Candidacy: P - 1972.

Scott, Winfield - N.J. (Whig) June 13, 1786–May 29, 1866; general-in-chief of U.S. Army, 1841–1861. Candidacy: P - 1852.

Sergeant, John - Pa. (National-Republican) Dec. 5, 1779–Nov. 23, 1852; House, 1815–1823, 1827–1829, 1837–1841. Candidacy: VP - 1832.

Sewall, Arthur - Maine (Democratic) Nov. 25, 1835–Sept. 5, 1900; Democratic National Committee member, 1888–1896. Candidacy: VP - 1896.

Seymour, Horatio - N.Y. (Democratic) May 31, 1810–Feb. 12, 1886; governor, 1853–1855, 1863–1865. Candidacy: P - 1868.

Sherman, James Schoolcraft - N.Y. (Republican) Oct. 24, 1855–Oct. 30, 1912; House, 1887–1891, 1893–1909; U.S. vice president, 1909–1912. Candidacies: VP - 1908, 1912. (Died during 1912 campaign; Nicholas Murray Butler replaced Sherman on the Republican ticket.)

Shriver, Robert Sargent Jr. - Md. (Democratic) Nov. 9, 1915– ; director, Peace Corps, 1961–1966; director, Office of Economic Opportunity, 1964–1968; ambassador to France, 1968–1970. Candidacy: VP - 1972. (Replaced Thomas F. Eagleton on Democratic ticket Aug. 8.)

Smith, Alfred Emanuel - N.Y. (Democratic) Dec. 30, 1873–Oct. 4, 1944; governor, 1919–1921, 1923–1929. Candidacy: P - 1928.

Smith, William - S.C., Ala. (Independent Democratic-Republican) Sept. 6, 1762–June 26, 1840; Senate, 1816–1823, 1826–1831. Candidacies: VP - 1828, 1836.

Sparkman, John Jackson - Ala. (Democratic) Dec. 20, 1899–Nov. 16, 1985; House, 1937–1946; Senate, 1946–1979. Candidacy: VP - 1952.

Stevenson, Adlai Ewing - Ill. (Democratic) Oct. 23, 1835–June 14, 1914; House, 1875–1877, 1879–1881; assistant postmaster general, 1885–1889; U.S. vice president, 1893–1897. Candidacies: VP - 1892, 1900.

Stevenson, Adlai Ewing II - Ill. (Democratic) Feb. 5, 1900–July 14, 1965; assistant to the secretary of Navy, 1941–1944; assistant to the secretary of state, 1945; governor, 1949–1953; ambassador to United Nations, 1961–1965. Candidacies: P - 1952, 1956.

Stockton, Richard - N.J. (Federalist) April 17, 1764–March 7, 1828; Senate, 1796–1799; House, 1813–1815. Candidacy: VP - 1820.

Taft, William Howard - Ohio (Republican) Sept. 15, 1857–March 8, 1930; secretary of war, 1904–1908; U.S. president, 1909–1913; chief justice of United States, 1921–1930. Candidacies: P - 1908, 1912.

Talmadge, Herman Eugene - Ga. (Independent Democratic) Aug. 9, 1913–March 21, 2002; governor, 1947, 1948–1955; Senate, 1957–1981. Candidacy: VP - 1956.

Taylor, Glen Hearst - Idaho (Progressive) April 12, 1904–April 28, 1984; Senate, 1945–1951. Candidacy: VP - 1948.

Taylor, Zachary - La. (Whig) Nov. 24, 1784–July 9, 1850; major general, U.S. Army; U.S. president, 1849–1850. Candidacy: P - 1848.

Tazewell, Littleton Waller - Va. (Democratic) Dec. 17, 1774–May 6, 1860; House, 1800–1801; Senate, 1824–1832; president pro tempore of the Senate, 1832; governor, 1834–1836. Candidacy: VP - 1840.

Telfair, Edward - Ga. (Democratic-Republican) 1735–Sept. 17, 1807; Continental Congress, 1778, 1780–1782; governor, 1789–1793. Candidacy: 1789.

Thomas, Norman Mattoon - N.Y. (Socialist) Nov. 20, 1884–Dec. 19, 1968; Presbyterian minister, 1911–1931; author and editor. Candidacies: P - 1928, 1932, 1936, 1940, 1944, 1948.

Thurman, Allen Granberry - Ohio (Democratic) Nov. 13, 1813–Dec. 12, 1895; House, 1845–1847; Ohio Supreme Court, 1851–1856; Senate, 1869–1881; president pro tempore of the Senate, 1879, 1880. Candidacy: VP - 1888.

Thurmond, James Strom - S.C. (States' Rights Democrat) Dec. 5, 1902–June 26, 2003; governor, 1947–1951; Senate, 1954–1956, 1956–2003; president pro tempore of the Senate, 1981–1987; 1995–2003. Candidacies: P - 1948.

Tilden, Samuel Jones - N.Y. (Democratic) Feb. 9, 1814–Aug. 4, 1886; governor, 1875–1877. Candidacy: P - 1876.

Tompkins, Daniel D. - N.Y. (Democratic-Republican) June 21, 1774–June 11, 1825; elected to the House for the term beginning in 1805 but resigned before taking seat; governor, 1807–1817; U.S. vice president, 1817–1825. Candidacies: VP - 1816, 1820.

Truman, Harry S. - Mo. (Democratic) May 8, 1884–Dec. 26, 1972; Senate, 1935–1945; U.S. vice president, 1945; U.S. president, 1945–1953. Candidacies: VP - 1944; P - 1948.

Tyler, John - Va. (Whig) March 29, 1790–Jan. 18, 1862; governor, 1825–1827; Senate, 1827–1836; U.S. vice president, 1841; U.S. president, 1841–1845. Candidacies: VP - 1836, 1840.

Van Buren, Martin - N.Y. (Democratic, Free Soil) Dec. 5, 1782–July 24, 1862; Senate, 1821–1828; governor, 1829; secretary of state, 1829–1831; U.S. vice president, 1833–1837; U.S. president, 1837–1841. Candidacies: VP - 1824, 1832; P - 1836, 1840, 1848.

Wallace, George Corley - Ala. (American Independent) Aug. 25, 1919–Sept. 13, 1998; governor, 1963–1967, 1971–1979, 1983–1989. Candidacy: P - 1968.

Wallace, Henry Agard - Iowa (Democratic, Progressive) Oct. 7, 1888–Nov. 18, 1965; secretary of agriculture, 1933–1940; U.S. vice president, 1941–1945; secretary of commerce, 1945–1946. Candidacies: VP - 1940; P - 1948.

Warren, Earl - Calif. (Republican) March 19, 1891–July 9, 1974; governor, 1943–1953; chief justice of United States, 1953–1969. Candidacy: VP - 1948.

Washington, George - Va. (Federalist) Feb. 22, 1732–Dec. 14, 1799; First and Second Continental Congresses, 1774, 1775; commander-in-chief of armed forces, 1775–1783; president of Constitutional Convention, 1787; U.S. president, 1789–1797. Candidacies: P - 1789, 1792, 1796.

Watson, Thomas Edward - Ga. (Populist) Sept. 5, 1856–Sept. 26, 1922; House, 1891–1993; Senate, 1921–1922. Candidacies: VP - 1896; P - 1904, 1908.

Weaver, James Baird - Iowa (Greenback, Populist) June 12, 1833–Feb. 6, 1912; House, 1879–1881, 1885–1889; Candidacies: P - 1880, 1892.

Webster, Daniel - Mass. (Whig) Jan. 18, 1782–Oct. 24, 1852; House, 1813–1817, 1823–1827; Senate, 1827–1841, 1845–1850; secretary of state, 1841–1843, 1850–1852. Candidacy: P - 1836.

Wheeler, Burton Kendall - Mont. (Progressive) Feb. 27, 1882–Jan. 6, 1975; Senate, 1923–1947. Candidacy: VP - 1924.

Wheeler, William Almon - N.Y. (Republican) June 30, 1819–June 4, 1887; House, 1861–1863, 1869–1877; U.S. vice president, 1877–1881. Candidacy: VP - 1876.

White, Hugh Lawson - Tenn. (Whig) Oct. 30, 1773–April 10, 1840; Senate, 1825–1835, 1835–1840. Candidacy: P - 1836.

Wilkins, William - Pa. (Democratic) Dec. 20, 1779–June 23, 1865; Senate, 1831–1834; minister to Russia, 1834–1835; House, 1843–1844; secretary of war, 1844–1845. Candidacy: VP - 1832.

Willkie, Wendell Lewis - N.Y. (Republican) Feb. 18, 1892–Oct. 8, 1944; utility executive, 1933–1940. Candidacy: P - 1940.

Wilson, Henry - Mass. (Republican) Feb. 16, 1812–Nov. 22, 1875; Senate, 1855–1873; U.S. vice president, 1873–1875. Candidacy: VP - 1872.

Wilson, Woodrow - N.J. (Democratic) Dec. 28, 1856–Feb. 3, 1924; governor, 1911–1913; U.S. president, 1913–1921. Candidacies: P - 1912, 1916.

Wirt, William - Md. (Anti-Masonic) Nov. 8, 1772–Feb. 18, 1834; attorney general, 1817–1829. Candidacy: P - 1832.

Wright, Fielding Lewis - Miss. (States' Rights Democratic) May 16, 1895–May 4, 1956; governor, 1946–1952. Candidacy: VP - 1948.

★ SELECTED BIBLIOGRAPHY

Abbott, David W., and James P. Levine. *Wrong Winner: The Coming Debacle in the Electoral College.* New York: Praeger, 1991.

Abramowitz, Alan, and Larry Sabato. *The 2008 Elections.* New York: Longman, 2009.

Abramson, Paul R., John H. Aldrich, and David W. Rohde. *Change and Continuity in the 2004 and 2006 Elections.* Washington, D.C.: CQ Press, 2007.

Aldrich, John H. *Before the Convention: Strategies and Choices in Presidential Nomination Campaigns.* Chicago: University of Chicago Press, 1980.

American Enterprise Institute. *Direct Election of the President.* Washington, D.C.: AEI Press, 1977.

Ansolabehere, Stephen, and Shanto Iyengar. *Going Negative: How Political Ads Shrink and Polarize the Electorate.* New York: Free Press, 1995.

Archer, J. Clark, Stephen J. Lavin, Kenneth C. Martis, and Fred M. Shelley. *Historical Atlas of U.S. Presidential Elections 1788–2004.* Washington, D.C.: CQ Press, 2006.

Asher, Herbert. *Presidential Elections and American Politics: Votes, Candidates, and Campaigns since 1952.* 5th ed. Pacific Grove, Calif.: Brooks-Cole, 1992.

Barber, James D. *The Presidential Character: Predicting Performance in the White House.* 4th ed. New York: Pearson/Longman, 2009.

Bartels, Larry M. *Presidential Primaries and the Dynamics of Public Choice.* Princeton, N.J.: Princeton University Press, 1988.

Bennett, Robert W. *Taming the Electoral College.* Stanford, Calif.: Stanford Law and Politics, 2006.

Berns, Walter, ed. *After the People Vote: A Guide to the Electoral College.* 3rd ed. Washington, D.C.: AEI Press, 2004.

Best, Judith. *The Choice of the People? Debating the Electoral College.* Lanham, Md.: Rowman and Littlefield, 1996.

Bickel, Alexander M. *Reform and Continuity: The Electoral College, the Convention, and the Party System.* New York: Harper and Row, 1971.

Black, Earl, and Merle Black. *The Vital South: How Presidential Elections Are Won.* Cambridge, Mass.: Harvard University Press, 1992.

Blumenthal, Sidney. *The Permanent Campaign.* Rev. ed. New York: Simon and Schuster, 1982.

Boiler, Paul F., Jr. *Presidential Campaigns.* Rev. ed. New York: Oxford University Press, 1996.

Buchanan, Bruce. *The Policy Partnership: Presidential Elections and American Democracy.* New York: Routledge, 2004.

———. *Presidential Campaign Quality: Incentives and Reform.* Upper Saddle River, N.J.: Pearson Prentice Hall, 2004.

———. *Renewing Presidential Politics: Campaigns, Media, and the Public Interest.* Lanham, Md.: Rowman and Littlefield, 1996.

Buell, Emmett H., and William G. Mayer. *Enduring Controversies in Presidential Nominating Politics.* Pittsburgh: University of Pittsburgh Press, 2004.

Buell, Emmett H., and Lee Sigelman. *Attack Politics: Negativity in Presidential Campaigns since 1960.* Lawrence: University Press of Kansas, 2008.

Burnham, Walter D. *Critical Elections and the Mainsprings of American Politics.* New York: Norton, 1971.

Butler, Roger L. *Claiming the Mantle: How Presidential Nominations Are Won and Lost before the Votes Are Cast.* Cambridge, Mass.: Westview Press, 2004.

Byrne, Gary C., and Paul Marx. *The Great American Convention: A Political History of Presidential Elections.* Palo Alto, Calif.: Pacific Books, 1977.

Campbell, James E. *The American Campaign: U.S. Presidential Campaigns and the National Vote.* 2nd ed. College Station: Texas A&M University Press, 2008.

Ceaser, James W. *Presidential Selection: Theory and Development.* Princeton, N.J.: Princeton University Press, 1979.

Ceaser, James W. and Andrew Busch. *Upside Down and Inside Out: The 1992 Elections and American Politics.* Lanham, Md.: Rowman and Littlefield, 1993.

Ceaser, James W., Andrew Busch, and John J. Pitney. *Epic Journey: The 2008 Elections and American Politics.* Lanham, Md.: Rowman and Littlefield, 2009.

Chase, James S. *Emergence of the Presidential Nominating Convention: 1789–1832.* Urbana: University of Illinois Press, 1973.

Cohen, Marty. *The Party Decides: Presidential Nominations before and after Reform.* Chicago: University of Chicago Press, 2008.

Congressional Quarterly. *Selecting the President: From 1789–1996.* Washington, D.C.: Congressional Quarterly, 1997.

Cook, Rhodes. *The Presidential Nominating Process: A Place for Us?* Lanham, Md.: Rowman and Littlefield, 2004.

———. *Race for the Presidency: Winning the 2008 Nomination.* Washington, D.C.: CQ Press, 2008.

———. *United States Presidential Primary Elections, 2000–2004: A Handbook of Election Statistics.* Washington, D.C.: CQ Press, 2007.

———. *U.S. Presidential Primary Elections, 1968–1996.* Washington, D.C.: CQ Press, 2000.

CQ Press. *National Party Conventions, 1831–2008.* Washington, D.C.: CQ Press, 2009.

Craig, Stephen C. *The Electoral Challenge: Theory Meets Practice.* Washington, D.C.: CQ Press, 2006.

Cravit, Lawrence. *The Forty-Year Parallel in Presidential Elections.* New York: Vantage Press, 1980.

Davis, James W. *National Conventions in an Age of Party Reform.* Westport, Conn.: Greenwood, 1983.

———. *U.S. Presidential Primaries and the Convention System: A Sourcebook.* Westport, Conn.: Greenwood, 1997.

Denton, Robert E., Jr., ed. *The 2008 Presidential Campaign: A Communication Perspective.* Lanham, Md.: Rowman and Littlefield, 2009.

DiClerico, Robert E. *The American President.* 5th ed. Englewood Cliffs, N.J.: Prentice Hall, 2000.

———. *Political Parties, Campaigns and Elections*. Upper Saddle River, N.J.: Prentice Hall, 2000.

DiClerico, Robert E., and James W. Davis. *Choosing Our Choices: Debating the Presidential Nominating Process*. Lanham, Md.: Rowman and Littlefield, 2000.

Eaton, Herbert. *Presidential Timber: A History of Nominating Conventions, 1868–1960*. New York: Free Press, 1964.

Edwards, George C. *Why the Electoral College Is Bad for America*. New Haven, Conn.: Yale University Press, 2005.

Ewing, Cortez A.M. *Presidential Elections from Abraham Lincoln to Franklin Roosevelt*. Westport, Conn.: Greenwood Press, 1972.

Farnsworth, Stephen J., and S. Robert Lichter. *The Nightly News Nightmare: Television's Coverage of U.S. Presidential Elections, 1988–2004*. Lanham, Md.: Rowman and Littlefield, 2007.

Fenno, Richard F., Jr. *The Presidential Odyssey of John Glenn*. Washington, D.C.: CQ Press, 1990.

Fortier, John C., and Walter Berns. *After the People Vote: A Guide to the Electoral College*. Washington, D.C.: AEI Press, 2004.

Friedenberg, Robert V. *Communication Consultants in Political Campaigns: Ballot Box Warriors*. Westport, Conn.: Praeger, 1997.

Glennon, Michael J. *When No Majority Rules: The Electoral College and Presidential Succession*. Washington, D.C.: Congressional Quarterly, 1992.

Goldstein, Michael L. *Guide to the 2004 Presidential Election*. Washington, D.C.: CQ Press, 2003.

Green, John Clifford. *The Faith Factor: How Religion Influences American Elections*. Westport, Conn.: Praeger, 2007.

Hacker, Kenneth L., ed. *Presidential Candidate Images*. Lanham, Md.: Rowman and Littlefield, 2004.

Haskell, John. *Fundamentally Flawed: Understanding and Reforming Presidential Primaries*. Lanham, Md.: Rowman and Littlefield, 1996.

Havel, James T. *U.S. Presidential Candidates and the Elections: A Biographical and Historical Guide*. New York: Macmillan Library Reference, 1996.

Haworth, Paul L. *The Hayes-Tilden Disputed Presidential Election of 1876*. 1906. Reprint. New York: AMS Press, 1979.

Heale, M.J. *The Presidential Quest: Candidates and Images in American Political Culture, 1787–1852*. New York: Longman, 1982.

Herzke, Allen D. *Echoes of Discontent: Jesse Jackson, Pat Robertson, and the Resurgence of Populism*. Washington, D.C.: CQ Press, 1993.

Hillygus, D. Sunshine, and Todd G. Shields. *The Persuadable Voter: Wedge Issues in Presidential Campaigns*. Princeton, N.J.: Princeton University Press, 2008.

Huckfeldt, Robert, and John Sprague. *Citizens, Politics, and Social Communication: Information and Influence in an Election Campaign*. New York: Cambridge University Press, 1995.

Hull, Christopher C. *Grassroots Rules: How the Iowa Caucus Helps Elect American Presidents*. Stanford, Calif.: Stanford Law and Politics, 2008.

Jackson, John S., and William Crotty. *The Politics of Presidential Selection*. New York: HarperCollins, 1996.

Jamieson, Kathleen Hall. *Electing the President, 2008: The Insiders' View*. Philadelphia: University of Pennsylvania Press, 2009.

———. *Packaging the Presidency: A History and Criticism of Presidential Campaign Advertising*. 3rd ed. New York: Oxford University Press, 1996.

Jensen, Merrill, ed. *The Documentary History of the First Federal Elections, 1788–1790*. Madison, Wis.: Madison House, 1991.

Johnson, Donald B. *National Party Platforms*. Rev. ed. Urbana: University of Illinois Press, 1978.

Just, Marion R., et al. *Crosstalk: Citizens, Candidates, and the Media in a Presidential Campaign*. Chicago: University of Chicago Press, 1996.

Kamarck, Elaine C. *Primary Politics: How Presidential Candidates Have Shaped the Modern Nominating System*. Washington, D.C.: Brookings Institution Press, 2009.

Kapeluck, Branwell D., Laurence W. Moreland, and Robert P. Steed. *A Paler Shade of Red: The 2008 Presidential Election in the South*. Fayetteville: University of Arkansas Press, 2009.

Keech, William R., and Donald R. Matthews. *The Party's Choice*. Washington, D.C.: Brookings Institution Press, 1976.

Kessel, John H. *Presidential Campaign Politics*. 4th ed. Pacific Grove, Calif.: Brooks-Cole, 1992.

Key, V.O., Jr. *The Responsible Electorate: Rationality in Presidential Voting, 1936–1960*. Cambridge, Mass.: Harvard University Press, 1966.

Kleppner, Paul. *Who Voted? The Dynamics of Electoral Turnout, 1870–1980*. New York: Praeger, 1982.

Kleppner, Paul, and Walter D. Burnham. *The Evolution of American Electoral Systems*. Westport, Conn.: Greenwood Press, 1982.

Kraus, Sidney. *Televised Presidential Debates and Public Policy*. 2nd ed. Mahwah, N.J.: Lawrence Erlbaum Associates, 2000.

Lazarsfeld, Paul Felix, Bernard Berelson, and Hazel Gaudet. *The People's Choice: How the Voter Makes Up His Mind in a Presidential Campaign*. Ann Arbor: UMI, 2005.

Longley, Lawrence D., and Neal R. Peirce. *The Electoral Primer*. New Haven, Conn.: Yale University Press, 1996.

Magleby, David B., J. Quin Monson, and Kelly D. Patterson. *Dancing without Partners: How Candidates, Parties, and Interest Groups Interact in the Presidential Campaign*. Lanham, Md.: Rowman and Littlefield, 2007.

Maisel, L. Sandy. *Parties and Elections in America: The Electoral Process*. 5th ed. Lanham, Md.: Rowman and Littlefield, 2008.

Mayer, William G. *The Making of the Presidential Candidates 2008*. Lanham, Md.: Rowman and Littlefield, 2008.

———, ed. *In Pursuit of the White House 2000: How We Choose Our Presidential Nominees*. Chatham, N.J.: Chatham House, 1999.

Mayhew, David R. *Divided We Govern: Party Control, Lawmaking and Investigations, 1946–2002*. 2nd ed. New Haven, Conn.: Yale University Press, 2005.

McCubbins, Matthew D., ed. *Under the Watchful Eye: Managing Presidential Campaigns in the Television Era*. Washington, D.C.: CQ Press, 1992.

McGillivray, Alice V. *Presidential Primaries and Caucuses: 1992, A Handbook of Election Statistics*. Washington, D.C.: Congressional Quarterly, 1992.

McKee, Thomas H. *The National Conventions and Platforms of All Political Parties, 1789–1905: Convention, Popular and Electoral Vote*. New York: AMS Press, 1971.

Menefee-Libey, David. *The Triumph of Campaign-Centered Politics*. New York: Chatham House, 2000.

Miller, Arthur H., and Bruce E. Gronbeck, eds. *Presidential Campaigns and American Self Images*. Boulder, Colo.: Westview, 1994.

Miller, Warren E., and Teresa E. Levitin. *Leadership and Change: Presidential Elections from 1952 to 1976*. Cambridge, Mass.: Winthrop, 1976.

Minow, Newton N., and Craig L. LaMay. *Inside the Presidential Debates: Their Improbable Past and Promising Future*. Chicago: University of Chicago Press, 2008.

Moore, John L. *Elections A to Z*. Washington, D.C.: CQ Press, 1999.

Nelson, Michael, ed. *The Elections of 2008.* Washington, D.C.: CQ Press, 2009.

———, ed. *The Elections of 2004.* Washington, D.C.: CQ Press, 2005.

———, ed. *Guide to the Presidency.* 4th ed. Washington, D.C.: CQ Press, 2008.

———, ed. *Historical Documents on Presidential Elections, 1787–1988.* Washington, D.C.: Congressional Quarterly, 1991.

———, ed. *The Presidency and the Political System.* 7th ed. Washington, D.C.: CQ Press, 2009.

———, ed. *The Presidency, the Public, and the Parties.* 3rd ed. Washington, D.C.: CQ Press, 2008.

Nimmo, Dan. *The Political Persuaders: The Technique of Modern Election Campaigns.* Englewood Cliffs, N.J.: Transaction Publishers, 1999.

Norrander, Barbara. *Super Tuesday: Regional Politics and Presidential Primaries.* Lexington: University Press of Kentucky, 1992.

Panagopoulos, Costas. *Rewiring Politics: Presidential Nominating Conventions in the Media Age.* Baton Rouge: Louisiana State University Press, 2007.

Peters, Gerhard, John T. Woolley, and Michael Nelson, eds. *The Presidency A to Z.* Washington, D.C.: CQ Press, 2008.

Pika, Joseph H., and Richard Watson. *The Presidential Contest.* 5th ed. Washington, D.C.: CQ Press, 1995.

Polsby, Nelson W., Aaron Wildavsky, and David A. Hopkins. *Presidential Elections: Strategies and Structures of American Politics.* 12th ed. Lanham, Md.: Rowman and Littlefield, 2008.

Pomper, Gerald M., et al. *The Election of 2000: Reports and Interpretations.* Chatham, N.J.: Chatham House, 2001.

Price, Tom. *Political Conventions: Have They Outlived Their Usefulness?* Washington, D.C.: CQ Press, 2008.

Ragsdale, Lyn. *Vital Statistics on the Presidency: George Washington to George W. Bush.* 3rd ed. Washington, D.C.: CQ Press, 2009.

Robinson, Edgar E. *The Presidential Vote, 1896–1932.* Stanford, Calif.: Stanford University Press, 1947.

———. *They Voted for Roosevelt: The Presidential Vote, 1932–1944.* Stanford, Calif.: Stanford University Press, 1947.

Roseboom, Eugene H. *A History of Presidential Elections: From George Washington to Jimmy Carter.* 4th ed. New York: Macmillan, 1979.

Rosenstone, Steven J., Roy L. Behr, and Edward Lazarus. *Third Parties in America: Citizen Response to Major Party Failure.* Princeton, N.J.: Princeton University Press, 1984.

Runyon, John H. *Source Book of American Presidential Campaign and Election Statistics, 1946–1968.* New York: Ungar, 1971.

Sabato, Larry. *Get in the Booth!: A Citizen's Guide to the 2008 Election.* New York: Pearson Longman, 2009.

Sanders, Arthur B. *Losing Control: Presidential Elections and the Decline of Democracy.* New York: Peter Lang, 2007.

Scammon, Richard M. *America Votes: A Handbook of Contemporary Election Statistics.* Vols. 1–2. New York: Macmillan, 1956–58. *America Votes.* Vols. 3–5. Pittsburgh: University of Pittsburgh, 1959–64. *America Votes.* Vols. 6–11. Washington, D.C.: Congressional Quarterly, 1966–1975.

Scammon, Richard M., and Alice V. McGillivray. *America Votes.* Vols. 12–21. Washington, D.C.: Congressional Quarterly, 1977–1995.

Scammon, Richard M., Alice V. McGillivray, and Rhodes Cook. *America Votes.* Vols. 22–28. Washington, D.C.: CQ Press, 1997–2009.

Schantz, Harvey L., ed. *American Presidential Elections: Process, Policy, and Political Change.* Albany: State University of New York Press, 1996.

Schlesinger, Arthur M., Jr. *The Coming to Power: Critical Presidential Elections in American History.* New York: Chelsea House, 1981.

———, ed. *Running for President: The Candidates and Their Images.* New York: Simon and Schuster, 1994.

Schlesinger, Arthur M., Fred L. Israel, and William P. Hansen. *History of American Presidential Elections, 1789–2001.* Philadelphia: Chelsea House, 2002.

Schroeder, Alan. *Presidential Debates: Fifty Years of High-Risk TV.* New York: Columbia University Press, 2008.

Shafer, Byron. *Bifurcated Politics: Evolution and Reform in the National Party Convention.* Cambridge, Mass.: Harvard University Press, 1988.

Singer, Aaron, ed. *Campaign Speeches of American Presidential Candidates, 1928–1972.* New York: Ungar, 1976.

———. *Campaign Speeches of American Presidential Candidates, 1948–1984.* New York: Ungar, 1985.

Smith, Steven S., and Melanie J. Springer. *Reforming the Presidential Nomination Process.* Washington, D.C.: Brookings Institution Press, 2009.

Squire, Peverill, ed. *The Iowa Caucuses and the Presidential Nominating Process.* Boulder, Colo.: Westview, 1989.

Stephenson, D. Grier, Jr. *Campaigns and the Court: The U.S. Supreme Court in Presidential Elections.* New York: Columbia University Press, 1999.

Sullivan, Denis G., Jeffrey L. Pressman, and F. Christopher Arterton. *Explorations in Convention Decision-Making: The Democratic Party in the 1970s.* San Francisco: Freeman, 1974.

Tenpas, Kathryn D. *Presidents as Candidates: Inside the White House for the Presidential Campaign.* New York: Garland, 1997.

Thurber, James A., and Candice J. Nelson, eds. *Campaigns and Elections American Style.* 2nd ed. Boulder, Colo.: Westview, 2004.

Troy, Gil. *See How They Ran: The Changing Role of the Presidential Candidate.* Rev. ed. Cambridge, Mass.: Harvard University Press, 1996.

Tugwell, Rexford G. *How They Became President: Thirty-Five Ways to the White House.* New York: Simon and Schuster, 1965.

Wattenberg, Martin P. *The Rise of Candidate-Centered Politics: Presidential Elections of the 1980s.* Cambridge, Mass.: Harvard University Press, 1991.

Wayne, Stephen J. *The Road to the White House 2008: The Politics of Presidential Elections.* Belmont, Calif.: Wadsworth/Thomson Learning, 2008.

Wayne, Stephen J., and Clyde Wilcox. *The Election of the Century and What It Tells Us About the Future of American Politics.* Armonk, N.Y.: M.E. Sharpe, 2002.

West, Darrell M. *Air Wars: Television Advertising in Election Campaigns, 1952–2008.* 5th ed. Washington, D.C.: CQ Press, 2009.

White, Theodore H. *America in Search of Itself: The Making of the President, 1956–1980.* New York: Harper and Row, 1982.

Witcover, Jules. *No Way to Pick a President.* New York: Farrar, Straus, and Giroux, 1999.

★ ILLUSTRATION CREDITS AND ACKNOWLEDGMENTS

1. Introduction

2 AP Images; 7 UPI Bettmann/Corbis; 8 AP Images; 11 Library of Congress

2. Chronology of Presidential Elections

19 Library of Congress; 21 Collection of the New-York Historical Society; 26 Library of Congress; 27 Library of Congress; 36 The Bettmann Archive/Corbis; 37 Library of Congress; 38 Library of Congress; 40 Library of Congress; 44 Library of Congress; 46 Library of Congress; 51 Library of Congress; 54 Courtesy of the Franklin D. Roosevelt Library; 55 Library of Congress; 56 The Bettmann Archive/Corbis; 58 Courtesy of the Franklin D. Roosevelt Library; 61 Library of Congress; 66 The Bettmann Archive/Corbis; 70 AP Images; 73 The Bettmann Archive/Corbis; 76 AP Images; 79 Library of Congress; 81 AP Images; 82 AP Images; 84 MTV; 85 AP Images; 87 AP Images; 90 Reuters/Jeff Mitchell; 91 AP Images; 97 AP Images

3. Presidential Primaries

110 Corbis/Wally McNamee; 112 AP Images; 117 Reuters/Jim Bourg

5. The Electoral College

202 AP Images

★ INDEX

Illustrations are indicated by italic page numbers. Boxes, notes, and tables are indicated with b, n, and t following the page number.